The New Book
of Lists

The New Book of Lists

The Original Compendium of Curious Information

David Wallechinsky
and
Amy Wallace

CANONGATE

Edinburgh · New York · Melbourne

First published in the United States in 1977 by William Morrow

Printed in the United States of America

ISBN-10: 1-84195-719-4
ISBN-13: 978-1-84195-719-7

Canongate
841 Broadway
New York, NY 10003

06 07 08 09 10   10 9 8 7 6 5 4 3

*This book is dedicated to the memory of
our father, Irving Wallace, who was*

1 of a Kind

Contents

Acknowledgments

The authors warmly thank Flora Wallechinsky for long hours of typing, organizing, and troubleshooting; Elijah and Aaron Wallechinsky and Macho Boubekour for help with typing; and Jaime Loucky for his creative research. Our love and thanks to our mother for her support and encouragement. To Chris Fishel, for his wonderful work and ingenuity as staff writer; to Danny Biederman, for organizing the celebrity lists; to Scott Bradley, for his work as researcher and writer of celebrity biographies and as editor with Amy; to Allison Berry, for abstracting texts and research. Warm thanks to Jamie Byng, our publisher at Canongate, whose vision and enthusiasm inspired us throughout. And with gratitude to Canongate's wonderful and enthusiastic staff, including our two editors, Helen Bleck and Nick Rennison. Thanks also to our agents, Ed Victor, for his long, long support of *The Book of Lists* series, and Wendy Shmalz, the model of equanimity and humor. And special thanks to Jeremy Beadle for being available for consultations, for providing good advice, and for always being a friend in need.

Amy would like to extend special thanks to Allison Berry for helping to keep her life running; to Scott Bradley for having saved his school lunch money at 13 to buy *The Book of Lists*, only to grow up to become part of its creation; and to Richard Jennings for support and keeping the wolves from the door.

This edition would not have been possible without the many people who worked on previous editions of *The Book of Lists*, in particular Vicki Baker, Carol Orsag-Madigan, Anita Taylor, Helen Ginsburg, Elizabethe Kempthorne, Judy Knipe, Fern Bryant, Rodger Fadness, Lee Clayton, and Torene Svitil.

Most of all, we wish to thank the millions of readers who wondered and the many who asked, "When is the next *Book of Lists* coming out?" We welcome ideas and contributions from our readers for future editions and thank you all for helping us create a genre that has lasted for three decades and is more popular than ever.

The authors can be reached at viciousgnu@aol.com.

Contributors

A.E.	Ann Elwood	K.H.J.	Kristine H. Johnson
A.K.	Aaron Kass	K.P.	Karen Pedersen
A.T.	Alan Tigay	L.B.	Linda Bosson
A.W.	Amy Wallace	L.C.	Linda Chase
B.F.	Bruce Felton	L.K.L.	Linda K. Laucella
B.F.G.	Bryan F. Griffin	L.K.S.	Laurie K. Strand
C.D.	Carol Dunlap	L.O.	Laurel Overman
C.F.	Chris Fishel	M.B.T.	Marguerite B. Thompson
C.O.M.	Carol Orsag-Madigan	M.J.H.	Michael J. Hayes
C.R.M.	Claude R. Mowry	M.J.T.	Michael J. Toohey
C.Ro.	Christopher Rouse	M.W.	Mike Ward
C.S.	Carl Sifakis	N.C.S.	Nancy C. Sorel
D.B.	Danny Biederman	N.R.	Nicholas Rennison
D.L.	Don Lessem	P.F.	Pamela Fields
D.P.M.	David P. Monahan	P.R.	Patrick Robertson
D.W.	David Wallechinsky	P.S.H.	Paul S. Hagerman
D.W.B.	David W. Barber	R.A.	Randy Alfred
E.F.	Ed Fishbein	R.C.B.	Richard C. Brown
E.H.C.	Ernest H. Corfine	R.H.	Robert Hendrickson
E.N.	Edward Nizalowski	R.J.F.	Rodger J. Fadness
F.B.	Fern Bryant	R.K.R.	R. Kent Rasmussen
F.H.	Frank Henry	R.S.	Ray Spangenburg
H.A.K.	H. Arthur Klein	R.T.	Richard Trubo
I.W.	Irving Wallace	R.W.S.	Roy W. Sorrels
J.Ba.	James Barnett	S.B.	Sue Berkman
J.Be.	Jeremy Beadle	S.C.B.	Scott C. Bradley
J.B.M.	Joseph B. Morris	S.R.	Steven Raichlen
J.F.	Josh Fishel	S.S.	Steven Sherman
J.Hu.	Jannika Hurwitt	T.A.W.	T. A. Waters
J.R.L.	James R. Longacre	T.C.	Tim Conaway
K.A.	Kayti Adkins	T.D.	Tom Dodds
K.A.M.	Kenneth A. Michaelis	W.A.D.	William A. DeGregorio
K.A.R.	Karla Rosenbusch	W.D.	Wendy Dreskin

Lists without initials were written by A.W. and D.W.

Introduction

As Oscar Wilde observed, the only sin is to be bored. If the great wit was correct, the authors and millions of *Book of Lists* readers are quite unblemished by sin: for we place a high value on curiosity.

We believe that it is an equal sin to be boring. As children, we were brought up on reference books in school that were dry as dust. At home, on our parents' bookshelves, we happily found a world of delights. The dry facts and cold equations of the dreary school books were toppled by our discoveries; according to the books in our family library, life was strange, unexpected, funny, tragic, mysterious, moving, absurd, and *always* astonishing.

Making lists can be a soothing endeavor or a riotously funny one. The everyday lists we all make are a balm to a cluttered mind; list making puts things in order, it clarifies, it helps coax truth from the cracks of the universe, and it invites our favorite question: "What if . . . ?"

The original 1977 volume of *The Book of Lists*, and its all new sequels, inspired nearly 200 imitation volumes. These have included books of lists about movies, rock 'n' roll, Judaism, the Bible, general sports, and countless other subjects. The books spawned games, toilet paper with lists on it, CD-ROMs, calendars, and television shows. We had no idea that *The Book of Lists* would become a best seller, let alone a phenomenon. We thought we were just having fun.

The *Book of Lists* rose to #1 on the best-seller lists and was published all over the world. Young readers wrote to tell us they'd bought our book for fun and were using it to spice up their schoolwork. Older readers locked themselves in bathrooms with it, curled up in bed with it, took it to parties, and demanded more editions. We invited their contributions, which came pouring in, and we featured many in the editions that followed.

Although we are pleased to have popularized a genre that so many people enjoy, we do not pretend to have been its founders. That honor goes to the Reverend Nathaniel Wanley, author of *Wonders of the Little World*, a book of lists first published in 1678. We didn't know about the Reverend Wanley when we wrote our own *Book of Lists*, but a glance through his table of contents shows striking similarities: "Of such People and Nations as have been scourged and afflicted by small and contemptible things," "Of such as having been extremely Wild, and Prodigal, or Debauched in their Youth, have afterwards proved excellent Persons," "Of such as have been seized with an extraordinary joy, at what hath followed there-upon."

The trend never died down and in recent years has had a dazzling renaissance. We appear to live in an age in which the volume of information available to us is far too overwhelming for our minds to process. Lists help us wend our way through the thicket of facts with whimsy and wisdom.

In the present volume, we have updated our readers' favorite lists, prepared an array of new material, and included lists from a wide variety of notables and celebrities. In all cases, lists make us think and sharpen minds dulled by television and hours spent staring at computer screens. We wish our readers happy foraging through the useful and the useless, the serious and the sublimely funny between these covers.

We owe much of the inspiration for this volume to our father, Irving Wallace, who always hoped we'd continue to compile new editions. Whenever possible, we have concentrated on lists that cause readers to laugh out loud, gasp, shake their heads in wonder, or call out, "Wait until you hear this!" To quote Mark Twain's introduction to *The Adventures of Huckleberry Finn*: "Persons attempting to find a motive in this narrative will be prosecuted; persons attempting to find a moral in it will be banished; persons attempting to find a plot in it will be shot."

CHAPTER ONE

People

11 TATTOOED CELEBRITIES

AGES OF 32 PEOPLE HAD THEY LIVED TO THE YEAR 2006

7 PEOPLE WHOSE NAMES WERE
CHANGED BY ACCIDENT

10 PEOPLE WITH THE MOST SQUARE MILES OF THE
EARTH'S SURFACE NAMED AFTER THEM

9 PEOPLE WITH EXTRA LIMBS AND DIGITS

20 FAMOUS PEOPLE WHO WERE EXPELLED
FROM SCHOOL

8 UNNAMED WOMEN OF THE BIBLE

15 MEN WHO CRIED IN PUBLIC

IF 29 FAMOUS MEN WERE KNOWN BY
THEIR MOTHER'S MAIDEN NAME

12 UGLY DUCKLINGS

6 FAKE *DE*S

9 DISPARAGING SOBRIQUETS

17 MEETINGS BETWEEN FAMOUS PEOPLE
AND PEOPLE NOT YET FAMOUS

30 ACHIEVERS AFTER THE AGE OF 86

FRANCISCO LENTINI - THREE-
LEGGED MAN WITH ONE OF HIS
FIVE CHILDREN. MR. LENTINI
WAS WITH RINGLING FOR 19
STRAIGHT SEASONS

**FRANCESCO LENTINI, THE THREE-LEGGED MAN—
WITH ONE OF HIS CHILDREN**

11 Tattooed Celebrities

1. **NICOLAS CAGE**
   On his back is a monitor lizard wearing a top hat.

2. **WINSTON CHURCHILL**
   Had an anchor on his arm. His mother, Jennie, had a snake on her right wrist.

3. **JOHNNY DEPP**
   Included in Depp's collection of tattoos is one that used to read "Winona Forever," in honor of his relationship with Winona Ryder. When the two separated, Depp had the message altered so that it now says, "Wino Forever."

4. **EMINEM**
   The singer has several tattoos, including one on his wrist that says "Slit Here," three in honor of his daughter, and an open grave with the words "Rot in Pieces" dedicated to his ex-wife.

5. **JANET JACKSON**
   Just below her bikini line she has what appears to be Mickey Mouse and Minnie Mouse having sex.

6. **PETER JACKSON**
   When the actors in *The Lord of the Rings* were tattooed with an Elfish design for "The 9" to represent the Fellowship of the Ring, director Jackson was tattooed with an Elfish "10."

7. **ANGELINA JOLIE**
   Jolie sports at least a dozen tattoos. Among them are one on her stomach that reads "Quod Me Nutrit Me Destruit" (Latin for "That Which Nourishes Me Also Detroys Me") and one on the inside of her left forearm that is a quote from Tennessee Williams: "A prayer for the wild at heart, kept in cages."

8. **JOHN MELLENCAMP**
   The singer has Jesus on his right arm and Woody Woodpecker on his left.

9. **CHARLIE SHEEN**
   Among his dozen tattoos are an open zipper with an eyeball peering out and, on his chest, a note that says "Back in 15 minutes."

10. **GEORGE SCHULTZ**
    The U.S. secretary of state had a tiger inscribed on his posterior in honor of his alma mater, Princeton University.

11. MIKE TYSON
    Besides the obvious Maori-style tattoo on his face, Tyson has pictures of
    Mao Tse-tung on his right arm, tennis player Arthur Ashe on his left
    arm, Che Guevara on his stomach, and his second wife, Dr. Monica
    Turner, on his left forearm.

Ages of 32 People Had They Lived to the Year 2006

1. John F. Kennedy (1917–1963), U.S. president	89
2. Judy Garland (1922–1969), singer and actress	84
3. Jack Kerouac (1922–1969), writer	84
4. Rocky Marciano (1923–1969), boxer	83
5. Lenny Bruce (1925–1966), comedian	81
6. Robert Kennedy (1925–1968), politician	81
7. Malcolm X (1925–1965), civil rights activist	81
8. Marilyn Monroe (1926–1962), actress	80
9. Ernesto "Che" Guevara (1928–1967), revolutionary leader	78
10. Anne Frank (1929–1945), diarist	77
11. Martin Luther King, Jr. (1929–1968), clergyman and civil rights leader	77
12. James Dean (1931–1955), actor	75
13. Elvis Presley (1935–1977), musician	71
14. Buddy Holly (1936–1959), musician	70
15. Michael Landon (1936–1991), actor	70
16. John Lennon (1940–1980), musician	66
17. Bruce Lee (1940–1973), martial artist and actor	66
18. Otis Redding (1941–1967), musician	65
19. Richie Valens (1941–1959), musician	65
20. Jimi Hendrix (1942–1970), musician	64
21. Jerry Garcia (1942–1995), musician	64
22. Janis Joplin (1943–1970), musician	63
23. Jim Morrison (1943–1971), musician	63
24. Bob Marley (1945–1981), musician	61
25. Marc Bolan (1947–1977), musician	59
26. John Belushi (1949–1982), comedian	57
27. Douglas Adams (1952–2001), science fiction writer	54
28. Princess Diana (1961–1997), British royalty	45
29. Kurt Cobain (1967–1994), musician	39
30. River Phoenix (1970–1993), actor	36
31. Tupac Shakur (1971–1996), musician	35
32. Biggie Smalls aka Notorious B.I.G. (1972–1997), musician	34

7 People Whose Names Were Changed by Accident

1. IRVING BERLIN (1888–1989), songwriter
   He was born Israel Baline, but the sheet music for his first composition, "Marie from Sunny Italy," credited the song to "I. Berlin." Baline preferred the mistake over his actual name.

2. WILLIAM FAULKNER (1897–1962), novelist
   After William Falkner's first book, *The Marble Faun* (1924), was published, he discovered that a *u* had been inserted into his last name. He decided to live with the new spelling rather than go through the hassle of correcting the error.

3. ULYSSES S. GRANT (1822–1885), general and U.S. president
   The future Civil War general was born Hiram Ulysses Grant. The prospect of entering the U.S. Military Academy with the initials "H.U.G." embarrassed him, so the new cadet reversed the order of his names and started signing himself U. H. Grant. He soon learned that Rep. Thomas L. Hamer, who had sponsored his appointment to West Point, had mistakenly enrolled him as Ulysses Simpson Grant, "Simpson" being the maiden name of Grant's mother. Finding nothing objectionable in the initials "U.S.G.," he adopted the new name.

4. BUDDY HOLLY (1936–1959), singer and songwriter
   When Charles "Buddy" Holley signed his first contract with Decca Records, his last name was misspelled as "Holly." Reasoning that others in the recording industry would make the same error, Buddy kept the new spelling.

5. JOHN KANE (1860–1934), artist
   He was born John Cain in Scotland. Shortly after he emigrated to the United States, a banker's misspelling changed his last name.

6. DIONNE WARWICK (1940–), singer
   When her first record, "Don't Make Me Over," was released in 1962, a printing error made Dionne Warrick over into Dionne Warwick.

7. OPRAH WINFREY (1954–), television personality
   Her parents intended to name her "Orpah" after Ruth's sister-in-law in the Old Testament, but the name was misspelled "Oprah" on her birth certificate. Winfrey has used it ever since.

Honorable Mention: HAKEEM OLAJUWON (1956–), basketball player
Because the *H* is silent, the Nigerian-born basketball star's first name
was misspelled as "Akeem" when he enrolled at the University of
Houston in 1980. Olajuwon politely ignored the error until 1991, when
he announced that he preferred the correct Arabic spelling, "Hakeem"
(which means "wise one").

C.F.

10 People with the Most Square Miles of the Earth's Surface Named After Them

Honoree	Square Miles
1. AMERIGO VESPUCCI, Italian explorer	
North America	9,360,000
South America	6,883,000
Total area	16,243,000
2. VICTORIA, British queen	
Queensland (Australia)	666,790
Victoria (Australia)	227,620
Great Victoria Desert (Australia)	127,000
Victoria Island (Canada)	83,000
Victoria Island (Antarctica)	60,000
Lake Victoria (Africa)	26,000
Victoria Strait (Canada)	6,000
Total area	1,196,410
3. MAUD, Norwegian queen	
Queen Maud Land (Antarctica)	1,081,000
Queen Maud Mountains (Antarctica)	15,000
Queen Maud Gulf (Canada)	6,000
Total area	1,102,000
4. JAMES WEDDELL, British seal hunter and explorer	
Weddell Sea (Antarctica)	1,080,000
5. ABEL JANSZOON TASMAN, Dutch explorer	
Tasman Sea (Pacific Ocean)	900,000
Tasmania (Australia)	24,900
Tasman Peninsula (Australia)	200
Total area	925,100

6. CHRISTOPHER COLUMBUS, Italian explorer

Colombia	440,830
British Columbia (Canada)	365,950
Columbia Plateau (U.S.)	100,000
District of Columbia and 10 U.S. counties (combined area)	6,790
Colon department (Honduras)	3,430
Colon department (Panama)	3,150
Total area	920,150

7. VITUS BERING, Russian explorer

Bering Sea (Arctic Ocean)	879,000

8. IBN-SAUD, Saudi king

Saudi Arabia	865,000

9. CHARLES WILKES, U.S. naval officer

Wilkes Land (Antarctica)	660,000

10. WILLEM BARENTS, Dutch explorer

Barents Sea (Arctic Ocean)	592,000
	C.F.

9 People with Extra Limbs and Digits

1. MYRTLE CORBIN (1868–unknown)
"The woman from Texas with four legs" was the only freak who could challenge the "King of Freaks," Frank Lentini, as a box-office attraction. ("Freak" expresses dramatic physical deviation from the norm and was not offensive to those in the sideshows.) The body of a twin grew from between Myrtle's legs, well developed from the waist down and completely functional. Myrtle was married and, according to her billing, had five children—three from her own body and two from her twin's.

2. JEAN BAPTISTA DOS SANTOS (1843–unknown)
Born in Cuba, Jean (or Juan) was a good-looking, well-proportioned boy who happened to have two fully functioning penises and an extra pair of legs behind and between his own, united along their length. His mental and physical capacities were considered above normal and so, according to one report, was his "animal passion" and sexual functioning. He was exhibited in Havana in 1865 and later in Paris, where he is alleged to have had an affair with the three-legged courtesan Blanche Dumas, who had two vaginas.

3. FOLDI FAMILY

Written up in the book *Anomalies and Curiosities of Medicine* in 1896, the Foldi family was described as living in the tribe of Hyabites in "Arabia" for many generations. Each member of the large family had 24 digits. They confined their marriages to other members of the tribe, so the trait was usually inherited. In fact, if a baby was born with only 10 fingers and 10 toes, it was sacrificed as the product of adultery.

4. LOUISE L. (1869–unknown)

Known as "La Dame á Quatre Jambes" ("The Lady with Four Legs"), Louise was born in France. Attached to her pelvis was a second, rudimentary pelvis from which grew two atrophied legs. There were two rudimentary breasts where the legs joined her body. In spite of this handicap, Louise not only married but also gave birth to two healthy daughters.

5. LALOO (1874–1905)

Laloo was a Muslim born in Oovonin, Oudh, India. He had an extra set of arms, legs, and sex organs from a headless twin attached to his body at the neck. He traveled with carnivals and circuses in the U.S. and Europe and was written up in many medical textbooks. He married in Philadelphia in 1894, and his wife traveled with him. His "parasitic twin" was male, but the circuses liked to advertise it as female to add to Laloo's strangeness.

6. FRANCESCO LENTINI (1889–1966)

For years acknowledged as the "King of Freaks," Frank Lentini had three legs, two sets of genital organs, four feet, and 16 toes. In order to counter his depression at being deformed, Lentini's parents took him to an institution for handicapped children, where he saw boys and girls who were far worse off than he was. "From that time to this," he would later recall, "I've never complained. I think life is beautiful, and I enjoy living it." He could use the third leg, which grew out of the base of his spine, as a stool. In his circus act he used it to kick a football the length of the sideshow tent. Born in Rosolini, Sicily, he came to the U.S. at the age of nine. He married and raised four children.

7. JEAN LIBBERA (1884–1934)

"The Man with Two Bodies" was born in Rome. He traveled with several circuses displaying his miniature "twin," named Jacques. Jacques had hips, thighs, arms, and legs. A German doctor using x-rays found a rudimentary structure resembling a head inside Jean's body. Jean covered Jacques with a cape when he went out. Walking with his wife and four children, he looked just like any other family man.

8. SHIVSHANKARI YAMANAPPA MOOTAGERI (1978–)
A young woman from Karnataka, India, Shivshankari has a third leg
with nine toes growing out of the middle of her body. She views her
anomaly as a divine blessing and supports her family by exhibiting
herself locally.

9. BETTY LOU WILLIAMS (1932–1955)
Betty Lou Williams was the daughter of poor black sharecroppers. She
looked pretty and shapely in her two-piece bathing suit on the sideshow
stage—but growing out of her left side was the bottom half of a body,
with two legs and one misplaced arm. Betty, who died at the age of 23,
made a good living during the depression. Her friends said she died of a
broken heart, jilted by a man she loved, but the more probable cause of
her death was complications from an asthma attack, aggravated by the
second head inside her body.

P.F. & D.W.

20 Famous People Who Were Expelled from School

1. TORI AMOS (1963–), singer and songwriter
At age five, Amos was the youngest person accepted to the Peabody
Conservatory in Baltimore, Maryland. Six years later, she was expelled
for refusing to read sheet music. The experience inspired the title of her
first album, *Y Kant Tori Read?*

2. JOHN BARRYMORE (1882–1942), actor
American actor John Barrymore was 16 when he was expelled from
Georgetown Academy in Washington, D.C. A faculty member recognized
him, in the company of several other young men, entering a bordello,
where they had gone to celebrate Washington's Birthday. The next day,
when asked to name the other men, Barrymore refused and was expelled.

3. HUMPHREY BOGART (1899–1957), actor
The son of a successful physician with inherited wealth, young Bogart
was sent to Phillips Academy of Andover, Massachusetts, and after a
year was thrown out for "irreverence" and "uncontrollable high
spirits." Since attending Yale was suddenly out of the question, Bogie
joined the U.S. Navy.

4. RICHARD BOONE (1917–1981), actor
Boone's career at Stanford came to an end in 1937, when he and
his Theta Xi fraternity brothers devised an ingenious prank. They

fashioned a dummy out of rags and bottles and laid it in the street. When the next passing car ran over it, Boone cried out, "You killed my brother!" Unfortunately, the car's driver was Mrs. Herbert Hoover, wife of the former U.S. president, who sprained her ankle during the resultant confusion. Boone later became an actor, best known for his role as Paladin in the TV series *Have Gun, Will Travel*.

5. TINA BROWN (1953–), magazine editor
Former editor-in-chief of *Vanity Fair* and of *The New Yorker*, Brown was expelled from three boarding schools by the time she was 16. "I got other girls to run away," she recalled, "and I organized protests because we weren't allowed to change our underpants." At one school the headmistress found her diary "and opened it where I had described her bosom as an unidentified flying object."

6. JACKIE COLLINS (1941–), novelist
At 16, Collins was expelled from Francis Holland School in England for (among other crimes) truancy, smoking behind a tree during lacrosse, selling readings from her diary of naughty limericks, and waving at the neighborhood flasher. Says Collins, "I was a *bad* girl." She later sent her daughters to the same school.

7. SALVADOR DALI (1904–1989), artist
In 1926, Spanish ultramodernist painter Salvador Dali was expelled from the Escuela Nacional de Bellas Artes de San Fernando in Madrid when he refused to allow his professors to critique his paintings.

8. ROGER DALTREY (1944–), musician
Daltrey was expelled from Acton County Grammar School in England. "I was an evil little so-and-so," he remembers. "I didn't fit in." The headmaster who expelled him commented, "When you have five hundred boys in uniform, and one in a teddy boy outfit, no wonder he didn't fit in."

9. GUSTAVE FLAUBERT (1821–1880), author
The 18-year-old Flaubert was first in his philosophy class at the College Royal. But he led a revolt against a substitute teacher, and when the noisy students were ordered to copy a thousand lines of poetry as punishment, he organized a petition in protest. The headmaster was unmoved, and Flaubert and two other boys were expelled.

10. WILLIAM RANDOLPH HEARST (1863–1951), plutocrat
In 1885, American newspaper publisher William Randolph Hearst was expelled from Harvard, halfway through his junior year. He had given each of his professors a chamber pot adorned with the recipient's name and picture.

11. JEAN-CLAUDE KILLY (1943–), ski champion
Killy began skiing at the age of three, and by the time he was a teenager, he often cut school to attend competitions. "Once you start racing in France," he said, "your schooling is finished." He was expelled at 15 because of chronic truancy.

12. BENITO MUSSOLINI (1883–1945), dictator
At age nine, Mussolini was sent 20 miles from home to a boarding school in Faenza, Italy, run by Salesian priests. The recalcitrant youth was nearly expelled for throwing an inkpot at a teacher who had struck him with a ruler. Finally, he went too far—he stabbed a fellow student in the buttocks with a knife. The future dictator was permanently dismissed.

13. DIANA NYAD (1949–), long-distance swimming champion and journalist
Nyad went through what she called a "late adolescence" in college and was "a real basket case." She attended Emory University in Atlanta, where she undertook such pranks as parachuting from a fourth-floor dormitory window. During her sophomore year, she was asked to leave. "It was kind of scary being kicked out of college," she recalled. "I began to wonder if maybe there really wasn't something wrong with me."

14. EDGAR ALLAN POE (1809–1849), author
In 1831, American author and poet Edgar Allan Poe was expelled from West Point when he refused to attend drills and classes for several weeks.

15. RICHARD PRYOR (1940–), comedian
Pryor was expelled from a Catholic grammar school in Peoria, Illinois, when the nuns discovered that his grandmother ran a string of brothels. At 16, he was expelled from Central High School for punching a science teacher named Mr. Think.

16. PERCY BYSSHE SHELLEY (1792–1822), poet
In 1811, while a student at Oxford, the poet Shelley and his close friend Thomas Jefferson Hogg sent a pamphlet entitled "The Necessity of Atheism," a summary of the arguments of John Locke and David Hume, to the heads of the colleges. When both students refused to answer questions about the pamphlet, they were summarily expelled.

17. LEON TROTSKY (1879–1940), political leader
At approximately the age of 10, Russian Communist leader Leon Trotsky was expelled from secondary school in Odessa, Russia, after he incited his classmates to howl at their teacher. He was the school's best pupil, however, and was readmitted the following year.

18. LUCINDA WILLIAMS (1953–), singer and songwriter
    Williams was expelled from a New Orleans high school when she
    protested the Vietnam War by refusing to pledge allegiance to the flag.
    Afterward, her father, a professor of English, taught her at home, with
    the help of the students in his creative writing class.

19. OWEN WILSON (1968–), actor and screenwriter
    Wilson was expelled from prep school after he and two friends stole the
    answers to a math exam. "I got called into the headmaster's office, and
    he handed me a geometry problem and told me to do it. When I
    couldn't, he pointed out I had just completed a similar one on the
    exam." The next year, Wilson was enrolled in the New Mexico Military
    Institute, where, he noted, "I learned to follow rules, even the ones I
    thought were stupid."

20. ORVILLE WRIGHT (1871–1948), inventor
    In 1883, during the sixth grade, American inventor and aviator Orville
    Wright was expelled from his elementary school in Richmond, Indiana,
    for mischievous behavior.

                                                            R.J.F. & the Eds.

8 Unnamed Women of the Bible

1. NOAH'S WIFE
   She is mentioned five times in the Book of Genesis but only in the
   context of being one of a group. This is surprising considering how
   talented and efficient she must have been to have been suddenly
   uprooted from her home and asked to set up housekeeping in a
   gopherwood ark filled with birds, snakes, insects, and full-grown
   animals of every species. This woman, who kept everything in order
   in the ark for 12 months, is known to us today only as "Noah's wife"
   (Gen. 6:18; 7:7, 13; 8:16, 18).

2. THE PHARAOH'S DAUGHTER
   Her father, probably Ramses II, decreed that it was necessary to kill
   all male children born to the Hebrews because the Hebrew population
   in Egypt was growing too quickly. One day the pharaoh's daughter
   was bathing in the Nile with her attendants when she noticed a basket
   containing a three-month-old baby boy. She realized that he was a
   Hebrew child and decided to raise him rather than allow him to be
   killed by her father. The baby's sister, Miriam, was standing nearby
   and offered to find a Hebrew woman to suckle the child. The baby's
   mother, Jochebed, also conveniently close at hand, was summoned
   and hired as a nurse to care for the child. The pharaoh's daughter

later named the baby Moshe, or Moses, and he grew up to become the
greatest leader and teacher in the history of the Jews. The woman who
saved his life and raised and educated him was known in various
history books as Thermuthis, Myrrina, and Mercis. However, the
authors of the Bible referred to her only as "the pharaoh's daughter"
(Exod. 2:5–10).

3. THE WOMAN PATRIOT OF THEBEZ
Abimelech was a tyrant who ruled over Shechem for three years during
the twelfth century BC. Having taken power by slaughtering 69 of his
79 brothers, he continued his bloody ways by killing the entire population of the town of Shechem when they revolted against him. Moving on
to the neighboring town of Thebez, he was about to set it ablaze when
"a certain woman" appeared on the roof of the town tower and dropped
a piece of a millstone on Abimelech's head, crushing his skull. Humiliated by the prospect of being killed by a woman, Abimelech ordered
one of his followers to run him through with a sword. With Abimelech
dead, his supporters dispersed and Thebez was saved (Judg. 9:50–55).

4. THE WISE WOMAN OF ABEL
When Sheba, the son of Bichri, led a revolt against King David, David
sent his commander-in-chief, Joab, to track down the rebel and kill
him. Joab finally found the culprit hiding in the walled city of Abel.
Joab and his soldiers began the destruction of the city but stopped
when a wise woman called out to them to discuss the situation. Joab
explained that if the people of Abel turned over to him the rebel Sheba,
he and his soldiers would leave them alone. The wise woman easily
convinced her people that this was a good deal. Sheba was quickly
decapitated, his head was thrown over the wall to Joab, and the city of
Abel was saved (II Sam. 20:15–22).

5. BARZILLAI'S DAUGHTER
When this Gileadite woman married, she retained her own name rather
than take her husband's. In fact, her husband, a priest, took *her*
family's name. Despite this early display of feminism, or perhaps
because of it, the Bible authors do not tell us her name, but refer to her
merely as "one of the daughters of Barzillai" (Neh. 7:63).

6. THE SHULAMITE SWEETHEART
According to some scholars, the Song of Songs tells the story of a young
Shulamite maiden who attracted the attention of King Solomon. He
forced her to come to Jerusalem and tried to convince her to marry
him, but she resisted him and insisted on remaining faithful to her
shepherd lover. Eventually, Solomon gave up and allowed her to return
home, while he was forced to continue living with the 700 women he had
already married (Song of Solomon).

7. **HERODIAS'S DAUGHTER**
   Known to the historian Josephus as Salome, this most famous of all dancers is not given a name in the New Testament. King Herod was so impressed by the dancing of Herodias's daughter that he offered her any gift, including half his kingdom. After consulting her mother, who was angry with John the Baptist for publicly denouncing her as an incestuous adulterer, she asked for the head of John the Baptist on a platter. She got it and promptly turned over the grisly prize to her mom (Matt. 14:6; Mark 6:22).

8. **THE ADULTEROUS WOMAN**
   Caught in the act of adultery, this woman was brought before Jesus by the scribes and Pharisees, who pointed out that the law required such an offense to be punished by stoning. Jesus ignored them at first and then said, "He that is without sin among you, let him first cast a stone at her." One by one her accusers slithered away, and she was not punished (John 8:3–11).

12 Men Who Cried in Public

1. **JEFF BLATNICK, wrestler**
   In July 1982, Blatnick was diagnosed as suffering from Hodgkin's disease, a form of cancer. His spleen and appendix were removed, and he received radiation therapy. Two years later, he won an Olympic gold medal in Greco-Roman wrestling. After his final match, which he dedicated to his deceased brother, Blatnick fell to his knees and burst into tears for the first time since his brother's death seven years earlier.

2. **JESUS CHRIST, religious leader**
   After Lazarus died, Jesus led his disciples to visit Lazarus's sisters, Mary and Martha. When the friends of Lazarus agreed to show Jesus the cave where Lazarus's body was laid, Jesus wept.

3. **BILL CLINTON, U.S. president**
   On the morning of his first inauguration, President Clinton and his family attended services at Washington's Metropolitan African Methodist Episcopal Church. As the choir sang hymns, tears rolled down Clinton's cheeks.

4. **DAVID, warrior king**
   When David and his troops returned to the city of Ziklag after being sent home by the princes of the Philistines, they discovered that the Amalekites had invaded the city and taken captive all of the women and children, including David's two wives. David and his followers immediately "lifted up their voices and wept until they had no more power to weep."

5. **LOU GEHRIG**, baseball player
One of the most dramatic moments in baseball history took place in Yankee Stadium in New York on July 4, 1939. Lou Gehrig, a humble and popular star, had been diagnosed as having amyotrophic lateral sclerosis, a terminal disease. Between the games of a Fourth of July doubleheader, Gehrig appeared at home plate and delivered an emotional farewell speech. After telling the crowd, "I'm the luckiest man on the face of the earth," he stepped away from the plate for the last time and wiped the tears from his eyes. Twenty-three months later, he died at the age of 38.

6. **JOHN LEE HOOKER**, musician
Hooker, the revered American blues musician, told an interviewer in 1998, "You can't get no deeper than me and my guitar. I open my mouth, and it's there. I get so deep the teardrops come to my eyes. That's why I wear my dark glasses, so you won't see the teardrops."

7. **MICHAEL JORDAN**, basketball player
According to Tom Lutz's *Crying: The Natural & Cultural History of Tears*, Michael Jordan cried openly when, while playing with the Chicago Bulls, he won his first NBA title in 1991, and that drew no comment from the press. When he won his fourth title in 1996, he wept once more, falling onto the floor in a fetal position and sobbing when the game ended. TV announcers explained that Jordan's father had been murdered a year and a half before; the game was played on Father's Day, and Jordan had made an incredible comeback after retiring for two years.

8. **EDMUND MUSKIE**, U.S. senator
Muskie was the leading contender for the 1972 Democratic Party presidential nomination, but his campaign was derailed when, angered by a vicious attack on his wife by New Hampshire newspaper editor William Loeb, he cried while speaking in her defense. It was later revealed that the newspaper attack was part of a "dirty tricks" campaign orchestrated by Richard Nixon's reelection committee. One of those who accused Muskie of lacking "stability" because he cried was Republican National Committee chairman Bob Dole. However, four years later, Dole himself began crying in public on a regular basis, going so far as to weep at Richard Nixon's funeral. There is no record of Dole ever apologizing to Muskie.

9. **RICHARD NIXON**, U.S. president
During a 1977 television interview, Nixon told David Frost, "I never cry—except in public." Nixon's most famous public weep occurred in 1952 after he made his notorious "Checkers speech" and Dwight Eisenhower decided to allow him to remain on the Republican ticket as the vice presidential candidate. Watching that performance, Nixon's

college drama coach, Albert Upton, who had taught the future politician how to cry, remarked, "Here goes my actor."

10. **JOHNNIE RAY**, singer
Known as "The Nabob of Sob" and "The Crying Crooner," Ray became one of the 1950s' biggest singing stars with the release of "Cry" in 1951. It was the first single to have its A and B sides reach numbers one and two on *Billboard*'s charts. The B side was "The Little White Cloud That Cried."

11. **JIMMY SWAGGART**, evangelist
On February 21, 1988, tears streaming down his face, Swaggart confessed on television and before a crowd of 6,000 to having committed "a sin," later revealed to be the hiring of prostitutes.

12. **PATRICK SWAYZE**, actor
Swayze was in the middle of a 1988 televised interview with Barbara Walters when he expressed regret that his father had not lived to see him become a star. Suddenly, Swayze burst into tears. "It's like a water faucet when I talk about him," he later explained, "because I have so many things I wanted to say to him."

If 29 Famous Men Were Known by Their Mother's Maiden Name

In our society, a married woman loses part of her identity through taking her husband's family name. Should her children happen to become famous, her husband's family is immortalized, while her own family is consigned to oblivion. (Picasso was one of the few famous men who chose to use their mother's name, partly because it was less common than Ruiz, his father's name.) It seems fitting to turn the spotlight, for once, upon the maternal branch responsible for contributing half the genetic endowment of the world's immortals and mortals.

1. William Arden (Shakespeare)
2. Isaac Ayscough (Newton)
3. Johann Sebastian Lämmerhirt (Bach)
4. George Ball (Washington)
5. Thomas Randolph (Jefferson)
6. Johann Wolfgang Textor (von Goethe)
7. Wolfgang Amadeus Pertl (Mozart)
8. Napoleon Ramolino (Bonaparte)
9. Ludwig Keverich (van Beethoven)
10. Abraham Hanks (Lincoln)

11. Charles Wedgwood (Darwin)
12. Charles Barrow (Dickens)
13. Giuseppe Uttini (Verdi)
14. Karl Pressburg (Marx)
15. Thomas Alva Elliot (Edison)
16. Sigmund Nathanson (Freud)
17. George Bernard Gurly (Shaw)
18. Winston Jerome (Churchill)
19. Albert Koch (Einstein)
20. Charlie Hill (Chaplin)
21. Ernest Hall (Hemingway)
22. Frank Garaventi (Sinatra)
23. Mick Scutts (Jagger)
24. Sylvester Labofish (Stallone)
25. Stephen Pillsbury (King)
26. Arnold Jedrny (Schwarzenegger)
27. Michael Scruse (Jackson)
28. Osama Ghanem (bin Laden)
29. Tiger Punsawad (Woods)

M.B.T. & the Eds.

12 Ugly Ducklings

1. JAMES BALDWIN (1924–1987), U.S. writer
   Baldwin grew up in New York's Harlem, and the person who had the greatest impact on him was his stepfather, David Baldwin ("He formed me, and he raised me, and he did not let me starve"). However, David Baldwin also labeled his son "ugly" and was ruthless in pointing out James's big, prominent eyes and frail body. In grade school, the kids called him "Frog Eyes," which only reinforced his father's taunting. One day, the young Baldwin excitedly yelled to his mother to come and look out the window at a woman he had spotted in the street. "Look, there's someone who's uglier than you and me." Baldwin grew up to become a much-admired and accomplished writer, but he was never able to shake the physical image of his childhood. In his best seller *Go Tell It on the Mountain*, the boy character (based on Baldwin) dreamed of being "beautiful, tall and popular," a boy who would become "a poet or a college president or a movie star."

2. BRIGITTE BARDOT (1934–), French actor
   No one would have guessed that the young Bardot would grow up to be an international sex symbol. Her hair was thin and frizzy, and she always seemed to be suffering from allergic rashes. She wore wire-rimmed eyeglasses because of an astigmatism and braces to straighten her

teeth. Bardot saw herself as homely, but in reality she was just plain. By the time she was fifteen, however, she was able to see the body and face that would make her famous. Nonetheless, she has never been satisfied with her appearance and once said, "My nose is a very bad nose. When I meet a man, it wrinkles up, as if I was sniffing a bowl of milk. My mouth is not a good mouth. My upper lip is heavier and more swollen than the other. My cheeks are too round, and my eyes are too small."

3. **J. M. BARRIE (1860–1937), English writer**
The man who created Peter Pan ("the boy who would not grow up"), Barrie was the runt of his family and extremely sensitive about his small stature. In school, the girls voted him "the sweetest smile" in the class, but none was attracted to the frail-looking boy. When no one was looking, Barrie would sneak off and scrawl his name along with a girl's name on the walls of the school. Many years later, when he was both rich and famous, he wrote, "Six feet three inches . . . If I had really grown to this it would have made a great difference in my life. I would not have bothered turning out reels of printed matter. My one aim would have been to become a favorite of the ladies which between you and me has always been my sorrowful ambition. The things I could have said to them if my legs had been longer. Read that with a bitter cry." Barrie's adult height was barely five feet.

4. **DALE CARNEGIE (1888–1955), U.S. writer**
The son of a poor farmer in Missouri, Carnegie was a skinny and gawky boy with a dimpled chin and huge ears. One of his classmates, Sam White, constantly made fun of his ears and threatened to cut them off. Terrified that the bully would carry out the threat, the young Carnegie endured many sleepless nights and never forgot the name of his tormentor. Unable to afford new clothes, he wore hand-me-downs that never fit and often made him look silly. Of being called to the chalkboard to solve a math problem, he once told his mother, "I can only think of the fact that people are probably laughing at my clothes." But he was determined to make up for his lack of physical assets with his speaking abilities. A powerful orator, he won many public speaking contests, feats that transformed him from social failure to intellectual leader. The ungainly boy from Missouri would go on to write *How to Win Friends and Influence People*, one of the biggest nonfiction best sellers of all time.

5. **GEORGE ELIOT (1819–1880), English writer**
Her real name was Marian Evans, and she would become one of the foremost English novelists of the nineteenth century; her best-known work is *Silas Marner*. When she was 10 years old, Marian said, "I don't like to play with children. I like to talk to grown-up people." Behind that comment was a young girl who was not very popular with her classmates. They called her "Little Mama." Although she was an

excellent student, Marian was a serious child and not terribly attractive. She had a large fleshy nose, prominent chin, full lower lip, dull complexion, and dark, clinging hair. As an adult, she wrote, "When I was quite a little child I could not be satisfied with the things around me; I was constantly living in a world of my own creation, and was quite contented to have no companions that I might be left to my own musings and imagining scenes in which I was chief actress."

6. ALFRED HITCHCOCK (1899–1980), English-born U.S. film director
He called himself "an uncommonly unattractive young man." Film director and master of the suspense thriller, Hitchcock preferred not to talk about his childhood. He was pudgy, very plain, and a loner. Girls were never an important part of his life, and he ended up marrying the first girl he ever dated. Always unhappy with his overweight body, he learned to joke about it: "A New York doctor once told me that I'm an adrenal type. That apparently means that I'm all body and only vestigial legs. But since I'm neither a mile runner nor a dancer, and my present interest in my body is almost altogether from the waist up, that didn't bother me much." Oddly enough, his unattractive body turned out to be an incredible publicity tool and helped to make him a worldwide celebrity. Movie fans eagerly awaited the short cameo appearance he made in each of his films. And his television series, *Alfred Hitchcock Presents*, opened with a silhouetted image of Hitchcock stepping into a profile sketch.

7. JANIS JOPLIN (1943–1970), U.S. singer
She tried hard to "fit in" in high school. At first, she conformed by wearing the "right" clothes and makeup and joining the right clubs. But she was always self-conscious about her underdeveloped body, her "pig" eyes, and her recurring bouts of acne. Joplin once remarked that she was unhappy in school "'cause I didn't have tits at age fourteen." When she failed to break into the popular groups in school, she changed course and created her own brand of popularity. She dyed her hair orange, donned a black leather jacket, and became known for her mastery of cuss words. Her code of nonconformity would later carry her into the hippie subculture of San Francisco and launch her career as a singer. Her most successful album was *Pearl*, which contains her number one hit "Me and Bobby McGee." Known for her loud, raspy vocal renditions, she said, "I'd rather not sing than sing quiet."

8. ABRAHAM LINCOLN (1809–1865), U.S. president
The sixteenth president of the United States was six feet tall by the time he was 15 (his adult height was six feet, four inches). As a teenager, he was admired for his strength and athletic abilities. In addition, he was a glib talker, a good joke teller, and a natural leader among the boys. The girls, however, paid him no attention. One of his schoolmates, Kate Ruby, said that all the girls made fun of his appearance, and she

described him as follows: "His skin was shriveled and yellow. His shoes, when he had any, were low. He wore buckskin breeches, linsey-woolsey shirt and a cap, made from the skin of a squirrel or coon. His breeches were baggy and lacked by several inches meeting the tops of his shoes, thereby exposing his shin-bone, sharp, blue and narrow." Abe, however, didn't seem too bothered by his lack of popularity with the girls. He said, "A woman is the only thing I am afraid of that I know can't hurt me."

9. ELEANOR ROOSEVELT (1884–1962), U.S. first lady
The opening sentence of her memoir is: "My mother was one of the most beautiful women I have ever seen." Unfortunately, her mother, Anna Hall Roosevelt, thought Eleanor was far from beautiful. In front of friends and relatives, Anna called her daughter "Granny" because she was so serious, awkward, and old-fashioned. Anna cautioned her daughter, "You have no looks, so see to it that you have manners." Eleanor's mother died when she was eight, and after her father died two years later, Eleanor moved in with her grandmother, Mary Hall. Eleanor's cousin, Alice Roosevelt, once said, "Eleanor was always making herself out to be an ugly duckling, but she was really rather attractive. Tall, rather coltish-looking, with masses of pale, golden hair rippling to below her waist, and really lovely blue eyes. It's true that her chin went in a bit, which wouldn't have been so noticeable if only her hateful grandmother had fixed her teeth." The future first lady of the United States was never able to erase the negative image her mother had placed upon her, however, and it would forever affect her self-esteem.

10. STENDHAL (1783–1842), French novelist
Marie Henri Beyle (Stendhal) was always self-conscious about his appearance. As an adolescent, his only redeeming qualities were his expressive eyes and curly black hair; he had an oversized head, a thick nose, short legs, fat cheeks, and a heavyset, stocky body. His outgoing personality and vivid imagination won over his classmates, however, and he never lacked friends. As an adult, he made fun of his appearance, saying, "I'd rather be a chameleon than an ox." Yet he let it be known that he always longed to be a tall, blond German.

11. BARBRA STREISAND (1942–), U.S. singer, actor, and film director
In grade school, her classmates called her names—"Big Beak," "Cross-Eyes," and "Mieskeit" (Yiddish for "ugliness"). Although she was an excellent student, the young Barbra was small and thin, awkward, and had a rather large nose. When she graduated from high school and tried to get work as an actress, most casting directors thought she had talent but were unimpressed with her looks. Undaunted, she trans-

formed herself with clothes, makeup, and a new hairstyle, taking full advantage of her striking blue eyes and long, slender neck. When the Broadway show *Funny Girl* made her a celebrity overnight, the homely Streisand suddenly found herself one of the world's most beautiful and glamorous entertainers. Women flocked to beauty salons to ask for the "Streisand look."

12. WOODROW WILSON (1856–1924), U.S. president
The son of an extremely handsome Presbyterian minister, Woodrow was a homely boy with a long, drawn face, big ears, and a thrusting jaw. In addition, at age eight, he was forced to wear eyeglasses. Wilson once told his cousin that if he had his father's looks, nobody would care what he said or did. As a child, he often recited the following limerick: "For beauty, I am not a star / There are others more handsome by far / But my face, I don't mind it / You see, I'm behind it / It's the people in front that I jar." Even after he became the twenty-eighth president of the United States, Wilson was somewhat camera-shy, telling reporters that he didn't like "pictorial publicity."

Source: When They Were Kids by Carol Orsag Madigan and Ann Elwood (Random House Reference, 1998).

6 Fake *DE*s

1. HONORÉ DE BALZAC
   The great French novelist was the son of a civil servant named Balzac. He added the aristocratic "de" to his name and passed it on to his son.

2. PIERRE-AUGUSTIN CARON DE BEAUMARCHAIS
   The author of *The Barber of Seville*, the most popular comedy of the eighteenth century, Caron was the son of a watchmaker. He married a widow and took over her husband's position in court, as well as his properties. One of those properties was in Beaumarchais, which name he then appended to his own.

3. DANIEL DEFOE
   Born Daniel Foe, he had already adopted his "de" before he wrote his famous novels, *Robinson Crusoe* and *Moll Flanders*.

4. FABRE D'EGLANTINE
   Born Philippe Fabre, he was a popular playwright and politician who is credited with creating the names of the months and days that were used in the French Revolutionary calendar. Accused of "moderacy," he was guillotined on April 5, 1794.

5. ANDRÉ DE TOTH

Born Andreas Toth in Hungary, he transformed himself into a "de," moved to Hollywood, and became a successful director of violent Westerns and action dramas. He also directed the 3-D classic *House of Wax* (1953).

6. DAME NINETTE DE VALOIS

Born Edris Stannus and married to Arthur Connell, she was known as a dancer, a choreographer, and the founder of what became England's Royal Ballet, as well as the Royal Ballet School. She died March 8, 2001, at the age of 92.

9 Disparaging Sobriquets

1. **CHARLES THE SIMPLE (879–929), king of the Franks**
Son of Louis the Stammerer, Charles III owes his nickname to his policy of making concessions to the Norse invaders to prevent the complete disintegration of his kingdom. In one concession, he gave Rollo, the Norse chieftain, the fiefdom of Normandy and his daughter in marriage. This act, among others, was unpopular with his barons, who later deposed and imprisoned him.

2. **LOUIS THE SLUGGARD (966?-987), king of the Franks**
Louis V's short reign (986–987) marked the end of the Carolingian line. Noted for his self-indulgence, Louis died at an early age due to a hunting accident. He was also known as Louis the Do-Nothing—but historians have noted that since the power of the kingdom was in the hands of the noblemen, there was little that he *could* do.

3. **ETHELRED THE UNREADY (968–1016), king of England**
Ethelred II's sobriquet is a result of his inability to repel the Danish invasion of England. At first, he paid tribute to the Danes, but their raids continued, and he was forced to abandon England for Normandy in 1013. In a more generous vein, he has also been called Ethelred the Ill-Advised.

4. **LOUIS THE FAT (1081–1137), king of France**
Like his father, Philip I, Louis VI was fat. At the age of 46, because of his extreme corpulence, he was unable to mount his horse. Yet he was a popular Capetian monarch and was also referred to as Louis the Wide-Awake because of the peace and prosperity of his reign.

5. **LOUIS THE QUARRELER (1289–1316), king of France**
Louis le Hutin can be translated as Louis the Stubborn or Louis the Quarreler. Louis X's brief reign (1314–1316) ended when he died of

pleurisy caused by overindulging in cold wine after becoming over-heated playing ball.

6. CHARLES THE BAD (1332–1387), king of Navarre
Charles II was "bad" because of his treacherous nature. His notoriety grew during the Hundred Years' War, when he forced John II of France to grant him lands in Normandy, one of several attempts to further his ambition to occupy the French throne.

7. FERDINAND THE INCONSTANT (1345–1383), king of Portugal
Ferdinand I earned his sobriquet by jilting the daughter of the king of Castile for the more beautiful Leonora Telles, a Portuguese noblewoman. He was also inconsistent in his political policies toward England and Castile.

8. CHARLES THE MAD (1368–1422), king of France
Charles VI assumed the throne at age 12, when he was referred to as Charles the Well-Beloved. In 1392 he took ill, suffering fever and convulsions—the first of 44 attacks he would subsequently endure. The bouts of madness, in which he sometimes tore his clothing and broke furniture, continued to plague him sporadically for the last 30 years of his reign.

9. IVAN THE TERRIBLE (1530–1584), czar of Russia
As a young ruler, Ivan IV tortured animals and tossed dogs from rooftops. Torture and executions were common throughout his reign. In 1570, he marched on Novgorod and killed thousands in a five-week binge—some of them children, who were thrown into the icy river. In 1580, he killed his own son in a mad rage.

D.P.M.

17 Meetings Between Famous People and People Not Yet Famous

1. NEW YORK, CITY, 1789. GEORGE WASHINGTON IS INTRODUCED TO WASHINGTON IRVING
As the president browsed in a Broadway shop, a servant of the Irving family spotted him from the street and hustled inside with six-year-old Washington Irving in tow. Informed that the lad had been named after him, the chief executive stroked the head that later would conjure up Rip Van Winkle and wished the boy well. *Note:* This pat on the head has been passed on through generations of Americans to the present-day recipient. An older Washington Irving bestowed it upon his

publisher, George Putnam, who in turn gave it to young Allan Nevins, the future Pulitzer Prize–winning historian. Years later, at an informal gathering at the Irving Wallace home, Nevins conferred the historic pat on 10-year-old Amy Wallace, saying, "Amy, I pat you on behalf of General George Washington." Amy refused to wash her hair for a week afterward. As *The Book of Lists* was going to print, she bestowed the historic pat upon baby Daniel, son of the owners of Clementines, one of Los Angeles's most popular restaurants.

2. LONDON, 1836. ELIZABETH BARRETT BROWNING ATTENDS A DINNER FOR WILLIAM WORDSWORTH
Elizabeth Barrett, not yet either married to Robert Browning or very well known, was a great admirer of Wordsworth. John Kenyon, a friend of the Barrett family, arranged for her to attend a dinner in the poet's honor. Although she was nervous (she said that she trembled "in my soul and my body") about being seated next to Wordsworth, he was kind and even recited one of Dante's sonnets for her entertainment. Eight years later, Barrett paid tribute to Wordsworth by mentioning him in "Lady Geraldine's Courtship."

3. BOSTON, MASSACHUSETTS, 1860. RALPH WALDO EMERSON PROOFREADS A SCHOOL PAPER FOR OLIVER WENDELL HOLMES, JR.
While a student at Harvard, young Holmes wrote a 15-page critical essay on Plato and took it to Emerson, an old family friend, for review. The great essayist, then 57 years old and with his best work behind him, read it and gave the future Supreme Court justice this advice: "When you shoot at a king, you must kill him." Holmes chucked the piece into a trash can.

4. ÉTRETAT, FRANCE, 1868. ALGERNON CHARLES SWINBURNE MEETS GUY DE MAUPASSANT
The 18-year-old Maupassant, later one of France's greatest writers, witnessed the near drowning of a swimmer, who turned out to be the eccentric English poet Swinburne. (According to some versions of the incident, including Maupassant's own, he was actually in on the rescue, but this is disputed by more objective accounts.) When Maupassant introduced himself, the poet invited him to dinner at his villa. Swinburne's guest was shocked by the main dish—roast monkey—and the presence of a large ape, which pushed the young Frenchman's head aside whenever he tried to drink.

5. WASHINGTON, D.C., 1887. GROVER CLEVELAND MAKES A WISH FOR FRANKLIN ROOSEVELT
On a visit to the nation's capital with his parents, five-year-old Franklin Roosevelt was taken to the White House to meet the president. Accord-

ing to FDR, Cleveland looked down at his eventual successor and said, "My little man, I am making a strange wish for you. It is that you may never be president of the United States."

6. PALO ALTO, CALIFORNIA, 1894. BENJAMIN HARRISON COUGHS UP 25¢ FOR HERBERT HOOVER
While serving as a guest lecturer at Stanford University, former President Benjamin Harrison inadvertently slipped into a college baseball game without paying the 25¢ admission. Unwilling to grant a freebie even to so distinguished a fan, the student manager of the home team, 19-year-old future president Herbert Hoover, caught up with Harrison and politely asked him to pay up. He did.

7. INDIANAPOLIS, INDIANA, 1895. LEW WALLACE WARNS BOOTH TARKINGTON OF THE DANGERS OF BREAKING INTO PRINT
During a visit to his hometown a decade before his death, Wallace, the author of *Ben Hur*, met Tarkington, then 26. Tarkington was wallowing in rejection slips and four years away from publishing his first book. "The publication of my first novel was almost enough to ruin my law practice," said the lawyer-turned-author to the wide-eyed Tarkington. "As soon as the jury of farmers and village merchants heard the word *novel*, they uttered heavy guffaws. . . . I might as well have appeared in court dressed as a circus clown." Despite the warning, Tarkington went on to write many best sellers, including *The Magnificent Ambersons* and *Seventeen*.

8. LEGHORN, ITALY, 1897. ENRICO CARUSO SINGS FOR GIACOMO PUCCINI
Near the beginning of his career, Caruso was hired by Arturo Lisciarelli to star as Rudolfo in a production of Puccini's *La Boheme*. Lisciarelli took advantage of Caruso's eagerness to sing the part by booking him for a mere 15 lire per performance, but he added, rather vaguely, that the fee would be increased to 1000 lire if Puccini liked him. When Caruso found out that Puccini lived nearby, he made a 25-mile trip to see the composer at his villa. After Caruso sang several measures, Puccini exclaimed, "Who sent you? God?" Despite the composer's praises, Lisciarelli held Caruso to the terms of his contract.

9. WASHINGTON, D.C., 1905. TEDDY ROOSEVELT SENDS FOR EDWIN ARLINGTON ROBINSON
Favorably impressed by Robinson's *Children of the Night*, a collection of poetry, President Roosevelt sent for the young writer, who was nearly destitute, and offered him a clerkship in the New York Custom House, with this admonition: "I expect you to think poetry first and

customs second." The post provided Robinson with a livelihood for four years while he continued to write.

10. NEW YORK CITY, 1910. SARAH BERNHARDT MEETS LILLIAN GISH IN THE WINGS

Before going west to become a star in D. W. Griffith's epic films, Miss Gish landed a dancing role in Sarah Bernhardt's show. As they waited together in the wings for the opening curtain, the Divine Sarah stroked the young girl's delicate curls admiringly and uttered something to her in French, a language Miss Gish had never before heard.

11. AKRON, OHIO, 1921. HARVEY FIRESTONE GIVES WENDELL WILLKIE A PARTING PREDICTION

After serving a couple of years as legal counsel to Firestone Tire and Rubber Company, 29-year-old Willkie decided to switch to private practice. In saying good-bye to the young attorney, Firestone, 53, spoke bluntly: "I like you, young man, but I don't think you will ever amount to a great deal." "Why not?" asked Willkie. "Because I understand you are a Democrat, and no Democrat can ever amount to much," Firestone replied. Nineteen years later, Willkie ran for U.S. president—as a Republican.

12. MIDDLEBURY, VERMONT, 1925. B. F. SKINNER MEETS ROBERT FROST

In 1925, "Fred" Skinner was a college student and aspiring author. While attending the Bread Loaf School of English that summer, he met Pulitzer Prize–winning poet Robert Frost, who asked Skinner to send him some samples of his writing. After reading Skinner's short stories, Frost responded with high praise: "You are worth more than anyone else I have seen in prose this year." Greatly encouraged, Skinner spent a year and a half unsuccessfully pursuing a literary career before concluding that he "had nothing important to say." He instead moved on to a career in science, becoming famous and controversial as the main proponent of behaviorism.

13. NEW YORK CITY, ca. 1945. NANCY REAGAN DATES CLARK GABLE

Gable dated the future first lady—then known as Nancy Davis and an aspiring actress—on three occasions during a visit to New York. Although gossip columnists speculated about a possible marriage, the relationship was never particularly romantic. Gable simply enjoyed seeing the town with Nancy and making her laugh, while she hero-worshipped Gable and wondered how long it would last. Once when they attended a party, she was convinced that Gable would leave her the moment a more glamorous woman appeared. When he stayed, it gave her self-confidence a great boost.

14. **NEW HAVEN, CONNECTICUT, 1948. GEORGE BUSH MEETS BABE RUTH**

Ruth was in New Haven to donate a signed manuscript of *The Babe Ruth Story* to the Yale library. He presented the book to the captain of the Yale baseball team, first baseman George Bush. Later that day, with the Sultan of Swat watching from the stands, the future U.S. president went two for four and led Yale to a 14–2 blowout over Princeton.

15. **GAINESVILLE, FLORIDA, 1962. TOM PETTY MEETS ELVIS PRESLEY**

When future rock star Petty was 11 years old, Elvis arrived in his hometown to shoot scenes for the movie *Follow That Dream*. Since his uncle was involved with making the film, Petty was able to visit the set and meet the king of rock 'n' roll. Petty remembered, "He didn't have much to say to us, but for a kid at an impressionable age, he was an incredible sight." Straightaway, Petty traded his slingshot for a friend's collection of Elvis records.

16. **WASHINGTON, D.C., 1963. BILL CLINTON SHAKES HANDS WITH JOHN F. KENNEDY**

In the summer of 1963, Clinton was named one of the delegates to Boys Nation, an American Legion program in which a select group of high school juniors traveled to Washington to watch national politics in action. The highlight of the trip was the delegates' visit to the White House, where a gangly, crew-cut Clinton briefly shook hands with President Kennedy. The moment was recorded for posterity (and future Clinton campaigns) in a photo and on film. When Clinton returned home to Arkansas, he was set on a political career. His mother, Virginia Kelley, remembered, "I'd never seen him so excited about something. When he came back from Washington, holding this picture of himself with Jack Kennedy, and the expression on his face—I just knew that politics was the answer for him."

17. **CHELTENHAM, ENGLAND, LITERARY FESTIVAL, 1963. JOHN FOWLES MEETS IRIS MURDOCH**

When best-selling author John Fowles was on the verge of success, but was not yet famous, he was a panelist at the Cheltenham Festival. He was prepared to attack the famous authoress Iris Murdoch, but instead found her "a gentle creature with a good mind." Mrs. Fowles felt Murdoch ignored them. Years later, when Fowles's fame was enormous, Murdoch invited the Fowleses to lunch. He recorded the following exchange in his diary:

I.M.: Are you religious?

J.F.: Not at all . . .

I.M.: Nor am I.

J.F.: in the normal sense of the word.

I.M.: Ah. (long Pinter-like silence, contemplation of the lawn outside.) I expect you have a nice intellectual circle at Lyme Regis? [The extremely remote country area where Fowles lived.]
J.F.: Are you mad?

W.A.D. & C.F.

30 Achievers After the Age of 86

1. At 100, Grandma Moses was painting.
2. At 99, David Eugene Ray of Franklin, Tennessee, started to learn to read.
3. At 99, Mieczyslaw Horszowski, the classical pianist, recorded a new album.
4–5. At 99, twin sisters Kin Marita and Gin Danie recorded a hit CD single in Japan and starred in a television commercial.
6. At 98, ceramist Beatrice Wood exhibited her latest work.
7. At 97, Martin Miller of Indiana was working full-time as a lobbyist for senior citizens.
8. At 96, Gus Langner swam the 1,500-meter freestyle in 47 minutes, 30.40 seconds.
9. At 96, Kathrine Robinson Everett was practicing law in North Carolina.
10. At 95, choreographer Martha Graham prepared her dance troupe for their latest performance.
11. At 94, Bertrand Russell was active in international peace drives.
12. At 94, comedian George Burns performed at Proctor's Theater in Schenectady, New York—63 years after he first played there.
13. At 94, Portuguese filmmaker Manoel de Olveira directed *A Talking Picture*—61 years after he directed his first feature.
14. At 93, actress Dame Judith Anderson gave a one-hour benefit performance.
15. At 93, George Bernard Shaw wrote the play *Farfetched Fables*.
16. At 93, Lillian Gish costarred with Bette Davis in the film *The Whales of August*. It was her ninety-sixth screen role and came 75 years after her acting debut.
17. At 93, mystery writer Phyllis Whitney published her seventy-sixth book, *Amethyst Dreams*.
18. At 92, Fauja Singh completed the London Marathon in 6 hours, 2 minutes, 43 seconds. Five months later, in Toronto, he ran a marathon in 5 hours, 40 minutes, 1 second.
19. At 91, Hulda Crooks climbed Mt. Whitney, the highest mountain in the continental United States.
20. At 91, Armand Hammer actively headed Occidental Petroleum.
21. At 91, Adolph Zukor was chairman of Paramount Pictures.
22. At 90, Eamon de Valera served as president of Ireland.
23. At 90, Pablo Picasso was producing drawings and engravings.

24. At 89, Arthur Rubinstein gave one of his greatest recitals in New York's Carnegie Hall.
25. At 89, Albert Schweitzer headed a hospital in Africa.
26. At 88, Pablo Casals was giving cello concerts.
27. At 88, Michelangelo prepared architectural plans for the Church of Santa Maria degli Angeli.
28. At 88, Konrad Adenauer was chancellor of Germany.
29. At 88, Doris Eaton Travis graduated from the University of Oklahoma with a degree in history.
30. At 87, Mary Baker Eddy founded the *Christian Science Monitor*.

CHAPTER TWO

MOVIES

21 MOVIE STARS AND HOW THEY WERE DISCOVERED

12 MOVIE STARS WHO FELL IN LOVE ON THE SET

8 MEMORABLE LINES ERRONEOUSLY ATTRIBUTED TO FILM STARS

24 ACTORS AND ACTRESSES WHO TURNED DOWN GREAT ROLES

MARY ASTOR'S 10 GREATEST MOVIE ACTRESSES

GLENDA JACKSON'S 10 ACTRESSES WHO MOST INFLUENCED HER

OLIVER STONE'S 12 BEST POLITICAL FILMS

PATRICK ROBERTSON'S 12 MORE TALES OF THE MOVIES

JOHN WAYNE'S 5 BEST MOTION PICTURES

THE 7 FILMS IN WHICH JOHN WAYNE DIED

GRACE DE MONACO'S 5 BEST MOTION PICTURES

JANE FONDA'S 4 BEST MOTION PICTURES OF ALL TIME

SEAN CONNERY'S 10 FAVORITE MOVIES OF ALL TIME

ROBERT DUVALL'S 10 FAVORITE MOVIES OF ALL TIME

15 FILM SCENES LEFT ON THE CUTTING ROOM FLOOR

11 MOVIES THAT WERE PART OF HISTORY

FEDERICO FELLINI'S 10 FAVORITE FILMS

WILLIAM WYLER'S 10 GREATEST FILMS OF ALL TIME

ROBERT WISE'S 5 BEST MOTION PICTURE DIRECTORS OF ALL TIME

PEDRO ALMODÓVAR'S 10 BEST FILMS OF ALL TIME

ROGER CORMAN'S 10 FAVORITE MOVIES

WILLIAM FRIEDKIN'S 10 FAVORITE MOVIES

STEPHEN KING'S 6 SCARIEST SCENES EVER CAPTURED ON FILM

JOHN WATERS'S 10 FAVORITE OVERLOOKED MOVIES

WALTER MATTHAU'S 10 FAVORITE COMEDIES

41 FAMOUS WRITERS WHO WORKED FOR THE MOVIES

HENRY MANCINI'S 10 HARDEST FILMS TO SCORE

15 COMMERCIAL FILM TITLES THAT MIGHT AS WELL BE PORNO TITLES

SEABISCUIT INFLATABLE EXTRAS
© The Inflatable Crowd Company, Inc.

21 Movie Stars and How They Were Discovered

1. **RICHARD ARLEN**
He was working as a film lab runner at Paramount Studios in 1922 when he was struck by a company car and hospitalized with a broken leg. Studio executives took notice and offered him a chance to act.

2. **FATTY ARBUCKLE**
The hefty comedian got his first break due to a blocked drain. Working as a plumber's assistant, he was summoned to unclog Mack Sennett's pipes in 1913, and the producer immediately offered him a job in his Keystone Kops comedies.

3. **MARY ASTOR**
She was unexpectedly brought to the attention of Harry Durant of the story department at Famous Players–Lasky Corporation in New York in 1920. Her father was applying for a script translator job when Durant spotted some photos of Mary that Mr. Astor had in his possession.

4. **WALTER BRENNAN**
He got his start in Hollywood in 1932, when he did a voice-over for a donkey. The actor volunteered to help a film director who was having difficulty getting the animal to bray on cue.

5. **ELLEN BURSTYN**
She was cast in her first major role in *Tropic of Cancer* (1969) on the basis of a political speech that director Joseph Strick heard her deliver.

6. **GARY COOPER**
Working as a stunt man, he was noticed by director Henry King on the set of *The Winning of Barbara Worth* at Samuel Goldwyn Studios in 1926.

7. **ANDY DEVINE**
Clad in a Santa Clara University football sweater, Devine was walking down Hollywood Boulevard in 1925 when he passed a Universal Studios casting director. He was recruited on the spot to play an athlete in a studio serial.

8. **FARRAH FAWCETT**
She was a freshman at the University of Texas in 1968, when she was voted a winner in the Ten Most Beautiful Contest. Photos of the winners were sent to Hollywood and came to the attention of publicist

David Mirisch, who persuaded Fawcett's parents to allow her to come to Hollywood.

9. **ERROL FLYNN**

He was discovered by Cinesound Studios casting director John Warwick in Sydney, Australia, in 1932. Warwick found some amateur footage of Flynn taken in 1930 by Dr. Herman F. Erben, a filmmaker and tropical-disease specialist who had chartered navigator Flynn's schooner for a tour of New Guinea headhunter territory.

10. **ROCK HUDSON**

Hudson, whose original name was Roy Fitzgerald, was working as a truck driver for the Budget Pack Company in 1954, when another driver offered to arrange a meeting between him and agent Henry Willson. In spite of Fitzgerald's professed lack of faith in his acting abilities, Willson took the aspiring actor under his wing, changed his name to Rock Hudson, and launched his career.

11. **JANET LEIGH**

She was a psychology student, when MGM star Norma Shearer happened to see a photo of her at a ski lodge in Northern California, where her parents were employed. Shearer took it to the studio with the result that Leigh was given a role in *The Romance of Rosy Ridge* (1947).

12. **GINA LOLLOBRIGIDA**

An art student in Rome, she was stopped on the street by director Mario Costa. She let loose a torrent of abuse about men who accost defenseless girls, and only when she paused for breath was he able to explain that he wanted to screen-test her for *Elisir d'Amore* (1946). She won the part.

13. **CAROLE LOMBARD**

She met director Allan Dwan in Los Angeles in the spring of 1921. Dwan watched 12-year-old Carole—then tomboy Jane Alice Peters—playing baseball outside the home of his friends Al and Rita Kaufman.

14. **MYRNA LOY**

She was singled out by Rudolph Valentino in 1923, when Henry Waxman at Warner Brothers Studios showed him several photographs of chorus girls.

15. **IDA LUPINO**

She was introduced to director Allan Dwan in England in 1933, while he was casting a film, *Her First Affair*. Forty-one-year-old Connie Emerald was trying out for a part, but Dwan found her 15-year-old daughter Ida better suited for the role.

16. **MAE MARSH**

One of the first actresses to achieve screen stardom without previous stage experience, Marsh was a 17-year-old salesgirl when she stopped by the Biograph Studios to see her sister, Marguerite Loveridge. She was spotted by director D. W. Griffith, who was having problems because none of his contract players was willing to play the lead in *Man's Genesis* (1912) with bared legs. Marsh had no such inhibitions when Griffith offered her the part.

17. **RYAN O'NEAL**

He was befriended by actor Richard Egan in 1962 at the gymnasium where they both worked out. "It was just a matter of Ryan himself being so impressive," said Egan.

18. **TELLY SAVALAS**

He was teaching adult education classes in Garden City, New Jersey, when an agent asked him if he knew an actor who could speak with an European accent. He tried out himself and landed a part in *Armstrong Circle Theater* on television.

19. **CHARLIZE THERON**

The South African–born actress studied dance and modeled in Milan and New York before heading to Los Angeles to pursue her dream of acting. After several difficult months in L.A., she was discovered in a Hollywood Boulevard bank. When a teller refused to cash an out-of-town check for her, she threw an enormous tantrum, which caught the attention of veteran talent manager John Crosby, who happened to be standing nearby. Crosby handed her his business card as she was being thrown out of the bank. After signing with Crosby, Theron landed a star-making role as a sexy assassin in 1996's *2 Days in the Valley*. She ended her association with Crosby in 1997 and has starred in such films as *The Cider House Rules, The Italian Job,* and *Monster,* which won her the Best Actress Oscar in 2004 for her portrayal of serial killer Aileen Wuornos.

20. **LANA TURNER**

She was spotted in Currie's Ice Cream Parlor across the street from Hollywood High School in January 1936. Billy Wilkerson, editor of the *Hollywood Reporter*, approached her while she was drinking a Coke.

21. **JOHN WAYNE**

He was spotted by director Raoul Walsh at Hollywood's Fox lot in 1928. Walsh was on his way to the administration building when he noticed Wayne—then Marion Morrison, a studio prop man—loading furniture from a warehouse onto a truck.

D.B. & C.F.

12 Movie Stars Who Fell in Love on the Set

1–2. VIVIEN LEIGH AND LAURENCE OLIVIER

Cast as lovers in *Fire over England* (1937), Leigh and Olivier had little difficulty playing the parts convincingly. They were both married when they became powerfully infatuated with each other. Leigh was the opposite of Olivier's cool, calm wife, and he was a contrast to her intelligent but rather dry and unromantic husband. The affair was ill-timed: Olivier's wife was about to give birth, and she guessed what was going on. At the christening party for his newborn son, Olivier stepped outside with Leigh and returned with lipstick on his cheek. On the set they were known as "the lovers." This was all too true for Olivier, who complained to another actor that he was exhausted. "It's not the stunts," he groaned. "It's Vivien. It's every day, two, three times. She's bloody wearing me out." He also felt guilty, "a really wormlike adulterer, slipping in between another man's sheets." Eventually, the two passionate actors divorced their respective spouses, and they married in 1940. Twenty years later, they divorced, and Olivier married his third wife, actress Joan Plowright.

3–4. RONALD REAGAN AND JANE WYMAN

Jane Wyman had a hard time getting going with Ronnie, as he was known on the set of *Brother Rat* (1938). Even before they were cast as lovers, she had noticed him around the studio and suggested, "Let's have cocktails at my place." He innocently replied, "What for?" Wyman didn't realize how straitlaced Ronnie was—although she was divorcing her husband, she was still officially married. When they finally began dating, they discovered they had little in common. She liked nightclubbing; he jabbered away about sports. Wyman loathed athletics, but she took up golf, tennis, and ice skating to be near Ronnie. "She's a good scout," Reagan told his mother after one date.

Reagan lived near his parents and visited them every day. Jane found his devotion and general goodness intimidating. It wasn't until the sequel to *Brother Rat*—*Brother Rat and a Baby* (1940)—that they began to date seriously. While their courtship was romantic, the proposal, Wyman recalled, "was about as unromantic as anything that ever happened. We were about to be called for a take. Ronnie simply turned to me as if the idea were brand-new and had just hit him and said, 'Jane, why don't we get married.'" They were wed in 1940 and divorced in 1948.

5–6. KATHARINE HEPBURN AND SPENCER TRACY

Having seen Tracy's work, Hepburn got him to act opposite her in MGM's *Woman of the Year* (1942), in which they would play feuding columnists who fall in love. The first time they met, she said, "I'm afraid I'm a little tall for you, Mr. Tracy." Their producer, Joseph Mankiewicz, turned to Hepburn and said, "Don't worry, Kate, he'll soon cut you down to size."

After a few days of sparring on the set—at first, Tracy referred to his costar as "Shorty" or "that woman"—an attraction began to develop between them. Tracy was married, although he lived apart from his wife, a Catholic who wouldn't consider divorce. As the pair fell in love, their relationship was treated with unusual respect by the gossip columnists and was rarely referred to in print. One of the great Hollywood love affairs, their romance lasted 25 years, until Tracy's death in 1967 of a heart attack.

Explaining the phenomenal success of their screen chemistry, Hepburn said, "Certainly, the ideal American man is Spencer. Sport-loving, a man's man . . . And I think I represent a woman. I needle him, I irritate him, and I try to get around him, yet if he put a big paw out, he could squash me. I think this is the sort of romantic ideal picture of the male and female in the United States." According to Hepburn biographers, the relationship was extremely dysfunctional.

7–8. LIZ TAYLOR AND RICHARD BURTON

The furor that attended the Burton-Taylor affair during the making of *Cleopatra* (1962) in Rome was as bombastic as the film they were starring in. Newspapers all over the world carried photos of the courting couple. Taylor was married at the time to Eddie Fisher, her fourth husband; Burton was also married.

In her memoirs, Taylor recalled their first conversation on the set. After the usual small talk, "he sort of sidled over to me and said, 'Has anybody ever told you that you're a very pretty girl?' And I said to myself, *Oy gevaldt*, here's the great lover, the great wit, the great intellectual of Wales, and he comes out with a line like that." Chemistry prevailed, however, and soon there was electricity on screen and off between the two stars. There were breakups and reconciliations, stormy fights and passionate clinches, public denials and private declarations, Liz's drug overdose and Richard's brief affair with a model. "Le Scandale," as Burton called it, grew so public that Liz was denounced by the Vatican and accused of "erotic vagrancy." Liz wondered, "Could I sue the Vatican?" During one love scene, director Joseph Mankiewicz yelled, "Cut! I feel as though I'm intruding."

Burton and Taylor married for the first time in 1964, divorced, remarried, and finally redivorced in 1976. Taylor said of *Cleopatra*, "It was like a disease. An illness one had a very difficult time recuperating from."

9–10. HUMPHREY BOGART AND LAUREN "BETTY" BACALL

When Bacall was cast opposite Bogart in *To Have and Have Not* (1944), she was disappointed. She was 19, and it was her first movie role. She said, "I had visions of playing opposite Charles Boyer and Tyrone Power. . . . But when [director Howard] Hawks said it was to be Bogart, I thought, 'How awful to be in a picture with that mug, that illiterate. . . . He won't be able to think or talk about anything.'" Bacall soon learned that she was confusing Bogey with the characters he played. She was so nervous the first day of shooting that her hands were shaking; Bogart was kind and amusing and teased her through it. Soon they were falling in love. He was 25 years her senior and unhappily married. Though the affair became serious, Bogart was reluctant to leave his wife. His friend Peter Lorre told him, "It's better to have five good years than none at all." Meanwhile, the courtship grew intensely romantic. In honor of Bacall's famous line in the movie, "If you want me, just whistle," Bogart gave her a small gold whistle. "Bogey," she said, "is the kind of fellow who sends you flowers." She is also rumored to have said "when he's drunk he thinks he's Bogart." They were married in 1945—he cried profusely at the wedding—and had 12 happy years until Bogart's death from cancer in 1957.

11–12. ANGELINA JOLIE AND BILLY BOB THORNTON

One of the twentieth century's most talked about bad-boy cinema stars, director-writer-actor Billy Bob Thornton struggled from poverty to worldwide acclaim with *Sling Blade* and a fast-and-furious series of roles and scripts. Equally fast and furious is his propensity for falling in and out of love. He was engaged to Laura Dern and professed happiness with his calm-at-last domestic life— he was finally spending time with his children by earlier mar-riages. Then, according to Dern, "I left our home to work on a movie, and while I was away, my boyfriend got married, and I've never heard from him again." Thornton and his bright, sexy costar Angelina Jolie were playing marrieds in 1999's *Pushing Tin*—in May 2000 they tied the knot in a quickie Las Vegas ceremony. The marriage was Thornton's fifth and was much publicized: The pair got complementary tattoos, exchanged vials of blood, and were notorious for their ribald public displays of affection. They adopted a Cambodian-born baby in June 2002, but 11 days after their son was brought to Los Angeles, Thornton abandoned his wife and child. Said Jolie, "It's clear to me that our priorities shifted overnight." Jolie had her tattoo removed; Thornton kept his. Laura Dern remarked in an interview that being dumped by Billy Bob was the best thing that could have happened to her.

8 Memorable Lines Erroneously Attributed to Film Stars

1. "Smile when you say that, pardner."
   What Gary Cooper actually said to Walter Huston in *The Virginian* (1929) was, "If you want to call me that, smile."

2. "Me Tarzan, you Jane."
   Johnny Weissmuller's first Tarzan role was in *Tarzan, the Ape Man* (1932). He introduced himself to costar Maureen O'Sullivan by thumping his chest and announcing, "Tarzan." He then gingerly tapped *her* chest and said, "Jane."

3. "You dirty rat."
   In fact, James Cagney never uttered this line in any of his roles as a hard-boiled gangster. It has often been used by impersonators, however, to typify his tough-guy image.

4. "Come with me to the Casbah."
   Charles Boyer cast seductive glances at Hedy Lamarr throughout *Algiers* (1938), but he never did make this suggestion. Delivered with a French accent, the line appeals to many Boyer imitators, who enjoy saying, "Come weez mee . . ."

5. "Why don't you come up and see me sometime?"
   Cary Grant found himself the recipient of Mae West's lusty invitation, "Why don't you come up sometime and see me?" in *She Done Him Wrong* (1933).

6. "Play it again, Sam."
   In *Casablanca* (1942) Ingrid Bergman dropped in unexpectedly at old lover Humphrey Bogart's nightclub, where she asked the piano player to "Play it, Sam," referring to the song "As Time Goes By." Although Bogart was shocked at hearing the song that reminded him so painfully of his lost love, he made Sam play it again—but the words he used were, "You played it for her, you can play it for me. . . . Play it."

7. "Judy, Judy, Judy."
   Cary Grant has never exclaimed this line in any film, but imitators often use it to display their Cary Grant–like accents.

8. "I want to be alone."
   In 1955, retired film star Greta Garbo—dispairing of ever being free of

publicity—said, "I want to be let alone." The melodramatic misinter-
pretation, however, is the way most people have heard and quoted it.

K.P.

24 Actors and Actresses Who Turned Down Great Roles

1. MARLON BRANDO
   Turned down the role of Frankie, the musician-junkie, in *The Man with the Golden Arm* (1955). Frank Sinatra got the part and reestablished his career with an electrifying performance.

2. JAMES CAGNEY
   Turned down the role of Alfred P. Doolittle in *My Fair Lady* (1964). The role went to Stanley Holloway. Cagney was offered $1 million but did not want to come out of retirement.

3. MONTGOMERY CLIFT
   Expressed enthusiasm for the role of the young writer in *Sunset Boulevard* (1950) but later turned it down, claiming that his audience would not accept his playing love scenes with a woman who was 35 years older. William Holden starred with Gloria Swanson in the widely acclaimed film.

4. SEAN CONNERY
   Long a fan-favorite to play Gandalf, the venerable wizard from J. R. R. Tolkien's *Lord of the Rings* trilogy, the star turned down the role because he did not want to spend 18 months filming in New Zealand. Sir Ian McKellen eventually played the role to wide acclaim. After the massive success of the first film, *The Fellowship of the Ring*, Connery said, "I had never read Tolkien, and the script when they sent it to me, I didn't understand . . . bobbits, hobbits."

5. BETTE DAVIS
   Turned down the role of Scarlett O'Hara in *Gone with the Wind* (1939). The role went to Vivien Leigh. Davis thought that her costar was going to be Errol Flynn, with whom she refused to work again, after the two had just finished shooting *The Private Lives of Elizabeth and Essex*.

6. KIRK DOUGLAS
   Turned down the role of Kid Shelleen in *Cat Ballou* (1965). The role won an Academy Award for Lee Marvin. Douglas's agent convinced him not to accept the comedic role of the drunken gunfighter.

7. **W. C. FIELDS**
Could have played the title role in *The Wizard of Oz* (1939). The part was written for Fields, who would have played the wizard as a cynical con man. But he turned down the part, purportedly because he wanted $100,000, and MGM offered him $75,000. However, a letter signed by Fields's agent asserts that Fields rejected the offer in order to devote all his time to writing *You Can't Cheat an Honest Man*. Frank Morgan ended up playing the wizard.

8. **JANE FONDA**
Turned down *Bonnie and Clyde* (1967). The role of Bonnie Parker went to Faye Dunaway. Fonda, living in France at the time, did not want to move to the United States for the role.

9. **CARY GRANT**
Producers Albert Broccoli and Harry Saltzman, who had bought the film rights to Ian Fleming's James Bond novels, originally approached Cary Grant about playing 007. Grant declined because he did not want to become involved in a film series. Instead, Sean Connery was cast as Bond, starting with *Dr. No* (1962). Fleming's comment on that casting choice: "He's not exactly what I had in mind."

10–11. **GENE HACKMAN AND MICHELLE PFEIFFER**
Orion Pictures acquired the film rights to *Silence of the Lambs* in 1988 because Gene Hackman had expressed an interest in directing and writing the screenplay for it. He would also star as serial killer Hannibal Lecter. By mid-1989, Hackman had dropped out of the project. Jonathan Demme took over as director and offered the female lead of FBI agent-in-training Clarice Starling to Michelle Pfeiffer, with whom he had worked in *Married to the Mob* (1988). Pfeiffer felt the film was too dark and declined the part. When *Silence of the Lambs* was made in 1990, the lead roles were played by Anthony Hopkins and Jodie Foster. Both won Academy Awards for their performances.

12. **ALAN LADD**
Turned down the role of Jett Rink in *Giant* (1956). The role went to James Dean. Ladd felt he was too old for the part.

13. **HEDY LAMARR**
Turned down the role of Ilsa in *Casablanca* (1942). Ingrid Bergman took over and, with Bogart, made film history. Lamarr had not wanted to work with an unfinished script.

14. **BURT LANCASTER**
Turned down the lead in *Ben-Hur* (1959). The role of Judah Ben-Hur went to Charlton Heston, who won an Academy Award and added another hit to his career of blockbusters.

15. MYRNA LOY

Turned down the lead (Ellie Andrews) opposite Clark Gable (Peter Warne) in *It Happened One Night* (1934). The role led to an Academy Award for Claudette Colbert. A previous film set on a bus had just failed, and Loy thought the film would not have a chance.

16. MICHAEL MADSEN

After his menacing performance in *Reservoir Dogs* (1992), Madsen was offered the role of Vincent Vega in Quentin Tarantino's follow-up, *Pulp Fiction* (1994). He turned it down because he was involved in the making of *Wyatt Earp* (1994), in which he was playing Virgil Earp. *Pulp Fiction* was an enormous success with audiences and critics. *Wyatt Earp* wasn't. John Travolta, who played Vincent Vega, found his career on the upswing, while Madsen found himself playing parts in a series of B pictures. "I wanted to take a walk down to the OK Corral," Madsen has been quoted as saying. "If I'd known how long a walk it was gonna be, I'd have taken a cab."

17–18. EWAN McGREGOR AND WILL SMITH

Both of these stars turned down the role of Neo in the blockbuster science fiction epic *The Matrix*, which eventually went to Keanu Reeves. McGregor starred as the young Obi-Wan Kenobi in *Star Wars: The Phantom Menace* instead, while Smith, who went on to star in the film version of Isaac Asimov's *I, Robot*, admitted, "I watched Keanu's performance—and very rarely do I say this—but I would have messed it up. I would have absolutely messed up *The Matrix*. At that point, I wasn't smart enough as an actor to let the movie be."

19. STEVE McQUEEN

When Paul Newman asked McQueen to star opposite him in *Butch Cassidy and the Sundance Kid* (1969), McQueen insisted on top billing. When his demand was turned down, he refused to appear in the film. Robert Redford played Sundance and became the most sought-after star of the '70s. McQueen turned down the lead role of Popeye Doyle in *The French Connection* (1971) because he felt the part was too similar to the tough cop he had played in *Bullitt* (1969). Gene Hackman got the part and won an Oscar for it. Finally, when director Francis Ford Coppola offered McQueen the starring role of Captain Willard in *Apocalypse Now* (1979), McQueen declined because he did not want to spend 16 weeks—Coppola's original shooting schedule—on location in the Philippine jungles, away from his new bride, Ali MacGraw. Martin Sheen, who accepted the role, ended up spending a year and a half on location and almost died from a massive heart attack during the filming. Nonetheless, he turned in an electrifying performance.

20. PAUL MUNI
Turned down the role of Roy Earle in *High Sierra* (1941). The role
went to Humphrey Bogart, who lifted the part to near-mythic quality.
Muni was tired of playing gangsters.

21. GREGORY PECK
The producer of *High Noon* (1952), Stanley Kramer, originally offered
the role of Will Kane, the retiring marshal who stays in town to con-
front the gunmen out to kill him, to Gregory Peck. Peck turned it down
because he thought it similar to the part of Jimmy Ringo, an aging
gunslinger haunted by his own reputation, which he had played in *The
Gunfighter* (1950). Several other actors, including Montgomery Clift,
Charlton Heston, and Marlon Brando, were approached before Gary
Cooper was signed to play Kane. He went on to win an Oscar for Best
Actor for his performance.

22. GEORGE RAFT
Turned down the main roles in *High Sierra* (1941), *The Maltese Falcon*
(1941), and *Casablanca* (1942), which became three of Humphrey
Bogart's most famous roles. Raft rejected the Sam Spade role in *The
Maltese Falcon* because he did not want to work with director John
Huston, an unknown at that time.

23. ROBERT REDFORD
Turned down the role of Ben Braddock in *The Graduate* (1967). The
role made an instant star of Dustin Hoffman. Redford thought he could
not project the right amount of naiveté.

24. EVA MARIE SAINT
Known for her selectivity in choosing roles, she turned down the central
role in *The Three Faces of Eve* (1957) after reading an early version of
the script. Joanne Woodward won an Oscar for her performance in the
film.

R.S. & C.F.

Mary Astor's
10 Greatest Movie Actresses
(Not Necessarily in This Order)

Born on May 3, 1906, in Quincy, Illinois, Mary Astor made her first screen
appearance at the age of 14. Perhaps best remembered for playing one of
the American crime film's greatest femme fatales, Brigid O'Shaughnessy in

The Maltese Falcon (1941), she appeared in numerous films, including *The Palm Beach Story* (1942), *Meet Me in St. Louis* (1944), and *Hush . . . Hush, Sweet Charlotte* (1964). She died of a heart attack in Woodland Hills, California, on September 25, 1987. Astor contributed the following list to *The Book of Lists* in 1983:

1. Greta Garbo
2. Lillian Gish
3. Sophia Loren
4. Jane Fonda
5. Vanessa Redgrave
6. Wendy Hiller
7. Maria Ouspenskaya
8. Bette Davis
9. Katharine Hepburn
10. Ingrid Bergman

Glenda Jackson's
10 Actresses Who Most Influenced Her

Born May 9, 1936, in the United Kingdom, Glenda Jackson first gained prominence for her performance in the Royal Shakespeare Company's 1964 production of *Marat/Sade* (she also appeared in the 1967 film version). Her numerous movie credits include *Women in Love* (1969) and *A Touch of Class* (1973), both of which earned her Oscars, as well as *Sunday Bloody Sunday* (1971), *Hopscotch* (1980), and *The Rainbow* (1989). In 1992, she was elected a member of Parliament for the Labor Party and was appointed junior transport minister in 1997.

1. Bette Davis
2. Joan Crawford
3. Barbara Stanwyck
4. Arletty
5. Marie Bell
6. Greta Garbo
7. Sybil Thorndike
8. Simone Signoret
9. Thelma Ritter
10. Kim Stanley

Oliver Stone's
12 Best Political Films

Born September 15, 1946, Oliver Stone served a tour of duty in Vietnam in 1967, during which he earned a Bronze Star and a Purple Heart. He won his first Academy Award for writing *Midnight Express* (1978); his other screenplay credits include *Conan the Barbarian* (1982), *Scarface* (1983), and *Year of the Dragon* (1985). As a director, he has won two Oscars, for *Platoon* (1986) and *Born on the Fourth of July* (1989). His other films include *Salvador* (1986), *The Doors* and *JFK* (both 1991), *Natural Born Killers* (1994), *Nixon* (1995), and *Alexander* (2004). He is also the author of a novel, *A Child's Night Dream,* which was published in 1997.

1. *Mr. Smith Goes to Washington* (1939)
   Idealism intersects reality.

2. *Z* (1969)
   The first conspiracy film that unfolds like a thriller.

3. *Fail-Safe* (1964)
   Intense Cold War dystopia done in stark television style.

4. *Dr. Strangelove or: How I Learned to Stop Worrying and Love the Bomb* (1964)
   Adds humor to the Cold War cocktail of dread.

5. *Seven Days in May* (1964)
   The coup d'état that actually occurred and is still unacknowledged—President John Kennedy himself said this would happen if he had another Bay of Pigs.

6. *The Manchurian Candidate* (1962)
   Brilliant Cold War paranoia from Richard Condon, and, as time has confirmed, it is true.

7. *Battleship Potemkin* (1925)
   First successful intersection of film and politics to create change.

8. *Viva Zapata!* (1952)
   My model for *Salvador*—revolutionary as hero, classic finale.

9. *Citizen Kane* (1941)
   Revolutionary as antihero undone by politics.

10. *The Battle of Algiers* (1965)
    Classic mix of documentary and drama, rigorous discipline in its
    perception of "objectivity."

Stone Notes: And two more with apologies: 11–12. *JFK* and *Salvador.*
Because I never thought either could get made, much less appreciated by a
large audience.

Patrick Robertson's
12 More Tales of the Movies

Patrick Robertson's earlier selections of movie lore appeared in *The Book
of Lists #3* and *The Book of Lists 90's Edition.* He is the author of *The
Book of Firsts* and the continuously updated *Guinness Movie Facts and
Feats,* both of which have appeared in many languages, and is currently
engaged on *The Book of American Firsts.*

1. DISNEY'S HOLY GRAIL
   The rarest and most sought-after cartoon film of all time was rediscovered in 1998 when a 16 mm print, bought in London for £2 from the
   disposal of the Wallace Heaton Film Library in the late 1970s, was
   identified as the only known copy of Walt Disney's first-ever production, the seven-minute *Little Red Riding Hood.* It was made in 1922 at
   Disney's Laugh-O-Gram Films, a small animation studio he established
   in Kansas City that went bankrupt within a year. *Little Red Riding
   Hood* is particularly notable to Disney buffs because, unlike the later
   Hollywood cartoons, such as Mickey Mouse, it was drawn by the 21-
   year-old fledgling filmmaker himself. The reason the unique print
   remained unidentified for so long was that the pirated copy bought by
   silent-movie collector David Wyatt had been retitled *Grandma Steps
   Out.* Only when he took it to the Disney company 20 years later was it
   revealed that the holy grail of animated films had been found at last.

2. DYNASTY
   Two families vie for the accolade of most generations of film stars, the
   Redgraves of England, Australia, and America and the Kapoors of
   India, each with four and counting. Roy Redgrave, father of revered
   thespian Sir Michael, acted in Australian movies from 1911 to 1920. Sir
   Michael Redgrave married actress Rachel Kempson, and their two
   daughters, Vanessa and Lynn, and son, Corin, all went into movies, as
   did Vanessa's daughters, Natasha and Joely Richardson, and Corin's
   daughter, Jemma Redgrave.

No fewer than 24 members of the Kapoor family have been screen actors since the debut of patriarch Prithviraj Kapoor in the 1929 silent film *Be Dhari Talwar*. His three sons, Raj, Shammi, and Shashi, all followed him into movies with spectacular success. The fourth generation is represented by Bollywood leading ladies Karishma and Kareena Kapoor, daughters of actor Randhir, son of Raj, and his actress wife, Babita.

So which of the families will be the first to produce a fifth generation of luminaries of the silver screen? My money is on the Redgraves. Word has it that Roy's teenage great-great-granddaughter Daisy is scoring straight As in acting class.

3. FATHER OF THE FEATURE

Every movie buff knows that in the early days of cinema, all films were one-reelers until D. W. Griffith came along and invented the full-length feature film with epics like *Birth of a Nation* (1915) and *Intolerance* (1916). Right? Wrong. The first full-length feature film was called *The Story of the Kelly Gang*, about desperado Ned Kelly, and it was made in Australia in 1906. Nor was this just a one-off. Other Australian features followed, with no fewer than 16 in 1911, the first year in which other countries began to make full-length movies, with France, Denmark, Germany, Italy, Poland, Russia, Serbia, and Spain in the vanguard. In 1912, Hungary made more features than any other country, and in 1913 it was Germany. With imports flooding in from France, Germany, Italy, and Denmark, American producers were finally forced to accept what they had steadfastly refused to believe: that the kind of unsophisticated people who frequented movie houses were able to concentrate on a story lasting as much as an hour and a half. There was an explosion of production in 1914, with the United States releasing no fewer than 212 features, of which one, *Judith of Bethulia*, was indeed by D. W. Griffith. But it is the long-forgotten Melbourne theatrical impresario Charles Tait, producer and director of *The Story of the Kelly Gang*, who should be honored as the true father of the feature-length movie.

4. THE CRYING GAME

Not all actresses can cry to order, and some directors have been known to resort to less than gentle measures to coax tears from the dry-eyed. Maureen O'Sullivan's tear ducts failed to respond in her deathbed scene as Dora in *David Copperfield* (1935) until director George Cukor positioned himself out of camera range of the bed and twisted her feet sharply and painfully. Victor Fleming achieved the same effect with Lana Turner, never noted as one of Hollywood's most accomplished thespians, by jerking her arm behind her back and giving it a vicious twist during the filming of *Dr. Jekyll and Mr. Hyde* (1941).

Kim Novak, unable to produce tears on demand in the waterfall scene with William Holden in *Picnic* (1955), asked director Joshua Logan to pinch her arms hard enough to make her cry. The scene took seven takes, and after each one a makeup artist swabbed Novak's arms to cover up the marks. Logan was so distressed by the need to inflict physical hurt on his star that he threw up afterward. Later, Novak accused him of un-prompted physical abuse when she recalled the episode.

Gregory La Cava was able to obtain convincing tears from Ginger Rogers in response to Katharine Hepburn's calla lilies speech in *Stage Door* (1937) only when he announced to her that a message had just come through saying that her home had been burned to the ground. Norman Taurog directed his own nephew, Jackie Cooper, in *Skippy* (1931). When he was unable to get the 10-year-old to cry on cue, he told him that he would have his dog shot. The ensuing waterworks helped young Cooper on his way to what would be the youngest Oscar nomina-tion for the next 40 years.

Otto Preminger stooped even lower when he needed spontaneous tears from a dozen small Israeli children in a scene in *Exodus* (1960) to show their fear of an imminent Arab attack. He told them that their mothers no longer wanted them and had gone away, never to return.

Whatever the vicissitudes of Hollywood, things were worse for child stars in Hong Kong. Veteran actress Josephine Siao Fong-Fong recalled her days as the colony's most famous juvenile of the 1950s: "If you were shooting a scene where you had to cry, and they were afraid you wouldn't be able to deliver, they simply beat you with a rattan cane till you did."

5. IRISH EYES WERE SMILING
Ireland had always been notorious for the vigilance of its censors. Surprisingly, though, Roman Polanski's 1962 debut feature, *Knife in the Water,* a film with strong homosexual overtones, passed unscathed. It was argued that homosexuality was quite unknown to the Irish and what they did not understand could not harm them. An earlier generation of censors had been less tolerant. In 1932, the Marx Brothers' slapstick comedy *Monkey Business* was banned, lest it provoke the Irish to anarchy.

6. MARRIED TO THE MOB
One of the most notorious examples of oppressive censorship occurred at the hands not of a censorship board but of what might be loosely described as a pressure group. The picture was *The Godfather;* those who were affronted were the Mafia; and the pressure group was the Italian American Civil Rights League, headed by Joseph Colombo. When the league attempted to halt production of the film, producer Albert S. Ruddy decided it would be in the interests of his personal well-being and prospects of longevity to meet with Mr. Colombo and others for a full and frank exchange of views. After protracted negotia-tions, during which the league asserted that the Mafia did not exist and was a figment of collective hysteria, they made him an offer he couldn't refuse. The film could go ahead with no fear of retribution from a

nonexistent underworld brotherhood, provided the word *Mafia* was wholly excised from the script. Ruddy declared that he had no wish to cast a slur on the blameless lives led by New York's Italian-American community and agreed to the league's suggestion. As it happened, Joseph Colombo was slain before the picture started, by persons alleged to belong to an organized crime syndicate composed of citizens of the same national origin as himself.

The Godfather (1972) was a sensation and became the top-grossing film of 1972 even without mention of the Mafia. But those who decried what they believed was a craven compromise with the mob were mistaken in their criticism. Mario Puzo, author of the original novel and scriptwriter of the film, wryly observed: "I must say that Ruddy proved himself a hard bargainer, because the word *Mafia* was never in the script in the first place."

7. PAY RAISE
Maybe you can't measure talent in dollars, but the moolah does say something about box-office appeal. While the second half of the 1990s saw a stable of male leads (Jim Carrey, Tom Cruise, Tom Hanks, Bruce Willis, Harrison Ford, Mel Gibson, Sylvester Stallone) crashing the $20 million barrier, on the distaff side the upfront fees for A-list leading ladies seemed pegged at a miserly $10 million. (What other profession is allowed to pay women half the rate of men in this day and age?) Then Demi Moore pushed the envelope with a $12.5 million paycheck for *Striptease*, but the picture bombed. Hard on her heels was Julia Roberts, who established herself as the undisputed number one female star with her hugely popular successes *Notting Hill* and *Runaway Bride*. For her next picture, the even bigger *Erin Brockovich*, the flame-haired beauty with the letter-box mouth became the first actress to join the $20 million upfront club. It had taken her 14 years since her debut in a long-forgotten 1986 flick called *Blood Red* to command a fee precisely 20,000 times the $1,000 she was paid on that one.

8. *SEABISCUIT* PICKED A WINNER
The 7,000 extras needed for the racetrack scenes in Universal's *Seabiscuit* (2003) would have put the movie into a severe budget bust at the standard fee of $50–60 per day. Savior of the movie was one Joe Biggins, the assistant to the unit production manager—not a role that normally wins plaudits from anyone other than the incumbent's mom. Biggins's inspiration was life-size inflatable dolls. Cheap to make and transport, they could be inflated three at a time with a portable pump in 12 seconds. Mixed in with a few live performers, the dolls could be computer-activated in postproduction to simulate crowd movement. With *Seabiscuit* in the can and on budget, a triumphant Biggins set up the Inflatable Crowd Co., offering 15,500 roll-up plastic "people" at $15 per week, compared with a $300-per-week tab for humans.

9. **SERGEANT VOSS'S PRIVATE ARMY**
Between 1923 and 1940, ex-sergeant Carl Voss commanded a private army. With a strength of 2,112 former World War I servicemen when it first appeared in the field of opposing American and German troops in *The Big Parade* (1925), the Voss Brigade took up arms again as Riff warriors, Hessians, Senegalese, Revolutionary Americans, Chinese, Romans, Maoris, and Crusaders in the years that followed. They not only would fight on both sides, but were equally adept as foot soldiers and cavalry; and as artillerymen it was said that there was no piece of ordnance they could not handle, from the Roman catapult to Big Bertha. Following a stint as Fascist troops in Chaplin's *The Great Dictator* (1940), their last battle was fought in *Four Sons* (1940), some ending as they had begun, as German soldiery, others as Czechs. On the eve of America's entry into World War II, the band of veterans was finally routed by the forces of bureaucracy. The Screen Actors Guild decreed that no agent could accept commission from an extra, and their commander Sergeant Voss was decreed to be acting as such. After 232 engagements without a serious casualty, the old soldiers faded away.

10. **WILLIAM WHO?**
In the United States before World War II, cinemas that had contracted to show a film had the right to pull out within a specified period. The number of cancellations for a big picture could be as few as 20, sometimes as high as 50. A spectacular new record was established in 1935 by Warner Bros.' star-studded *Midsummer Night's Dream*, with no fewer than 2,971 scratched contracts. It seemed that the booking agents had failed to reveal that this was a goddamn fairy story by a scripter from England, who had written it three hunnert and somp'n years ago, for chrissake.

11. **THE LAST STAR OF THE SILENTS**
Two actors who had starred in silent movies, and only two, were still performing in the twenty-first century. But with the death of Sir John Gielgud, who made his debut in *Who Is the Man* (1924) and his last screen appearance in David Mamet's *Catastrophe* (2000), only one survives. He is Mickey Rooney, who appeared at the age of five in *Not to Be Trusted* (1926) as a cigar-smoking midget, giving rise to an ongoing belief that he was a vertically challenged adult who played child roles. Starring as a teenaged, albeit diminutive, Andy Hardy with Judy Garland as his squeeze helped to lay the myth to rest, but MGM could not resist casting the 5' 3" Rooney opposite 6' 6" Dorothy Ford in *Love Laughs at Andy Hardy* (1947). These roles and the hundred or so that followed may not have had quite the gravitas of Sir John's, but Mickey outlived him to become not only the silent screen's last active survivor but one of twenty-first-century Hollywood's few actors of such unremitting energy that he puts in as many as four performances in a year.

12. MOST MARRIED

   The most married of many-times-wedded Hollywood stars was
   B-movie luminary Al "Lash" LaRue (1917–1996), who went to the
   altar and the divorce court on 10 occasions, finally ending a turbulent
   life—in which he had been charged with vagrancy, drunkenness,
   possession of marijuana (while practicing as an evangelist), and
   stealing candy from a baby in Florida, besides scripting porno
   movies—unmarried.

John Wayne's
5 Best Motion Pictures

Born Marion Morrison on May 26, 1907, in Winterset, Iowa, John "the
Duke" Wayne was one of the screen's most enduring and popular icons.
Best known for starring in classic Westerns such as John Ford's *The
Searchers* (1956) and Howard Hawks's *Rio Bravo* (1959), his diverse
filmography includes *The Longest Day* (1962), *The Man Who Shot Liberty
Valance* (1962), and numerous other features. Wayne was also the director-
producer (as well as star) of *The Alamo* (1960) and *The Green Berets*
(1968). He won the Academy Award for Best Actor in 1970 for his performance in *True Grit*. He eventually died of cancer; his final film appearance
was in *The Shootist* (1976), in which he played a gunfighter dying of cancer.
He contributed the following list to *The People's Almanac #2* in 1978,
shortly before his death:

1. *A Man for All Seasons*
2. *Gone with the Wind*
3. *The Four Horsemen of the Apocalypse*
4. *The Searchers*
5. *The Quiet Man*

The 7 Films in Which
John Wayne Died

John Wayne acted in 175 movies, specializing in the strong hero who saves
others and survives. But every now and then he did not manage to make
it out alive.

1. *Reap the Wild Wind* (1942)
2. *The Fighting Seabees* (1944)

3. *Wake of the Red Witch* (1949)
4. *Sands of Iwo Jima* (1949)
5. *The Alamo* (1960)
6. *The Cowboys* (1972)
7. *The Shootist* (1976)

Note: John Wayne also played the role of a corpse in *The Deceiver* (1931).

Grace De Monaco's
5 Best Motion Pictures

One of the cinema's greatest beauties, Grace Kelly (born in Philadelphia, Pennsylvania, in 1929) worked as a model and acted on stage before moving to Southern California to pursue a movie career. Her second film performance, opposite Gary Cooper in the classic Western *High Noon* (1952), proved to be a star-making break. Her other films included *The Country Girl* (for which she won the Best Actress Academy Award) and three collaborations with director Alfred Hitchcock (*Rear Window, Dial M for Murder*, and *To Catch a Thief*). At the height of her career, she married Prince Rainier III of Monaco and retired from acting. Princess Grace died in a road accident in Monaco on September 14, 1982. She contributed the following list to *The People's Almanac #2* in 1978:

1. *The Quiet Man*
2. *The Bicycle Thief*
3. *Gone with the Wind*
4. *La Grande Illusion*
5. *Some Like It Hot*

M.J.H.

Jane Fonda's
4 Best Motion Pictures of All Time

The daughter of actor Henry Fonda, Jane Fonda has been as controversial for her politics (especially her anti–Vietnam War activism) and her personal life (marriages to director Roger Vadim, activist Tom Hayden, and media mogul Ted Turner) as acclaimed for her roles in numerous films, including *The Chapman Report, Barbarella*, and Oscar-winning performances in *Klute* and *Coming Home*. She became an exercise guru in 1982 with the video *Jane Fonda's Workout*, which launched a fitness industry built around her name. In 2005, after more than a decade of semiretirement out of the public eye, Fonda reemerged with a best-selling autobiography, *My Life So Far*, and a new movie, *Monster-in-Law*.

1. *Citizen Kane*
2. *Les Enfants du Paradis*
3. *Paths of Glory*
4. *The Grapes of Wrath*

Sean Connery's
10 Favorite Movies of All Time

Born August 25, 1930, in Scotland, Sean Connery appeared on stage and in films like *Darby O'Gill and the Little People* before becoming a worldwide icon for his portrayal of suave secret agent James Bond in *Dr. No* (1962). His varied and acclaimed career includes not only seven Bond films, but also such movies as *The Molly Maguires, The Wind and the Lion, Highlander, The Untouchables* (which earned him an Oscar for Best Supporting Actor), and *The Rock*. He was knighted by Queen Elizabeth on New Year's Eve, 1999. A tireless performer, avid golfer, and male sex symbol, he was voted Sexiest Man of the Century by *People* magazine in 1999.

1. *The Seven Samurai*
2. *Seven Brides for Seven Brothers*
3. *Persona*
4. *The Best Years of Our Lives*
5. *Never on Sunday*
6. *On the Waterfront*
7. *The African Queen*
8. *Umberto D*
9. *The Gold Rush*
10. *Battleship Potemkin*

Robert Duvall's
10 Favorite Movies of All Time

Born on January 5, 1931, in San Diego, California, Robert Duvall served in the U.S. Army and studied acting in New York. He appeared on stage before landing his first film role in 1962, as Boo Radley in the classic movie adaptation of Harper Lee's *To Kill a Mockingbird*. His long and prestigious film career includes *M*A*S*H* (1970), *The Godfather* (1972), *The Godfather,*

Part II (1974), *Network* (1976), *Apocalypse Now* (1979), and *Tender Mercies* (1983). He has also acted to great acclaim on television in the miniseries *Lonesome Dove* (1989) and in the title role of the cable film *Stalin* (1992). Duvall has directed several films, including *The Apostle* (1997) and *Assassination Tango* (2002). In 1984, he won the Best Actor Academy Award for *Tender Mercies*.

1. *The Seven Samurai*
2. *Kes*
3. *The Godfather*
4. *Tomorrow*
5. *Pixote*
6. *The 400 Blows*
7. *Gunga Din*
8. *Alambrista!*
9. *The Great Dictator*
10. *Kagemusha*

Note: Kenneth Loach directed *Kes* (1970), a film about a young boy who trains a hawk. *Tomorrow,* a 1972 film directed by Joseph Anthony, stars Duvall in the story (adapted from William Faulkner) of a Mississippi cotton farmer who raises a child. *Pixote,* a 1981 movie by Brazilian director Hector Babenco, depicts the desperate lives of reform school boys who escape only to find that survival in the city is a lonely and dangerous business. *Alambrista!* first shown on TV in 1977, describes the plight of a Mexican farmworker who immigrates illegally to California. It was written, directed, and photographed by Robert M. Young.

15 Film Scenes Left on the Cutting Room Floor

1. FRANKENSTEIN (1931)
   In one scene, the monster (Boris Karloff) walks through a forest and comes upon a little girl, Maria, who is throwing flowers into a pond. The monster joins her in the activity but soon runs out of flowers. At a loss for something to throw into the water, he looks at Maria and moves toward her. In all American prints of the movie, the scene ends there. But as originally filmed, the action continues, to show the monster grabbing Maria, hurling her into the lake, and then departing in confusion when she fails to float as the flowers did. This bit was deleted because Karloff, objecting to the director's interpretation of the scene, felt that the monster should have gently put Maria into the lake. Though Karloff's intentions were good, the scene's omission

suggests a crueler death for Maria, since a subsequent scene shows her bloodied corpse being carried through the village by her father.

2. KING KONG (1933)

The original *King Kong* was released four times between 1933 and 1952, and each release saw the cutting of additional scenes. Though many of the outtakes—including the censored sequence in which Kong peels off Fay Wray's clothes—were restored in 1971, one cut scene has never been found. It is the clip in which Kong shakes four sailors off a log bridge, causing them to fall into a ravine, where they are eaten alive by giant spiders. When the movie—with spider sequence intact—was previewed in San Bernardino, California, in late January 1933, members of the audience screamed and either left the theater or talked about the grisly sequence throughout the remainder of the film. Said the film's producer, Merian C. Cooper, "It stopped the picture cold, so the next day back at the studio, I took it out myself."

3. TARZAN AND HIS MATE (1934)

Considered by many to be the best of the Tarzan films, *Tarzan and His Mate* included a scene in which Tarzan (Johnny Weissmuller), standing on a tree limb with Jane (Maureen O'Sullivan), pulls at Jane's scanty outfitand persuades her to dive into a lake with him. The two swim for a while and eventually surface. When Jane rises out of the water, one of her breastsis fully exposed. Because various groups, including official censors of the Hays Office, criticized the scene for being too erotic, it was cut by MGM.

4. THE WIZARD OF OZ (1939)

The Wizard of Oz originally contained an elaborate production number called "The Jitter Bug," which cost $80,000 and took five weeks to shoot. In the scene, Dorothy, the Scarecrow, the Cowardly Lion, and the Tin Man are on their way to the witch's castle when they are attacked by "jitter bugs"—furry pink and blue mosquito-like "rascals" that give one "the jitters" as they buzz about in the air. When, after its first preview, the movie was judged too long, MGM officials decided to sacrifice the "Jitter Bug" scene. They reasoned that it added little to the plot and, because a dance by the same name had just become popular, they feared it might date the picture. (Another number was also cut for previews because some felt it slowed the pacing, but it was eventually restored. Its title was . . . "Over the Rainbow.")

5. THE BIG SLEEP (1946)

This movie is famed as a classic despite its notoriously difficult-to-follow plot. As originally filmed, it included an aid for the viewer: Philip Marlowe (Humphrey Bogart) and a DA meet and have a conversation that summarizes the plot. The film was finished in 1945 but held out of release until the studio finished rolling out its backlog of World War II films. During the delay, the decision was made to reshoot several scenes to play up the chemistry between Bogart and Lauren Bacall. Also, a scene was added in which Bogart and Bacall meet in a nightclub and flirt while ostensibly talking about horse racing. In order to keep the running time of the film the same, the scene of Marlowe and the DA was cut.

6. SUNSET BOULEVARD (1950)
Billy Wilder's film classic about an aging Hollywood film queen and a down-on-his-luck screenwriter originally incorporated a framing sequence, which opened and closed the story at the Los Angeles County Morgue. In a scene described by Wilder as one of the best he'd ever shot, the body of Joe Gillis (William Holden) is rolled into the morgue to join three dozen other corpses, some of whom—in voice-over—tell Gillis how they died. *Eventually*, Gillis tells his story, which takes us to a flashback of his affair with Norma Desmond (Gloria Swanson). The movie was previewed with this opening, in Illinois and on Long Island. Because both audiences inappropriately found the morgue scene hilarious, the film's release was delayed six months so that a new beginning could be shot, in which police find Gillis's corpse floating in Norma's pool while Gillis's voice narrates the events leading to his death.

7. LIMELIGHT (1952)
Charlie Chaplin's film about a vaudeville comic on the decline features a scene in which Chaplin, as the elderly Calvero, makes his comeback in a music hall sketch. The routine, which originally ran 10 minutes, has Calvero performing on stage with an old colleague, played by Buster Keaton. It has been said that while Chaplin was good, Keaton was sensational. Consequently, Chaplin allowed only a small portion of the scene to remain in release prints.

8. THE SEVEN YEAR ITCH (1955)
Originally, the movie included a scene of Marilyn Monroe in the bathtub, getting her toe stuck in the faucet. Although Monroe remained covered by bubbles, the scene ran afoul of the Hollywood censors, so director Billy Wilder cut it.

9. SPARTACUS (1960)
Of the 167 days it took Stanley Kubrick to shoot *Spartacus*, six weeks were spent directing an elaborate battle sequence in which 8,500 extras dramatized the clash between Roman troops and Spartacus's slave army. Several scenes in the battle drew the ire of the Legion of Decency and were therefore cut. These included shots of men being dismembered. (Dwarfs with false torsos and an armless man with a phony "break-away" limb were used to give authenticity.) Seven years later, when the Oscar-winning film was reissued, an additional 22 minutes

were chopped out, including a scene in which Varinia (Jean Simmons) watches Spartacus (Kirk Douglas) writhe in agony on a cross. Her line "Oh, please die, my darling" was excised, and the scene was cut to make it appear that Spartacus was already dead.

10. SPLENDOR IN THE GRASS (1961)
As filmed, *Splendor in the Grass* included a sequence in which Wilma Dean Loomis (Natalie Wood) argues with her mother (Audrey Christie) while taking a bath. The bickering finally becomes so intense that Wilma jumps out of the tub and runs nude down a hallway to her bedroom, where the camera cuts to a close-up of her bare legs kicking hysterically on the mattress. Both the Hollywood censors and the Catholic Legion of Decency objected to the hallway display. Consequently, director Elia Kazan dropped the piece, leaving an abrupt jump from tub to bed.

11. DR. NO (1962)
The first of the James Bond films ended with Honey Ryder (Ursula Andress) being attacked by crabs when Bond (Sean Connery) rescues her. The crabs moved too slowly to look truly menacing, so the ending was reshot without them.

12. EVERYTHING YOU ALWAYS WANTED TO KNOW ABOUT SEX BUT WERE AFRAID TO ASK (1972)
"What Makes a Man a Homosexual?" was one of the many vignettes filmed for the Woody Allen movie using the title of Dr. David Reuben's best-selling book. The sequence stars Allen as a common spider anxious to court a black widow (Louise Lasser). After doing a mating dance on Lasser's web, Allen makes love to the widow, only to be devoured by her afterward. The scene was cut out of the film because Allen couldn't come up with a suitable way to end the piece.

13. BIG (1988)
In this film, Tom Hanks plays Josh, a 12-year-old who becomes an adult literally overnight when he makes a wish on a machine at a carnival. While an adult, Josh falls in love with a woman named Susan (Elizabeth Perkins), but he has to leave her behind when he makes another wish to become 12 again. In the original version, there was an additional scene at the end, in which Josh is back at school and a new girl named Susan arrives. The implication is that Susan went back to the carnival machine to make herself Josh's age. Due to negative audience feedback, the scene was cut from the movie.

14. JERRY MAGUIRE (1996)
Jerry Maguire originally included a fictional Reebok advertisement starring Rod Tidwell (Cuba Gooding, Jr.), which was cut from the film by director Cameron Crowe. However, when the movie was broadcast

on the Showtime cable network, the commercial was restored, playing under the closing credits. Reportedly, the scene was put back in because of a lawsuit filed by Reebok against Columbia Pictures over the terms of product placement in the film.

15. TITANIC (1997)

The film ends with Rose (Gloria Stuart) going to the deck of the research ship investigating the *Titanic* wreck, leaning over the railing, and dropping a necklace with the valuable "Heart of the Ocean" diamond into the ocean. As originally filmed, the crew members of the research ship see Rose, mistakenly believe that she is planning to jump overboard, and try to talk her out of committing suicide. When they realize what she is actually doing, they try to persuade her to preserve the necklace. Director James Cameron decided that he wanted the scene to focus on Rose, so he reshot it with her alone.

D.B. & C.F.

11 Movies That Were Part of History

1. MANHATTAN MELODRAMA (1934)

The film starred William Powell and Clark Gable as two street-wise city kids who grew up in opposite directions—one good, the other headed for the electric chair. The plot was old hat, even in 1934, but the film was enough to draw John Dillinger into the theater with the "lady in red." He had just left the theater when the tipped-off G-men sprang their trap and killed him in the ensuing fight.

2. LA GRANDE ILLUSION (1937)

Directed by pacifist Jean Renoir and starring Erich von Stroheim, this movie was being shown when the German army marched into Vienna in 1938. Not surprisingly, Nazi storm troopers invaded the theater and confiscated the World War I antiwar classic in midreel.

3. THE GREAT DICTATOR (1940)

Produced by, directed by, and starring Charlie Chaplin in 1940, the movie was a brilliant political satire on Nazi Germany. Hitler ordered all prints of the film banned, but when curiosity got the best of him, he had one brought in through Portugal and viewed it himself in complete privacy—not once, but twice. History does not record his views on the film.

4. FOXFIRE (1955)

Starring Jane Russell and Jeff Chandler, this film—a Universal production dealing with a dedicated mining engineer and his socialite wife—was playing in the tourist-section theater of the *Andrea Doria* on the foggy night in July 1956 when the liner collided with the *Stockholm*. The film was in its last reel when the collision occurred. Fifty people lost their lives in the tragedy.

5. ROCK AROUND THE CLOCK (1956)
This was a raucous celebration of rock 'n' roll starring Bill Haley and the Comets. In London, its young audience took the message to heart in September of 1956. After seeing the picture, more than 3,000 Teddy Boys left the theater to stage one of the biggest riots in recent British history.

6. CAN-CAN (1960)
A Twentieth Century-Fox production starring Frank Sinatra, Shirley MacLaine, and Maurice Chevalier, it was just a little too lavish for the taste of Soviet premier Nikita Khrushchev during his 1959 visit to the studio where it was being filmed. The Cold War heated up briefly when Khrushchev reacted with shocked indignation at the "perversity" and "decadence" of dancer MacLaine's flamboyantly raised skirts.

7. WAR IS HELL (1963)
A double bill featuring two B-style war movies was playing at the Texas Theatre in Dallas, where Lee Harvey Oswald was captured after the assassination of John F. Kennedy in 1963. *War Is Hell*, starring Tony Russell, had just begun, when Oswald called attention to himself by ducking into the theater without paying the 90¢ admission. He was apprehended by the police amid the sound of onscreen gunfire.

8. I AM CURIOUS (YELLOW) (1967)
The Swedish film starring Lena Nyman as a sexually active political sociologist was a shocking sensation in 1969. On October 6, 1969, though, Jackie Onassis was the one making headlines after she allegedly gave a professional judo chop to a New York news photographer who took pictures of her leaving the movie house showing the film.

9. MOHAMMED, MESSENGER OF GOD (1976)
Directed by Moustapha Akkad, this picture, which purported to be an unbiased, authentic study, evoked the wrath of the Hanafi Muslim sect, which assumed that the film would depict the image of the Prophet, an act they consider blasphemous. Demanding that the film be withdrawn from the Washington, D.C., theater where it was opening, small bands of Hanafi gunmen invaded the local city hall and two other buildings on March 10, 1977, killing one man and holding more than 100 hostages for two days before surrendering. Their protest turned out to be much ado about nothing. The Prophet was neither seen nor heard in the film; instead, actors addressed the camera as if it were the Prophet standing before them.

10. **THE DEER (GAVAZNHA) (1976)**

This Iranian film was being shown in the Cinema Rex theater in Abadan, Iran, on August 19, 1977, when arsonists set fire to the building, killing at least 377 people (an additional 45 bodies were discovered later in the charred ruins, but those were not included in the official government totals). Police arrested 10 members of a Muslim extremist group that opposed the shah's reforms and had been implicated in other theater and restaurant fires. However, another version of this incident was sent to the authors by an eyewitness who claims that police chained shut the theater doors and fended off the crowd outside with clubs and M16s. The fire department, only 10 minutes from the theater, reportedly did not arrive until the fire had burned itself out. Surprisingly, this witness found that most of the people had been burned to death in their seats.

11. **TAXI DRIVER (1976)**

John Hinckley, Jr., an underachiever from a well-to-do family, watched *Taxi Driver* (1976) more than a dozen times and became obsessed with Jodie Foster, who played a teenaged prostitute in the film. By this time, the actress was a student at Yale, where Hinckley left letters for her and tried to contact her by phone. Frustrated in his attempts to court Foster and apparently inspired by scenes in *Taxi Driver* in which Travis Bickle (Robert De Niro) plots to kill a presidential candidate, Hinckley began stalking President Jimmy Carter and then his successor, Ronald Reagan. On March 30, 1981, after writing a final letter of dedication to Foster, Hinckley pulled a revolver and shot Reagan outside the Washington Hilton. Reagan was wounded in the shooting, along with press secretary James Brady, Secret Service agent Timothy McCarty, and Washington, D.C., police officer Thomas Delaharty. At a jury trial the next year, Hinckley was found not guilty by reason of insanity. He was sent to St. Elizabeth's Hospital in Washington, D.C., where he still resides.

R.S.

Federico Fellini's
10 All-Time Favorite Films

Born in Rimini, Italy, on January 20, 1920, Federico Fellini began his film career as a screenwriter, coauthoring the scripts for *Open City* (1945) and *Paisan* (1946), both directed by Roberto Rossellini. Among the many classic films Fellini directed are four Academy Award winners—*La Strada* (1954), *The Nights of Cabiria* (1957), *8½* (1963), and *Amarcord*

(1974)—as well as *La Dolce Vita* (1959), *Juliet of the Spirits* (1965), and *Satyricon* (1969). Federico Fellini died in Rome on October 31, 1993. He contributed the following list to *The Book of Lists* in 1993:

1. Several Charles Chaplin pictures, in order by year: *The Circus* (1928), *City Lights* (1931), *Monsieur Verdoux* (1947)
2. *Stagecoach* (1939), by John Ford
3. A Marx Brothers picture or a Stan Laurel and Oliver Hardy picture
4. *Rashomon* (1950), by Akira Kurosawa
5. *Le Charme Discret de la Bourgeoisie* (*The Discreet Charm of the Bourgeoisie*, 1972), by Luis Buñuel
6. *2001: A Space Odyssey* (1968), by Stanley Kubrick
7. *Paisan* (1946), by Roberto Rossellini
8. *The Birds* (1963), by Alfred Hitchcock
9. *Smultronstället* (*Wild Strawberries*, 1957), by Ingmar Bergman
10. *8½* (1963), by Federico Fellini

William Wyler's
10 Greatest Films of All Time

Born Wilhelm Wyler in Germany on July 1, 1902, William Wyler had a career that spanned 45 years, during which he directed 70 feature films, ranging from historical epics such as *Ben-Hur* to literary adaptations such as *The Collector* (from the novel by John Fowles). His other acclaimed and award-winning films include *The Westerner, Mrs. Miniver, The Best Years of Our Lives*, and *Funny Girl*. Wyler was the recipient of three Academy Awards for Best Director and was nominated another nine times. He died of a heart attack on July 27, 1981, in Los Angeles. William Wyler contributed this list to *The Book of Lists* in 1977:

1. *The Cabinet of Dr. Caligari*
2. *The Battleship Potemkin*
3. *All Quiet on the Western Front*
4. Several Charlie Chaplin films
5. *Bridge on the River Kwai*
6. Marcel Pagnol's *Fanny* (not the musical)
7. *La Dolce Vita*
8. *The Treasure of the Sierra Madre*
9. *Dr. Strangelove*
10. and (with apologies) *The Best Years of Our Lives*

Robert Wise's
5 Best Motion Picture Directors of All Time

Born September 10, 1914, in Winchester, Indiana, Robert Wise began his cinematic career as a film editor, working on two of Orson Welles's classics, *Citizen Kane* and *The Magnificent Ambersons*. He made his directorial debut for RKO with *Curse of the Cat People* (1944). His prestigious and varied oeuvre includes the musical classics *West Side Story* and *The Sound of Music* (both of which won him Best Director Academy Awards), as well as *The Haunting* (1963), *The Sand Pebbles* (1966), *The Andromeda Strain* (1971), and *Star Trek: The Motion Picture* (1979). Wise died in Los Angeles September 14, 2005.

1. D. W. Griffith
2. Charles Chaplin
3. John Ford
4. Jean Renoir
5. William Wyler

Pedro Almodóvar's
10 Best Films of All Time

The most celebrated contemporary Spanish film director, Pedro Almodóvar was born on September 24, 1949. He made his first feature film in 1980 and gained international acclaim in 1988 with *Women on the Verge of a Nervous Breakdown*. His other films include *Tie Me Up! Tie Me Down!* (1990), *Live Flesh* (1997), *All About My Mother* (1999), and *Talk to Her* (2002). Regarding his profound relationship to the celluloid image, Almodóvar has said, "Cinema has become my life. I don't mean a parallel world, I mean my life itself. I sometimes have the impression that the daily reality is simply there to provide material for my next film."

1. *Viaggio in Italia (Journey to Italy)*, Roberto Rossellini
2. *Leave Her to Heaven*, John M. Stahl
3. *Opening Night*, John Cassavetes
4. *The Apartment*, Billy Wilder
5. *To Be or Not to Be*, Ernst Lubitsch
6. *El*, Luis Buñuel
7. *La Règle du Jeu (Rules of the Game)*, Jean Renoir
8. *The Quiet Man*, John Ford
9. *Out of the Past*, Jacques Tourneur
10. *North by Northwest*, Alfred Hitchcock

Roger Corman's
10 Favorite Movies

Born April 5, 1926, in Detroit, Michigan, Roger Corman is a director and producer whose name is synonymous with low-budget filmmaking outside the studio system. *The Little Shop of Horrors, The Intruder,* and a spate of Edgar Allan Poe adaptations (including *House of Usher, The Pit and the Pendulum,* and *The Raven*) are among his accomplishments as a director. As a producer, he helped launch the careers of such Hollywood notables as Francis Ford Coppola, Jack Nicholson, Peter Bogdanovich, Jonathan Demme, and James Cameron. Corman published his best-selling memoir, *How I Made a Hundred Movies in Hollywood and Never Lost a Dime,* in 1990.

1. *Battleship Potemkin,* Sergei Eisenstein, 1925
2. *La Grande Illusion,* Jean Renoir, 1937
3. *The Seventh Seal,* Ingmar Bergman, 1957
4. *I Vitelloni,* Federico Fellini, 1953
5. *Citizen Kane,* Orson Welles, 1941
6. *Lawrence of Arabia,* David Lean, 1962
7. *The 400 Blows,* François Truffaut, 1959
8. *The Grapes of Wrath,* John Ford, 1940
9. *Star Wars,* George Lucas, 1977
10. *An Outcast of the Islands,* Carol Reed, 1952

William Friedkin's
10 Favorite Movies

Born August 29, 1935, in Chicago, Illinois, William Friedkin began his career in television and documentaries before moving to features. His early films include such diverse movies as *Good Times* (1967), starring Sonny and Cher, and *The Birthday Party* (1968), adapted from the Harold Pinter play. In 1971, he directed *The French Connection* and became the youngest filmmaker in history to win the Best Director Oscar. In 1973, his adaptation of William Peter Blatty's horror novel *The Exorcist* became one of the most successful and controversial films in the history of cinema. His other films include *Sorcerer* (1977), *Cruising* (1980), *To Live and Die in L.A.* (1985), and *The Hunted* (2003). Friedkin is also a passionate classical music and opera fan and has directed productions of Alban Berg's *Wozzeck* in 1998 and Richard Wagner's *Tannhauser* in 2004. He lives in Los Angeles with his wife, producer Sherry Lansing.

1. *Citizen Kane*, Orson Welles
2. *All About Eve*, Joseph C. Mankiewicz
3. *The Treasure of the Sierra Madre*, John Huston
4. *Singin' in the Rain*, Stanley Donen and Gene Kelly
5. *The Band Wagon*, Vincente Minnelli
6. *Double Indemnity*, Billy Wilder
7. *2001*, Stanley Kubrick
8. *The Verdict*, Sidney Lumet
9. *Fatal Attraction*, Adrian Lyne
10. *Paths of Glory*, Stanley Kubrick

Stephen King's
6 Scariest Scenes Ever Captured on Film

One of the most popular, prolific, and influential writers in the history of American literature, Stephen King was born on September 21, 1947, in Portland, Maine. He attended college at the University of Maine at Orono, where he met his wife, Tabitha, who is also a best-selling author. Beginning with the 1974 publication of *Carrie*, King's best-selling output has included such novels as *The Stand, Pet Sematary, It, Misery, The Green Mile*, and *Bag of Bones*. Hit movies adapted from his works include *The Shining* (directed by Stanley Kubrick), *The Dead Zone* (directed by David Cronenberg), and *The Shawshank Redemption* (directed by Frank Darabont, and currently #2 on the Internet Movie Database's user poll of the top 250 films of all time). King himself has written and directed one film (*Maximum Overdrive*, based on his short story "Trucks") and undertaken several television projects, most recently 2004's *Kingdom Hospital*, a loose remake of Lars von Trier's *The Kingdom*. In June 1999, King suffered life-threatening injuries when struck by a van. He continued to write throughout his recovery; however, in January 2002, he announced that he would retire from publishing fiction after the completion of his massive horror-fantasy epic, *The Dark Tower*, the seventh and final volume of which was published in 2004. Shortly thereafter, King retracted his retirement with the announcement of a new novel, *The Colorado Kid*. In 2003, King was awarded the National Book Foundation Medal for Distinguished Contribution to American Letters. Stephen and Tabitha King have three grown children and live in Bangor, Maine.

1. *Wait Until Dark* (Terence Young). The moment near the conclusion, when Alan Arkin jumps out at Audrey Hepburn, is a real scare.

2. *Carrie* (Brian De Palma). The dream sequence at the end, when Sissy Spacek thrusts her hand out of the ground and grabs Amy Irving. I knew it was coming and still felt as if I'd swallowed a snow cone whole.

3. *I Bury The Living* (Albert Band). In this almost forgotten movie, there is a chilling sequence when Richard Boone begins to maniacally remove the black pins in the filled graveyard plots and to replace them with white pins.

4. *The Texas Chainsaw Massacre* (Tobe Hooper). The moment when the corpse seems to leap out of the freezer like a hideous jack-in-the-box.

5. *Night of the Living Dead* (George Romero). The scene where the little girl stabs her mother to death with a garden trowel in the cellar . . . "Mother, please, I can do it myself."

6. *Psycho* (Alfred Hitchcock). The shower scene, of course.

Source: Gabe Essoe, *The Book of Movie Lists* (Westport, Conn.: Arlington House, 1981).

John Waters's
10 Favorite Overlooked Movies

Born April 22, 1946, in Baltimore, Maryland, John Waters started his directorial career with such cult favorites as *Pink Flamingos* (1972), *Female Trouble* (1974), and *Desperate Living* (1977), before achieving a mainstream notoriety with movies like *Hairspray* (1988), *Pecker* (1998), and *A Dirty Shame* (2004). He is also the author of several books on pop and trash culture, including *Crackpot: The Obsessions of John Waters*. He has appeared as a guest voice on *The Simpsons* and acted in many films, including *Seed of Chucky* (2004). Waters continues to live in Baltimore, the setting for nearly all of his films.

1. *Tremors*, Ron Underwood
   Giant worms under the earth attack Kevin Bacon—it's great and somehow not cheesy.

2. *Rope*, Alfred Hitchcock
   Leopold and Loeb, sort of.

3. *Moon in the Gutter*, Jean-Jacques Beineix
   Beyond overlooked—*hated* by the public. My favorite lunatic art film.

4. *Story of Women*, Claude Chabrol
   Isabelle Huppert as the real-life abortionist who was guillotined in Vichy, France.

5. *Tucker*, Francis Ford Coppola
   Biography of the crackpot inventor of the "car of the future."

6. *Patty Hearst*, Paul Schrader
   The best legal defense she ever had.

7. *The Naked Kiss*, Sam Fuller
   A lurid melodrama in which a prostitute who teaches crippled children
   falls in love with the town's most outstanding citizen and discovers that
   he is a child molester.

8. *The Wannsee Conference*, Heinz Schirk
   Horrifying re-creation of the actual suburban Berlin meeting of Nazi
   leaders where the Final Solution was planned.

9. *Of Unknown Origin*, George Pan Cosmatos
   The best rat horror movie ever made.

10. *American Hot Wax*, Floyd Mutrux
    The definitive version of the Alan Freed story.

Walter Matthau's 10 Favorite Comedies

Born Walter Matthow on October 1, 1920, to Russian-Jewish immigrants in
New York City, Matthau was an amazingly versatile actor, best known for
his comedic performances in such hits as *The Odd Couple*, *The Bad News
Bears*, and *Grumpy Old Men*. He also played notable dramatic roles in a
variety of films, including *Fail-Safe*, *Charley Varrick*, and *JFK*. He re-
ceived Best Actor Oscar nominations for his work in *The Sunshine Boys* and
Kotch and won an Oscar for Best Supporting Actor in *The Fortune Cookie*.
Matthau died of a heart attack on July 1, 2000, just a few months after the
release of his final film, *Hanging Up*. He contributed this list to *The Book of
Lists* in 1983:

1. *The Odd Couple*
2. *The Producers*
3. *A New Leaf*
4. *Macbeth*
5. *City Lights*
6. *Wuthering Heights*
7. *Death of a Salesman*

8. *A Streetcar Named Desire*
9. *Horse Feathers*
10. *Hamlet*

41 Famous Writers Who Worked for the Movies

1. JAMES AGEE (novelist, 1909–1955)
   The Quiet One (1948), *The African Queen* (1951), *The Night of the Hunter* (1955)

2. MAXWELL ANDERSON (playwright, 1888–1959)
   All Quiet on the Western Front (1930), *Washington Merry-Go-Round* (1932), *Death Takes a Holiday* (1934), *Joan of Arc* (1948), *The Wrong Man* (1957)

3. MAYA ANGELOU (poet, 1928–)
   Georgia, Georgia (1972), *Poetic Justice* (1993)

4. RAY BRADBURY (science fiction writer, 1920–)
   Moby Dick (1956), *Something Wicked This Way Comes* (1983)

5. BERTOLT BRECHT (playwright, 1898–1956)
   Hangmen Also Die (1943)

6. CHARLES BUKOWSKI (poet and novelist, 1920–1994)
   The Killers (1984), *Barfly* (1987), *Lonely at the Top* (1993)

7. TRUMAN CAPOTE (novelist, 1924–1984)
   Beat the Devil (1954), *The Innocents* (1961)

8. RAYMOND CHANDLER (detective story writer, 1888–1959)
   And Now Tomorrow (1944), *Double Indemnity* (1944), *The Unseen* (1945), *The Blue Dahlia* (1946), *Strangers on a Train* (1951)

9. MICHAEL CRICHTON (novelist, 1942–)
   Westworld (1973), *Coma* (1978), *The Great Train Robbery* (1979), *Jurassic Park* (1993), *Rising Sun* (1993)

10. ROALD DAHL (author, 1916–1990)
    You Only Live Twice (1967), *Chitty Chitty Bang Bang* (1968), *Willy Wonka and the Chocolate Factory* (1971)

11. **THEODORE DREISER** (novelist, 1871–1945)
An American Tragedy (1931), *Tobacco and Men* (1935), *My Gal Sal* (1942)

12. **ROGER EBERT** (film critic, 1942–)
Beyond the Valley of the Dolls (1970), *Beneath the Valley of the Ultra-Vixens* (1979)

13. **WILLIAM FAULKNER** (novelist, 1897–1962)
Today We Live (1933), *Road to Glory* (1936), *To Have and Have Not* (1945), *The Big Sleep* (1946), *Land of the Pharaohs* (1955)

14. **F. SCOTT FITZGERALD** (novelist, 1896–1940)
A Yank at Oxford (1938), *Three Comrades* (1938), *Gone with the Wind* (1939), *The Women* (1939), *Madame Curie* (1943)

15. **CARLOS FUENTES** (novelist, 1928–)
Pedro Paramo (1967), *Muneca Riera* (1971)

16. **GRAHAM GREENE** (novelist, 1904–1991)
The Green Cockatoo (1937), *The Fallen Idol* (1948), *The Third Man* (1950), *Saint Joan* (1957), *Our Man in Havana* (1960), *The Comedians* (1967)

17. **DASHIELL HAMMETT** (detective story writer, 1894–1961)
City Streets (1931), *Mister Dynamite* (1935), *After the Thin Man* (1937), *Another Thin Man* (1939), *Watch on the Rhine* (1943)

18. **LILLIAN HELLMAN** (playwright, 1905–1984)
The Dark Angel (1935), *Dead End* (1937), *The Little Foxes* (1941), *The Children's Hour* (1961), *The Chase* (1966)

19. **ERNEST HEMINGWAY** (novelist, 1899–1961)
The Spanish Earth (1937), *The Old Man and the Sea* (1956)

20. **JAMES HILTON** (novelist, (1900–1954)
Camille (1936), *We Are Not Alone* (1939), *The Tuttles of Tahiti* (1942), *Mrs. Miniver* (1942), *Forever and a Day* (1944)

21. **ALDOUS HUXLEY** (novelist and essayist, 1894–1956)
Rage in Heaven (1941), *Forever and a Day* (1944), *The Loved One* (1965), *Frankenstein, the True Story* (1973)

22. **WILLIAM KENNEDY** (novelist, 1928–)
The Cotton Club (1984), *Ironweed* (1987)

23. NORMAN MAILER (novelist, 1923–)
Tough Guys Don't Dance (1987), *King Lear* (1987)

24. LARRY McMURTRY (novelist, 1936–)
The Last Picture Show (1971), *Falling from Grace* (1992)

25. ARTHUR MILLER (playwright, 1915– 2005)
Death of a Salesman (1951), *Let's Make Love* (1960), *The Misfits* (1961), *An Enemy of the People* (1977), *Everybody Wins* (1990)

26. CLIFFORD ODETS (playwright, 1906–1963)
The General Died at Dawn (1936), *None but the Lonely Heart* (1944), *Sweet Smell of Success* (1957), *The Story on Page One* (1960), *Wild in the Country* (1961)

27. DOROTHY PARKER (short story writer, 1893–1967)
Suzy (1936), *A Star Is Born* (1937), *Weekend for Three* (1941), *Saboteur* (1942), *The Fan* (1949)

28. S. J. PERELMAN (humorist, 1904–1979)
Horse Feathers (1932), *Sitting Pretty* (1933), *Florida Special* (1936), *Boy Trouble* (1939), *Around the World in 80 Days* (1956)

29. HAROLD PINTER (playwright, 1930–)
The Birthday Party (1968), *The Last Tycoon* (1976), *The French Lieutenant's Woman* (1981), *The Trial* (1993)

30. AYN RAND (novelist, 1905–1982)
Love Letters (1945), *You Came Along* (1945), *The Fountainhead* (1949)

31. GEORGE BERNARD SHAW (playwright, 1856–1950)
Pygmalion (1938), *Major Barbara* (1941), *Caesar and Cleopatra* (1946)

32. SAM SHEPARD (playwright, 1943–)
Zabriskie Point (1970), *Paris, Texas* (1984), *Silent Tongue* (1993)

33. NEIL SIMON (playwright, 1927–)
Barefoot in the Park (1967), *The Sunshine Boys* (1975), *The Goodbye Girl* (1977), *The Lonely Guy* (1984), *Brighton Beach Memoirs* (1986), *Lost in Yonkers* (1993)

34. JOHN STEINBECK (novelist, 1902–1968)
The Forgotten Village (1941), *The Pearl* (1948), *The Red Pony* (1949), *Viva Zapata* (1952).

35. TOM STOPPARD (playwright, 1937–)
   Brazil (1985), *Empire of the Sun* (1987), *The Russia House* (1990),
   Shakespeare in Love (1998)

36. GORE VIDAL (novelist, 1925–)
   I Accuse! (1958), *Suddenly, Last Summer* (1959), *Ben-Hur* (1959), *The
   Best Man* (1961), *Caligula* (1980)

37. EDGAR WALLACE (novelist, 1875–1932)
   King Kong (1933)

38. NATHANAEL WEST (novelist, 1903–1940)
   Ticket to Paradise (1936), *It Could Happen to You* (1937), *Five Came
   Back* (1939), *I Stole a Million* (1939), *Let's Make Music* (1940)

39. THORNTON WILDER (novelist and playwright, 1897–1975)
   The Dark Angel (1935), *Our Town* (1940), *Shadow of a Doubt* (1943)

40. TENNESSEE WILLIAMS (playwright, 1911–1983)
   A Streetcar Named Desire (1951), *Baby Doll* (1956), *Sweet Bird of
   Youth* (1962)

41. TOM WOLFE (journalist and novelist, 1937–)
   Three Ways to Love (1969), *The Right Stuff* (1983)

C.F. & F.B.

Henry Mancini's
10 Hardest Films to Score

Born in Cleveland, Ohio, in 1924, composer Henry Mancini won Academy
Awards (with Johnny Mercer) for "Moon River" from *Breakfast at Tiffany's*
and "Days of Wine and Roses" from the film of the same title. He also won
Academy Awards for best song and score for *Victor/Victoria*. Perhaps best
known for his signature themes for *The Pink Panther* and *Peter Gunn*, the
prolific composer died of cancer in 1994. In April 2004, Mancini was honored
with a U.S. Postal Service stamp, which featured a photo of the composer, a
list of his major credits, and the grinning cartoon image of the Pink Panther.
He contributed this list to *The Book of Lists* in 1993:

1. *Ghost Dad* (1990)
2. *The Great Impostor* (1960)
3. *Lifeforce* (1985)
4. *Mommie Dearest* (1981)

5. *Silver Streak* (1976)
6. *The Hawaiians* (1970)
7. *Soldier in the Rain* (1963)
8. *The Glass Menagerie* (1987)
9. *The Great Waldo Pepper* (1975)
10. *The White Dawn* (1974)

15 Commercial Film Titles That Might as Well Be Porno Titles

1. *Die Hard* (1988)
2. *Howard's End* (1992)
3. *Deep Impact* (1998)
4. *The Firm* (1993)
5. *Free Willy* (1993)
6. *Roger & Me* (1989)
7. *Enter the Dragon* (1973)
8. *Raising Victor Vargas* (2002)
9. *Snatch* (2000)
10. *In & Out* (1997)
11. *The 400 Blows* (1959)
12. *Shaft* (1971, 2000)
13. *Gone in 60 Seconds* (1974, 2000)
14. *The Fast and the Furious* (1954, 2001)
15. *The African Queen* (1951)

Music

THE ARTISTS FORMERLY KNOWN AS POLKA TURK
© Harry Goodwin/Redferns

23 Early Names of Famous Music Groups

In the music business, you have to hit not only the right chords but also the right name. Here's a quiz to test your knowledge:

1. Angels and the Snakes	a. Bangles
2. Composition of Sound	b. Beach Boys
3. Big Thing	c. Beatles
4. Artistics	d. Bill Haley and the Comets
5. Carl and the Passions	e. Black Sabbath
6. Primettes	f. Blondie
7. Tom and Jerry	g. Byrds
8. Johnny and the Moondogs	h. Champagne Music Makers (Lawrence Welk)
9. Caesar and Cleo	i. Chicago
10. Honolulu Fruit Gum Band	j. Creedence Clearwater Revival
11. Paramours	k. Depeche Mode
12. Polka Tulk	l. Journey
13. Bangs	m. Led Zeppelin
14. Beefeaters	n. Lynyrd Skynyrd
15. Falling Spikes	o. Mamas and the Papas
16. Sparrow	p. Righteous Brothers
17. My Backyard	q. Simon and Garfunkel
18. The New Journeymen	r. Sonny and Cher
19. The Elgins	s. Steppenwolf
20. The Four Aces of Western Swing	t. Supremes
21. The Golliwogs	u. Talking Heads
22. The New Yardbirds	v. Temptations
23. The Golden Gate Rhythm Section	w. Velvet Underground

Answers: 1 (f), 2 (k), 3 (i), 4 (u), 5 (b), 6 (t), 7 (q), 8 (c), 9 (r), 10 (h), 11 (p), 12 (e), 13 (a), 14 (g), 15 (w), 16 (s), 17 (n), 18 (o), 19 (v), 20 (d), 21 (j), 22 (m), 23 (l)

Dr. Demento's
19 Worst Song Titles

Disc jockey Dr. Demento was educated at UCLA, where he received his master's degree in music. His radio program, The *Dr. Demento Show*, is heard on 200 radio stations in the United States and on the Armed Forces Radio Network. His personal collection of more than 200,000 records is said to be one of the largest private collections in the world.

1. "I Scream, You Scream, We All Scream for Ice Cream," by Fred Waring & His Pennsylvanians

2. "They Needed a Songbird in Heaven (So God Took Caruso Away)," by Michael Hebbert

3. "Plant a Watermelon on My Grave, and Let the Juice Soak Through," by Doye O'Dell

4. "If the Man in the Moon Were a Coon," by Jack Leonard

5. "Where Did Robinson Crusoe Go with Friday on Saturday Night?", by Al Jolson

6. "How Could You Believe Me When I Said I Love You When You Know I've Been a Liar All My Life?", by Fred Astaire

7. "I've Got Those Wake Up Seven Thirty, Wash Your Ears They're Dirty, Eat Your Eggs and Oatmeal Rush to School Blues," by Jimmy Boyd

8. "Would You Rather Be a Colonel with an Eagle on Your Shoulder or a Private with a Chicken on Your Knee?", by Arthur Fields

9. "Mama Get Your Hammer (There's a Fly on Baby's Head)," by the Bobby Peterson Quintet

10. "When There's Tears in the Eyes of a Potato," by the Hoosier Hot Shots

11. "I Like Bananas Because They Have No Bones," by the Hoosier Hot Shots

12. "She Was Bitten on the Udder by an Adder," by Homer & Jethro

13. "A Bowl of Chop Suey and You-ey," by Sam Robbins & His Hotel McAlpin Orchestra

14. "I've Got Tears in My Ears from Lying on My Back in Bed While I Cry over You," by Homer & Jethro

15. "Santa Claus Has Got the AIDS This Year," by Tiny Tim

16. "I'd Rather Have a Bottle in Front of Me (Than a Frontal Lobotomy)," by Randy Hanzlick, M.D. (Dr. Demento adds: "[Hanzlick] is, or was as

of 1980, a real internist, practicing in Atlanta, writing songs for a hobby. This record had little commercial success but became, and remains, an often requested item on my show.")

17. "It's So Hard to Say I Love You (When You're Sitting on My Face)," by Marty and the Muff Tones

18. "Jesus Loves Me (but He Can't Stand You)," by the Austin Lounge Lizards

19. "Kill a Tree for Christ," by Celtic Elvis

12 Suggested Names for Religious Rap Groups

1. Ludachrist
2. Jera Maya
3. Dr. Dreidel
4. Holla 4 Allah
5. Notorious G.O.D.
6. EZ Kiel
7. Buddhalicious
8. V-Shnoop Dogg
9. Sheikh Yer Tailfeather
10. Judaizzle
11. G Zu$$
12. Kris Kross

M.W. & J.F.

Johnny Cash's 10 Greatest Country Songs of All Time

Johnny Cash, widely considered to be the greatest country music singer and composer in history, died in September 2003, at the age of 71. Known as "The Man in Black" (he always wore black), Cash was born the son of a poor sharecropper in Arkansas, in 1932, and he sang to himself while picking cotton for 10 hours a day. Cash recorded more than 1,500 songs. He toured worldwide, and he played for free in prisons throughout America. Among his greatest hits are "Ring of Fire" and "I Walk the Line." His 1975 autobiography, *Man in Black*, has sold more than 1.5 million copies. Cash's death was long and painful, and his last four albums are considered by many to be his greatest work, as they all examine a hardworking man coming to terms with the end of his life. Said Merle Kilgore, one of the coauthors of "Ring of Fire," "It's a sad day in Tennessee, but a great day in Heaven. The Man in Black is now wearing white as he joins his wife, June, in the angel band." June and Johnny were married for 35 years, and her death preceded his by four months. Cash contributed this list to *The Book of Lists* in 1977:

1. "I Walk the Line," Johnny Cash
2. "I Can't Stop Loving You," Don Gibson
3. "Wildwood Flower," Carter Family
4. "Folsom Prison Blues," Johnny Cash
5. "Candy Kisses," George Morgan
6. "I'm Movin' On," Hank Snow
7. "Walking the Floor over You," Ernest Tubb
8. "He'll Have to Go," Joe Allison and Audrey Allison
9. "Great Speckle Bird," Carter Family
10. "Cold, Cold Heart," Hank Williams

Benny Goodman's
7 Best Popular Songs of the 20th Century

Born Benjamin David Goodman in Chicago, Illinois, on May 30, 1909, the world-renowned "King of Swing" popularized jazz in the 1930s and 1940s and helped usher in the big-band era as a composer, orchestra conductor, and peerless clarinetist. One of his signature works, the rousing hit "Sing, Sing, Sing," was named one of the 100 Most Important American Musical Works of the 20th Century by National Public Radio. Goodman continued to play clarinet until his death at age 77 on June 13, 1986. He contributed the following list to *The Book of Lists* in 1980:

1. "Stardust" (1929) by Hoagy Carmichael and Mitchell Parish
2. "Sing, Sing, Sing" (1936) by Louis Prima
3. "Body and Soul" (1930) by Johnny Green, Ed Heyman, Robert Sour, and Frank Eyton
4. "Send in the Clowns" (1973) by Stephen Sondheim
5. "Begin the Beguine" (1935) by Cole Porter
6. "You are the Sunshine of My Life" (1973) by Stevie Wonder
7. "Alexander's Ragtime Band" (1911) by Irving Berlin

Alan Jay Lerner's
10 Best Modern Songwriters

Born August 31, 1918, in New York City, playwright and lyricist Alan Jay
Lerner grew up in a wealthy retailing family and began his career writing
advertising copy and radio scripts. He teamed with composer Frederick
Loewe in 1942, and by 1947 they had their first major Broadway hit,
Brigadoon. A string of successes followed until the team split in 1962 after
their final hit, *Camelot*. Lerner also worked extensively in film and earned
Oscars for his screenplays for *An American in Paris* and *Gigi*. He died of
lung cancer on June 14, 1986. He contributed the following list (in alphabetical order) to *The Book of Lists* in 1980:

 1. Burt Bacharach
 2. Leonard Bernstein
3–4. John Kander and Fred Ebb
 5. Burton Lane
 6. Richard Rodgers
 7. Paul Simon
 8. Stephen Sondheim
 9. Jule Styne
 10. Jimmy Webb

Andrew Motion's
Top 12 Dylan Lyrics

Motion notes: For my money, songs accumulate an even larger baggage of
associations than poems. The time I first heard them, the situations—intense
or otherwise—in which I have listened to them, the people who introduced
them to me, or who I know also like them: All these things become attached
to the lyrics as well as the melody, at once broadening the experience of
listening and making it more intimate. Turning over the pages of Bob
Dylan's *Lyrics 1962–85* is like opening a Pandora's Box crammed with my
life's delights, winces, blushes, broodings, geographies. Which in turn means
that reducing his titles to any kind of list is seriously difficult. One song
counted in means one (at least one) left out—and the choice is likely to
change from day to day.
　　On the day I'm writing this, May 24, 2004, my top 12, in album order,
are:

1. "Talkin' John Birch Paranoid Blues"—for the comedy in the anger and the wit in the satire.

2. "Tomorrow Is a Long Time"—for the tenderness and simplicity.

3. "The Times They Are A-Changin'"—for saying all the right (but still surprising) things at the right time and every time.

4. "All I Really Want to Do"—for the freedom it offers, and for knowing that freedom is difficult to give in fact.

5. "Love Minus Zero/No Limit"—for being so damn beautiful.

6. "It's All Over Now, Baby Blue"—for "Leave your stepping stones behind, something calls for you."

7. "Desolation Row"—for getting its arm round so much, with such a strange mixture of ease and effort.

8. "All Along the Watchtower"—for the economy of its mystery.

9. "Idiot Wind"—for its tender outrage.

10. "Hurricane"—for the accuracy of its anger.

11. "Man Gave Names to All the Animals"—for its jokes.

12. Oh, and (out of order) "Visions of Johanna"—for all of the above reasons, and more besides.

Allen Ginsberg's
11 Greatest Blues Songs

Born in New Jersey in 1926, Allen Ginsberg was educated at Columbia University in New York City, where he met fellow writers Jack Kerouac and William S. Burroughs, forming a creative triad that gave birth to the Beat Movement of the 1950s. Ginsberg's most famous work, *Howl and Other Poems,* was published in 1955, and its graphic, excoriating vision of the failure of the American Dream resulted in both literary acclaim and obscenity charges. Other books by Ginsberg include *Kaddish* (1961), *Reality Sandwiches* (1965), and *First Blues: Songs* (1982). Allen Ginsberg died in 1997. He contributed this list to *The Book of Lists* in 1993:

1. "James Alley Blues," by Richard "Rabbit" Brown
2. "Washington D.C. Hospital Center Blues," by Skip James
3. "Jelly Bean Blues," by Ma Rainey
4. "See See Rider Blues," by Ma Rainey
5. "Young Woman's Blues," by Bessie Smith
6. "Poor Me," by Charles Patton
7. "Black Girl," by Leadbelly
8. "Levee Camp Moan Blues," by Texas Alexander
9. "Last Fair Deal Gone Down," by Robert Johnson
10. "I'm So Lonesome I Could Cry," by Hank Williams, Sr.
11. "Idiot Wind," by Bob Dylan

Dizzy Gillespie's
10 Greatest Jazz Musicians

Jazz legend John Birks "Dizzy" Gillespie was born in Cheraw, South Carolina, October 21, 1917. After playing piano at age four, he taught himself to play the trombone but then switched to the trumpet before the age of twelve. The leading exponent of "bebop" jazz, Gillespie was famous for conducting big bands, for playing trumpet (many consider him the greatest trumpeter in history), and for his work with Earl "Fatha" Hines and Charlie Parker, among others. Gillespie's energy was so great that his career never stopped, and at least 10 biographies of the world-famous, beloved revolutionary of jazz have been published. Among his most famous compositions are "Salt Peanuts," "Bebop," "Guachi Guararo (Soul Sauce)", "Night in Tunisia," and "Manteca," a pioneering piece in Afro-Cuban style. Gillespie lived a stable private life and disdained the addictive drugs favored by so many jazz heroes. He remained humorous and charming until the end of his life. He died on January 6, 1993, at the age of 75, and the world mourned the loss of a true jazz giant. In 1980, he prepared this list for *The Book of Lists*:

1. Charlie Parker
2. Art Tatum
3. Coleman Hawkins
4. Benny Carter
5. Lester Young
6. Roy Eldridge
7. J. J. Johnson
8. Kenny Clarke
9. Oscar Pettiford
10. Miles Davis

Wynton Marsalis's
14 Greatest Jazz Musicians in History

Born October 18, 1961, in New Orleans, jazz great Wynton Marsalis began studying trumpet at the age of 12. At 18 he attended the Juilliard School of Music, and by 1980 he had been signed by Columbia Records. His self-titled debut album was released in 1983; his follow-ups have included *Think of One . . .*, *Hot House Flowers*, and *The Wynton Marsalis Quartet Live at Blue Alley*. He is the first musician to win Grammys in both the jazz and classical fields in one year. In 1997, Marsalis became the first jazz musician to win the Pulitzer Prize for his epic oratorio on slavery entitled *Blood on the Fields*.

1. Duke Ellington (and his orchestra)
2. Louis Armstrong
3. Jelly Roll Morton
4–5. Charlie Parker, Kenny Clarke
6. Art Tatum
7. Thelonious Monk
8-9. Jo Jones, Lester Young
10.-11. John Coltrane, Elvin Jones
12.-13. Miles Davis, Paul Chambers
14. Charles Mingus

Quincy Jones's
10 Favorite Jazz Recordings of All Time

Born on March 14, 1933, in Chicago, Illinois, Quincy Jones first teamed up with Ray Charles to form a combo in Seattle, then went on to steal the spotlight as trumpeter with Dizzy Gillespie and Lionel Hampton. He has arranged and conducted music for Count Basie, Sarah Vaughan, and Aretha Franklin, among others. He wrote the scores for such diverse films as *In Cold Blood*, *The Getaway*, and *The Wiz*. Jones is the all-time most-nominated Grammy artist, with a total of 77 nominations, and he has won 26 times. In addition to his musical work, he is a film and TV producer, with credits ranging from *The Color Purple* to *Mad TV*.

1. "Body and Soul" (Coleman Hawkins)
2. "Just Friends" (Charlie Parker)
3. "Miles Ahead" (Miles Davis)
4. "Rockin' in Rhythm" (Duke Ellington)

5. "Love You Madly" (Oscar Peterson)
6. "Giant Steps" (John Coltrane)
7. "I Can't Get Started" (Dizzy Gillespie)
8. "Sleep" (Benny Carter)
9. "The Midnight Sun Will Never Set" (Phil Woods)
10. "Anything" (Count Basie)

Kareem Abdul-Jabbar's
10 Greatest Jazz Artists in History

Born in 1947 in New York City, the 7'2", Kareem Abdul-Jabbar (formerly Lew Alcindor) was a star of the Los Angeles Lakers for 13 years. When he left the game in 1989, no NBA player had scored more points or won more MVP awards. He has also appeared in several films, including *Game of Death* (with Bruce Lee, under whom he studied the Jeet Kun Do martial art) and *Airplane!* Jazz has been Abdul-Jabbar's hobby since he first borrowed records from earlier basketball wizard Wilt Chamberlain.

1. Thelonious Monk
2. Miles Davis
3. John Coltrane
4. Dizzy Gillespie
5. Duke Ellington
6. Louis Armstrong
7. Lester Young
8. Billie Holiday
9. Charles Mingus
10. Charlie Parker

13 Blind Musicians

1. THOMAS ("BLIND TOM") BETHUNE (1848–1908)
   A natural mimic who learned to play the piano by ear and committed more than 700 songs to memory, Bethune was born blind to slaves in Georgia. Purchased by a Colonel Bethune, he played (and imitated machine and animal noises) for audiences throughout Europe and the United States.

2. ANDREA BOCELLI (1958–)
   Born with visually debilitating glaucoma, Bocelli went completely blind at age 12 after being hit in the head while playing soccer with friends.

He became a lawyer, then started studying opera. He has since sold more than 20 million albums worldwide, making him one of the most successful classical recording artists of all time.

3. RAY CHARLES (1930–2004)
The 1950s mix of gospel melodies and love lyrics by this renowned composer-singer-pianist was the birth of "soul." Blinded by glaucoma at age six, Grammy winner Charles remembers his mother's advice: "Just because you've lost your eyesight, you're not stupid."

4. JOSÉ FELICIANO (1945–)
A victim of congenital glaucoma, Puerto Rican–born Feliciano gained fame for his 1968 Latin-soul version of "Light My Fire." He taught himself guitar because "I didn't want to make chairs and mops and brooms."

5. ALLAN ("BLIND BOY") FULLER (1908–1941)
Blinded by a jealous girlfriend who put lye in the water in his washbasin, Fuller sometimes played his fast blues guitar with Blind Blake and Blind Gary Davis. However, he is best known for his work with prominent bluesmen Sonny Terry and Brownie McGee. McGee was sometimes called Blind Boy Fuller's No. 2.

6. JEFF HEALEY (1966–)
Healey went blind from eye cancer when he was only one year old. He first picked up a guitar at age three and was performing in public at age six. An accomplished blues, jazz, and pop player, Healey had a Top 5 hit with "Angel Eyes" from his platinum album *See the Light* in 1989.

7. ("BLIND") LEMON JEFFERSON (1897–1929)
Sightless from birth, Jefferson was one of the first to call his rough guitar stylings and high, loud singing the "blues." A blind street singer's bitterness shows in "Tin Cup Blues," but often he was bawdy, as in "Black Snake Moan." He recorded in Chicago, where he froze to death in a snowstorm.

8. WILLIAM ("BLIND WILLIE") JOHNSON (1902–1947)
An itinerant guitar-playing gospel minstrel who went blind at age seven, Johnson used a rich blend of gospel tunes and blues style, which is often copied. His prominent recordings include "Dark Was the Night" and "Lord, I Just Can't Keep from Crying."

9. RONNIE MILSAP (1945–)
An award-winning country-and-western vocalist and composer, Milsap isn't bitter about his lifelong blindness, sometimes quipping, "I remember names better than I do faces." His style is that of the honky-tonk love song.

10. **GEORGE SHEARING (1919–)**
   Blind from birth, jazz pianist-composer Shearing is a British émigré
   known as a master of the "locked hands" style. His best-known composition is
   "Lullaby of Birdland." When people offered to bequeath their eyes to him,
   he refused, saying, "I am a completely happy man. My life today suits me."

11. **TOM SULLIVAN (1947–)**
   Undeterred by lifetime blindness, Sullivan is not only a singer-
   composer-writer but also an actor and an athlete. He is known as well
   for his book (and subsequent movie) *If You Could See What I Hear*,
   about two years of his young adulthood.

12. **ARTHEL ("DOC") WATSON (1923–)**
   Born blind in Deep Gap, North Carolina, Watson is a virtual walking
   history of southern folk music. A master of flat picking and finger
   picking on guitar, he also plays banjo and fiddle at campus concerts
   and music festivals, where he is a regular. One of his most popular
   works is a version of "Tennessee Stud."

13. **STEVIE WONDER (1950–)**
   A premature baby, Wonder blames his blindness on "too much oxygen
   in the incubator." One of the outstanding composers and performers in
   soul-rock music, he catapulted to success at age 13 with his first hit,
   "Fingertips." In the recording studio, Wonder often takes on all the
   vocal, instrumental, and production responsibilities himself.

   T.C.

Bing Crosby's
10 Favorite Performers

Born Harry Lillis Crosby in Tacoma, Washington, on May 2, 1903, legendary
entertainer Bing Crosby began his career as a singer in dance bands. Soon he
was turning out million-seller records (including 38 #1 singles) and starring
in hit movie musicals such as *Pennies from Heaven* (1936), *Holiday Inn*
(1942), *White Christmas* (1954), and a series of popular team-ups with Bob
Hope (starting with 1940's *The Road to Singapore*). He also earned an Oscar
for Best Actor in 1945 for his role in *Going My Way*. Bing Crosby died at age
74 in Madrid, Spain. He contributed this list to *The Book of Lists* in 1977:

1. Al Jolson
2. Ethel Waters
3. James Barton
4. Frank Sinatra

5. Lena Horne
6. Louis Armstrong
7. Nat Cole
8. Mel Tormé
9. Judy Garland
10. Victor Borge

Jonathan Richman's 11 Favorite Singers

Born May 16, 1951, in Natick, Massachusetts, Jonathan Richman first gained fame with the proto-punk band the Modern Lovers; during that period, he wrote the song "Roadrunner," for which he is well known. His records include *I, Jonathan; Having a Party with Jonathan Richman; Jonathan Goes Country;* and *You Must Ask the Heart.* In 1998, Richman earned his biggest mainstream exposure yet with his appearance in the Farrelly Brothers' smash-hit comedy *There's Something About Mary.* He currently lives in Northern California.

1. Van Morrison
2. Marty Robbins
3. Skeeter Davis
4. John Lee Hooker
5. Nicolas Reyes of the Gypsy Kings
6. Dion
7. Ted Hawkins (sings on the boardwalk in Venice, California)
8. Nana Mouskouri
9. Desmond Dekker
10. Maurice Chevalier
11. Mary Wells

Richmond notes: In limiting this list to eleven singers, I've left out many of my favorites. I've left out lead singers for vocal groups; for example, Jay Siegel of the Tokens, Frankie Lymon and the Teenagers, Nolan Strong and the Diablos, etc., because that would be a whole other category.

9 Drummers of Note— Selected by Ben Schott

Ben Schott is the best-selling author of *Schott's Original Miscellany* and subsequent miscellanies on Food & Drink, and Sporting, Gaming, & Idling.

His drumming is mediocre at best, and he harbors ambitions to play the Hammond organ to the same standard. Below, in no particular order, are some of Schott's drummers of note:

1. **CLYDE STUBBLEFIELD**
   Stubblefield was James Brown's "Funky Drummer," and as such can claim to be the most sampled drummer in the world. Alongside fellow drummers Jabo Starks and Clayton Fillyau, Stubblefield pioneered the tight, crisp, and heavily syncopated snare and hi-hat riffs that defined the James Brown sound, and funk itself.

2. **JAMES BLADES**
   More a percussionist than a drummer, Blades deserves mention as the man who recorded the Morse code "V for Victory" signal for the BBC during World War II. The "dot-dot-dot-dash" rhythm was played on an African membrane drum with a timpani mallet and was broadcast up to 150 times a day to encourage the Resistance in Continental Europe. As if that were not enough, James Blades also recorded the famous J. Arthur Rank gong (on a small Chinese tam-tam) that was mimed by the boxer Bombardier Billy Wells.

3. **CHARLIE WATTS**
   Without doubt the most dapper of drummers, Watts merits a place in any drumming lineup for his bespoke suits alone. Like that of (the much-underestimated) Ringo Starr, the essence of Watts's skill lies in playing just enough for the song and no more. When asked what 25 years of rock 'n' roll with the Rolling Stones was like, Watts apparently replied: "It's been one year drumming, and 24 years hanging around."

4. **STEVE GADD**
   One of the most recorded drummers in history, Gadd has played with a stellar lineup of musicians, from Stanley Clark to Eric Clapton. His work with Paul Simon has justly received high praise: The groove on "Late in the Evening" and his fiendishly complex riff on "Fifty Ways to Leave Your Lover" typify his fluid and effortless style.

5. **JOHN "STUMPY" PEPYS**
   Tall, geeky, and bespectacled, Pepys was the first of six drummers for the band Spinal Tap. His formal technique might seem unsophisticated to modern ears, but he pioneered the simple pop sound of the early 1960s—best illustrated in his drumming on the 1965 Thamesmen track "Gimme Some Money." In 1969, Pepys died in a bizarre gardening accident that to this day remains a mystery.

6. **KEITH MOON**
   Setting aside Moon's antics (both real and apocryphal), his drumming for The Who was as stylish and clever as it was violent and anarchic.

Almost any Who track demonstrates the genius of Moon's drumming—from the simple power of "Substitute" to the flamboyance of "Won't Get Fooled Again."

7. RICHIE HAYWARD
The drummer for the American band Little Feat, Hayward has two apt nicknames: "The Beat Behind the Feat" and "Mr. Sophistifunk." On tracks like "Dixie Chicken" and "Sailin' Shoes," Hayward sits just behind the groove, seamlessly melding the styles of rock, zydeco, folk, and blues.

8. RONNIE VERRELL
Verrell was a stylish swing drummer who played with some of the great names of jazz, including Ted Heath, Syd Lawrence, David Lund, and Buddy Rich. More important than that, of course, is that he played Animal's drum solo on the theme to *The Muppet Show*.

9. JOHN BONHAM
Bonham was the typhonic drummer for '70s rock band Led Zeppelin (a band name suggested by Keith Moon, q.v.). Alongside bass player John Paul Jones, Bonham provided driving, relentless, and (for rock music) astonishingly complex riffs—perhaps best illustrated in "Fool in the Rain." The less said about the half-hour drum solo during "Moby Dick" the better.

Ian Rankin's 7 Great Gigs

Born in 1960, Ian Rankin held a variety of jobs—including grape picker, alcohol researcher, and punk musician—before turning his talents to the best-selling Inspector John Rebus novels, detailing the adventures of an Edinburgh cop described by the London *Sunday Telegraph* as "a compassionate, quick-tempered . . . loner." He has also written three thrillers under the pseudonym Jack Harvey (a combination of Rankin's son's first name and his wife Miranda's maiden name). A resident of Edinburgh, Scotland, Rankin hit the best-seller lists again in 2004 with the Inspector Rebus novel *A Question of Blood*.

1. I was just the right age for punk—17—in 1977. Of course, growing up in a traditional coal mining community, it didn't do to stand out, so we punks tended to congregate in each other's bedrooms, listening to records and the John Peel show on Radio 1. Then a club opened at the Station Hotel in nearby Kirkcaldy. It happened every Sunday night and was called the Pogo-a-Gogo. Basically, it was the hotel's upstairs

ballroom, with a bar serving fizzy lager. But there were also occasional live gigs. By this time, Fife had a punk band of its own—The Skids. The guitarist, Stuart Adamson, had been to the same school as me. There was no stage, band and audience becoming one, writhing on the floor or bouncing to the music. I'd sneak my punk clothes (a boiler-suit spattered with bleach) out of the house and change at a friend's, then his dad would drive us to Kirkcaldy. Great nights, and my first really great gig.

2. Of course, I'd been to gigs before. It had taken some persuading, but my parents finally agreed that I could accompany a friend to Edinburgh at the age of 16 to see Barclay James Harvest. I'd then have to stay the night at his house, as there was no way to get home. A huge adventure. I'd never heard any BJH albums (and, indeed, have never owned any since). It was also my first visit to the Usher Hall, a posh cavern of a place. Were Barclay James Harvest any good? Frankly, no, but that didn't matter. They had dry ice and a light show and amps turned up to the requisite 11. Tom Robinson was in the support band, and I came home with a program, poster, and badge. They say you never forget the first time. . . .

3. Though BJH was my first gig, I'd been lying to pals at school. As far as they were concerned, I'd previously trekked alone to the wilds of Dundee's Caird Hall to see Hawkwind. I made the whole thing up, of course, wanting to impress with my solo efforts. I duly scrawled some signatures on a Hawkwind album sleeve, then crushed and tore it a bit to make it look like there'd been a fracas of sorts. And around this fake artifact I spun the story of my trip. I explained the light show, the nude female dancers, the sonic wondrousness of it all, until I almost began to believe that I really had been there. All in all, a brilliant night, which exists only in my imagination.

4. While a student in Edinburgh, I saw many great gigs (Pere Ubu, Iggy Pop, The Kinks, Ramones, Bauhaus . . .). I also missed a few. A mate tried to get me to go see The Buzzcocks, all because of the support act, a new band called Joy Division. I stayed home and wrote an essay instead and have regretted it ever since. I also missed out on the Stones at the Playhouse because I had an exam the next day. But one concert that stays with me is U2. They were playing in a disco in Tollcross. I think their first album had just been released. A few hundred sweaty fans, dancing for a solid 90 minutes, and a gang of young men on stage, playing for their professional lives. They were brilliant. And to think, I only went because my mate's girlfriend let him down and he had a ticket going spare.

5. After uni, I moved to London. I'd pretty much stopped going to gigs by that time, apart from jazz nights in Hoxton. But I did make the trip to a pub in Finsbury Park to see a new outfit called The Proclaimers. Until that night, I'd never realized how many Scots had made the move south. The place was awash with familiar accents and football scarves—everything from Partick to Aberdeen. The twins won me over that night—they were electrifying. It was a pretty rough and drunken crowd, but they had them eating out of their hands. After the gig, I decided to walk home rather than take the tube: That way, I'd have more time to reflect on what I'd just seen and sing a few of the numbers to myself. That's how good a gig it was: It made me want to walk through the rummer parts of nighttime London.

6. I had to wait a while for my next outstanding London gig. It happened in 2003, in another fairly small venue, the Astoria on Charing Cross Road. I'd managed to miss having dinner with two thirds of REM (which is another story in itself) and was gutted. Taking pity, my publisher found me a ticket to a secret Rolling Stones gig. This was supposed to be for fan club members and took place in the sweltering confines of the Astoria nightclub. The audience had come from the four corners of the globe to see the Stones on home ground, playing a set much like the ones they'd have played when they first started. The stage was only about six feet off the ground, with no props or gimmicks. Just a band playing out of their skins. At last, I could discern that Keith really is a good guitarist, and that Jagger has the stamina of a man half his age.

7. Back home in Edinburgh, one of my favorite venues is the Queen's Hall, not so much for the acoustics (iffy) or the views of the stage (even iffier), but for the quality of music it seems to attract. I've seen bands as different as The Residents and the Art Ensemble of Chicago . . . musicians as different as Dick Gaughan and Lloyd Cole, The Durutti Column and Plainsong. But the gig that stands out for me was another recent one—Mogwai. Young men with attitudinal guitars and no need to keep the noise in perspective, as there's no singer to drown out. Their show there in 2003 was colossal, and for the first time I really felt my age. As the volume increased, I found myself at the very back of the hall, plaster falling around me. This was a really, really loud gig. Loud and great. It felt as though the whole hall might elevate, rise from its pinnings into the sky, propelled like a rocket. Which is what the best gigs should do—transport you.

15 Composers Who Died in Unusual Circumstances

1. **JEAN-BAPTISTE LULLY (1632–1687)**
   Creator of French grand opera, Lully was a great favorite of King Louis XIV's. It was Lully's custom to conduct ensembles by pounding the floor with a large pointed cane. While conducting a Te Deum for the king's benefit, he accidentally struck his foot so violently with the cane that he developed an infection. Gangrene set in, followed by blood poisoning, which led to his death.

2. **ALESSANDRO STRADELLA (1645?–1682)**
   Singer, violinist, and composer of more than 200 chamber cantatas, Stradella led a life of mystery and intrigue that has been glorified in eight operas and at least one novel. In 1677, a Venetian senator hired men to murder Stradella after he eloped with the senator's fiancée. Legend has it that the would-be killers refused to carry out their assignment after hearing one of Stradella's oratorios. Five years later, a second assassination attempt proved successful.

3. **MICHAEL WISE (1648–1687)**
   A multitalented Englishman known for his quick temper, Wise once began playing the organ in the middle of a religious service attended by King Charles II, simply to express displeasure with the lengthy sermon. On the night of August 24, 1687, Wise quarreled with his wife. In a rage, he rushed out into the street, where he was accosted by a night watchman. Wise struck him and in return received a blow from the watchman's club, which fatally fractured his skull.

4. **JEAN-MARIE LECLAIR (1697–1764)**
   Leclair was composer and ballet master to both the French court and the court of the Netherlands. Early one morning, he was found murdered in a Paris street near his home. Although the crime was never officially solved, evidence indicated that he may have been killed by his estranged wife.

5. **JOHANN SCHOBERT (1720–1767)**
   A popular composer of chamber music, Schobert died in his Paris home after eating mushrooms that were in fact toadstools. One of his friends, as well as a servant and all the members of his immediate family, with the exception of one young child, also died from ingesting the poisonous mushrooms.

6. **FRANZ KOTZWARA (1750?–1793)**

Born in Prague, Kotzwara spent much of his life traveling and finally settled in London. A versatile musician, he is best known for his sonata *The Battle of Prague*. He led a dissipated private life, and he was particularly fond of a very unusual sexual practice: being hanged and nearly strangled, a practice known as *jeu de coupe-corde*, or "game of cutting the rope." He usually paid young women to hang him from the ceiling for five minutes and then cut the rope. On February 2, 1793, he was discovered dead in a house of ill repute in Covent Garden. Susannah Hill, his accomplice, had not been able to revive him after cutting the rope. She was arrested, tried for murder, and acquitted.

7. **CHARLES-VALENTIN MORHANGE ALKAN (1813–1888)**

Alkan was noted for his novel—and often bizarre—piano works, composed in a harmonically daring musical style. He lived reclusively and was crushed to death when he accidentally pulled a bookcase over on himself while reaching for a copy of the Talmud.

8. **PYOTR ILICH TCHAIKOVSKY (1840–1893)**

On October 28, 1893, the illustrious Russian composer conducted the first performance of his Symphony no. 6 in B Minor in St. Petersburg. Called the *Pathetic* Symphony because of its melancholic air, it was not well received. Four days later, Tchaikovsky—already feeling ill—knowingly drank a glass of unboiled water, though a cholera epidemic was raging throughout the city. His death on November 6 set off a flurry of rumors that, despondent over the reaction to his symphony, he had committed suicide by purposely contracting cholera.

9. **ERNEST CHAUSSON (1855–1899)**

Chausson was a wealthy man who switched from the study of law to the composition of introspective chamber music. His career was cut short when he lost control of his bicycle while riding down a steep slope near his home in Limay, France. He crashed into a wall and died instantly.

10. **ENRIQUE GRANADOS CAMPIÑA (1867–1916)**

One of the foremost composers of Spanish nationalist music, Granados overcame his terror of deep water and sailed to New York City to hear an operatic adaptation of his piano compositions. He braved the return journey as a passenger on the S.S. *Sussex* and was drowned in the English Channel when the ship was torpedoed by a German submarine. The tragedy was compounded because, by agreeing to play at a reception given by President Wilson, Granados missed the boat on which he was originally scheduled to return to Spain.

11. ALEXANDER SCRIABIN (1872–1915)

This innovative Russian composer developed a pustule on his lip in the spring of 1915 but elected to ignore it. Soon the pustule developed into a carbuncle, which disfigured much of his face. Bedridden with a fever of 106°F (41° Celsius), Scriabin allowed surgeons to lance his lip several times, but blood poisoning set in and he was dead within hours. No death mask could be cast because of the hideous scarring caused by the emergency surgery.

12. MIECZYSLAW KARLOWICZ (1876–1909)

Considered the greatest Polish composer of the late Romantic era, Karlowicz blended aspects of nationalist music with the ultra-Romantic tradition of Richard Strauss. He was also one of the first of his countrymen to popularize skiing. On one of his frequent solo skiing expeditions in the Tatra Mountains, he was buried by an avalanche.

13. ANTON VON WEBERN (1883–1945)

A brilliant composer whose unconventional music was banned by the Nazis in 1938, Webern was killed because of a tragic mistake. While staying with his daughter in the small Austrian town of Mittersill, he inadvertently failed to respond to a wartime curfew warning and was shot by an overzealous American soldier. The guilt-ridden soldier spent his last years in an asylum.

14. ALBAN BERG (1885–1935)

An outstanding student of Arnold Schönberg, Berg—like Scriabin—died from blood poisoning caused by a carbuncle. In Berg's case, the abscess was located in the small of his back and was the result of an insect bite.

15. WALLINGFORD RIEGGER (1885–1961)

One of the first American composers to employ Schönberg's system of composition, Riegger met his end when he became entangled in the leashes of two fighting dogs. He fell to the ground and sustained a serious head injury. Emergency brain surgery proved futile, and he died shortly thereafter.

D.W.B. & C.Ro.

Isaac Stern's
10 Best Violinists in History

Born in Kreminiecz, Russia, in 1920, violinist Isaac Stern came with his parents to the United States when he was 10 months old. He began playing the violin at the age of 8, made his debut with the San Francisco Symphony

Orchestra in 1931 at age 11, and went on to become one of the world's great violinists. He was also passionately dedicated to helping younger musicians; among his discoveries were Itzhak Perlman and Yo-Yo Ma. He was also the solo violinist for the film *Fiddler on the Roof* (1971) and played the movie's memorable theme song. Stern died on September 22, 2001, of heart failure. He contributed this list to *The Book of Lists* in 1980:

1. Niccolò Paganini (1782–1840)
2. Antonio Vivaldi (1678–1741)
3. Ludwig (Louis) Spohr (1784–1859)
4. Henri Vieuxtemps (1820–1881)
5. Henri Wieniawski (1835–1880)
6. Pablo de Sarasate y Navascués (1844–1908)
7. Joseph Joachim (1831–1907)
8. Eugène Ysaye (1858–1931)
9. Bronislaw Hubermann (1882–1947)
10. Jascha Heifetz (1901–)

Yehudi Menuhin's 10 Greatest Violinists

Born in 1916 in New York, legendary violinist Yehudi Menuhin made his debut at Carnegie Hall at age 11. He studied music in Paris and during World War II played over 500 concerts for Allied soldiers; after the war, he played concerts for liberated concentration camp inmates. In 1963, he opened the Yehudi Menuhin School for musically gifted children. He also began conducting in the mid-1960s. In addition to his musical work, Menuhin authored several books, including *Violin: Six Lessons* (1972) and his autobiography, *Unfinished Journey* (1977). He died in Berlin, Germany, on March 12, 1999. He contributed the following list to *The Book of Lists* in 1983:

1. Arcangelo Corelli (1653–1713), Italian
2. Antonio Vivaldi (1678–1741), Italian
3. Pietro Locatelli (1695–1764), Italian
4. Niccolò Paganini (1782–1840), Italian
5. Jean-Marie Leclair (1697–1764), French
6. Giuseppe Tartini (1692–1770), Italian
7. Ludwig Spohr (1784–1859), German
8. Henri Vieuxtemps (1820–1881), Belgian
9. Henryk Wieniawski (1835–1880), Polish
10. Pablo de Sarasate (1844–1908), Spanish

Stirring Opening Lines
of 11 National Anthems

1. ALGERIA
   We swear by the lightning that destroys,
   By the streams of generous blood being shed
   By the bright flags that wave
   That we are in revolt . . .

2. BOLIVIA
   Bolivians, propitious fate has crowned our hopes . . .

3. BURKINA FASO
   Against the humiliating bondage of a thousand years
   Rapacity came from afar to subjugate them
   For a hundred years.
   Against the cynical malice in the shape
   Of neocolonialism and its petty local servants,
   Many gave in and certain others resisted.

4. GUINEA-BISSAU
   Sun, sweat, verdure and sea,
   Centuries of pain and hope;
   This is the land of our ancestors.

5. LUXEMBOURG
   Where slow you see the Alzette flow,
   The Sura play wild pranks . . .

6. OMAN
   O Lord, protect for us Our Majesty the Sultan
   And the people in our land,
   With honor and peace.
   May he live long, strong and supported,
   Glorified by his leadership.
   For him we shall lay down our lives.

7. PARAGUAY
   To the peoples of unhappy America,
   Three centuries under a scepter oppressed.
   But one day, with their passion arising,
   "Enough," they said and broke the scepter.

8. **SENEGAL**

   Everyone strum your koras,
   Strike the balafons,
   The red lion has roared,
   The tamer of the bush with one leap,
   Has scattered the gloom.

9. **TAIWAN**

   The three principles of democracy our party does revere.

10. **URUGUAY**

    Eastern landsmen, our country or the tomb!

11. **USSR**

    Unbreakable union of freeborn republics,
    Great Russia has welded forever to stand;
    Thy might was created by will of our peoples,
    Now flourish in unity, great Soviet land!

Arts

FLORENCE FOSTER JENKINS
© People's Almanac Photographic Archives

That's Entertainment?
7 Perfectly Wretched Performers

1. HADJI ALI

   Billed as the Amazing Regurgitator, Hadji Ali enjoyed an improbably widespread popularity at the beginning of the twentieth century as a vaudeville drawing card. His act consisted of swallowing a series of unlikely objects—watermelon seeds, imitation jewels, coins, peach pits—and then regurgitating specific items as requested by his audience. It was impressive, if tasteless, stuff—but his grand finale brought down the house every night. His assistant would set up a tiny metal castle on stage while Ali drank a gallon of water, chased down by a pint of kerosene. To the accompaniment of a protracted drumroll, he would eject the kerosene across the stage in a 6-foot arc and set the castle afire. Then, as flames shot high into the air, he would upchuck the gallon of water and extinguish the blaze.

2. THE CHERRY SISTERS

   When impresario Oscar Hammerstein found himself in a financial hole, he decided to try a new approach. "I've been putting on the best talent, and it hasn't gone over," he told reporters. "I'm going to try the worst." On November 16, 1896, he introduced Elizabeth, Effie, Jessie, and Addie Cherry to New York audiences at his Olympic Theatre. A sister act that had been treading the vaudeville boards in the Midwest for a few years, the girls strutted onto the Olympia's stage garbed in flaming red dresses, hats, and woolen mittens. Jessie kept time on a bass drum while her three partners did their opening number:

   Cherries ripe Boom-de-ay!
   Cherries red Boom-de-ay!
   The Cherry Sisters
   Have come to stay!

   New York audiences sat transfixed, staring goggle-eyed in disbelief, but they proved more merciful than audiences in the Midwest had. They refrained from pelting the girls with garbage and overripe tomatoes at first. Eventually, the Cherry sisters had to put up a wire screen to protect themselves from the inevitable hail of missiles showered on them by their outraged audiences. In later years, they denied that anything had ever been thrown at them. Said a writer in the *New York Times:* "It is sincerely hoped that nothing like them will ever be seen again." Another critic wrote, "A locksmith with a strong rasping file could earn steady wages taking the kinks out of Lizzie's voice." Despite their reputation as the world's worst act, they played consistently to SRO crowds, wowing their fans with such numbers as "The Modern Young Man" (a recitation), "I'm out upon the Mash, Boys," "Curfew

Must Not Ring Tonight," and "Don't You Remember Sweet Alice, Ben Bolt?"

3. RONALD COATES

This nineteenth-century British eccentric may well have been the worst actor in the history of the legitimate theater. A Shakespearean by inclination, Coates saw no objection to rewriting the Bard's great tragedies to suit his own tastes. In one unforgettable reworking of *Romeo and Juliet,* in which he played the male lead, he tried to jimmy open his bride's casket with a crowbar. Costumed in a feathered hat, spangled cloak, and billowing pantaloons—an outfit he wore in public, as well—he looked singularly absurd. He was frequently hooted and jeered off stage for his inept, overblown performances. Quite often he had to bribe theater managers to get a role in their productions, and his fellow thespians, fearing violence from the audience, demanded that he provide police protection before they would consent to appear on stage with him. He was slandered and laughed at throughout the British Isles and often threatened with lynching, but he persisted in his efforts to act. During one dramatic performance, several members of the audience were so violently convulsed with laughter that they had to be treated by a physician. Coates was struck and killed by a carriage—but not until 1848, when he was 74.

4. SADAKICHI HARTMANN

It seemed like a good idea at the time. Billing himself as a Japanese-German inventor, Hartmann was, briefly, a fixture in the New York theater in the early 1900s, offering soon-to-be-jaded audiences what he called "perfume concerts." Using a battery of electric fans, he blew great billowing clouds of scented smoke toward his audience, meanwhile explaining in thickly accented English that each aroma represented a different nation. Hartmann, who frequently had trouble with hecklers, rarely made it beyond England (roses) or Germany (violets) before being hooted from the stage.

5. FLORENCE FOSTER JENKINS

A taxi collision in 1943 left would-be diva Florence Foster Jenkins capable of warbling a higher F than she'd ever managed before. So delighted was she that she waived legal action against the taxi company, presenting the driver with a box of imported cigars instead—an appropriately grand gesture for the woman universally hailed as the world's worst opera singer. The remarkable career of this Pennsylvania heiress was for many years an in-joke among cognoscenti and music critics—the latter writing intentionally ambiguous reviews of the performances she gave regularly in salons from Philadelphia to Newport. "Her singing at its finest suggests the untrammeled swoop of some great bird," Robert Lawrence wrote in the *Saturday Review.* Edward Tatnall Canby spoke of a "subtle ghastliness that defies description." But *Newsweek* was the most graphic, noting: "In high notes, Mrs. Jenkins sounds as if she was afflicted with low, nagging backache." On October 25, 1944, Mrs. Jenkins engineered the most daring coup of her career: a recital before a packed Carnegie Hall. That concert, like her others, saw the well-padded matron, then in her seventies, change costume numerous times. She appeared variously as the tinsel-winged "Angel of Inspiration"; the Queen of the Night from Mozart's *Magic Flute;* and a Spanish coquette, draped in a colorful shawl, with a jeweled comb and a red rose in her hair. Inevitably, she seasoned her "coquette" rendition by tossing rose petals plucked from a wicker basket to the audience. On at least one occasion she inadvertently tossed the basket, as well. But she always made certain to retrieve the petals for the next performance.

6. MRS. ELVA MILLER

While growing up in Kansas, Elva figured that with practice and training she might have a shot at a career in singing. Her friends and family thought otherwise. However, she made the high school glee club and the church choir and even studied voice at Pomona College in Claremont, California. But with it all, her voice was reminiscent of cockroaches rustling in a garbage can at dawn. In the 1960s—by now a fiftyish California housewife—she recorded on her own a few favorite melodies "just for the ducks of it." She persuaded a local disc jockey to give her an airing and finally cut a nightmarish 45 single of the hit song "Downtown." It sold 250,000 copies in barely three weeks and made "The Kansas Rocking Bird," as she was dubbed, the darling of TV variety shows. "Her tempos, to put it charitably, are free form," said *Time* magazine. "She has an uncanny knack for landing squarely between the beat, producing a new ricochet effect that, if nothing else, defies imitation. . . . [She] also tosses in a few choruses of whistling for a change of pace."

7. WILLIAM HUNG

Hung, a 21-year-old engineering student from the University of California at Berkeley, auditioned for the 2004 season of the *American Idol* television show. After he sang a tuneless, but enthusiastic, rendition of Ricky Martin's song "She Bangs," judge Simon Cowell observed, "You can't sing, you can't dance, so what do you want me to say?" Despite the rejection, repeated showings of the *Idol* clip turned Hung into a cult star. Soon the "Real American Idol" was giving off-key performances on talk shows ranging from the *Today* show to *The Tonight Show*, singing at a nationally televised NBA game, and sharing the stage with the likes of Janet Jackson, OutKast, and Lenny Kravitz at the Wango Tango Music Festival at the Rose Bowl in Pasadena, California. He signed a contract with Koch Entertainment and recorded an album, *Inspiration*, that sold more than 200,000 copies—outselling the debut album by *Idol*'s season-one runner-up, Justin Guarini.

B.F.

13 Art Riots

1. **THE "OLD PRICE" RIOTS, COVENT GARDEN THEATRE, 1809**
   After the Covent Garden Theatre burned to the ground in 1808, a new building was put up the following year and the management of the theater took the opportunity to raise prices from six to seven shillings for boxes, and from three shillings and sixpence to four shillings for most other seats. Outraged by the rise, the audience at the first performance in the new theater constantly interrupted the playing of *Macbeth* with loud shouts of "Old prices! Old prices!" Soldiers were sent into the gallery to quell the disturbances, but the gallery-goers, further angered by the fact that in the badly designed new theater they could see little more than the legs of the actors, continued to cause mayhem. In fact, they continued to do so at every performance for three months, bringing rattles, whistles, trumpets, and farmyard animals into the theater to cause maximum disruption. Eventually, the management, under the famous actor and impresario John Philip Kemble, bowed to the pressure and returned to the old prices.

2. **THE APPEARANCE OF WILLIAM MACREADY, ASTOR PLACE OPERA HOUSE, NEW YORK, MAY 10, 1849**
   William Macready, a close friend of Charles Dickens, was the most famous English actor of his day. When he traveled to the United States to perform, he fully expected to receive the kind of acclaim he was used to in London. Instead, he found himself at the center of a fierce controversy involving a rival actor, the American Edwin Forrest. Patriotic Americans championed Forrest over Macready, whom they saw as an arrogant, patronizing foreigner. On May 10, 1849, 15,000 Forrest supporters gathered outside the Astor Place Opera House, where Macready was due to perform. They hurled stones at the building and at police attempting to protect it. As the violence grew worse, the militia were summoned and eventually opened fire on the crowd. Twenty-three people were killed and hundreds injured.

3. **PREMIERE PERFORMANCE OF THE MARQUISE DE MORNY'S PANTOMIME PLAY *RÊVE D'ÉGYPTE*, MOULIN ROUGE, PARIS, JANUARY 3, 1907**
   Set in the pharaohs' Egypt, this pantomime featured the controversial French writer and music hall actress Colette and her friend and inamorata, the Marquise de Morny. The women portrayed reunited lovers, with the marquise playing the male role. Colette said, "I become my parts," and she did that night, for when the lovers embraced in a long kiss, Colette, almost nude, displayed uninhibited passion. The marquise's husband, his friends, and the audience were outraged. When the curtain came down, the audience was in an ugly mood, and its

outrage boiled over into a riotous affair, with people throwing objects at the performers and beating each other with their umbrellas.

4. **PREMIERE PERFORMANCE OF ARNOLD SCHÖNBERG'S** *PIERROT LUNAIRE*, **BERLIN, 1912**
In 1912, Schönberg had yet to develop his 12-tone system, but his composing had already evolved toward music severe in style, terse in form, and atonal, with melodies that were somber and unadorned. *Pierrot Lunaire* was such a work, and it provoked hostility, riots, and scandal. Blows were traded amid hysteria and laughter. One critic wrote, "If this is music, then I pray my Creator not let me hear it again." Even years later, repercussions were felt, as a man from the premiere audience brought assault charges against another man. In court, a physician testified that the music had been so jarring as to awaken peculiar neuroses.

5. **PREMIERE PERFORMANCE OF IGOR STRAVINSKY'S** *RITE OF SPRING* **AND THE ACCOMPANYING BALLET BY NIJINSKY, THÉÂTRE DES CHAMPS ÉLYSÉES, PARIS, MAY 29, 1913**
The music performed that night was so revolutionary in concept that many in the audience perceived it as musical anarchy. Also, Nijinsky's dancing was too sensual for the moral and aesthetic palates of many upper-class ballet lovers. Together, the music and dance shocked the audience. Whistling and catcalls rocked the theater, and sympathetic patrons tried, unsuccessfully, to silence the upheaval. Fistfights cropped up in the aisles, and gendarmes arrived to expel the worst of the offenders, but pandemonium soon broke out anew and continued until the end of the performance. Years later, the composer-conductor Pierre Boulez referred to the *Rite* as "the cornerstone of modern music."

6. **VIOLIN RECITAL BY FRITZ KREISLER, CORNELL UNIVERSITY, DECEMBER 1919**
After being wounded in World War I and subsequently released from the Austrian army, Kreisler traveled to the United States for a concert tour. With war sentiment running high, many of his concerts were canceled—one by a director of public safety, another by a women's club, and yet another due to protests. In December 1919, more than a year after the Armistice, he played at Cornell University, even though the mayor of Ithaca exhorted citizens not to attend. During the performance, irate American Legionnaires cut the electric wires, but Kreisler played on in the blackout for 40 minutes. Disturbances escalated to riotous proportions, and the police were summoned.

7. **PERFORMANCE OF MUSIC FOR PIANO BY GEORGE ANTHEIL, THE PHILHARMONIE, BUDAPEST, 1923**
A composer of avant-garde music that was considered antiromantic and antiexpressive, Antheil often met with hostile audiences. As a result, he

began carrying a gun hidden in a shoulder holster whenever he performed. His opening concert in Budapest provoked the audience because of its harsh and unfamiliar sounds, and a riot broke out. The following night, determined that his music be heard, Antheil ordered the ushers to lock all the doors. Then, with the audience's full attention on him, he pulled out his gun and placed it on the piano, where it remained for the rest of an uninterrupted performance.

8. **INITIAL SCREENINGS OF LUIS BUÑUEL AND SALVADOR DALI'S *L'ÂGE D'OR*, PARIS, DECEMBER 1930**
A film that bombards the viewer with violent and erotic surrealistic imagery, *L'Âge d'Or* is concerned with the malice and hypocrisy of man; it vigorously scorns the conventions and institutions of bourgeois society. As expected, bourgeois society was not delighted with the film. One newspaper called it "obscene, repellent, and paltry," and another commented that "country, family and religion are dragged through the mud." An article in an extreme rightist paper incited reactionary young Frenchmen, and they launched an attack on the theater that did not stop for six days. By that time, 120,000 francs' worth of damage had been done. Due to the violent controversy, the film was not shown again publicly for more than 35 years.

9. **UNVEILING OF MURAL BY DIEGO RIVERA, HOTEL DEL PRADO, MEXICO CITY, JUNE 1948**
Diego Rivera's mural *Sunday in the Alameda,* commissioned for the dining room of the new Hotel Del Prado in 1948, showed Mexican historian Ignacio Ramirez holding an open book. The words "Dios no existe" ("God does not exist") were clearly printed on one page. Consequently, Archbishop L. M. Martinez refused to bless the government-owned structure, and a mob of youths stormed into the dining room and scraped away the words with a knife. When Rivera restored the words with a fountain pen, local students threatened to obliterate them as often as he replaced them. The hotel had the mural covered, and while its fate remained in limbo, Rivera was denied entrance to a movie house and his home was vandalized. Eventually, a priest who preferred to remain anonymous quietly blessed the hotel.

10. **CONCERT BY PAUL ROBESON, PEEKSKILL, NEW YORK, SEPTEMBER 4, 1949**
As the Cold War intensified, Robeson came under increasing fire for his leftist political views. A benefit concert for the Civil Rights Congress by Robeson and other liberal singers in Peekskill, New York, scheduled for August 27, 1949, had to be canceled when a mob of anti-Communists reinforced by the Ku Klux Klan smashed chairs and beat concertgoers. Robeson returned on September 4 to sing for a crowd of 10,000 in a field outside of Peekskill. Supporters formed a human shield around him as he

performed songs such as "Go Down Moses" and "Old Man River." At the end of the show, concertgoers had to run a gauntlet of rock throwers lining the exit. Singer Pete Seeger used the rocks thrown at his car to build a chimney for his house. Hundreds were injured trying to leave the show. A year later, Robeson was blacklisted after he refused to sign an affidavit disclaiming his membership in the Communist Party.

11. UNAUTHORIZED EXHIBIT OF MODERN ART, MOSCOW, SEPTEMBER 15, 1974
A group of Russian artists whose paintings were in many styles—except Social Realism, the official art of the USSR—were unable to obtain either permission or a building for an exhibit, so one was set up in a muddy field in southeast Moscow. Soviet police met the challenge by driving bulldozers and high-pressure water trucks through the exhibit grounds, sending men, women, and children fleeing in panic. Plain-clothesmen trampled many paintings underfoot, and the police burned others. Thirty foreign diplomats watched while artists were beaten up, journalists were manhandled, and U.S. consul Leonard F. Willems was shoved around. The police defended these actions, saying that the bulldozers and trucks were building "a park of rest and culture." Two weeks later, to appease the United States—its détente partner—and to court world opinion, the Soviet government gave permission for a similar exhibit.

12. "BLOOD AND HONEY" EXHIBITS, SERBIA, JUNE–AUGUST 2002
A series of confrontations occurred when "Blood and Honey," a collection of pictures taken on the battlefields of the former Yugoslavia by American photographer Ron Haviv, was displayed in Serbian cities. On June 5, 2002, a group of 40 people disrupted the exhibition in Uzice, protesting that the pictures were anti-Serb. A month later, in Cacak, a gang of skinheads burst into the gallery during the opening of the exhibition and attacked organizer Ivan Zlatic, leaving him badly injured. When the exhibit opened in Kragujevac in August, protestors, many wearing T-shirts declaring war criminal Radovan Karadzic a "Serbian hero," greeted visitors with shouts of "Traitors!" Police arrived on the scene but did not react as the demonstrators continued to hurl insults at people entering the gallery. Exhibit organizers decided to postpone the opening to avoid a major confrontation.

13. "CAUTION! RELIGION" EXHIBITION, SAKHAROV MUSEUM, MOSCOW, JANUARY 18, 2003
Items on display at the Sakharov Museum included a church made of vodka bottles and an image of Christ on a Coca-Cola ad with the words, "Coca-Cola. This is my blood." After the works had been on display for four days, Russian Orthodox demonstrators vandalized the museum, breaking some items and spray-painting "Sacrilege" and "You hate

orthodoxy" on others. Six rioters were arrested after being locked in the gallery by a custodian. Russian Orthodox archpriest Alexander Shargunov, founder of a movement called "For the Moral Revival of the Fatherland," led a publicity campaign that got charges dropped against the vandals. Instead, the government charged museum director Yuri Samodurov, exhibition organizer Lyudmila Vasilovskaya, and artist Anna Mikhalchuk with "inciting religious hatred," a charge that carried a potential five-year sentence. The three went on trial on June 15, 2004, but their indictment was dismissed as "flawed" by the court.

E.H.C. & C.F.

Ricky Jay's
10 Most Unusual Variety Acts of All Time

(In No Particular Order)
Ricky Jay is an author, actor, sleight-of-hand artist, and scholar of the unusual. Most of the performers listed here are included in his histories of remarkable entertainers, *Learned Pigs & Fireproof Women* and *Jay's Journal of Anomalies.*

1. TOMMY MINNOCK
   Shortly before the turn of the century this "human horse," a subject able to withstand excruciating pain, was literally nailed to a cross in a Trenton, New Jersey, music hall. While he was crucified, he regaled the audience with his rendition of the popular tune "After the Ball Is Over."

2. THEA ALBA
   This German schoolgirl wrote with both hands, both feet, and her mouth, simultaneously; for a finale, she wrote 10 different numerals at the same time with pieces of chalk extending from pointers on each of her fingers.

3. DANIEL WILDMAN
   This eighteenth-century equestrian beekeeper rode around the circus ring on the back of a horse while swarms of bees surrounded his face and then moved away to specific locations at his command.

4. MATHEW BUCHINGER
   Born in Germany in 1674, this remarkable man was one of the best-known performers of his day. He played a dozen musical instruments, danced the hornpipe, and was an expert pistol shot, bowler, calligrapher, and magician. His accomplishments seem even more remarkable when one realizes he stood only 28 inches high and had no arms or legs.

5. ORVILLE STAMM

Billed as "The Strongest Boy in the World," he played the violin with an enormous bulldog suspended from the crook of his bowing arm. For an encore, he lay on the ground and a piano was placed on his chest; a keyboardist stood on his thighs and pounded out the accompaniment as Orville sang "Ireland Must Be Heaven 'Cause Mother Comes from There."

6. SIGNORA GIRARDELLI

In the early nineteenth century, she entertained audiences by cooking eggs in boiling oil held in her palm, running a red-hot poker over her limbs, and attending to baked goods while inside a blazing oven.

7. ARTHUR LLOYD

This vaudevillian astounded fans by producing from his capacious pockets any item printed on paper. Admission tickets to the White House, membership cards to the Communist Party, and ringside tickets to the Dempsey-Carpentier championship fight were among the 15,000 items he could instantly retrieve from his clothing.

8. JEAN ROYER

A seventeenth-century native of Lyon, he swallowed an enormous quantity of water and then spewed it out in continuous graceful arcs for as long as it took to walk 200 paces or recite the Fifty-first Psalm.

9. CLARENCE WILLARD

As "Willard, the Man Who Grows," he had an act that consisted of his growing six inches in height while standing next to a volunteer from the audience. A master of manipulating his body, Willard used no trick apparatus of any kind.

10. JOSEPH PUJOL

"Le Petomane," as he was called, was the legendary French musical farter who issued sonorous—and odorless—notes from his body's most secret orifice.

Lucille Ball's
10 Favorite TV Series

One of the best-loved comediennes in history, Lucille Ball was born on August 6, 1911, in Jamestown, New York. After years of mostly small parts in films, she found her real success on television, costarring with her real-life husband Desi Arnaz in *I Love Lucy*, which became widely regarded as one of the greatest sitcoms in TV history and ran from 1951 to 1957. She starred in several other TV series and became an extremely successful producer. She also starred in a number of movies, including *The Long, Long Trailer* (1954) and *Yours, Mine and Ours* (1968). She died in Beverly Hills, California, on April 26, 1989. She contributed the following list to *The Book of Lists* in 1983:

1. *M*A*S*H*
2. *The Carol Burnett Show*
3. *The Honeymooners*
4. *The Dick Van Dyke Show*
5. *The Mary Tyler Moore Show*
6. *The Jack Benny Show*
7. *National Geographic* shows
8. *The Milton Berle Show*
9. *Hallmark Theatre*
10. And, of course, *I Love Lucy*

Chris Golden's
10 Favorite Supernatural Television Series

Born and raised in Massachusetts, where he still lives with his family, Christopher Golden is the best-selling author of such horror and fantasy novels as *The Boys Are Back in Town, The Ferryman*, and *Strangewood*. He has also written original novels tied in to such popular film and television franchises as *Buffy the Vampire Slayer, Angel, X-Men, Hellboy*, and Peter Jackson's remake of *King Kong*. Stephen King wrote that Golden's most recent book, *Wildwood Road*, "is a brilliant novel of supernatural suspense that reminded me of the early classics by Ira Levin—think *Rosemary's Baby* and you won't be disappointed." Golden is currently at work on a dark fantasy trilogy for Bantam Books entitled *The Veil*.

1. THE TWILIGHT ZONE: Rod Serling's classic anthology series combined the supernatural, science fiction, and social commentary in five seasons of one of the greatest television series of all time. Many of its episodes are among the finest programs to ever grace the small screen. The 1980s update gets an honorable mention for a handful of stunning hours, some of which held up to the best of the originals.

2. KOLCHAK—THE NIGHT STALKER: Darren McGavin was utterly convincing as the curmudgeonly reporter who stumbled upon chilling supernatural mysteries week after week. Though it lasted only one season, the series was an inspiration to writers of novels, films, and television, including *X-Files* creator Chris Carter.

3. **BUFFY THE VAMPIRE SLAYER:** Joss Whedon's landmark series brought a new wave of female empowerment to television, added a whole new cadence to American language, and became a worldwide phenomenon, despite being seen by only five or six million people per week in the United States. It offered monsters who mirrored the troubles of the teenage experience and characters whose relationships were the source of boundless passion on the part of the series' faithful.

4. **TWIN PEAKS:** David Lynch's ingenious television series had one of the most wonderfully creepy first episodes in the history of television and was layered with murder and magic. Its weirdness gave rise to one of the earliest Internet fan communities. Unfortunately, it fell apart in season two, spinning away into oblique surreality.

5. **THE X-FILES:** Chris Carter promised us that the truth was out there, and that one day everything would be explained. Sadly, it turned out that the producers of the show had no more idea how it all fit together than the viewers did. When Mulder and Scully were on, however, and particularly in supernatural-based episodes, *The X-Files* was riveting.

6. **BEWITCHED:** This charming comedy about a hapless advertising executive married to a witch may be here simply because the nine-year-old in me will always be in love with Elizabeth Montgomery's "Samantha." Or perhaps it really was as wonderful as I remember it.

7. **ANGEL:** Joss Whedon's *Buffy* spinoff was a gem all its own, beginning as a hard-boiled detective series about a vampire attempting to redeem his soul, morphing into a show about a law firm whose clients are all monsters—human and otherwise—and finally becoming a show about a motley group of troubled people who are the only chance the world has against cosmic evil. Its final episode may have been its very best. There's nothing like going out on top.

8. **MIRACLES:** This recent, short-lived series starring Skeet Ulrich—about a Vatican expert on the supernatural—lasted only half a dozen episodes (seven additional episodes are available on the DVD edition), but each one is a breathtaking masterpiece. Wonderful television series are canceled all the time, but few leave the kind of impression that *Miracles* did.

9. **CARNIVALE:** HBO's tale of a dustbowl-era conflict between good and evil—with a righteous minister becoming the tool of evil and a troubled carnival worker given a divine touch—was unsettling, terrifying, and beautifully crafted. It was also unique in the history of television.

10. **OUTER LIMITS, BORIS KARLOFF'S THRILLER, NIGHT GALLERY, TALES FROM THE DARKSIDE:** While none can compare to

The Twilight Zone, each of these wonderful anthology series produced some extraordinary supernatural television, episodes that were harrowing originals, as well as some adapted from the works of classic horror, fantasy, and science fiction writers.

Gene Kelly's
11 Greatest Dancers

Born Eugene Curran Kelly in Pittsburgh, Pennsylvania, on August 23, 1912, he came to Hollywood at age 30 after starring in the hit Broadway show *Pal Joey* in 1941. He quickly became one of the silver screen's most enduring stars in such musical hits as *Anchors Aweigh* (1945), *An American in Paris* (1951), *Brigadoon* (1954), and *Singin' in the Rain* (1952), which he codirected with Stanley Donen. He also directed *Gigot* (1962) and *Hello, Dolly!* (1969). In 1952 he received a special Academy Award for his innovative contributions to choreography in film, and in 1985 he was awarded the Life Achievement Award by the American Film Institute. Gene Kelly died in Beverly Hills, California, on February 2, 1996. He contributed this list to *The Book of Lists* in 1977:

1. Salome
2. Master Juba (19th century), minstrel dancer, born William Henry Lane
3. Isadora Duncan
4. Nijinsky
5. Carlotta Grisi (19th century), Italian ballerina
6. Maria Taglioni (19th century), Italian ballerina
7. Fanny Cerito (19th century), Italian ballerina
8–9. Doris Humphrey and Charles Weidman (20th century), U.S. dancing duo
10. John Bubbles (1940s), U.S. tap dancer
11. Bill Robinson

John Gielgud's
6 Greatest Hamlets

Born in London on April 14, 1904, Sir John Gielgud was trained at the Royal Academy of Dramatic Arts and distinguished himself as an actor early on, playing his first Hamlet at age 26 and quickly becoming one of the great Shakespearean actors of the century. His production of *Much Ado About Nothing* in 1950 was considered a theatrical landmark. His extensive film credits included work with such noted and varied directors as Alfred Hitchcock (*Secret Agent*, in which he played W. Somerset Maugham's famous spy Ashenden), David Lynch (*The Elephant Man*), and Peter Greenaway (*Prospero's Books*), as well as his Best Supporting Actor Oscar–winning turn in the hit comedy *Arthur*. He directed Richard Burton in *Hamlet* in 1964. Gielgud was knighted by Queen Elizabeth in 1996, and he died of natural causes on May 21, 2000. He contributed this list to *The Book of Lists* in 1983:

1. Richard Burbage (1567?–1619)
2. Thomas Betterton (1635?–1710)
3. Edwin Booth (1833–1893)
4. Sir Henry Irving (1838–1905)
5. Sir Johnston Forbes-Robertson (1853–1937)
6. John Barrymore (1882–1942)

Charles M. Schulz's
10 Greatest Cartoon Characters

Charles (aka "Sparky") M. Schulz, the creator of *Peanuts*, the most popular comic strip in the world, took a correspondence course in cartooning. His cast of characters, led by Charlie Brown, included Linus, Lucy, and, of course, Snoopy, based on his own mixed-breed dog, Spike. A warm, loving, and generous man, Schulz brought the expression "Good grief!" into popular use and introduced the expression "security blanket" into the English language. He confessed to having a pessimistic streak, saying that Charlie Brown was based on himself as a young man, when he always expected the worst. Regarding his success, Schulz said, "Well, frankly, I did expect success because it was something I had planned for since I was six years old." He wrote more than 1,400 books, and his comics ran in 2,600 papers and were read by 355 million people in 75 countries. Schulz died on February 12, 2000, at the age of 77, after 50 years of doing what he loved. He died on the eve of his last cartoon strip, which included a farewell letter. He contributed this list to *The Book of Lists* in 1977:

1. CHARLIE BROWN and SNOOPY
   Charlie Brown is the wishy-washy but likable star of *Peanuts*. His dog, Snoopy, often steals the show by parading as a World War I flying ace, a baseball player, or a novelist.

2. BLONDIE and DAGWOOD
   Chic Young's comic strip deals with the domestic misadventures of this happily but crazily married couple.

3. POPEYE and WIMPY

Popeye, the spinach-eating sailor, and Wimpy, his hamburger-eating buddy, are the prime characters of the popular *Popeye* cartoon created by Elzie Segar.

4. KRAZY KAT

The playful romance between the lovesick Krazy Kat and Ignatz Mouse, who throws bricks at Krazy, is the subject of this universally acclaimed comic strip created by George Herriman.

5. WASH TUBBS and CAPTAIN EASY

Wash Tubbs, a funny little guy who liked big women, and his sidekick, a soldier of fortune named Captain Easy, were developed by Roy Crane.

6. SUPERMAN

Faster than a speeding bullet and blessed with x-ray vision, Superman was the brainchild of two teenagers, Jerry Siegel and Joe Shuster.

7. SKIPPY

Skippy, a misanthropic 10-year-old developed by Percy Crosby, starred in one of the first comics in which children adopted adult reactions to the world around them.

8. SKEEZIX

The prime character of Frank King's *Gasoline Alley* was the first character to grow from infancy to adulthood in a comic strip in the same number of years it would take a real person to grow up.

9. LITTLE ORPHAN ANNIE

Created by Harold Gray, this curly-haired, redheaded orphan with blank eyes crept into the hearts of millions.

10. DICK TRACY

Developed by Chester Gould, *Dick Tracy* was the first realistic detective comic strip.

10 People Who Hated Portraits of Themselves

1–5. JACOB VON LOON, VOLCKERT JANZ, WILLEM VON DOEYENBURG, JACHEM DE NEVE, AERNOUT VAN DER MEIJE

Rembrandt's group portrait of the board of directors of the cloth makers guild, although judged by modern critics to be a great painting, was thought by its conservative subjects to be too radical in approach. Today it serves as a trademark for a cigar company.

6. MARY RIDDLE (d. 1892)
Mrs. Riddle, a cousin of Mary Cassatt, once gave the artist a blue and white china tea set. In gratitude, Cassatt painted a portrait of Riddle seated at a table on which the set was prominently displayed. The Riddle family refused to accept the portrait, complaining that Mrs. Riddle's nose was too large. Cassatt, who noted, "You may be sure it was like her," put the picture away in storage until 1915. *Lady at the Tea Table* now hangs in the Metropolitan Museum of Art in New York City.

7. WINSTON CHURCHILL (1874–1965), British statesman
"Disgusting," said Lord Hailsham, Churchill's good friend, of Graham Sutherland's portrait. "A beautiful work," said Nye Bevan, Churchill's bitter foe. Churchill called it "a remarkable example of modern art." Churchill hated modern art. So did Lady Churchill. In 1955, she retrieved the portrait, valued at $300,000, from its hiding place behind a cellar boiler, smashed it to the floor, and then tossed it in the incinerator. Another portrait of Sir Winston, done by his painting instructor, Sir Walter Sickert, also met with her disfavor. She put her foot through it.

8. LYNDON JOHNSON (1908–1973), U.S. president
LBJ called Peter Hurd's portrait "the ugliest thing I ever saw in my whole life." Lady Bird Johnson hoped she would never see another like it if she "lived to be a thousand." Nevertheless, the Johnsons were unable to prevent it from being hung in the Smithsonian Portrait Gallery in Washington, D.C.

9. PHILIP MOUNTBATTEN (1921–), British prince consort
The prince was not pleased with Pietro Annigoni's portrait. One observer who looked at it said, "If he is really like that, I shouldn't like to meet him in the dark."

10. HENRY KISSINGER (1923–), U.S. secretary of state
Gardner Cox's portrait was to have hung in the State Department, but Kissinger felt he had been "reduced." A spokesman at State said it "made him look something like a dwarf." Cox rejected the offer to rework the portrait, forfeiting his $12,000 commission, saying he liked the painting the way it was.

R.W.S.

10 Artists Whose Works Were Painted Over

1. **UNKNOWN ARTIST** (10th century), *Kuan Lin Holding Lotus Blossom*
   In 1953, officials of the esteemed Nelson Gallery of Art in Kansas City received a valuable twelfth-century Chinese wall painting that had been damaged during shipping. The horror of the officials was to be short-lived, for as restorer James Roth worked on the mural, he discovered a trace of blue paint underneath a layer of mud and rice husks. After careful, detailed work, a gracious goddess was exposed and identified as an outstanding example of tenth-century painting. It was hailed as one of the greatest Oriental art discoveries in recent years.

2. **GIOVANNI BELLINI** (1430?–1516), *Feast of the Gods*
   It had long been known that the renowned Renaissance painter Titian (1488–1576) had altered *Feast of the Gods,* a painting by his teacher, Giovanni Bellini. When the painting was x-rayed in the 1950s, it was discovered that Titian had also painted over several principal figures, altered the composition, and in essence changed the very content of the masterpiece. Art historians now view the two masters' artistry as enhancing the value of the canvas and consider the painting as two original works in one.

3. **SANDRO BOTTICELLI** (1444?–1510), *Three Miracles of St. Zenobius*
   During the cleaning of this fifteenth-century masterpiece, restorers at the New York Metropolitan Museum of Art noted that a central portion of the painting had been painted over. Technicians using x-rays to examine the area discovered an image of two preserved skeletons lying in a coffin. As the painting had previously been owned by Sir William Abdy of London, it is believed that he had the skeletons painted over in deference to Victorian tastes.

4. **LUCAS CRANACH** (1472–1553), *Charity*
   In this painting of a nude woman nursing her child, puritanical sentiment triumphed over the artist's intentions when a restorer painted a complete set of clothes on the woman. Later, the clothing was removed, leaving the painting in its original state.

5. **MICHELANGELO** (1475–1564), charcoal drawings
   The world's only group of mural sketches by the great Renaissance painter, sculptor, and architect was found in late 1975 when chapel director Paolo Dal Poggetto was trying to devise an alternate route for moving tourist traffic through Florence's Medici Chapel. Before opening up a storeroom as an exit to the street, restorer Sabino Giovannoni performed tests on the walls. Under several layers of whitewash and grime, he discovered more than 50 large drawings of the human form and

one of a horse's head, evidently Michelangelo's record of past works and preliminary sketches of future projects. Art historians believe that Michelangelo, an outspoken Republican, may have rendered the sketches while hiding out from an assassin hired by the Medicis, who were purging Florence of political opposition.

6. BARTOLOMEO DA VENETO (1502–1546), *St. Catherine of Alexandria*
Bartolomeo's *St. Catherine* had been in the collection of the Stadel Museum in Frankfurt, Germany, under that name since 1840. In 1991, when the painting was taken to the lab to have blemishes removed, chief restorer Peter Waldeis noticed inconsistencies and peculiarities. A scientific examination revealed that the ratchets on the wheel on which Catherine was to die and the pearls and embroidery on her cloak were the result of overpainting. Once it was removed, the "wheel" on which "Catherine" rested her fingers was "in fact the stone edge of a pool or fountain," Waldeis noted. Also, "the garment looked coarser and more masculine, as did the hair." Waldeis and Jurg Sander, the chief art historian of the Stadel, concluded that the subject of the painting actually was Narcissus, the youth of Greek mythology who pined away longing for his reflection in a pool. Waldeis speculated that the changes had been made in the early nineteenth century, when religious themes were particularly popular. Presumably, the person who altered the picture thought he could get a better price for a portrait of St. Catherine.

7. PAUL CÉZANNE (1839–1906), *Portrait of a Peasant*
After recovering a stolen Cézanne, *The Artist's Sister*, in 1962, the St. Louis City Art Museum decided to have the painting cleaned and relined. Art conservator James Roth discovered another portrait on the back of the canvas. Painted while Cézanne was in his early twenties, the new portrait of a peasant raised the value of the original by $75,000. The canvas is mounted so that both portraits can be viewed.

8. MAURICE UTRILLO (1883–1955), *Execution des Generaux Lecomte & Clement Thomas par les Communards a la Caserne de Chateau Rouge* (aka *La Caserne*)
The painting, an atypical work for Utrillo, provides a dispassionate view of two figures facing a firing squad during the 1871 Paris Commune uprising. The work was bought in Paris in April 1994 for $87,400 and sold in June at Christie's in London for $109,000. During the two intervening months, the rifles of the firing squad were painted over, apparently to eliminate the reference to an execution. Although Christie's claimed that Utrillo experts Gilbert Petrides and Jean Fabris had authenticated *La Caserne*, both denied having been consulted before the London sale. Fabris added, "In my opinion, it's a fake, as it was tampered with."

9. ARSHILE GORKY (1905–1948), aviation murals
   Two murals of an original 10 painted by Armenian-born artist Arshile
   Gorki were recovered in 1973 due to the efforts of Mrs. Ruth Bowman,
   a Newark, New Jersey, art historian. Five years after the completion of
   the 10 murals—commissioned by the Works Progress Administration in
   1937—the Army Air Corps took over Newark Airport, which housed
   the murals, and put the first of 14 coats of whitewash over them. Every
   major art text published since 1948 claimed the murals had been lost,
   but Mrs. Bowman decided to investigate the walls further and found
   two murals intact. The other eight paintings were destroyed when walls
   were torn down to expedite the installation of new radiators.

10. DAVID SALLE (1952–), *Jump*
    In September 1980, the artists David Salle and Julian Schnabel traded
    paintings. The painting that Salle gave Schnabel, *Jump*, consists of two
    canvases mounted side by side. The right side portrayed a woman and a
    baby in a bedroom, the left side featured birds. Schnabel decided that
    the work was incomplete, so he painted Salle's face in orange on the left
    panel. Salle was not initially pleased with Schnabel's handiwork. When
    Schnabel first showed him the painting, Salle jumped up and wrestled
    him to the floor. They later reconciled and sold *Jump* as a joint work to
    collector Eugene Schwartz.

                                                               E.H.C. & C.F.

Andrew Wyeth's
8 Greatest American Paintings in History

Born in 1917, the great realist artist Andrew Wyeth was taught to paint by his
father, the famed illustrator N. C. Wyeth, and is often referred to as "Painter
of the People." His work can be seen in the National Gallery of Art, the
Smithsonian American Art Museum, and the Fine Arts Museum of San
Francisco. When asked to explain his worldwide popularity, Wyeth answered:
"It's because I happen to paint things that reflect the basic truths of life: sky,
earth, friends, the intimate things."

1. *Fox Hunt* (1893) by Winslow Homer
2. *Riverdale* (1863) by Fitz Hugh Lane
3. *Colonel George Washington* (1772) by Charles Willson Peale
4. *Hunting* (1874) by Thomas Eakins
5. *The Race Track* (1910) by Albert Pinkham Ryder
6. *Daughters of Revolution* (1932) by Grant Wood
7. *Noah's Ark* (1846) by Edward Hicks
8. *Fur Traders Descending the Missouri* (1845) by George Caleb Bingham

9 Valuable Art Works Found Unexpectedly

1. **IN A FARMER'S FIELD**
   In 1820, a Greek peasant named Yorgos was digging in his field on the island of Milos when he unearthed several carved blocks of stone. He burrowed deeper and found four statues—three figures of Hermes and one of Aphrodite, the goddess of love. Three weeks later, the Choiseul archaeological expedition arrived by ship, purchased the Aphrodite, and took it to France. Louis XVIII gave it the name *Venus de Milo* and presented it to the Louvre in Paris, where it became one of the most famous works of art in the world.

2. **BENEATH A STREET**
   On February 21, 1978, electrical workers were putting down lines on a busy street corner in Mexico City when they discovered a 20-ton stone bas-relief of the Aztec night goddess, Coyolxauhqui. It is believed to have been sculpted in the early fifteenth century and buried prior to the destruction of the Aztec civilization by the Spanish conquistadors in 1521. The stone was moved 200 yards from the site to the Museum of the Great Temple.

3. **IN A HOLE IN THE GROUND**
   In 1978, more than 500 motion pictures dating from 1903 to 1929 were dug out of a hole in the ground in Dawson City, Yukon, where they had been used as landfill. Under normal circumstances, the 35 mm nitrate films would have been destroyed, but the permafrost had preserved them perfectly. Included in the trove were films starring Harold Lloyd, Douglas Fairbanks, and Pearl White.

4. **UNDER A BED**
   Joanne Perez, the widow of vaudeville performer Pepito the Spanish Clown, discovered the only existing copy of the pilot for the TV series *I Love Lucy* when she cleaned out the area underneath her bed. Pepito had coached Lucille Ball and had guest-starred in the pilot. Ball and her husband, Desi Arnaz, had given the copy to Pepito as a gift in 1951, and it had remained under the bed for 30 years.

5. **ON A WALL**
   A middle-aged couple in a suburb of Milwaukee, Wisconsin, asked an art prospector to appraise a painting in their home. While he was there, he examined another painting that the couple had thought was a reproduction of a work by Vincent van Gogh. It turned out to be an 1886 original. On March 10, 1991, the painting *Still Life with Flowers* sold at auction for $1,400,000.

6. IN A TRUNK IN AN ATTIC

In 1961, Barbara Testa, a Hollywood librarian, inherited six steamer trunks that had belonged to her grandfather, James Fraser Gluck, a Buffalo, New York, lawyer who died in 1895. Over the next three decades she gradually sifted through the contents of the trunks, until one day in the fall of 1990 she came upon 665 pages that turned out to be the original handwritten manuscript of the first half of Mark Twain's *Huckleberry Finn*. The two halves of the great American novel were finally reunited at the Buffalo and Erie County Public Library.

7. AT A FLEA MARKET

A Philadelphia financial analyst was browsing at a flea market in Adamstown, Pennsylvania, when he was attracted by a wooden picture frame. He paid four dollars for it. Back at his home, he removed the old torn painting in the frame and found a folded document between the canvas and the wood backing. It turned out to be a 1776 copy of the Declaration of Independence—one of 24 known to remain. On June 13, 1991, Sotheby's auction house in New York sold the copy for $2,420,000.

8. ABOVE A COPYING MACHINE

For 60 years, a painting of Niagara Falls had hung unappreciated in Eno Memorial Hall in Simsbury, Connecticut, most recently above a copying machine. In April 1991, a local gallery owner walked into the building and recognized it as a previously unknown work by John Frederick Kensett. After a dispute over ownership, the 1855 oil was acquired, in 2002, by the Wadsworth Atheneum Museum of Art in Hartford, Connecticut, which paid an undisclosed sum to the city of Simsbury.

9. MASQUERADING AS A BICYCLE RACK

For years, employees of the God's House Tower Archaeology Museum in Southampton, England, propped their bikes against a 27-inch black rock in the basement. In 2000, two Egyptologists investigating the museum's holdings identified the bike rack as a seventh-century BC Egyptian statue portraying King Taharqa, a Kushite monarch from the region that is modern Sudan. Karen Wordley, the Southampton city council's curator of archaeological collections, said it was a "mystery" how the sculpture ended up in the museum basement.

CHAPTER FIVE

Health and Food

10 REALLY UNUSUAL MEDICAL CONDITIONS

10 AFFLICTIONS AND THEIR PATRON SAINTS

RATING THE EFFECTS OF 51 PERSONAL CRISES

19 NEW NEUROSES

5-YEAR SURVIVAL RATES FOR 25 TYPES OF CANCER

13 PEOPLE WHO SUCCEEDED AFTER HAVING A STROKE

14 PROMINENT PEOPLE WHO DIED WHILE EXERCISING

29 ACTIVITIES AND THE CALORIES THEY CONSUME

12 DRINKS NAMED AFTER PEOPLE

15 NOTABLE EVENTS THAT HAPPENED UNDER THE
INFLUENCE OF ALCOHOL

8 GREAT SAUSAGE EVENTS

11 MAMMOTH CHEESES

14 HIGHLY UNUSUAL RECIPES

16 PEOPLE WHO BECAME FOODS

JULIA CHILD'S 10 FAVORITE COOKBOOKS

10 FAMOUS INSOMNIACS

14 HEALTHY INSOMNIA CURES

21 HEALTH EXPERTS AND HOW THEY DIED

12 SUFFERERS OF TINNITUS

5 BODY PARTS NAMED AFTER ITALIANS

9 BODY PARTS YOU DIDN'T KNOW HAD NAMES

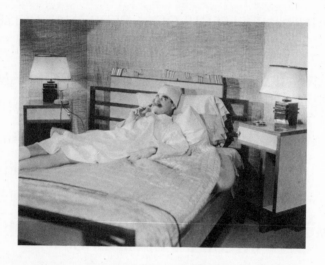

MR. MARX PREPARES FOR THE LAND OF NOD
© Corbis

10 Really Unusual Medical Conditions

Nothing is too wonderful to be true. —Michael Faraday

1. ART ATTACK
   Fine art can really make you sick. Or so says Dr. Graziella Magherini,
   author of *The Stendhal Syndrome*. She has studied more than a
   hundred tourists in Florence, Italy, who became ill in the presence of
   great works. Their symptoms include heart palpitations, dizziness, and
   stomach pains. The typical sufferer is a single person between the ages
   of 26 and 40 who rarely leaves home. Dr. Magherini believes the
   syndrome is a result of jet lag, travel stress, and the shock of an overwhelming sense of the past. "Very often," she says, "there's the anguish
   of death." The disorder was named after the nineteenth-century
   French novelist, who became overwhelmed by the frescoes in Florence's
   Santa Croce Church. Particularly upsetting works of art include
   Michelangelo's statue of David, Caravaggio's painting of Bacchus, and
   the concentric circles of the Duomo cupola.

2. HULA HOOP INTESTINE
   On February 26, 1992, Beijing worker Xu Denghai was hospitalized
   with a "twisted intestine" after playing excessively with a hula hoop.
   His was the third such case in the several weeks since a hula hoop craze
   had swept China. The Bejing *Evening News* advised people to warm up
   properly and avoid hula-hooping immediately after eating.

3. CARROT ADDICTION
   In its August 1992 issue, the highly respected *British Journal of
   Addiction* described three unusual cases of carrot dependence. One
   forty-year-old man had replaced cigarettes with carrots. He ate as
   many as five bunches a day and thought about them obsessively.
   According to two Czech psychiatrists, when carrots were withdrawn, he
   and the other patients "lapsed into heightened irritability."

4. CUTLERY CRAVING
   The desire to eat metal objects is comparatively common. Occasionally,
   there is an extreme case, however, such as that of 47-year-old Englishman
   Allison Johnson. An alcoholic burglar with a compulsion to eat silverware,
   Johnson has had 30 operations to remove strange things from his stomach.
   As of 1992, he had eight forks and the metal sections of a mop head lodged
   in his body. He has repeatedly been jailed and then released, each time
   going immediately to a restaurant and ordering lavishly. Unable to pay, he
   would then tell the owners to call the police and eat cutlery until they
   arrived. Johnson's lawyer said of his client, "He finds it hard to eat and
   obviously has difficulty going to the lavatory."

5. DR. STRANGELOVE SYNDROME

Alien hand syndrome is caused by damage to certain parts of the brain and afflicts thousands of people. This bizarre neurological disorder causes one of a person's hands to act independently of the other and of its owner's wishes. For example, the misbehaving hand may do the opposite of what the normal one is doing: If a person is trying to button a shirt with one hand, the other will follow along and undo the buttons. If one hand pulls up trousers, the other will pull them down. Sometimes the hand may become aggressive—pinching, slapping, or punching the patient; in at least one case, it tried to strangle its owner. Says neurologist Rachelle Doody, "Often a patient will sit on the hand, but eventually it gets loose and starts doing everything again."

6. MUD WRESTLER'S RASH

Within 36 hours after twenty-four men and women wrestled in calf-deep mud at the University of Washington, seven wrestlers were covered with patches of "pus-filled red bumps similar to pimples," and the rest succumbed later. Bumps were on areas not covered by bathing suits—one unlucky victim had wrestled in the nude. The dermatitis palaestrae limosae, or "muddy wrestling rash," may have been caused by manure-tainted mud.

7. ELECTRIC PEOPLE

According to British paranormalist Hilary Evans, some people are "upright human [electric] eels, capable of generating charges strong enough to knock out streetlights and electronic equipment." Cases of "electric people" date back to 1786; the most famous is that of 14-year-old Angelique Cottin, whose presence caused compass needles to gyrate wildly. To further investigate this phenomenon, Evans founded SLIDE, the Street Lamp Interference Data Exchange.

8. MARY HART EPILEPSY

The case of Dianne Neale, 49, appeared in the *New England Journal of Medicine:* In a much-publicized 1991 incident, Neale apparently suffered epileptic seizures upon hearing the voice of *Entertainment Tonight* cohost Mary Hart. Neale experienced an upset stomach, a sense of pressure in her head, and confusion. Laboratory tests confirmed the abnormal electrical discharges in her brain, and Neale held a press conference to insist that she was not crazy and resented being the object of jokes. She said she bore no hard feelings toward Hart, who apologized on the air for the situation.

In another bizarre case, the theme from the show *Growing Pains* brought 27-year-old Janet Richardson out of a coma. She had been unresponsive for five days after falling out of bed and hitting her head, until, according to her sister, the TV theme "woke her up."

9. FOREIGN ACCENT SYNDROME

There are about 50 recorded cases of foreign accent syndrome, in which people who have suffered strokes or other injuries adopt a new accent. For example, Tiffany Roberts of Florida suffered a stroke and then began speaking with an English accent. She even adopted such Anglicisms as "bloody" and "loo." Roberts had never been to Great Britain and was not a fan of British television shows.

Perhaps the oddest case concerned a Norwegian woman who fell into a coma after being hit on the head by shrapnel during an air raid in 1941. When she woke up, she spoke with a thick German accent and was ostracized by her neighbors.

10. UNCOMBABLE HAIR SYNDROME

Also known as "hair felting," this condition causes hair to form a tangled mass. In a case reported in 1993 in the *Archives of Dermatology*, a 39-year-old woman's hair fell out and was replaced by dry, coarse, curly hair so tangled that it was impossible to comb. It lacked knots, kinks, or twists that would explain the tangling. The hairs themselves were strangely shaped: The cross-sections were triangular, grooved, or shaped like kidneys instead of circular. The usual solution to this problem is to cut off the solidified mass of hair. In one case, a woman from Indiana wanted to keep her hair, having spent 24 years growing it. After two and a half months of lubricating her hair with olive oil and separating the strands with knitting needles, the hair became normal.

A.W. & C.F.

10 Afflictions and Their Patron Saints

1. CANCER

A young fourteenth-century Italian, Peregrine Laziosi, once demonstrated against the papacy but was converted and became famous for his preaching and his holiness. When he developed cancer on his foot and doctors were about to amputate, he prayed all night and was miraculously cured. He became the patron saint of cancer victims.

2. EPILEPSY

St. Vitus expelled an evil spirit from a Roman emperor's child, and so he became the patron of people suffering from diseases typified by convulsions—epilepsy, chorea (St. Vitus's dance), and other neurological disorders. He is also considered the patron saint of dancers, comedians, and actors.

3.–4. HEMORRHOIDS AND VENEREAL DISEASE

St. Fiacre, a seventh-century holy man who set up a hospice for travelers in France, was known for miraculously healing his visitors of a variety of ills, including venereal disease and hemorrhoids. Cabdrivers also call on him as their protector because the Hôtel St. Fiacre in Paris was the first establishment to offer coaches for hire.

5. MENTAL ILLNESS

The remains of St. Dympna, a seventh-century Irish princess murdered by her father when she tried to escape his incestuous desires, are kept in a church in Gheel, Belgium. Dympna became the patron saint of the mentally ill when many insane and retarded people were cured after visiting her shrine.

6. PARALYSIS

St. Giles, a hermit who lived near Arles, France, in the seventh century, became the patron of the lame and the crippled. He had protected a deer that was being hunted and took an arrow that was meant for the animal.

7. RABIES

According to legend, St. Hubert (eighth century) converted to Christianity when during a hunt he saw a stag bearing a cross in its antlers. He became the patron saint of hunters and—because of his connection with wild animals—rabies victims.

8. SKIN DISEASES

The patron saint of pig herders, St. Anthony, was also the fourth-century Egyptian monk who established the world's first Christian monastery. Because pork fat was used to dress wounds, he became the intercessor for people with skin problems. One type of skin inflammation is known as St. Anthony's fire.

9. THROAT INFECTIONS

St. Blaise (fourth century) cured a young boy who was near death from a fish bone caught in his throat. To this day, Catholics celebrate the blessing of throats. Blaise is also the patron saint of wool combers (his enemies used iron combs on his flesh) and of wild animals (he once lived in a cave among animals).

10. TOOTHACHES

The intercessor for those with toothaches (and the patron saint of dentists) is St. Apollonia. She lived in Alexandria, Egypt, during the third century, at a time when gangs roamed the city and tortured Christians. When artists draw her, they show her holding either a gold tooth or a set of pincers—her teeth were pulled out by a mob when she refused to give up her Christianity.

Rating the Effects of 51 Personal Crises

In the 1920s, Dr. Walter Cannon began recording connections between stressful periods in a person's life and the appearance of physical ailments. A decade later, Dr. Adolf Meyer compiled a "life chart," which specifically correlated health problems with a person's life circumstances at the time. This process was refined during the 1950s and 1960s and resulted in the creation of the Social Readjustment Rating Scale (SRRS), which ranks 43 life crises on a scale of Life Change Units (LCUs). The ratings were arrived at by researchers who used in-depth interviewing techniques on an international sample of 5,000 people from Europe, the United States, Central America, Oceania, and Japan. Because of the consistency with which marriage was rated as one of the most significant life changes, it was given a value of 50 on the scale, and 42 other life crises were judged in relation to it. Some cultural differences surfaced (for example, the Japanese ranked minor law violations near the middle of the list and jail terms second from the top), but on the whole there was a remarkable uniformity of results, cutting across all national and socioeconomic identifiers. SRRS supporters contend that there is a direct correlation between annual LCUs and stress-related diseases. One of their studies found that with a "mild" stress level (150 to 199 LCUs in a single year), health problems increased 37 percent above the average; with a moderate level (200 to 299 LCUs), the increase was 51 percent; and with a major crisis level (300 LCUs and above), 79 percent more health problems occurred. The researchers noted that what counted was the cumulative total, not whether the life changes in themselves were positive or negative. The original chart, produced in 1964 by T. H. Holmes and T. H. Rahe, has been updated to reflect changing values as well as cross-cultural differences.

Rank	Life Event	LCU Value
1.	Death of spouse/mate	87
2.	Death of close family member	79
3.	Major injury/illness to self	78
4.	Detention in jail or other institution	76
5.	Major injury/illness to close family member	72
6.	Foreclosure on loan/mortgage	71
7.	Divorce	71
8.	Being a victim of crime	70
9.	Being a victim of police brutality	69
10.	Infidelity	69
11.	Experiencing domestic violence/sexual abuse	69
12.	Separation [from] or reconciliation with spouse/mate	66
13.	Being fired/laid-off/unemployed	64
14.	Experiencing financial problems/difficulties	62
15.	Death of a close friend	61

16.	Surviving a disaster	59
17.	Becoming a single parent	59
18.	Assuming responsibility for sick or elderly loved one	56
19.	Loss of or major reduction in health insurance/benefits	56
20.	Self/close family member being arrested for violating the law	56
21.	Major disagreement over child support/custody/visitation	53
22.	Experiencing/involved in auto accident	53
23.	Being disciplined at work/demoted	53
24.	Dealing with unwanted pregnancy	51
25.	Adult child moving in with parent/parent moving in with adult child	50
26.	Child develops behavior or learning problem	49
27.	Experiencing employment discrimination/sexual harassment	48
28.	Attempting to modify addictive behavior of self	47
29.	Discovering/attempting to modify addictive behavior of close family member	46
30.	Employer reorganization/downsizing	45
31.	Dealing with infertility/miscarriage	44
32.	Getting married/remarried	43
33.	Changing employers/careers	43
34.	Failure to obtain/qualify for mortgage	42
35.	Pregnancy of self/spouse/mate	41
36.	Experiencing discrimination/harassment outside the workplace	39
37.	Release from jail	39
38.	Spouse/mate begins/ceases work outside the home	38
39.	Major disagreement with boss/coworker	37
40.	Change in residence	35
41.	Finding appropriate child care/day care	34
42.	Experiencing a large unexpected monetary gain	33
43.	Changing positions (transfer, promotion)	33
44.	Gaining a new family member	33
45.	Changing work responsibilities	32
46.	Child leaving home	30
47.	Obtaining a home mortgage	30
48.	Obtaining a major loan other than home mortgage	30
49.	Retirement	28
50.	Beginning/ceasing formal education	26
51.	Receiving a ticket for violating the law	22

19 New Neuroses

1. ACQUIRED SITUATIONAL NARCISSISM
Adult-onset form of narcissism characterized by grandiosity, lack of

empathy, rage, isolation, and substance abuse. Mainly afflicts celebrities, who tend to be surrounded by enablers.

2. ANGLOLALIA
The uncontrollable urge to affect a British accent, most often afflicting celebrities (Madonna, Faye Dunaway, Sammy Davis, Jr., Jessye Norman) and, for some reason, Reform rabbis.

3. BIGOREXIA
Preoccupation, especially among bodybuilders, with imaginary physical shortcomings. Just as anorexics look in the mirror and see a fat person, bigorexics, no matter how massive or chiseled, look in the mirror and see a 98-pound weakling.

4. CELEBRIPHILIA
Pathological desire to have sex with a celebrity.

5. CELL YELL
Loud talking on cell phones in public places by people with the neurotic need to invade their own privacy.

6. CYBERCHONDRIA
Hypochondria resulting from seeing one's symptoms on a medical Web site.

7. HATHOS
Pleasurable hatred of someone or something, especially politicians or powerful organizations.

8. HOLLOW-TOOTH SYNDROME
Compulsion to torture oneself mentally, based on the principle that nothing fixes a thing so intensely in the memory as the wish to forget it. The masochistic urge to revisit past embarrassment, sometimes called mnemophobia, causes some sufferers to actually cry out the instant the memory occurs.

9. HURRIED-CHILD SYNDROME
The neurotic result of parents pushing their children to excel academically while overscheduling their free time with countless extracurricular activities, i.e., hurrying them into adulthood.

10. INFORMATION SICKNESS
Anxiety produced by information overload, especially from television newscasts, with their guiding programming principle, "If it bleeds, it leads." Symptoms can include sleep disturbance, substance abuse, and compassion fatigue.

11. **INTERNET ADDICTION DISORDER**
Term coined by Ivan Goldberg in 1996 as a parody of America's
obsession with addiction but now used earnestly to describe people
who are unable to control the amount of time they spend online
engaging in chat rooms, auction shopping, pornography, gambling,
day-trading, etc.

12. **MOUSE TERROR**
Fear of potential health hazards from food additives and pesticides
engendered by published experiments purporting to show harm to
laboratory mice from exposure to these substances, even though the
scientific validity of comparing mice to people is questionable because
(a) mice aren't people, and (b) exposure does not equal toxicity (i.e.,
dosage is everything). One such experiment concluded that "new-car
smell" is toxic, and another showed that dimes cause cancer (when
affixed to the shaved backs of lab mice).

13. **NANNY ENVY**
1. Resentment of your nanny because of all the time she spends with
your children when you can't. 2. Envy of your friends who can afford a
nanny when you can't.

14. **PLASTIC SURGERY ADDICTION**
Disorder in which the addict must have more and more "work" (breast
augmentation, liposuction, fat grafting, collagen or Botox injections)
done to obtain the desired rush of reassurance. These "slaves of the
scalpel," according to *Mademoiselle* contributor Jill Neimark, are
"caught in the same cycle of elation and despair one finds in obsessive
dieters or bodybuilders."

15. **PRONOIA**
The irrational belief that people like you.

16. **RELATIONAL AGGRESSION**
Constellation of catty behaviors, including ridicule, ostracism, gossip-
mongering, and even some body language, whereby adolescent girls vent
their mutual hostilities. Studies have shown that teenage females, though
less physically aggressive than males, are more socially aware, and they
use that savvy to covertly but ruthlessly jockey for pack position.

17. **RETAIL THERAPY**
Shopping as a means of comfort, relaxation, or mood elevation, or to
mask emotional problems; merchandise as medication. Retail therapy
can range from the palliative novelty of buying a new handbag to the
purchase of useless items from the Home Shopping Network, to the
attempt to buy your way into the future, as when an ambitious young

executive buys a car he can't afford hoping it will enhance his prospects for promotion to a higher-paying job (which will allow him to afford the car).

18. ROAD RAGE BY PROXY
Vicarious road rage resulting from merely witnessing a traffic incident, as when one driver becomes incensed from seeing another cut off by a third. In 1997, a Durham, North Carolina, driver-education teacher was forced to resign after ordering a student to chase down a motorist who had cut them off, at which point the instructor jumped from the car and punched the other driver.

19. TELEPHILIA
Term coined by critic Frank Rich to describe the pathological longing of Americans, no matter how talentless, to be on television.

Source: Encyclopedia Neurotica by Jon Winokur, copyright 2005 by Jon Winokur. Reprinted by permission of the author.

5-Year Survival Rates for 25 Types of Cancer

Cancer Type	Total Survival (%)
1. Prostate	99.8
2. Thyroid	96.6
3. Testis	96.0
4. Melanoma	91.6
5. Breast	88.2
6. Corpus uteri	85.3
7. Lymphoma (Hodgkin)	85.3
8. Urinary bladder	81.8
9. Cervix uteri	73.3
10. Leukemia (lymphocytic)	71.4
11. Larynx	65.6
12. Rectum	64.7
13. Kidney and renal pelvis	64.6
14. Colon	63.9
15. Lymphoma (non-Hodgkin's)	60.2
16. Gum and other oral cavity	60.0
17. Ovary	44.6
18. Brain and nervous system	33.3
19. Myeloma	32.4
20. Leukemia (myeloid and monocytic)	25.6
21. Stomach	23.2

22. Lung and bronchus	15.3
23. Esophagus	14.9
24. Liver	9.7
25. Pancreas	4.6

Source: SEER Cancer Statistics Review 1995–2001, National Cancer Institute.

13 People Who Succeeded After Having a Stroke

1. **GEORGE FRIDERIC HANDEL** (1685–1759), composer
   Suffered a stroke in 1737, at age 52. Five years later, he composed *The Messiah*, and he continued to compose until his death.

2. **WALT WHITMAN** (1819–1892), poet
   Suffered his first stroke in 1858 and made a complete recovery. After the stroke, he made several revisions and enlargements of *Leaves of Grass*, the poetry volume first published in 1855. A second stroke in 1873 left him partially paralyzed, but he continued revising the book, which did not begin to resemble its final form until 1881. His last revision was published the year of his death.

3. **LOUIS PASTEUR** (1822–1895), chemist and microbiologist
   Permanently paralyzed on his left side by a stroke in 1868, Pasteur did most of his immunology research afterward, developing vaccines for anthrax and chicken cholera in 1881 and for rabies in 1885.

4. **WINSTON CHURCHILL** (1874–1965), British prime minister/ statesman
   Suffered his first stroke in 1949 and a second in 1953. He served as prime minister from 1951 until his resignation in 1955 and remained active in Parliament until 1959. Among his accomplishments after his second stroke were supervision of the development of the British hydrogen bomb in 1955 and the publication of his four-volume *History of the English-Speaking Peoples* in 1956–1958.

5. **DWIGHT D. EISENHOWER** (1890–1969), general and U.S. president
   Made a quick and complete recovery from a stroke in 1955. The following year, he was reelected, and he completed a second presidential term. In retirement, he remained active in Republican Party politics and wrote three books. An avid golfer, he scored his only hole in one in 1968, 13 years after his stroke and a year before his death.

6. AGNES DE MILLE (1905–1993), choreographer
Suffered a stroke in 1974. She described her return from near death to an active life in *Reprieve*, one of five books she wrote afterward. In addition, she choreographed four new ballets after her stroke: *Texas Fourth* (1976), *A Bridegroom Called Death* (1978), *The Informer* (1988), and *The Other* (1992).

7. ELLEN CORBY (1913–1999), actress
Suffered a near-fatal stroke in 1976. Corby, who portrayed Grandma Walton on the popular television series *The Waltons*, was never written out of the script of the popular series; instead, she was referred to as being hospitalized. In 1978, partially paralyzed and with impaired speech, she returned to *The Waltons* as a regular.

8. KIRK DOUGLAS (1916–), actor
Suffered a stroke in 1995. He returned to acting in *Diamonds* (1999), playing a stroke sufferer undergoing speech therapy. He subsequently was nominated for an Emmy in 2000 for a guest appearance in *Touched by an Angel*.

9. ED KOCH (1924–), politician
While serving his third term as mayor of New York City, Koch suffered a stroke, in 1987. He recovered and served the rest of his term. After retiring from politics, he wrote two biographies and a series of mysteries; commented on politics for newspapers, radio, and TV; was named an adjunct professor at New York University; and served a year as the judge on the TV program *The People's Court*.

10. PATRICIA NEAL (1926–), actress
Suffered a series of near-fatal strokes in 1965. Though pregnant at the time of the first stroke, she bore a normal child. She resumed acting in 1968 and received an Academy Award nomination for Best Actress in *The Subject Was Roses*.

11. ROBERT GUILLAUME (1927–), actor
Best known for his Emmy-winning role in *Benson*, he suffered a stroke in 1999, while appearing in the critically acclaimed series *Sports Night*. When he returned to the show four months later, the effects of his stroke were written into the show.

12. DELLA REESE (1931–), singer and actress
She collapsed from a stroke while singing at a taping of *The Tonight Show* in 1979. She went on to costar in the series *Touched by an Angel* from 1994 to 2003. Reese observed, "People in my generation thought if you had a stroke, it was the end of the world and there was nothing you could do about it. Well, I'm sitting here as living proof that there is help available."

13. QUINCY JONES (1933–), musician, composer, and producer
Suffered a stroke in 1974. He survived two open-brain surgeries, despite a 90 percent risk of death. After the stroke, he had to give up playing the trumpet. His successes since then include winning a Grammy for album of the year for *Back on the Block* (1990) and producing such best sellers as Michael Jackson's *Thriller* (1982) and the all-star charity single "We Are the World" (1985).

A.T. & C.F.

14 Prominent People Who Died While Exercising

1. SONNY BONO (1935–1998)
The singer-turned-congressman died while skiing at a Lake Tahoe resort. He had left the trails to ski the deeper powder in a wooded area when he lost control and struck a tree.

2. JEFF BUCKLEY (1966–1997)
Buckley, a singer best known for his alternative rock hit album *Grace,* died when he took an impromptu swim in the Mississippi River. He apparently drowned when he was swamped by the wake of a passing boat.

3. BING CROSBY (1904–1977)
The Crooner, an avid golfer, had just completed 17 holes of golf at La Moralejo Golf Club in Spain when he fell to the ground. His golf partners thought he had merely slipped, but he had had a massive heart attack. He died en route to a hospital in Madrid.

4. TED DEMME (1963–2002)
Demme, film director and creator of the show *Yo! MTV Raps,* collapsed during a charity basketball game. He suffered a cocaine-induced cardiac arrest.

5. JIM FIXX (1932–1984)
A 220-pound, two-pack-a-day smoker until age 35, Fixx became the guru of marathoners in the 1970s when he wrote *The Complete Book of Running.* He died of a massive heart attack at age 52, during one of his daily 10-mile runs.

6. ZANE GREY (1875–1939)
The famous author of Westerns suffered a fatal heart attack after working out on weight equipment in his home. As a record-holding

deep-sea fisherman, he used the weights to stay in shape for his fishing expeditions.

7. HAROLD E. HOLT (1908–1967)
Holt, the prime minister of Australia, drowned near his home outside Melbourne while skin diving in the ocean in search of crayfish. His doctor had earlier advised him to cut down on swimming and tennis.

8. BRIAN JONES (1944–1969)
Guitarist Jones had quit the Rolling Stones only one month before taking what turned out to be a fatal midnight swim. Friends who found him at the bottom of his pool were unable to revive him.

9. KIRSTY MacCOLL (1959–2000)
Singer-songwriter MacColl, well known for "Fairytale of New York," a duet with Shane Megowan of The Pogues, drowned while on vacation at the Mexican resort of Cozumel. She was struck by a speedboat that illegally entered an area reserved for swimmers.

10. JOSEF MENGELE (1911–1979)
The infamous doctor of the Auschwitz concentration camp, Mengele was responsible for some 400,000 deaths. After World War II, he escaped justice and lived under an assumed name in Brazil. He drowned in 1979, suffering a stroke while swimming. His death wasn't confirmed until a team of forensics experts examined his remains in 1985.

11. NICO (1938–1988)
Nico, the German-born vocalist who sang with the Velvet Underground, died of a cerebral hemorrhage while riding her bicycle in Ibiza, Spain. She had performed in Berlin four weeks before.

12. THEODORE ROETHKE (1908–1963)
Though overweight, the Pulitzer Prize–winning poet was a good swimmer, tennis player, and dancer. However, a few minutes after he dived into a swimming pool, friends found him floating facedown, dead of a heart attack.

13. CARROLL ROSENBLOOM (1907–1979)
Sports entrepreneur and owner of the Rams football team, Rosenbloom drowned while swimming in the surf near his rented Florida vacation home. He was caught in a severe undertow.

14. JEAN TROISGROS (1926–1983)
Troisgros, one of the great chefs of Europe, died of a heart attack while playing tennis at Vittel, a French spa.

C.F. & The Eds.

29 Activities and the Calories They Consume

Activity	Calories per Hour
1. Making mountains out of molehills	500
2. Running around in circles	350
3. Wading through paperwork	300
4. Pushing your luck	250
5. Eating crow	225
6. Flying off the handle	225
7. Jumping on the bandwagon	200
8. Spinning your wheels	175
9. Adding fuel to the fire	150
10. Beating your head against the wall	150
11. Climbing the walls	150
12. Jogging your memory	125
13. Beating your own drum	100
14. Dragging your heels	100
15. Jumping to conclusions	100
16. Beating around the bush	75
17. Bending over backward	75
18. Grasping at straws	75
19. Pulling out the stoppers	75
20. Turning the other cheek	75
21. Fishing for compliments	50
22. Hitting the nail on the head	50
23. Pouring salt on a wound	50
24. Swallowing your pride	50
25. Throwing your weight around (depending on your weight)	50–300
26. Passing the buck	25
27. Tooting your own horn	25
28. Balancing the books	23
29. Wrapping it up at day's end	12

Source: Bulletin, Columbus Industrial Association, July 11, 1977.

12 Drinks Named After People

1. ALEXANDER
Made with crème de cacao, gin, or brandy and cream, this cocktail was named for Alexander the Great, centuries after his death.

2. BLOODY MARY

Ferdinand L. Petiot, bartender at Harry's New York Bar in Paris, mixed vodka and tomato juice in 1920; American entertainer Roy Barton gave it the name Bucket of Blood after the club in Chicago. The drink was renamed the Red Snapper when Petiot spiced it up with salt, pepper, lemon, and Worcestershire sauce. Though it has been said that this "queen among drinks" was named after Mary, Queen of Scots, it was Queen Mary I of England who was known as Bloody Mary.

3. BRONX COCKTAIL

The drink was labeled in 1919 in honor of a New York City borough—the Bronx—which, in turn, was named after Jonas Bronck, a Dane who first settled the area for the Dutch West India Company in 1641.

4. DOM PÉRIGNON

Dom Pérignon (1638–1715) entered the religious life at age 15. A blind man, his acute senses of taste and smell aided him in making and improving the wines of the Benedictine monastery near Épernay, France, where he was a cellarmaster. It was Dom Pérignon who perfected the process of fermenting champagne in the bottle—he put in the all-important bubbles. Moët et Chandon vineyards later honored Pérignon's accomplishments by naming its finest vintage after him.

5. GIBSON

Toward the beginning of the twentieth century, a bartender at the New York Players Club was fixing a martini for artist Charles Dana Gibson. When he discovered that there were no more olives, the bartender substituted a pearl onion and named the drink after his customer.

6. GIMLET

Believing that straight gin harmed the health of naval officers, British naval surgeon Sir T. O. Gimlette created the "healthy cocktail" by diluting gin with lime juice in 1890.

7. GROG

British vice admiral Sir Edward Vernon was called Old Grog because he wore an impressive grogram coat on deck in all kinds of weather. When in 1740 he ordered that all rum rations be diluted with water to curb drunken brawling aboard ships, incensed old sea dogs dubbed the diluted rum "grog," which later came to mean any cheap liquor.

8. HARVEY WALLBANGER

California surfer Tom Harvey (c. 1970) had a great passion for the "Italian screwdriver" (orange juice, vodka, Galliano). After a day of surfing, Harvey still couldn't stay off the waves. He would rush to his favorite bar, overindulge himself—and then walk into a wall when it came time to go home.

9. MARGARITA
There are at least eight different stories relating to the creation of the tequila-based margarita. The most commonly accepted one is that the drink was concocted in 1938 or 1939 by Carlos Herrera, a Mexican bartender who named the drink in honor of a showgirl named Marjorie King, who was allergic to all hard liquor except tequila.

10. MICKEY FINN
Mickey Finn was apparently the name of a bartender who worked in Chicago around 1896–1906. He served knockout drinks (which probably contained chloral hydrate) to his customers so that they could be robbed.

11. ROB ROY
This concoction of Scotch whiskey, sweet vermouth, and bitters, topped with a maraschino cherry, bears the nickname of the legendary eighteenth-century Scottish freebooter Robert Macgregor.

12. TOM COLLINS
This drink was named after a nineteenth-century bartender at Limmer's Old House in London who was famous for his Gin Sling—a tall drink that resembles the Collins mixture of gin, lemon, sugar, and soda water.

R.H. & D.B.

15 Notable Events That Happened Under the Influence of Alcohol

1. HANGING OF CAPTAIN KIDD (1701)
Captain William Kidd was sentenced to death for murder and piracy and led to the gallows at London's Execution Dock on May 23, 1701. The execution itself was a fiasco. As a large group of spectators sang a series of ballads in honor of the pirate, a very drunk public executioner attempted to hang Kidd, who was so smashed that he could hardly stand. Then the rope broke, and Kidd fell over into the mud. Though a second attempt at hanging the prisoner succeeded, the sheriff in charge was later harshly criticized in a published editorial for the bungled performance.

2. BOSTON TEA PARTY (1773)
In Boston, Massachusetts, 50 colonials and members of the Committee of Correspondence met at the home of a printer named Benjamin Edes

at about 4:00 p.m. on December 16, 1773. Later that evening, they intended to destroy the tea aboard three ships in Boston Harbor as a protest against the British government's taxation of the American colonies. To bolster their resolve, Edes filled a massive punch bowl with a potent rum concoction. Edes's son Peter had the job of keeping the bowl filled, which proved to be an almost impossible task because of the ardor with which the patriots drank. Shortly after 6:00 p.m., the men, most of whom were now in a noisy, festive mood, with a few staggering noticeably, departed and marched to Griffin's Wharf, where the tea ships were anchored. For the next three hours they sobered up, a number becoming violently ill, as they dumped heavy tea chests into the harbor—and set off the American Revolution.

3. NAT TURNER REBELLION (1831)
On the night of August 21, 1831, black slave-prophet Nat Turner launched a rebellion in Southampton County, Virginia, that left more than 50 whites and more than 120 blacks dead. Although Turner never touched alcohol, his six followers had feasted on roast pig and apple brandy that night. At the first plantation they attacked, the rebels drank hard cider before massacring the whites living there. Through the night and into the next day, the insurgents raided plantations, killed whites, and confiscated horses, weapons, and brandy. By noon, Turner's army had expanded to approximately 60 men, but many of them were so intoxicated they kept falling off their horses. When Turner caught up with one advance party, they were relaxing in the brandy cellar of a plantation. Learning that a group of whites was approaching, Turner rallied his men and put the whites to flight. But the next day, an alarm scattered his new recruits, and he had only 20 men left to fight 3,000 armed white militiamen and volunteers. The rebellion was crushed.

4. VICE PRESIDENTIAL INAUGURATION OF ANDREW JOHNSON (1865)
As Abraham Lincoln's running mate in the 1864 U.S. presidential election, Johnson campaigned incessantly across the country, until he became exhausted and contracted malaria. When he awoke on March 4, 1865, the day of his inauguration as vice president, he could barely get out of bed. To fortify himself, he drank "medicinal" whiskey and quickly became intoxicated because of his weakened condition. When he began to ramble drunkenly through his inauguration address, officials interrupted him and administered the oath of office. Because he slurred his words and repeated his lines incorrectly, this took a considerable amount of time, after which Johnson launched into yet another bout of inebriated oratory. Finally, a Supreme Court justice mercifully led him away.

5. LINCOLN'S ASSASSINATION (1865)
   On April 14, 1865, actor John Wilkes Booth began drinking at 3:00 p.m. in the Kirkwood House bar in Washington, D.C. At 4:00 p.m., he arrived at Deery's Saloon and ordered a bottle of brandy. Two hours later, he was drinking whiskey at Taltavul's Saloon, next door to Ford's Theatre. Having made the final arrangements for his impending crime, Booth returned at 9:30 to Taltavul's, where President Abraham Lincoln's valet, Charles Forbes; his coachman, Francis Burns; and his bodyguard, John Parker, an alcoholic policeman, were all drinking. At 10:15, while Parker continued to imbibe—thus leaving the president unprotected—Booth left, went next door to Ford's Theatre, and shot Lincoln. Meanwhile, George Atzerodt, Booth's fellow conspirator, who was supposed to assassinate Vice President Andrew Johnson, had become so intoxicated and frightened that he abandoned the plan.

6. BATTLE OF THE LITTLE BIGHORN (1876)
   A controversy still rages over the extent and level of intoxication of the officers and men of the U.S. 7th Cavalry Regiment at the Battle of the Little Bighorn. It is known that Custer's second-in-command, Major Marcus Reno, had a half-gallon keg of whiskey with him on the expedition. When they reached the Rosebud River four days before the battle, the 7th Cavalry troopers may have replenished their supplies of alcohol from a steamboat carrying whiskey. According to Indian veterans of the battle, numerous canteens half full of whiskey were found with the bodies of Custer's men. It is a fact that Reno, who was probably an alcoholic, was drunk when besieged by Indians the night after Custer was defeated.

7. REPUDIATION OF THE CAÑON DE LOS EMBUDOS TREATY (1886)
   On March 27, 1886, in the Cañon de los Embudos in Sonora, Mexico, U.S. Army general George Crook and the Chiricahua Apache leader Geronimo negotiated a peace treaty whereby Geronimo and his followers would surrender and be returned to the San Carlos Reservation in Arizona. Unfortunately, the night the treaty was concluded, the Apaches were sold a large quantity of whiskey and mescal by a Swiss-American bootlegger. As the Indian warriors became increasingly intoxicated, they had second thoughts about the agreement. Late in the evening, an inebriated Geronimo declared that he would never surrender to the white man and repudiated the treaty he had just signed. Accompanied by 20 warriors, Geronimo rode away that night to continue the bloody Apache War until he was tracked down five months later.

8. SULLIVAN-KILRAIN FIGHT (1889)
   A champagne-loving alcoholic and the bare-knuckle boxing champion, American heavyweight John L. Sullivan met Jake Kilrain—also a heavy

drinker—in a title fight on July 8,1889, in Richburg, Mississippi. At first, Sullivan's manager refused to let his man drink any alcohol. Eventually, to combat exhaustion and the effects of the 112°F temperature, Sullivan was allowed to drink cold tea laced with whiskey after the forty-third round. Unfortunately, the whiskey made him violently ill, and he vomited in the center of the ring. After the thirty-sixth round, Kilrain, who was taking a terrible beating, was given shots of bourbon between rounds by one of the timekeepers, William "Bat" Masterson. By the time he conceded defeat after the seventy-fifth round, Kilrain had consumed an entire bottle of bourbon.

9. THIRD BATTLE OF THE AISNE RIVER (1918)
   In May 1918, during World War I, General Erich Ludendorff's German troops reached the Marne River at Château-Thierry only 37 miles from Paris during the third battle of the Aisne River. On the verge of capturing Paris, but after living without any luxuries for years, the German soldiers invaded France's champagne provinces, where well-stocked wine cellars abounded. Drunkenness quickly spread through the ranks; even the German military police joined the revelries. In the village of Fismes on the morning of May 30, the bodies of soldiers who had passed out littered the streets, making it difficult for trucks to drive through the town on their way to the front lines. The intoxication and subsequent hangovers afflicting the Germans slowed their advance and halted it completely in certain sectors. This enabled the French and Americans to establish new defensive lines, counterattack, and end Ludendorff's offensive, which proved to be the Germans' last chance for victory in WWI.

10. FOUNDING OF ALCOHOLICS ANONYMOUS (1935)
    Alcoholics Anonymous came into existence when a New York stockbroker named Bill W. (an AA member uses only his last initial), an alcoholic who had stopped drinking as a result of a spiritual experience, helped a physician named Doctor Bob to quit drinking. During a business trip to Akron, Ohio, Bill W. met Doctor Bob and shared with him his own experiences as an alcoholic and his method of recovering from the disease of alcoholism. Suffering from a severe hangover, the still woozy Doctor Bob had his last drink on June 10, 1935. The next day, with Bill W., he founded the organization Alcoholics Anonymous. Neither Bill W., who lived until 1971, nor Doctor Bob, who lived until 1950, ever drank again. The fellowship they founded, which is based on the concept of alcoholics helping other alcoholics, now has more than two million members.

11. FILMING OF *MY LITTLE CHICKADEE* (1940)
    As in almost all of his films, W. C. Fields was toasted throughout the production of *My Little Chickadee*. After drinking from two to four

martinis with his breakfast each morning, he arrived at Universal Studios with a cocktail shaker full of martinis. Apparently at his comic best when drunk, he consumed two bottles of gin each day during the filming. Fields's inebriated behavior often infuriated his costar, Mae West, especially once when, in an overly affectionate mood, he prodded and pinched her generous figure and called her "my little brood mare." Although he often required an afternoon nap to diminish the effects of his drinking, Fields was never incapacitated by alcohol during his performance in the movie.

12. WRITING OF *A CLOCKWORK ORANGE* (1962)

Even though his work sometimes dealt with projected future worlds, English author Anthony Burgess developed his novels from his personal experiences. For example, the brutal rape scene in *A Clockwork Orange* was derived from an assault on his wife during World War II, which resulted in the death of their expected child. While writing *A Clockwork Orange*, Burgess became so emotionally involved that he frequently had to calm himself by drinking. He later admitted, "I had to write *A Clockwork Orange* in a state of near drunkenness, in order to deal with material that upset me so much."

13. *EXXON VALDEZ* OIL SPILL (1989)

After striking a reef, the *Exxon Valdez* spilled 250,000 barrels of oil into Alaska's Prince William Sound, forming a slick that covered 2,600 square miles and washed onto 1,000 miles of coastline. At the time of the accident, Captain Joseph Hazelwood was belowdecks, having left Third Mate Gregory Cousins at the helm. Cousins was not certified to pilot the tanker in the Sound. After the collision, Hazelwood attempted to pilot the tanker off the reef despite warnings that the ship might break up if he succeeded. He failed to sound a general alarm. Also, Hazelwood was seen chain-smoking on the bridge until Coast Guard officers arrived and warned him that he could set the whole ship on fire. One of the Coast Guard officers who boarded the ship two and half hours after the collision stated that Hazelwood's breath smelled of alcohol. When a blood test was administered—a full nine hours after the accident—Hazelwood's blood alcohol level was above the legal level to operate a ship. Although Hazelwood admitted that he had been drinking while ashore earlier that day (witnesses spotted him drinking in two different bars), he denied being impaired at the time of the accident and insisted that the blood alcohol test was inaccurate. Indeed, although a jury convicted Hazelwood on misdemeanor negligence charges (later overturned on a technicality), he was acquitted of operating a ship while under the influence of alcohol. On the other hand, an investigation by the National Transportation Safety Board concluded that he had left the bridge because of "impairment from alcohol."

14. **FAILED SOVIET COUP (1991)**
    In a last-ditch attempt to undo the reforms of glasnost, on August 19, 1991, Communist Party hardliners attempted to overthrow Soviet premier Mikhail Gorbachev. The coup collapsed two days later in the face of resistance led by Boris Yeltsin, president of the Russian Republic. The plotters' failure to act decisively against Yeltsin caused the coup to fail. Heavy drinking contributed to the ineptitude of the plotters. Former Soviet vice president Yanayev, the front man for the coup, drank heavily throughout the affair and was found "in an alcoholic haze" in his office when the coup collapsed. Another plotter, former prime minister Pavlov, began drinking the first night of the coup, by his own admission. When Pavlov tried unsuccessfully to convince the government to declare a state of emergency, he appeared sick "or more likely drunk," according to Deputy Prime Minister Shcherbakov. The failed coup ultimately led to the complete disintegration of the Soviet Union.

15. **DEATH OF PRINCESS DIANA (1997)**
    On August 31, 1997, Diana; her boyfriend, Dodi al-Fayed; and their driver, Henri Paul, were killed in a car crash in a tunnel in Paris. Paul had been driving at more than 100 mph when he apparently clipped another car and lost control. An investigation found that his blood alcohol level was three times the legal limit. There were also traces of antidepressants in his blood. Conspiracy theorists—including Dodi's father, Mohammed al-Fayed—have disputed the blood test results. They note that two bodyguards who were with Paul shortly before the crash said that he did not appear drunk and acted normally.

    R.J.F. & C.F.

8 Great Sausage Events

1. **COMIC SAUSAGE**
   Epicharmus, a Greek dramatist who lived during the golden age of Sophocles and Aeschylus, wrote a comedy titled *Orya* (*The Sausage*) around 500 BC. Because the play exists today only as a fragment, we will never know exactly what the Greeks thought was funny about sausage.

2. **HEATHEN SAUSAGE**
   The ancient Romans were so fond of pork sausage spiced with pine nuts and pepper that the dish became a staple of the annual Lupercalian and Floralian festivals. Since those pagan celebrations usually degenerated into orgiastic rites, the early Christians looked upon them with

disapproval. When Constantine the Great, a Christian, became emperor in 324 AD, he outlawed production and consumption of the sinful sausage. But the Romans refused to cooperate and developed a flourishing black market in it. They continued to eat the bootlegged delicacies throughout the reigns of several Christian emperors until the ban was finally lifted.

3. FATAL SAUSAGE

At a simple peasant meal in Wildbad, Germany, in 1793, 13 people shared a single sausage. Within hours, they became seriously ill, and 6 of them died. Their disease became known as botulism—a word coined from the Latin for sausage, *botulus*. The powerfully toxic bacteria Clostridium botulinum inside the sausage could have easily been killed by boiling it for two minutes. Once in the body, botulism toxins attack the nervous system, causing paralysis of all muscles, which brings on death by suffocation.

4. HUMAN SAUSAGE

Adolph Luetgert, a Chicago sausage maker, was so fond of entertaining his mistresses that he had a bed installed in his factory. Louisa Luetgert was aware of her husband's infidelities, and, in 1897, their marriage took a dramatic turn for the worse. Louisa subsequently disappeared, and when the police arrived to search Luetgert's factory, they found human teeth and bones—as well as two gold rings engraved "L.L."—at the bottom of a sausage vat. During his well-publicized trial, Luetgert maintained his innocence, but he was convicted of murder and spent the rest of his life in prison.

5. MUCKRAKING SAUSAGE

Upton Sinclair's novel *The Jungle,* an exposé of conditions in the Chicago stockyards and meat industry, contained shocking descriptions: "There was never the least attention paid to what was cut up for sausage ... there would be meat stored in great piles ... thousands of rats would race about on it ... these rats were nuisances, and the packers would put poisoned bread out for them; they would die, and then rats, bread, and meat would go into the hoppers together." Americans were deeply alarmed by the filth described, and in the same year the book was published, Congress passed the Pure Food and Drug Act of 1906.

6. INSOLENT SAUSAGE

In October 1981, Joseph Guillou, an engineer on the Moroccan tanker *Al Ghassani,* was arrested, fined £50, and sentenced to two years in jail for insulting Morocco's King Hassan. Guillou's offense was hanging a sausage on the hook normally reserved for a portrait of the monarch. A sausage, said Guillou, was "more useful than a picture of the king."

7. VICTIM SAUSAGE

During home games at Miller Park, the Milwaukee Brewers baseball team holds "sausage races," in which people costumed as different types of sausages run around the park between innings. During a game on July 9, 2003, as the runners passed the visiting team's dugout, Randall Simon, the first baseman for the Pittsburgh Pirates, struck the Italian sausage, Mandy Block, with his bat, knocking her to the ground. After the game, Simon was handcuffed by Milwaukee County sheriff's deputies, taken to a police station, and fined $432 for disorderly conduct. The sausage whacking was broadcast repeatedly, but Block ignored the controversy, accepting Simon's apology. When he returned to Miller Park later in the season, Simon bought Italian sausages for a section of fans. Block was recognized by the National Hot Dog and Sausage Council with a certificate of bravery. "I'm proud of it," Block said. "I didn't even know there was a hot dog council."

8. SPEEDING SAUSAGE

In Finland, traffic fines are calculated according to the offender's income. In early 2004, Jussi Salonoja was caught driving double the speed limit in downtown Helsinki. Because Salonoja, age 27, was the heir to a large sausage business and had an annual income of $8.9 million, he was fined $216,900, breaking the previous record for a speeding fine of $101,700.

K.P.

11 Mammoth Cheeses

1. THE 28½ -TON CHEDDAR

The world's largest block of cheese was 6 feet high, 32 feet long, and 4½ feet wide. It was commissioned in 1995 by Loblaws Supermarket and made by the Agropur dairy cooperative of Quebec, Canada. At 57,508 pounds, the giant cheddar was equivalent to the amount of cheese eaten by 2,500 Canadians in one year.

2. THE 20-TON CHEDDAR

Known as the Belle of Wisconsin, it was made in 1988 by Simon's Specialty Cheese. It was taken on tour in a refrigerated Cheese-Mobile.

3. THE 17½-TON CHEDDAR

Known as the Golden Giant, this enormous chunk of cheese was 14½ feet long, 6½ feet wide, and 6 feet high. Produced in 1964 by Steve's Cheese of Denmark, Wisconsin, for the Wisconsin Cheese Foundation, it required 183 tons of milk—the daily production of 16,000 cows. After its manufacture, the cheese was shipped via a special tractor-trailer called the Cheese-Mobile to the Wisconsin Pavilion at the New York World's Fair. A refrigerated glass enclosure remained its home until 1965. It was then cut up into 2-pound pieces that were put on display until 1968, when they were sold for $3 per package. At the 1978 Wisconsin Cheese Makers' Association convention, the two remaining pieces of the cheese were auctioned off for $200 each.

4. THE 11-TON CHEDDAR
Twelve Canadian cheesemakers collaborated to make a cheese for display at the 1893 Chicago World's Fair. The "Canadian Mite" was 6 feet tall and 28 feet in circumference. When the Mite was put on display at the fair's Canadian Pavilion, it broke through the floor and had to be placed on reinforced concrete at the agricultural building. In 1943, a concrete replica of the cheese was unveiled alongside the railroad tracks in Perth, Ontario, to commemorate the fiftieth anniversary of the cheese. For the hundredth anniversary in 1983, Perth organized a week-long celebration.

5. THE 6-TON CHEDDAR
This giant was produced by upstate New York cheesemakers under the direction of W. L. Kilsey for the 1937 New York State Fair at Syracuse. Production began on July 12, 1937. It took seven weeks to cure and had to be turned frequently to ensure even ripening. It used the milk of 6,000 cows.

6. THE 4-TON CHEDDAR
Made by Canadian cheesemakers, this 7,000-pound-plus giant excited spectators at the 1883 Toronto Fair. Mortician-poet James McIntyre immortalized it in the following cheesy verses:
We have thee, mammoth cheese,
Lying quietly at your ease;
Gently fanned by evening breeze,
Thy fair form no flies dare seize.

7. THE 1,400-LB. CHEDDAR
Bestowed upon U.S. president Andrew Jackson by a New York State cheesemaker in 1837, this three-quarter-ton monster ripened in the vestibule of the White House for nearly two years. It was served to the entire city of Washington, D.C., when Jackson threw open the doors of the White House to celebrate Washington's Birthday. According to eyewitnesses, the whole atmosphere for a half-mile around was infected with cheese. The birthday cheddar was devoured in less than two hours. Only a tiny morsel was saved for the president.

8. THE 1,200-LB. CHESHIRE
In 1801 President Thomas Jefferson received this cheddarlike tribute from the tiny town of Cheshire in the Berkshire Mountains of Massachusetts. Named the Ultra-Democratic, Anti-Federalist Cheese of

Cheshire, it was shipped to Washington, D.C., by sled, boat, and wagon to honor Jefferson's triumph over the Federalists. The originator of the cheese was a preacher named John Leland, who took advantage of all the fuss and publicity to proselytize for his church. Duly impressed, Jefferson donated $200 to Leland's congregation.

9. THE 1,100-LB. CHEDDAR
The Great Pennard Cheese, 9 feet in diameter, was a wedding gift to Queen Victoria in 1840. Puzzled and somewhat embarrassed by not knowing what to do with it, the queen was relieved when its makers asked if they could borrow it to exhibit it around England. But when they tried to return the grubby, show-worn cheese, Victoria refused to accept it. After lengthy quarrels over its disposition, the cheddar was finally surrendered to the British Chancery, where it gradually disappeared. In 1989, John Green of West Pennard re-created the Great Pennard Cheese, but added 100 pounds. The modern Pennard was displayed at the May Festival of British Food and Farming.

10. THE 1,000-LB. LUNI CHEESE
One of the lesser-known wonders of the ancient world, the 1,000-pound Luni cheese, named after an ancient town in northern Italy, was reported by Pliny in his *Natural History* about 77 AD. Manufactured in what is now Tuscany, near the famous Carrara marble quarries in central Italy, the Luni cheese was probably made from a mixture of cow's and goat's milk. It is supposed to have tasted like a cross between cheddar and Parmesan.

11. THE 1,000-LB. CHEDDAR
The largest cheese to travel halfway around the world, this half-ton cheddar was taken to London all the way from New Zealand. It was the star attraction at the Wembley Exposition of 1924.

S.R. & C.F.

14 Highly Unusual Recipes

Calvin W. Schwabe is a professor of epidemiology and veterinary medicine at the University of California at Davis. Among his goals are helping people overcome existing prejudices about food and introducing international ways of eating to the Western world. Schwabe serves as an adviser on numerous international committees devoted to nutrition. In 1979, he wrote the groundbreaking work *Unmentionable Cuisine*, published by the University of Virginia Press.

1. BRAIN TACOS, Italy (*Cevello di agnello alla napoletana*)
Put olive oil in earthenware casserole. Add halved, parboiled lambs'

brains, turn over, and coat with oil, add salt and pepper, capers, crushed garlic, pitted ripe olives, and bread crumbs. Bake in 400-degree oven for 10–15 minutes. Brain Casserole, Algeria (*Mokh*) is an alternative. In Turkey, brain salad is commonly eaten.

2. STUFFED KID, Saudi Arabia (*Kharuf mahshi*)
This popular dish is not only a temptation for frustrated parents. Rub a skinned, eviscerated kid inside and out with chopped nuts, parsley or coriander, chopped fresh ginger, salt, and pepper. Stuff the kid with cooked rice, mixed nuts (pistachios, almonds, pignolias), sultana raisins or seedless grapes, plus residue of kid rubbing mix. Sew up opening, paint with melted butter, roast on a spit over charcoal (or in a 270–300-degree oven) until brown and tender. Serve on a mound of the stuffing. Guests sit on the floor and dig in.

3. STIR-FRIED HEART, China (*Nan Chow Sin*)
Trim beef or pork heart, cut into one-eighth-inch pieces. Julianne. Marinate with sections of scallions in a mix of cornstarch, water, soy sauce, sherry, sugar, salt, and minced ginger. Drain vegetables and stir-fry medium hot. Pork heart must be thoroughly cooked.

4. UTERUS SAUSAGE, Ancient Rome (*Vulvulae botelli*)
"For the cook," writes Professor Schwabe, "who has successfully subjugated most of the family's food prejudices . . . " Stuff a pig uterus with cumin, leeks, pepper, garum, pounded pork meat, and pine nuts. Cook sausage in water and oils with some garum, dill, and leeks.

5. STUFFED DORMICE, Ancient Rome
Prepare a stuffing of dormouse meat or pork, pepper, and pine nuts, a tasty broth, asafetida, and some garum. Stuff the dormice and sew them up. Bake in oven on a tile. (In 1972, an enterprising chef in Britain revived this recipe, hoping to acquaint modern diners with cuisine of ancient Rome. The results of his mission remain unknown.)

6. FISH SPERM CREPES, France (*Pannequets aux laitances*)
Spread unsweetened crepes with a mixture of chopped fish sperm and mushrooms bound with fish-based béchamel sauce. Roll crepes and set in a buttered dish, sprinkle with Parmesan cheese and melted butter; heat dish in a 350-degree oven until top browns.

7. STUFFED PIG RECTUM SAUSAGE, France (*Andouilles de troyes*)
Soak a calf's mesentery with the udder of a young beef in cold water, blanch for 30 minutes in boiling water. Dry and cut into small pieces. Sauté a generous amount of chopped mushrooms and some chopped parsley and shallots. Add salt, pepper, nutmeg, and a glass of white

wine. Remove from heat, and thicken with five egg yolks. Stir in the meat and stuff the mixture into the pig rectum. Tie off both ends, poach sausage for 45 minutes in stock mixed with white wine. Allow to cool in pot.

8. **BRAIN FRITTERS, France (*Subrics de cervelle*)**
Mix small cubes of poached beef brains, chopped buttered spinach (spinach goes well with brain), a crepe batter, and pepper and salt. Fry spoonfuls in hot oil until browned on both sides.

9. **RED ANT CHUTNEY, India (*Chindi Chutney*)**
Collect ants in leaf cups, put directly into the hot ashes of a fire for just a few minutes. Remove ants and make into a paste. Add salt and ground chilies; then bake. (This chutney is said to have "a sharp, clean taste" and is eaten with cocktails and other curries.)

10. **FERMENTED SHARK, Iceland (*Hakerl*)**
Schwabe allows that this recipe "sounds weird" and suggests as an introduction for the family "shark fillets à la meuniere." The recipe for fermented shark: Eviscerated sharks are buried in the sand or kept in an open bowl for three years to ferment. The much-prized result resembles in taste a ripe cheese.

11. **BEE GRUBS IN COCONUT CREAM, Thailand (*Mang non won*)**
Marinate grubs, sliced onions, and citrus leaves in coconut cream with some pepper. Wrap in pieces of linen and steam; serve over rice.

12. **KANGAROO RAT RAVIOLI, United States**
Debone kangaroo rats, pass meat through fine blade of grinder. Sauté with bacon fat and garlic. Add chopped cooked spinach or watercress, salt and pepper, and stuff raviolis. (In New Orleans, Louisiana, an enterprising local cooks a variant, alligator and cream cheese ravioli, for his friends.)

13. **CATERPILLAR PRETZELS, Mexico (*Gusitanitos di maguey*)**
Caterpillars of skipper butterflies, which live on the maguey cactus, are toasted or fried and eaten with mescal. Since the maguey is the source of pulque and tequila, "caterpillar pretzels" are a favorite in Mexico, even available canned.

14. **DRAGONFLY NYMPHS, Laos (*Mang Por*)**
Boil dragonfly nymphs. Eat them.

16 People Who Became Foods

1. **SAMUEL BENEDICT**
   After a long, hard night of partying in 1894, New York socialite Samuel Benedict confronted the Waldorf-Astoria maître d'hôtel and asked for the following hangover remedy: a piece of buttered toast topped with a poached egg, bacon, and hollandaise sauce. The maître d' complied but substituted an English muffin for the toast and ham for the bacon. Since then, Eggs Benedict has become a popular dish more for its flavor than for its medicinal properties.

2. **CAESAR CARDINI**
   The name of the Caesar Salad does not refer to the Roman conqueror but to its creator, the Tijuana, Mexico, restaurateur Caesar Cardini. He created the salad over the Fourth of July weekend in 1924. He served it as finger food, arranging garlic-scented leaves on platters. Later, he shredded the leaves into bite-sized pieces. The salad became a hit with the Hollywood movie stars who visited Tijuana and was soon added to the menus of trendy restaurants such as Chasen's and Romanoff's.

3. **FRANÇOIS RENÉ DE CHATEAUBRIAND**
   As a young man, Chateaubriand (1768–1848) witnessed the storming of the Bastille and fought on the side of the Royalists in the French Revolution. He journeyed to America, where he explored the Mississippi and Ohio rivers. On his return to Europe, he earned fame as a novelist, playwright, and social critic. Ironically, in spite of all his adventures and accomplishments, Chateaubriand is best remembered today for a cut of meat prepared for him by his chef, Montmireil. Beefsteak Chateaubriand is a thick cut of tenderloin from the center of the filet mignon, usually served with a béarnaise sauce.

4. **ROBERT COBB**
   Cobb was the owner of the Brown Derby restaurant in Hollywood. One evening in 1936, he let himself in late after everyone else had gone home. Having had no dinner, he made a salad out of leftovers in the restaurant refrigerators. He liked the results so much that he added the Cobb Salad to the menu.

5. **ALFREDO DE LILLEO**
   De Lilleo was an Italian chef. When his wife was weak after giving birth, he prepared her a sauce made of cream, butter, and Parmesan cheese for nourishment, and served it over fettuccine to aid her digestion. The new dish, Fettuccine Alfredo, became popular in the U.S. after Douglas Fairbanks and Mary Pickford dined on it at de Lilleo's restaurant during their honeymoon in Rome.

6. SYLVESTER GRAHAM

Graham (1794–1851) was America's premier health food exponent. During the 1840s, he traveled far and wide denouncing both white bread and meat and extolling the benefits of fruits, vegetables, and whole grains and their inevitable consequence—bowel regularity. He was frequently harassed by bakers and butchers, whose livelihoods were threatened by such rhetoric as "Meat is a powerful constipator which stimulates sexual excess." The nutritional guru and his true believers—among them Horace Greeley, Thomas Edison, and Mormon prophet Joseph Smith—would no doubt feel vindicated today, since many of Graham's theories have proved correct. However, the whole wheat crackers that he developed and named after himself have evolved into sugary treats containing bleached flour and preservatives.

7–8. JAMES LOGAN AND RUDOLF BOYSEN

During the late 1850s, Indiana-born schoolteacher James Logan (1841–1921) drove an ox team west to California, where the young man found fortune in a law practice and fame in horticulture. He developed the loganberry by planting California blackberries between Texas Early blackberries and Red Antwerp raspberries. In the early 1900s, a Californian named Rudolf Boysen (1895–1950) combined the hybrid loganberry with the blackberry and raspberry to produce a new variety of trailing blackberry, which he called the boysenberry.

9. JOHN MACADAM

The macadamia was first described botanically by Baron Ferdinand Jakob Heinrich von Mueller. The Baron named the plant for his friend John Macadam (1827–1865), a doctor of medicine, chemist, and member of Parliament in Australia. Macadam is not to be confused with John MacAdam, who gave his name to the macadam road.

10. NELLIE MELBA

Australian-born Helen Porter Mitchell (1861–1931) did not study opera until age 21, yet she quickly earned worldwide fame under the stage name Nellie Melba. While staying at the Savoy Hotel in London, Dame Nellie was accidentally served burnt toast. To the chef's surprise, the diva found the crisp slices of bread delicious. With this endorsement, Melba Toast was put on the menu in her honor. A peach, raspberry, and ice cream dessert was also named after the singer.

11. JOHN MONTAGU, 4TH EARL OF SANDWICH

According to legend, Montagu (1718–1792) was in the middle of a card game when he asked a servant to place some cold roast beef between two pieces of toast, so he could eat with one hand while he played cards with the other. Revisionists have argued that the earl was actually writing or hunting when he ordered the first sandwich, but the card-game story is the most plausible. Forty-eight-hour card games were among the earl's more wholesome pursuits. As a member of the notorious Hellfire Club, he was an enthusiastic participant in drunken orgies and Black Masses. It is not known whether Montagu found the sandwich a convenient snack to accompany his other vices as well.

12. ANNA PAVLOVA

In 1929, ballerina Anna Pavlova (1882–1931) toured Australia and caused a sensation. Six years later, Bert Sachse, chef at the Esplanade Hotel, created a new dessert based on beaten egg whites stiffened with cornstarch. The dessert got its name when it was presented to the owners for approval. The hotel manager declared, "It is as light as Pavlova."

13. SUZANNE REICHENBERG

Suzanne Reichenberg was an actress who worked professionally under the name Suzette. In 1897, she appeared in the Comédie Française in the role of a maid. The play featured a meal in which she served crepes. To attract the attention of the audience—as well as to reheat the crepes for the actors who had to eat them—they were served flambé. The crepes were provided for each performance by Monsieur Joseph, the proprietor of the nearby Restaurant Marivane. When Joseph moved on to the trendsetting Savoy Hotel in London, he brought his now-famous Crepes Suzette with him.

14. JOHN D. ROCKEFELLER

By 1899, oil tycoon John D. Rockefeller (1839–1937) was well on his way to his first billion. So when a diner at Antoine's restaurant in New Orleans proclaimed that a new oyster dish was "as rich as Rockefeller," it was no faint praise. Thereafter, the recipe for oysters broiled with vegetables and seasonings on a bed of rock salt was called Oysters Rockefeller.

15. JAMES H. SALISBURY

In 1886, this New York physician prescribed a cure-all for pulmonary tuberculosis, hardening of the arteries, gout, colitis, asthma, bronchitis, rheumatism, and pernicious anemia. He stipulated that well-done ground beef be eaten three times a day and that a glass of hot water be drunk before and after each meal. The so-called Salisbury Steak—basically a hamburger without a bun—is hardly the gourmet dish it sounds. During both World Wars, patriotic extremists fought a stateside campaign to substitute "Salisbury Steak" for the German word "hamburger," but their efforts largely failed. However, the term "Salisbury Steak" endures, since it looks better on a menu than "hamburger, plain."

16. **MARIA ANN SMITH**

An elderly widow working on a farm near Sydney, Australia, Maria Ann Smith noticed a seedling growing in a part of her garden where she had dumped a bunch of rotten apples. She decided to save the little tree, which eventually bore large green apples with a tart flavor. Smith's neighbors, impressed, asked for cuttings. By the time she died in 1870, the apples had become well known locally. Twenty-five years later, they were first exported. The "Granny Smith" apple quickly became popular in the British Isles and United States.

M.J.T. & C.F.

Julia Child's
10 Favorite Cookbooks (Besides Her Own!)

Chef Julia Child delighted millions with her hit PBS television show *The French Chef* and with her many cookbooks (most notably *Mastering the Art of French Cooking*, coauthored with Simone Beck and Louisette Bertholle). She was born in Pasadena, California, on August 15, 1912. During World War II, prior to her culinary career, Child served with the Office of Strategic Services (the forerunner of the CIA) in Washington, Sri Lanka, and China, before going to Paris to study cooking. Julia Child died of complications from kidney failure at the age of 91 on August 13, 2004. Her kitchen has been preserved as a permanent exhibit at the Smithsonian Institution. She contributed the following list to *The Book of Lists* in 1980:

1. *The Classic Italian Cook Book* and its sequel by Marcella Hazan
2. *The Art of Eating* by M. F. K. Fisher
3. *Larousse Gastronomique*
4. *La Technique* by Jacques Pépin
5. *The Cuisines of Mexico* and its sequel by Diana Kennedy
6. *American Cooking* and *The Theory and Practice of Good Cooking* by James A. Beard
7. *The Key to Chinese Cooking* by Irene Kuo
8. *The Art of Making Sausages, Patés, and Other Charcuterie* by Jane Grigson
9. *The Joy of Cooking* by Irma Rombauer and Marion Becker
10. *French Provincial Cooking* by Elizabeth David

10 Famous Insomniacs

1. **MARLENE DIETRICH, actress**

Dietrich said that the only thing that lulled her to sleep was a sardine-and-onion sandwich on rye.

2. **AMY LOWELL**, poet
Whenever she stayed in a hotel, Lowell would rent five rooms—one to sleep in, and empty rooms above, below, and on either side, in order to guarantee quiet.

3. **W. C. FIELDS**, actor
The aging Fields resorted to unusual methods to go to sleep. He would stretch out in a barber's chair (he had always enjoyed getting haircuts) with towels wrapped around him, until he felt drowsy. Sometimes he could only get to sleep by stretching out on his pool table. On his worst nights, he could only fall asleep under a beach umbrella being sprinkled by a garden hose. He told a friend that "somehow a moratorium is declared on all my troubles when it is raining."

4. **ALEXANDRE DUMAS**, author
Dumas suffered from terrible insomnia, and after trying many remedies, he was advised by a famous doctor to get out of bed when he couldn't sleep. He began to take late-night strolls and eventually started to sleep through the night.

5. **JUDY GARLAND**, actress
As a teenager, Garland was prescribed amphetamines to control her weight. As the years went by she took so many that she sometimes stayed up three or four days running. She added sleeping pills to her regime, and her insomnia and addiction increased. She eventually died of a drug overdose.

6. **TALLULAH BANKHEAD**, actress
Bankhead suffered from severe insomnia. She hired young homosexual "caddies" to keep her company, and one of their most important duties was to hold her hand until she drifted off to sleep.

7. **FRANZ KAFKA**, author
Kafka, miserable with insomnia, kept a diary detailing his suffering. For October 2, 1911, he wrote, "Sleepless night. The third in a row. I fall asleep soundly, but after an hour I wake up, as though I had laid my head in the wrong hole."

8. **THEODORE ROOSEVELT**, president
His insomnia cure was a shot of cognac in a glass of milk.

9. **GROUCHO MARX**, comic actor
Marx first began to have insomnia when the stock market crashed in 1929 and he lost $240,000 in 48 hours. When he couldn't sleep, he would call people up in the middle of the night and insult them.

10. **MARK TWAIN, author**
    An irritable insomniac, Twain once threw a pillow at the window of his bedroom while he was a guest in a friend's house. When the satisfying crash let in what he thought was fresh air, he fell asleep at last. In the morning he discovered that he had broken a glass-enclosed bookcase.

14 Healthy Insomnia Cures

Do not use these cures without consulting your health practitioner, as every body is different.

1. **DRINK A CUP OF CHAMOMILE TEA,** unless you have an allergy to plants in the ragwort family.

2. **TAKE THE DIETARY SUPPLEMENT MELATONIN.** In the UK, melatonin is a prescription drug; in America, it is available at natural food stores and pharmacies. It is widely considered an effective and safe sleep aid.

3. **TAKE THE AMINO ACID GABA.** This safe sleep aid can cause some people to itch the way the B-vitamin niacin does. Most people, however, find gaba very soothing.

4. **A MUG OF HOT MILK WITH HONEY AND/OR A FEW DROPS OF BRANDY.** Though health experts argue, this is a time-honored remedy, which may be effective because it is so comforting.

5. **TO NAP OR NOT TO NAP?** In certain countries, like Mexico and Italy, napping is a part of life and seems to be healthy. In America, a person who naps is often regarded as weak or lazy. Naps are usually recommended to be not over two hours, and if you do nap, the important thing is that it be regular.

6. **DOZE, REST, AND MEDITATE.** If you can't fall asleep, these practices are highly restorative for our brains and bodies.

7. **MORNING AND EVENING RITUALS.** Do you like to read when you wake up or before bed? Sew buttons? Play solitaire? Whatever you do, have it be regular.

8. **TAKE CALCIUM, MAGNESIUM, AND POTASSIUM.** These sleep aids, found at pharmacies and natural food stores, are soothing and can stop restless leg syndrome, which keeps millions of people awake. You can also rub organic balms into your legs.

9. AVOID STIMULANTS SUCH AS TEA AND COFFEE IN THE EVENING—unless you're used to an after-dinner coffee and it doesn't bother you. Never disrupt a schedule that works.

10. LEARN IF YOU HAVE SLEEP APNEA. Overweight people and those with sinus problems may have *sleep apnea*, a term describing cessation of breath during the night, usually accompanied by heavy snoring. Consult your health practitioner, because there are cures, and sleep apnea prevents you from getting the levels of REM sleep we all need to function healthily.

11. EAT POTATOES, WARM OR ROOM TEMPERATURE, BEFORE BED. Many studies show this to be a wonderful insomnia cure, as is pasta or a single candy. Other studies argue that one should not eat anything three hours before sleep.

12. USE WHITE NOISE. Boxes are available that produce what is called white noise, said to be highly effective for some. Alternatively, tapes of tides or soft sounds of nature can send you to sleep.

13. AVOID ANY STRENUOUS EXERCISE THREE HOURS BEFORE BED. Studies have shown that that is the wrong time for aerobic exercise, which will keep you awake.

14. DON'T GO TO SLEEP WITH AN ARGUMENT UNSETTLED. American comedienne Phyllis Diller is often credited with this bit of wisdom, but in truth it is as old as the hills. Do all you can to make up your fight before sleeping, or at least one of you is likely to have insomnia or even nightmares.

21 Health Experts and How They Died

1. STUART M. BERGER (1953–1994) Age at death: 40
The 6'7" Berger successfully reduced his weight from 420 to 210 pounds. He described his techniques in such best sellers as *The Southampton Diet* (1984) and *Dr. Berger's Immune Power Diet* (1986). He claimed that his diet would boost the immune system and promote longevity. He died in his New York City apartment from a heart attack brought on by cocaine abuse and obesity: At the time of his death, he weighed 365 pounds.

2. EDWARD BACH (1886–1936) Age at death: 50
A respected bacteriologist and homeopath, Bach was convinced that the underlying causes of illness always reflected abnormal mental or emotional states. He found remedies for these negative attitudes in

38 different wildflowers. When in the presence of any one of these healing plants, he experienced peace of mind. Mustard, for example, seemed to dispel gloom, and heather worked against feelings of loneliness. A month after his fiftieth birthday, Bach became so weak that he was confined to bed. Apparently, he was unafraid of his impending death, for he believed that an important part of his work could be accomplished only after he had shed his physical body. He died quietly in his sleep.

3. JIM FIXX (1932–1984) Age at death: 52
A former 220-pound, two-pack-a-day smoker, Fixx hardly seemed likely to inspire the jogging craze of the late 1970s. He took up running at age 35, quit smoking, and lost 61 pounds. In 1977, he wrote *The Complete Book of Running*, which was on the best-seller lists for more than a year. Seven years later, Fixx collapsed during his daily 10-mile run and died from a heart attack. An autopsy revealed scars on his heart muscle that indicated he had suffered three undetected heart attacks in the preceding weeks. Fixx may have relied too heavily on jogging to improve his health, while ignoring possible changes in his diet. During a 1979 interview with the *London Daily Mail*, he boasted that he had breakfasted on fried eggs, sausage, bacon, buttered toast, and coffee with cream. He managed to stay thin while eating such foods, but the fats eventually clogged his arteries. The autopsy showed that one coronary artery was 90 percent obstructed, another 80 percent blocked, and the third 70 percent.

4. ARNOLD EHRET (1866–1922) Age at death: 56
As a young man, Ehret was beset by illnesses, including Bright's disease, a heart disorder, and bronchial weakness. He gradually regained his health by alternating between a fruit-based diet and periodic fasting, a regimen that he claimed rid the body of mucus—a substance he attributed to disease. Thus was born Ehret's Mucusless Diet Healing System. His career as a health lecturer came to an abrupt end after he delivered a successful speech in Los Angeles on October 8, 1922. Ehret, who had hiked thousands of miles to demonstrate his renewed strength and vigor slipped, while stepping into the street and fell backward, hitting his head on the curb. He suffered a basal fracture of the skull and died within minutes, never regaining consciousness.

5. SYLVESTER GRAHAM (1794–1851) Age at death: 57
A clergyman and temperance leader, Graham believed that good health could be achieved through a strict regime that included cold showers, daily exercise, and a vegetarian diet. In 1847 he spoke to an audience in Boston and triggered a near riot by butchers and bakers who were angered by his advocacy of vegetarianism and homemade bread. He was deeply shaken by the attack, and his health began to decline. Treatment with stimulants, mineral water, and tepid baths proved to be of no lasting help, and he died broken in body and spirit. He is

remembered today chiefly for his creation of the graham cracker, though the present-day commercial product—containing bleached flour sugar and preservatives—would have horrified him.

6. EUGENE SANDOW (1867–1925) Age at death: 58
Through the application of scientific methods of muscle development, Sandow transformed himself from a weak youth into the "world's strongest man," as show business promoter Florenz Ziegfeld billed him at the 1893 World's Columbian Exposition in Chicago. In 1911, Sandow was appointed professor of physical culture to King George V. However, his primary concern was to convince the average man that anyone could achieve strength and vigor by exercising for as little as 20 minutes a day. The strongman pushed himself beyond even his immense capacities when, without any assistance, he lifted a car out of a ditch after an accident. He suffered severe strain and died soon afterward from a burst blood vessel in the brain. However, some believe that he died of syphilis.

7. PHILIP HANDLER (1917–1982) Age at death: 64
Handler, a former head of the National Academy of Sciences, was an internationally recognized authority on the connection between nutrition and disease. Principal among his discoveries was the link between vitamin-B deficiency and pellagra, a disease common among people who eat a corn-based diet. Handler died of cancer complicated by pneumonia.

8. ÉMILE COUÉ (1857–1926) Age at death: 69
Trained as a pharmacist, Coué became interested in hypnotism and developed a health treatment based on autosuggestion. He told his patients that their health would improve dramatically if, morning and evening, they would repeat faithfully: "Every day and in every way, I am becoming better and better." Prior to World War I, an estimated 40,000 patients flocked to his clinic each year, and Coué claimed a 97 percent success rate. He kept up a demanding schedule. After one of his lecture tours he returned to his home in Nancy, France, and complained of exhaustion. There, he died of heart failure.

9. NATHAN PRITIKIN (1915–1985) Age at death: 69
Pritikin was diagnosed with heart disease in his mid-forties. Although he did not have a background in medicine, he spent the next 20 years researching diet and nutrition. He developed a low-fat, low-cholesterol, and high-fiber diet that he credited with reversing his heart disease. In 1976, he opened the Pritikin Longevity Center in California to spread the word. He also published eight books on diet and exercise. His program gained credibility in 1984 when the National Institutes of Health concluded that lowering cholesterol reduced the risk of heart disease. Unfortunately, at the same time, Pritikin developed leukemia.

The chemotherapy he underwent to fight the cancer brought about anemia, kidney failure, and severe pain. On February 21, 1985, Pritikin committed suicide in his hospital bed, slashing his wrists with a razor. The leukemia had probably been caused by a dubious medical technique underwent in 1957. His doctor prescribed x-ray treatments to destroy a fungal infection causing a skin rash. Afterward, Pritikin was diagnosed with an elevated white blood cell count, a frequent precursor to leukemia.

10. ADELE DAVIS (1904–1974) Age at death: 70

"You are what you eat," claimed Davis, the well-known American nutritionist who advocated a natural diet rich in fresh fruits and vegetables along with large doses of vitamins. When she was diagnosed with bone cancer at age 69, her first reaction was disbelief. "I thought this was for people who drink soft drinks, who eat white bread, who eat refined sugar, and so on," she said. Eventually, she came to accept her illness as a delayed reaction to the "junk food" eating habits she had acquired in college, which had lasted until the 1950s. Her hope was that those who had faith in her work would not be disheartened by her fatal illness.

11. ROBERT ATKINS (1930–2003) Age at death: 72

On April 17, 2003, the famous "low-carb diet doctor" died after falling on an icy street and hitting his head. In 1972, Dr. Atkins—who had a history of heart disease—had published the best-selling *Dr. Atkins' Diet Revolution*, which advocated consuming meat, eggs, and cheese while shunning all carbohydrates, including wheat bread, all rice, and fruits. His books sold more than 15 million copies and became the subject of heated debate. Many respected dieticians advise the opposite approach—fruit, fresh vegetables, and a largely vegetarian diet. A group of doctors, severely critical of Atkins's plan, maintain that his program leads to weight gain and heart disease. Atkins supporters insist that his death was the result of his stay in a hospital, where, in a coma, he gained 70 pounds in fluid retention. Upon entering the hospital, the 6-foot Atkins weighed 195 pounds—which made him overweight by the standards of the Center for Heart Disease. He died eight days later at the formidable weight of 265 pounds. Defenders of the diet vigorously claim the cause was bloat. His books continue to sell.

12. J. I. RODALE (1898–1971) Age at death: 72

The head of a multimillion-dollar publishing business, Rodale used his popular magazines *Organic Gardening* and *Prevention* to promulgate his belief in "organic food" (food free from chemicals and artificial additives) supplemented by natural vitamins. He was at the height of his fame when he appeared on *The Dick Cavett Show* on June 9, 1971. After describing the dangers of milk, wheat, and sugar, Rodale proceeded to say, "I'm so healthy that I expect to live on and on." Shortly after the conclusion of the interview, he slumped in his chair, the victim of a fatal heart attack.

13. FRANZ MESMER (1734–1815) Age at death: 80
Mesmer believed that a person became ill when his "animal magnetism" was out of balance. To correct that condition, the Viennese doctor made use of magnets and held séance-like therapeutic sessions for his patients. Hounded out of Vienna on charges of practicing magic, Mesmer moved to Paris, where a royal commission (whose members included Benjamin Franklin and Antoine Lavoisier) concluded that Mesmer's "cures" were due solely to his patients' imaginations. Mesmer was convinced that he would die in his eighty-first year, as a Gypsy woman had foretold. Her prediction came true two months before his eighty-first birthday, when he succumbed to an extremely painful bladder condition that had troubled him for years.

14. ANN WIGMORE (1909–1993) Age at death: 83
Wigmore wrote more than 35 books advocating a "living food" diet that emphasized fresh fruits and vegetables and frequent drinks of wheatgrass juice. She claimed that wheatgrass juice had cured her of various maladies, including arthritis, colon cancer, and a gangrenous leg. In 1988, she ran into legal trouble. Wigmore had to sign a decree after being sued by the state of Massachusetts for misrepresenting herself as a medical doctor who claimed that her regime could cure AIDS. Wigmore remained vigorous and active until her death, February 16, 1993, of smoke inhalation following a fire in her home.

15. D. C. JARVIS (1881–1966) Age at death: 85
This country doctor became an overnight sensation in 1958 with the publication of *Folk Medicine: A Vermont Doctor's Guide to Good Health.* Part of his appeal derived from the simplicity of his remedies. For example, he suggested that one could stay healthy through a daily dose of two teaspoons each of honey and apple cider vinegar in a glass of water. Jarvis had many supporters, in spite of a Harvard professor's comment that "this claptrap is strictly for those gullible birds stung by the honey bee." Jarvis died in a nursing home in Vermont after suffering a cerebral hemorrhage.

16. F. MATTHIAS ALEXANDER (1869–1955) Age at death: 86
As a young actor, Alexander solved the problem of losing his voice during performances by paying careful attention to how he held his head and used his throat muscles. Thus he developed the Alexander technique, a postural system to improve health. His students included George Bernard Shaw, Aldous Huxley, and John Dewey. In 1947, he

injured himself in a fall, then suffered a stroke, paralyzing his left side. He recovered quickly and was soon teaching again, amazing his students with his suppleness and agility. He remained active for eight more years until, after a day at the races, he caught a chill and died.

17. BERNARR MACFADDEN (1868–1955) Age at death: 87
Billing himself as a kinestherapist, Macfadden ran a chain of health food restaurants and sanitariums that pushed his program of exercise, fresh air, personal hygiene, and wholesome diet. He also published the popular but controversial magazine *Physical Culture*, which featured photos of men and women posing nearly naked. Throughout his long life, Macfadden was almost always in the news—his marriages; his attacks on the medical establishment; his founding of a new religion, the Cosmotarian Fellowship. He celebrated his eighty-third birthday by parachuting 2,500 feet into the Hudson River. He finally succumbed to a urinary tract blockage that he had unsuccessfully tried to cure by fasting.

18. SAMUEL HAHNEMANN (1755–1843) Age at death: 88
A German physician, Hahnemann developed what was in his day a radical philosophy, homeopathy. Its basic tenet is that a drug that produces symptoms of illness in a healthy person will cure a sick person who exhibits those symptoms when that drug is administered in minute doses. Hahnemann died from an inflammation of the bronchial tubes, which had plagued him for 20 years. Although he had come to terms with death ("My earthly shell is worn out," he stated), his wife was less accepting of the inevitable. She kept his embalmed corpse with her for nine days before giving it up for burial.

19. J. H. KELLOGG (1852–1943) Age at death: 91
A Seventh-Day Adventist and lifelong vegetarian, Dr. Kellogg ran a sanitarium in Battle Creek, Michigan, where he made his patients' diets more palatable by devising new vegetarian products. His brother Will marketed some of these products, including the now famous Kellogg's Cornflakes. (Another breakfast food magnate, C. W. Post, was one of Kellogg's patients.) J. H. Kellogg died from pneumonia shortly after waging a successful court battle to keep the Adventists from assuming control of his sanitarium.

20. LINUS PAULING (1901–1994) Age at death: 93
The only person to win two unshared Nobel Prizes (for Chemistry and Peace, not Medicine), Pauling wrote a book in 1970 arguing that large doses of vitamin C could cure the common cold. Over the years, he expanded on his claim, declaring that vitamin C would extend a person's life by decades and ward off cancer and heart disease. Pauling himself took 18,000 mg of vitamin C a day (the recommended daily

allowance for adults is 60 mg). He was diagnosed with prostate cancer in December of 1991. He died of complications at his ranch in Big Sur, California, two years later.

21. ANCEL KEYS (1904–2004) Age at death: 100
A public health scientist at the University of Minnesota, Keys developed the K-rations consumed by millions of soldiers in World War II. After the war, he initiated a study of Minnesota businessmen that first demonstrated a strong link between the consumption of saturated fats and heart disease. In 1958, he began the "Seven Countries Study," tracking the diets of 12,763 middle-aged men in the United States, Japan, Finland, the Netherlands, Yugoslavia, Greece, and Italy. Based on the results, he became an advocate of the "Mediterranean diet," emphasizing fruits, vegetables, pasta, fish, and the use of olive oil in place of animal fats. Keys, who considered himself a champion of "reasonably low-fat diets," died at his home in Minnesota, two months shy of his 101st birthday, after having suffered several strokes.

F.B. & C.F.

12 Sufferers of Tinnitus

Tinnitus is a ringing in the ears or other head noises which are perceived in the absence of any external noise source. It is estimated that one out of every five people experiences some degree of tinnitus.

1. LUDWIG VAN BEETHOVEN (1770–1827), German composer
In an 1801 letter noting that his hearing had become progressively weaker over the three previous years, Beethoven added, "Day and night I have a buzzing and singing in my ears." The most likely cause of his tinnitus and eventual deafness was otosclerosis, a gradual formation of tissue around his ear.

2. FRANCISCO GOYA (1746–1828), Spanish artist
At age 46, Goya suddenly was stricken by a mysterious and agonizing illness. In addition to relentless ringing in his ears, Goya suffered from a terrifying spectrum of symptoms: dizziness, nausea, impaired speech, hallucinations, convulsions, partial paralysis, and, no doubt most frightening to a painter, partial blindness. The illness nearly killed Goya, but it also revolutionized his art. He had been a conventional, talented painter—he became a creator of emotionally charged works of genius. Modern speculation about the cause of Goya's illness has included syphilis, infection with the rare Vogt-Koyanagi virus, and severe lead poisoning.

3. JOAN OF ARC (1412–1431), French heroine and Catholic saint
Some medical authorities believe that the heavenly voices Joan of Arc heard were the result of intermittent attacks of tinnitus. She told her English captors that she had been unable to understand the voices the first time she heard them. Joan also told the English that she felt compelled to kneel whenever she heard the voices, and one of her captors observed her becoming nauseated while being visited by the voices. This evidence suggests that she may have suffered from Ménière's disease, a serious disorder of the inner ear that frequently causes tinnitus, disorientation, vertigo, and nausea.

4. MARTIN LUTHER (1483–1546), German religious reformer
Through much of his life, Luther suffered from Ménière's disease and the resulting attacks of dizziness and tinnitus. During acute episodes, he became convinced that he was being visited by the devil, who would roar in his ears and spin so fast in his head that Luther fell out of his chair.

5 STEVE MARTIN (1945–), U.S. actor
Martin developed tinnitus as a result of exposure to loud noise while filming a pistol-shooting scene in 1986. He has borne the discomforts stoically, commenting, "You just get used to it, or you go insane."

6. ROBERT SCHUMANN (1810–1856), German composer
In 1846, Schumann's hearing troubles caused a 10-month delay in the completion of his Second Symphony. He complained that his head seemed to be spinning and that his ears were "peculiarly out of tune," a condition his wife Clara described as "constant singing and rushing." On February 10, 1854, Schumann suffered an extremely painful attack of his ear malady, which was followed by aural hallucinations, such as angels dictating a theme to him. Two weeks later, he attempted suicide and spent the rest of his life in asylums.

7. WILLIAM SHATNER (1931–), Canadian actor
Shatner's tinnitus was apparently caused by an explosion on the set of *Star Trek* (costar Leonard Nimoy developed a milder case). He said that his condition contributed to the breakup of his second marriage and even caused him to contemplate suicide. Shatner has since found relief using an electric masking device.

8. ALAN SHEPARD (1923–1998), U.S. astronaut
In 1961, Shepard became the first American in space. But he was grounded by NASA in 1963, when he began suffering from ringing in the ears, vertigo, and nausea, which were diagnosed as Ménière's disease. In 1969, he underwent surgery to have a tube installed in his inner ear to drain excess fluid. The operation was a success, and

Shepard was restored to full flight status. In 1971, he walked (and golfed) on the moon as part of the *Apollo XIV* mission.

9. BARBRA STREISAND (1942–), U.S. singer and actress
Streisand developed tinnitus at age seven: "One morning I woke up with a clicking noise in my ears which wouldn't go away. Later it developed into a continuous, unrelenting ringing noise. It has been with me ever since." She wears a masking device in order to sleep at night.

10. PETER TOWNSEND (1945–) , British rock musician and songwriter
Townsend was lead guitarist for The Who, one of the loudest bands in rock history. Thus, he developed tinnitus. He commented, "I've shot my hearing. It's painful, and it's frustrating when little children talk to you and you can't hear them."

11. VINCENT VAN GOGH (1853–1890), Dutch artist
Van Gogh suffered from intermittent attacks of vertigo, vomiting, hallucinations, and noises in his ears. Some think that those symptoms, and the artist's later insanity, were the result of his habit of eating his paints, which contained toxic chemicals. In 1990, Dr. I. Kaufman Arenberg suggested that van Gogh suffered from Ménière's disease.

12. NEIL YOUNG (1945–), Canadian singer and songwriter
The "Godfather of Grunge" developed tinnitus during his 1991 Ragged Glory tour. Afterward, he gave his ears a break by recording two acoustic albums, *Harvest Moon* and *MTV Unplugged*. He returned to louder rock in 1994, telling an interviewer, "I still have a bit of tinnitus, but fortunately now I'm not as sensitive to loud sounds. . . . My hearing's not perfect, but it's OK."

C.F.

5 Body Parts Named After Italians

1. ORGAN OF CORTI
The organ of hearing in the internal ear. Named after Alfonso Corti (1822–1878).

2. EUSTACHIAN TUBE
A tube leading from the middle ear to the throat. Its purpose is to equalize pressure in the ear. Named after anatomist Bartolommeo Eustachio (1524?–1574).

3. FALLOPIAN TUBES
The pair of tubes that conduct the egg from the ovary to the uterus in the female. Named after anatomist Gabriel Fallopius (1523–1562).

4. RUFFINI'S CORPUSCLES

Sensory nerve endings that respond to warmth. Named after anatomist Angelo Ruffini (1864–1929).

5. SERTOLI CELLS

Cells of the testis that serve to nourish sperm cells. Named after histologist Enrico Sertoli (1842–1910).

K.A.M.

9 Body Parts You Didn't Know Had Names

1. CANTHUS

The corner of the eye where the upper and lower eyelids meet.

2. EPONYCHIUM

Another term for the cuticle of the fingernail, a narrow band of epidermal tissue that extends over the margin of the nail wall.

3. FRENUM GLANDIS

Found in the male reproductive system, this delicate fold of skin attaches the foreskin to the undersurface of the glans penis.

4. GLABELLA

A flattened area of the frontal bone (forehead area) between the frontal eminences and the superciliary arches (eyebrows) just above the nose.

5. LUNNULE

The white crescent-shaped mark at the base of a fingernail.

6. OTOLITHS

Particles of calcium carbonate in the utricles and saccules of the internal ears. The otoliths respond to gravity by sliding in the direction of the ground and causing sensitive hairs to bend, thus generating nervous impulses important in maintaining equilibrium.

7. PHALANX

A bone of the fingers and toes. There are two phalanges in each thumb and great toe, while there are three phalanges in all other fingers and toes, making a total of fourteen in each hand and foot.

8. PHILTRUM

The vertical groove in the middle portion of the upper lip.

9. PUDENDUM

A collective name for the external genitalia of the female; also known as the vulva. It includes the mons pubis, the labia majora, and the labia minora.

K.A.M.

CHAPTER SIX

ANIMALS

10 MOST INTELLIGENT BREEDS OF DOGS

10 LEAST INTELLIGENT BREEDS OF DOGS

17 WINNERS OF THE DOG HERO OF THE YEAR AWARD

17 CHILDREN WHO MAY HAVE LIVED WITH WILD ANIMALS

11 EXAMPLES OF UNUSUAL ANIMAL MATING HABITS

AVERAGE ERECT PENIS LENGTHS FOR 10 SPECIES

8 EXAMPLES OF STRANGE ANIMAL BEHAVIOR

10 ANIMALS THAT HAVE EATEN HUMANS

11 LARGE ANIMALS DISCOVERED BY WESTERN
SCIENCE SINCE 1900

15 EXTINCT ANIMALS THAT ARE NO LONGER EXTINCT

5 OF THE WORLD'S MOST OFT-SIGHTED
LAKE AND SEA MONSTERS

12 PLACES WITH MORE SHEEP THAN HUMANS

4 PLACES WITH MORE PIGS THAN HUMANS

10 NATIONS WITH THE MOST CAMELS

MAXIMUM RECORDED LIFESPAN OF 58 ANIMALS

THE CAT CAME BACK: 15 CATS WHO TRAVELED
GREAT DISTANCES TO RETURN HOME

THE DAY OF EXTINCTION FOR 8 BIRDS

5 TIPS ON HOW TO SURVIVE AN ENCOUNTER WITH A BEAR

10 FUNGUSES THAT CHANGED HISTORY

24 MOLECULES AND AMOEBAS WITH FUNNY NAMES

PENGUINS MATING
© G. R. Guy

10 Most Intelligent Breeds of Dogs

In *The Intelligence of Dogs* (New York: The Free Press, 1994), Stanley Coren ranked breeds of dogs for working intelligence. The rankings were based on questionnaires completed by 199 obedience judges from the American and Canadian Kennel Clubs.

1. Border collie
2. Poodle
3. German shepherd
4. Golden retriever
5. Doberman pinscher
6. Shetland sheepdog
7. Labrador retriever
8. Papillon
9. Rottweiler
10. Australian cattle dog

10 Least Intelligent Breeds of Dogs

1. Afghan hound
2. Basenji
3. Bulldog
4. Chow chow
5. Borzoi
6. Bloodhound
7. Pekingese
8. Mastiff
9. Beagle
10. Basset hound

17 Winners of the Dog Hero of the Year Award

In 1954, Ken-L Ration began honoring canine heroes by awarding a Dog Hero of the Year medal. In recent years, other sponsors have taken responsibility for the awards. Each year, a panel of judges selects the dog who has shown the greatest courage in saving life or property. Here are the remarkable stories of 17 of the winners:

1. TANG (1954)

   The first Ken-L Ration Dog Hero of the Year was a collie owned by Air Force Captain and Mrs. Maurice Dyer of Denison, Texas. While the Dyers were stationed at air force bases in Alaska and Texas, the friendly dog saved at least five youngsters from being hit by military vehicles. On another occasion, Tang planted himself in front of a parked truck, howling and barking, until the driver discovered a two-year-old stowaway. Had she not been found, the little girl would have fallen to the pavement the moment the truck began to move. Tang was a familiar and well-loved sight in Denison, and when he was awarded the Ken-L Ration gold medal, the neighborhood children had a parade in his honor.

2. TAFFY (1955)

   This cocker spaniel was owned by Mr. and Mrs. Ken Wilson of Coeur d'Alene, Idaho. Taffy was selected for saving three-year-old Stevie Wilson from drowning in an icy lake. The boy was supposed to stay with a neighbor while his father was trying out a saddle horse in a corral near a lake. But the child and his dog went out to play, and Stevie fell into the lake and sank to the bottom. Taffy bounded up to the corral barking excitedly and racing about Wilson's horse. When this did not attract the man's attention, Taffy dashed into the lake, barking at the top of her lungs, and then came out and nipped at the horse's legs until Wilson was almost thrown from his mount. He then leaped off his horse and raced after Taffy to the lake. Wilson saw Stevie's red mackinaw floating on the surface, dove into the four-foot-deep water, and lifted his unconscious son from the bottom. Six hours later, Stevie regained consciousness. The first thing he saw was his dog Taffy, crouched in a prayerful attitude beside his head. The attending physician said that just a few more moments at the bottom of the lake probably would have proved fatal.

3. BUDDY (1964)

   A collie owned by Mr. and Mrs. Matthew S. Crinkley, Jr., of Budd Lake, New Jersey, was the first Dog Hero of the Year to be chosen because of heroism that led to the saving of animal life. The Crinkleys ran a goat dairy farm, and one cold January morning before dawn, a fire broke out in the farm's maternity barn. While his master was sleeping, Buddy took charge and herded the entire flock of 70 pregnant goats out of the barn to safety, suffering severe burns on his paws and nasal damage from smoke inhalation. The Crinkleys were finally awakened by Buddy's frantic barks and rushed to a window, only to see the walls and roof of the now-empty barn tumble into a flaming pile of ruin. The warning of this dedicated farm dog allowed the Crinkleys just enough time to wet down the roof of a second barn and save the 30 remaining goats.

4. RINGO (1968)

The Saint Bernard mix owned by Mrs. Raymond Saleh of Euless, Texas, saved two-year-old Randy Saleh from being hit by traffic on a busy road. Randy wandered away from home one day, and a two-hour police search failed to locate the boy. About three quarters of a mile away from the Saleh home, Harley Jones, a school maintenance employee, came upon a traffic jam that motorists said was caused by a "mad dog in the road ahead." Jones parked his car and went to the head of the line, where Ringo, resolutely stationed in the center of the road, was protecting Randy, who was playing in the center of the heavily traveled roadway. Ringo would block the oncoming cars and then rush back to Randy and nudge him to the side of the road. But thinking it was a game, Randy would immediately return to the center of the road. Jones spoke soothingly to Ringo and finally calmed him down, but the dog did not relax and allow cars to pass until Randy was safely out of the traffic.

5. TOP (1969)

The Great Dane owned by Axel Patzwaldt of Los Angeles saved two children from death or severe injury by performing two heroic deeds within eight weeks. The dog's exploits began in April when an 11-year-old neighbor girl took him for a walk. A short distance from home, she started across the street, not noticing that a large truck was swiftly approaching. Top barked loudly, jumped in front of her, and pushed her out of the way. She was unhurt, but Top was hit by the truck, which broke his right rear leg. One week after his seven-week stint in a cast, Top found two-year-old Christopher Conley, another neighbor's child, at the bottom of a nearby swimming pool. Top alerted his master by barking wildly and then led him to the scene. A former lifeguard, Patzwaldt pulled Christopher out and began mouth-to-mouth resuscitation on the child, who resumed breathing in a short time.

6. GRIZZLY BEAR (1970)

This Saint Bernard, owned by Mr. and Mrs. David Gratias of Denali, Alaska, battled and finally chased away a grizzly bear that had attacked the dog's mistress behind their cabin home. Mrs. Gratias had discovered a young grizzly bear cub in the backyard. Assuming that the mother must be near, the woman raced back to close the front door in an effort to protect her napping two-year-old daughter, Theresa. As she rounded the corner of the house, she came face to face with the mother grizzly. The huge beast raised itself up to its eight-foot height and grabbed Mrs. Gratias, who slipped on the icy ground and lay stunned by the fall. Instantly upon her, the grizzly raked her cheek with one paw while it sank the other one deep into her shoulder. Before the bear could inflict a possibly fatal bite, she suddenly staggered backward as the Saint Bernard—aptly named Grizzly Bear—lunged with all of his

180 pounds. Maneuvering and slashing at the beast with his teeth and paws, Grizzly Bear protected his helpless owner until the bear wandered off, exhausted.

7. MIMI (1972)

The first miniature poodle to become the Dog Hero of the Year, Mimi was owned by Mr. and Mrs. Nicholas Emerito of Danbury, Connecticut. This tiny canine helped save the lives of eight members of one family when fire broke out in their home. Mr. Emerito had fallen asleep in front of the TV. Wakened by Mimi's barking and scratching at his chest, he found the living room in flames. While he ran to awaken his wife and small son in a first-floor bedroom, Mimi raced up the stairs and aroused five other children. Two of the teenage boys were trapped by the flaming stairway, but they leaped to safety from the roof. All were saved, but the house was completely destroyed.

8. CHESTER (1978)

The twenty-fifth Ken-L Ration Dog Hero of the Year was a Chesapeake Bay retriever owned by Mr. and Mrs. Gary Homme of Livingston, Montana. Nicknamed Chessie, the heroic dog pulled five-year-old Kenny Homme from a surging creek. Mrs. Homme was washing dishes at the time and periodically looked out of her kitchen window to check on the boy, who was playing outside. Suddenly, Mrs. Homme noticed that he was gone. She ran outside and heard him shouting, "Help me! Save me!" The boy had slid down a steep hill and fallen into a creek that was swollen and surging with a powerful current. Chester was in the water trying to save the child. As the dog swam toward Kenny, the water pulled the boy into a culvert. Chester battled the raging water for 10 minutes. Kenny grabbed onto Chester's fur twice but lost his grip both times. Then he grabbed on top of the dog's back and was carried out of the tunnel to safety. "If we didn't have Chessie, we wouldn't have a son," Mrs. Homme said.

9. WOODIE (1980)

A collie mix owned by Rae Anne Knitter of Cleveland, Woodie leapt off an eighty-foot cliff to rescue Knitter's fiancé, Ray Thomas, from drowning. One afternoon, Rae Anne, Ray, and Woodie were walking along a nature trail in the Rocky River Reservation, when Ray, an amateur photographer, decided to capture a spectacular view from atop a steep shale cliff. Rae Anne and Woodie waited on the path while Ray disappeared over the top of the hill. Suddenly, the usually well-behaved Woodie began twisting and tugging to escape from Rae Anne. She let go of him, and he raced ahead. When Rae Anne reached the brink, she saw Ray lying unconscious in a stream 80 feet below. Woodie, who broke both hips in the jump, was by his side, nudging Ray's face to keep it out of the water. Both Ray and Woodie survived.

10. **KING (1981)**

   On the morning of December 26, 1981, the Carlson family of Granite
   Falls, Washington, was asleep, when a fire broke out in their utility room.
   King, a German shepherd mix, was sleeping in the adjoining family room.
   Instead of escaping through a door that had been left open for him, he
   clawed and chewed his way through the plywood door that separated him
   from the utility room. Then he charged through the burning room into
   the bedroom where 16-year-old Pearl Carlson was sleeping. He woke her,
   and the two rushed to her parents' bedroom to alert them. Howard
   Carlson had a lung condition and could not move as quickly as his wife
   and daughter, but King remained by him until the man was safely
   outside. King was badly burned on his paws and had a gash on his back
   and splinters in his mouth, but he made a full recovery.

11. **BO (1982)**

   Bo, a Labrador retriever, was rafting on the Colorado River with a
   puppy named Dutchess and their owners, Laurie and Rob Roberts of
   Glenwood Springs, Colorado, when an eight-foot wave flipped the raft.
   Rob and Dutchess were thrown free, but Laurie and Bo were trapped
   underneath. Bo finally emerged but then dived back under the raft. He
   reappeared towing Laurie by the hair. Once she was free of the raft,
   Laurie grabbed Bo's tail and let the dog pull her across the strong
   current to shore.

12. **VILLA (1983)**

   During a severe blizzard in Villas, New Jersey, 11-year-old Andrea
   Anderson was blown into a large snowdrift about 40 feet from her
   home. Disoriented, blinded by snow being blown by 60-mile-an-hour
   winds, and unable to pull herself out, she began to scream for help.
   Villa, a one-year-old black Newfoundland puppy belonging to Mrs.
   Lynda Veit, heard Andrea's cries and, for the first time in her life, leapt
   over the five-foot fence surrounding her run. Villa ran 80 feet to the
   snowdrift, found Andrea, and licked her face reassuringly. Then she
   circled the girl to clear the snow entrapping her. Once Andrea was free,
   Villa cleared a path for her through the blinding snow and led her to
   the front door of her house.

13. **LEO (1984)**

   Leo, a four-year-old standard poodle from Hunt, Texas, was playing
   near the Guadalupe River with eleven-year-old Sean Callahan and
   Sean's nine-year-old sister, Erin. Suddenly, Leo and the two children
   stumbled upon a five-and-a-half-foot rattlesnake. Leo lunged between
   the snake and Sean, allowing his young master to escape. Leo received
   six poisonous bites to the head. He almost died, but made a remarkable
   recovery.

14. REONA (1989)

On October 17, 1989, a devastating earthquake hit Northern California. After the first jolt, Reona, a two-and-a-half-year-old rottweiler owned by Jim Patton of Watsonville, heard screams from across the street. She bolted out the door, jumped three fences (something she had never done), and raced into the home of five-year-old Vivian Cooper. The terrified child was standing in the kitchen when Reona pushed her against the cabinets and sat on her. Seconds later, a large microwave oven on top of the refrigerator came crashing down where Vivian had been standing.

15. WILLY (1991)

Betty Souder of Los Alamos, New Mexico, was sleeping soundly when she was awakened by her nine-year-old Weimaraner, Willy. "I couldn't seem to wake up," she later recalled. But Willy persisted. When Souder finally stood, she felt dizzy and noticed that Willy was weaving, too. Almost too weak to pick up the telephone, Souder finally managed to place a call to a friend. It turned out that a faulty furnace had leaked, filling the house with poisonous carbon monoxide gas. Had Souder slept a few minutes longer, she probably would not have been able to make her lifesaving call.

16. WEELA (1993)

Eleven-year-old Gary Watkins was chasing lizards in his backyard when Weela, the family pit bull, jumped on him and sent him flying. Seconds later, a rattlesnake sank its fangs into Weela's face. Weela saved Gary from the rattlesnake attack, but that incident was not the one that earned Weela the Dog Hero of the Year award. Years later, in January 1993, the Tijuana River Valley in Southern California was hit by flooding when heavy rains caused a dam to break. Weela and the Watkins family spent six hours fighting strong currents and floating debris to reach a friend's ranch and rescue 12 dogs. Over the following month, Weela, carrying 30 to 50 pounds of dog food in a harnessed backpack, made repeated trips across the flooded river to bring help to seventeen dogs and puppies and one cat who were stranded on an island. On one occasion, Weela led a rescue team to thirteen horses who were stranded. Finally, while carrying food to the stranded dogs and cat, Weela came across thirty people who were trying to cross the floodwaters. By barking and running back and forth, she guided the group to a different point, where the water was shallower. By the time the floodwaters subsided, Weela had saved thirty people, twenty-nine dogs, thirteen horses, and one cat.

17. BLUE (2002)

On the evening of July 21, 2001, 85-year-old Ruth Gay of LaBelle, Florida, took her family dog for a walk. Blue was a 35-pound Australian blue heeler. Gay slipped on wet grass and fell, breaking her nose and dislocating her shoulder. As she cried for help, an alligator in a nearby canal sensed her vulnerability and headed in her direction. Blue intercepted the alligator, fought it off, and kept it at bay until Gay's family arrived home 45 minutes later. Blue received a stomach wound but survived.

17 Children Who May Have Lived with Wild Animals

1–2. ROMULUS AND REMUS (8th century BC)
Twin brothers Romulus and Remus were allegedly raised by a wolf after being abandoned in the countryside by their uncle. A number of years later, they were rescued by a shepherd, and they went on to found the city of Rome in 753 BC. Scholars long considered their childhood adventures to be mythical, but recent studies of children known to have lived with animals have demonstrated that there could well be an element of truth to the Romulus and Remus legend.

3. HESSIAN WOLF-BOY (1344)
In 1344, hunters in the German kingdom of Hesse captured a boy between 7 and 12 years of age who had been living in the wild. Wolves had brought him food and dug holes to shelter him at night. The boy ran on all fours and had an extraordinary ability to leap long distances. Treated as a freak by his human captors, he died shortly after his return to civilization because of an enforced diet of cooked food.

4. LITHUANIAN BEAR-BOY (1661)
In 1661, in a Lithuanian forest, a party of hunters discovered a boy living with a group of bears. The hunters captured him, even though he resisted by biting and clawing them. Taken to Warsaw, Poland, and christened Joseph, the boy continued to eat raw meat and graze on grass. Although he never dropped the habit of growling like a bear, he did acquire a limited vocabulary and became the servant of a Polish nobleman.

5. IRISH SHEEP-BOY (1672)
In 1672, a 16-year-old boy was found trapped in a hunter's net in the hills of southern Ireland. Since running away from his parents' home as a young child, the boy had lived with a herd of wild sheep. He was healthy and muscular even though he ate only grass and hay. After his capture, he was taken to the Netherlands, where he was cared for in Amsterdam by Dr. Nicholas Tulp. The boy never learned human speech and continued to bleat like a sheep throughout his life.

6. FRAUMARK BEAR-GIRL (1767)

In 1767, two hunters captured a girl who attacked them after they shot her bear companion in the mountains near the village of Fraumark, Hungary. The tall, muscular, 18-year-old girl had lived with bears since infancy. She was locked up in an asylum in the town of Karpfen because she refused to wear clothes or eat anything but raw meat and tree bark.

7. WILD BOY OF AVEYRON (1800)

In 1800, hunters captured a 17-year-old boy who had lived alone in the forest of Aveyron, France, since he was an infant. Given the name Victor, the boy was not happy living in civilized society and repeatedly tried to escape. He growled and gnashed his teeth at first, but later became adjusted to being with humans. When he died at the age of 40, he had learned only three words: "Peter" and "King George."

8. DINA SANICHAR (1867)

In 1867, a hunting party found a seven-year-old boy living with wolves in a cave in the jungles of Bulandshahr, India. Taken to the Sekandra Orphanage near Agra and given the name Dina Sanichar, the boy refused to wear clothes and sharpened his teeth by gnawing on bones. For 28 years, he lived at the orphanage, but he never learned to talk. In 1895, he died of tuberculosis aggravated by the one human habit he had adopted—smoking tobacco.

9. WILLIAM MILDIN (1883)

An intriguing but not fully substantiated case is that of Englishman William Mildin, the Fourteenth Earl of Streatham. (One authority believes the name of this child was actually William Russell.) Shipwrecked on the West African coast at the age of 11 in 1868, Mildin lived with apes for 15 years before being discovered and returned to England. He may have inspired Edgar Rice Burroughs to create his most famous character—Tarzan of the Apes.

10–11. AMALA AND KAMALA (1920)

In October 1920, the Reverend J. A. L. Singh captured two girls, one about three years old and the other about five, who had lived with a pack of wolves near the village of Midnapore, India. Named Amala and Kamala by Singh, the girls were mute except for occasional growling sounds, walked on all fours, and loved to eat raw meat. After a year in civilization, Amala died. Kamala eventually acquired a 45-word vocabulary before her death in 1929.

12. CACHARI LEOPARD-BOY (1938)

In 1938, an English sportsman found an eight-year-old boy living with a leopard and her cubs in the north Cachar Hills of India. The boy, who had been carried off by the leopard five years earlier, was returned to his family of peasant farmers. Although nearly blind, he could identify individuals and objects by his extremely well-developed sense of smell.

13. **MISHA DEFONESCA (1945)**
When she was seven years old, Misha's mother and father were seized by Nazis. She was hidden in a safe house, but, worried that she might be turned over to the Germans, she ran off and lived in the wild. For the next four years, as World War II raged, Defonesca wandered through Europe, covering more than 3,000 miles. During this time, she lived on raw berries, raw meat, and food stolen from farmhouses. On occasion, she lived with packs of wolves. She later recalled, "In all my travels, the only time I ever slept deeply was when I was with wolves. . . . The days with my wolf family multiplied. I have no idea how many months I spent with them, but I wanted it to last forever—it was far better than returning to the world of my own kind. . . . Those were the most beautiful days I had ever experienced."

14. **SAHARAN GAZELLE BOY (1960)**
In September 1960, Basque poet Jean Claude Armen discovered and observed a boy who was approximately eight years old living with a herd of gazelles in the desert regions of the Western Sahara. For two months, Armen studied the boy, who he speculated was the orphaned child of some nomadic Saharan Moorish family. The boy traveled on all fours, grazed on grass, dug roots, and seemed to be thoroughly accepted by the gazelles as a member of the herd. Since the boy appeared happy, Armen left him with his gazelle family. American soldiers unsuccessfully attempted to capture the boy in 1966 and 1970.

15. **SHAMDEO THE WOLF BOY (1972)**
This boy was taken to the Catholic mission at Sultanpur, a town in Punjab, India, by a man who allegedly had found him living in a forest with wolves. The boy, estimated to be three or four years old at the time, was covered with matted hair and had calluses on his elbows, palms, and knees. According to Father Joseph de Souza, Shamdeo learned to stand upright in five months and within two years was doing chores around the mission. He communicated with sign language. Father Joseph noted that the boy no longer caught and ate live chickens, but he was still drawn by the scent of blood. That Shamdeo actually had lived with wolves has not been authenticated.

16. **JOHN SSEBUNYA (1991)**
In 1991, Ugandan villagers treed and captured a little boy living with a pack of monkeys. One of the villagers identified the child as John Ssebunya, who had fled the village three years earlier when his father had murdered his mother and then disappeared. John was adopted by

Paul and Molly Wasswa, who ran an orphanage. Several experts who studied John were convinced that he really had lived with monkeys. When left with a group of monkeys, he approached them from the side with open palms in classic simian fashion. He also had an unusual lopsided gait and pulled his lips back when he smiled. He tended to greet people with a powerful hug, the way monkeys greet each other. After some time in the orphanage, John learned to talk and to sing. In 1999, he visited Great Britain as part of the Pearl of Africa Children's Choir. That same year, he was the subject of a BBC documentary, *Living Proof.*

17. BELLO OF NIGERIA (1996)

In 1996, a boy about two years old was found by hunters living with chimps in the Falgore forest in Nigeria. He was taken to the Tudan Maliki Torrey children's home, where the staff named him Bello. Mentally and physically disabled, with a misshapen forehead, sloping right shoulder, and protruding chest, he was apparently abandoned by his parents, members of the nomadic Fulani tribe. When he arrived at the home, Bello walked like a chimp, moving on his hind legs and dragging his hands on the ground. As of 2002, he still could not speak but made chimplike noises.

R.J.F. & C.F.

11 Examples of Unusual Animal Mating Habits

1. PENGUINS

Penguins prefer to be "married," but they suffer long separations due to their migratory habits. When reunited, a pair will stand breast to breast, heads thrown back, singing loudly, with outstretched flippers trembling. Two weeks after a pair is formed, their union is consummated. The male makes his intentions known by laying his head across his partner's stomach. They go on a long trek to find privacy, but the actual process of intercourse takes only three minutes. Neither penguin will mate again that year. The male Adele penguin must select his mate from a colony of more than a million, and he indicates his choice by rolling a stone at the female's feet. Stones are scarce at mating time because many are needed to build walls around nests. It becomes commonplace for penguins to steal them from one another. If she accepts his gift, they stand belly to belly and sing a mating song.

2. HIPPOPOTAMI

Hippos have their own form of aromatherapy. They attract mates by marking territory, urinating and defecating at the same time. Then, an enamored hippo will twirl its tail like a propeller to spread this delicious slop in every direction. This attracts lovers, and a pair will begin foreplay, which consists of playing by splashing around in the water before settling down to business.

3. MALE UGANDA KOB

Exhaustion is the frequent fate of the male Uganda kob, an African antelope. Like many species of birds and mammals, the kob roams in a social group until the mating season, when the dominant male establishes a mating territory, or lek. But the females decide which territory they wish to enter and pick the male they think most attractive. He then mates with all the females until he is too weak to continue (usually due to lack of food) and is replaced by another.

4. SQUID

Squid begin mating with a circling nuptial dance. Teams revolve around a "spawning bed" 200 meters in diameter. At daybreak, they begin having sex and continue all day long—they take a break only so the female can dive down and deposit eggs. When she returns to the circle, she and her partner go at it again. As twilight falls, the pair go offshore to eat and rest. At the first sign of sunlight, they return to their spot and do it all over again. This routine can last up to two weeks, ensuring a healthy population of squid.

5. PORCUPINES

The answer to one of our oldest jokes, "How do porcupines do it?" "Veeery carefully!" is not quite true. The truth is more bizarre than dangerous. Females are only receptive for a few hours a year. As summer approaches, young females become nervous and then excited. Next, they go off their food, stick close by the males, and mope. Meanwhile, the male becomes aggressive with other males and begins a period of carefully sniffing every place the female of his choice urinates, smelling her all over. This is a tremendous aphrodisiac. While she is sulking by his side, he begins to "sing." When he is ready to make love, the female runs away if she's not ready. If she is in the mood, they both rear up and face each other, belly to belly. Then males spray their ladies with a tremendous stream of urine, soaking their loved one from head to foot—the stream can shoot as far as seven feet. If they're not ready, females respond by 1) objecting verbally, 2) hitting with front paws like boxers, 3) trying to bite, 4) shaking off the urine. When ready, they accept the bath. This routine can go on for weeks. Six months after the beginning of courtship, the female will accept any male she has been close to. The spines and quills of both go relaxed and flat, and the male enters from behind. Mating continues until the male is worn out. Every time he tries to stop, the female wants to continue. If he has given up, she chooses another partner, only now she acts out the male role. To "cool off," females engage in the same courtship series, step by step, in reverse order. It is advised never to stand close to a cage that contains courting porcupines.

6. GEESE
Two male geese may form a homosexual bond and prefer each other's company to any female's. Sometimes, however, a female may interpose herself between them during such a courtship and be quickly fertilized. They will accept her, and weeks later the happy family of three can be seen attending to its tiny newborn goslings.

7. WHITE-FRONTED PARROTS
These birds, native to Mexico and Central America, are believed to be the only species besides humans to kiss. Before actually mating, male and female will lock their beaks and gently flick their tongues together. If kissing is satisfying for both parties, the male boldly takes the next step, by regurgitating his food for his girlfriend, to show his love. White-fronted parrots also share parenting, unlike many other species. When the female lays her one egg, both parents take turns incubating it. When the baby hatches, the couple feed and care for their offspring together.

8. GRASSHOPPERS
Why are grasshoppers so noisy? It's because they're singing to woo their partners. They have as many as 400 distinct songs, which they sing during their courtship and mating cycles. Some males have a different song for each distinct mating period—for example, there may be a flirting song, then a mating song.

9. SEAGULLS
Lesbian mating is practiced by between 8 percent and 14 percent of the seagulls on the Santa Barbara islands, off the California coast. Lesbian gulls go through all the motions of mating and lay sterile eggs. Homosexual behavior is also known in geese, ostriches, cichlid fish, squid, rats, and monkeys.

10. RED-SIDED GARTER SNAKES
These snakes are small and poisonous and live in Canada and the northwestern United States. Their highly unusual mating takes place during an enormous orgy. Twenty-five thousand snakes slither together in a large den, eager to copulate. In that pile, one female may have as many as 100 males vying for her. These "nesting balls" grow as large as two feet high. Now and then a female is crushed under the heavy mound—and the males are so randy that they continue to copulate, becoming the only necrophiliac snakes!

11. LYNX SPIDERS

When a male lynx spider feels the urge, he will capture his beauty in his web and wrap her in silk. Offering her this elegant meal (the silken web) is his way of wooing. When the mood is right, the female, distracted by her feast, will allow her suitor to mount her and begin mating. Oblivious, she ignores him and enjoys her supper.

Average Erect Penis Lengths for 10 Species

Animal	Average Erect Penis Length
1. Humpback whale	10 ft.
2. Elephant	5 to 6 ft.
3. Bull	3 ft.
4. Stallion	2 ft. 6 in.
5. Rhinoceros	2 ft.
6. Pig	18 to 20 in.
7. Man	6 in.
8. Gorilla	2 in.
9. Cat	¾ in.
10. Mosquito	1/100 in.

Note: The Argentine lake duck averages 16 inches from head to foot. However, its erect penis size is 17 inches. Primary Source: Leigh Rutledge, *The Gay Book of Lists* (Boston: Alyson Publications, 1987).

8 Examples of Strange Animal Behavior

1. GENTLE CROCODILES

Nile crocodiles, although physically and morally capable of killing humans, are tender guardians of their own babies. Newborn crocodiles average twenty-eight centimeters (eleven inches) in length and weigh a hundred grams (three and a half ounces)—tempting prey for a wide range of predators. To protect them when they emerge from their shells, a mother crocodile delicately picks up the hatchlings with her deadly jaws and slips them into a pouch inside her mouth. Then she carries the chirping babies to the water, where they are greeted by a roaring chorus from the adult males.

2. TRANSFORMER FROGS

The female gastric brooding frog (*Rheobatrachus silus*), which flourished in Queensland, Australia, until its recent extinction, swallowed her fertilized eggs, transformed her stomach into a uterus, carried the developing tadpoles in her stomach, and gave birth to fully formed young through her mouth.

3. FARMER ANTS

Aphids produce a sugary excrement, which has come to be known as honeydew. Some ants obtain this honeydew by licking the leaves and stems on which it has fallen. But some ant species have learned to gather the aphids into their nests, feed them, and then when the ants are hungry, to stroke the aphids with their feelers so that they produce the honeydew, which the ants then drink fresh.

4. INCESTUOUS MITES

The female mite known as *Histiostoma murchiei* creates her own husband from scratch. She lays eggs that turn into adults without needing to be fertilized. The mother then copulates with her sons within three or four days of laying the eggs, after which the sons die rather quickly.

5. NON-NURTURING CUCKOOS

Female cuckoos deposit their eggs in the nests of other birds, who then incubate the eggs and raise the offspring until they are able to fly away on their own. Curiously, each individual cuckoo mother chooses the same species to adopt all of her children and is able to lay eggs that resemble the eggs of the foster family.

6. CODEPENDENT ANGLER FISH

As soon as they mature sexually, male angler fish begin a desperate search to find a mate in the dark water 6,000 feet below the surface. As soon as they locate likely prospects, certain species of angler fish attach themselves to the females—literally. The male latches on to the much larger female and never lets go for the rest of his life. In fact, their vascular systems become united, and the male becomes entirely dependent on the female's blood for nutrition. In exchange, the male provides the female with sperm.

7. CHILD-LABORING ANTS

Several species of tree ants in southeast Asia have evolved a bizarre method for building their nests. While one brigade of ants holds two leaves together, another brigade grabs hold of ant larvae and squeezes out of their young bodies a sticky thread that is used to bind the edges of the leaves.

8. TORTURING MURDEROUS WASPS
   Ichneumon wasps are the sort of beings that inspire horror films. At the
   worst, an ichneumon mother picks a victim, usually a caterpillar, and
   injects her eggs into the host's body. Often she also injects a poison that
   paralyzes the victim without killing it. When the eggs hatch, the wasp
   larvae begin eating the caterpillar. Because a dead caterpillar would be
   useless to developing wasps, they contrive to keep the unfortunate
   victim alive as long as possible by eating its fatty deposits and digestive
   organs first and saving the heart and central nervous system for last.

10 Animals That Have Eaten Humans

1. BEARS
   The North American bear, although smaller and less aggressive than
   the grizzly, can be deadly and has been responsible for many harmful
   attacks on humans. In 1963, when the Alaskan blueberry crop was
   poor, hungry black bears attacked at least four people, one of whom
   they killed.

2. CROCODILES
   Estuarine crocodiles are the most prolific man-eaters on earth, killing
   approximately 2,000 people a year. On the night of February 19, 1945,
   they were responsible for the most devastating animal attack on human
   beings in recorded history. British troops had trapped 1,000 Japanese
   infantrymen, many of whom were wounded, in a swampy area in the
   Bay of Bengal. The noise of gunfire and the smell of blood attracted
   hundreds of crocodiles, and by evening the British could hear terrible
   screams. The following morning, only 20 Japanese were found alive.

3. GIANT SQUID
   The giant squid is the most highly developed of the invertebrates. Its
   eyes are almost exact replicas of human eyes. It has 10 arms, and its
   body can reach up to 65 feet in length. Often confused with the octopus,
   which attacks humans only when threatened, the giant squid is a
   carnivorous predator. One notable incident occurred on March 25,
   1941, when the British ship *Britannia* sank in the Atlantic Ocean. As a
   dozen survivors clung to their lifeboat, a giant squid reached its arms
   around the body of a man and pulled him below. Male squid sometimes
   eat the female after mating.

4. KOMODO DRAGON
   The world's largest lizard, the Komodo dragon can reach 10 feet in
   length and weigh more than 300 pounds. They are the top predators on
   the handful of Indonesian islands where they live. Their prey normally

consists of deer, wild goats, and pigs, but they will eat anything they can catch, which includes the occasional human. Komodo dragons devour their prey completely, including the bones. All that was left of a French tourist killed in 1986 was his bloodstained shoes. A German tourist eaten in 1988 left only his mangled glasses.

5. LEOPARDS

Considered one of the most dangerous animals to hunt, the leopard is quick and stealthy and seldom observed. In the central provinces of India, leopards have been known to invade native huts to find their prey. One, known as the Panawar man-eater, is reputed to have killed 400 people. It was shot in 1910 by Jim Corbett, who also killed the Champawat man-eating tigress the following year.

6. LIONS

Like tigers, lions do not usually attack humans. Man-eating lions usually hunt in prides, or groups, although occasionally single lions and pairs have become man-eaters. In October 1943, a lone lion was shot in the Kasama district of what is now Zambia after it had killed 40 people.

7. PUMA (MOUNTAIN LION)

Pumas have been known to catch prey seven to eight times their own size: A 100-pound female has been seen killing an 800-pound bull elk. In recent years, as people have built subdivisions in the mountains of the western United States, attacks by pumas on humans have exploded. Since 1970, there have been more than forty attacks, at least seven of them fatal. In 1994, two female joggers in California were killed and partly consumed by female pumas.

8. PYTHON

Pythons are quite capable of killing people, and several incidents have been reported since they became a trendy pet in the 1990s. However, most reports of pythons actually eating humans have proven untrue. A picture circulating on the Internet of a boy allegedly recovered from a python's digestive tract is a hoax. However, there is at least one credible report. In 1992, a group of children playing in a mango plantation near Durban, South Africa, were attacked by a 20-foot rock python, which swallowed one of them. Craig Smith, the owner of a snake park, declared, "I've dealt with a few cases like this and I always dispel them as absolute rubbish. But in my opinion this one did happen."

9. SHARKS

Of the 200 to 250 species of shark, only 18 are known to be dangerous to humans. The most notable are the great white, the mako, the tiger, the white-tipped, the Ganges River, and the hammerhead. The best known of all individual "rogue" shark attacks occurred on July 12,

1916. Twelve-year-old Lester Stilwell was swimming in Matawan Creek, New Jersey, 15 to 20 miles inland, when he was attacked by a great white shark. Both he and his would-be rescuer were killed. In 10 days, four people were killed over a 60-mile stretch of the New Jersey coast. Two days after the last attack, an 8½-foot great white was netted just four miles from the mouth of the creek. According to the Florida Museum of Natural History, between 1670 and 2003, there were 833 confirmed unprovoked shark attacks in the United States, 52 of which were fatal.

10. TIGERS
A tigress known as the Champawat man-eater killed 438 people in the Himalayas in Nepal between 1903 and 1911. Tigers do not usually hunt humans, unless the animals are old or injured or have become accustomed to the taste of human flesh.

Note: AND TWO WHO WOULD NOT. While it is almost certain that wolves have preyed on human beings at some time in history, there are no confirmed reports of unprovoked attacks upon humans by North American wolves. Likewise, there are no confirmed reports of piranha-caused deaths. Observers in the river regions of northeastern South America do report that many natives have lost fingers, toes, or penny-sized chunks of flesh while bathing in piranha-infested waters. A school of piranhas can strip a wounded alligator of flesh in five minutes, but they are generally sluggish in their movements.

D.L. & C.F.

11 Large Animals Discovered by Western Science Since 1900

In 1812, the Father of Paleontology, Baron Georges Cuvier, rashly pronounced that "there is little hope of discovering a new species" of large animals and that naturalists should concentrate on extinct fauna. In 1819, the American tapir was discovered, and since then a long list of "new" animals have disproved Cuvier's dictum.

1. OKAPI
By saving a group of Congolese pygmies from a German showman who wanted to take them to the 1900 Paris Exhibition, Sir Harry Johnston immediately gained their trust. He then began hearing stories about the okapi, a mule-sized animal with zebra stripes. In 1901, Sir Harry sent a whole skin, two skulls, and a detailed description of the okapi to London, and it was found that the okapi had a close relationship to the giraffe. In 1919, the first live okapi were brought out of the Congo

River basin, and in 1941, the Stanleyville Zoo witnessed the first birth of an okapi in captivity. The okapis, striking in appearance, are now rare but popular attractions at the larger, more progressive zoological parks of the world.

2. **MOUNTAIN NYALA**
First discovered in the high mountains of southern Ethiopia in 1910, the mountain nyala remains a relatively unknown species. The male has gently twisting horns almost 4 feet long and can weigh up to 450 pounds. His coat is grayish brown, with white vertical stripes on the back. After it was described by Richard Lydekker, the eminent British naturalist, it was ruthlessly hunted by field biologists and trophy seekers through some of the most inhospitable terrain in existence. The mountain nyala lives in the Arussi and Bale mountains at heights above 9,000 feet, where the sun burns hot in the day and temperatures fall to freezing at night. Its existence is presently threatened by illegal hunting.

3. **PYGMY HIPPOPOTAMUS**
Karl Hagenbeck, a famous German animal dealer, established a zoological garden near Hamburg that was the prototype of the modern open-air zoo. In 1909, he sent German explorer Hans Schomburgk to Liberia to check on rumors about a "giant black pig." After two years of jungle pursuit, Schomburgk spotted the animal 30 feet in front of him. It was big, shiny, and black, but the animal clearly was related to the hippopotamus, not the pig. Unable to catch it, he went home to Hamburg empty-handed. In 1912, Hans Schomburgk returned to Liberia and, to the dismay of his critics, came back with five live pygmy hippos. A full-grown pygmy hippopotamus weighs only about 400 pounds, one tenth the weight of the average adult hippopotamus.

4. **KOMODO DRAGON**
These giant monitor lizards are named for the rugged volcanic island of Komodo, part of the Lesser Sunda Islands of Indonesia. Unknown to science until 1912, the Komodo dragon can be up to 12 feet long and weigh over 350 pounds. The discovery of the giant lizard was made by an airman who landed on Komodo island and brought back incredible stories of monstrous dragons eating goats and pigs, and even attacking horses. At first, no one believed him, but then the stories were confirmed by Major P. A. Ouwens, director of the Buitenzorg Botanical Gardens in Java, who offered skins and photographs as proof. Soon live specimens were caught and exhibited. The world's largest living lizard is now a popular zoo exhibit.

5. **CONGO PEACOCK**
Some animal discoveries are made in museums. In 1913, the New York Zoological Society sent an unsuccessful expedition to the Congo in an

attempt to bring back a live okapi. Instead, one of the team's members, Dr. James P. Chapin, brought back some native headdresses with curious long reddish brown feathers striped with black. None of the experts could identify them. On another of his frequent visits to the Congo, in 1934, Chapin noticed similar feathers on two stuffed birds at the Tervuren Museum. They were labeled "Young Indian Peacocks," but he knew that was not what they were. As it turned out, a mining company in the Congo had donated them to the museum and labeled them. Chapin soon discovered that they were a new species. The following year, he flew down to the Congo and brought back seven birds. He confirmed them as the first new bird genus discovered in 40 years. They were not peacocks at all, but pheasants. The Congo peacock is now commonly found in European and North American zoos.

6. **KOUPREY**
   The kouprey is a large wild ox that was found along the Mekong River in Cambodia and Laos and has been the source of much controversy. It first came to the attention of Western scientists in 1936, when it showed up as a hunting trophy in the home of a French veterinarian. The following year, the director of the Paris Vincennes Zoo, Professor Achille Urbain, went to northern Cambodia and reported that a new wild ox, unlike the gaur and the banteng, was to be seen in Cambodia. Other naturalists felt he was wrong and suggested that the kouprey might be just a hybrid of the gaur and the banteng. Finally, in 1961, a detailed anatomical study of the kouprey proved it to be so different from the area's other wild oxen that it might belong in a new genus, although many scientists continue to insist that it does not. Urbain's 1937 discovery was upheld. The Vietnam War was responsible for the death of many koupreys. A 1975 New York Zoological Society expedition was unable to capture any, although they did see a herd of 50. The kouprey has not been observed by scientists since 1988, although kouprey skulls occasionally show up at local markets. It is now considered critically endangered.

7. **COELACANTH**
   This 5-foot-long, 127-pound, large-scaled, steel-blue fish was brought up in a net off South Africa in December, 1938. The huge fish crawled around on deck for three hours before it died. Marjorie Courtenay-Latimer and ichthyologist James Smith of Rhodes University, South Africa, identified the coelacanth after it was already dead and had begun to decay. The problem was the coelacanth was supposed to have been extinct for 60 million years. Professor Smith then began years of searching for a second living coelacanth and was finally rewarded in December 1952, when a fishing trawler off the Comoro island of Anjouan, near Africa's east coast, brought up an excellent specimen. Dr. Smith was soon shocked to learn that the local inhabitants of the Comoros had been catching and eating the "living fossils" for generations.

8. BLACK-FACED LION TAMARIN MONKEY

Brazilian scientists found the black-faced lion tamarin monkey in June 1990 on the island of Superagui, along Brazil's heavily populated Atlantic coast, where less than 5 percent of the country's original Atlantic forest remains. The amazing discovery led biologist Dr. Russell Mittermeier, president of Conservation International, to say, "It's almost like finding a major new species in a suburb of Los Angeles." The monkey has a lionlike head and a gold coat. Its face, forearms, and tail are black. Prior to its discovery, there were only three known species of the lion tamarin monkey. It is estimated that fewer than two dozen of the new species exist. In 1992, two years after this species' discovery, another new species of monkey, the Maues marmoset, was found in Brazil—this time in a remote part of the Amazon rain forest. First spotted near the Maues River, a tributary of the Amazon, by Swiss biologist Marco Schwarz, the tiny monkey has a pink koala-like face and faint zebralike stripes.

9. SAO LA

According to British biologist John MacKinnon, who discovered the sao la in May 1992, the mammal "appears to be a cow that lives the life of a goat." Skulls, horns, and skins of the sao la were found by MacKinnon in the Vu Quang Nature Reserve, a pristine 150,000-acre rain forest in northwestern Vietnam near the Laotian border, during an expedition sponsored by the World Wildlife Fund. Known to the local Vietnamese as a "forest goat," the sao la—also called the Vu Quang ox—weighs about 220 pounds. Smaller than a cow but larger than a goat, the mammal has a dark brown, shiny coat with white markings on its face. It has daggerlike straight horns about 20 inches long and two-toed concave hooves that enable it to maneuver through slippery and rugged mountain areas. While the animal had occasionally been spotted, trapped, and eaten by local hunters, scientists did not get to see a live example of the new species until June 1994, when a four-month-old female calf was captured. Unfortunately, the calf, and another adolescent sao la that was subsequently captured, died in October 1994; both died from an infection of the digestive system. MacKinnon estimates that only a few hundred sao las still exist, and the Vietnamese government has outlawed hunting or trapping the animal. However, the enormous publicity surrounding the discovery of the sao la caused numerous scientists and reporters to travel to Vietnam in search of the animal. Some television crews reportedly offered a huge bounty to local farmers to entice them to capture a sao la; four more sao las were found in 1994, but all eventually died. Environmentalists fear that the sao la could become extinct—a victim of its popularity. In 1998, the sao la population was estimated at 120 to 150.

10. GIANT MUNTJAC DEER

Muntjacs, or barking deer, are a common food in Vietnam. But in April 1994, the World Wildlife Fund and the Vietnamese Ministry of Forestry announced that a new species of the mammal—the giant muntjac deer—was discovered in Vu Quang Nature Reserve, the same rain forest where the sao la had been found two years earlier. One and a half times larger than other muntjacs, the deer weighs about a hundred pounds and has eight-inch antlers that are bowed inward. It has a reddish coat and large canine teeth. While the initial identification of the giant muntjac was made from skulls and skins, a live animal was captured in Laos by a team of researchers working for the Wildlife Conservation Society. In August 1997, another montjac, the truong son, or dwarf muntjac, was located in the Vu Quang Nature Reserve. Weighing only thirty pounds, it has black fur and extremely short antlers. It is expected that other new species of animals will be found in the Vu Quang Nature Reserve, which miraculously survived bombing and herbicide spraying during the Vietnam War. British biologist John MacKinnon calls the area "a corner of the world unknown to modern science" and "a biological gold mine."

11. BONDEGEZOU

This large, black and white, whistling tree kangaroo was first described by zoologist Dr. Tim Flannery in 1995. Although previously unknown to science, the local Moni tribe in West Papua (Irian Jaya) on the island of New Guinea had long revered the bondegezou as their ancestor.

L.C. & C.O.M.

15 Extinct Animals That Are No Longer Extinct

1. CAHOW

This ocean-wandering bird nested exclusively on the islets of Bermuda. Also known as the Bermuda petrel, the last of the cahows was believed to have been killed during the famine of 1615, when British colonists built cook fires into which the unwary cahows flew by the thousands. On January 8, 1951, the cahow was rediscovered by Bermuda's conservation officer, David Wingate. Under his protection, the existing 18 birds were encouraged to breed and now number more than 150.

2. DIBBLER

A marsupial mouse, the dibbler was listed as extinct in 1884. In 1967 an Australian naturalist hoping to trap live honey possums caught instead a pair of dibblers. The female of the captured pair soon produced a litter of eight, and they were then bred in captivity.

3. **DWARF LEMUR**
The last known dwarf lemur was reported in 1875, and it was afterward regarded as extinct. Then, in 1966, the small tree-dwelling marsupial was once again seen, near the city of Mananara, Madagascar.

4. **MOUNTAIN PYGMY POSSUM**
This small marsupial was considered to have been extinct for 20,000 years until Dr. Kenneth Shortman caught one in the kitchen of his skiing lodge on Mount Hothan in southeast Australia in 1966. Three more of the tiny possums were discovered in 1970.

5–6. **TARPAN and AUROCHS**
A primeval forest horse of central Asia, long extinct, the tarpan was re-created by brothers Lutz and Heinz Heck, curators of the Berlin and Munich zoos, respectively. By selective crossbreeding of Polish primitive horses with Swedish Gotlands, Icelandic ponies, and Polish Konik mares, they created a strain of wild horse identical in appearance to what we know of the mouse-gray tarpan. The first colt was born May 22, 1933. By this same method, the auroch, a European wild ox that died out in Poland in 1627, has also been duplicated.

7. **WHITE-WINGED GUAN**
A flower-eating South American bird, the guan was thought extinct for a century until sighted in September of 1977. An American ornithologist and his Peruvian associate located four of the pheasant-sized birds in remote northwestern Peru.

8. **CEBU FLOWERPECKER**
Considered extinct since 1906, this bird native to the Philippines was rediscovered in 1992 living in a tiny (500-acre) patch of forest. The Philippines Wetland and Wildlife Conversation Foundation has initiated projects to preserve the remnants of Cebu's forests, but the Cebu flowerpecker is considered one of the most endangered bird species in the world.

9. **FOREST SPOTTED OWLET**
One of India's most mysterious bird species, the owlet had last been reported in 1884. Then in 1997, a team led by Dr. Pamela Rasmussen from the National Museum of Natural History in Washington, D.C., videotaped two forest spotted owlets in wooded country northeast of Bombay. This was the second time the species had been thought rediscovered, but the first instance was later discounted as a hoax. In 1914, Colonel Richard Meinertzhagen claimed to have recently shot a

specimen in the wild and produced a stuffed example as his proof. Experts later declared that it was the same stuffed owlet that had earlier disappeared from London's Natural History Museum.

10. **GILBERT'S POTOROO**

This small marsupial was last reported in 1869 and regarded as extinct. But in 1994, while trapping for quokkas in the Two Peoples Bay Nature Reserve on Australia's southern coast, Elizabeth Sinclair captured several potoroos. It is thought that there are about 30 remaining potoroos.

11. **JERDON'S COURSER**

Despite several searches, this ploverlike bird had last been seen in 1900. In January 1986, a living specimen was caught by a local hunter in the Pennar Valley of the Chuddash district of Andhra Pradesh, India. The rediscovery was hailed as one of the most significant ornithological events of the decade.

12. **MACGILLIVRAY'S PETREL**

This small black and brown bird native to Fiji had last been seen in 1855. In May 1984, British naturalist Dick Watling's year-long search for the bird came to a successful end as one of the petrels, attracted by lures, crashed into Watling's head.

13. **PYGMY BLUE TONGUE LIZARD**

Last seen in 1959, this lizard was thought to be extinct until it was rediscovered near Burra, Australia, in 1992. Amateur herpetologist Graham Armstrong discovered one of the lizards in the stomach of a squashed snake that he found on the highway.

14. **WOOLLY FLYING SQUIRREL**

Discovered in the Himalayas in 1888, the woolly flying squirrel was thought to be extinct, not having been seen since 1924. However, after a two-year search, Peter Zahler and Chantal Dietemann found a living female of this largest member of the squirrel family in 1997.

15. **IVORY-BILLED WOODPECKER**

Described by John James Audubon as the "great chieftain of the woodpecker tribe," the ivory-billed woodpecker was, with a wingspan of 30 inches, the largest American woodpecker. Once found throughout the Southeast and in Cuba, the ivory-bill began to decline as forest land disappeared. The last confirmed sighting of an ivory-bill in the United States was in Louisiana in 1944. Then, on February 11, 2004, amateur birdwatcher Gene Sparling was kayaking in the Cache River National Wildlife Refuge in Arkansas, when he spotted an unusually large red-crested woodpecker flying toward him. A second sighting a mere 16 days later appeared to confirm the discovery. Scientists kept the good news secret for a year in order to plan for the protection of the bird. Some ornithologists remained skeptical, pending production of an actual photograph of the ivory-bill.

D.L. & C.F.

5 of the World's Most Oft-Sighted Lake and Sea Monsters

1. NESSIE—The Loch Ness Monster
"Nessie," the world-famous serpentlike creature of Loch Ness, Scotland, was first photographed in 1933, after decades of rumors that something odd lived in the lake. Since then, "Nessie watching" has become an international sport, and there now exist a variety of photographs, an official Loch Ness Monster Fan Club, and numerous theories. One of the most popular theories is that the snakelike neck and lizardlike head point to this beast's being one of a race of as many as 30 remaining pleiosaurs, a type of dinosaur previously believed to be extinct. However, the Loch Ness could not provide sustenance for a pleiosaur, and other theories are hotly debated. Naysayers believe all the photos to be of no more than bark, driftwood, and seaweed. The latest theory, proposed by cryptozoologist Jon Downes, is that Nessie is actually a European eel, grown to an enormous size. Occasionally, these eels become sterile and lose their biological imperative to move from a lake to the Sargasso Sea and breed—thus they are called "eunuch eels." Downes proposes that there is something in the waters of Loch Ness and nearby lakes that causes this condition. These eels can cross long distances on land, which might account for the numerous out-of-water sightings. Nessie may, after all, be a "he."

2. CHAMP—The Monster of Lake Champlain
This creature apparently lives in a lake that knifes from New York to Canada. Only a few photographs and videos of "Champ" exist— however, a 1977 photo, taken by Sandra Mansi, is considered the most impressive photo of any sea or lake "monster." Ms. Mansi was watching children in the lake when she saw a disturbance in the water. She assumed it was a scuba diver. Then she "saw the head come up . . . then the neck, then the back." Her fiancé, upon seeing Champ, began to scream, "Get the kids out of the water!" Sandra had the wherewithal to take a picture, which she tucked away in the family album for four years. When the snapshot came to the attention of cryptozoologists, it was published in the *New York Times*. Since then, over 130 sightings have been reported. Books, seminars, and arguments followed, and many strongly believe Ms. Mansi took a photo of a piece of driftwood.

Arguing against this is her statement that "the mouth was open when it came up, and water came out." Champ is believed to be dark in color, about 30 feet long, and is most often seen on early summer mornings.

3. OGOPOGO

Canada is said to be home to numerous famous lake monsters. There are usually several sightings a year of the Ogopogo, said to live in the Okanagan Lake in British Columbia. An Ogopogo timeline, compiled by author Mary Moon, lists hundreds of sightings, beginning in the late 1700s. The creature is 30–50 feet long, (9–15 meters), with an undulating, serpentlike body; a long, thin neck; and a rather horselike head. It is reputed to swim extremely fast, appearing as several humps, or arches, on the water's surface. Occasionally it is reported to look like an upturned boat. It is believed to live mainly on fish and weeds, and Native American legends tell of the Ogopogo attacking humans, and some swimmers in the lake have disappeared without a trace.

4. THE KRAKEN

Sea monster lore includes a wide variety of giant squid, the most famous of which is the terrifying Kraken, the subject of Norse myth and a poem by Lord Alfred Tennyson—"There hath he lain for ages and will lie / Battening upon huge sea worms in his sleep." Modern scientists have speculated that the Kraken is actually a school of giant squid breaking the surface, or several schools, fanning out together.

5. CADBOROSAURUS—"Caddy and Amy"

Cadboro Bay in British Columbia supposedly sports a pair of aquatic reptiles nicknamed Caddy and Amy. Caddy's overall length is estimated at 40–70 feet (12–20 meters) There have been more than 50 years of sightings, beginning in the 1940s and continuing with at least half a dozen a year. In 1946, sightings were so common that a plan was developed to catch one of the creatures and put it on display in Vancouver's swimming pool; happily, Caddy and Amy's friends vetoed the idea. In 1994, Dr. Ed Bousfield published a book about Caddy—*Cadborosaurus: Survivor from the Deep*—having collected over 200 accounts.

12 Places with More Sheep Than Humans

Place	Sheep	Humans
1. Australia	94,500,000	20,090,000
2. Sudan	48,000,000	40,187,000
3. New Zealand	40,049,000	4,035,000
4. Turkmenistan	13,150,000	4,952,000

5.	Mongolia	12,000,000	2,791,000
6.	Uruguay	9,508,000	3,416,000
7.	Mauritania	8,850,000	3,087,000
8.	Ireland	4,850,100	4,016,000
9.	Namibia	2,900,000	2,031,000
10.	Falkland Islands	690,000	3,000
11.	Iceland	470,000	297,000
12.	Faeroe Islands	68,100	47,000

Note: The world sheep population: 1,058,800,770. Source: Food and Agriculture Organization of the United Nations, FAOSTAT, July 15, 2005.

4 Places with More Pigs Than Humans

Place		Pigs	Humans
1.	Denmark	13,233,235	5,432,000
2.	Samoa	201,000	187,000
3.	Wallis and Futuna Islands	25,000	16,000
4.	Tuvalu	13,500	11,600

Note: The world pig population is 947,801,201. Source: Food and Agriculture Organization of the United Nations, FAOSTAT, July 15, 2005.

10 Nations with the Most Camels

Nation		Camels (2004 estimate)
1.	Sudan	3,300,000
2.	Mauritania	1,300,000
3.	Kenya	830,000
4.	Pakistan	800,000
5.	Chad	735,000
6.	India	635,000
7.	Mali	472,000
8.	Ethiopia	468,390
9.	Niger	420,000
10.	Mongolia	272,000

Note: Egypt ranks 18th with 135,000. The world camel population is 19,039,934. Source: Food and Agriculture Organization of the United Nations, FAOSTAT, July 15, 2005.

Maximum Recorded Lifespan
of 58 Animals

1.	Tortoise	188 years
2.	Lake sturgeon	152 years
3.	Human	122 years 5 months
4.	Fin whale	116 years
5.	Blue whale	110 years
6.	Humpback whale	95 years
7.	Elephant	80 years
8.	Turtle (eastern box)	75 years
9.	Parrot (African gray)	73 years
10.	Chimpanzee	71 years
11.	Alligator	66 years
12.	Horse	62 years
13.	Orangutan	59 years
14.	Eagle (eastern imperical)	56 years
15.	Seal (Baikal)	56 years
16.	Hippopotamus	54 years 4 months
17.	Gorilla	54 years
18.	Camel	50 years
19.	Dolphin	50 years
20.	Grizzly bear	50 years
21.	Rhinoceros (Indian)	49 years
22.	Brown bear	47 years
23.	Condor (California)	45 years
24.	Goldfish	43 years
25.	Hyena (spotted)	41 years 1 month
26.	Boa constrictor	40 years 3 months
27.	Vulture	40 years
28.	Polar bear	38 years 2 months
29.	Giraffe	36 years 4 months
30.	Rhinoceros (Sumatran)	35 years
31.	Cat	34 years
32.	Frog	30 years 4 months
33.	Ant (queen)	30 years
34.	Kangaroo (red)	30 years
35.	Panda (giant)	30 years
36.	Dog	29 years 6 months
37.	Lion	29 years
38.	Porcupine (Old World)	27 years 4 months
39.	Tiger	26 years 4 months
40.	Wombat	26 years 1 month
41.	Aardvark	24 years

42. Sheep	24 years
43. Jaguar	22 years
44. Raccoon	20 years 7 months
45. Koala	20 years
46. Porcupine (normal)	20 years
47. Vampire bat	19 years 6 months
48. Pigeon	18 years 6 months
49. Rabbit	18 years
50. Duck-billed platypus	17 years
51. Guinea pig	14 years 10 months
52. Hedgehog	14 years
53. Shrew (nonhuman)	12 years
54. Hamster	10 years
55. Gopher (eastern pocket)	7 years 2 months
56. Anchovy	7 years
57. Partridge	5 years 2 months
58. Mole	5 years

Primary source: Longevity Records: Life Spans of Mammals, Birds, Amphibians, Reptiles, and Fish, James R. Carey and Debra S. Judge (Odense University Press, 2000), http://www.demogr.mpg.de/

The Cat Came Back:
15 Cats Who Traveled Long Distances to Return Home

1. SUGAR—1,500 miles
   Sugar, a two-year-old part-Persian, had a hip deformity that made her uncomfortable during car travel. Consequently, she was left behind with a neighbor when her family left Anderson, California, for Gage, Oklahoma. Two weeks later, Sugar disappeared. Fourteen months after that, she turned up in Gage on her old owner's doorstep—having traveled 100 miles a month to reach a place she had never been. The case was investigated in person by the famous parapsychologist J. B. Rhine, who observed the cat and interviewed witnesses.

2. MINOSCH—1,500 miles
   In 1981, Mehmet Tunc, a Turkish "guest worker" in Germany, went home with his cat and family for a vacation. At the Turkish border, Minosch disappeared. Sixty-one days later, back on the island of Sylt, in northern Germany, the family heard a faint scratching at the door. It was a bedraggled Minosch.

3. SILKY—1,472 miles
Shaun Philips, and his father, Ken, lost Silky at Gin Gin, about 200 miles north of Brisbane, Australia. That was in the summer of 1977. On March 28, 1978, Silky turned up at Philips's house in a Melbourne suburb. According to his owner, "He was as thin as a wisp and stank to high heaven."

4. HOWIE—1,200 miles
In 1978, this three-year-old Persian walked home from the Gold Coast in Queensland, Australia, to Adelaide—a trip that took a year. Said his owner, 15-year-old Kirsten Hicks, "Although its white coat was matted and filthy and its paws were sore and bleeding, Howie was actually purring."

5. RUSTY—950 miles
Rusty distinguished himself by setting an American all-time speed record for a cat return. In 1949, this ginger tom traveled from Boston, Massachusetts, to Chicago, Illinois, in 83 days. It is speculated that he hitched rides on cars, trucks, and trains.

6. NINJA—850 miles
Brent Todd and his family moved from Farmington, Utah, to Mill Creek, a suburb of Seattle, Washington, in April 1996, taking with them their eight-year-old tomcat, Ninja. After a week, Ninja jumped over the fence of the new yard and disappeared. More than a year later, on May 25, 1997, Ninja turned up on the porch of the Todds' former home in Farmington, waiting to be let inside and fed. He was thin and scraggly, but his distinctive caterwaul was recognized by the Todds' former neighbors, Marilyn and John Parker. Mrs. Parker offered to send Ninja back to the Todds, but they decided to let him stay.

7. ERNIE—600 miles
In September 1994, Ernie jumped from the truck of Chris and Jennifer Trevino while it was traveling 60 mph down the highway 600 miles west of their home. A week later, Ernie showed up at the Trevinos' home in Victoria, Texas. When Mrs. Trevino called the cat by name, he came forward and rubbed his face against her leg.

8. GRINGO—480 miles
The Servoz family lost their pet tom, Gringo, from their home in Lamarche-sur-Seine, France, in December 1982. The following July, they learned that the cat had moved to the French Riviera. Wishing to escape the cold winter, he had made the journey south in a week and appeared at their summer home, where neighbors took care of him.

9. MUDDY WATER WHITE—450 miles
On June 23 or 24, 1985, Muddy Water White jumped out of a van
driven by his owner, Barbara Paule, in Dayton, Ohio. Almost exactly
three years later, he returned to his home in Pennsylvania. "He came
and just flopped down like he was home," said Mrs. Paule. She fed him
for three days before realizing who he was. His identification was later
confirmed by the local vet.

10. MURKA—400 miles
In 1987, Murka, a stray tortoiseshell, was adopted by Vladimir Donsov
in Moscow. Murka killed his canary; a year later, she unlocked the bird
cage and killed another one. She was banished to live with Mr. Donsov's
mother in Voronezh but disappeared after two years. On October 19,
1989, Mr. Donsov found her in his Moscow apartment building, hungry,
dirty, pregnant, and missing the tip of her tail. She ate a large meal and
slept for three days.

11. SKITTLES—353 miles
Skittles, a two-year-old tomcat, disappeared on September 3, 2001,
from the Dells area of Wisconsin, where Charmin Sampson and her son
Jason were living in a trailer while working at a water park during the
summer. Twenty weeks later, on January 14, 2002, Skittles appeared at
the Sampsons' home in Hibbing, Minnesota. "I knew it was Skittles,"
said Jason. "The cat is orange, with white paws and he's got a look to
him—a unique look."

12. CHICHI—300 miles
The Reverend J. C. Cox of Blanchard, Louisiana, gave his 17-year-old
cat to his granddaughter, who lived in a suburb of New Orleans. Chichi
missed Reverend Cox and, to everyone's astonishment, crossed the
Mississippi and Red rivers in three weeks and arrived home in time for
Christmas.

13. POOH—200 miles
The Reverend and Mrs. James Daves moved from Long Island to
Georgia in 1973. Because their daughter was allergic to animal fur, they
gave her two-year-old white tom, Pooh, to a friend, but he soon ran
away. In May, the family moved to South Carolina. On April 18, 1975,
Pooh showed up at the home he had never been to before.

14. RANULPH—300 miles
Ranulph, an eight-year-old black tomcat, was named after the explorer
Ranulph Fiennes. He justified his name after his owner Gill Bray gave
him to a friend in Consett in County Durham, Scotland. He disappeared but showed up a year and a half later on the doorstep of Bray's

home in Archiestown on Speyside. He arrived just before his former owner was going to move to a new house closer to her work in Glasgow. He had lost about half his weight.

15. BORIS—8 miles
Boris trekked back twice in 1990 to his old home in Berkshire, England—a short trip but one that involved crossing two superhighways, the M4 and the A34.

The Day of Extinction for 8 Birds

1. GREAT AUK, JUNE 3, 1844
The great auk was a large, flightless bird that lived in the Arctic regions of the North Atlantic. It was the first bird known as a "penguin," but, when explorers from the Northern Hemisphere came across the similar but unrelated species in the Antarctic, they transferred the name to the new bird. The last recorded breeding place of the great auk was Eldey Island, off the coast of Iceland. On June 3, 1844, three men, part of an expedition funded by an Icelandic bird collector called Carl Siemsen, landed on the island. They found and killed two auks among other birds gathered on the island's cliffs and took away an egg, which was later sold to an apothecary in Reykjavik. Since then there has been no confirmed sighting of a great auk on Eldey Island or anywhere else.

2. LABRADOR DUCK, DECEMBER 12, 1872
A small black and white duck indigenous to North America, the Labrador was considered to be a strong and hardy species, and its decline is still mysterious. The duck bred on the east coast of Canada but flew as far south as Philadelphia in the summer. Hunting no doubt contributed to its demise. The last reported Labrador duck was shot down over Long Island on December 12, 1872.

3. GUADALUPE ISLAND CARACARA, DECEMBER 1, 1900
A large brown hawk with a black head and gray striped wings, the caracara was last seen alive and collected by R. H. Beck December 1, 1900. One of the few cases in which a bird was deliberately exterminated, the caracara was poisoned and shot by goatherds, who thought it was killing the kids in their herds.

4. PASSENGER PIGEON, SEPTEMBER 1, 1914
These brownish gray pigeons were once so numerous that a passing flock could darken the sky for days. As recently as 1810, an estimated 2,230,272,000 pigeons were sighted in one flock. But massive hunting by

settlers and a century of forest destruction eliminated the passenger and its native forest habitat. In 1869, 7,500,000 pigeons were captured in a single nesting raid. In 1909, a $1,500 reward was offered for a live nesting pair, but none could be found. Martha, the last of the passenger pigeons, died of old age September 1, 1914, in the Cincinnati Zoo.

5. CAROLINA PARAKEET, FEBRUARY 21, 1918

The striking green and yellow Carolina parakeet was once common in the forests of the eastern and southern United States, but because of the widespread crop destruction it caused, farmers hunted the bird to extinction. The last Carolina parakeet, an old male named Incas, died in the Cincinnati Zoo February 21, 1918. The zoo's general manager believed it died of grief over the loss of Lady Jane, its mate of 30 years, the previous summer.

6. HEATH HEN, MARCH 11, 1932

An East Coast U.S. relative of the prairie chicken, the heath hen was once so common around Boston that servants sometimes stipulated before accepting employment that heath hen not be served to them more than a few times a week. But the bird was hunted to extinction, and the last heath hen, alone since December 1928, passed away on Martha's Vineyard on March 11 at age eight, after the harsh winter of 1932.

7. EULER'S FLYCATCHER, SEPTEMBER 26, 1955

Known only from two specimens and one sighting, Euler's flycatcher was an 8½-inch olive and dusky yellow bird. It was believed by James Bond (the authority on Caribbean birds, not Ian Fleming's 007) to have perished on Jamaica during Hurricane Janet September 26, 1955.

8. DUSKY SEASIDE SPARROW, JUNE 18, 1987

This sparrow was once common in the marshes of Merritt Island, Florida, and along the nearby St. John's River. In the 1960s, Merritt Island was flooded to deal with the mosquito problem at the Kennedy Space Center, while the marshes along the St. John's were drained for highway construction. Pesticides and pollution also contributed to the bird's demise. In 1977, the last five dusky seaside sparrows were captured. Unfortunately, they were all male, with no female to perpetuate the species. The five were relocated to Disney World's Discovery Island to live out their last days. The last one, an aged male blind in one eye, named Orange Band, died 10 years later, on June 18, 1987.

D.L.

5 Tips on How to Survive
an Encounter with a Bear

The following situations may occur anywhere in bear country. This recommended behavior is generally advised, but is no guarantee of averting a mishap. Above all, remain calm and give the bear the opportunity to learn that your intentions are not hostile.

1. **NEVER RUN**
   Do not run. Bears can run faster than 30 miles per hour (50 kilometers per hour)—faster than Olympic sprinters. Running can elicit a chase response from otherwise nonaggressive bears.

2. **AN UNAWARE BEAR**
   If the bear is unaware of you, detour quickly and quietly away from it. Give the bear plenty of room, allowing it to continue its own activities undisturbed.

3. **AN AWARE BEAR**
   If the bear is aware of you but has not acted aggressively, back away slowly, talking in a calm, firm voice while slowly waving your arms. Bears that stand up on their hind legs are usually just trying to identify you and are not threatening.

4. **AN APPROACHING BEAR**
   Do not run; do not drop your pack. A pack can help protect your body in case of an attack. To drop a pack may encourage the bear to approach people for food. Bears occasionally make "bluff charges," sometimes coming to within 10 feet of a person before stopping or veering off. Stand still until the bear stops and has moved away, then slowly back off. Climbing trees will not protect you from black bears, and may not provide protection from grizzlies.

5. **IF A BEAR TOUCHES YOU**
   If a grizzly bear does actually make contact with you, curl up in a ball, protecting your stomach and neck, and play dead. If the attack is prolonged, however, change tactics and fight back vigorously. If it is a black bear, do not play dead; fight back.

Source: Denali National Park and Preserve, Denali Park, Alaska.

10 Funguses That Changed History

1. THE YELLOW PLAGUE (*Aspergillus flavus*)
   A. flavus is an innocent-looking but deadly yellowish mold also called
   aflatoxin. Undoubtedly the cause of countless deaths throughout
   history, it was not suspected of being poisonous until 1960. That year, a
   mysterious disease killed 100,000 young turkeys in England, and
   medical researchers traced the "turkey-X disease" to *A. flavus* growing
   on the birds' peanut meal feed. Hardy, widespread, and lethal, aflatoxin
   is a powerful liver cancer agent. People have long cultivated it—in
   small amounts—as part of the manufacturing process of soy sauce and
   sake, but it can get of control easily. It thrives in warm, damp conditions, and as it breeds—sometimes to lethal proportions within 24
   hours—the mold produces its own heat, which spurs even faster
   growth. Some of its favorite dishes are stored peanuts, rice, corn, wheat,
   potatoes, peas, cocoa, cured hams, and sausage.

2. THE MOLD THAT TOPPLED AN INDUSTRY (*Aspergillus niger*)
   This common black mold, most often found on rotting vegetation,
   played a key role in the collapse of a major industry. Until the early
   1920s, Italy produced about 90 percent of the world's citric acid, using
   low-grade lemons. Exported mainly to the United States as calcium
   citrate, this citric acid was a costly ingredient—about a dollar a
   pound—used in food, pharmaceutical, and industrial processing. When
   American chemists discovered that *A. niger*, the most ordinary of
   molds, secreted citric acid as it grew in a culture medium, they seized
   the opportunity to perfect citric acid production using the easily grown
   mold. Charles Pfizer & Co., of Brooklyn, New York, became known as
   the "world's largest lemon grove"—without a lemon in sight. Hard-
   worked acres of *A. niger* were soon squirting out such quantities of
   citric acid that by 1923 the price was down to 25¢ a pound, and the
   Italians were out of business.

3. ST. ANTHONY'S FIRE (*Claviceps purpurea*)
   A purplish black, spur-shaped mass, *C. purpurea* is a formidable and
   even frightening fungus that has long plagued humankind. But it has
   valuable medical uses if the greatest care is taken to use tiny amounts.
   The fungus is a powerful muscle contractor and can control bleeding,
   speed up childbirth, and even induce abortion. It is also the source of
   the hallucinogenic LSD-25. In doses larger than microscopic, *C.
   purpurea*—commonly called ergot—produces ergotamine poisoning, a
   grisly condition known in the Middle Ages as St. Anthony's fire. There
   is still no cure for this hideous, often fatal disease caused by eating
   fungus-infected rye. The victim suffers convulsions and performs a
   frenzied "dance." This is often accompanied by a burning sensation in

the limbs, which turn gangrenously black and fall off. Some victims of medieval ergotism went insane, and many died. In 994 AD, more than 40,000 people in two French provinces died of ergotism, and in 1722 the powerful fungus forced Peter the Great of Russia to abandon his plan to conquer Turkey when, on the eve of the Battle of Astrakhan, his entire cavalry and 20,000 others were stricken with ergotism. The last recorded outbreak of ergot poisoning was in the French village of Pont-Saint-Esprit in 1951.

4. **THE NOBEL MOLD** (*Neurospora crassa*)
The humble bread mold *N. crassa* provided the means for scientists to explore the most exciting biological discovery of the twentieth century: DNA. As anyone with an old loaf of bread in the bread box knows, *N. crassa* needs only a simple growing medium, and it has a short life cycle. With such cooperative qualities, this reddish mold enabled George Beadle and Edward Tatum to win the Nobel Prize in Medicine/Physiology in 1958 for discovering the role that genes play in passing on hereditary traits from one generation to the next. By x-raying *N. crassa*, the researchers produced mutations of the genes, or components of DNA, and then found which genes corresponded with which traits.

5. **THE BLUISH GREEN LIFESAVER** (*Penicillium notatumchrysogenum*)
A few dots of a rather pretty bluish green mold were Dr. Alexander Fleming's first clue to finding one of the most valuable lifesaving drugs ever developed. In 1928, he noticed that his petri dish of staphylococcus bacteria had become contaminated with symmetrically growing, circular colonies of *P. notatum*. Around each speck, all the bacteria were dead. Fleming found that the mold also killed pneumonia, gonorrhea, and diphtheria germs—without harming human cells. The unassuming bluish green mold was beginning to look more interesting, but Fleming could not isolate the active element. In 1939, Howard Florey and Ernst Chain identified penicillin, a secretion of the growing mold, as the bacteria killer. The first important antibiotic, penicillin revolutionized treatment of many diseases. Fleming, Florey, and Chain won the Nobel Prize in Physiology or Medicine in 1945 for their pioneering work with the common fruit mold that yielded the first "miracle drug."

6. **THE GOURMET'S DELIGHT** (*Penicillium roquefortii*)
According to an old legend, a French shepherd forgot his lunch in a cave near the town of Roquefort, and when he found it weeks later, the cheese had become blue-veined and was richly flavored. No one knew why this happened until American mycologists discovered the common blue mold *P. roquefortii* in 1918. All blue cheeses—English stilton, Italian gorgonzola, Norwegian gammelost, Greek kopanisti, and Swiss paglia—derive their tangy flavor from the energetic blue mold, which grows rapidly in the cheese, partially digesting it and eventually turning the entire cheese

into mold. Of course, it's more appetizing to say that *P. roquefortii* ripens the cheese instead of rotting it, but it's the same process.

7. THE FAMINE MAKER (*Phytophthona infestans*)

The political history of the world changed as a result of the unsavory activity of *P. infestans*, a microscopically small fungus that reduced Ireland to desperate famine in 1845. Hot, rainy July weather provided perfect conditions for the white fungus to flourish on the green potato plants—most of Ireland's food crop—and the bushes withered to brown, moldy, stinking clumps within days. The entire crop was devastated, causing half a million people to starve to death, while nearly two million emigrated, mostly to the United States. *P. infestans* dusted a powdery white death over Ireland for six years. The fungus spread rapidly, and just one bad potato could infect and ruin a barrel of sound ones. British prime minister Robert Peel tried to get Parliament to repeal tariffs on imported grain, and while the MPs debated, Ireland starved. Relief came so slowly and inadequately that Peel's government toppled the next year, in 1846.

8. THE TEMPERANCE FIGHTER (*Plasmopara viticola*)

A soft, downy mildew infecting American-grown grapes was responsible for nearly ruining the French wine industry. In 1872, the French unwittingly imported *P. viticola* on grafting stock of wine grapes grown in the United States. Within 10 years, the mild-mannered mildew had quietly decimated much of France's finest old vineyards. But in 1882, botanist Pierre-Marie-Alexis Millardet discovered a miraculous cure for the ravages of *P. viticola*. He noticed that Médoc farmers painted their grape leaves with an ugly paste of copper sulfate, lime, and water—to prevent theft. Called the Bordeaux mixture, this paste was the first modern fungicide. The vineyards of France recovered, and the entire world sighed with relief.

9. MERCHANT OF DEATH (*Saccharomyces cerevisiae*)

Ordinary brewer's yeast, *S. cerevisiae*, used to leaven bread and make ale, was once employed as a wartime agent of death. During WWI, the Germans ran short of both nitroglycerin and the fat used in its manufacture. Then they discovered that the usually friendly fungus *S. cerevisiae* could be used to produce glycerin, a necessary ingredient in explosives. Fermenting the fungus together with sucrose, nitrates, phosphates, and sodium sulfite, the Germans produced more than 1,000 tons of glycerin per month. According to some military sources, this enabled them to keep their war effort going for an additional year.

10. THE TB KILLER (*Streptomyces griseus*)

A lowly mold found in dirt and manure piles, *S. griseus* nevertheless had its moment of glory in 1943, when Dr. Selman Waksman discovered that it yields the antibiotic streptomycin, which can cure tuberculosis.

Waksman went to the United States in 1910 as a Russian refugee, and by 1918 he had earned his doctorate in soil microbiology. He had worked with S. *griseus* before, but not until a crash program to develop antibiotics (a word coined by Dr. Waksman himself) was launched did he perceive the humble mold's possibilities for greatness. Streptomycin was first used successfully on human beings in 1945, and in 1952 Dr. Waksman was awarded the Nobel Prize in Physiology/Medicine.

K.P.

24 Molecules and Amoebas with Funny Names

1. **APATITE**
   This is not a hungry amoeba. It is widely used as a phosporus fertilizer.

2. **BIPLANENE (or LEPIDOPTERENE)**
   These molecules look like butterflies. When the two wings are directly on top of each other, they resemble a World War 1 biplane, thus their name.

3. **CACADYL**
   This molecule's name is derived from the Greek *kakodes,* which means "stinking." It has a very strong manure odor, with a delicate hint of garlic. It is most famous for being one of the compounds Robert Bunsen (of Bunsen burner fame) worked on.

4. **SNOUTENE**
   This amoeba looks exactly like an animal's nose or snout. There are no reports of it being smelly.

5. **FURFUYL FURFURATE**
   Very smelly. A cousin of this molecule is used in building space shuttles.

6. **BETWEENANEENES (also SCREWENES)**
   These are shaped liked rugs joined together. The original name, screwenes, became unpopular.

7. **DRACULIN**
   This is the anticoagulant formula found in vampire bat saliva. It is made from 411 amino acids.

8. **NONANONE (or NONANON)**
   In most countries, this molecule is spelled without an *e* at the end. Nonanon is the only palindromic molecule, both in spelling and in structure.

9. FUKUGETIN (or FUCKUGISIDE)

This is from the bark of the Gacenia species of tree, otherwise known as Fukugiside.

10. SPAMOL

Well, you can't eat spamol out of a can. It has antispasmodic, therapeutic properties.

11. WINDOWPANE

These molecules look like a set of windows and go colloquially by the name "broken window."

12. GODNOSE

This is a trick entry, because it didn't turn out to be the official name. The scientist who discovered it mistakenly thought it was a sugar but did not properly understand its structure. A journal editor refused to accept ignose (the original name)—because he did not consider it to be sensible. The founder suggested Godnose. The editor, lacking any sense of irony, thought this was a much more "proper" name. Eventually, it was named ascorbic acid, then vitamin C.

13. DIABOLIC ACID

This class of compounds was named after the Greek *diabollo*, which means to mislead, because these were difficult molecules to work with. One of the inventors thought the acid had "horns like the devil."

14. DOMPERIDONE

No, it's not a champagne. It's an antiemetic drug.

15. URANATE

A family of molecules that has been described as sounding like "the entry fee for a toilet after 8:00 p.m."

16. ANTIPAIN

Despite its promising name, this toxic compound causes severe pain and itching when it touches skin.

17. ANOL

Anol is used in the flavor industry. Asks one researcher, "Are compounds that bind strongly to this molecule anally retentive?"

18. ANGELIC ACID

Another ill-named molecule, made from a plant, that is a beetle defense substance.

19. **CLITORIN**

Little is known of this intriguingly named molecule, which is a flavenol glycoside. It is touch-sensitive.

20. **CONSTIPATIC ACID**

It is a mystery how this molecule got its name. It is a constituent of certain Australian lichens.

21. **PENGUINONE**

Its 2-D structure looks like a penguin, but this charming effect is lost in the 3-D model.

22. **PAGADENE**

This compound resembles two Japanese pagodas back to back.

23. **DEAD**

Also known as "dead cat," this an acronym for diethyl azodiacarboxilate. This orange light-sensitive molecule is toxic, probably carcinogenic, and an eye, skin, and respiratory irritant.

24. **MIRASORVONE**

A recently discovered molecule that forms part of the chemical defensive system of a type of beetle. It was named after the actress Mira Sorvino because of her appearance in the film *Mimic*, in which she plays an entomologist who inadvertently inflicts a mutant insect on the world.

Source: http://www.bristol.ac.uk/Depts/Chemistry/MOTM/silly/sillymols.htm

CHAPTER SEVEN

America

19 POSSIBLE EXPLORERS OF AMERICA
BEFORE COLUMBUS

9 CLOSE ENCOUNTERS WITH RICHARD NIXON

15 PRESIDENTS WHO WON WITH LESS
THAN 50% OF THE VOTE

12 PRESIDENTS RANKED BY POPULARITY

36 GREAT SLIPS OF THE TONGUE
IN AMERICAN POLITICS

13 UNEXPECTED EXPENSES IN
THE UNITED STATES BUDGET

THE REAL PEOPLE BEHIND
6 POPULAR AMERICAN IMAGES

15 AMERICAN THOROUGHFARES WITH UNUSUAL
NAMES

4 NOTEWORTHY INTERSECTIONS

14 ARAB AMERICANS

10 LEADING SOURCES OF OIL FOR THE UNITED STATES

OOPS: 6 CASES OF FOREIGNERS MISTAKENLY
KILLED BY THE AMERICAN MILITARY

RICHARD NIXON WITH FRIENDS BEBE REBOZO
AND ROBERT ABPLANALP
© UPI

19 Possible Explorers of America before Columbus

1–2. HSI and HO (c. 2640 BC), Chinese
Based on evidence derived from the geography text *Shan Hai Ching T'sang-chu* and the chronicle *Shan Hai Jing*, it is argued that the Chinese imperial astronomers Hsi and Ho were the first explorers of America, in the twenty-seventh century BC. Ordered by the Emperor Huang Ti to make astronomical observations in the land of Fu Sang—the territories to the east of China—the two men sailed north to the Bering Strait and then south along the North American coastline. They settled for a while with the "Yao people," ancestors of the Pueblo Indians living near the Grand Canyon, but eventually journeyed on to Mexico and Guatemala. Upon returning to China, they reported their astronomical studies and geographic discoveries to the emperor. A short time later, they were both executed for failing to predict a solar eclipse accurately.

3–6. VOTAN, WIXEPECOCHA, SUME, AND BOCHIA (c. 800–400 BC), Indian
According to Hindu legends and to Central American tribal legends, seafaring Hindu missionaries reached the Americas more than 2,000 years before Columbus. Sailing from India to Southeast Asia, they voyaged to the Melanesian and Polynesian islands and then across the Pacific to South and Central America. Votan was a trader from India who lived among the Mayans as a historian and chieftain, while his contemporary, Wixepecocha, was a Hindu priest who settled with the Zapotecs of Mexico. Two more Hindu emigrants were Sume, who reached Brazil and introduced agriculture to the Cabole Indians, and Bochia, who lived with the Muycas Indians and became the codifier of their laws.

7. HUI SHUN (458 AD), Chinese
Using official Chinese imperial documents and maps from the Liang dynasty, scholars have reconstructed the travels of the Chinese explorer and Buddhist priest Hui Shun and proposed that he arrived in North America in the fifth century. Sailing from China to Alaska in 458, Hui—accompanied by four Afghan disciples—continued his journey on foot down the North American Pacific coast. Reaching Mexico, he taught and preached Buddhism to the Indians of central Mexico and to the Mayans of the Yuçatán. Allegedly, he named Guatemala in honor of Gautama Buddha. After more than 40 years in America, he returned to China, where he reported his adventures to Lord Yu Kie and Emperor Wu in 502.

8. ST. BRENDAN (c. 550), Irish
Two medieval manuscripts, *The Voyage of Saint Brendan the Abbot* and the *Book of Lismore*, tell of an Irish priest who, with 17 other

monks, sailed west from Ireland and reached the "Land Promised to the Saints." Employing a curragh—a leather-hulled boat still in use in Ireland—Brendan and his companions made a sea pilgrimage that lasted seven years during the sixth century AD. They traveled to Iceland, Greenland, and Newfoundland, and one authority asserts that Brendan reached the Caribbean island of Grand Cayman, which he called the Island of Strong Men. He returned safely to his Irish monastery and reported on his travels but died soon after. In 1977, Timothy Severin, sailing a modern curragh, retraced Brendan's voyage to America.

9. BJARNI HERJULFSSON (986), Norse
According to two medieval Icelandic narratives, the *Flateyjarbok* and *Hauk's Book*, a young Norse merchant named Bjarni Herjulfsson sailed from Iceland toward Greenland to visit his father, who lived there, but was blown off course by a gale. When the storm ended, Bjarni sighted a hilly, forested land, which is now thought to have been Cape Cod. Wanting to reach the Norse settlements on Greenland before winter, he did not drop anchor and send men ashore to explore. Instead, he sailed north to Greenland. He was criticized by the Greenlanders for not investigating the new land, and his discoveries stimulated further exploration of North America.

10. LEIF ERICSON (1003), Norse
In 1003, Leif bought Bjarni Herjulfsson's ship and, with a 35-man crew, sailed for North America. While most scholars agree that Ericson did land in North America, there is disagreement about where he landed. The only Viking site ever found in the New World is L'Anse aux Meadows in Newfoundland, which was discovered in 1960 and excavated for the next eight years by Helge Ingstad, a Norwegian explorer. According to Ingstad, Ericson's first landing was at Baffin Island, which he named Helluland; his second was at Labrador, which he called Markland; and finally he reached Newfoundland, which he christened Vinland. To Leif and his companions, Vinland was an abundant country, rich in game, wild wheat, and timber, and its climate was mild compared to Iceland and Greenland. The explorers spent the winter in Vinland, where they constructed a village of "big houses." In 1004, Leif returned to Greenland, where he was given the honorary name of Leif the Lucky.

11. THORVALD ERICSON (1004), Norse
The Icelandic sagas record that, soon after Leif Ericson returned to Greenland, he gave his ship to his brother Thorvald. In the autumn of 1004, Thorvald sailed to Leif's Vinland settlement and wintered there. The next summer, while exploring the St. Lawrence region, Thorvald and his crew attacked a band of Indians, killing eight of them. In

retaliation, the Indians ambushed the Norsemen, and Thorvald was killed in the ensuing battle. In 1007, the expedition's survivors returned to Greenland and took with them Thorvald's body, which was delivered to Leif for burial.

12. **THORFINN KARLSEFNI (1010), Norse**
The Greenlanders' Saga and *Karlsefni's Saga* are the two medieval sources that give accounts of the Icelander Thorfinn Karlsefni's attempt to establish the first permanent European settlement in America. In 1010, with 60 men and 5 women, Thorfinn—who was Leif Ericson's brother-in-law—sailed to Leif's Vinland camp, which he planned to colonize. In Vinland, Thorfinn's wife gave birth to a son—the first European child born in America—who was named Snorri. Thorfinn explored extensively, traveling as far south as Long Island and the Hudson River and, possibly, Chesapeake Bay. Four years later, he and the Norse settlers returned to Greenland because of Indian attacks and because of violent internal discord caused by the shortage of women.

13. **PRINCE MADOG AB OWAIN GWYNEDD (1170, 1190), Welsh**
The Atlantic voyages of this Welsh prince were recorded by the medieval historian Gymoric ap Grono Guntyn Owen and by the seventeenth-century chroniclers Thomas Herbert and Richard Hakluyt. Because of political conflicts with his brothers, Prince Madog sailed from Abergwili, Wales, in 1170. He voyaged westward across the Atlantic and landed somewhere in the Americas, where he built and fortified a settlement. After several years, he returned to Wales, leaving 120 men behind in the new colony. In 1190, he again crossed the Atlantic to discover that most of his men had been annihilated, presumably by Indians. Madog himself died in the New World a short time later. The actual site of his settlement is disputed. Possible locations are the Florida peninsula; Mobile, Alabama; and the West Indies.

14. **KING ABUBAKARI II (1311), Malian**
According to medieval Arab historical and geographical documents and Malian oral epics, King Abubakari II of Mali, a Black Muslim, sailed from West Africa to northeastern South America. After learning from Arab scholars that there was land on the west side of the Atlantic, King Abubakari became obsessed with the idea of extending his kingdom into these as yet unclaimed lands. He mobilized the resources of his empire to hire Arab shipbuilders from Lake Chad to build a fleet. (Their descendants were employed by Thor Heyerdahl to construct his reed boat, *Ra I*.) In 1311, the king and his crew sailed down the Senegal River and across the Atlantic. It is believed that while he sighted the north coast of South America, he made his first landfall in Panama. Then King Abubakari and his entourage supposedly traveled south from Panama and settled in the Inca Empire.

15. **PAUL KNUTSON (1356), Norwegian**
In a letter dated 1354, King Magnus of Norway and Sweden ordered the Norwegian sea captain Paul Knutson to journey to Greenland to restore the Christian faith to the Norsemen still living there. Knutson sailed to Greenland in 1355 and, the next year, to Vinland, where he established a camp on the North American coast. His camp was probably at Newport, Rhode Island, where a tower believed to have been constructed by his party still stands. One group of Knutson's men, who explored Hudson Bay and the territory to the south of it, is thought to be responsible for the Kensington Stone, a rock with possible Norse runes carved on its surface, which was found in central Minnesota. Most of the members of the expedition, including Knutson, died in America. A few survivors returned to Norway in 1364.

16. **HENRY ST. CLAIR (1398), Scottish**
The voyage of St. Clair, the Prince of Orkney and Earl of Rosslyn, is described in the fifteenth-century *Zeno Narrative*, allegedly written by the grandnephew of St. Clair's Venetian navigator, Antonio Zeno. During a trip to Iceland and Greenland in 1393, St. Clair reportedly learned of a land to the west. Five years later, he led an expedition consisting of 13 ships and 200–300 men that landed in Nova Scotia. He left behind a group of settlers, who may have traveled as far south as New England. St. Clair died in a battle at Kirkwall in August 1400, just after his return from America. His sudden death severed all links with the colony in the New World.

17–18. **JOHANNES SCOLP and JOÃO VAZ CORTE REAL (1476), Danish and Portuguese**
In 1475, King Alfonso of Portugal and King Christian I of Denmark arranged a joint expedition to North America to find a sea route to China. Danish sea captain Johannes Scolp and a Portuguese nobleman named João Vaz Corte Real were appointed as commanders of the combined fleet. They sailed from Denmark across the North Atlantic to the Labrador coast and explored Hudson Bay, the Gulf of St. Lawrence, and the St. Lawrence River. Failing to find a sea passage to Asia, they returned to Denmark, where their discoveries were largely ignored.

19. **ALONSO SANCHEZ DE HUELVA (1481), Spanish**
De Huelva reportedly landed in the West Indies at Santo Domingo after being blown off course by a tempest. He returned to Madeira with a handful of survivors. According to some, Columbus learned about the New World from de Huelva. Martin Alonzo Pinzon, Columbus's second in command, had earlier been de Huelva's first mate.

R.J.F.

9 Close Encounters with Richard Nixon

1. **CAB CALLOWAY**
   On April 29, 1969, President Nixon held a black-tie dinner in honor of pianist-composer Duke Ellington's seventieth birthday. Among the show business personalities invited to attend the affair was big band leader and jazz great Cab Calloway. Calloway passed down the reception line, shaking hands with such dignitaries as the Shah of Iran, and finally reached Nixon, who gave him a big smile as he approached. Nixon grasped Calloway's hand in both of his and said, "Ah, Mr. Ellington, it's so good you're here. Happy, happy birthday. Pat and I just love your music." Not wanting to embarrass the president of the United States, Calloway smiled, thanked him, and moved on.

2. **A SMALL GIRL**
   President Nixon was shaking hands and talking with members of a crowd at an airport when a little girl shouted to him, "How is Smokey the Bear?" referring to the famous fire-fighting symbol who was then residing at the Washington Zoo. Nixon smiled at the girl and turned away, but she kept waving and asking her question. Unable to make out her words, Nixon sought help from his aide-de-camp, Steve Bull. Bull whispered, "Smokey the Bear, Washington National Zoo." Nixon walked over to the little girl, shook her hand, and said, "How do you do, Miss Bear?"

3. **ANTIWAR PROTESTORS**
   Following the invasion of Cambodia and the death of four students at Kent State University in 1970, thousands of people poured into Washington, D.C., in preparation for a major antiwar demonstration. Unable to sleep the morning of May 9, Nixon called his valet, Manolo Sanchez, and asked him if he had ever seen the Lincoln Memorial after dark. Sanchez had not, so Nixon said, "Let's go." Accompanied by several Secret Service agents, they toured the memorial and emerged at about 5:00 a.m. On the steps outside, they encountered a small group of students from New York's Alfred State College, who had been talking politics with a park policeman. Nixon chatted amiably with the young people, and soon a crowd of 40 or 50 sleepy protestors had gathered. When the protestors began asking political questions, the president became vague and somewhat evasive, preferring to launch into a long monologue about his world travels instead. When one student said he was from California, Nixon talked about surfing; when three others said they were from Syracuse, he remarked, "Oh, the Orangemen, that's a good football team." Some protestors became so discouraged that they walked away. One Syracuse student, Lynn Shatzkin, commented, "He didn't look anyone in the eyes; he was mumbling; when people asked

him to speak up, he would boom one word and no more. . . . I always thought Nixon was just a man who disagreed with me, but that's not what he is. He's obviously a very sick person who's had too much pressure and cracked. I'm just wondering who's running the country."

After the conversation, Nixon had breakfast at the Mayflower Hotel and ate corned beef hash with a poached egg for the first time in five years.

4–5. DON LEADBETER AND FRENCH GENDARME
On October 28, 1970, motorcycle policeman Don Leadbeter was leading a presidential motorcade in St. Petersburg, Florida, when he was hit by a truck and severely injured. Nixon rushed over to express his sympathies. Leadbeter replied by apologizing for delaying the motorcade. Then, after an awkward silence, the president blurted out, "Do you like the work?"

In 1974, in Paris to attend the funeral of Georges Pompidou, Nixon asked the same question of a French policeman who was struggling to hold back an enthusiastic crowd. Unfortunately, the beleaguered gendarme did not understand English.

6. RICH LITTLE
The comedian, famed for his realistic impersonations of Richard Nixon, attended a reception for the president at his estate in San Clemente, California. After actress Debbie Reynolds was introduced to Nixon, she turned to Little and said, "Go ahead, Rich, do your impression of Nixon." The president watched politely, shook Little's hand, and continued greeting people in the receiving line. Later Nixon asked an aide, "Who was that fellow with the strange voice imitating?"

7. ELVIS PRESLEY
When Elvis learned that a certain Hollywood celebrity was an undercover agent for the Federal Narcotics Bureau, he decided that he, too, wanted to be an agent. If that could not be arranged, then he at least wanted a Federal Narcotics Bureau badge. Uninterested in the honorary shield offered by Deputy Narcotics Director John Finlator, Elvis took his case straight to the president, who invited him to the Oval Office. When Nixon saw Elvis's costume, he said, "Boy, you sure do dress kind of wild, don't you?" To which Elvis replied, "Mr. President, you've got your show to run, and I've got mine." After offering to help Nixon with his antidrug campaign, Elvis got his badge but failed to curb his own fatal drug addictions.

8. ANTHONY CALOMARIS
Calomaris was a teenager who lived next door to J. Edgar Hoover on Thirtieth Place in Washington, D.C. One night in April 1974, during a newspaper strike, Hoover held a secret dinner party for Nixon.

However, word of the president's visit to the home of the FBI director leaked out, and when Nixon prepared to leave, he was shocked to discover TV cameramen waiting for him outside. Calomaris was also there, and when the president emerged, the young man asked for his autograph. It was Calomaris's lucky night; he ended up with four autographs of Richard Nixon. "He didn't seem to want to talk to the television people," said Calomaris, "and when I gave him my writing pad, he just kept turning the pages and signing his name."

9. STANLEY ROCKWELL

Mr. Rockwell, an insurance salesman from West Hartford, Connecticut, was standing at a pay phone in Nantucket in mid-September 1980, talking to his wife, Betty, when he noticed Richard Nixon step off a nearby yacht. Calling out to the ex-president, Rockwell asked Nixon if he wouldn't say a few words to his wife. Glad to oblige, Nixon picked up the phone, and said, "Betty, who's this woman your husband's with?" Then he smiled at Rockwell and walked away.

15 Presidents Who Won with Less Than 50% of the Vote

Year	Candidates	Popular Vote	% of Popular Vote
1824	JOHN QUINCY ADAMS	108,740	30.5
	Andrew Jackson	153,544	43.1
	Henry Clay	47,136	13.0
	William H. Crawford	46,979	12.9
1844	JAMES K. POLK	1,338,464	49.6
	Henry Clay	1,300,097	48.1
	James G. Birney	62,300	3.3
1848	ZACHARY TAYLOR	1,360,967	47.4
	Lewis Cass	1,222,342	42.5
	Martin Van Buren	291,263	2.3
1856	JAMES BUCHANAN	1,832,955	45.3
	John C. Frémont	1,339,932	33.1
	Millard Fillmore	871,731	21.6
1860	ABRAHAM LINCOLN	1,865,593	39.8
	Stephen A. Douglas	1,382,713	29.5
	John C. Breckenridge	848,356	18.1
	John Bell	592,906	12.6

1876	RUTHERFORD B. HAYES	4,036,572	48.0
	Samuel Tilden	4,284,020	51.0
1880	JAMES A. GARFIELD	4,453,295	48.5
	Winfield Hancock	4,414,082	48.1
	James B. Weaver	308,578	3.4
1884	GROVER CLEVELAND	4,879,507	48.5
	James G. Blaine	4,850,293	48.2
	Benjamin F. Butler	175,370	1.8
	John P. St. John	150,369	1.5
1888	BENJAMIN HARRISON	5,447,129	47.9
	Grover Cleveland	5,537,857	48.6
	Clinton B. Fisk	249,506	2.2
	Anson J. Streeter	146,935	1.3
1892	GROVER CLEVELAND	5,555,426	46.1
	Benjamin Harrison	5,182,690	43.0
	James B. Weaver	1,029,846	8.5
	John Bidwell	264,133	2.2
1912	WOODROW WILSON	6,296,547	41.9
	Theodore Roosevelt	4,118,571	27.4
	William Howard Taft	3,486,720	23.2
	Eugene V. Debs	900,672	6.0
	Eugene W. Chafin	206,275	1.4
1916	WOODROW WILSON	9,127,695	49.4
	Charles Evans Hughes	8,533,507	46.2
	A. L. Benson	585,113	3.2
	J. Frank Hanly	220,506	1.2
1948	HARRY S. TRUMAN	24,105,812	49.5
	Thomas E. Dewey	21,970,065	45.1
	J. Strom Thurmond	1,169,063	2.4
	Henry Wallace	1,157,172	2.4
1960	JOHN F. KENNEDY	34,227,096	49.9
	Richard M. Nixon	34,108,546	49.6
	Harry F. Byrd	440,298	0.6
1968	RICHARD M. NIXON	31,785,480	43.4
	Hubert Humphrey	31,275,165	42.7
	George Wallace	9,906,473	13.5

1992	WILLIAM CLINTON	44,909,889	42.9
	George H. Bush	39,104,545	37.4
	H. Ross Perot	19,742,267	18.9
1996	WILLIAM CLINTON	47,402,357	49.2
	Robert Dole	39,198,755	40.7
	H. Ross Perot	8,085,402	8.4
2000	GEORGE W. BUSH	50,456,002	47.8
	Albert Gore	50,999,897	48.4
	Ralph Nader	2,882,995	2.7

Note: In the 1896 presidential election, William McKinley won with 50.2 percent of the popular vote; in 1976, Jimmy Carter won with 50.1 percent; in 1980, Ronald Reagan won with 50.8 percent; and in 2004, George W. Bush won with 50.6 percent.

12 Presidents Ranked by Popularity

	Median Approval Rating During Presidency
1. John F. Kennedy	72.5
2. George Bush, Sr.	66
3. Dwight Eisenhower	65
4. Franklin Roosevelt (1938–1943)	60
5. Bill Clinton	57
6. George W. Bush (through August 30, 2005)	57
7. Lyndon Johnson	55
8. Ronald Reagan	52
9. Richard Nixon	52
10. Gerald Ford	46
11. Jimmy Carter	42
12. Harry Truman	39

Source: The Gallup Poll.

36 Great Slips of the Tongue in American Politics

1. "The United States has much to offer the third world war."
   (Ronald Reagan, speaking in 1975 on third world countries; he repeated the error nine times.)

2. "Thank you, Governor Evidence."
   (President Richard Nixon, referring to Washington governor Dan Evans in a speech during the Watergate scandal in 1974)

3. "That is a discredited president."
   (President Richard Nixon, meaning "discredited precedent," in a speech during the Watergate scandal in 1974)

4. "I hope that Spiro Agnew will be completely exonerated and found guilty of the charges against him."
   (John Connally, attempting to defend the scandal-plagued vice president in a speech in 1973)

5. "My heart is as black as yours."
   (Mario Procaccino, Democratic candidate for mayor of New York, addressing a group of black voters in 1969)

6. "Get this thing straight once and for all. The policeman isn't there to create disorder. The policeman is there to preserve disorder."
   (Mayor Richard J. Daley of Chicago, defending the actions of his policemen during the Democratic convention in 1968)

7. "They have vilified me, they have crucified me. Yes, they have even criticized me."
   (Mayor Richard J. Daley, attacking his opponents)

8. "Many Americans don't like the simple things. That's what they have against we conservatives."
   (Republican presidential candidate Barry Goldwater, speaking during the 1964 campaign)

9. "The right to suffer is one of the joys of a free economy."
   (Howard Pyle, adviser to President Eisenhower, philosophizing during the 1956 presidential campaign)

10. "The police are fully able to meet and compete with the criminals."
    (John F. Hylan, mayor of New York, commenting on a crime wave in 1922)

11. "We may be finding that in some blacks when it [the chokehold] is applied, the veins or arteries do not open up as fast as they do on normal people."
    (Los Angeles police chief Daryl Gates, 1982)

12. "How are you, Mr. Mayor? I'm glad to meet you. How are things in your city?"

(Ronald Reagan, failing to recognize Samuel Pierce, his secretary of housing and urban development, at a White House reception for U.S. mayors, 1981)

13. "It's wonderful to see all these beautiful white faces . . . I mean black and white faces."
(Nancy Reagan, 1980 presidential campaign)

14. "Don't confuse me with the facts. I've got a closed mind."
(Representative Earl Landgrebe, R-Ind., upon being told of the "smoking gun" Watergate tape, 1974)

15. "The president is aware of what is going on in Southeast Asia. That is not to say anything is going on in Southeast Asia."
(Nixon press secretary Ron Ziegler, during an embargo on news about South Vietnam when asked if U.S. troops were about to invade Laos, 1971)

16. "We will once again have an administration that is inept in putting up with problems."
(Mario Procaccino, trying to convince voters to elect him mayor of New York, 1969)

17. "I don't think anyone in his right mind would say he wanted a bloodbath."
(Paul Beck, press secretary of California governor Ronald Reagan, commenting on Reagan's statement, "If it takes a bloodbath" to silence campus radicals, "let's get it over with. No more appeasement." 1970)

18. "A fellow like myself would never be mayor of this great city without a Democratic Party."
(Chicago mayor Richard Daley, 1967)

19. "Facts are stupid things."
(Ronald Reagan, addressing the Republican National Convention in 1988. He was misquoting John Adams, who in 1770 wrote, "Facts are stubborn things." Reagan repeated the mistake several times.)

20. "I hope I stand for antibigotry, anti-Semitism, antiracism. That is what drives me."
(George Bush, Sr. in 1988; New York governor Mario Cuomo remarked that Bush at least had not offended Italians by declaring himself antipasto.)

21. "We have had triumphs, we have made mistakes, we have had sex."
(George Bush, Sr. in 1988, speaking of his eight years as vice president under Reagan, meant to say "we have had setbacks.")

22. "If Lincoln were alive today, he'd roll over in his grave."
(Newly inaugurated president Gerald Ford)

23. "My first qualification for mayor of the city of New York is my monumental ingratitude to each and all of you."
(Fiorello La Guardia, on the night of his first election victory)

24. "Outside of the killings, we have one of the lowest crime rates."
(Marion Barry, mayor of Washington, D.C., in 1989)

25. "Now, the simple truth is those Democrats who are here are probably here because, like millions I've met across the country, they have found they can no longer follow the leadership of the Republican Party, which has taken them down a course that leads to ruin."
(Ronald Reagan in 1986, campaigning on behalf of Republican candidate Jim Santini)

26. "Now we are trying to get unemployment to go up, and I think we are going to succeed."
(Ronald Reagan in 1982)

27. "The first black president will be a politician who is black."
(L. Douglas Wilder, governor of Virginia, in 1992)

28. "This is Pearl Harbor Day. Forty-seven years ago to this very day, we were hit and hit hard at Pearl Harbor."
(George Bush, Sr. addressing the American Legion in Louisville, Kentucky, on September 7, 1988, three months off target)

29. "I didn't go down there with any plan for the Americas, or anything. I went down to find out from them and [learn] their views. You'd be surprised. They're all individual countries."
(Ronald Reagan in 1982, responding to a question about whether his Latin American trip had changed his outlook on the region)

30. "Boy, they were big on crematoriums, weren't they?"
(George Bush, Sr. in 1987, after a visit to the Auschwitz death camp)

31. "What a waste it is to lose one's mind—or to not have a mind. How true that is."
(Dan Quayle in 1989, addressing the United Negro College Fund)

32. "I stand by all the misstatements."
(Dan Quayle in 1989, on his oratorical slipups)

33. "Those who survived said, 'Thank God, I'm still alive,' but of course those who died . . . well, their lives will never be the same." (Representative Barbara Boxer, D-Cal., November 1989)

34. "I think we agree the past is over." (Candidate George W. Bush, May 10, 2000)

35. "We need an energy bill that encourages consumption." (President George W. Bush, September 23, 2002)

36. "You're free. And freedom is beautiful. And it'll take time to restore chaos and order . . ." (President George W. Bush to the people of Iraq, April 13, 2003)

Primary source: David Olive, *Political Babble* (New York: John Wiley & Sons, copyright 1992). Reprinted by permission of John Wiley & Sons, Inc.

E.F.

13 Unexpected Expenses in the United States Budget

Each year, each member of Congress tries to secure as much money as possible for his or her district or state. Sometimes members of Congress request funding for projects that please their constituents or their backers but look a bit bizarre when seen from outside the district. Here are a few prime examples from fiscal year 2005:

1. Research at Auburn University in Alabama to develop new vaccines for fish and a means for mass vaccination of fish: $1,000,000

2. Grant to the Iowa Central Community College dental hygiene program to address the "grave" shortage of dental hygienists in north-central Iowa: $500,000

3. Support of industry-directed research to increase the competitiveness of Hawaii's cut flower and foliage industry: $355,000

4. Feasibility study for the world's first indoor motor speedway, to be built in Ohio's Mahoning Valley: $300,000

5. Research to reduce labor costs in the asparagus industry by replacing human harvesters with mechanical harvesting: $278,000

6. Funding to improve facilities at the YMCA in Franklin County, Kentucky: $250,000. The funding was originally approved for 2004, but

because of a typing error the money went instead to the *town* of Franklin, Kentucky, in Simpson County, which used the windfall to build a new YMCA.

7. Funding to connect the North Creek Ski Bowl in Warren County, New York, to the Gore Mountain Resort in order to better compete with resorts in Vermont and New Hampshire: $250,000

8. Grant to Ocean Spray, a cranberry and grapefruit growers' cooperative, to market cranberry juice in Great Britain: $225,000

9. Grant to the Chaldean Cultural Center in West Bloomfield, Michigan, to promote Chaldean language, history, and culture: $200,000

10. Grant to the Grammy Foundation in Santa Monica, California, to cultivate the appreciation of recorded music: $150,000

11. Curriculum development for the study of mariachi music in Clark County, Nevada: $25,000

12. Grant to provide audio and video capabilities to the Web site of the Birthplace of Country Music Award, enabling web visitors to listen to short clips of artists from Upper East Tennessee: $10,000

13. Creation of a musical theater production in Sunnyside, New York, that celebrates the history and art of the tango: $10,000

The Real People Behind
6 Popular American Images

1. UNCLE SAM
Samuel Wilson (1766–1854) was a self-made man who founded a meat-packing business in Troy, New York, in 1970. By the time of the War of 1812, he had become a prominent citizen and so won a contract to supply meat to the U.S. Army. During a tour of his plant on October 2, 1812, Governor Daniel Tompkins of New York noticed the initials "EA-US" on the barrels of meat waiting to be shipped to the army. When he asked what that meant, he was told "EA" stood for Elbert Anderson, the contractor for whom Wilson worked. The "US" was an abbreviation for United States, but a workman joked that it stood for "Uncle Sam" Wilson. The story spread, and because Wilson had a reputation for being honest and hardworking, by the end of the war, Uncle Sam had become a symbol of the national character and the federal government.

2. THE STATUE OF LIBERTY

The famous statue in New York harbor was sculpted by France's Frédéric Auguste Bartholdi. Originally called *Liberty Enlightening the World*, it was dedicated in 1886 and became popularly known as the Statue of Liberty. At the time that Bartholdi was working on Liberty, he was in love with a young woman named Jeanne-Émilie Baheux de Puysieux, a dressmaker's assistant from Nancy. He used Baheux de Puysieux as the model for the statue's arms. When it came to fashioning Liberty's face, he felt that Jeanne-Émilie was too beautiful. He wanted someone who looked strong, trustworthy, and long-suffering to symbolize the perseverance needed to achieve liberty. He chose his mother, Charlotte Bartholdi.

3. INDIAN HEAD–BUFFALO NICKEL

The Buffalo nickel was minted between 1913 and 1938. On one side is the head of an American Indian. Previous designs of Indian head coins had used white models, but James Earle Fraser, the world-renowned sculptor who got the job to do the five-cent piece, chose real Native Americans. Chief John Big Tree of the Iroquois nation was the model for the nose and forehead. Two Tail, one of the Sioux warriors who defeated General Custer at the Little Big Horn, modeled for the cheek and chin. For the buffalo, Fraser traveled to the wilds of Central Park Zoo in New York City and sketched an old buffalo named Black Diamond. Two years after the coin bearing his likeness was issued, Black Diamond was slaughtered and sold for $100. His body yielded 750 pounds of meat, his hide was turned into a robe, and his head became a trophy.

4. AMERICAN GOTHIC

Grant Wood's 1930 painting portrays a somber-faced Iowa farmer holding a pitchfork and his even more somber-faced daughter. The daughter was modeled after the artist's sister, Nan Wood Graham, who later said that the fame she gained saved her from "a very drab life as the world's worst stenographer." The model for the farmer was Byron McKeeby, a local dentist.

5–6. BARBIE AND KEN

Ruth Handler watched her daughter, Barbie, play with paper dolls and thought that little girls would rather own a fashion doll with a large wardrobe and hair they could comb. In 1959, she and her husband, Elliot, the founders of Mattel Inc., introduced the Barbie doll. Three years later, they added a boy doll and named it after their son, Ken. By the time the dolls were marketed, the real Barbie was a teenager and too old to play with dolls. Between them, the real Barbie and Ken had three daughters, but none of them played with Barbie and Ken dolls, either.

15 American Thoroughfares with Unusual Names

1. TYMAN PLACE in Faribault, Minnesota

2. ROAD TO HAPPINESS in Vermilion, Ohio

3. NONE SUCH PLACE in New Castle, Delaware

4. ALMOSTA ROAD in Darby, Montana

5. EWE TURN in Kaysville, Utah

6. FAMILY CIRCLE in Sandy, Utah

7. MEMORY LANE in Salt Lake City, Utah

8. THE LIVING END in Austin, Texas

9–11. DAMN IF I KNOW,
DAMN IF I CARE,
DAMN IF I WILL in Boca Grande, Florida

12–15. STAYA WAY,
GETTA WAY,
KEEPA WAY,
OUTATHA WAY in Mocksville, North Carolina

4 Noteworthy Intersections

1. HAVETEUR WAY and UNIDA PLACE in San Diego, California

2. GRINN DRIVE and BARRET ROAD in West Chester, Ohio

3. ANTONIO PARKWAY and AVENIDA DE LAS BANDERAS in Santa Margarita, California

4. HICKORY AVENUE and DICKORY AVENUE intersect with DOCK STREET in Harahan, Louisiana

R.C.B. & the Eds.

14 Arab Americans

Arab is a cultural, not a racial or religious, designation, and it applies to anyone who is from an Arabic-speaking country or is the product of Arab culture. More than one million Americans are of Arab ancestry.

1. Paula Abdul, singer and choreographer
2. F. Murray Abraham, actor
3. Paul Anka, popular singer
4. William Peter Blatty, author of *The Exorcist*
5. Dick Dale, king of the surf guitar
6. Dr. Michael E. De Bakey, renowned heart surgeon
7. Shannon Elizabeth, actress
8. Doug Flutie, football quarterback
9. Salma Hayek, actress
10. Ralph Nader, consumer advocate and politician
11. Tony Shalhoub, actor
12. Danny Thomas, actor and entertainer
13. Helen Thomas, White House correspondent for UPI
14. Frank Zappa, singer and songwriter

C.F. & the Eds.

10 Leading Sources of Oil for the United States

Country	Thousand barrels/day (2004)
1. Canada	1,616
2. Mexico	1,598
3. Saudi Arabia	1,495
4. Venezuela	1,297
5. Nigeria	1,078
6. Iraq	655
7. Angola	306
8. Kuwait	241
9. United Kingdom	238
10. Ecuador	232

Source: Energy Information Administration.

Oops: 6 Cases of Foreigners Mistakenly Killed by the American Military

The annual budget for the United States military is equal to the military budgets of all the other nations in the world combined. As the police of the world, American soldiers sometimes make mistakes and kill innocent men, women, and children. Here are a few examples:

1. **MENTAL PATIENTS IN GRENADA**
   On October 23, 1983, suicide bombers attacked a Marines barrack in Beirut, Lebanon, killing 241 people. To deflect attention from this humiliating tragedy, President Ronald Reagan ordered the invasion, two days later, of the small Caribbean island nation of Grenada. As military actions go, this was an easy one. Grenada's army and militia had little interest in fighting, so the 8,500 U.S. troops met with serious resistance only from the 784 Cubans who were on the island building an airfield— and only 44 of them were actually soldiers. However, the "crisis" on Grenada was created so hastily that planning and execution were confusing. At one point, a U.S. Army lieutenant had to use a pay phone and credit card to call in air support. Of the 19 Americans who died during the invasion, only 9 were killed by enemy fire. The Americans did kill 21 Grenadian fighters and 24 Cubans, only 2 of whom were professional soldiers. However, they also ended the lives of 18 Grenadian mental patients when they mistakenly bombed a mental hospital.

2. **PASSENGERS ON IRANIAN COMMERCIAL AIRPLANE**
   Between 1980 and 1988, Iran and Iraq fought a bloody war that took the lives of about 365,000 people and left a million wounded. Midway through the war, the United States, under President Ronald Reagan, chose to support Iraq. Reagan provided Saddam Hussein with weapons and intelligence. U.S. forces also attacked Iranian ships and oil platforms. On July 3, 1988, the USS *Vincennes*, a $1.2 billion U.S. Navy guided missile cruiser, crossed into Iranian territory to chase a group of Iranian gunboats. In the midst of the exchange of fire, sailors on board the *Vincennes* spotted an Iranian airplane and shot it down. Unfortunately, it turned out to be a commercial passenger plane in its normal air corridor during a scheduled flight between Iran and Dubai. Two hundred ninety civilians from six nations were killed, including 65 children. The incident was quickly forgotten in the United States, but in the Islamic world, it was another story. Because both President Reagan and the next U.S. president, George Bush, Sr., refused to apologize or even to accept responsibility for the deaths of the innocent civilians, anti-American sentiment spread. Only seven weeks after the plane was shot down, Iran and Iraq signed a ceasefire ending their eight-year conflict.

3. SKIERS IN ITALY
    Four U.S. Marines flying an EA-6B Prowler on a training mission in the
    Italian Alps on February 3, 1998, dropped to about 370 feet in a valley
    and clipped a cable supporting a ski lift gondola. Twenty skiers from six
    countries fell to their deaths. Although the pilot, Captain Richard
    Ashby, was flying 104 mph above the speed limit and way below the
    authorized altitude, he was acquitted by a military jury. Ashby did
    serve six months in prison when it was discovered that he and his
    navigator, Joseph Schweitzer, had destroyed a videotape made from the
    plane during the incident.

4. JAPANESE FISHERMEN
    U.S. Navy officials asked Captain Scott Waddle, commanding officer of
    the USS *Greeneville*, a nuclear attack submarine operating out of Pearl
    Harbor, to show off the sub's capabilities to a group of sixteen mildly
    distinguished visitors on February 9, 2001. To give the visitors a thrill,
    Waddle demonstrated a "main ballast blast," an emergency maneuver
    in which the submarine rapidly rushes to the surface from a depth of
    400 feet. As it reached the surface, the 6,080-ton *Greeneville* ripped
    through a Japanese fishing school training ship, the *Ehime Maru*. On
    board the Japanese vessel were 35 crew members and students. Nine
    Japanese were killed, including four 17-year-old students. A year later,
    a memorial to the victims was dedicated in Honolulu's Kaka'ako
    Waterfront Park.

5. AFGHAN ENGAGEMENT PARTIES
    During the invasion of Afghanistan in 2002, American forces pursued a
    strategy of swift and extreme force that favored the use of air strikes.
    This policy led to numerous mistakes in which noncombatant civilians
    were killed. One of the most tragic episodes occurred on July 1, when
    an American AC-130 gunship attacked four villages near Kakrak in
    Oruzgan Province. U.S. pilots claimed they had been fired on, but
    locals said that two engagement parties were being celebrated and that,
    according to tradition, some Afghani men had fired rifles into the air.
    The Americans killed 54 celebrants, most of them women and children,
    and wounded at least 120. U.S. officials later admitted that they had
    made a mistake. It is estimated that at least 3,500 innocent Afghans
    were killed by U.S. bombers, more than the number of innocent
    Americans killed in the terrorist attacks of September 11, 2001.

6. IRAQI WEDDING PARTY
    The United States government has refused to release figures for the
    number of civilians killed by American forces during the war in Iraq.
    However, it is known that many mistakes have been made. On May 19,
    2004, American forces bombed what they claimed was an insurgent
    dormitory in the village of Makr al-Deeb near the Syrian border, killing

42 people. When video emerged showing a wedding party in the village and matching one of the musicians to one of the corpses, Brigadier General Mark Kimmet conceded, "Bad people have celebrations, too." The nearest hospital reported that a majority of the dead were women and children. The U.S. military was more forthcoming about an incident near Mosul on January 8, 2005, when they admitted dropping a 500-pound bomb on the wrong house, killing 14 members of one family.

Work and Money

MICROSOFT CORPORATION, 1978

42 Very Odd Jobs

1. ANT CATCHER
   Digs up live ants for use in plastic ant farms.

2. BACK WASHER
   Tends machine that washes, rinses, and dries fiber (called sliver) in the textile industry.

3. BALL PICKER
   Picks up unclaimed baseballs, golf balls, and the like to keep recreation areas clean.

4. BONE CRUSHER
   Tends the machine that crushes animal bones used in the manufacture of glue.

5. BONER
   Inserts stays (bones or steels) into prepared pockets of women's foundation garments, such as corsets and brassieres.

6. BOSOM PRESSER
   Clothing presser who specializes in pressing bosoms of blouses and shirts.

7. BOTTOM BLEACHER
   Applies bleaching liquid to bottom of leather outsoles of lasted shoes, using brush or cloth, to lighten color outsoles.

8. BRAIN PICKER
   Places animal head on a table or on hooks in a slaughterhouse, splits the skull, and picks out the brains.

9. CAN CATCHER
   Stands at end of conveyor belt and catches falling cans in hands in order to keep cans from colliding with and denting each other.

10. CAR CHASER
    Directs the movement of grain-freight railroad cars.

11. CHICK SEXER
    Inserts a light to examine the sex organs of chicks, then separates the males from the females. A university degree in chick sexing is offered in Japan.

12. DEBUBBLIZER

Tends high-pressure heating equipment that removes internal solvent bubbles from nitrocellulose rod stock in the plastic industry.

13. DOPE SPRAYER

Sprays a solution, known as dope, on tanned hides in leather manufacturing.

14. EASTER BUNNY

Impersonates Easter Bunny to promote sales activity in retail stores, at conventions and exhibits, and to amuse children at hospitals, amusement parks, and private parties.

15. EGG BREAKER

Separates yolks and whites of eggs for use in food products by striking eggs against a bar. Pours contents of broken eggs into an egg-separating device.

16. EGG SMELLER

Smells eggs after they are broken open to check for spoilage.

17. FINGER WAVER

Hairdresser who sets waves in with fingers.

18. FISH HOUSEKEEPER

Cleans, dresses, wraps, labels, and stores fish for guests at resort establishments.

19. FOOT STRAIGHTENER

Straightens and screws into place the feet on watch and clock dials during assembly.

20. HEEL GOUGER

Tends the machine that cuts a cavity to form the seat for a heel in shoe manufacturing.

21. HOOKER INSPECTOR

Inspects cloth in a textile mill for defects by using a hooking machine that folds the cloth.

22. IMPREGNATOR

Tends vacuum or pressure tank that impregnates powdered-metal parts with lubricating oil or molten plastic.

23. KISS MIXER

Mixes the ingredients used in processing Candy Kisses.

24. **LEGEND MAKER**
Arranges and mounts letters, logos, and numbers on paper backing to make signs and displays.

25. **MANGLER**
Tends a machine that shapes and smoothes knitted garments.

26. **MASHER**
Operates cooker and mashing tub to combine cereal and malt in the preparation of beer.

27. **MOTHER REPAIRER**
Repairs metal phonograph record "mother" by removing dirt and nickel particles from soundtrack grooves. Records are mass-produced by being pressed by the metal mother record.

28. **MUCKER**
Shovels muck and other debris from work areas and ditches around construction sites and in mines.

29. **NECKER**
Feeds cardboard and fabric into a machine that wraps them around each other to form the neck of a jewelry box. The neck is the filler between the case and the fabric lining.

30. **PILLOWCASE TURNER**
Tends machine that turns pillowcases right side out and stretches material to remove wrinkles.

31. **PRUNE WASHER**
Tends machine that washes prunes preparatory to canning, packaging, or making specialty foods.

32. **QUEEN PRODUCER**
Raises queen bees.

33. **REEFER ENGINEER**
Operates refrigeration or air-conditioning equipment aboard ships.

34. **SLIME-PLANT OPERATOR**
Tends agitation tanks that mix copper or slime and acid solution preparatory to precipitation of copper.

35. **SNIFFER**
Sniffs people's body parts to test the effectiveness of foot and underarm deodorants.

36. **SUCKER-MACHINE OPERATOR**
Tends machine that automatically forms lollypops of specified shape on ends of wooden sticks.

37. **THRILL PERFORMER**
Entertains audiences at fairs, carnivals, and circuses by performing daredevil feats, such as diving from a high diving board into a tank of water, parachuting from an airplane, or being shot from a cannon onto a net.

38. **TOE PUNCHER**
Tends toe-punching machine that flattens toe seams of knitted seamless socks.

39. **TOP SCREW**
Supervises cowboys—called screws.

40. **UPSETTER**
Sets up and operates a closed-die forging machine that expands the ends of hot metal bars.

41. **VAMP CREASER**
Tends the machine that creases shoe vamps, the part of the shoe over the instep.

42. **WEED FARMER**
Grows weeds for sale to universities and chemical companies to be used in herbicide research.

Early Careers of 7 Self-Made Billionaires

1. WARREN BUFFETT (1930–)
The son of a U.S. representative from Nebraska, Buffett was an energetic paperboy for the *Washington Post* when he was growing up, covering several routes simultaneously. He also retrieved lost golf balls from a suburban course and sold them. When he was 11 years old, he and his sister began playing the stock market on a modest scale. A year later, he published a horse-racing handicapping sheet, and, while in high school, he and a fellow student were partners in a small pinball machine business that grossed $50 a week.

As a business major (he earned a BS from the University of Nebraska and an MBA from Columbia), Buffett studied with Benjamin Graham, who taught students to seek out undervalued stocks and wait patiently for them to rise. After Buffett formed his own investment fund, he scored one of his first big coups by following Graham's advice. In 1963, shares of American Express were selling cheaply because the company, then the victim of a major swindle, was considered near bankruptcy by many on Wall Street. Buffett, noticing that customers at Omaha shops and restaurants were using their American Express cards just as much as before the scandal broke, ignored the Wall Street gossip and bought 5 percent of the company's stock. Over the next five years, the value of the stock quintupled. Buffett's fortune has since grown to $44 billion.

2. MICHAEL DELL (1965–)

When he was 12 years old, Dell used the money he earned working at a Chinese restaurant to start a stamp collection. He then made $2,000 reselling the stamps through mail order. By the time he was 16, he had saved enough money to buy an Apple computer. He used the computer in his next business venture, selling subscriptions to the *Houston Post*. Reasoning that many new subscribers would be people setting up new households, such as newlyweds, he obtained lists of marriage license applicants from local courthouses. Then, using the computer, he sent out personalized letters with subscription offers. He earned $17,000, which he used to buy his first BMW.

Dell's parents wanted Michael to become a doctor. When he entered the University of Texas in 1983, he obliged his parents by enrolling in premed courses. But he began a new business on the side—selling computers. Operating out of his dorm room, he bought remaindered IBM and IBM-clone computers from local dealers, upgraded them, and sold them both door to door and through mail order. When his parents found out, they were upset and asked him to quit. A compromise was reached: Dell would put his business on hold until he finished the school year; if sales during his summer break weren't good, he would return to school. During the last month of his break, Dell sold $180,000 worth of computers. He dropped out of college, set up shop in Austin, Texas, and achieved sales of $6 million in his first year. He soon pioneered the concept of "direct selling" to customers, which established computer companies had resisted in the belief that buyers of expensive equipment would not be willing to make a purchase without a hands-on inspection. Dell Computers grew into the third-largest computer seller in the United States, and Michael Dell's net worth is now $16 billion.

3. BILL GATES (1955–)

Gates attended Lakeside School, a private Seattle establishment with rigorous academic standards. In 1967, the school's mothers club used the proceeds of a rummage sale to buy a digital training terminal that was linked by phone to a computer at a local company. Gates was hooked immediately and, with three like-minded friends, formed the

Lakeside Programming Group and hung out at the computing center day and night. He and his friends were so enamored of computers that they rummaged through the trash bins at the nearby Computing Center Corporation (CCC), looking for scraps of paper left by the programmers. After searching for errors in the company's programs, the group produced a 300-page manual, *The Problem Report Book*, that landed them on the CCC payroll. Later, the members of the Lakeside Programming Group formed their own company, Traf-O-Data, to sell a traffic monitoring program. Within a year, Traf-O-Data had earned $20,000, but business fell off when customers learned that Gates, the company president, was only 14 years old. During his senior year of high school, Gates was permitted to suspend his studies to accept a position as a programmer for TRW.

In 1975, Gates, who had enrolled at Harvard as a prelaw major, and Paul Allen, a former member of the Lakeside Programming Group who was working for Honeywell, set about designing software programs for the Altair 8800, the first commercially available microprocessor. They contacted the president of MITS, the manufacturer of the Altair, and told him they had successfully adapted the computer language BASIC for the Altair, even though they had yet to begin. When the president asked to see their program, they started working day and night in Gates's dorm room. Although neither Gates nor Allen had ever seen the Altair 8800 firsthand, their program worked and became the industry standard for the next six years. Gates dropped out of Harvard to form Microsoft with Allen. The company was so successful that he became a self-made billionaire at 31. He is now the world's second-richest man, worth $46 billion.

4. STEVE JOBS (1955–)

While he was in high school, Jobs attended lectures at the Hewlett-Packard electronics plant in Palo Alto, California. One day he phoned William Hewlett, the company president, and asked for parts to build a frequency counter for a school project. Hewlett not only complied, he also gave Jobs a summer job.

In college, Jobs teamed up with his future partner in Apple Computers, Stephen Wozniak, to sell "blue boxes" that allowed people to illegally make free long-distance calls. Jobs supplied the parts, Wozniak provided the labor, and they sold hundreds of the devices for $150 each in University of California dorms and through a friend in Beverly Hills. After dropping out of Reed College, Jobs landed a job as a technician at Atari. One of his first tasks was engineering the computer game Breakout. When Jobs was unable to meet the deadline, he asked Wozniak for help. "Steve wasn't able to design anything that complex," said Wozniak later. "I designed the game thinking that he was going to sell it to Atari for $700 and that I would receive $350. It wasn't until years later that I learned that he had actually sold the game for $7,000." Jobs used the money he received to travel to India, searching for spiritual enlightenment. Back in the United States, he spent time at an Oregon farm commune. After returning to California in 1975, he met up with Wozniak again and suggested that they start their own computer company. To raise the $1,000 they needed, Wozniak sold his prized HP-65 calculator, while Jobs sold his VW van. The Apple Computer company set up shop in the Jobs family garage. Their Apple II was the first computer designed for home use and set off the personal computer revolution. Although Jobs had a contentious relationship with Apple—he was forced out of the company in the late 1980s, then brought back in 1998—the company remains the center of his $3 billion fortune.

5. ROSS PEROT (1930–)

Perot got his first job at the age of six, working for his father, a cotton dealer and horse trader, breaking horses to the saddle for a dollar or two apiece. At 12, he worked out a deal with the *Texarkana Gazette* by which he would establish a paper route in the city's predominately black slum area and in return would receive 70 percent, rather than the standard 30 percent, of subscription fees collected. Setting out on horseback at 3:30 each morning, Perot covered 20 miles a day and was soon earning $40 a week.

After high school, he attended Texarkana Junior College for a year before obtaining an appointment to the U.S. Naval Academy in 1949. Although he loved the navy, he was less than enamored of the promotion and seniority systems and so decided not to sign on for another hitch. While serving aboard the aircraft carrier *Leyte*, Perot had been invited by an IBM executive to look him up after his discharge. Perot did so and got a job selling computers. During his fifth year at IBM, he sold his entire quota for the year before January was over and was promoted to a desk job at the corporation's Dallas office. While there, he became convinced that there was a market for a company that would design, install, and operate processing systems on a contract basis. He quit his IBM job to strike out on his own and, on his thirty-second birthday, used $1,000 of savings to found Electronic Data Systems. Perot's net worth is now $4.3 billion.

6. TED TURNER (1938–)

Turner's father, Ed, ran a successful outdoor advertising company, for which Ted worked a 40-hour week during the summer, cutting grass around billboards and creosoting poles. As a student at Brown University, he was bitterly disappointed when his father insisted that he continue working summers for the family business, forcing him to turn down a job offer from the Norton (Connecticut) Yacht Club that included an opportunity to race in a fleet of lightning boats. After two stints in the Coast Guard after being suspended, then expelled, from Brown, Ted became general manager of the Turner Advertising

Company's branch in Macon, Georgia, in 1960. In 1963, Ed Turner, facing financial difficulties after overextending his business, killed himself. Ted took over at age 24 and successfully revived the faltering company.

In 1970, over the protests of his financial advisers, Turner purchased Channel 17, an independent Atlanta UHF station, and then used the revenues from the billboard business to ride out losses of $2 million and grind down the local competition. The station became the start of an entertainment and broadcasting empire—including WTBS, CNN, the Atlanta Braves baseball team, and the Atlanta Hawks basketball team—that made Turner worth $2 billion.

7. SAM WALTON (1918–1992)
After graduating from the University of Missouri with a BA in economics in 1940, Sam Walton took his first job in retailing as a JCPenny sales trainee. A few years later, he and his brother James became franchisees of the Ben Franklin variety store chain. As a franchisee (the brothers eventually ran 15 stores in Arkansas and Missouri), he traveled throughout the eastern and midwestern United States and noticed that the large retail chains always placed their stores in or near large cities. Walton felt that smaller towns could successfully support a large retailer, but he received no encouragement from Ben Franklin's management when he brought up the idea. Undaunted, he launched the project himself, and in 1962 opened the first Wal-Mart in Rogers, Arkansas. Although the chain struggled early on—David Glass, who later became Wal-Mart's CEO, called the second Wal-Mart "the worst retail store I had ever seen"—by 1991, Wal-Mart had passed Sears as America's largest retailer, and Walton was worth more than $8 billion.

C.F.

17 Household Items and When They Were Introduced

1. Pressure cooker—1690 (called a steam digester by its inventor, physicist Denis Papin)

2. Tin can—1810 (the first patented tin cans were expensive because they were made by hand)

3. Adhesive postage stamp—1840 (first used in England)

4. Mechanical dishwasher—1879 (invented by Illinois housewife Josephine Cochrane, who was upset by the number of dishes her kitchen help broke)

5. Contact lenses—1887 (designed by a German glassblower; plastic lenses became available about 50 years later)

6. Electric oven—1889 (first installed in a Swiss hotel)

7. Lipstick—1915 (marketed in a metal cartridge-type case)

8. Radio—c. 1920 (date available for use in the home)

9. Kleenex—1924 (the first disposable handkerchiefs were originally called Celluwipes)

10. Electric blender—1936 (inventor Stephen Poplawski's blender was successfully marketed by bandleader Fred Waring)

11. Nylon-bristle toothbrush—1938 (the toothbrush was originally developed in China around 1500)

12. Microwave oven—1946 (discovered when microwaves melted candy in scientist Percy Spencer's pocket)

13. Transistor radio—1955 (the first inexpensive transistor offered)

14. Aluminum can—1960 (tab tops came three years later)

15. Felt-tip pen—1960 (first marketed by a Japanese stationery firm)

16. Electric toothbrush—1961 (first manufactured by Squibb)

17. Sony Walkman—1979 (the portable personal tape player)

Source: *The New York Public Library Book of Chronologies* by Bruce Wetterau, copyright 1990 by Bruce Wetterau, Stonesong Press, and the New York Public Library. Used by permission of the publisher, Prentice Hall Press, a division of Simon & Schuster, New York.

19 Little-Known Inventors of Common Things

1. MARGARET KNIGHT—FLAT-BOTTOMED PAPER BAG (1869)
   A grade school dropout who lived in Springfield, Massachusetts, Margaret Knight loved mechanical devices and machinery. From 1867 to 1869, she devised the heavy machinery necessary to produce the modern flat-bottomed paper bag. The practicality of Knight's bag was far superior to the existing paper bag, whose origin is unknown. For the

paper bag and dozens of other inventions, she received little compensation. At her death, her estate was valued at a mere $275.05.

2. **WILLIAM PAINTER—CROWN BOTTLE CAP (1892)**
A Quaker who lived in Baltimore, Maryland, William Painter invented the bottle cap, the machinery to manufacture it, and the method to attach it to bottles. An engineer, he formed the Crown Cork and Seal Company to exploit his invention, which eventually made him a millionaire. Painter's bottle cap was the only one used for decades, until the appearance of the twist-off cap in the 1960s.

3. **WHITCOMB L. JUDSON—ZIPPER (1893)**
On August 29, 1893, Whitcomb Judson of Chicago patented the zipper—two thin metal chains that could be fastened by pulling a metal slider up between them. Intended for use on shoes and boots, Judson's zipper was marketed in 1896 as the "universal fastener." However, the zipper as we know it today was designed by a Swedish engineer from Hoboken, New Jersey, Gideon Sundback. In 1913, Sundback patented his "separable fastener," the first zipper with identical units mounted on parallel tapes.

4. **JOHAN VAALER—PAPER CLIP (1900)**
Vaaler, a Norwegian, patented the paper clip in Germany in 1900. In 1989, a 22½-foot paper clip was erected in his honor in Oslo.

5. **CECIL BOOTH—VACUUM CLEANER (1902)**
Cecil Booth's first commercially produced vacuum cleaner was so large that it was mounted on wagon wheels and parked in the street outside the house to be cleaned. Hoses as long as 800 feet were passed through the windows, and the cleaning was done by Booth's own operators. Fashionable ladies in London would hold vacuum-cleaning parties at which guests could actually watch the transmission of the dirt, since Booth had thoughtfully inserted glass-covered apertures at intervals in the sides of the hose. Portable vacuum cleaners that could be purchased for home use appeared in America in 1905, but even those machines weighed a formidable 92 pounds.

6. **JACQUES BRANDENBERGER—CELLOPHANE (1908)**
As a hobby, aristocratic Swiss chemist and businessman Jacques Brandenberger spent nearly 10 years experimenting with the machinery needed to mass-produce cellophane, a material he had invented. In 1908, he patented the manufacturing process, and three years later he began to sell his product. At first, the transparent sheets were expensive and were used only as wrapping paper for luxurious gifts. Today cellophane is produced cheaply and is used primarily by the food industries. The enormous success of cellophane enabled Brandenberger to retire comfortably and collect Louis XV antiques.

7. **WALLACE HUME CAROTHERS—NYLON (1934)**
An extremely emotional, shy, and humorless man, Wallace Hume Carothers worked as a research chemist for E. I. Du Pont de Nemours & Company. At Du Pont, Carothers invented the first nylon thread in 1934 by squeezing a chemical solution through a hypodermic needle. Originally known as Polymer 66, nylon was first used for stockings and toothbrushes. In 1937, depressed over the death of his sister and feeling himself a failure as a scientist, even though he had been elected to the National Academy of Sciences, Carothers committed suicide. He never realized the full potential of his creation.

8–9. **CARLTON MAGEE AND GERALD HALE—PARKING METER (1935)**
In the late 1920s, Carlton Magee, a newspaperman and member of the Oklahoma City Chamber of Commerce, asked mechanical engineering professor Gerald Hale to devise a timing mechanism to regulate parking. Fascinated with the project, Hale invented the parking meter. In 1935, 150 were installed on streets in Oklahoma City. People disliked the new invention, and when similar meters were put on the street in Mobile, Alabama, that same year, a group of concerned citizens chopped them down with axes.

10. **SYLVAN GOLDMAN—SHOPPING CART (1937)**
Oklahoma City supermarket owner Sylvan Goldman looked at a pair of folding chairs in his office and was inspired to invent the shopping cart. On June 4, 1937, he used the first shopping carts in his own Standard Supermarkets. At first, customers balked at using them, so Goldman hired male and female models to walk around his store pretending to use them. The concept caught on, and Goldman became a millionaire.

11. **CHESTER CARLSON—XEROGRAPHIC COPIER (1938)**
The son of a Swedish immigrant barber, physicist Chester Carlson invented the dry, or xerographic, method of copying in the back room of his mother-in-law's beauty salon in Queens. The patent royalties of the invention, which was bought by the Haloid Company (later Xerox) in 1947, made Carlson a multimillionaire. His first copier is now on display at the Smithsonian Institution in Washington, D.C.

12. **GEORGE DE MESTRAL—VELCRO (1941)**
One day in 1941, De Mestral, a Swiss mechanical engineer, went hunting in the Jura Mountains with his Irish pointer. When he tried to remove the cockleburs that had stuck to his dog's coat and to his own wool pants, he was amazed by the strength of the seedpods. He took one home, examined it under a microscope, and discovered that the burrs contained hundreds of tiny hooks. Ten years later, he patented the Velcro fastener, which gained wide success in the fashion industry and was used to keep the boots of astronauts stuck to the floor in a

weightless environment. The name Velcro is derived from two French words: *velour*, a kind of fabric, and *crochet*, or hook.

13. **PERCY LEBARON SPENCER—MICROWAVE OVEN (1945)**
Percy LeBaron Spencer of the Raytheon Company in Waltham, Massachusetts, conceived the idea of the microwave one day when he happened to stand in front of a radar power tube in the factory and found, when he reached into his pocket, a gooey brown mess where formerly there had been a candy bar. The next day, he put an egg in a kettle with a hole cut in the side and placed it in front of the power tube. One of Spencer's colleagues passed by, lifted the lid of the kettle to see what lay inside, and received a faceful of half-cooked egg as the shell exploded under pressure. The first microwave oven to go on sale was marketed by Raytheon at $3,000 in 1947 as the Radar Range—it was, after all, simply a radar set you could use for cooking.

14. **ROBERT ABPLANALP—AEROSOL VALVE (1949)**
A 27-year-old mechanical engineer and machine shop owner, Robert Abplanalp revolutionized the aerosol spray can industry in 1949 with his seven-part leakproof valve. He started the Precision Valve Corporation to manufacture, market, and sell the valve, which has since earned him well over $100 million. Every year, Precision Valve manufactures one billion aerosol valves in the United States and a half billion in ten foreign countries. Abplanalp, one of President Richard Nixon's closest friends, commented on his success: "Edison said genius was 99 percent perspiration and 1 percent inspiration. I say it's 2 percent inspiration, 8 percent work, and 90 percent luck. I'm a lucky guy." But the world may not be so lucky. Some scientists believe that the fluorocarbons used in spray cans for almost 30 years are destroying the earth's protective ozone layer.

15. **CHARLIE DOUGLASS—LAUGH TRACK (1950s)**
During the 1950s, when television programs were performed before live audiences, Charlie Douglass (1910–2003), an engineer working as a technical director for live shows, had the idea to create a "laugh machine" that would simulate the real reactions of an audience. His Laff Box proved a great success, as studies showed that home audiences really did laugh more if a show was accompanied by a laugh track. Decades later, laugh machines are still used, but now they bring together hundreds of human sounds, including the laughter of a wide range of cultures.

16. **BETTE NESMITH GRAHAM—TYPING CORRECTION FLUID (1956)**
Bette Nesmith Graham's success story would not have happened had she been a better typist. Prone to making errors in her typing as a secretary at Texas Bank and Trust in Dallas, she needed a surefire way of correcting them without leaving smudges. Her solution was inspired,

even though it did not require any inventive skills. She simply poured white tempera water-based paint into a small bottle and took it to work, along with an eyebrow brush. When other typists began asking for her "correcting fluid," she began bottling it in the garage with the help of her son Michael. (He was later to achieve fame and fortune as Michael Nesmith of the pop group The Monkees.) Bette achieved her fame and fortune with what was to become Liquid Paper, a hugely successful venture that was worth $47 million when she sold it to Gillette in 1979.

17. ERMAN CLEON FRAZE—PULL-TAB OPENER (1959)
In 1959, Fraze, an engineer, was on a family picnic near his hometown of Dayton, Ohio, when he had to use a car bumper to open a beer because he had forgotten to bring a can opener. Thinking that there must be an easier way to open cans, he invented the pull tab and obtained a patent in 1963. By 1990, over 150 billion pull-tab cans were being manufactured every year.

18. ARTHUR J. MINASY—ANTISHOPLIFTING TAG (1966)
When Arthur J. Minasy was growing up in Astoria, Queens, he shoplifted marbles and tennis balls from the local Woolworth's five-and-ten. By the early 1960s, he was working as a consultant for the New York City Police Department, trying to solve the growing problem of shoplifting. In 1964, he beat out other inventors by creating in his garage an electronic tag that would set off an alarm when it passed through a security system near the door. A prototype of Minasy's invention, which he called the Knogo (as in no-go) and upon which his international Knogo Corporation was founded, was accepted into the permanent collection of the Smithsonian's National Museum of American History in 1991.

19. ARTHUR FRY—POST-IT NOTES (1979)
The special gum that enables the ubiquitous little paper rectangles to "stick without sticking" was developed by chance in 1973 by Dr. Spencer Silver of the Minnesota Mining & Manufacturing (3M) Company. Nobody could think of a use for it until his colleague Arthur Fry, a member of a local choir, used the unwanted gum to make markers for his music book that would not fall out. The market for bookmarkers, however efficient they may be, is limited. But one day, Fry had occasion to make a brief comment on a report. He used one of his markers to write a note, stuck it on the report, and sent it to his boss. The boss's reply came back written on the same note. This was the moment of revelation—the stickers could be marketed as notelets for short comments, instructions, or reminders. But when they were sales-tested as Press 'n' Peel pads, there was no demand. Only when 3M bombarded Boise, Idaho, with a campaign it called the "Boise Blitz" and changed the name of the product to the catchier Post-it did it take off.

R.J.F. & P.R.

5 Unfortunate Product Names and 1 Honorable Mention

A corporate or product name can symbolize more than intended, especially when that name is used in other lands. Today's multinational markets require sensitivity to other cultures, as many companies have learned the hard way.

1. GROS JOS
   Hunt-Wesson introduced its Big John products in Canada before realizing that the name, which translated to *Gros Jos,* was French-Canadian slang for "big breasts." However, sales did not suffer from the translation.

2. PINTO
   The Ford Pinto suffered image problems when it went on sale in Brazil—*pinto* is Portuguese slang for "small male genitals." For Brazilian buyers, Ford changed the name to Corcel, which means "horse."

3. BITE THE WAX TADPOLE
   When Coca-Cola expanded to China in the 1920s, the company chose Chinese characters that, when pronounced, would sound like the English name for the drink. Those particular Chinese letters, though, actually translated to "bite the wax tadpole" or "wax-flattened mare." The company switched to characters meaning "good mouth, good pleasure" or "happiness in the mouth."

4. PLEDGE
   The Johnson Company retained the American name of the wax product when it was introduced in the Netherlands. Unfortunately, in Dutch it means "piss," making it difficult for shoppers to ask for Pledge. The product survived because most Dutch retail stores converted to self-service.

5. BUICK LaCROSSE
   When General Motors introduced this car for the 2005 model year, it discovered that "lacrosse" was a slang term for masturbation among teenagers in French-speaking Quebec. The car was renamed the Allure for the Canadian market.

Honorable Mention:
   The Yokohama Rubber Company was forced to withdraw hundreds of tires from the sultanate of Brunei when Islamic authorities complained that the tread design resembled the word for Allah.

12 Early Cars with Unusual Names

1. **CAR WITHOUT A NAME**
   T. S. Fauntleroy, H. R. Averill, and E. H. Lowe of Chicago formed an automotive firm in 1909. As the start of production neared, they still had not settled on a name for the new vehicle and began to call it "The Car Without a Name." The designation stuck until 1910, when the three men decided to change it to F.A.L., their last initials. The F.A.L. was built until 1914, and the company estimated total production at 65,000 units, although the figures were probably exaggerated.

2. **MYSTERY CAR**
   This one-of-a-kind vehicle was exhibited at the Auditorium Hotel during the 1925 Chicago Automobile Show. The five-passenger touring model was priced at around $500, according to the sign on its windshield. Not only was the car a mystery, the builder was as well. *The American Motorist* said that the man behind the venture was reportedly "one of the most spectacular merchandising geniuses in the country, a man who has been strangely silent." He was never identified, and the car never entered regular production.

3. **BEN HUR**
   Produced between 1917 and 1918 in Willoughby, Ohio, the Ben Hur was built by fledgling automaker L. L. Allen. He chose the name because it sounded far more dramatic than "the Allen." Approximately 40 cars were produced before the company entered receivership in May 1918.

4. **DOLLY MADISON**
   As a tribute to the late U.S. first lady, the Madison Motor Company of Anderson, Indiana, named its first cars Dolly Madison in 1915. Unfortunately, they didn't do enough research—President Madison's wife spelled her name "Dolley." The firm's later cars were called Madison and were produced until 1919.

5. **AVERAGE MAN'S RUNABOUT**
   George Adam of Hiawatha, Kansas, produced the Average Man's Runabout for only one year—1906. Apparently, its name was sadly apt, as the car had nothing remarkable about it. But the public wanted status symbols, so few of the cars were produced.

6. **MILLIONAIRE'S CAR**
   Officially named the Orson, the Millionaire's Car—as it was more popularly known—was built in Springfield, Massachusetts, in 1911. The

company was backed by 100 of the most prominent bankers in New York City, who were to take delivery of the first 100 vehicles built. Unfortunately, financial mismanagement and expensive lawsuits killed the company within two years.

7. SEVEN LITTLE BUFFALOES
William Andrew DeSchaum of Buffalo, New York, began production of a car under his own name in 1908. Sales were extremely poor, so DeSchaum decided that a name change to the more whimsical Seven Little Buffaloes might help. It didn't. Production ended in 1909.

8. PICKLE
The Pickle, named for its inventor, Fred Pickle, was a one-of-a-kind car built in Greenville, Michigan, in 1906. The unusual-looking car used ordinary bicycle wheels and a small 3½-horsepower engine.

9. BIG BROWN LUVERNE
The Luverne auto was built in Luverne, Minnesota, from 1904 through 1916. Its most popular model was the Big Brown Luverne. An exceptionally large car with a 130-inch wheelbase, the model featured a distinctive solid silver radiator, many coats of "Luverne brown" paint, and special upholstery of—according to the sales literature—"old Spanish brown leather with all hair filling."

10. AMERICAN CHOCOLATE
William Walter owned the American Chocolate Machinery Company in New York City. In 1902, he decided to expand his business into automotive production by building cars in his factory. While he called his car the Walter, much of the public knew it as the sweeter-sounding American Chocolate. Production was relatively successful and continued until 1909.

11. GRUBB
William I. Grubb produced steam cars in Pottstown, Pennsylvania, between 1901 and 1902. Known as both the Grubb and the Light Steamer, only two examples were assembled.

12. ECK
James Eck of Reading, Pennsylvania, built steam-powered vehicles under the model name of Boss from 1897 to 1909. Production was rather haphazard over the years, and a total of only 22 cars were manufactured.

K.A.R

15 Famous People Who Worked in Bed

1. **KING LOUIS XI (1423–1483)**
   This French king was ugly, fat, and sickly but also ruthless and clever, earning the title of the "universal spider." He introduced the custom of the *lit de justice* (bed of justice), a ceremonial appearance of the monarch, in bed, before *le parlement*, with the princes of the realm on stools, the greater officials standing, and the lesser ones kneeling. No one is sure exactly why he began the practice, but it caught on and lasted until the French Revolution. Fontanelle, a critic of Louis XV, was asked on the eve of the Revolution, "What, sir, is a 'bed of justice'?" He replied, "It is the place where justice lies asleep."

2. **LEONARDO DA VINCI (1452–1519)**
   Leonardo earned unique fame as an artist and scientist, and according to his *Notebooks*, he spent some time each night "in bed in the dark to go over again in the imagination the main outlines of the form previously studied . . . it is useful in fixing things in the memory."

3. **CARDINAL DE RICHELIEU (1585–1642)**
   In the last year of his life, the diabolically clever and scheming cardinal took to his bed and stayed there because of his rapidly deteriorating health. This did not prevent him from working—he directed his highly efficient secret police in exposing the treasonous machinations of the youthful royal favorite Cinq Mars. Nor did it hinder the peripatetic cardinal from traveling—his servants carried him about in his bed, and if the door of the house he wanted to stay in was too narrow, they would break open the walls.

4. **THOMAS HOBBES (1588–1679)**
   Hobbes, the great British political philosopher renowned for his mathematical approach to natural philosophy, found bed a comfortable and handy place to work on his formulas. He wrote the numbers on the sheets and, when he ran out of room, on his thighs. He wrote his 1661 *Dialogue on Physics or On the Nature of Air* entirely in bed. Hobbes also sang in bed because (according to Aubrey's *Brief Lives*) "he did believe it did his lungs good, and conduced much to prolong his life."

5. **HENRY WADSWORTH LONGFELLOW (1807–1882)**
   Throughout his life, Longfellow suffered from periodic bouts of severe insomnia. Out of desperation he decided to put his sleepless nights to some good use, and he began to write poetry in bed—including his 1842 classic "The Wreck of the Hesperus."

6. MARK TWAIN (1835–1910)

Twain loved the luxurious comfort of writing in bed and there composed large portions of *Huckleberry Finn*, *The Adventures of Tom Sawyer*, and *A Connecticut Yankee in King Arthur's Court*. He seems to have been the first person to point out that working in bed must be a very dangerous occupation, since so many deaths occur there.

7. IGNACE FANTIN-LATOUR (1836–1904)

Best known for his portrait groups, especially *Homage á Delacroix*, this French painter worked in bed out of necessity when he could not afford wood for a fire. William Gaunt, in *The Aesthetic Adventure*, describes him propped up in bed, "shivering, mournful, persistent . . . in a threadbare overcoat, a top hat over his eyes and a scarf round his mouth, balancing a candle on the edge of his drawing board and sketching with numbed, gloved hand."

8. ROBERT LOUIS STEVENSON (1850–1894)

For years, Stevenson was wracked by coughing spells caused by tuberculosis, and consequently he wrote most of *Kidnapped* and *A Child's Garden of Verses* in bed at his home in Bournemouth, England. Bed sometimes brought him inspiration in the form of dreams. One night his subconscious mind spun "a fine bogey tale," as he called it, based on a real-life criminal he had read about. Stevenson's dream became *Dr. Jekyll and Mr. Hyde*.

9. EDITH WHARTON (1862–1937)

Pulitzer Prize–winning author Edith Wharton (*Age of Innocence*, 1920) wrote primarily about the upper class into which she was born, often writing tragedies of rich people becoming destitute. She also wrote about lower-class life, however, her most famous works in the genre being *Ethan Frome* (1911) and *Summer* (1917), which Wharton described as the "hot Ethan." She wrote in the mornings, finding inspiration in the comfort of her bed. So accustomed was she to this routine that she once suffered a fit of hysterics because her hotel room bed did not face the light.

10. MARCEL PROUST (1871–1922)

Bundled in sweaters, a hot-water bottle at his feet, the French author worked to refine his series of novels called *A la Recherche du Temps Perdu* (*In Search of Lost Time*) while lying virtually flat in bed in a cork-lined room. He had all the necessities within arm's reach—more than a dozen pens (if he dropped one, he refused to pick it up because of dust); all of his notes, notebooks, and manuscripts; even fumigation powder, which he believed helped his asthma. In spite of all his precautions, he died of pneumonia at age 51.

11. **WINSTON CHURCHILL (1874–1965)**

    Churchill loved to lie abed in comfort each morning for several hours while dictating letters and going through the boxes of official state papers. Although he much preferred to write his books while standing up, declining health in his later years forced him to write and correct most of *The Second World War* and *History of the English-Speaking Peoples* in bed.

12. **MAE WEST (1892–1980)**

    The legendary sex queen with the hourglass figure was famous for her double entendres. She wrote several of her own screenplays, including *Diamond Lil,* and in 1959 she published her autobiography, *Goodness Had Nothing to Do with It.* She did all her writing in bed, she reported, noting, "Everybody knows I do my best work in bed."

13. **MAMIE EISENHOWER (1896–1979)**

    While in the White House, First Lady Mamie Eisenhower did away with an office but not with the office routine. She held conferences, dictated to her secretary, paid the bills, and signed letters while ensconced in her pink-ruffled bed.

14. **F. SCOTT FITZGERALD (1896–1940)**

    During the last two years of his life, while writing *The Last Tycoon,* Fitzgerald found that he could work longer hours by staying in bed. He would retire to bed with a dozen Coca-Colas (having given up alcohol) and prop himself up on pillows. Using a lapboard, he'd work for about five hours a day. A fatal heart attack prevented him from completing *The Last Tycoon.*

15. **HUGH HEFNER (1926–)**

    It seems appropriate that a man who made his fortune in sex should have done so in bed. For decades, Hefner controlled the Playboy empire from a massive bed in his Chicago mansion, where he stayed awake for 60-hour stretches, fueled by amphetamines and Pepsi.

    R.W.S. & the Eds.

11 Famous People Who Were Dentists

1. **GEORGE W. BEERS (1825–1903)**

    In 1867, Beers created the official set of rules for lacrosse.

2. **EDGAR BUCHANAN (1902–1979)**

    This American character actor starred in the TV series *Petticoat Junction,* which ran from 1963 to 1969.

3. LEMAIRE D'AUGERVILLE (?–?)

A Paris dentist, d'Augerville is credited with patenting, in 1828, the first "swimming belt" diving apparatus that led to the development of scuba diving.

4. ZANE GREY (1875–1939)

Before he attended dental school, this U.S. novelist was a "traveling tooth puller" and treated patients in small towns—at the same time that he played baseball for a Baltimore, Ohio, team. In 1892, Grey entered the University of Pennsylvania, graduating in 1896 and opening his first dental office in 1898 in New York. He quit dentistry in 1904 to write full-time. Grey's most popular western novel was *Riders of the Purple Sage.*

5. DOC HOLLIDAY (1851–1887)

A notorious gunslinger of the Old West, Holliday practiced dentistry first in Atlanta, Georgia, then in Griffin, Georgia. In 1873, he moved his office to Dallas, Texas, hoping to improve his poor health. A victim of tuberculosis, he suffered from a chronic cough that scared away many patients. He was arrested for the first time in 1875, after which his medical career ended.

6. MAHLON LOOMIS (1826–1886)

A pioneer in wireless telegraphy, Loomis transmitted the first aerial wireless signals a distance of 18 miles in 1868, thus beating Marconi by 27 years. He patented his discovery in 1872 but was unable to make further refinements due to a lack of money.

7. CARY MIDDLECOFF (1921–1998)

A professional golfer, Middlecoff won the U.S. Open in 1949 and 1956 and the Masters Tournament in 1955.

8. KERSTIN PALM (1946–)

Fencer Kerstin Palm is the only woman to have competed in seven Summer Olympics. She was also Sweden's youngest-ever dental surgeon.

9. CHARLES WILLSON PEALE (1741–1827)

Peale was an eighteenth-century portrait artist who painted George Washington.

10. PAUL REVERE (1735–1818)

Revere rode from Charleston to Lexington in 1775 to warn American colonists of the approach of British troops—a feat immortalized in Longfellow's poem "Paul Revere's Ride." In 1768, however, he was a practicing dentist in Boston, who advertised his services in the *Boston*

Gazette. He gave up his practice in 1783, after the American Revolution, to engage in the manufacture of silverware.

11. THOMAS WELCH (1825–1903)
    Welch originated unfermented, bottled grape juice and founded the
    Welch Grape Juice Co.

    R.T.

14 Librarians Who Became Famous in Other Fields

1. GOTTFRIED VON LEIBNIZ (1646–1716)
   German philosopher, mathematician, diplomat, and intellectual giant of
   his time, Leibniz was appointed librarian at Hanover in 1676 and at
   Wolfenbüttel in 1691.

2. DAVID HUME (1711–1776)
   British philosopher, economist, and historian Hume spent the years
   1752–1757 as librarian at the Library of the Faculty of the Advocates
   at Edinburgh, where he wrote his *History of England.*

3. GIOVANNI GIACOMO CASANOVA (1725–1798)
   At the age of 60, the inestimable womanizer began 13 years as librarian
   for Count von Waldstein in the chateau of Dux in Bohemia.

4. AUGUST STRINDBERG (1849–1912)
   The Swedish author of the classic drama *Miss Julie* was made assistant
   librarian at the Royal Library in Stockholm in 1874.

5. POPE PIUS XI (Ambrogio Damiano Achille Ratti; 1857–1939)
   After 19 years as a member of the College of Doctors of the Ambrosian
   Library in Milan, he was appointed chief librarian. In 1911, he was
   asked to reorganize and update the Vatican Library. From 1922 until
   his death in 1939, the former librarian served as pope.

6. MARCEL DUCHAMP (1887–1968)
   Before launching his art career, Duchamp worked as a librarian at the
   Bibliotheque Sainte-Genevieve in Paris.

7. MARIANNE MOORE (1887–1972)
   The poet was an assistant in the Hudson Park Branch of the New York
   Public Library from 1921 to 1925.

8. BORIS PASTERNAK (1890–1960)
After the Russian Revolution, the future author of *Doctor Zhivago* was employed by the library of the Soviet Commissariat of Education.

9. ARCHIBALD MacLEISH (1892–1982)
Playwright, poet, lawyer, assistant secretary of state, winner of three Pulitzer prizes, and a founder of the United Nations Educational, Scientific, and Cultural organization (UNESCO), MacLeish was appointed by President Franklin D. Roosevelt as librarian of Congress in 1939 for five years.

10. MAO ZEDONG (1893–1973)
In 1918, he worked as an assistant to the chief librarian of the University of Beijing. Overlooked for advancement, he decided to get ahead in another field and eventually became chairman of the Chinese Communist Party.

11. J. EDGAR HOOVER (1895–1972)
His first job as a young man was that of messenger and cataloger in the Library of Congress.

12. GOLDA MEIR (1898–1978)
While attending Milwaukee Teachers' Training College, the future prime minister of Israel worked as a librarian at a local branch library and taught part-time in a neighborhood Yiddish folk school.

13. JORGE LUIS BORGES (1899–1986)
After his father's death in 1938, Borges (who later became Argentina's most famous author) started his first regular job, as an assistant in a small municipal library in Buenos Aires. In 1946, he was fired for signing an anti-Peron manifesto. After Juan Peron was overthrown in 1955, Borges was named director of the National Library of Argentina.

14. LAURA BUSH (1946–)
The future first lady worked for the Kashmere Gardens Branch of the Houston Public Library from 1973 to 1974. From 1974 until 1977, she was a teacher and librarian at Dawson Elementary School in Austin, Texas.

S.S. & C.F.

Women's Wages Compared to Men's for 20 Occupations

Occupation	Median Weekly Earnings, 2004 ($)		
	Women	Men	%
1. Mail clerks and mail machine operators except postal service	479	433	110.6
2. Dining room and cafeteria attendants and bartender helpers	356	326	109.2
3. Receptionists and information clerks	463	454	102.0
4. Food preparation workers	323	319	101.3
5. Secretaries and administrative assistants	550	598	92.0
6. Registered nurses	895	1,031	86.8
7. Elementary and middle school teachers	776	917	84.6
8. Cashiers	313	380	82.4
9. Waiters and waitresses	327	399	82.0
10. Designers	646	818	79.0
11. Postsecondary teachers	886	1,162	76.2
12. Accountants and auditors	757	1,016	74.5
13. Lawyers	1,255	1,710	73.4
14. Chief executives	1,310	1,875	70.0
15. Loan counselors and officers	695	1,001	69.4
16. Retail salespersons	386	597	64.7
17. Insurance sales agents	615	970	63.4
18. Financial managers	839	1,397	60.1
19. Securities, commodities, and financial services sales agents	651	1,168	55.7
20. Physicians and surgeons	978	1,874	52.2
U.S. national average	573	713	80.4

Source: "Median Weekly Earnings of Full-Time Wage and Salary Workers by Detailed Occupation and Sex," Bureau of Labor Statistics Web site, ftp:// ftp.bls. gov/pub/special.requests/lf/aat39.txt

22 Famous People Who Went Bankrupt

1. P. T. BARNUM (1810–1891)
   Barnum, who made more than $2 million hawking freaks and wild animals, allegedly said, "There's a sucker born every minute." However, he often played the fool himself by making embarrassingly bad investments. The final humiliation came in 1855, when he invested more

than $500,000 in the Jerome Clock Co., only to find out he had been swindled again. The loss plunged him into bankruptcy and caused him to briefly contemplate suicide. It also provided a theme for countless moralistic editorial writers.

2. KIM BASINGER (1953–)
Basinger was forced into bankruptcy in 1993 after losing a lawsuit and being ordered to pay $7.4 million for failing to honor a verbal contract to star in the movie *Boxing Helena*. As a result, she lost the Georgia town of Brazelton, which she had purchased in 1989 for $20 million. Her partners in the deal got Brazelton.

3. LORRAINE BRACCO (1949–)
The actress racked up more than $2 million in legal bills during a six-year custody battle with actor Harvey Keitel over their daughter, Stella. The debts forced her to declare bankruptcy in 1999. Despite that, 1999 ended up as a good year for Bracco—she was cast in HBO's *The Sopranos*, which she described as "a big turning point. It allowed me to put myself back on my feet."

4. TONI BRAXTON (1967–)
The singer filed for bankruptcy in 1998, with debts of more than $1 million. Although she had sold more than 15 million records, she claimed that her deal with her recording label left her earning far less than most multiplatinum artists. Since Braxton had filed a lawsuit against LaFace Records in 1997, some observers suggested that her bankruptcy was really a legal maneuver to terminate her contract so she could renegotiate a better deal.

5. GARY COLEMAN (1968–)
When he starred in *Different Strokes* in the 1980s, Coleman earned $64,000 a week, making him the highest-paid child star of his day. Although he found few roles after the series went off the air, he still had $7 million as of 1990. A bitter legal battle with his adoptive parents (he accused them of stealing as much as $1 million) and ongoing medical problems (he underwent two kidney transplants) drained his bank account. In 1995, he filed for bankruptcy, unable to pay $72,000 in debts. "I can spread the blame all the way around," Coleman said, "from me to accountants to my adoptive parents, to agents to lawyers and back to me again."

6. FRANCIS FORD COPPOLA (1939–)
The Oscar-winning director observed, "As they say, cash doesn't stay in my pockets very long." In 1992, he filed for bankruptcy with assets of $53 million dwarfed by liabilities of $98 million. Coppola came back financially in 1993, when he earned $10 million for directing *Bram Stoker's Dracula*.

7. **ALEISTER CROWLEY (1875–1947)**
   In 1934, the bisexual author and poet who claimed proficiency in black magic and blood sacrifice was brought into a London court to face his creditors. With Crowley's liabilities set at £5,000, the court receiver declared him bankrupt.

8. **DOROTHY DANDRIDGE (1924–1966)**
   In March 1963, the actress filed for bankruptcy in Los Angeles. Although she had once commanded six-figure movie contracts, she now claimed $5,000 in assets against $128,000 in debts. She blamed her insolvency on bad investments, such as $150,000 worth of dry oil wells, and an ex-husband who had run up his share of the bills.

9. **WALT DISNEY (1901–1966)**
   In 1921, Disney started the Laugh-O-Gram Corp. in Kansas City, Missouri, with $15,000 from investors. But he was forced to file for bankruptcy two years later when his backers pulled out because of problems with New York distributors of his animated fairy tales. In July 1923, Disney left for Hollywood with all his belongings: a pair of pants, a coat, one shirt, two sets of underwear, two pairs of socks, and some salvaged drawing materials.

10. **EDWARD III, KING OF ENGLAND (1312–1377)**
    Not content with the English crown, King Edward itched to rule France, too. His ambition led to the Hundred Years War and to his own financial ruin. Unable to repay a $7 million loan in 1339, he was brought under a petition of bankruptcy. He was the first national ruler to go bankrupt.

11. **EDDIE FISHER (1928–)**
    In 1972, exactly three decades after he began his singing career on Skipper Dawes's radio show in his native Philadelphia, Fisher was declared bankrupt in a federal court in San Juan, Puerto Rico. His debts totaled nearly $1 million.

12. **CHARLES GOODYEAR (1800–1860)**
    During the 1830s, it had almost become a sport for creditors to take poor Goodyear to court, have him declared bankrupt, and toss him into debtors' prison in Philadelphia, New Haven, or Boston. Still, his wife's unshakable loyalty and his own pluck saw him through the bad times. It was between stays in jail that he discovered how to vulcanize rubber. But when he died, he left his family $200,000 in debt.

13. **ULYSSES S. GRANT (1822–1885)**
    Late in life, Grant became a partner in a banking house called Grant and Ward. In 1884, the firm went bankrupt, and the ensuing stock

market crash left Grant so buried in debt that he was forced to hand over all his property, including his swords and trophies. Broke and dying of cancer, he spent his remaining days writing his memoirs to provide an income for his widow. Mark Twain published the book, and 300,000 copies were sold door to door. Twain generously offered the former president 70 percent of the net profits; after Grant died, his wife received $350,000 in royalties.

14. **DOROTHY HAMILL (1956–)**
After winning a gold medal at the 1976 Winter Olympics, figure skater Hamill became the first female athlete to sign a $1 million-per-year contract—with the Ice Capades. After the Ice Capades went bankrupt, she bought it in 1993, but she was unable to halt the skating tour's continuing slide into financial chaos. She sold it to televangelist Pat Robertson and filed for bankruptcy in 1996 with debts of $1.6 million.

15. **HAMMER (1962–)**
His *Please Hammer Don't Hurt Them* (1990) remains the best-selling rap album of all time. Hammer earned $33 million in 1991 alone. He spent equally lavishly, buying 17 cars, a Boeing 747, and a racehorse. In 1996, he filed for bankruptcy with debts of $13.7 million. He had to sell his $10 million mansion, which came with two bowling alleys and an indoor basketball court, at half its purchase price.

16. **ISAAC HAYES (1942–)**
This Academy Award–winning singer-composer filed bankruptcy on behalf of his wife and himself in 1976, listing debts of $6 million. Hayes, who won a 1971 Oscar for writing the score for *Shaft*, gave up all his business ventures, including a fast-food endeavor called Hot Buttered Soul Ltd. The largest of his debts was said to be a $1.7 million loan he had secured at a Memphis bank.

17. **BURT REYNOLDS (1936–)**
Reynolds was Hollywood's top star from 1978 to 1982. In 1996, he filed for bankruptcy with assets of $6.65 million and debts of $11.2 million. His creditors ranged from the IRS to the firm supplying his hairpieces. Reynolds blamed his financial troubles on an expensive divorce from actress Loni Anderson. "I'm paying the third-highest alimony and child support in the world," he told NBC's *Dateline*. "And the only two ahead of me are sheiks." In addition, the divorce hurt his reputation, costing him endorsement deals with Quaker State Oil and the Florida Citrus Commission.

18. **DEBBIE REYNOLDS (1932–)**
Actress Reynolds fulfilled a longtime dream in 1993 when she opened a casino-hotel in Las Vegas that also served as a showcase for her collec-

tion of movie memorabilia, including 3,000 costumes and 36,000 square feet of props. Things went sour after the hotel lost its casino when the company running it pulled out in 1996, citing a lack of profits. Losses from the hotel forced Reynolds into bankruptcy in 1997.

19. **MICKEY ROONEY (1920–)**
In 1962, the actor filed for bankruptcy in Los Angeles with $1,500 in assets against $463,513.12 in liabilities. Although he had grossed $12 million during his career up to that time, bad investments, multiple alimony payments, a disastrous partnership, and gambling had gobbled it up. His creditors ranged from a grocer clamoring for $385 to a furrier demanding a $1,900 balance due on his wife's leopard coat, to a bank calling in $25,000 that Rooney had borrowed to invest in a pay-television operation, to a production company that he was obligated to for $168,000.

20. **MARK TWAIN (1835–1910)**
Twain lost around half a million dollars on a wide range of inventions that included steam generators and marine telegraphs. But his downfall came when he decided not to invest $5,000 in Alexander Graham Bell's telephone company, because he saw possibilities in the Paige typesetting machine. Ultimately, he backed its inventor with more than $250,000. The machine complicated rather than simplified the typesetting process, and in 1894, Twain's losses caused him to declare bankruptcy.

21. **MIKE TYSON (1966–)**
The youngest heavyweight champion in boxing history, Tyson earned an estimated $300 million during his career. He spent extravagantly on mansions, automobiles, gifts for his entourage, even a pair of Bengal tigers. In 2003, he filed for bankruptcy with $23 million in debts, including $13.4 million to the IRS, $4 million to the British tax authorities, $300,000 to a limo service, and $173,000 to a Las Vegas jeweler.

22. **JAMES ABBOTT McNEILL WHISTLER (1834–1903)**
Whistler often had to borrow money or pawn his pictures to pay his debts. When a bill collector would come and carry off one of his chairs or beds, Whistler did not get upset. He simply drew a picture of the missing piece of furniture on the floor where it had stood. Once a bailiff who had taken possession of Whistler's house was joshed into dressing up as a butler and serving tea for Whistler and his friends. But such madcap antics could not prevent the inevitable, and on May 8, 1879, Whistler became bankrupt with debts of $10,000.

C.F., W.A.D., A.K. & L.K.L.

20 Famous Gurus and Their Former Jobs

1. **MARSHALL APPLEWHITE (1931–1997), U.S. cofounder of Heaven's Gate**
   The son of a Presbyterian minister, Applewhite graduated as a philosophy major from Austin College in Texas in 1952. After brief stays in seminary school and the Army Signal Corps, he decided to pursue a career in music. While obtaining a master's degree in music from the University of Colorado, he appeared in a number of operas produced in Houston, Texas, and Boulder, Colorado. During the 1960s, Applewhite taught music at St. Thomas University, a small Catholic school in Houston. He was fired in 1970 for having an affair with a student. Depressed, he checked into a psychiatric hospital the next year. There he met nurse Bonnie Nettles, who convinced Applewhite that the two of them were aliens from a higher level of reality. They opened an occult bookstore in Houston. After it failed in 1973, they took to the road to recruit followers. Their movement underwent several changes before evolving into Heaven's Gate.

2. **SHOKO ASAHARA (1955–), Japanese founder of Aum Shinrikyo**
   Asahara (born Chizuo Matsumoto) was born blind in one eye and raised in government-run boarding schools for the visually impaired. After graduating from high school, he went to Tokyo and spent years studying to enter Tokyo University, a virtual prerequisite for Japan's ruling elite. He told friends that he wanted to join the nation's conservative party and perhaps one day become prime minister. But Asahara failed and returned to his hometown of Kumamoto to work in a massage parlor. At age 23, he went back to the capital, married a 19-year-old student, and opened an acupuncture clinic. Soon after, he had his first run-in with the law—for peddling a fake herbal medicine. He had better luck teaching yoga classes and became interested in spiritual enlightenment. After a religious retreat in India, he claimed to have gained visionary powers. Asahara renamed his yoga school Aum Shinrikyo ("Supreme Truth") and began preaching a faith based on elements of Buddhism, Hinduism, Christianity, and New Age ideas. In 1995, his group attacked the Tokyo subway system with sarin nerve gas, killing 12 people. Asahara was sentenced to death for the attacks.

3. **SRI AUROBINDO (1872–1950), Indian founder of the Vedanta Society**
   After an extensive education in England, Aurobindo returned to India and became a lecturer in French and a professor of English at Baroda College. During this time, he was a noted poet and served as coeditor of the *Bandemataram*, a paper that became the mouthpiece of the Indian nationalist movement. He published two more nationalist papers, the *Karmayogin* and the *Darma*, before political pressures forced him to flee to Pondicherry, where he established his ashram.

4. YOGI BHAJAN (1929–), Sikh religious leader
After working as a bodyguard for the president of India, Bhajan
became a captain in the Indian army. He then served as an intelligence
officer in the customs service. He traveled to Canada in 1968 and
worked in a factory in Montreal. Before long, he had founded 3HO
(Healthy, Happy, Holy Organization) and become the best-known
exponent of the Sikh religion in America.

5. HELENA PETROVNA BLAVATSKY (1831–1891), Russian cofounder
of the Theosophical Society
The high-strung Russian mystic claimed that she reaped a fortune
selling ostrich feathers in Africa in the 1850s. Returning to Russia, she
supported herself and her lover in the late 1860s by making and selling
artificial flowers. In 1873, she sailed to the United States, where she
designed advertising cards for a shirt and collar factory before establishing the Theosophical Society with Henry Steel Olcott in 1875.

6. CARLOS CASTANEDA (1925—1999), Peruvian author
Castaneda left home in his twenties with the goal of achieving academic
success in the United States. He was a self-avowed chronic liar, something he eventually called a spiritual practice. His best sellers, such as
The Teachings of Don Juan: A Yaqui Way of Knowledge (1968) and *A
Separate Reality: Further Conversations with Don Juan* (1971), made
him a household name in the late 1960s and early 1970s, and his
reclusiveness added to his fame. He had harems and cult followers in
numerous countries. Castaneda had real jobs, probable jobs, and
possible jobs—he obscured much of his pre-guru history. The real jobs
included being a sculptor—in the '60s, a large statue of his in downtown
Los Angeles was torn down during a renovation. He drew stencils for an
art company, was a barber, a teacher's assistant at UCLA, and then a
full professor, teaching anthropology. He claimed to have walked on
bodybuilder Jack La Lanne's back for pay (Castaneda was short and
small) at a Hollywood gym. He also did carpentry, made jewelry, and
claimed to have done interviews of mental patients, which he then
transcribed (rumor has it that he was a patient). He often bragged that
he worked as a for-hire assassin and was a soldier of fortune but never
explained whom he worked for. When his first book became a best
seller, he turned to writing full-time (rumor persists that some of his
work was ghost-written, or at least heavily rewritten) and became a
professional guru until his death, enjoying the guru-benefit of selecting
hundreds of women to sleep with, claiming his sperm was magical.

7. WERNER ERHARD (1935–), U.S. founder of est
Born John Paul Rosenberg, Erhard worked as a construction supervisor
after graduating from high school. About 1960, he moved to St. Louis,
Missouri, and became a used-car dealer, operating under the business

name of Jack Frost. Another move took him to California, where he established himself as a top-notch door-to-door encyclopedia salesman for the Parents Cultural Institute of *Parents'* magazine. He became a vice president at the institute in 1967. When it went out of business in 1969, he landed a job as division manager for the Grolier Society, Inc., another encyclopedia sales company. He left Grolier in 1971 to found est.

8. GEORGE IVANOVITCH GURDJIEFF (1872–1949), Russian mystic
   As a young man, Gurdjieff worked at many jobs, including train stocker, ship's hand, hypnotist, corset merchant, organizer of cattle drives, and trader in carpets and antiques. He made money at whatever he turned his hand to. One of his more ingenious schemes was selling live sparrows, dyed and clipped to look like American canaries. It is rumored that he spent a decade in Tibet, serving as a Russian spy and tutoring the Dalai Lama.

9. L. RON HUBBARD (1911–1986), U.S. founder of the Church of Scientology
   In the 1930s, Hubbard wrote Westerns for pulp magazines, using the name Winchester Remington Colt. He switched to the field of science fiction after World War II and published nearly 80 stories under the pseudonyms of Kurt Von Rachen and Rene Lafayette. His best-known science fiction was published under his own name.

10. JIM JONES (1931–1978), U.S. founder of the People's Temple
    Jones worked as an orderly at Reid Memorial Hospital in Richmond, Indiana, and served briefly as a Methodist pastor before establishing his own church in 1953. He helped finance his church by selling monkeys door to door. After four years as the Indianapolis human relations commissioner, he moved to California, and in 1976, he was appointed chairman of the San Francisco Housing Authority by Mayor George Moscone. The following year Jones left for Guyana.

11. LI HONGZHI (1952–), Chinese founder of Falun Gong
    The self-styled spiritual leader has claimed that he started learning qigong, a form of meditation and breathing exercises, at age four and that he was taught by a Taoist immortal at age twelve. The reality was far more mundane. Teachers and classmates remembered him as an unexceptional student whose principal talent was for playing the trumpet. At 17, he went to work at a People's Liberation Army stud farm. He later worked as a trumpeter in a police band, a guesthouse attendant, and a clerk in a grain store. He began studying qigong in 1988 and founded Falun Gong four years later.

12. MAHARISHI MAHESH YOGI (1918–), Indian founder of Transcendental Meditation (TM)
    In 1940, the maharishi earned a bachelor's degree in physics from

Allahabad University. After graduation, he immersed himself in the study of spiritual science, and in 1955, he began the TM movement.

13. MEHER BABA (1894–1969), Indian mystic
While still a young boy in Poona, India, Meher Baba earned a small amount of money writing mystery stories that were published in England's *Union Jack* magazine. He went on to attend Deccan College and at age 19 met Hazrat Babajan, an elderly Muslim woman who became his first spiritual teacher.

14. SUN MYUNG MOON (1920–), Korean founder of the Unification Church
Educated at Tokyo's Waseda University, Moon worked as an engineer before founding his underground church in North Korea in 1946. After several years in a Communist concentration camp, he fled to South Korea and earned money as a dock worker from 1950 to 1954 while developing his religious philosophy.

15. SRI NISARGADATTA MAHARAJ (1890–1981), Indian religious leader
Born in the slums of Bombay, India, "Marutti" (his family nickname) worked first as a farmer on the family's small plot of land. Later, he worked as a clerk in his own store, selling odds and ends and Indian hand-rolled cigarettes known as *bidis*. With the guidance of a guru, Marutti achieved his quest for inner peace and walked barefoot through the Himalayas for three years. Upon returning to his family (a wife and three children) he opened a *bidi* shop, which he ran by day until his death—while at night he gave free talks and answered questions about philosophy and spirituality. His crowd of visitors quickly grew, coming from around the world. (After his death, numerous transcriptions of the dialogues were published as *I Am That*.) His work continues to deeply inspire readers, and the message is simple, put in various intriguing ways: The basis of Nisargadatta's beliefs is that we have the answers to our questions about all suffering within ourselves. He gives instruction about how to quiet the mind and listen to our own wisdom.

16. PETER DEMIANOVITCH OUSPENSKY (1878–1947), Russian mystic
After studying math at Moscow University, Ouspensky became a noted journalist and author. In 1909, he published *The Fourth Dimension*, a critically acclaimed book dealing with abstract mathematical concepts.

17. SWAMI PRABHUPADA (1896–1977), Indian founder of the International Society for Krishna Consciousness
A graduate of Calcutta University, Prabhupada managed a large pharmaceutical firm in Calcutta, then began his own highly successful chemical factory in Allahabad. Although he became a spiritual leader in the 1930s, he remained in the pharmaceutical business until 1954.

18. BABA RAM DASS (1931–), U.S. teacher of Hindu mysticism
Born Richard Alpert, he obtained his PhD in psychology and taught at
Stanford University, the University of California at Berkeley, and
Harvard. In 1963, he was dismissed from Harvard for allegedly involv-
ing undergraduates in experiments with the drug psilocybin.

19. SWAMI SATCHIDANANDA (1914–2002), Indian mystic
Born into a wealthy family, Satchidananda was a prosperous businessman who managed machine shops, worked in the automobile and
motion picture industries, and supervised factories. When his wife died,
he abandoned his business interests and devoted himself to the attain-
ment of spiritual enlightenment.

20. ALAN WATTS (1915–1973), British writer and lecturer on Zen
Buddhism
In 1945, Watts received a theological degree from Chicago's Northwest-
ern University. He was ordained an Episcopal priest and served at the
Northwestern campus until he left the church in 1950. Six months later,
he affiliated himself with the American Academy of Asian Studies in
San Francisco, where he functioned as a teacher and an administrator
during the next six years.

J.Hu., C.F. & the Eds.

12 Unusual Items Actually Sold on eBay

1. Pierre Omidyar (eBay's Founder) broken laser pointer; sold for $14
   (Fall 1995)

2. Honus Wagner "T206" baseball card (rarest, most valuable trading
   card in the world; sold for $1.3 million) (July 2000)

3. Gulfstream private business jet (most expensive item ever sold on eBay;
   sold for $4.9 million) (August 2001)

4. Oldest known pair of Levi's jeans; sold for $46,432 (May 2001)

5. Man's entire life's possessions (www.allmylifeforsale.com) (Summer
   2001)

6. Justin Timberlake's partially-eaten French toast; sold for $1,025
   (March 2000)

7. Britney Spears's chewed bubble gum; sold for $511.04 (September
   2004)

8. Grilled cheese sandwich with purported image of the Virgin Mary; sold for $28,000 (November 2004)

9. Woman's deceased father's walking cane (his ghost included); sold for $65,100 (December 2004)

10. Three tablespoons of water from a cup used by Elvis Presley; sold for $455 (December 2004)

11. Texas snowball (fell on Christmas Day; first time snow had fallen in Texas in 109 years); sold for $92 (January 2005)

12. Man's forehead for advertising space; sold for $37,375 (January 2005)

CHAPTER NINE

Sex, Love, and Marriage

HOW 11 FAMOUS PEOPLE MET THEIR MATES

GEORGE BURNS'S 5 TIPS FOR MEETING WOMEN

8 CELEBRITY COUPLES MARRIED
THREE WEEKS OR LESS

9 UNLIKELY COUPLES

6 INCESTUOUS COUPLES OF THE BIBLE

32 FAMOUS PEOPLE'S THOUGHTS ABOUT MARRIAGE

BENJAMIN FRANKLIN'S 8 REASONS TO MARRY
AN OLDER WOMAN

12 FOODS CLAIMED TO BE APHRODISIACS

22 MEMORABLE KISSES

6 POSITIONS FOR SEXUAL INTERCOURSE

MEMBERS OF SOCIETY: PRESERVED SEX ORGANS
OF 5 FAMOUS MEN

RUDOLPH VALENTINO'S 10 ATTRIBUTES
OF THE PERFECT WOMAN

13 MOTHERS OF INFAMOUS CHILDREN

DEAR ABBY READERS' 7 MOST
UNUSUAL PROBLEMS

ANN LANDERS READERS' 10 MOST
UNUSUAL PROBLEMS

THE MTV CELEBRITY KISSFEST, 2003
© Frank Micelotta/Getty Images

How 11 Famous People Met Their Mates

1. **JOHN LENNON AND YOKO ONO**
   According to biographers, avant-garde artist Ono pursued Lennon
   relentlessly. At the time they met, she was showing her work at London's
   Indica Gallery. Lennon saw the show, which impressed him, but did not
   respond immediately to her advances, which included pleas for sponsor-
   ship of her art, hanging around outside his door, and bombarding him
   with notes. Eventually, the couple divorced their respective spouses and
   married in 1969 on the Rock of Gibraltar.

2. **OLIVER HARDY AND VIRGINIA LUCILLE JONES**
   Jones was a script girl on *The Flying Deuces*, starring Laurel and
   Hardy. One day on the set, she tripped over a rolled-up carpet, struck
   her head on the arc light, and was taken to the hospital. While she was
   unconscious, Hardy was struck by her beauty. He courted her by
   sending flowers and notes to the hospital. They were married in 1940.

3. **LYNDON BAINES JOHNSON AND CLAUDIA "LADY BIRD" TAYLOR**
   Future U.S. president Johnson met Lady Bird in the office of a friend
   in Austin, Texas, in 1934. Within three minutes of their introduction,
   Johnson asked her for a date. She turned him down. He barraged her
   with telegrams and phone calls until she relented, and two months later
   they were married.

4. **OZZY OSBOURNE AND SHARON ARDEN**
   Heavy-metal rocker Osbourne met his wife-to-be when she was working
   as a receptionist for her father, a London music agent. He walked into
   her office barefoot, with a water faucet dangling from his neck, and sat
   on the floor. "I was terrified," she recalled. The couple wed two years
   later, in 1981, and had three children together.

5. **RUTH WESTHEIMER AND MANFRED "FRED" WESTHEIMER**
   The diminutive sex therapist met her third husband on a ski trip in the
   Catskills in 1966. Her boyfriend, Hans, was six feet tall, and an uncomfortable match on the ski-lift T-bar. At the top, she told Hans, "I'm
   going up with that short man," pointing to the five-foot Westheimer.
   They married less than a year later. Westheimer sometimes called his
   wife "my skiing accident."

6. **THE DUKE OF WINDSOR AND MRS. WALLIS SIMPSON**
   The Duke of Windsor was introduced to Mrs. Wallis Simpson—the
   woman for whom he eventually gave up the throne—at a house party.
   He asked whether she missed American central heating. She replied,
   "I'm sorry, sir, but you disappoint me. . . . Every American woman that

comes to your country is always asked the same question. I had hoped for something more original from the Prince of Wales."

7. **DWIGHT D. EISENHOWER AND MAMIE DOUD**
In 1915, Eisenhower met his future wife, Mamie Doud, at a dinner dance. When he asked her for a date, she told him to call in a month. Instead, he called her every fifteen minutes the next day, until she agreed to see him that night. He arrived four hours early, and they were engaged within three months.

8. **PAMELA ANDERSON AND TOMMY LEE**
Baywatch actress Anderson met the Motley Crue drummer at a New Year's party. "He sat with me and kept licking my face," she recalled. "When I left, he was begging me for my phone number. I said no way. But then I gave him my number because he was interesting." After a five-day courtship at the resort of Cancun, Mexico, the couple was wed on the beach.

9. **JULIE ANDREWS AND BLAKE EDWARDS**
Their romance began after Andrews heard that movie director Edwards had described her as "so sweet she probably has violets between her legs." Amused by this remark, she sent him a bunch of violets and a note. They soon began dating and were married in 1969.

10. **TINA BROWN AND HARRY EVANS**
Brown, the future editor of *Vanity Fair* and *The New Yorker,* was a 22-year-old Oxford coed when she decided to meet Evans, the 47-year-old editor of the venerable *Times* of London. She camped outside his door and refused to move until he agreed to see her. Four years later, Evans divorced his wife and married Brown.

11. **DOLLY PARTON AND CARL DEAN**
On her first day in Nashville in 1964, Parton took a suitcase of dirty clothes to a Laundromat. Dean drove by and honked his truck's horn at the pretty blonde. Parton cheerfully waved back, and he stopped. They chatted, began dating, and fell in love. After Dean got out of the army two years later, he and Parton married . . . and they have been together ever since.

The Eds. & C.F.

George Burns's 5 Tips for Meeting Women

Born Nathan Birnbaum in 1896, George Burns began his entertainment career singing on street corners in New York City at the age of seven. After more than 30 years of comedy partnership with his wife, Gracie Allen, he continued performing solo after her death in 1964. He appeared in a number of movies, including *Oh, God!* (1977) and *The Sunshine Boys* (1975), for which he won an Academy Award. The venerable entertainer, rarely seen without his trademark cigar, lived to be 100 years old, dying on March 9, 1996, of natural causes. He contributed the following list to *The Book of Lists* in 1993:

1. Be sure to wear a good cologne, a nice aftershave lotion, and a strong underarm deodorant. And it might be a good idea to wear some clothes, too.

2. If a real beauty comes your way walking her dog, stop and pet it. That makes you her friend, and before you know it, she'll be introducing herself and shaking your hand—unless her dog is a pit bull. Then she'll just introduce herself.

3. Bump into her rear end. I mean, if she's driving ahead of you. This may cost you a hundred, but you'll have her name, address, and phone number. The rest is up to you.

4. Making the scene in a sporty convertible with the top down still gets results. I was doing fine last week until the girl had to jump out to bring my hair back.

5. If all of the above fails, book yourself on a cruise. And if you strike out there, forget my tips on how to meet women, but I've got some great ones on how to make a fortune in the stock market.

8 Celebrity Couples Married Three Weeks or Less

1. RUDOLPH VALENTINO (actor) and JEAN ACKER (actress)—6 hours
   Married November 5, 1919, Hollywood's smoldering Great Lover was locked out on his wedding night by his lovely bride. His first marriage lasted less than six hours.

2. ZSA ZSA GABOR (professional celebrity) and FELIPE DE ALBA (socialite)—1 day
   After surviving her one-day marriage, Gabor commented, "I'm a wonderful housekeeper. Whenever I leave a man, I keep his house."

3. JEAN ARTHUR (actress) and JULIAN ANKER (nice Jewish boy)—1 day
   Before she gained fame in such films as *Mr. Deeds Goes to Town*, *Mr. Smith Goes to Washington*, and *Shane*, Arthur fell in love with "a nice

Jewish boy" named Julian Anker because "he looked like Abraham Lincoln." They married on a whim, but both sets of parents were horrified, and the couple filed for annulment the following day.

4. BRITNEY SPEARS (singer) and JASON ALEXANDER (childhood friend)—2 days
Pop superstar Britney Spears was married for 48 hours to an old Kentwood, Louisiana, buddy. The marriage took place in Las Vegas at the Little White Wedding Chapel. The bride wore a baseball cap and torn jeans. Both were 22 years old and claimed they were not intoxicated at the time. Said the groom, "It was just crazy, man. We said, 'Let's do something wild. Let's get married, for the hell of it.'" Spears made no comment. Calling it "a mistake," the couple had a judge annul the marriage, which took two hours.

5. GLORIA SWANSON (actress) and WALLACE BEERY (actor)—3 weeks
Married in Hollywood in March 1916, Swanson and Beery separated three weeks later. Said Beery: "She wanted the fancy life—to put on airs and all of that. Me, I like huntin' and fishin' and the simple life." Said Swanson: "I wanted to have a baby, and Wally didn't want that responsibility."

6. GERMAINE GREER (writer and feminist) and PAUL DE FEU (model)—3 weeks
The first male nude centerfold model for the London edition of *Cosmopolitan* magazine, De Feu lured Greer into marriage in May 1968. In Greer's words, "The marriage lasted three weeks. Three weekends, to be precise."

7. DREW BARRYMORE (actress) and JEFFREY THOMAS (Welsh barman)—3 weeks
In 1994, the pair was married for three weeks. Barrymore later admitted that she was trying to help Thomas obtain a green card to stay in the United States.

8. DARVA CONGER (reality TV contestant) and RICK ROCKWELL (reality TV contestant)—3 weeks
On Valentine's Day, 2000, Fox Television broadcast *Who Wants to Marry a Multimillionaire,* a special in which 50 women competed to win the hand of a millionaire and wed him on live TV. At the end of the show, real estate developer Rick Rockwell chose emergency room nurse Darva Conger to be his bride. The couple spent all but one day of their honeymoon in separate rooms. After 21 days, Conger filed for an annulment, calling the marriage a "mutual mistake . . . entered into solely for an entertainment purpose." By then Rockwell's image had

taken a beating. The Smoking Gun Web site revealed that in 1991, a judge had issued a restraining order against Rockwell after his ex-fiancée accused him of hitting her and threatening to kill her. It also turned out that he was not a millionaire real estate developer: He was a stand-up comedian and occasional motivational speaker with far less than the $2 million in assets the show had claimed. After the annulment became final, Conger cashed in on her 15 minutes of fame by posing in *Playboy* for $500,000.

9 Unlikely Couples

1. **DANNY KAYE AND LAURENCE OLIVIER**
   Kaye met Olivier and his wife, Vivian Leigh, at a Hollywood party in 1940. From then on, he visited and entertained them constantly, lavishing attention on his new friend, whom he nicknamed Lally. Kaye was married but apparently had an arrangement with his wife. The Olivier-Leigh marriage was more volatile—Olivier found his wife too sexually demanding. When the men began an affair, according to biographer Donald Spoto, it was no secret to Leigh. Nevertheless, the Oliviers continued to socialize with Kaye. On one occasion, Kaye disguised himself as a customs inspector in order to strip-search Olivier when he entered the United States on a 1953 trip. Their liaison lasted 10 years, until Olivier's next wife, Joan Plowright, strongly objected to it.

2. **JIM BROWN AND GLORIA STEINEM**
   Brown, football hero and actor, claims in one of his memoirs to have had a fling with feminist Steinem. They met in 1968, when she interviewed him for a magazine profile. The affair caused Brown's then girlfriend, Eva Bohn-Chin, to become jealous, which led to a quarrel during which Brown was arrested for allegedly throwing her off a balcony.

3. **GYPSY ROSE LEE AND OTTO PREMINGER**
   Lee, the famous and flamboyant stripper, instigated an affair with the Hollywood filmmaker in order to have a child by him. She selected him over other men "in spite of his reputation" for being a brute. She "sensed he was a good man" and admired his mind. Once she was pregnant, she brushed him off. Their son, Erik, did not know who his real father was until he was an adult. After Lee's death, Preminger legally adopted Erik, and the two became close friends.

4. **AIMEE SEMPLE MCPHERSON AND MILTON BERLE**
   In 1930, four years after her infamous "kidnapping," the flamboyant evangelist met Berle—then a rising young comic—at a charity show.

The two had a brief affair. Berle found her a worldly, passionate woman who enjoyed making love in her apartment in front of a home-made altar, complete with candles and crucifix.

5. **IMELDA MARCOS AND BENIGNO AQUINO, JR.**
When she won the Miss Manila beauty contest in 1953, Imelda Romualdez attracted several suitors. Among them was the young journalist Benigno Aquino, whom she dated for a time. But it was another of her suitors, politician Ferdinand Marcos, whom she married. Nearly 30 years later, the assassination of Aquino brought down the Marcos government and swept the widowed Corazon Aquino into power.

6. **BARBARA WALTERS AND ROY COHN**
Cohn, a rabid "red-baiter" during the anti-Communist witch hunts of the 1950s, dated Walters when she was in college. Friends believe that, at the time, she was unaware of his homosexuality. Said one, "Barbara felt that the only problem with Roy was that he was very tied to his mother." Acquaintances believe that the affair was never consummated, even though Cohn asked Walters more than once to marry him.

7. **MARLENE DIETRICH AND GENERAL GEORGE S. PATTON**
During World War II, Dietrich devoted herself wholeheartedly to entertaining the Allied troops at the front. Traveling together, Patton and Dietrich began an intense affair. This unlikely passion was eventually replaced by an even hotter liaison—between Dietrich and the handsome General James A. Gavin.

8. **JANIS JOPLIN AND WILLIAM BENNETT**
When he was a graduate student at the University of Texas, future U.S. antidrug czar and self-appointed arbiter of virtue Bennett was set up on a blind date for a barbeque with Janis Joplin, who was then at the height of her career. Although Bennett and the uninhibited rock singer may not seem to have had anything in common, he was a bit wilder in his youth. At his fraternity, he earned the nickname "Ram" by head-butting down a door that his girlfriend had locked on him. When asked what he and Janis did on their date, Bennett responded, "Hey, that is really none of your business." On another occasion, he said that they "sat under the Texas sky, talked, and had a couple of beers."

9. **ERROL FLYNN AND TRUMAN CAPOTE**
In 1947, Flynn visited Capote at his tiny walk-up apartment. The two had a one-night stand while they were both drunk. "If it hadn't been Errol Flynn," Capote later noted, "I wouldn't have remembered."

6 Incestuous Couples of the Bible

1–2. LOT AND HIS DAUGHTERS

After the destruction of Sodom and Gomorrah, the only survivors, Lot and his two virgin daughters, lived in a cave. One night, the daughters plied their father with wine, and the elder daughter seduced him in order to "preserve the seed of [their] father." The following night, they got him drunk again, and the younger daughter took her turn. Lot apparently had no memory of the events, although nine months later his daughters gave birth to two sons, Moab and Ben-ammi. (Gen. 19:30–38)

3. ABRAHAM AND SARAH

Abraham and Sarah had the same father but different mothers. Sarah married her half brother in Ur, and they remained together until she died at the age of 127. (Gen. 20:12)

4. NAHOR AND MILCAH

Abraham's brother, Nahor, married his niece, the daughter of his dead brother Haran and the sister of Lot. (Gen. 11:27, 29)

5. AMRAM AND JOCHEBED

Amram married his father's sister, and Aunt Jochebed bore him two sons, Aaron and Moses. (Exod. 6:20)

6. AMNON AND TAMAR

Amnon raped his half sister Tamar and was murdered in revenge two years later by Tamar's full brother Absalom. (II Sam. 13:2, 14, 28–29)

32 Famous People's Thoughts About Marriage

1. "Marriage, *n.* The state or condition of a community consisting of a master, a mistress and two slaves, making in all, two." —Ambrose Bierce

2. "A man may be a fool and not know it—but not if he is married." —H. L. Mencken

3. "For a while we pondered whether to take a vacation or get a divorce. We decided that a trip to Bermuda is over in two weeks, but a divorce is something you always have." —Woody Allen

4. "My parents want me to get married. They don't care who anymore, as long as he doesn't have a pierced ear; that's all they care about. I think

men who have a pierced ear are better prepared for marriage. They've experienced pain and bought jewelry." —Rita Rudner

5. "The happiest time of anyone's life is just after the first divorce." —John Kenneth Galbraith

6. Heinrich Heine bequeathed his estate to his wife on the condition that she marry again, because, according to Heine, "There will be at least one man who will regret my death."

7. "American women expect to find in their husbands a perfection that English women only hope to find in their butlers." —W. Somerset Maugham

8. "I've only slept with the men I've been married to. How many women can make that claim?" —Elizabeth Taylor

9. "Take it from me, marriage isn't a word—it's a sentence." —King Vidor

10. "Marrying a man is like buying something you've been admiring for a long time in a shop window. You may love it when you get it home, but it doesn't always go with everything else in the house." —Jean Kerr

11. "I don't think I'll get married again. I'll just find a woman I don't like and give her a house." —Lewis Grizzard

12. "The only charm of marriage is that it makes a life of deception necessary for both parties." —Oscar Wilde

13. "By all means marry; if you get a good wife, you'll be happy. If you get a bad one, you'll become a philosopher." —Socrates

14. "Marriage is neither heaven nor hell; it is simply purgatory." —Abraham Lincoln

15. "It destroys one's nerves to be amiable every day to the same human being." —Benjamin Disraeli

16. "Marriage is based on the theory that when a man discovers a brand of beer exactly to his taste he should at once throw up his job and go to work in the brewery." —George Jean Nathan

17. "We would have broken up except for the children. Who were the children? Well, she and I were." —Mort Sahl

18. "She has buried all her female friends; I wish she would make friends with my wife." —Martial

19. "Wives are people who feel they don't dance enough." —Groucho Marx

20. "A man's mother is his misfortune, but his wife is his own fault."
—Walter Bagehot

21. "My wife doesn't care what I do when I'm away, as long as I don't have
a good time." —Lee Trevino

22. "If you want to sacrifice the admiration of many men for the criticism
of one, go ahead, get married." —Katharine Hepburn

23. "Married men live longer than single men. But married men are a lot
more willing to die." —Johnny Carson

24. "Why do Jewish divorces cost so much? Because they're worth it."
—Henny Youngman

25. "Gettin' married's a lot like getting into a tub of hot water. After you
get used to it, it ain't so hot." —Minnie Pearl

26. "Sex when you're married is like going to a 7-Eleven. There's not as
much variety, but at three in the morning, it's always there." —Carol
Leifer

27. "Sex in marriage is like medicine. Three times a day for the first week.
Then once a day for another week. Then once every three or four days
until the condition clears up." —Peter De Vries

28. "My wife and I were happy for twenty years. Then we met." —Rodney
Dangerfield

29. "It is a sad fact that 50 percent of marriages in this country end in
divorce. But hey, the other half end in death. You could be one of the
lucky ones!" —Richard Jeni

30. "Only choose in marriage a woman whom you would choose as a friend
if she were a man." —Joseph Joubert

31 "Whatever you may look like, marry a man your own age—as your
beauty fades, so will his eyesight." —Phyllis Diller

32. "All men make mistakes, but those who are married find out about
them sooner." —Red Skelton

Primary source: A Curmudgeon's Garden of Love, compiled and edited by
Jon Winokur, copyright 1991 by Jon Winokur. Reprinted by permission of
the author.

Benjamin Franklin's
8 Reasons to Marry an Older Woman

1. Because they have more Knowledge of the world, and their Minds are better stored with Observations; their Conversation is more improving, and more lastingly agreeable.

2. Because when Women cease to be handsome, they study to be good. To maintain their Influence over Men, they supply the Diminution of Beauty by an Augmentation of Utility. They learn to do a thousand Services, small and great, and are the most tender and useful of all Friends when you are sick. Thus they continue amiable. And hence there is hardly such a thing to be found as an old Woman who is not a good Woman.

3. Because there is no hazard of children, which irregularly produced may be attended with much inconvenience.

4. Because through more Experience they are more prudent and discreet in conducting an Intrigue to prevent Suspicion. The Commerce with them is therefore safer with regard to your reputation; and with regard to theirs, if the Affair should happen to be known, considerate People might be rather inclined to excuse an old Woman, who would kindly take care of a young Man, form his manners by her good Councils, and prevent his ruining his Health and Fortune among mercenary Prostitutes.

5. Because in every Animal that walks upright, the Deficiency of the Fluids that fill the Muscles appears first in the highest Part. The Face first grows lank and wrinkled; then the Neck; then the Breast and Arms; the lower parts continuing to the last as plump as ever; so that covering all above with a Basket, and regarding only what is below the Girdle, it is impossible of two Women to know an old one from a young one. And as in the Dark all Cats are grey, the Pleasure of Corporal Enjoyment with an old Woman is at least equal and frequently superior; every Knack being by Practice capable of improvement.

6. Because the sin is less. The Debauching of a Virgin may be her Ruin, and make her Life unhappy.

7. Because the Compunction is less. The having made a young Girl miserable may give you frequent bitter Reflections; none of which can attend making an old Woman *happy*.

8th & lastly. They are so grateful!!!

Source: Advice to a Young Man (Philadelphia, June 25, 1745).

12 Foods Claimed to Be Aphrodisiacs

1. ASPARAGUS
   Asparagus contains a diuretic that increases the amount of urine excreted and excites the urinary passages. The vegetable is rich in potassium, phosphorus, and calcium—all necessary for maintenance of a high energy level. However, it also contains aspartic acid, which neutralizes excess amounts of ammonia in one's body and may cause apathy and sexual disinterest.

2. CAVIAR
   In addition to being nutritious (30 percent protein), caviar has been considered an aphrodisiac because of its obvious place in the reproductive process. All fish and their by-products have been linked to the myth of Aphrodite, the goddess of love who was born from the foam of the sea. Supposedly, anything that came from the sea world partook of Aphrodite's power.

3. EEL
   Eel, like most fish, is rich in phosphorus and has an excitant effect on the bladder. In addition to its general associations with the aphrodisiac effect of fish, it has probably been favored as an aphrodisiac because of its phallic appearance.

4. GARLIC
   Both Eastern and Western cultures have long regarded garlic as an aphrodisiac. The Greeks and Romans sang its praises, and oriental lovers claimed to be towers of strength because of eating it.

5. GINSENG
   The Chinese call ginseng the "elixir of life" and have used it for more than 5,000 years. Although medical opinion is sharply divided as to its merits, Russian experiments claim that ginseng increases sexual energy and has a general healing and rejuvenating influence on the body.

6. GREEN M&M'S
   Mars, the manufacturers of M&M's, have consistently denied that green M&Ms have any effect on the libido, and nobody is sure how the rumor started. However, in 1996, Mars ran a commercial cashing in on the rumor. In it, comedian Dennis Miller asks a female green M&M, "Is it true what they say about the green ones?"

7. HONEY
   Honey is highly nutritious and rich in minerals, amino acids, enzymes, and B-complex vitamins. Galen, Ovid, and Sheikh Nefzawi, author of

The Perfumed Garden, believed that honey has outstanding aphrodisiac powers.

8. LOBSTER
The lobster has been described as an amatory excitant by many writers, including Henry Fielding in *Tom Jones*. In addition, it shares the Aphrodite-derived power attributed to all seafood.

9. OYSTERS
Oysters are one of the most renowned aphrodisiac foods. Like other seafoods, they are rich in phosphorus. Although they are not a high source of energy, they are easily digestible. Among the eminent lovers who have vouched for oysters was Casanova, who called them "a spur to the spirit and to love."

10. PEACHES
"Venus owns this tree . . . the fruit provokes lust . . . ," wrote herbalist Nicholas Culpeper. The Chinese considered the fruit's sweet juices symbolic of the effluvia of the vagina, and both Chinese and Arabs regard its deep fur-edged cleft as symbolic of the female genitalia. A "peach house" was once a common English slang term for a house of prostitution, and the term "peach" has been used almost universally to describe a pretty or sexually appealing girl.

11. TOMATOES
When they were first brought from South America to Europe, tomatoes were thought to be the forbidden fruit of Eden. They were also celebrated as a sexual stimulant and nicknamed "love apples."

12. TRUFFLES
Truffles, the expensive underground fungi, are similar to oysters in that they are composed mostly of water and are rich in protein. Rabelais, Casanova, George Sand, Sade, Napoleon, and Mme. Pompadour are a few of the many notables who have praised the truffle's aphrodisiac powers. An ancient French proverb warns: "Those who wish to lead virtuous lives should abstain from truffles."

R.H.

22 Memorable Kisses

1. THE KISS OF LIFE
It was a kiss from God that infused the "spirit of life" into man, according to the account of Genesis (2:7). God is said to have formed Adam from slime and dust and then breathed a rational soul into him. This

concept of divine insufflation, which surfaces frequently in religious teachings, is often viewed through the kiss metaphor.

2. THE BETRAYAL KISS OF JUDAS (c. 29 AD)
   As told in the New Testament, Judas Iscariot used the kiss as a tool of betrayal when he embraced Jesus Christ in the Garden of Gethsemane. Jewish leaders under the high priest Caiaphas had paid Judas 30 pieces of silver to identify Jesus. With a kiss, Judas singled him out. Jesus was arrested, charged with blasphemy, and condemned to death.

3. THE KISS THAT AWAKENED SLEEPING BEAUTY (17th century)
   In the classic fairy tale *Sleeping Beauty*, it is with a kiss that the handsome prince awakens the enchanted princess. This kiss first appeared in Charles Perrault's version of 1697, "La Belle au bois dormant." But in fact, *Sleeping Beauty* dates back to two earlier romances, *Perceforest* and *Pentamerone*. In those stories, the handsome prince finds the sleeping beauty, falls in love with her, rapes her, and leaves.

4. THE KISS THAT COST THOMAS SAVERLAND HIS NOSE (1837)
   At the dawn of the Victorian Era in Great Britain, Thomas Saverland attempted to kiss Caroline Newton in a lighthearted manner. Rejecting his pass, Miss Newton not so lightheartedly bit off part of his nose. Saverland took Newton to court, but she was acquitted. "When a man kisses a woman against her will," ruled the judge, "she is fully entitled to bite his nose, if she so pleases." "And eat it up," added a barrister.

5. *THE KISS* BY FRANÇOIS AUGUSTE RODIN (1886)
   One of the most renowned pieces of sculpture in the Western world is *The Kiss*, sculpted by French artist François Auguste Rodin in 1886. Inspired by Dante, the figure of two nude lovers kissing brought the era of classical art to an end. Rodin described *The Kiss* as "complete in itself and artificially set apart from the surrounding world."

6. THE FIRST KISS RECORDED ON FILM (1896)
   The first kiss ever to be recorded in a motion picture occurred in Thomas Edison's film *The Kiss* between actor John C. Rice and actress May Irwin in April 1896. Adapted from a short scene in the Broadway comedy *The Widow Jones*, *The Kiss* was filmed by Raff and Gammon for nickelodeon audiences. Its running time was less than 30 seconds.

7. THE MOST OFTEN KISSED STATUE IN HISTORY (late 1800s)
   The figure of Guidarello Guidarelli, a fearless sixteenth-century Italian soldier, was sculpted in marble by Tullio Lombardo (c. 1455–1532) and put on display at the Academy of Fine Arts in Ravenna, Italy. During the late 1800s, a rumor started that any woman who kissed the

reclining, armor-clad statue would marry a wonderful gentleman and settle down with him. More than five million superstitious women have since kissed Guidarelli's cold marble lips. Consequently, the soldier's mouth has acquired a faint reddish glow.

8. **THE MOVIE WITH 191 KISSES (1926)**
In 1926, Warner Brothers Studios starred John Barrymore in *Don Juan*. During the course of the film (2 hours 47 minutes), the amorous adventurer bestows a total of 191 kisses on a number of beautiful senoritas—an average of one every 53 seconds.

9. **THE LONGEST KISS ON FILM (1941)**
The longest kiss in motion picture history is between Jane Wyman and Regis Toomey in the 1941 production of *You're in the Army Now*. The Lewis Seiler comedy about two vacuum cleaner salesmen features a scene in which Toomey and Wyman hold a single kiss for 3 minutes and 5 seconds (or 4 percent of the film's running time).

10. **THE VJ-DAY KISS (1945)**
When the news of Japan's surrender was announced in New York City's Times Square on August 14, 1945, *Life* photojournalist Alfred Eisenstaedt photographed a jubilant sailor clutching a nurse in a back-bending passionate kiss to express his joy. The picture became an icon of the cathartic celebration that erupted over the end of the war. Over the years, at least three nurses and ten sailors have claimed to be the people in the photo. Since Eisenstaedt had lost his notes and negatives by the time the claimants came forward, he was never able to say definitively who was in the photo.

11. **THE KISS AT L'HOTEL DE VILLE (1950)**
A famous 1950 photograph of a young couple kissing on the streets of Paris—"Le Baiser de l'Hotel de Ville"—found itself under an international media spotlight when, four decades after the picture was taken, the photo became a commercial success, drawing out of the woodwork dozens of people who claimed to have been the photo's unidentified kissers. The black-and-white snapshot—originally taken for *Life* magazine by Robert Doisneau as part of his series on the Parisian working class—made Doisneau wealthy when, between 1986 and 1992, it became a best seller through poster and postcard reprints. Among those who subsequently identified themselves as the kissers were Denise and Jean-Louis Lavergne, who sued Doisneau for $100,000 after he rejected their claim. They lost their case when it was determined, in 1993, that the kissers were actually two professional models (and real-life lovers), Françoise Bornet and Jacques Cartaud.

12. **THE FIRST INTERRACIAL KISS ON U.S. TELEVISION (1968)**
NBC's *Star Trek* was the first program to show a white man kissing a black woman. In the episode "Plato's Children," aliens with psychic powers force Captain Kirk (William Shatner) to kiss Lieutenant Uhura (Nichelle Nichols).

13. **THE MAJORCA, SPAIN, KISS-IN (1969)**
In 1969, an effort was made to crack down on young lovers who were smooching in public in the town of Inca on the island of Majorca. When the police chief began handing out citations that cost offenders 500 pesetas per kiss, a group of 30 couples protested by staging a kiss-in at the harbor at Cala Figuera. Following a massive roundup by police, the amorous rebels were fined 45,000 pesetas for their defiant smooching and then released.

14. **THE HOMOSEXUAL KISS IN *SUNDAY BLOODY SUNDAY* (1971)**
One cinema kiss that turned heads among the movie-going public was between two male actors, Peter Finch and Murray Head, in the 1971 film *Sunday Bloody Sunday*. The British tale of a bisexual love triangle included a medium close-up shot of this kiss in a scene originally planned to have featured only an embrace from afar. Director John Schlesinger commented that Finch and Head "were certainly less shocked by the kiss than the technicians on the set were. When Finch was asked about the scene by somebody on TV, he said, 'I did it for England.'"

15. **THE KISS OF HUMILITY (1975)**
In an unprecedented gesture of humility, Pope Paul VI kissed the feet of Metropolitan Meliton of Chalcedon, envoy of Patriarch Demetrios I, who was head of the Eastern Orthodox Church, during a Mass at the Sistine Chapel in Rome in 1975. The two men were commemorating the tenth anniversary of the lifting of excommunications that the churches of Constantinople and Rome had conferred on each other during the eleventh century. Taken aback by the pontiff's dramatic action, Meliton attempted to kiss the pope's feet in return but was kept from doing so by Paul. Meliton kissed the pope's hand, instead.

16. **THE KISS THAT DIDN'T HAPPEN (1975)**
King Faisal of Saudi Arabia was beginning a meeting with the Kuwait oil minister when the king's nephew, Prince Faisal ibn Mussa'id Abdel Aziz, slipped into the office unannounced. The king stood and, assuming that the prince wished to offer him holy greetings for Mohammed's birthday, lowered his head and waited for the traditional kiss. It never arrived. Instead, the prince fired a bullet into the king's head and another into his neck, killing him.

17. **THE KISS THAT COST $1,260 (1977)**
Ruth van Herpen visited an art museum in Oxford, England, in 1977 and kissed a painting by American artist Jo Baer, leaving red lipstick stains on the $18,000 work. Restoration costs were reported to be as much as $1,260. Appearing in court, van Herpen explained, "I only kissed it to cheer it up. It looked so cold."

18. **THE KISSED THAT CAUSED A CENSORSHIP DEBATE (1978)**
The first kiss to reach the movie screen in India was between actor Shashi Kapoor and actress Zeenat Aman in the 1978 Indian film *Love Sublime*. This landmark kiss, a product of new film guidelines, triggered a nationwide debate over censorship. Kapoor felt that the increased creative freedom would only add logic to Indian love stories and result in less cinema violence. Chief minister and film actor M. G. Ramachandran called for a mass protest, labeling the kissing scenes "an insult."

19. **THE FIRST LESBIAN KISS ON AMERICAN COMMERCIAL TELEVISION (1991)**
The first visible kiss between two women on an American network television series took place in 1991 on the show *L.A. Law* when Michelle Greene kissed Amanda Donohoe. However, it was a later kiss, on the March 1, 1994, ABC-TV broadcast of the situation comedy *Roseanne* that caused a sensation. In a controversial scene well publicized in the press, guest star Mariel Hemingway kissed series star Roseanne Arnold on the mouth. The kiss occurred in a "gay bar" setting, and Hemingway portrayed a lesbian stripper whose kiss caused Roseanne to question her own sensibilities. The episode (whose script originally included a second kiss between two other women) became the subject of much high-profile bickering between ABC executives and series producers Tom and Roseanne Arnold during the weeks before it aired. Up to the eleventh hour, inclusion of the kiss appeared to remain in question, prompting protests by gay rights organizations. ABC finally let the kiss happen, but added a viewer warning at the start of the episode.

20. **THE SEXUAL HARASSMENT KISS (1996)**
Six-year-old Johnathan Prevette, a first grader at Southwest Elementary School in Lexington, North Carolina, kissed a classmate on the cheek. A teacher saw the September 19, 1996, incident and reported it to the school principal, Lisa Horne, who punished Johnathan by keeping him from attending an ice cream party and ordering him to spend a day in a disciplinary program. But Johnathan's mother called a local radio talk show, word of the incident spread, and within six months the U.S. Department of Education had rewritten its sexual harassment guidelines to omit kisses by first graders. For the record, Johnathan said that the girl had asked him for a kiss.

21. THE MTV CELEBRITY KISSFEST (2003)

For the opening number of the 2003 MTV Video Music Awards, Britney Spears and Christina Aguilera sang Madonna's 1984 hit "Like a Virgin" while wearing white wedding gowns. As the music segued into Madonna's latest hit, "Hollywood," Madonna stepped out of a wedding cake wearing a tuxedo. What followed was a drag show of sorts with Madonna playing the groom and Britney and Christina the virginal brides. The performance climaxed with a French kiss between Madonna and Britney and then between Madonna and Christina. The kisses overshadowed the awards themselves and were front-page news around the world.

22. BIG BROTHER IN BAHRAIN (2004)

In 2004, Bahrain-based MBC-TV attempted to introduce a Middle Eastern version of the voyeuristic reality show *Big Brother* to Arabic-speaking audiences. A few minutes into the first episode, Abdel Hakim of Saudi Arabia kissed Kawthar of Tunisia. This ran so counter to cultural tradition that public protests broke out and the show was canceled after only two weeks.

D.B.

6 Positions for Sexual Intercourse—In Order of Popularity

Gershon Legman, an American who wrote about sex, calculated that there are more than four million possible ways for men and women to have sexual intercourse with each other. Most of these "postures," as he called them, are probably variations on the six main positions that Alfred C. Kinsey used as categories in the questionnaires on sexual habits that were the basis for his *Kinsey Report*s in 1948 and 1953.

The *Kama Sutra*, a Hindu love manual written sometime between 300 and 540 AD, lists many imaginative and acrobatic variations on these positions—for example, the Bamboo Cleft, the Crab, the Wild Boar; some *Kama Sutra* experts suggest that people try out difficult positions in the water first. Chinese pillow books, written more than 400 years ago, show more feasible positions with titles like Two Dragons Exhausted by Battle and name the parts of the body equally poetically—the penis is called the Jade Stem and the clitoris, the Pearl on the Jade Step.

According to these sources, interpretations of ancient art, and anthropological studies, humans have changed their preference rankings of sexual positions—the "missionary" (man-on-top) position, overwhelmingly the number one choice of the Americans Kinsey studied, was not that high on the lists of ancient Greeks and Romans, primitive tribes, and many other groups.

The advantages and disadvantages of each position are taken from Albert Ellis's *The Art and Science of Love* and from *Human Sexual Inadequacy* by William H. Masters and Virginia E. Johnson.

1. MAN ON TOP

   To many people this is the only position considered biologically "natural," though other primates use the rear-entry position almost exclusively. Called the "missionary" position because it was introduced to native converts—who liked to make fun of it—by Christian missionaries who regarded other positions as sinful.

   Advantages: Allows face-to-face intimacy, deep thrusting by male, pace setting by male.

   Disadvantages: Does not allow good control for the premature ejaculator, or freedom of movement for the woman.

   Chances for conception: Good.

2. WOMAN ON TOP

   Shown in ancient art as most common position in Ur, Greece, Rome, Peru, India, China, and Japan. Roman poet Martial portrayed Hector and Andromache in this position. Generally avoided by those at lower educational levels, according to Kinsey, because it *seems* to make the man less masculine, the woman less feminine.

   Advantages: Allows freedom of movement for women, control for premature ejaculators, caressing of female by male. Most often results in orgasm for women. Good when the man is tired.

   Disadvantage: Too acrobatic for some women.

   Chances for conception: Not good.

3. SIDE BY SIDE

   From Ovid, a poet of ancient Rome: "Of love's thousand ways, a simple way and with the least labor, this is: to lie on the right side, and half supine withal."

   Advantages: Allows manipulation of clitoris, freedom of movement for man and woman. Good for tired or convalescent people and premature ejaculators, as well as pregnant women.

   Disadvantage: Does not allow easy entry.

   Chances for conception: Okay.

4. REAR ENTRANCE

   Frequently used by 15 percent of married women. Favored by primates and early Greeks. Rejected by many Americans because of its "animal origins" and lack of face-to-face intimacy.

   Advantages: Allows manual stimulation of clitoris. Exciting for men who are turned on by female buttocks. Good for pregnant women, males with small penises, women with large vaginas.

Disadvantages: Does not allow easy entry or face-to-face intimacy. Penis tends to fall out.

Chances for conception: Good.

5. SITTING

According to Kinsey, learned by many while "making out" in backseats of cars.

Advantages: Allows clitoral contact with male body, free movement, intimacy. Good for male who wants to hold off orgasm, pregnant women.

Disadvantages: Does not allow vigorous thrusting. Sometimes tiring. Penetration may be too deep.

Chances for conception: Poor

6. STANDING

Has echoes of a "quickie" against alley wall with prostitute, therefore exciting. Indian lotus position: Each stands on one leg, wraps other around partner.

Advantages: Allows caressing. Exciting, can flow from dancing, taking shower.

Disadvantages: Does not allow much thrusting. Entry difficult, particularly when one partner is taller than the other. Tiring. Not good for pregnant women.

Chances for conception: Poor.

A.E.

Members of Society:
Preserved Sex Organs of 5 Famous Men

1. GENERAL KANG PING

In the time of the Ming dynasty, when Emperor Yung Lo ruled China (1402–1424), his best friend and favorite military leader was General Kang Ping. Forced to leave the capital for a journey to another city, the emperor left Kang Ping in charge of protecting his palace and the beautiful women of his harem who lived inside. Since Kang Ping knew that the mercurial emperor might worry about the faithfulness of his harem concubines and the loyalty of his army staff, he decided he must anticipate any future accusations of disloyalty. The paranoid emperor went off on his travels, and when he returned to the capital he immediately accused Kang Ping of seducing several of his concubines. The general denied the accusation and said he could prove his loyalty. He pointed to the saddle horse the emperor had used on the journey and asked the emperor to look in the hollow of the saddle. The emperor

looked, and there he found Kang Ping's penis. The general had castrated himself, preserved his penis, and secretly sent it off with his
ruler so that he would later be able to prove his loyalty. So moved was
the emperor by his friend's gesture that he elevated him to chief
eunuch, and upon Kang Ping's death had a temple built to him and
venerated him as patron saint of all eunuchs.

2. NAPOLEON BONAPARTE

When the exiled former emperor of France died of stomach cancer on
May 5, 1821, on the remote island of St. Helena, a postmortem was held.
According to Dr. C. MacLaurin, "His reproductive organs were small and
apparently atrophied. He is said to have been impotent for some time
before he died." A priest in attendance obtained Napoleon's penis. After a
secret odyssey of 150 years, the severed penis turned up at Christie's Fine
Art Auctioneers in London around 1971. The one-inch penis, resembling a
tiny sea horse, an attendant said, was described by the auction house as "a
small dried-up object." It was put on sale for £13,300, then withdrawn
from bidding. Shortly afterward, the emperor's sex organ (along with bits
of his hair and beard) was offered for sale in Flayderman's Mail Order
Catalogue. There were no buyers. In 1977, Napoleon's penis was sold to an
American urologist for about $3,800. Today, Napoleon's body rests in the
crypt at the Invalides, Paris—sans penis.

3. GRIGORY RASPUTIN

In 1968, in the St. Denis section of Paris, an elderly White Russian
female émigré, a former maid in czarist St. Petersburg and later a
follower and lover of the Russian holy man Rasputin, kept a polished
wooden box, 18 by 6 inchs in size, atop her bedroom bureau. Inside the
box lay Rasputin's penis. It "looked like a blackened, overripe banana,
about a foot long, and resting on a velvet cloth," reported Rasputin
biographer Patte Barham. In life, this penis, wrote Rasputin's daughter
Maria, measured "a good 13 inches when fully erect." According to
Maria's account, in 1916, when Prince Felix Yussupov and his fellow
assassins attacked Rasputin, Yussupov first raped him, and then fired a
bullet into his head, wounding him. As Rasputin fell, another young
nobleman pulled out a dagger and "castrated Grigory Rasputin, flinging
the severed penis across the room." One of Yussupov's servants, a
relative of Rasputin's lover, recovered the penis and turned the severed
organ over to the maid. She fled to Paris with it.

4. JOHN DILLINGER

One of the controversial legends of the twentieth century concerns the
disposition of bank robber and badman John Dillinger's private parts.
When Dillinger was shot to death by the FBI in front of a Chicago
movie theater in 1934, his corpse was taken to the morgue for dissection
by forensic pathologists. That was where the legend began. The

gangster's penis—reported as 14 inches flaccid, 20 inches erect—was supposedly amputated by an overenthusiastic pathologist. Despite rumors to the contrary, Dillinger's penis is not in the collection of the Smithsonian Institution.

5. ISHIDA KICHIZO
Kichizo was a well-known Tokyo gangster, and his mistress was a young Japanese geisha named Abe Sada. They were involved in a long, passionate, sadomasochistic love affair. He enjoyed having her try to strangle him with a sash cord as she mounted him. Kichizo could make love to Abe Sada only at intervals, because he was married and had children. She could not stand their separations. He offered to set her up in a teahouse and drop in on her once in a while. She suggested they run away together or commit suicide together. On the night of May 18, 1936, fearing he was going to leave her forever, she started to play their strangling game with her pajama cord, then really strangled him until he was dead. Now she wouldn't have to share him with anyone. Yet she wanted to possess part of him. Taking a butcher knife, she cut off Kichizo's penis and testicles, wrapped them in his jacket, and placed the bundle in a loincloth she tied around her kimono. She then fled her geisha house and took hotel rooms, fondling Kichizo's penis and pressing it against her body constantly. Eventually, the police caught her and confiscated the penis she had been preserving. She was tried for her crime, found guilty, and sentenced to jail. She languished in prison for eight years, all through World War II, until the American army of occupation moved into Tokyo. The Americans released all Japanese political prisoners—including Abe Sada by mistake. In 1947, an "aging but vivacious" Abe Sada owned a bar near Tokyo's Sumida River. A sensational film, *In the Realm of the Senses* (1976), was made about the affair, which made Abe and Kichizo—and his penis—legend in Japan.

I.W.

Rudolph Valentino's 10 Attributes of the Perfect Woman

Idolized as the great lover of the screen in the 1920s, Rudolph Valentino starred in such romantic epics as *The Sheik, Blood and Sand,* and *The Eagle.* His death in 1926 caused worldwide hysteria, several suicides, and riots at his funeral. Each year, on the anniversary of his death, hundreds of the faithful gather at his burial site to pay tribute.

1. Fidelity
2. The recognition of the supreme importance of love
3. Intelligence

4. Beauty
5. A sense of humor
6. Sincerity
7. An appreciation of good food
8. A serious interest in some art, trade, or hobby
9. An old-fashioned and wholehearted acceptance of monogamy
10. Courage

Source: Cleveland Amory, *Vanity Fair.* Copyright 1926, 1954 by The Conde Nast Publications Inc.

13 Mothers of Infamous Children

1. AGRIPPINA, THE YOUNGER (mother of NERO, monstrous Roman emperor)
Raised by her grandmother, Agrippina was accused of having had incestuous relations with her brother Caligula. Lucius Domitius Ahenobarbus (later called Nero) was the product of her first marriage. She was believed to have poisoned her second husband before embarking upon a third marriage, which was to her uncle, Emperor Claudius I. She held such sway over Claudius that she convinced him to set aside his own son and make her son Nero heir to the throne. When Nero was 16, she poisoned Claudius, thus setting the stage for Nero to be proclaimed emperor. Resentful of his mother's continuing interference, Nero later arranged to have her assassinated.

2. HANNAH WATERMAN ARNOLD (mother of BENEDICT ARNOLD, American traitor in Revolutionary War)
Hannah belonged to a prominent family, and when, as a young widow, she married Benedict Arnold III, she brought with her considerable wealth inherited from her first husband. Unfortunately, her new husband squandered this fortune, and as his ineptitude increased, Hannah assumed a dominant position in the household. She achieved a reputation as a long-suffering, pious woman, and she was pitied by her neighbors. When her young son, Benedict Arnold IV, was sent away to school, she wrote him long letters advising him as to proper Christian behavior. Hannah lost five of her seven children in a yellow fever epidemic, and thereafter she was obsessed by fears of death. She continually exhorted young Benedict and his sister to submit to God's will and urged them to be prepared to die at any moment. Hannah herself died when her son Benedict was 18.

3. MARY ANN HOLMES BOOTH (mother of JOHN WILKES BOOTH, assassin of Abraham Lincoln)

Eighteen-year-old Mary Ann was a London flower girl when she met Junius Brutus Booth, a talented but dissolute tragedian. Already legally married, Junius fell madly in love with the gentle, warmhearted Mary Ann. In 1821, he accompanied her to the United States. Eventually, she bore him 10 children; John Wilkes was her ninth and favorite child. Although she was acknowledged as his wife in America, Mary Ann's existence was kept secret from Junius's legal wife in England. However, in 1846 his double life was exposed, and in 1851 he obtained a divorce and at last wed Mary Ann. John Wilkes was devoted to his mother, and it is reputed that his dying words after he had assassinated Abraham Lincoln were "Tell Mother . . . tell Mother . . . I died for my country."

4. BARBARA BUSH (mother of GEORGE W. BUSH, president of the United States)
Born on June 8, 1925, Barbara Pierce grew up in Rye, New York, a wealthy suburb of New York City. Her father was an executive in the publishing industry. When Barbara was 16 years old, she met George Bush at a country club dance. Three years later, she dropped out of Smith College so that they could marry. While her husband pursued a career in the oil industry and eventually entered politics, Barbara gave birth to six children, of whom George W. was the oldest. (A daughter, Robin, died of leukemia at the age of four.) George W. was not a perfect son. Saddled with a serious alcohol problem until the age of 40, he was arrested at least three times, once for stealing a wreath, once for public rowdiness at a Yale-Princeton football game, and once, when he was 30 years old, for driving under the influence of alcohol. As First Lady of the United States, Barbara Bush worked hard to promote literacy programs.

5. TERESA CAPONE (mother of AL CAPONE, U.S. gangster)
Born in Italy, Teresa immigrated with her husband to New York City, in 1893, where she worked as a seamstress to help support her family in Brooklyn's Italian colony. Alfonso, her fourth son, was forced to take over as head of the household when his father died in 1920. By that time, Al had already begun to establish his underworld connections. Later, during the periods when he was imprisoned, Teresa visited him regularly and she always maintained, "Al's a good boy."

6. MARIE ÉLÉNORE MAILLÉ DE CARMAN (mother of the MARQUIS DE SADE, noted debauchee and author)
Marie Élénore, lady-in-waiting in a royal family related to the de Sades, married the Count de Sade in 1733 and gave birth to a son, the future Marquis de Sade, in 1740. By 1750, the count had become increasingly difficult to live with, and as a result Marie Élénore removed herself to a Carmelite convent in Paris, where she remained until her death in 1777. Despite her pleas to the king, her son was imprisoned numerous times for his debauchery. Upon hearing of his mother's impending

death, he escaped from prison and hurried to Paris. Unfortunately, he arrived too late and was rearrested through the efforts of his mother-in-law. During his subsequent 13 years in prison, the marquis wrote the books that made him infamous.

7. **VANNOZZA DEI CATTANEI** (mother of CESARE BORGIA, ruthless Renaissance politician)
Vannozza was the mistress of Cardinal Rodrigo Borgia (who later became Pope Alexander VI) and bore him at least four children, of whom Cesare was reputedly the first. During the course of her life Vannozza also had four husbands, the last one hand-picked by the pope. Always known for her piety, by the time of her death in 1518, she had left so much money to the church where she was buried that Augustine monks were still saying masses for her soul 200 years later.

8. **EKATERINA GELADZE DZHUGASHVILI** (mother of JOSEPH STALIN, dictator of USSR)
Born in 1856 in a Georgian village, Ekaterina was the daughter of serfs. After her marriage to Beso Dzhugashvili, she supported her new family by working as a washerwoman and seamstress. When her son Joseph was born, she hoped he would become a priest, and throughout her life she was disappointed at his choice of a different career. Ekaterina never learned to speak Russian, and even after her son's rise to power, she had no desire to leave her home in the Caucasus.

9. **ALIA GHANEM** (mother of OSAMA BIN LADEN, Saudi terrorist leader of al-Qaeda)
The daughter of a Syrian merchant, Alia Ghanem married Mohammed bin Laden, a prominent Saudi citizen of Yemeni origin, when she was 22 years old. Having experienced a more worldly society, she did not fit in to the bin Laden family and was known sarcastically as "the Slave." Osama, who was mockingly called "the Son of the Slave," was her only child by bin Laden. Pushed to the outskirts of the bin Laden clan, Alia had to watch as her son was raised by others. Mohammed died when Osama was 10 years old, and it was only then that he was sent to live with his mother. They lived together for only a few months, after which Osama went back to live with an uncle. Alia Ghanem later married another Saudi businessman, but she remained in contact with her son.

10. **KLARA PÖLZL HITLER** (mother of ADOLF HITLER, Nazi dictator)
A simple, uneducated Bavarian girl, 18-year-old Klara joined the household of her second cousin, "Uncle" Alois Hitler, whose mistress she became and whom she eventually married. Three of her children died in infancy prior to the birth of Adolf, and Klara was always fearful of his death, as well. Disappointed in her marriage, she pinned all hopes

on her surviving son. When she died of breast cancer in 1908, Hitler was overcome with grief.

11. **ZERELDA COLE JAMES** (mother of JESSE JAMES, U.S. bandit)
Married at the age of 17, Zerelda went west with her husband, Robert, to homestead in Missouri in the early 1840s. Jesse was their second son. The elder James died while Jesse was still a boy, and Zerelda then married a man named Simms. That marriage failed, and she embarked upon a third marriage, to Dr. Reuben Samuels. Throughout the bank-robbing careers of Jesse and his younger brother Frank, Zerelda remained loyal to her sons. A pious woman, she would often attend church in Jesse's company. She was described by a newspaper reporter who interviewed her in later years as "graceful in carriage and gesture, calm and quiet in demeanor, with a ripple of fire now and then break-ing through the placid surface." Perhaps it was that fire that she had imparted to her sons.

12. **SUBHA TULFAH AL-MUSSALLAT** (mother of SADDAM HUSSEIN, dictator of Iraq)
Subha's husband, Hussein al-Majid, either died or abandoned the family before Saddam's birth. Subha considered having an abortion, but was talked out of it by a midwife. She gave birth to Saddam in a mud-brick house outside of Tikrit belonging to her brother, Khairallah al-Talfa. Subha, in a deep depression, could not take care of her newborn son, so she left him with Khairallah. Saddam did not live with his mother until he was three years old, when Khairaillah was impris-oned for taking part in an anti-British, pro-Nazi uprising. By this time, Subha had married her first cousin, Hassan al-Ibrahim, known as "Hassan the Liar." Hassan refused to send his stepson to school and forced him to steal chickens and sheep. At age 10, Saddam, wanting to go to school and fed up with his stepfather's abuse, ran away from home to live with his uncle Khairallah. Despite her indifferent parenting, when Subha died in 1982, her son ordered a huge shrine built in Tikrit at government expense to honor the "Mother of Militants."

13. **ROSA MALTONI MUSSOLINI** (mother of BENITO MUSSOLINI, Italian dictator)
Born in a small Italian village in 1858, Rosa Maltoni was known for her retiring and gentle disposition. While employed as a schoolteacher in the village of Dovia, she met and married the village blacksmith, Alessandro Mussolini. Benito, their first child, was constantly in trouble and the source of much anxiety to Rosa. She was worn out and dis-heartened when she died of meningitis in 1905.

F.B. & D.W.

Dear Abby Readers'
10 Most Unusual Problems

Dear Abby, aka Jeanne Phillips, is the most widely syndicated newspaper columnist in any genre in the world. Dear Abby commands a client list of about 1,4000 newspapers worldwide, with a daily readership of more than 110 million people.

The Dear Abby column was founded in 1956 by Jeanne's mother, Pauline Phillips. From the age of 14, to earn her allowance, Jeanne worked for her mother, helping to answer letters from young people. In the years that followed, Jeanne edited and then cowrote the column before assuming all the writing responsibilities in 1987.

In 2002, the Phillips family made the sad announcement that Pauline had Alzheimer's disease. At that time, Jeanne took over the complete role of Dear Abby, adopting the pen name of Abigail Van Buren. Since the announcement about her mother, Jeanne has stepped forward to play an important advocacy role for the Alzheimer's Association.

1. "I'm a bus driver and want some information on how to become a shepherd."

2. "I want to have a child but don't even have a boyfriend. Can you line me up with somebody?

3. "I hear there is life after death. If that is true, can you put me in touch with my Uncle LeRoy Albert from Victoria, Texas?"

4. "Will you please send me all the information you have on the rhythm method? I'm learning how to dance."

5. "I'm a 50-year-old widow and my doctor says I need a husband or the equivalent. Would it be all right?

6. "My husband burns the hair out of his nose with a lighted match. And he thinks I'm crazy because I voted for Goldwater."

7. "I can't trust my husband. He cheats so much I'm not even sure my last baby is HIS."

8. "I've been married only three months, and ever since our honeymoon our sex life has become anonymous."

9. "Is it okay for the mother-in-law of the bride to give her a shower? She could sure USE one!"

10. "I heard there's a sex revolution going on. Can you tell me where it is and how to get there?"

Ann Landers Readers'
10 Most Unusual Problems

One of the best-known and most popular newspaper advice columnists in the history of journalism, Ann Landers (born Esther Pauline Friedman in Sioux City, Iowa) began writing her column for the *Chicago Sun-Times* in 1955 after winning a contest to replace the original Ann Landers, who had died. Her twin sister, Pauline Esther Friedman Phillips, also became an advice columnist, writing "Dear Abby" under the name Abigail Van Buren. Landers died of bone marrow cancer on June 22, 2002, at the age of 83. She contributed the following list to *The Book of Lists* in 1977:

1. The man who hid his wife's dentures so she couldn't go out and vote for a Democrat.

2. The bride who phoned her mother on her honeymoon to say she was on her way home. Her husband was a mortician and confessed that he could enjoy sex only with women who were dead or pretended to be. He instructed her to lie in a bathtub filled with very cold water for at least 20 minutes, then come to bed and pretend she was dead.

3. The man who wanted to be buried in his 1939 Dodge.

4. The man who was unable to urinate in public bathrooms.

5. The girl who had a leg crippled by polio and wanted to have it amputated and replaced by an artificial limb so she wouldn't limp at her wedding.

6. The woman who wrote to inquire about who owned the walnuts from the tree that grew on her property but very close to the neighbor's property. Most of the nuts were falling on the neighbor's property, and she felt that since it was her tree that produced the nuts, she was entitled to them. (Answer: The neighbor could use the nuts that fell on her property, but couldn't sell them.)

7. The woman whose husband was going to have a transsexual operation. She wanted to know what the children should call their father after the operation. "Daddy" didn't seem appropriate for a "woman." (Answer: They can call him "Bob" or "Bill" or whatever he changes his name to—probably "Mary" or "Sue.")

8. The totally bald woman who used to remove her wig at poker games and place it on her chips for luck.

9. The man who kept a pig in his apartment and insisted the pig was a wonderful "watchdog." The neighbors complained.

10. The woman who did her housework in the nude and enjoyed it thoroughly until one day she went to the basement to do her laundry and was surprised by the meter man.

CHAPTER TEN

Crime

33 STUPID THIEVES AND 3 DISHONORABLE MENTIONS

20 UNDERWORLD NICKNAMES

11 POSSIBLE ALTERNATIVE GUNMEN IN
THE ASSASSINATION OF JOHN F. KENNEDY

10 DEFENDANTS FROM HISTORY ALAN DERSHOWITZ
WOULD LIKE TO HAVE DEFENDED

19 INNOCENT AMERICANS WHO
WERE ALMOST EXECUTED

22 UNUSUAL STOLEN OBJECTS

CLIFFORD IRVING'S 10 BEST FORGERS OF ALL TIME

ABBIE HOFFMAN'S 10 HEROES WHO GOT AWAY WITH IT

38 UNUSUAL LAWSUITS

WHAT 12 FAMOUS OR INFAMOUS PEOPLE
WERE DOING WHEN ARRESTED

8 CREATIVE LEGAL DEFENSES

10 TRIAL VERDICTS THAT CAUSED RIOTS

22 CASES OF ANIMALS AND INSECTS
BROUGHT BEFORE THE LAW

WITTICISMS OF 9 CONDEMNED CRIMINALS

**MAFIA BOSS JOSEPH AIUPPA—
IRONICALLY THEY CALLED HIM "HA HA"**

33 Stupid Thieves and
3 Dishonorable Mentions

1. SHOWING OFF HIS BOOTY
   Charles Taylor of Wichita, Kansas, was arrested for robbing a shoe
   store at knifepoint and stealing a $69 pair of size 10½ tan hiking boots
   on December 18, 1996. At his trial three months later, Taylor arro-
   gantly rested his feet on the defense table. He was wearing a pair of size
   10½ tan hiking boots. The judge, James Fleetwood, was incredulous. "I
   leaned over and stared," he later said. "Surely nobody would be so
   stupid as to wear the boots he stole to his trial." But it turned out that
   one person was that stupid. Taylor was convicted of aggravated robbery and sent back to jail in his stocking feet.

2. WRONG PLACE, WRONG TIME
   On November 29, 1978, David Goodhall and two female accomplices
   entered a home supplies shop in Barnsley, South Yorkshire, intending
   to engage in a bit of shoplifting. After stuffing a pair of curtains into a
   plastic carrier bag, the threesome attempted to leave by separate exits.
   However, they were apprehended immediately by several store detectives. Goodhall and his cohorts had failed to notice that the shop, at
   that very moment, was hosting a convention of store detectives.

3. DOUBLE-SEXED FORGER
   Houston pawnbroker Ted Kipperman knew something was wrong when a
   man entered his store on April 8, 1982, and attempted to cash a $789 tax-
   refund check, claiming his name was "Ernestine and Robert Hayes." He
   explained that his mother had expected twins. When only one child
   showed up, she gave him both names. Kipperman took the stolen check
   and the makeshift ID and then told the man that the police had just come
   by looking for the check, which caused the would-be customer to flee.
   Kipperman located the real Ernestine and Robert Hayes, a couple who
   lived in southeastern Houston, and gave them back their tax-refund check.

4. CHECKING OUT
   Eighteen-year-old Charles A. Meriweather broke into a home in
   northwest Baltimore on the night of November 22–23, 1978, raped the
   woman who lived there, and then ransacked the house. When he
   discovered she had only $11.50 in cash, he asked her, "How do you pay
   your bills?"
   She replied, "By check," and he ordered her to write out a check
   for $30. Then he changed his mind and upped it to $50.
   "Who shall I make it out to?" asked the woman, a 34-year-old
   government employee.

"Charles A. Meriweather," said Charles A. Meriweather, adding, "It better not bounce, or I'll be back."

Meriweather was arrested several hours later.

5. SELF-INFLICTED CAPITAL PUNISHMENT

On August 7, 1975, John Anthony Gibbs, described by witnesses as "very nervous," entered a restaurant in Newport, Rhode Island, flashed a gun, and demanded cash. After collecting $400, he put the money in a bag and tried to stuff the bag into his shirt pocket. Unfortunately, he was holding his gun in the same hand as the bag. The gun went off under his chin and Gibbs, 22, was killed instantly.

6. JUST REWARD

Every night, Mrs. Hollis Sharpe of Los Angeles took her miniature poodle, Jonathan, out for a walk so that he could do his duty. A responsible and considerate citizen, Mrs. Sharpe always brought along with her a newspaper and a plastic bag to clean up after Jonathan. "You have to think of your neighbors," she explained. On the night of November 13, 1974, Jonathan had finished his business and Mrs. Sharpe was walking home with the bag in her right hand when a mugger attacked her from behind, shoved her to the ground, grabbed her plastic bag, jumped into a car, and drove off with the spoils of his crime. Mrs. Sharpe suffered a broken arm but remained good-humored about the incident. "I only wish there had been a little more in the bag," she said.

7. A MINOR DETAIL

Edward McAlea put on a stocking mask, burst into a jewelry store in Liverpool, and pointed a revolver at the three men inside. "This is a stickup," he said. "Get down." None of them did, since all of them noticed the red plastic stopper in the muzzle of McAlea's toy gun. After a brief scuffle, McAlea escaped, but not before he had pulled off his mask. The jeweler recognized him as a customer from the day before, and McAlea was apprehended.

8. GOLDILOCKS

When Thomas Schimmel of Tawas City, Michigan, went home from work for lunch on the afternoon of November 1, 1978, he was surprised to discover that someone had entered his home, eaten a bowl of cereal and some chicken, and left. A sheriff's deputy was called and a report was filed, after which Schimmel went back to work. Returning home at 6:30 p.m., he immediately fell asleep on the couch and did not awaken until 11:45 p.m. He then went to his bedroom, where he discovered that the thief had not only returned but was in fact asleep in Mr. Schimmel's bed. Schimmel called the police, who woke the burglar and charged him with breaking and entering.

9. BARK BIGGER THAN BITE

A 14-year-old would-be burglar in south Phoenix, Arizona, managed to chop his way through a brick wall of the State Market on East Broadway on the night of April 3, 1980. However, he tripped an alarm in the process. The store was soon surrounded by police officers, but the boy refused to surrender. Then Officer Steve Gregory had a stroke of inspiration and called out to the boy that they were about to send in the K-9 Corps. Officer Al Femenia supported this threat by barking loudly.

"Don't let the dog come in," cried the burglar, "I'm coming out!" The young man was greatly disturbed when he learned that a policeman had been doing the barking, not a dog.

10. A PETTY THIEF

Things didn't work out quite the way Clay Weaver had planned on the night of February 16, 1982. The 19-year-old entered Hutchinson's Fine Foods in West Valley City, Utah, at 9:00 p.m., intending to rob the store. He waved a gun at the clerk, who laughed because she thought it was a toy. The gun was quite small, but it was in fact real—a two-bullet derringer. Weaver cocked the gun, but the bullet dribbled out onto the counter. Weaver then fled but got into an argument with his accomplice, Gary Hendrickson, who pushed Weaver away and drove off without him. Finally, he was chased down and hauled back to Hutchinson's by two store employees who happened to be members of the high school wrestling team. Weaver later confessed to 14 other robberies he had miraculously managed to commit.

11. KEEP THE CHANGE

In 1977, a thief in Southampton, England, came up with a clever method of robbing the cash register at a local supermarket. After collecting a basketful of groceries, he approached the checkout area and placed a £10 note on the counter. The grocery clerk took the bill and opened the cash register, at which point the thief snatched the contents and ran off. It turned out to be a bad deal for the thief, since the till contained only £4.37—he ended up losing £5.63.

12. THE WELD-PLANNED ROBBERY

On the night of August 23–24, 1980, a well-organized gang of thieves began their raid on the safe of the leisure-center office in Chichester, Sussex, in England by stealing a speedboat. Using water skis to paddle across the lake, they picked up their equipment and paddled on to the office. However, what they thought were cutting tools turned out to be welding gear, and they soon managed to seal the safe completely shut. The next morning, it took the office staff an hour to hammer and chisel the safe open again.

13. THE HAMBURGLAR

During the early morning hours of May 6, 1982, Carlos Aralijo attempted to burglarize a McDonald's restaurant in midtown Los Angeles by sliding down an oven flue. What the 28-year-old Aralijo discovered too late was that although the vent was 14 inches square at the roof, it narrowed to 8 inches square above the stove. Aralijo became stuck in the pipe, which was heavily coated with hot grease, and spent four or five hours screaming for help before someone heard him. It took fire fighters and paramedics 30 minutes to free him, by which time he had suffered first- and second-degree burns on his feet and lower legs.

14. WHO WAS THAT MASKED MAN?

Clive Bunyan ran into a store in Cayton, near Scarborough, England, and forced the shop assistant to give him £157 from the till. Then he made his getaway on his motorbike. To hide his identity, Bunyan had worn his full-face helmet as a mask. It was a smooth, successful heist, except for one detail. He had forgotten that across his helmet, in inch-high letters, were the words, "Clive Bunyan—Driver." Bunyan was arrested and ordered to pay for his crime by doing 200 hours of community service.

15. BURGLARY BY THE NUMBER

Terry Johnson had no trouble identifying the two men who burglarized her Chicago apartment at 2:30 a.m. on August 17, 1981. All she had to do was write down the number on the police badge one of them was wearing and the identity number on the fender of their squad car. The two officers—Stephen Webster, 33, and Tyrone Pickens, 32—had actually committed the crime in full uniform, while on duty, using police department tools.

16. BELATED COVER-UP

Gregory Lee Cornwell had everything in order when he planned to rob the Continental Bank in Prospect Park, Pennsylvania, in 1978: a car for the getaway, a ski mask to conceal his identity, an army knapsack for the money, and a sawed-off shotgun to show he was serious. On August 23, he parked his car in front of the bank and went inside. Displaying his shotgun, he threw the knapsack on the counter and demanded money. Then he put on his mask. Although he managed to leave the bank with $8,100, Cornwell was apprehended quickly and easily identified.

17. THE WORST LAWYER

Twenty-five-year-old Marshall George Cummings, Jr., of Tulsa, Oklahoma, was charged with attempted robbery in connection with a purse-snatching at a shopping center on October 14, 1976. During the trial the following January, Cummings chose to act as his own attorney.

While cross-examining the victim, he asked, "Did you get a good look at my face when I took your purse?" Cummings later decided to turn over his defense to a public defender, but it was too late. He was convicted and sentenced to 10 years in prison.

18. STUPID THIEF MAKES GOOD

Just because a person is a stupid thief does not mean that he is doomed to a life of failure. A good example is country music singer-songwriter Merle Haggard. In December 1957, Haggard and a friend named Micky Gorham got very drunk one night in Bakersfield, California, and decided at about 3:00 a.m. to break into a local restaurant on Highway 99. After ripping off the screen on the back door, Haggard began prying the lock with a crowbar. Just as the door opened, he heard the voice of the owner, a man Haggard knew well.

"What are you boys doing? Why don't you boys come around to the front door like everybody else?" What Haggard and Gorham had failed to realize was that it wasn't 3:00 a.m., at all. In fact, it was barely 10:00 p.m., and the restaurant was still open, with customers inside. Haggard was convicted of burglary and eventually served a prison term at San Quentin. In 1972, he received a full and unconditional pardon from California governor Ronald Reagan.

19. SAFE AT LAST

On the night of June 12, 1991, John Meacham, Joseph Plante, and Joe Laattsch were burgling a soon-to-be-demolished bank building in West Covina, California, when Meacham came upon an empty vault. He called over his accomplices and invited them inside to check out the acoustics. Then he closed the vault door so they could appreciate the full effect. Unfortunately, the door locked. Meacham spent forty minutes trying to open it, without success. Finally, he called the fire department, who called the police. After seven hours, a concrete-sawing firm was able to free the locked-up robbers, after which they were transported to another building they could not get out of.

20. BIG MOUTH

Dennis Newton was on trial in 1985 for armed robbery in Oklahoma City. Assistant District Attorney Larry Jones asked one of the witnesses, the supervisor of the store that had been robbed, to identify the robber. When she pointed to the defendant, Newton jumped to his feet, accused the witness of lying, and said, "I should have blown your —ing head off!" After a moment of stunned silence, he added, "If I'd been the one that was there." The jury sentenced Newton to 30 years in prison.

21. INCONVENIENCE STORE

In December 1989, three 15-year-old boys stole a car in Prairie Village, Kansas, and stopped off at the nearest convenience store to ask directions back to Missouri. Except that it wasn't a convenience store—it was a police station. At the same moment, a description of the stolen vehicle was broadcast over the police station public address system. The car thieves tried to escape but were quickly apprehended.

22. A REAL DRAG
When Silver's lock and safe shop of Canoga Park, California, moved in October 1990, they had to leave behind a 6,000–pound safe until they could rent a forklift to transport it. In the meantime, a rumor spread that the safe contained $6,000. This was too much of a temptation for James Richardson and Jeffrey Defalco, who got the brilliant idea of stealing the safe. In the dead of night, they tied a nylon strap around the safe and attached the strap to their car. Then they made their getaway. Unfortunately for Richardson and Defalco, the scraping of the safe on the asphalt street created showers of sparks that could be seen for blocks, not to mention a deafening roar that woke up the entire neighborhood. The two would-be thieves were easily tracked and arrested. The safe turned out to be empty.

23. WRONG FENCE
Stephen Le and two juvenile companions tried to break into a parked pickup truck in Larkspur, California, on the night of September 27, 1989. But the owner caught them in the act, chased them, and hailed a police car. Le and one of his friends climbed a fence and ran. It soon became apparent that they had chosen the wrong fence—this one surrounded the property of San Quentin prison. The suspects were booked for investigation of auto burglary and trespassing on state property, although charges were never filed. "Nothing like this has ever happened here before," said Lieutenant Cal White. "People just don't break into prison every day."

24. MURPHY'S LAW
On June 3, 1984, Charles Murphy of Long Beach, California, tried to hold up a Safeway supermarket. But he became so nervous that he ran out of the store without a penny and went straight home. It didn't take a Sherlock Holmes to find Murphy. Twenty-five minutes before his bungled robbery attempt, he had entered the same store, gone up to the same window, and filled out an application for a check-cashing identity card, using his correct name and address.

25. STUPID GANG OF THIEVES
This complex and well-planned robbery took place in the Silverlake district of Los Angeles on June 7, 1990. A gang of 10 to 12 men from Chula Vista, some of them armed with guns, drove up to the lot of the Shipping Company, a company that shipped cars across the United States. The robbers kidnapped the security guard, picked out nine cars,

and drove them away. What the thieves failed to realize was that all the cars had been drained of all but a gallon of gasoline. The gang raced to the freeway, but one by one they ran out of gas, sputtered, and stopped. One of them even suffered a flat tire.

26. MOST PHOTOGENIC
Vernon Brooks, 34, thought he was being a clever thief when he robbed a RadioShack in Raleigh, North Carolina, in July 1992. Before leaving the store, he disconnected the video surveillance camera and took it with him. However, he forgot to take the recorder to which the camera had been connected. Police found a perfect full-face shot of Brooks on the tape and had little difficulty identifying him. After he was released from jail, Brooks was again captured on film by a surveillance camera, this time while robbing a grocery store.

27. PENNY-WISE, DOLLAR DUMB
On January 6, 1990, David Posman lured an armored car driver away from his truck in Providence, Rhode Island. Posman knocked him on the head with a bottle, then ran back to the truck and grabbed four 30-pound bags of loot and staggered away. The weight of the bags greatly slowed his escape, and police had little trouble capturing him in a nearby parking garage. The bags all contained pennies.

28. TOO HEAVY TO HEIST
In the early morning hours of April 8, 1993, 21-year-old Michael Foster and a 17-year-old companion broke into a tavern in Monroe County, Wisconsin, and hauled away a seven-foot-tall electronic dart machine. They managed to load the enormous machine into the back of their pickup truck, but it was so heavy that when they tried to drive away, the truck sank into the mud in the tavern's parking lot. Unable to extract it, Foster and his friend decided they needed a tow. So they called the local sheriff's department, who towed the truck—and arrested them.

29. BIRDBRAINED THIEVES
During a midnight raid in May 1997, thieves climbed a six-foot fence at the home of Bob Hodgson in Ryton, England. They broke open two locks and stole forty homing pigeons worth £1,000. It was a clever, well-organized robbery—except for one minor problem: Homing pigeons fly home. That is exactly what all but the eight youngest pigeons did.

30. RETURNING TO THE SCENE OF THE CRIME
While training to become a military police officer, U.S. Army Private Daniel Bowden was taught how criminals commit bank robberies. As it turned out, Bowden was not a very good student. In May 1997, he robbed a federal credit union in Fort Belvoir, Virginia, making away

with $4,759 in cash. The following week, Bowden, who had not worn a mask during the commission of his crime, returned to the same bank and tried to deposit the money into his personal account. He was immediately recognized by a teller, who alerted the military police.

31. WHAT A DRAG

James Tamborella thought he had planned well when he attempted to rob a bank in Kenner, Louisiana, on February 8, 1999. In order to disguise himself, he donned women's clothing, put on makeup, and carried a purse. But he overlooked one critical detail: The holdup note that he handed the teller was written on the back of a personal check that included his name and address. Tamborella left the bank before he collected any money, but police had no trouble tracking him down.

32. STUCK FOR LIFE

There is a whole subgenre of stupid thieves who get stuck trying to sneak into buildings through chimneys and air vents that turn out to be narrower at the bottom than at the top. However, none has quite met the fate that befell Calvin Wilson of Natchez, Mississippi. A burglar with a criminal record, Wilson disappeared in 1985. The following year, a body found on the banks of the Mississippi River was identified—incorrectly, as it turned out—as that of Wilson. Fifteen years later, in January 2001, masons renovating a historic building in Natchez discovered a fully clothed skeleton in the chimney. Lying next to the skeleton was a wallet belonging to Calvin Wilson. Adams County sheriffs theorized that Wilson had tried to enter the building, which was then a gift shop, through the chimney, fallen in headfirst, and become stuck in the chimney, unable to call for help.

33. SHOOTING HIMSELF IN THE FOOT

In February 2004, Carlos Henrique Auad of Petropolis, Brazil, broke into a bar near his home and stole a television set. A few nights later, he tried to break into the same bar through the roof. This time, carrying a gun, he slipped and fell and shot himself in the right foot. Auad went straight home, but failed to notice that he left a trail of blood that led right to his door. He was arrested by police, who found the television set.

3 DISHONORABLE MENTIONS

1. STUPID DRUG DEALER

Alfred Acree, Jr., was sitting in a van in Charles City, Virginia, on April 7, 1993, with three friends and at least 30 small bags of cocaine. When sheriff's deputies surrounded the van, Acree raced into a dark, wooded area by the side of the road. He weaved in and out of the trees in an attempt to evade his pursuers. He thought he had done a pretty good job—and was amazed when the deputies caught him (and found $800 worth of cocaine in his pockets). What he had forgotten was that he was wearing L.A. Tech sneakers that sent out a red light every time they struck the ground. While Acree was tiring himself out zigzagging through the forest, the sheriffs were calmly following the blinking red lights.

2. STUPID TERRORIST
In early 1994, an Islamic fundamentalist group in Jordan launched a terrorist campaign that included attacks against secular sites such as video stores and supermarkets that sold liquor. During the late morning of February 1, Eid Saleh al Jahaleen, a 31-year-old plumber, entered the Salwa Cinema in the city of Zarqa. The cinema was showing soft-core pornographic films from Turkey. Jahaleen, who was apparently paid $50 to plant a bomb, had never seen soft-core porn and became entranced. When the bomb went off, he was still in his seat. Jahaleen lost both legs in the explosion.

3. STUPID DRUG TRAFFICKERS
Drug traffickers Edward Velez and José Gonzales were transporting two pounds of methamphetamine by airplane on the night of December 7, 1994. They had planned to land at a small airport in Turlock, California, but Velez, the pilot, miscalculated and touched down at a different airport 20 miles away. Unfortunately for Velez and Gonzales, the airport was part of the Castle Air Force Base, where pilots were practicing night touch-and-go landings. Security police intercepted the plane as soon as it landed.

20 Underworld Nicknames

1. FRANK "THE DASHER" ABBANDANDO
A prolific hit man for Murder, Inc.—organized crime's enforcement arm in the 1930s—and with some 50 killings to his credit, Frank Abbandando once approached a longshoreman on whom there was a "contract." Abbandando fired directly into his victim's face, only to have the weapon misfire. The chagrined executioner dashed off—and circled the block so fast that he came up behind his slowly pursuing target and this time managed to shoot him dead, picking up his moniker in the process.

2. TONY "JOE BATTERS" ACCARDO
Tough Tony Accardo was a Chicago syndicate boss for many decades who prided himself on never having spent a day in jail. He was sometimes called Joe Batters, harking back to his earlier days of proficiency with a baseball bat when he was one of Al Capone's most dedicated sluggers.

3. **JOSEPH "HA HA" AIUPPA**

An old-time Capone muscle-man, Joseph Aiuppa rose to become the Mafia boss of Cicero, Illinois. Because he was a notorious scowler not given to smiling, he was called Ha Ha.

4. **ISRAEL "ICEPICK WILLIE" ALDERMAN**

This Minneapolis gangster liked to brag about the grotesque murder method that earned him his nickname. Alderman (also known as Little Auldie and Izzy Lump Lump) ran a second-story speakeasy where he claimed to have committed 11 murders. In each case, he deftly pressed an icepick through his victim's eardrum into the brain; his quick technique made it appear that the dead man had merely slumped into a drunken heap on the bar. Icepick Willie would then laughingly chide the corpse as he dragged it to a back room, where he dumped the body down a coal chute leading to a truck in the alley below.

5. **LOUIS "PRETTY" AMBERG**

Louis Amberg, the underworld terror of Brooklyn from the 1920s to 1935—when he was finally rubbed out—was called Pretty because he may well have been the ugliest gangster who ever lived. Immortalized by Damon Runyon in several stories as the gangster who stuffed his victims into laundry bags, Amberg was approached when he was 20 by Ringling Brothers Circus, which wanted him to appear as the missing link. Pretty turned down the job but often bragged about the offer afterward.

6. **MICHAEL "UMBRELLA MIKE" BOYLE**

Business agent of the mob-dominated electrical workers union in Chicago in the 1920s, Michael J. Boyle gained the title of Umbrella Mike because of his practice of standing at a bar on certain days of the week with an unfurled umbrella. Building contractors deposited cash levies into that receptacle and then magically were not beset by labor difficulties.

7. **LOUIS "LEPKE" BUCHALTER**

Louis Buchalter—who died in the electric chair in 1944—was the head of Murder, Inc. He was better known as Lepke, a form of "Lepkeleh." This was the affectionate Yiddish diminutive, meaning "Little Louis," that his mother had used. Affectionate, Lepke was not. As one associate said, "Lep loves to hurt people."

8. **"SCARFACE" AL CAPONE**

Al Capone claimed that the huge scar on his cheek was from a World War I wound suffered while fighting with the lost battalion in France, but he was never in the armed service. He had been knifed by a hoodlum named Frank Galluccio during a dispute over a woman while working as a bouncer in a Brooklyn saloon-brothel. Capone once visited the editorial offices of William Randolph Hearst's *Chicago American* and convinced that paper to stop referring to him as "Scarface Al."

9. VINCENT "MAD DOG" COLL

Vincent "Mad Dog" Coll was feared by police and rival gangsters alike in the early 1930s because of his utter disregard for human life. Once he shot down several children at play while trying to get an underworld foe. When he was trapped in a phone booth and riddled with bullets in 1932, no one cried over his death, and police made little effort to solve the crime.

10. JOSEPH "JOE ADONIS" DOTO

Racket boss Joseph Doto adopted the name of Joe Adonis because he considered his looks the equal of Aphrodite's famous lover.

11. CHARLES "PRETTY BOY" FLOYD

Public enemy Charles Arthur Floyd hated his nickname, which was used by prostitutes of the Midwest whorehouses he patronized, and in fact he killed at least two gangsters for repeatedly calling him Pretty Boy. When he was shot down by FBI agents in 1934, he refused to identify himself as Pretty Boy Floyd and with his dying breath snarled, "I'm Charles Arthur Floyd!"

12. CHARLIE "MONKEY FACE" GENKER

A mainstay of the Chicago whorehouse world for several decades after the beginning of the twentieth century, Charlie "Monkey Face" Genker achieved his moniker not simply for a countenance lacking in beauty but also for his actions while employed by Mike "de Pike" Heitler (a piker because he ran a 50-cent house). Monkey Face matched the bounciness of his jungle cousins by scampering up doors and peeking over the transoms to get the girls and their customers to speed things up.

13. JAKE "GREASY THUMB" GUZIK

A longtime devoted aide to Al Capone, Jake Guzik continued until his death in 1956 to be the payoff man to the politicians and police for the Chicago mob. He often complained that he handled so much money he could not get the inky grease off his thumb. This explanation of the Greasy Thumb sobriquet was such an embarrassment to the police that they concocted their own story, maintaining that Jake had once worked as a waiter and gained his nickname because he constantly stuck his thumb in the soup bowls.

14. "GOLF BAG" SAM HUNT

Notorious Capone mob enforcer Golf Bag Hunt was so called because he lugged automatic weapons about in his golf bag to conceal them when on murder missions.

15. ALVIN "KREEPY" KARPIS

Bank robber Alvin Karpis was tabbed Kreepy by fellow prison inmates in the 1920s because of his sallow, dour-faced looks. By the time he became public enemy number one in 1935, his face had become even creepier, thanks to a botched plastic surgery job that was supposed to alter his appearance.

16. GEORGE "MACHINE GUN" KELLY

Somehow a blundering bootlegger named George R. Kelly became the feared public enemy Machine Gun Kelly of the 1930s. His criminally ambitious wife, Kathryn, forced him to practice with the machine gun she gave him as a birthday present, while she built up his reputation with other criminals. Kelly was not a murderer, however, nor did he ever fire his weapon in anger with intent to kill.

17. CHARLES "LUCKY" LUCIANO

Charles Luciano earned the name Lucky when he was taken for a ride and came back alive, although a knife wound gave him a permanently drooping right eye. Luciano told many stories over the years about the identity of his abductors—two different criminal gangs were mentioned, as well as the police, who were trying to find out about an impending drug shipment, but the most likely version is that he was tortured and mutilated by the family of a cop whose daughter he had seduced. Luciano parlayed his misfortune into a public relations coup, since he was the one and only underworld figure lucky enough to return alive after being taken for a one-way ride.

18. THOMAS "BUTTERFINGERS" MORAN

The acknowledged king of the pickpockets of the twentieth century, Butterfingers Moran picked his first pocket during the 1906 San Francisco earthquake and his last in 1970 at 78—some 50,000 pockets in all. He could, other practitioners acknowledged rather jealously, "slide in and out of a pocket like pure butter."

19. LESTER "BABY FACE" NELSON

The most pathological public enemy of the 1930s, Lester Gillis considered his own name nonmacho and came up with Big George Nelson instead—a ridiculous alias considering the fact that he was just 5 feet 4 inches tall. He was called Baby Face Nelson behind his back and in the press, which constantly enraged him.

20. BENJAMIN "BUGSY" SIEGEL

Alternately the most charming and the most vicious of all syndicate killers, Benjamin Siegel could thus be described as being "bugsy." No one called him that to his face, however, since it caused him to fly into a

murderous rage. His mistress, Virginia Hall, likewise clobbered newsmen who called her man by that offensive sobriquet.

C.S.

11 Possible Alternative Gunmen
in the Assassination of John F. Kennedy

According to the Warren Commission, Lee Harvey Oswald was the lone
assassin in the killing of President Kennedy. However, a large majority of
the public believes that the assassination was the result of a conspiracy. The
CIA, the FBI, the Mafia, the military, pro-Castro Cubans and anti-Castro
Cubans have all been cited as possible forces behind the scenes. Among the
people accused of doing the actual shooting are the following:

1. **LUCIEN SARTI AND TWO CORSICAN HIT MEN**
   According to jailed French mobster Christian David, Kennedy was shot
   by three Corsican assassins. David named the deceased Sarti as one of
   the gunmen and offered to reveal the identities of the others if he was
   given his freedom. According to him, the two unnamed assassins were in
   buildings to the rear of the president, while Sarti fired from the grassy
   knoll in front of the motorcade. The British television documentary *The
   Men Who Killed Kennedy* identified Sarti as the man in a police
   uniform apparently firing a rifle on the grassy knoll who's visible in a
   computer-enhanced enlargement of a photo taken by Mary Moorman at
   the moment of the fatal shot.

2. **CHARLES V. HARRELSON**
   Harrelson—the father of *Cheers* actor Woody Harrelson—has been
   serving a life sentence since 1979 for murdering federal judge John H.
   Wood, Jr. During a six-hour standoff before his arrest, Harrelson held
   a gun to his head and confessed to shooting Kennedy. He later retracted
   the statement, saying he had been high on cocaine at the time.

3. **"CARLOS" AND OTHERS**
   Minister Raymond Broshears reported that David Ferrie—a bizarre
   individual often suspected of involvement in the assassination who had
   ties to Oswald, the CIA, and the Mafia—would, after getting drunk,
   often talk about his role in the conspiracy. He reportedly said his job
   was to wait in Houston for two gunmen, one of them a Cuban exile
   Ferrie referred to as Carlos, and then fly them on the second leg of an
   escape route that was to take the assassins to South Africa via South
   America. Ferrie told Broshears the plan fell apart when the assassins,

flying in a light plane, decided to skip the stop in Houston and press on to Mexico. They allegedly died when their plane crashed near Corpus Christi, Texas.

4. LUIS ANGEL CASTILLO
According to assassination researcher Penn Jones, Castillo has stated under hypnosis that "he was on the parade route with a rifle that day . . . [with] instructions to shoot at a man in a car with red roses." Jackie Kennedy was the only person in the motorcade with red roses; all the other women had been given yellow Texas roses.

5. ELADIO DEL VALLE AND LORAN HALL
According to "Harry Dean" (the "war name" of a man who claims to be a former CIA agent), as quoted by W. B. Morris and R. B. Cutler in *Alias Oswald*, the assassins were anti-Castro activists Hall and del Valle, who were hired by the John Birch Society. Although Hall says he was at his home in California on November 22, 1963, he allegedly told the *Dallas Morning News* in 1978 that, a month before the assassination, right-wing activists working with the CIA tried to recruit him for a plot to kill Kennedy. As for del Valle, he died under suspicious circumstances in 1967. He was being sought as a possible witness in the Clay Shaw conspiracy trial when he was discovered shot through the heart and with his head split open by a machete.

6. "BROTHER-IN-LAW" AND "SLIM"
In 1992, Kerry Thornley appeared on the television show *A Current Affair* and said he had been part of a conspiracy to kill President Kennedy. His coconspirators were two men he called Brother-in-Law and Slim. Thornley denied framing Oswald, whom he had befriended in the Marines: "I would gladly have killed Kennedy, but I would never have betrayed Oswald." He added, "I wanted [Kennedy] dead. I would have shot him myself." Thornley has also claimed that he and Oswald were the products of a genetic engineering experiment carried out by a secret neo-Nazi sect of eugenicists called the Vril Society and that the two of them had been manipulated since childhood by Vril overlords.

7. JEAN RENE SOUTRE
Soutre, a terrorist in the French Secret Army Organization, is believed by some researchers to have been recruited by the CIA to serve as an assassin. According to CIA documents obtained under the Freedom of Information Act by researcher Mary Ferrell, French intelligence reported that Soutre was in Fort Worth on the morning of November 22, 1963, and in Dallas that afternoon. He was picked up by U.S. authorities in Texas within 48 hours of the assassination and expelled from the country.

8. ROSCOE WHITE, "SAUL," AND "LEBANON"

In 1990, Ricky White claimed that his father, Roscoe, a Dallas police officer, who died after being burnt in an industrial fire in September 1971, had been one of President Kennedy's assassins. According to Ricky, a detailed description of the conspiracy could be found in Roscoe's diary, which had disappeared after it was taken by the FBI for inspection. Two other gunmen, referred to in the diary only by the code names Saul and Lebanon, were also involved. In addition, Roscoe's widow, Geneva, told journalist Ron Laytner that she had overheard Roscoe and Jack Ruby plotting to kill Kennedy, adding, "We at first thought the assassination was more Mob [but later realized] it was more CIA." Fifteen years before Ricky and Geneva White went public, Hugh McDonald, in *Appointment in Dallas*, identified one of the killers as a professional assassin known as Saul. McDonald claimed to have tracked down Saul, who admitted to having been paid $50,000 to shoot the president. Saul claimed to have fired from the Dallas County Records Building—which was also described in Roscoe White's diary as one of the locations the assassins had shot from. Despite these similarities, there are some inconsistencies in the plots described by McDonald and Ricky White. Most notably, Roscoe White in his diary and Saul in his meeting with McDonald each allegedly claimed to have fired the fatal shot.

9. GEORGE HICKEY, JR.

According to Bonar Menninger's book *Mortal Error*—based on 25 years of research by ballistics expert Howard Donahue—Kennedy was accidentally killed by Hickey, a Secret Service agent in the car behind the presidential limo. According to this theory, when Oswald began shooting, Hickey reached for his rifle and slipped off the safety. As he tried to stand in the backseat of the car to return fire, he lost his balance and accidentally pulled the trigger, firing the shot that killed the president. Hickey himself told the Warren Commission that he did not even pick up his rifle until after the fatal shot.

10. FRANK STURGIS AND OPERATION 40

Marita Lorenz, a CIA operative who had been Fidel Castro's mistress, told the *New York Daily News* in 1977 that she had accompanied Lee Harvey Oswald and an assassination squad to Dallas a few days before Kennedy was killed. She identified her companions on the trip as CIA operative (and future Watergate burglar) Frank Sturgis and four Cuban exiles: Orlando Bosch, Pedro Diaz Lang, and two brothers named Novis. The men were members of Operation 40, a group of about 30 anti-Castro Cubans and their American advisers originally formed by the CIA in 1960 for the Bay of Pigs invasion. Lorenz later stated that Sturgis had been one of the actual gunmen and that he told her after the assassination, "You could have been part of it—you know, part of history. You should have stayed. It was safe. Everything was covered in advance. No arrests, no real newspaper investigation. It was all covered, very professional." Sturgis denies that there is any truth to Lorenz's story. However, he once said that the FBI questioned him about the assassination right after it happened, because, the agents said, "Frank, if there's anybody capable of killing the president of the United States, you're the guy who can do it."

11. **JAMES FILES AND CHARLES NICOLETTI**
In 1996, Files claimed that he and Nicoletti, a Mafia hit man, had been on the grassy knoll at Dealey Plaza and that they had shot President Kennedy at the same time. Files said that he was paid $30,000 and had orders not to hit Jacqueline Kennedy. He added that Nicoletti took his order from Sam "Momo" Giancana, who in turn answered to Anthony "Big Tuna" Accardo. Since all three mobsters had been murdered between 1975 and 1977, there was no one to corroborate Files's story. The FBI dismissed the story, noting that Files was serving a 50-year sentence in Illinois for murdering a policeman and thus had little to lose by "confessing" and gaining his 15 minutes of fame.

C.F.

10 Defendants from History Alan Dershowitz Would Like to Have Defended

Professor Alan Dershowitz of Harvard Law School has been described as a "feisty civil libertarian," "defense attorney extraordinaire," and "the top lawyer of last resort in the country." His high-profile clients have included Claus von Bulow, Leona Helmsley, Mike Tyson, and Patricia Hearst; he was also a member of the legal "Dream Team" that defended O. J. Simpson. A frequent guest expert on legal matters for TV and radio, Dershowitz is also the author of numerous books, including *Reversal of Fortune* (about the von Bulow case), *Supreme Injustice: How the High Court Hijacked Election 2000*, and *Shouting Fire: Civil Liberties in a Turbulent Age.*

1. JESUS OF NAZARETH
   Think how much difficulty would have been avoided if a Jewish lawyer had successfully defended Jesus.

2. SOCRATES
   I would have urged him to appeal rather than taking the hemlock.

3. **GALILEO GALILEI**
Whose innocence for espousing the heliocentric theory—that the earth revolves around the sun—was finally acknowledged by the Catholic Church, 350 years after he copped a plea to avoid being burned.

4. **SHOELESS JOE JACKSON**
The baseball star who took the fall for Charles Comiskey, the crooked owner of the Chicago Black Sox, who knew the World Series of 1919 was fixed.

5. **JOHN BROWN**
Who was hanged for trying to free the slaves, but whose truth goes marching on.

6. **OSCAR WILDE**
I would have advised him not to sue for defamation unless he was willing to come out of the closet.

7. **THE SALEM WITCHES**
What a challenge! To defend in front of judges who genuinely believed in witches!

8. **JOHN T. SCOPES**
I would have loved to make monkeys out of politicians who forbade teachers from teaching evolution.

9. **MENDEL BEILIS**
A Jew charged with the "blood libel"—that Jews kill Christian children to use their blood for ritual purposes—in Russia in 1911. What a great opportunity to expose one of the most pernicious frauds in history.

10. **KING CHARLES I OF ENGLAND**
I always wanted to defend a king.

19 Innocent Americans Who Were Almost Executed

1–2. **WILLIAM JENT AND EARNEST MILLER**—minus 16 hours
Half brothers Jent and Miller were convicted of rape and murder in 1980. Three years later, they came within 16 hours of being executed before a federal judge issued a stay. In 1986, the victim's identity was finally established, and suspicion shifted to her boyfriend. In 1988, Jent and Miller were released from prison, and in 1991 they

were judged to be victims of corruption of witnesses and incompetent police. They were awarded $65,000 in compensation by the Pasco County, Florida, sheriff's department.

3. JOSEPH GREEN BROWN—minus 13 hours
In 1974, Brown and a partner, Ronald Floyd, committed a robbery together in Florida. Brown turned himself in and implicated Floyd. As revenge, Floyd claimed that Brown had confessed to a murder that took place the day after the robbery. Brown was convicted of first-degree murder and sentenced to death. A new trial was ordered in 1986, 13 hours before Brown was due to be executed. A year later, the state dropped all charges, and Brown was released.

4. EDWARD LARKMAN—minus 10 hours
Larkman was convicted of the August 12, 1925, murder of the paymaster of the Art Metal Shop in Buffalo, New York. Ten hours before his scheduled execution, Governor Alfred Smith commuted his sentence to life imprisonment. Two years later, a Buffalo gangster confessed to the crime. However, it was not until 1933 that Larkman was pardoned, after it was revealed that the police, knowing the killer had worn sunglasses, forced Larkman to put on a pair of sunglasses and stand alone at the lineup, where an eyewitness identified him.

5. WILLIAM LINDLEY—minus several hours
On August 18, 1943, 13-year-old Jackie Hamilton was raped and murdered in Yuba City, California. As she lay dying, she turned to her father and whispered, "Don't let that old redheaded man get me, Daddy." There were two redheaded men living nearby. Local police chose 49-year-old "Red" Lindley, an illiterate farm worker who had served time in a Texas prison for burglary. Although the trial was delayed a year on the grounds that Lindley was mentally incompetent, he was eventually tried, convicted, and sentenced to death. While Lindley was awaiting execution, the famous mystery writer Erle Stanley Gardner began researching the case and discovered that Lindley had an excellent alibi that was never presented in court—he was with the victim's father at the time of the crime! Despite this new evidence, Lindley was almost executed on three occasions in 1946. Once he was reprieved a few hours before he was to enter the gas chamber, and another time, two days before. Finally, in April 1947, Governor Earl Warren commuted his sentence to life imprisonment. Unfortunately, by this time Lindley's ordeal had destroyed him emotionally. He lived out his days in a prison for the criminally insane.

6. AYLIFF DRAPER—minus several hours
Draper and a friend, Roy House, committed a robbery in which the victim was murdered. House claimed that Draper had done the killing.

Both men were convicted and sentenced to death. In 1936, with a few hours to go before their execution, House confessed that he, not Draper, had committed the murder and proved it by directing police to the murder weapon. House was executed, but in 1938 Draper was released.

7. LLOYD MILLER—minus 7½ hours
In November 1955, Miller was arrested for the murder of an eight-year-old girl in Canton, Illinois. Two days later, after intense police pressure, he signed a confession. Between 1958 and 1963, he was scheduled for electrocution seven times, once coming within seven and a half hours of execution. A crucial piece of evidence used against him was the discovery of bloodstained Jockey shorts. Reexamination of the evidence showed not only that Miller did not wear Jockey shorts, but also that the "blood" was really paint, a fact that the prosecution had known but never revealed. Miller was finally released in 1967.

8. RALPH RENO—minus 7 hours
Reno was convicted of a 1925 double murder in Illinois and sentenced to death; however, the judge considered the evidence insufficient and ordered a new trial. Again, Reno was convicted and sentenced to death. Seven hours before his scheduled execution, he was granted a stay and allowed an appeal, thanks to the efforts of the first judge, who considered him innocent. At a third trial, he was finally acquitted when the only witness changed her testimony. Reno was released from prison in 1928.

9. TOM JONES—minus 5 hours
In 1936, Jones was convicted of murdering his wife, even though he claimed that the gun had gone off while he was struggling to prevent her from committing suicide. Five hours before his scheduled execution, a stay was granted. Two thousand citizens of Kentucky, including the original jurors, signed petitions for clemency, and the conviction was eventually reversed.

10. GANGI CERO—minus 4 hours
Cero was convicted of the June 11, 1927, Boston murder of Joseph Fantasia and sentenced to death. He claimed mistaken identity. He was reprieved four hours before his execution because his brother found a witness who identified Cero's boss, Samuel Gallo, as the murderer. Gallo was tried and convicted. Then both men were tried together in a bizarre trial during which they implicated each other. Eventually, both Cero and Gallo were acquitted.

11. ANASTACIO VARGAS—minus 4 hours
Vargas, of Austin, Texas, was convicted of murder in 1925 and sentenced to life imprisonment. The conviction was reversed on appeal. At

the retrial, he was again found guilty, but this time he was sentenced to death. Vargas's head had already been shaved and he had already been served his last meal when a look-alike confessed to the murder. Vargas was pardoned and released in 1929. Thirty-five years later, he sued the state for damages and was awarded $20,000.

12–13. EDGAR LABAT AND CLIFTON PORET—minus 3 hours
Labat and Poret, both of whom were black, were convicted of raping a white woman in Louisiana in 1953. After their lawyers gave up on them, the two men smuggled out an appeal for help that ran as an ad in the *Los Angeles Times*. A reader hired a new attorney on their behalf, and in 1960 their ninth stay of execution was granted, this one a mere three hours before the end. At this point, the state's case began to unravel, and a new trial was ordered. To avoid the embarrassment of an acquittal, the Louisiana courts resentenced Labat and Poret to time served and released them—after they had spent 16 years on death row for a crime they did not commit.

14. ISADORE ZIMMERMAN—minus 2 hours
In 1937, Zimmerman was arrested in New York for providing the guns that were used in a robbery during which a police detective was killed. Zimmerman was barely mentioned during the high-profile trial, which included five defendants, twelve defense attorneys, and eighty-four witnesses. Nonetheless, he was convicted and sentenced to death. On January 26, 1939, he ate his last meal, had his head shaved, and said good-bye to his family. Then, two hours before he was to be electrocuted, he learned that Governor Herbert Lehman had commuted his sentence to life imprisonment. But Zimmerman continued to maintain his complete innocence. Finally, in 1962, he won the right to a new trial and was subsequently released. He demanded compensation for the 24 years he had spent in prison. On June 30, 1983, Zimmerman was vindicated at last when he won an award for $660,000 (after expenses). Three and a half months later, he died of a heart attack.

15. CHARLES STIELOW—minus 40 minutes
A farmhand in Shelby, New York, Stielow was convicted of the 1915 murder of his boss and the boss's housekeeper. He received five stays of execution. On July 29, 1916, he had already been sent to the execution chamber and was 40 minutes away from electrocution. Two weeks later, another man confessed to the killings, but it was 20 months before Stielow was finally released from prison.

16. GUS COLIN LANGLEY—minus 25 minutes
In 1932, Langley was convicted of killing a gas station attendant in Asheville, North Carolina, even though he was 400 miles away at the

time of the crime. He came so close to being executed that when the chaplain appeared at his cell door, Langley thought he was being led away to the electric chair. Instead, he was granted a stay because of a technical error. After six more reprieves, including another one with only minutes to spare, the state of North Carolina admitted that Langley was innocent. He was pardoned and released in 1936.

17. CHARLES BERNSTEIN—minus several minutes

In 1919, Bernstein was convicted of a robbery he did not commit. He spent nine years in prison. Four years after his release, he was again arrested for a crime he did not commit. This time it was the April 21, 1932, murder of a gambler in Washington, D.C. Despite the testimony of six witnesses who said that he was in New York at the time of the crime, the unfortunate Bernstein was convicted and sentenced to death by electrocution. Minutes before his scheduled execution in 1935, President Franklin Roosevelt commuted his sentence to life in prison. In 1940, Roosevelt commuted the sentence to time served, and on April 30, 1945, Bernstein was granted a full pardon by President Harry Truman.

18. WILLIAM WELLMAN—minus 2 minutes

Wellman, who was black, was sentenced to death for the 1941 rape of an elderly white woman in Iredell County, North Carolina. In fact, he had been at work in Virginia, 350 miles away, at the time of the crime. Wellman was already seated in the electric chair when Governor J. Melville Broughton issued a reprieve upon learning that another man had confessed to the crime. After an investigation showed that Wellman had signed a payroll receipt in Virginia on the day of the rape, he was granted a full pardon and released from custody.

19. J. B. BROWN—minus 1 minute

A railroad worker, Brown was convicted of murdering an engineer in Florida on October 17, 1901. As he was standing on the gallows with a rope around his neck, the death warrant was read, and it was discovered that, by mistake, the name of the jury foreman had been written in instead of Brown's name. The hanging was canceled, and in 1902, Brown's sentence was commuted to life imprisonment. In 1913, the real murderer confessed, and Brown was granted a pardon. In 1929, the state of Florida awarded him a relief fund of $2,492.

Primary source: In Spite of Innocence by Michael Radelet, Hugo Bedau, and Constance Putnam (Boston: Northeastern University Press, 1992).

22 Unusual Stolen Objects

1. **MARLA MAPLES'S SHOES**
   When the girlfriend of entrepreneur Donald Trump discovered that more than 40 pairs of her high-heeled shoes were missing, she installed a video camera in her bedroom closet to catch the culprit. On July 15, 1992, the camera reportedly recorded Maples's publicist, Chuck Jones, filching another pair. New York police raided Jones's office and recovered the shoes, as well as a copy of *Spike,* a pornographic magazine for shoe fetishists. Jones pleaded not guilty to the charges.

2. **GEORGE WASHINGTON'S WALLET**
   One hundred ninety-one years after his death in 1799, George Washington's battered wallet was stolen from an unlocked case in the Old Barracks Museum in Trenton, New Jersey. The wallet was later returned to police. In a separate incident in 1986, a lock of Washington's hair was taken from a museum in France. Five years later, it was recovered, along with a lock of hair belonging to the Marquis de Lafayette, by French police during a raid on a drug dealer's hideout.

3. **BULL SEMEN**
   In October 1989, $10,000 worth of frozen bull semen and embryos was taken from the dairy building at California Polytechnic University in San Luis Obispo, California. The embryos were later found, but despite a $1,500 reward, the semen was never recovered.

4. **CHURCH PULPIT**
   On August 2, 1992, congregation leaders of the First Missionary Baptist Church in Houston, Texas, voted to oust their pastor, the Reverend Robert L. White. The Reverend White retaliated by loading most of the church's property into three cars, a pickup, and a 14-foot U-Haul truck. Included in his take were furniture, an organ, curtains, speakers, amplifiers, and even the pulpit. He left behind the church's piano because it was still being paid for.

5. **HALF A HUMAN HEAD**
   Jason Paluck, a premedical student at Adelphi University on Long Island, was arrested in May 1992 after his landlord discovered half of a human head in a plastic bag while evicting Paluck from his Mineola, New York, apartment. Paluck admitted that he had taken the head from one of his classes.

6. **KATEY SAGAL'S PUSH-UP BRA**
   On the night of April 30, 1992, Jim B., a 24-year-old art student in Los Angeles, drove into Hollywood to observe the fires and looting

that followed the acquittal of four police officers in the beating of Rodney King. Jim B. joined the crowd looting Frederick's of Hollywood, the famous purveyor of exotic lingerie. He headed straight for its lingerie museum, intent on grabbing Madonna's bustier. It had already been stolen, so he settled for Ava Gardner's bloomers and a push-up bra worn by Katey Sagal on the television comedy *Married . . . with Children.* A couple of days later, a repentant Jim B. handed over the stolen items to the Reverend Bob Frambini, the pastor at the Church of the Blessed Sacrament, who returned them to Frederick's. Madonna's bustier is still on the missing list. However, she donated a replacement in exchange for a contribution to a charity that provides free mammograms for the poor.

7. **20-FOOT INFLATABLE CHICKEN**
To mark the March 1990 debut of a new franchise in Sherman Oaks, California, the El Pollo Loco fast-food chain installed a 20-foot inflatable rubber chicken in front of the restaurant. Two weeks later, it was stolen. "Don't ask me what someone would do with it," said Joe Masiello, director of operations for Chicken Enterprises, Ltd. "If you put it in your yard, someone would notice it." The restaurant's owners offered a reward of 12 free chicken combos for its return, but the thieves didn't bite.

8. **BUTTONS**
Felicidad Noriega, the wife of Panamanian dictator Manuel Noriega, was arrested in a Miami-area shopping mall in March 1992. She and a companion eventually pleaded guilty to stealing $305 worth of buttons, which they had removed from clothes in a department store.

9. **15-TON BUILDING**
In August 1990, businessman Andy Barrett of Pembroke, New Hampshire, reported the unexpected loss of an unassembled fifteen-ton prefabricated structure, complete with steel girders and beams thirty-five feet long and three feet thick.

10. **MANHOLE COVERS**
In July 1990, Los Angeles police broke the case of the Great Manhole Theft Caper when they arrested two culprits who later confessed to stealing 300 manhole covers weighing as much as 300 pounds each. The Manhole Men were selling the covers for $6 each to scrap dealers. They could have made 30 times as much money by recycling the same weight in aluminum soft-drink cans. Two years later, manhole mania hit Lillehammer, Norway, site of the 1994 Winter Olympics, after local officials began stamping the covers with the Olympic logo. Three of the 140-pound covers were stolen, but one was returned after the thief "sobered up."

11. **SACRED CHIN**
Saint Anthony's jawbone and several teeth were taken from a basilica in Padua, Italy, in October 1991 but were later found near Rome's international airport at Fiumicino.

12. **BIRD'S NESTS**
Burglars in Hong Kong stole $250,000 worth of bird's nests from a restaurant during the night of May 1, 1992. The nests are a main ingredient in a popular Chinese soup.

13. **GODZILLA**
In March 1992, a 132-pound rubber model of Godzilla was stolen from a Tokyo movie studio. Ten days later, it was found in a bamboo thicket outside the city.

14. **VINTAGE AIRPLANE**
Israeli Air Force Reserve Major Ishmael Yitzhaki was convicted in February 1992 of stealing a World War II Mustang fighter plane and flying it to Sweden, where he sold it for $331,000. He had managed to remove the plane from the Air Force Museum by saying it needed painting.

15. **GENE KELLY'S LAMPPOST**
Bryan Goetzinger was part of the labor crew that cleared out the Metro-Goldwyn-Mayer film company vaults when MGM ceded its Culver City, California, lot to Lorimar Telepictures in 1986. Among the items scheduled to be trashed was the lamppost that Gene Kelly swung on in the Hollywood musical classic *Singin' in the Rain*. Goetzinger brought the lamppost home and installed it in the front yard of his Hermosa Beach home. Four years later, it was stolen. It was never recovered.

16. **MARY'S LITTLE LAMB**
A life-size statue of Mary's famous little lamb was erected in Sterling, Massachusetts, the hometown of Mary Sawyer, who was the inspiration for the nursery rhyme, written in 1830 by Sarah J. Hale. During the night of June 30, 1990, the unfortunate lamb was stolen from the town commons. Happily, it was later returned.

17. **SOFA BALLOON**
When Nadar Almasi, the manager of Krause's Sofa Factory in Fremont, California, reported the theft of a sofa from his store, Fremont police laughed. The sky-blue sofa, known as Maxine, was actually a 31-foot, 500-pound forced-air balloon that had adorned the store's rooftop until the Independence Day weekend of 1989. Maxine was recovered a few weeks later.

18. **FAKE BISON TESTICLES**
    In celebration of the 2001 World Championships in Athletics, the host city of Edmonton, Canada, erected statues of bison, painted in colors representing the competing nations. Twenty of the statues were vandalized, with thieves removing the testicles from the bison. Although two vandals were caught red-handed in August, police considered the remaining cases unsolved. Ric Dolphin, chairman of the project that erected the statues, suggested that if the vandals were caught, "Let the punishment fit the crime."

19. **18-TON BRIDGE**
    In May 1998, thieves in Bytow, Poland, stole an 18-ton nineteenth-century steel bridge that led to a riverside cottage. The scrap value of the bridge was estimated to be $1,200.

20. **CABIN**
    Kay Kugler and her husband, B. J. Miller, bought 40 acres in California's El Dorado County and erected a 10-by-20-foot prefabricated cabin on the property, which they used as a vacation home. In July 2003, they arrived at their property to discover that the cabin was gone. In their absence, someone had stolen the cabin, a shed, a generator, an antique bed, a well pump, and a 2,600-gallon water tank.

21. **CONDOM MACHINE**
    Keith Bradford, 34, drank three beers at the Irish Tavern in Waterford, Michigan, in November 1994, headed into the men's room, and ripped a condom machine from the wall. Numerous witnesses saw him walk away with the machine, so the police followed him home and recovered the machine, 48 condoms and 127 quarters.

22. **USED COOKING GREASE**
    During the spring of 2004, thieves in Edmond, Oklahoma, stole almost 5,000 pounds of used cooking grease from three different restaurants. Local police speculated that they were familiar with the recycled grease industry and estimated that the loot was worth about $380.

Clifford Irving's
10 Best Forgers of All Time

Born in New York City on November 5, 1930, the son of cartoonist Jay Irving, Clifford Irving attended Cornell University and became a full-time writer, publishing such novels as *On a Darkling Plain, The Losers, The Valley, The 38th Floor,* and a widely read nonfiction book, *Fake!* In 1971 and 1972, he became world-famous by selling an autobiography purportedly written by reclusive billionaire industrialist and aviator Howard Hughes (with Irving's assistance) to McGraw-Hill publishers. The book proved to be a complex and fantastic forgery that, when exposed, led to Irving's being sentenced to two and a half years in federal prison. After his incarceration, he relocated to Mexico and continued to write books, including the highly acclaimed 1982 historical novel *Tom Mix and Pancho Villa*. In his list of the greatest forgers of all time, contributed to *The Book of Lists* in 1977, Irving picked himself as one of them and told his own version of the Hughes caper, which he expanded into a book-length account entitled *The Hoax* in 1999.

1. **THE SEE OF ROME**
   For audacity, simplicity, and widespread effect over the centuries, no forgery can equal that of the *Constitutum Constantini*, the so-called *Donation of Constantine*. Constantine, the first Roman emperor to become a Christian, not only legalized his religion throughout the empire but, sometime between 315 and 325 AD, gave the See of Rome spiritual command over the entire world and secular authority over Europe. He did this in a 3,000-word document, the *Donation*, although, oddly, it was not made public by the Church until the ninth century, when Rome was at odds with the Eastern Orthodox Church. The *Donation* was cited by various popes throughout the Middle Ages and used to buttress many of the Church's temporal claims. The first doubts were cast in the fifteenth century, and by the eighteenth century, Voltaire could openly and without serious contradiction call it "that boldest and most magnificent forgery." For one thing, it had come to light that Constantine had given Rome authority over his capital, New Rome (which later became Constantinople and, still later, Istanbul), at least a decade before New Rome was founded. The actual author of the text of the *Constitutum Constantini* remains unknown.

2. **WILLIAM HENRY IRELAND (1777–1835)**
   The son of a London printer and Shakespearean scholar, young Ireland, at the age of 19, "discovered" in an English country manor an extraordinary treasure: love letters from Shakespeare to his mistress, a new version of *King Lear*, a fragment of *Hamlet*, various legal and other documents, and, even more marvelously, in time, two "lost" and unknown complete Shakespearean plays, *Vortigern*, a love story of the Saxon conquest, and *Henry II*—both handwritten by the Bard. Most scholars, including James Boswell, examined them and were ecstatic. *Vortigern* was performed in 1796, but somehow by then, doubts had arisen, and the public at the Drury Lane Theatre howled with scorn toward the end of the performance. It was a one-night stand, and within a year Ireland had confessed that the entire collection of Shakespeareana was a forgery, composed and written by him on old paper stained with a clear dye to simulate even greater age.

Ireland received no punishment other than the angry disdain of critics when he went on to publish several novels.

3. ALCIBIADES SIMONIDES (1818–1890)
An Albanian artist and chemist, this little-known but prolific forger wins the prize for industriousness and perseverance in the face of constant exposure. He began his career in 1853 by selling an ancient manuscript of Homer to the king of Greece, who consulted scholars at the University of Athens before making his purchase. The Homer was soon discovered to be a forgery, but by then Simonides had vanished. Some years later, he sold to a consortium of Turkish scholars, for the then handsome sum of $40,000, a collection of ancient Greek, Assyrian, and Egyptian manuscripts. Microscopic examination in Berlin determined that they were fake, but by then Simonides had excavated rare manuscripts in Turkey and sold them to local pashas. Finally, he turned up in London with letters reputedly written by Belisarius to the Emperor Justinian and by Alcibiades to Pericles, for which the Duke of Sutherland eventually paid over $4,000. They were found to be forgeries, but again Simonides had vanished. He was banished once from Spain, but never imprisoned, and he died old.

4. CHARLES DAWSON (1864–1916)
This English attorney and amateur geologist was the discoverer of Piltdown man, the bones of the so-called missing link between man and ape that were unearthed in 1912 from a gravel pit near Piltdown Common in East Sussex, England. Experts from the British Museum authenticated the find, and the scientific world was so thrilled—for it seemed a confirmation of basic Darwinian theory—that it bestowed upon Dawson a high honor by naming the new species *Eoanthropus dawsoni*. In 1949, however, the English geologist Kenneth Oakley subjected the famous Piltdown bones to some new chemical tests and announced that there was doubt as to their authenticity. Finally, in 1953, newer and more sophisticated tests proved that the jaw of *Eoanthropus dawsoni* was that of an orangutan; its teeth had been filed with modern instruments and then stained in a crucible. Piltdown man was one of the more amusing forgeries of history. Charles Dawson—one might think, luckily—died many years before its exposure.

5. FRITZ KREISLER (1875–1962)
The famous Viennese violinist, clearly a genius as an interpretive performer, was also the most successful known musical forger. Because he believed that the concert violinist's repertory of unaccompanied pieces was too small, and therefore insufficient to display his talents, Kreisler created a repertory of his own. Beginning in the late 1890s, he wrote pieces and ascribed them to then little-known composers such as Couperin, Pugnani, Francoeur, Padre Martini, Porpora—even

Vivaldi—claiming that he had found the hitherto unknown manuscripts "in libraries and monasteries while visiting Rome, Florence, Venice, and Paris." Critics called them "little masterpieces." In 1935, casually, he confessed his brilliant forgeries to Olin Downes, music critic of the *New York Times*. There was an uproar but, of course, no penalty.

6. HANS VAN MEEGEREN (1889–1947)

The forgeries of this erratic, hardworking Dutch painter might never have been revealed had it not been for a quirk of fate: Reichsmarschall Hermann Göring owned one of them, which had been bought for him in the Netherlands during World War II. Called *Christ and the Adulteress*, it was signed Jan Vermeer, and it was one of 14 seventeenth-century Dutch "masterpieces" by Vermeer and Pieter de Hooch that had been laboriously painted and most carefully aged by Hans van Meegeren. Dutch authorities accused van Meegeren of collaboration with the Nazi enemy in selling works of national importance. He was jailed, and, to evade the consequences of the worse crime, he confessed to the lesser: forgery. To prove his point, in his prison cell he painted one more Vermeer and, in addition, produced some of the rare pigments he had used in the forgeries. Van Meegeren had been paid the astounding sum of over $3 million in Dutch gulden for his paintings, and six of his Vermeers hung in museums and galleries. At his trial, he was given a year's imprisonment, but before the sentence could be carried out, frail, penniless, and depressed, he died of a heart attack.

7. ARTURO ALVES REIS (1896–1955)

Labeled by one biographer as *The Man Who Stole Portugal*, mild-mannered, visionary Alves Reis was indisputably history's boldest known forger of money. With several confederates, including a then famous Dutch actress, he forged documents and letters that convinced the famous London firm of Waterlow & Sons, which printed money for the Bank of Portugal, that he was empowered to personally receive over $10 million worth of Portuguese 500-escudo banknotes destined—he said—for the Portuguese colony of Angola. Alves Reis said that his company would stamp the notes with the word "Angola" so that they could not be used in Portugal, but they never did so. The money flowed so smoothly and steadily into Alves Reis's hands that he not only founded his own private bank in Lisbon, but also with the forged notes, bought so many shares in the Bank of Portugal that in time he threatened to become its majority stockholder. A duplication of serial numbers led to his arrest in 1925. He finally confessed in 1930, spent the next 15 years in prison, and died a pauper.

8. ELMYR DE HORY (1906–1976)

Born Joseph Hoffman, and also known as Louis Raynal, Jean Cassou, and Elmyr Dory-Boutin, this Hungarian Jewish émigré homosexual was probably the greatest and certainly the most prolific art forger of all time. He was a failed expressionist painter, but hundreds of his works hang in famous museums and art galleries throughout the world, and thousands are in private collections; they are all signed Matisse, Modigliani, Dufy, Chagall, Derian, Picasso, Vlaminck, Gauguin, Braque, or Cézanne. He was the subject of a biography, *Fake!* by Clifford Irving, and a 1976 feature-length documentary film by Orson Welles. After 1962, de Hory lived and painted on the island of Ibiza, Spain. He was finally exposed in 1967 through the greed and flamboyance of two men who had sold 44 of his fake postimpressionist canvases to a Texas oil millionaire. In 1976, harassed, constantly threatened by the two men who had grown rich as salesmen of his fakes, and facing almost certain extradition to France, where he feared he would die of cold in a prison cell, de Hory killed himself on Ibiza with an overdose of barbiturates. At the time of his death, the market value of his lifework was estimated at over $30 million.

9. CLIFFORD IRVING (1930–)
A novelist, Irving perpetrated the most widely publicized hoax of the twentieth century when, in 1971, he convinced his New York publisher, McGraw-Hill, that he had been commissioned to ghostwrite the autobiography of the famous elusive billionaire Howard Hughes. With Richard Suskind, a friend and author of children's books, Irving not only wrote a wildly imaginative 1,200-page book "by Hughes" that veteran newsmen and men who knew Hughes well swore "had to be authentic," but also forged over 20 pages of handwritten letters and contracts by Hughes to buttress his claim. Those forgeries, done by a complete amateur who had never seen an original specimen of the handwriting he was reproducing, were submitted to five of the finest handwriting experts in the U.S., who, after close examination, unanimously declared them to be genuine. For Irving to have forged such a mass of material, said expert Paul Osborn, "would be beyond human ability." Despite the furor and publicity, Irving's essentially absurd scheme would never have been discovered and proved a hoax if Swiss banks had not broken their traditional secrecy and revealed that the holder of a Zurich bank account in the name of H. R. Hughes was in fact a woman—Irving's wife. The author returned what was left of the $765,000 he had received from McGraw-Hill and went to prison for 17 months.

10. MR. X (?–?)
By definition, the identity of the greatest forger of all time, whether man or woman, is unknown to us. For he (or she) must have been—or must be—far too clever and skillful ever to have been suspected or exposed. Caveat emptor.

Abbie Hoffman's
10 Heroes Who Got Away with It

Born on November 30, 1936, Abbott "Abbie" Hoffman was a cofounder of the Youth International Party ("Yippies") and one of the elder statesmen of the protest and antiwar movements of the 1960s. He was also one of the Chicago Seven, a group of political activists arrested for their protests during the 1968 Democratic Convention in Chicago, whose trial became a legendary media circus. He published a number of books, the most famous of which is *Steal This Book* (1971). Busted in 1973 for allegedly dealing cocaine, Hoffman lived for years as a fugitive under the alias Barry Freed. He died in 1989, an apparent suicide. He contributed this list to *The Book of Lists* in 1980, while still a fugitive from law enforcement:

1. **B. TRAVEN** (1882?–1969; 1890?–1969; 1894?–1969; 1901?–1969)
   The man who called himself B. Traven was the world's greatest fugitive, as well as the best working-class novelist ever to pick up a pen. He authored over 30 books, including the classic novel *The Treasure of the Sierra Madre*, while on the run from at least four governments. He began his career in Germany as an actor and anarchist, using the name Ret Marut. He was put on trial in 1919 for treason in Munich and was sentenced to death but escaped. He fled to Moscow, fought with Stalin, and then fled to France. Next he became a sailor on "death ships" for the American merchant marine that were sunk to collect insurance money. (His 1934 best seller was *The Death Ship: The Story of an American Sailor*.) In 1923, he made his way to the oil fields of Mexico, where, with Wobbly organizers, he agitated for unions. This activity led to his being hunted as "El Rubio," an enemy of the state. Hiding out in Mexico, he began an immensely successful career as the novelist B. Traven. In addition, he became a firmly established photographer, working under the name Traven Torsven. He was also a respected archaeologist and was considered a great medicine healer by the Chiapas Indians. *Life* magazine once offered $5,000 to anyone who could find the elusive author. Late in the 1950s, he emerged from hiding, married, settled down in Mexico City, and successfully managed to blur the facts of his early life. Just before he died, he burned most of his personal papers, but books remain a proud legacy from a noble champion of freedom.

2. **KIM PHILBY** (1912–1988)
   Born Harold Adrian Philby, this Britisher was recruited into the British Secret Service in 1939. A brilliant spy, he was quickly promoted to lead the Soviet section during World War II. In 1949, he was assigned to be chief liaison between all Anglo-American intelligence

operations. He won praise from Roosevelt, Truman, and Churchill and was often mentioned as a likely candidate to head British Intelligence. What no one knew was that in 1933, Philby had been recruited as a Russian agent. Until 1951, he successfully eluded suspicion. In that year, the British Secret Service learned that two of their agents, Guy Burgess and Donald MacLean, were double agents working for the Russians. Before they could be arrested, the two fled to Moscow. Someone had informed them of their impending arrest, and suspicion fell upon Philby. For 10 years, the British tried unsuccessfully to prove that Philby was a double agent. Finally in 1961, when Philby was working as a foreign correspondent in Beirut, Lebanon, a Russian spy named George Blake was arrested and confirmed what the British had suspected. On the night of January 23, 1963, Philby slipped away from pursuing agents on his way to a dinner party. Disguised as an Arab, he walked 300 miles through Syria to Turkey, to surface in Moscow six months later.

3. GÜNTER WALLRAFF (1942–)
Born in Cologne, Germany, Wallraff is the world's best undercover reporter. The author of several books and articles, he has championed the working class by exposing—in a variety of inventive ways—Nazis in positions of power, government spying, and illegal business practices. For four years, he posed successfully as a migrant worker, a derelict, a mental patient, a Turkish laborer, a steel worker, and a postal clerk. What emerged were two fascinating exposés of squalid conditions. In 1976, posing as an official in the Bonn government, he managed to arrange a secret arms deal with Portuguese archconservative General Antonio Spinola. In 1977, he infiltrated Germany's largest newspaper, the right-wing *Bild Zeitung*. He documented the fabrication of anti-worker articles. On other occasions, he posed as the valet to the bishop of Bavaria, as a police informer, and as a napalm manufacturer. He has been in prison several times, and the courts have ordered numerous censorings of his books. A man of a thousand faces, Europe's most popular reporter carries out his missions undetected. [The 1990 film *The Man Inside* is based on Wallraff's life.]

4. HARRY HOUDINI (1874–1926)
Houdini perhaps got away from it more than with it. He literally could not be locked up. He escaped from a water tank manacled upside down by his ankles and from hundreds of jails and bank vaults. He was the world's greatest escape artist. Extraordinarily dexterous, he could tie and untie a knot with the toes of one foot. He made elaborate plans to communicate with the living 50 years after his death. Several close friends are convinced he managed even that. Rumor has it that he is currently a TV repairman living in Paterson, New Jersey.

5. FRANCISCO VILLA (1877–1923)

"Pancho" Villa, the fabled Mexican revolutionary, led the last army to get away with invading the United States. It happened on March 9, 1916, at Columbus, New Mexico. President Wilson ordered General Pershing to track the rebel force into Mexico. Leading the pursuit was George Patton. They failed to capture Pancho Villa, who led them on a madcap chase through the mountains. Villa escaped many close calls during the Mexican Revolution. On July 20, 1923, after he had retired to a ranch in Durango, he was ambushed and shot while driving his automobile.

6. HENRI CHARRIÈRE, aka "PAPILLON" (1907–1973)

Henri Charrière was one of the few to escape from the dreaded French penal colony on Devil's Island. Convicted of murder in France in 1931, Charrière, alias Papillon, was sentenced to hard labor for life. He was sent with hundreds of others on a prison ship to St. Laurent, French Guiana, where he began a series of daring escapes and recaptures. He was finally transferred from the mainland prison to the brutal Devil's Island, after serving three years and nine months in solitary confinement. He made his escape from Devil's Island riding two sacks of coconuts through a shark-infested sea to the mainland. His story became a best-selling book in 1970, and the French government subsequently pardoned him for his original crime.

7. D. B. COOPER (1926?–?)

Little is known about this modern-day legend. In 1971, D. B. Cooper boarded a plane in Los Angeles with a briefcase he claimed was rigged as a bomb and a request for $200,000. The extortion was the first of its nature; out of it emerged the word *skyjacker*. He ordered the plane to land in Seattle, where he collected the $200,000 and four parachutes and let the passengers go. The crew remained on board and flew him south. FBI agents guarded every airport on the West Coast. The plane was under continued close scrutiny. Cooper bailed out somewhere over Washington and foiled all attempts to follow him. Although low-level officials claim he perished in the woods, no body or other trace of him was ever found. What no one knows is that D. B. Cooper lost all of the money investing in Arizona real estate and is currently collecting unemployment in Phoenix.

8. RONALD BIGGS (1930–)

England's greatest modern rogue, Ronnie Biggs seems to lead a charmed life. On August 8, 1963, he and his cohorts robbed a Royal Mail train and successfully made off with $7.3 million, for a new world's record. Later that year, Scotland Yard cracked the case, and Biggs and company were arrested and sent to jail. Much of the money, however, remained at large. Biggs engineered a successful prison escape from England's top-security prison and eventually made his way to Brazil.

There he got a woman pregnant, and—according to Brazilian law—being the father of a Brazilian citizen, he was not subject to extradition. His English wife allowed him to marry the Brazilian woman. A popular punk-rock group called the Sex Pistols signed up Biggs as lead singer early in 1978. A smash hit and a movie role followed. [After running out of money in 2001, Biggs returned to England for medical treatment and was immediately arrested.]

9. RICHARD MILHOUS NIXON (1913–1994)
Nixon was born on January 9, 1913, in Yorba Linda, California, and died the following day. He got away with so much for so long I just couldn't resist including him. Because of the events that occurred during his administration, Nixon will be remembered long after all other presidents of the twentieth century become names in trivia contests.

10. ANONYMOUS
Obviously, the ones who got away with the most are unknown. They're smiling when they read this, knowing that compared to them, the above nine are amateurs.

38 Unusual Lawsuits

1. PRAY FOR RAIN
In hopes of ending a drought in upstate New York in the 1880s, a Presbyterian minister named Duncan McLeod organized a mass prayer session to take place on a Saturday in August. At noon, people through-out the area stopped their activities and prayed for rain. By one o'clock, clouds had appeared; by two, a gusty wind was blowing; by three, the temperature had dropped 20 degrees; and by four, a thunderstorm had arrived. The storm, which dropped almost two inches of rain, washed out a bridge and completely destroyed a barn, which burned to the ground after being struck by lightning.
    As it happened, the barn belonged to Phineas Dodd, the only farmer in Phelps, New York, who had refused to join the collective prayer. Many thought that Dodd had been a victim of divine justice, but Dodd had other ideas: When he heard that Reverend McLeod was accepting congratulations for ending the drought, he sued the minister for $5,000 to cover the damages to his property. The minister was put in a difficult situation: After repeatedly telling his followers that God had answered their prayers, he could hardly back down and say that the storm was just a coincidence. Fortunately for McLeod, his lawyer was able to convince the judge that the mass prayers had requested only rain and that the thunder and lightning had been a bonus provided by God for which McLeod and his parishioners were not responsible.

2. THE KABOTCHNICKS SPEAK ONLY TO GOD

The elite status of the Cabot family of New England is summarized in the old ditty:

> Here's to the city of Boston,
> The land of the bean and the cod,
> Where the Lowells speak only to the Cabots,
> And the Cabots speak only to God.

In August 1923, the Cabots received a bit of a jolt when Harry and Myrtle Kabotchnick of Philadelphia filed a petition to have their last name changed to Cabot. Immediate objections were raised by several prominent members of the Cabot family, as well as by the Pennsylvania Society of the Order of Founders and Patriots of America. However, Judge Audendried ruled in favor of the Kabotchnicks, and a new branch was grafted onto the Cabot family tree.

3. A CABLE CAR NAMED DESIRE

The case of Gloria Sykes caused a sensation in San Francisco throughout the month of April 1970. A devout Lutheran and college graduate from Dearborn Heights, Michigan, the 23-year-old Sykes had been involved in a cable car accident. The Hyde Street cable car had lost its grip and plunged backward, throwing Sykes against a pole. She suffered two black eyes and several bruises, but worst of all, claimed her lawyer, she was transformed into a nymphomaniac. Although she had had sex back in Michigan, she became insatiable after the accident and once engaged in sexual intercourse 50 times in five days. This inconvenience caused her to sue the Municipal Railway for $500,000 for physical and emotional injuries. The jury of eight women and four men was basically sympathetic and awarded Sykes a judgment for $50,000.

4. SUING A FOREIGN PRINCE

In 1971, Gerald Mayo filed suit at the U.S. district court in Pennsylvania against Satan and his servants, claiming they had placed obstacles in his path that caused his downfall. On December 3, Mayo's complaint was denied on the grounds that the defendant did not reside in Pennsylvania.

5. COUNTING HIS BLESSINGS

On September 7, 1971, Hugh McNatt of Miami donated $800 to the Allapattah Baptist Church after hearing Pastor Donald Manuel promise that "blessings, benefits, and rewards" would come to anyone who tithed 10 percent of his or her wealth to the church. Three years passed without any blessings, benefits, or rewards, so McNatt, an unemployed electrical worker, sued the church. Before the case could come to trial, a Texas businessman named Alton S. Newell read about McNatt's predicament and sent him a check for $800, whereupon McNatt agreed to drop the suit.

6. **SHARPER THAN A SERPENT'S TOOTH IS A THANKLESS CHILD**
   In April 1978, 24-year-old Tom Hansen of Boulder, Colorado, sued his
   parents, Richard and Shirley, for "parental malpractice." Young
   Hansen claimed that his parents had done such a bad job of rearing
   him that he would be forced to seek psychiatric care for the rest of his
   life. He asked for $250,000 in medical expenses and $100,000 in
   punitive damages. In explaining his reasons for filing the suit, Hansen
   said it was an alternative to his desire to kill his father: "I felt like
   killing my father for a long time. I guess I found a more appropriate
   way of dealing with it." The suit was subsequently dismissed by the
   district court and later by the Colorado Court of Appeals.

7. **STANDING UP FOR THE STOOD UP**
   Tom Horsley, a 41-year-old accountant from Campbell, California, was
   quite upset in May 1978, when his date for the night, 31-year-old
   waitress Alyn Chesselet of San Francisco, failed to show up. He was so
   upset, in fact, that he sued her for "breach of oral contract." His lawyer
   explained that Mr. Horsley is "not the type of man to take standing up
   lying down." Horsley asked for $38 in compensation: $17 for time lost
   at his hourly wage of $8.50, $17 in travel expenses, and $4 in court
   costs. Chesselet, in her defense, said she had attempted to call Horsley
   about her change in plans, which was due to having to work an extra
   shift, but he had already left his office. Judge Richard P. Figone ruled
   against Horsley, who remained philosophical. "I feel good about the
   whole thing," he said. "It raised people's consciousness about this
   problem. . . . There's too much of this thing, broken dates. It shows
   people are not sincere."

8. **WORSE THAN CAPITAL PUNISHMENT**
   In 1978, convicted murderer Ralph E. Dodson claimed that his sentence of life imprisonment in an all-male prison was cruel and unusual
   punishment because it imposed upon him a lifetime of celibacy. He
   requested transfer to a women's prison, instead. The Indiana Supreme
   Court rejected his appeal on the grounds that he had forfeited his right
   "to pursue his amorous pleasures as if he were a free man" when he was
   convicted of first-degree murder. Three years later, Dodson was
   charged with murdering a fellow prisoner.

9. **THE MISPLACED CORPSE**
   Beatrice Daigle, 73, of Woonsocket, Rhode Island, filed a $250,000 suit
   when she learned that she had been praying at the wrong grave for
   17 years. After her husband died on January 28, 1961, the Church of
   the Precious Blood in Woonsocket sold Mrs. Daigle a plot at St. John the
   Baptist Cemetery in Bellingham, Massachusetts. Mrs. Daigle visited the
   grave frequently to pray for the repose of her dead husband's soul. On
   April 26, 1978, workers opened the grave in order to move Mr. Daigle's

body to another plot and discovered instead the body of a woman, Jeanne Champagne. Three more graves had to be dug up before Mr. Daigle's body was located. Mrs. Daigle, who was present at the exhumation, suffered "severe emotional trauma and distress" because of the mistake. In November 1979, the case was dismissed.

10. DEMON LIQUOR

On February 5, 1979, Woodrow W. Bussey filed a $2 million suit in Oklahoma County District Court claiming that the Adolph Coors Co. and a local tavern had caused him to become an alcoholic by failing to warn him that the 3.2 beer served in Oklahoma is actually an intoxicating beverage. Bussey said that Coors beer had done irreparable damage to his brain, "pickling his mind" and preventing him from thinking clearly. In 1988, reacting to the reparations paid to Japanese-Americans who were interned during World War II, he sued the United States government for uprooting his Cherokee ancestors during the 1838 forced march known as the Trail of Tears.

11. THE WANDERING BELLY BUTTON

Virginia O'Hare, 42, of Poughkeepsie, New York, filed a malpractice suit against plastic surgeon Howard Bellin after her navel ended up two inches off center following surgery in November 1974 to give her "a flat sexy belly." Dr. Bellin had previously performed successful operations on O'Hare's nose and eyelids. He argued that O'Hare's navel (which was later returned to its proper position by another plastic surgeon) had been misplaced by only a half inch, which he called "not cosmetically unacceptable." In May 1979, a state supreme court jury awarded O'Hare $854,219, including $100,000 for pain and suffering, $4,219 for the corrective surgery, and $750,000 for loss of earnings. Not surprisingly, Dr. Bellin appealed the verdict but later agreed to pay Mrs. O'Hare $200,000.

12. EXTRASENSORY PAIN

Martha Burke's twin sister, Margaret Fox, was one of the 580 people killed in the plane disaster at Tenerife in the Canary Islands on March 27, 1977. Consequently, Mrs. Burke sued Pan American—not for the wrongful death of her sister, but for her own injuries, which she sustained because of the "extrasensory empathy" that is common among identical twins. At the moment of the collision, Mrs. Burke, sitting in her home in Fremont, California, suffered burning sensations in her chest and stomach and a feeling of being split. On February 21, 1980, federal court judge Robert Ward ruled against her, explaining that legally she had to be physically present at the accident to collect damages.

13. THE POORLY TRAINED SPY

Maria del Carmen y Ruiz was married to one of Fidel Castro's intelligence chiefs when, in 1964, she was approached by the CIA in Cuba and asked to be a spy. She worked diligently at her new job, but in January 1969, she was caught by Cuban counterintelligence agents and sentenced to 20 years in prison. After serving eight and a half years, she became the first convicted American spy to be released from Cuban custody. In May 1980, Ruiz, remarried and known as Carmen Mackowski, sued the CIA for inadequate training. She also charged that the CIA had misled her into believing that if she was detected, it would arrange for her immediate release. U.S. district court judge Dickinson Debevoise of Trenton, New Jersey, ruled in favor of the CIA, because, as one newspaper put it, federal judges "do not have authority to intervene in CIA employment matters that might result in the release of intelligence information."

14. X-RATED SHRUBBERY
In September 1980, in La Jolla, California, the "Grand Old Man of Divorce Law," John T. Holt, and his wife, Phyllis, filed suit against their neighbors, William and Helen Hawkins. The Holts claimed that the Hawkins had trimmed their hedges into obscene shapes. The Holts named 20 other neighbors as coconspirators. They asked $250,000 in punitive damages and demanded removal of trees and hedges that had been shaped "to resemble phallic symbols." The case was finally dismissed in January 1982.

15. THE MUMMY'S CURSE
Police officer George E. La Brash, 56, suffered a stroke on September 23, 1979, while guarding the 3,300-year-old golden mask of King Tutankhamen when it was on display in San Francisco. La Brash claimed that he was a victim of the famous Curse of King Tut, which had caused the sudden death of numerous people involved in the 1923 discovery of Tut's tomb. For this reason, he contended that the stroke was job-related and that he was entitled to $18,400 in disability pay for the eight months of his recuperation. On February 9, 1982, superior court judge Richard P. Figone denied La Brash's claim.

16. L-A-W-S-U-I-T
The two finalists in a contest to decide who would represent Los Altos School in the 1987 Ventura County, California, spelling bee were Steven Chen, 13, and Victor Wang, 12. Victor spelled *horsy* h-o-r-s-y, while Steven spelled it h-o-r-s-e-y. Contest officials ruled that Steven's spelling was incorrect and advanced Victor to the county finals. But when Steven went home, he found both spellings in his dictionary and returned to the school to lodge a protest. It turned out that the officials had used an inadequate dictionary, so it was decided that both boys could advance. At the county finals, Steven defeated defending champion Gavin McDonald, 13, and advanced to the National Spelling Bee. Gavin's father sued the county event's sponsor, the

Ventura County Star–Free Press, charging mental distress, and asked for $2 million in damages. He claimed that Steven Chen should not have been allowed to compete because each school was allowed only one entrant. A superior court judge and a state court of appeals dismissed the suit, stating that the major reason Gavin McDonald lost the Ventura County Spelling Bee was not that the contest was poorly run but that he had misspelled *iridescent.*

17. **NERDS NOT ALLOWED**
Two cases filed in Los Angeles challenged the right of fashionable nightclubs to deny entrance to would-be patrons because they are not stylishly dressed. In the first case, settled in 1990, Kenneth Lipton, an attorney specializing in dog-bite cases, was barred from entering the Mayan nightclub because a doorman judged his turquoise shirt and baggy olive pants to be "not cool." Owners of the club were forced to pay Lipton and three companions $1,112 in damages. The following year, the California State Department of Alcoholic Beverage Control won its suit against Vertigo, another trendy club that refused admittance to those people it claimed had no fashion sense. Administrative law judge Milford Maron ruled that Vertigo would lose its license if it continued to exclude customers based on a discriminatory dress code and the whim of door-men. Vertigo's owners chose to close the club in December 1992.

18. **FALSE PREGNANCY**
"World's Oldest Newspaper Carrier, 101, Quits Because She's Pregnant," read the headline in a 1990 edition of the *Sun,* a supermarket tabloid. The accompanying article, complete with a photograph of the sexually active senior, told the story of a newspaper carrier in Stirling, Australia, who had to give up her job when a millionaire on her route impregnated her. The story was totally false. Stirling, Australia, doesn't even exist. But, as it turned out, the photo was of a real, living person—Nellie Mitchell, who had delivered the *Arkansas Gazette* for 50 years. Mitchell wasn't really 101 years old—she was only 96, young enough to be humiliated when friends and neighbors asked her when her baby was due. She sued the *Sun,* charging invasion of privacy and extreme emotional distress. John Vader, the editor of the *Sun,* admitted in court that he had chosen the picture of Mitchell because he assumed she was dead. Dead people cannot sue. A jury awarded Mitchell $850,000 in punitive damages and $650,000 in compensatory damages. In 1993, a federal district court judge reduced the amount of compensatory damages to $150,000.

19. **A HARD CASE**
On the surface, *Plaster Caster v. Cohen* was just another lawsuit concerning disputed property. What made the case unusual was the nature of the property. In 1966, Cynthia Albritton was, in her own words, "a teenage virgin dying to meet rock stars." She was also a

student at the University of Illinois. When her art teacher gave her an assignment to make a plaster cast of "something hard," she got an idea. She began approaching visiting rock groups and asking if she could make plaster casts of their penises. She had no problem finding girlfriends to help her prepare her models. At first, she used plaster of paris, then a combination of tinfoil and hot wax, before settling on an alginate product used for tooth and jaw molds. Her project gained underground notoriety, and she changed her name to Cynthia Plaster Caster. In 1970, her home in Los Angeles was burglarized, so she gave 23 of her rock members to music publisher Herb Cohen for safekeeping. Cohen refused to return them, claiming they were a payoff for a business debt owed him by Frank Zappa, who had employed Plaster Caster. In 1991, Plaster Caster filed suit against Cohen, who countersued. Two years later, a Los Angeles superior court ruled in favor of Cynthia Plaster Caster, who regained control of her "babies," including Jimi Hendrix, Anthony Newley, and Eric Burdon.

20. ROTTHUAHUAS
Canella, a rottweiler living in Key Largo, Florida, was in heat, and her owner, Kevin Foley, had plans to mate her with "an acceptable male" and then sell the litter. But before he could do so, a neighboring Chihuahua named Rocky sneaked onto Foley's property and engaged Canella. Rocky and Canella were caught in the act, both by Foley, who snapped a photo of the incident, and by an animal control officer who happened to be passing by and stopped to watch the unusual coupling. A month later, Foley learned that Canella was pregnant. He terminated the pregnancy by hysterectomy and sued Rocky's owner, Dayami Diaz. On November 1, 1993, Monroe County judge Reagan Ptomey ruled in favor of Foley and ordered Diaz to pay him $2,567.50.

21. BANK ROBBER SUES BANK
On May 25, 1992, Amil Dinsio, Sr., his brother, his son, his nephew, and a friend who specialized in safecracking tried to break into the United Carolina Bank in Charlotte, North Carolina. They were stopped immediately because the FBI had received a tip about the heist and had been trailing the Dinsios for days. Caught red-handed, the gang members pleaded guilty. Federal sentencing guidelines allowed U.S. district court judge Robert Potter to take into account, when determining the robbers' sentences, the amount of money the bank might have lost if the robbery had been successful. He gave Amil Dinsio, Sr., and his brother, James, the maximum sentence—46 months in prison. Languishing in jail with nothing better to do, Amil sued United Carolina Bank, claiming it had inflated the potential-loss figures in an attempt to punish him. Amil lost his case and served out his sentence, but he didn't stay out of prison for long. In 1997, he and James were sentenced to 25 years to life for kidnapping a police officer at gunpoint and threatening his life.

22. DAMAGED BY BARRY MANILOW

It was with some reluctance that Arizona Court of Appeals judge Philip Espinosa accompanied his wife to a Barry Manilow concert on the fateful night of December 23, 1993. Not a Manilow fan to begin with, he nonetheless expected an endurable evening of "soft, amplified music." Instead, he found himself sitting through the loudest concert he had ever attended. It was so loud, in fact, that Espinosa was left with a constant and permanent ringing in his ears. He sued Manilow and others responsible for damages. The case was settled out of court in 1997, when Manilow agreed to donate $5,000 to an ear disorder association.

23. BREASTLASH

In honor of his upcoming wedding, Paul Shimkonis's friends threw a bachelor party for him at the Diamond Dolls topless club in Clearwater, Florida. As part of the show, he was asked to lean back in a chair with his eyes closed while dancer Tawny Peaks danced around him. In the words of the lawsuit that Shimkonis filed a year and a half later, "Suddenly, without warning and without Plaintiff's consent, [the dancer] jumped on the Plaintiff, forcing her very large breasts into his face, causing his head to jerk backwards." Shimkonis, a physical therapist, suffered head and neck injuries, incurred major medical bills, and still couldn't turn his head to the right. Finally, on June 29, 1998, he filed suit against Diamond Dolls, asking for $15,000 to cover his medical expenses and as compensation for "loss of capacity for the enjoyment of life." The case was brought before television's *People's Court* with former New York City mayor Ed Koch presiding. A female court officer examined Peaks's 69HH breasts in chambers and reported that although they were 20 percent silicone, they were soft and "not as dense as plaintiff described." Koch ruled in favor of Tawny Peaks and the club. In 2004, Peaks sold her breast implants on eBay for $16,766.

Surprising as it may seem, *Shimkonis v. Peaks* was not the only lawsuit to arise from a 1996 breast attack. In an unrelated case in Belleview, Illinois, Bennie Casson sued dancer Busty Heart (Susan Sykes) and P.T.'s Show Club in Sauget after he was assaulted by Heart's 88-inch breasts during a performance.

24. COKE ISN'T IT

Amanda Blake of Northampton, Massachusetts, had been working for Coca-Cola Bottling Company for eight years when, in 1985, Coca-Cola discovered that she had fallen in love with and become engaged to David Cronin, who worked for Pepsi. Blake was ordered to break off her engagement, persuade Cronin to quit his job, or quit herself. She refused and was fired for "conflict of interest." Blake sued Coca-Cola for damages and won a $600,000 settlement.

25. CORPORATE SPY?

For six weeks in the summer of 1989, Maritza and Stephen French of Costa Mesa, California, rented a room in their house to Takashi Morimoto, an employee of Nissan Motor Company who had been sent from Japan to study American automotive habits. Three months later, the French family read in an article in the *Los Angeles Times* that Mr. Morimoto's research had included a detailed study of the Frenches themselves, about whom he had taken copious notes. Feeling violated, the Frenches sued Morimoto and Nissan, claiming fraud, invasion of privacy, trespassing, and unfair business practices. However, they eventually dropped the lawsuit rather than face the stress of continued litigation.

26. TOO BIG TO BOOST

When 17-year-old Vicki Ann Guest was not chosen for the 1986 cheerleading squad at Fountain Valley High School in Southern California, she asked Jean Clower, the teacher in charge of the squad, what she had done wrong. Clower explained that Guest's problem was that her breasts were too large. She suggested that Guest, who had already received a scholarship to study dance, should undergo breast reduction surgery. Guest sued the school district, citing sex discrimination and emotional distress. The suit was settled out of court.

27. THE WRONG CHANNEL

New Age channeler J. Z. Knight made a fortune claiming she could pass on the thought of Ramtha, a warrior who lived 35,000 years ago on the lost continent of Atlantis. Besides charging for sessions with Ramtha, Knight and her husband, Jeffrey, marketed books, tapes, and survival gear. When the couple divorced in 1989, Jeffrey came away with a meager $120,000. He later claimed that Ramtha had bullied him into accepting the settlement. In 1992, Judge Bruce Cohoe of the Pierce County, Washington, Superior Court, rejected the charge of coercion but did order J. Z. to pay her ex-husband $720,000—half of the "goodwill value" of the Ramtha business, which had not been taken into account as part of the original settlement.

28. ACTING LIKE AN ASS

Former sex symbol Brigitte Bardot has devoted her post–film career years to promoting the rights of animals. Among the members of her personal menagerie in St. Tropez, France, were a thirty-two-year-old mare named Duchesse and a young donkey named Mimosa. In the summer of 1989, Bardot invited her neighbor's donkey, a three-year-old male named Charley, to graze alongside Duchesse and Mimosa. When Charley began to display a sexual interest in Duchesse, Bardot feared that if he was allowed to have his way with the elderly mare, it might prove fatal to Duchesse. So she called her vet and had Charley castrated. Charley's owner, Jean-Pierre Manivet, was out of town at the time. When he returned to St. Tropez, he was outraged by what had happened. Manivet sued Bardot, claiming that Charley had really been interested in Mimosa, not Duchesse. Bardot countersued, alleging that the bad publicity had harmed her reputation. Both suits were eventually rejected by the courts.

29. CHILD DIVORCES PARENTS

In a widely publicized case that was televised live in 1992, 12-year-old Gregory Kingsley of Florida filed a lawsuit to sever his legal relationship with his biological parents and asked to be adopted by his foster parents, George and Lizabeth Russ. Gregory's natural father, Ralph Kingsley, did not contest the lawsuit, but his natural mother, Rachel Kingsley, did. Circuit judge Thomas Kirk ruled that Mrs. Kingsley had been a neglectful parent and allowed Gregory to be adopted by the Russes.

30. SPRINTING TO THE COURTS

On August 28, 1988, the world championship cycling road race, held in Robse, Belgium, came down to a sprint between Steve Bauer of Canada and 1984 world champion Claude Criquielion of Belgium. But a mere 75 meters from the finish line, the two crashed, allowing Maurizio Fondriest of Italy to snatch an unexpected victory. In a case without precedent in professional cycling, Criquielion sued Bauer for assault and asked for more than $1.5 million in damages. Criquielion alleged that Bauer had swerved in front of him and elbowed him, thus denying him the glory and financial rewards that come with a world championship. The case dragged though the courts, but finally, three and a half years later, a Belgian judge ruled in favor of Bauer.

31. AN ARM AND A LEG

On the night of April 10, 1989, dishwasher Francisco Merino became so drunk that he fell onto the subway tracks at the 183rd Street IRT station in the Bronx and was hit by a northbound train. He lost his left arm in the accident and filed suit against the New York Transit Authority for failing to remove him from the platform when they noticed that he was intoxicated. Incredibly, in September 1990, a jury decided that the Transit Authority was responsible for all disabled passengers, including those disabled by alcohol. They awarded Merino $9.3 million in damages. The court threw out the judgment, declaring that the jury had acted "irrationally." The case was retried, and Merino was awarded $3.6 million, based on the failure of the Transit Authority to upgrade the lighting at the station. However, in 1996, that ruling, too, was overturned.

32. SORE LOSER

Toshi Van Blitter of El Macero, California, was not a good gambler. Playing blackjack at two Harrah's casinos in Nevada, she ran up $350,000 in debts. In 1985, she filed suit to have her debts canceled, charging that Harrah's had been negligent in failing to inform her that she was incompetent and in failing to suggest that she attend classes on how to play blackjack. Two federal courts rejected her claim.

33. BACKDOOR MAN AND WOMAN

In 1989, a Ft. Lauderdale, Florida, couple, Henrietta and Alfread Binns, were forced to file a lawsuit to seek permission to use their back door. The property manager for Bonaventure Condominiums ordered the Binns to stop using their back door because they were wearing a path in the lawn between their condo and the parking lot. NCSC Housing Management Corporation told the Binns that they were destroying the landscaping and creating an eyesore. The case was dismissed when NCSC sent the Binns a letter of apology, paid their legal fees, and agreed to let them continue to use their back door.

34. HELL HATH NO FURY LIKE A LAWYER SCORNED

When Maria Dillon broke off her engagement to Chicago corporate lawyer Frank Zaffere in 1992, the 45-year-old Zaffere responded by suing the 21-year-old restaurant hostess. He demanded that she repay the $40,310.48 he had spent courting her. The amount covered the costs of a fur coat, a car, a typewriter, a ring, and even the champagne he had used to toast her. Zaffere dropped the suit three months after he filed it.

35. THE BIG SPIN

On December 30, 1985, Doris Barnett of Los Angeles appeared on television to try her luck at the California lottery's Big Spin. She spun the lottery wheel and watched as her ball settled into the $3 million slot. Show host Geoff Edwards threw his hands in the air and shouted, "Three million dollars!" Barnett's children rushed out of the audience and joined her in celebration, whooping and jumping for joy. Then Edwards tapped Barnett on the shoulder and turned her attention back to the wheel. The ball had slipped out of the $3 million slot and into the $10,000 slot. Edwards explained that lottery rules required the ball to stay in the slot for five seconds. Barnett was hustled offstage, but she did not go meekly. She sued the California lottery. In 1989, after watching endless videos of other contestants being declared winners in less than five seconds, a jury awarded Barnett the $3 million, as well as an extra $400,000 in damages for emotional trauma. But the California lottery didn't go meekly either: It refused to pay. Eventually, "a mutually satisfactory settlement" was reached, with the agreement that the amount not be made public.

36. FLYING GLADS

Australian mega-star Dame Edna Everage (aka Barry Humphries) made a point of ending her public performances by tossing dozens of gladioli with cut stems into the audience. Unfortunately, at the end of a show in Melbourne in April 2000, the stem of one of Dame Edna's glads hit singing teacher Gary May in the left eye. May, who was taken away in an ambulance, sued for $40,000 Australian, but later reached an out-of-court settlement.

37. SNORE

In 1981, the city government of Davis, California, passed an antinoise ordinance aimed at loud parties and raucous drinkers. But in 1994, college student Chris Doherty called police to complain that he could not sleep because his neighbor, a mother of two named Sari Zayed, snored too loudly. The police woke Zayed and fined her $50. The citation was later dismissed, but Zayed sued the City of Davis for causing her stress and lost wages. The city settled out of court by paying Zayed $13,500.

38. HARD TO SWALLOW

In 1999, Dr. Richard Phillips and Dr. Sharon Irons of Chicago engaged in sex, after which Irons became pregnant. When the baby was born, Irons sued Phillips for child support and won. Phillips claimed that the couple had engaged in oral sex and that, unbeknownst to him, Irons had gone into the next room and impregnated herself with the sperm she had received. Phillips sued Irons for theft of private property and for emotional distress. The theft part of the case was dismissed on the basis that when Phillips delivered his sperm, it was a gift. However, the rest of the case was allowed to proceed.

What 12 Famous or Infamous People Were Doing When Arrested

1. HARVEY BAILEY (1889–?)

Bank robber Bailey had stolen $2 million in 1930—the largest robbery then on record. He was teeing off at the Old Mission Golf Course in Kansas City, Kansas, when FBI agents arrested him—and the other members of his golf foursome: bank robbers Tommy Holden, Francis Keating, and Frank Nash—in 1932.

2. MENAHEM BEGIN (1913–1992)

On September 20, 1940, the future prime minister of Israel, then active in the Zionist movement, was playing chess with his wife in their home in Lithuania when Russian police broke in and arrested him. As he was dragged away, he called out that he conceded the game.

3. ELMER "TRIGGER" BURKE (1917–1958)
In 1946, after robbing a New York City liquor store, syndicate killer Elmer Burke was standing outside the store holding a gun and thumbing through a wad of bills when a passing policeman arrested him.

4. ALEXANDER DUBČEK (1921–1992)
Dubček and other members of the Czech Presidium were meeting in Prague on August 20, 1968, when word came that the Soviets had invaded the country. Shortly after 4:30 the next morning, Russian parachutists entered the building and arrested Dubček while he was trying to answer a telephone call. The phone was torn from his hands, and the cord was cut.

5. PATRICIA HEARST (1954–)
On September 18, 1975, Patricia Hearst was standing in the kitchen of a San Francisco apartment, talking with fellow fugitive Wendy Yoshimura, when FBI agent Tom Padden stuck a gun through the back door window and yelled, "Don't move or I'll blast your head off." Hearst was so surprised that she wet her pants. She was allowed to change clothes before being taken into custody.

6. NINA HOUSDEN (1919–?)
In Toledo, Ohio, in 1947, Nina Housden was sleeping in the front seat of her car, which was being repaired in a service station, when police arrested her for murder. The attendant had discovered the dismembered corpse of her husband wrapped in Christmas paper in the backseat of the car.

7. JAMES EARL RAY (1928–1998)
In Chicago in 1952, James Earl Ray—who was convicted of assassinating Dr. Martin Luther King, Jr., 16 years later—robbed a cab driver of $11.09. Pursued by the police, he ran down a blind alley and jumped over a fence. However, he subsequently tripped and crashed through the basement window of a house—falling directly into a washtub, where police caught him.

8. MAXIMILIEN ROBESPIERRE (1758–1794)
In 1794, the French dictator Maximilien Robespierre was denouncing and demanding the arrest of his political enemies during a session of the Convention, revolutionary France's legislative assembly, when he was arrested for treason. The day after his arrest, he was guillotined.

9. JULIUS ROSENBERG (1918–1953)

On July 17, 1950, Julius and Ethel Rosenberg were listening to *The Lone Ranger* on the radio when FBI agents arrived and arrested Julius for spying for the Soviet Union. Ethel Rosenberg was arrested less than a month later.

10. MARQUIS DE SADE (1740–1814)

In 1801, when the police came to arrest him for writing pornography and committing lewd acts, the Marquis de Sade was consulting with his publisher, Nicolas Massé, who had informed the authorities that de Sade was in his office.

11. JOHN SEADLUND (1910–1938)

After kidnapping and murdering wealthy greeting card manufacturer Charles Ross in 1937, John Seadlund was placing a $10 bet at the Santa Anita Race Track in California when FBI agents arrested him in 1938.

12. OSCAR WILDE (1854–1900)

In 1895, Oscar Wilde was drinking hock and seltzer and talking to his friend Lord Alfred Douglas at the Cadogan Hotel in London when a Scotland Yard inspector arrested him for sodomy.

R.J.F.

8 Creative Legal Defenses

1. RAP MUSIC MADE THEM DO IT

On April 16, 1991, five drunk and stoned teenagers attacked and shot to death at random a 26-year-old stranger in Dodge City, Kansas. Defense attorneys for the accused claimed that their clients had been hypnotized by the music of the Geto Boys, a Houston-based rap group. The case is believed to be the first in which music-prompted insanity was used as a defense in a murder trial.

2. THE OUIJA BOARD MADE THEM DO IT

Vance Davis and five other U.S. Army intelligence analysts went AWOL from their Augsburg, Germany, base in July 1990. The six soldiers, all of whom had top-secret security clearances, were arrested five days later for driving with a broken taillight in Gulf Breeze, Florida. They refused to explain why they left their posts, and they were discharged from the army two weeks later. In 1992, Davis finally broke his silence. He revealed that a spirit had visited them through a Ouija board and told them to leave and to assume their role of preparing people for an impending world cataclysm.

3. DAN RATHER MADE HIM DO IT

James Campbell, a chemist at Virginia Tech, was caught in 1991 making methamphetamines—speed—in a university laboratory. He told police in Christiansburg, Virginia, that he needed the money to pay off debts. While watching TV's *48 Hours*, he saw Dan Rather explain how to make speed and decided to try it. Campbell received probation.

4. PMS MADE HER DO IT

One night in May 1979, Sandie Craddock was working in a pub west of London when she stabbed a fellow barmaid to death. Craddock had previously been convicted of 30 lesser crimes. When a doctor, Katharina Dalton, studied the pattern of Craddock's transgressions, she identified the outburst as being prompted by premenstrual syndrome. Craddock's charge was reduced to manslaughter, and she was released on probation with the stipulation that she receive progesterone treatment. She continued to commit crimes whenever her doses were reduced.

5. PHILADELPHIA MADE HIM DO IT

At a 1992 hearing before the Illinois Attorney Registration and Disciplinary Commission, Kenneth Solomon confessed to submitting 154 fake expense reports between 1982 and 1990. His excuse, supported by a psychologist's report, was that his behavior had been triggered by a "deep-seated resentment" at having to make frequent business trips to Philadelphia. A sympathetic hearing board voted two to one to suspend Solomon's law practice for only one year instead of the two years sought by prosecutors.

6. IT WAS REALLY BURIED TREASURE

When former first lady Imelda Marcos returned to the Philippines in November 1991, the Filipino government filed 54 civil and criminal suits against her and accused her and her husband, Ferdinand, of stealing $5 billion from the country. Mrs. Marcos claimed that it was all a misunderstanding. She and Ferdinand had not really robbed and looted the nation's treasury through graft and corruption; the source of the family fortune that the Marcoses so gaudily displayed was actually the fabled Yamashita treasure, which had been buried by Japanese general Tomoyuki Yamashita during World War II. Marcos claimed that her husband had found the treasure while he was a guerrilla fighting the Japanese. Filipino authorities were not convinced and refused to drop the charges.

7. THE TWINKIE DEFENSE

On November 27, 1978, Dan White, a former policeman and a member of San Francisco's board of supervisors, shot and killed the city's mayor, George Moscone, and its first openly homosexual supervisor,

Harvey Milk. At White's trial the following year, his attorneys brought in a battery of psychiatrists to testify on his behalf. One psychiatrist contended that White had taken his revolver and extra ammunition to City Hall that tragic morning not because he planned to murder Moscone and Milk, but because the gun represented a "security blanket" at a time when he felt emotionally threatened. Another psychiatrist stated that White entered the building by crawling through a basement window rather than going through the front door because he "didn't want to embarrass the police officer" at the door. Another expert testified that White shot Moscone because he was too moral to punch him in the nose, shooting being a more impersonal and, thus, more moral expression of anger. Yet another psychiatrist discussed White's near addiction to junk food, especially Twinkies, Coca-Cola, and potato chips, and how the resultant extreme variations in blood sugar levels exacerbated his manic depression and led to the killings. On May 21, 1979, White, who had been charged with murder, was instead convicted of involuntary manslaughter. He later committed suicide.

8. THE BURRITO DEFENSE

Less well known than Dan White's "Twinkie" defense was the burrito defense of Edward Vasquez, a student of criminal justice and sociology at California State University, Los Angeles. In September 1988, Vasquez was accused of shooting to death a security guard in a parking lot in central Los Angeles. The perpetrator was described as wearing a white T-shirt; Vasquez claimed that he had been wearing a green jacket and that when the shooting took place, he was on the other side of the parking lot buying a burrito from a canteen truck. Vasquez's jacket was seized as evidence and kept in law enforcement custody until his trial, which did not begin until almost two years later.

At the trial, Vasquez claimed that he had been wounded in the rear by a stray bullet. The prosecution contended that if Vasquez had been wearing the jacket, it would have been covered with blood, when, in fact, it was blood-free. Vasquez's lawyer, Jay Jaffe, noted that the jacket reached only to Vasquez's waist and had his client try on the jacket in front of the jury to prove his point. While the jury was deliberating the case, Vasquez contacted Jaffe and told the lawyer that when he tried on the jacket, he had felt "something heavy in the right pocket." The jury was brought back into the courtroom, the jacket was recalled from custody, and from the right pocket Jaffe produced an object wrapped in foil. The foil was unwrapped and the two-year-old burrito was revealed. Vasquez was acquitted.

10 Trial Verdicts That Caused Riots

1. **THE DREYFUS AFFAIR (1894–1906)**
   The conviction of a Jewish army officer for high treason in 1894
   unleashed a tidal wave of anti-Semitism and popular unrest in France.
   Alfred Dreyfus, the son of a manufacturer who lived in Alsace, a region
   annexed by Germany in 1871, had achieved the rank of captain and
   was the only Jew on the general staff when he was accused of selling
   military secrets to the Germans. On the basis of forged and falsified
   evidence, he was court-martialed and sentenced to life imprisonment
   on Devil's Island, the notorious prison of French Guiana. His trial
   polarized French society into two groups—the "revisionists" (liberals
   and anticlericals) and the "nationalists" (the army and the Catholic
   Church). Friendship and family ties were broken over the case, duels
   were fought, strikes occurred, and street fights broke out, bringing
   France to the verge of civil war. Novelist Émile Zola was convicted of
   criminal libel for writing a newspaper article that accused the authorities of framing Dreyfus. Retried in 1899—and again found guilty by the
   army—Dreyfus was pardoned by the president of France that year, but
   he was not restored to his former rank until 1906.

2. **MME. CAILLAUX (JULY 28, 1914)**
   In July 1914, the wife of France's minister of finance was tried for the
   murder of Gaston Calmette, the editor of *Le Figaro*. Lacking any legal
   means to stop Calmette's personal and professional attacks upon her
   husband, Henriette Caillaux had purchased a pistol, presented herself
   at the editor's office, and shot him to death. During her nine-day trial,
   she wept copiously and was subject to fainting spells, especially when
   her prenuptial love letters from the then married Caillaux were read in
   open court. After the verdict of acquittal was announced on July 28,
   pandemonium broke out in the courtroom and in the streets of Paris,
   reflecting the widespread feeling that power and wealth had subverted
   justice. Coincidentally, that very day Austria-Hungary declared war on
   Serbia, swallowing up the Caillaux verdict in the general onrush toward
   World War I.

3. **SACCO and VANZETTI (1921–1927)**
   In 1921, two Italian-born anarchists were convicted, on the basis of
   disputed evidence, of murdering a guard and a paymaster in a South
   Braintree, Massachusetts, payroll robbery. The six-year legal battle for
   the life of shoemaker Nicola Sacco and his friend Bartolomeo Vanzetti,
   a fishmonger, became an international cause célèbre. There were
   general strikes in South America, massive demonstrations in Europe,
   and protest meetings in Asia and Africa to affirm a worldwide belief in
   their innocence. Despite new evidence, the trial judge refused to reopen

the case, sending Sacco and Vanzetti to the electric chair on August 23, 1927, and sparking a new wave of riots all over the world. In the United States, important people and public facilities were placed under armed guard as a precaution, while thousands of mourners conducted the martyrs to their final resting place.

4. THE SCOTTSBORO BOYS (1931–1950)
Nine young blacks, aged 13–19, were charged with the rape of two white prostitutes who had been riding the rails with them. Hurriedly tried and convicted in the Alabama town of Scottsboro, all but the youngest boy received a death sentence in 1931. The case attracted the attention of the Communist Party, and workers throughout the United States soon demonstrated—at Communist instigation—against the conviction of the "Scottsboro boys." In Dresden, Germany, the U.S. Consulate was stoned by a crowd of Communist youths. In New York City's Harlem, 1,500 protestors led by Communists left so many signs and banners after their march that two dump trucks were needed to haul away the refuse. The U.S. Supreme Court twice ordered retrials, citing the inadequacy of defense counsel and the exclusion of blacks from southern juries. The Scottsboro boys were retried three times in all. It was 1950 before the last one—middle-aged by then—was released.

5. THE MARIA HERTOGH CUSTODY CASE (December 11, 1950)
Maria Hertogh was born in Indonesia to Dutch Roman Catholic parents. When the Japanese invaded in World War II, they interred Maria's parents. Che Amirah and her husband took charge of Maria, who was four and a half years old. She was renamed Nadra and raised as a Moslem. Later, the Amirahs moved to the British colony of Malaysia. After the war, Maria's parents tried to find her but were unable to locate her until 1949. Adeline Hertogh went to court to claim custody of Maria. A Singapore court ruled that Maria should be returned to her natural parents. After the verdict was announced, Maria cried, "Amirah is my mother. She has loved me, cared for me, and brought me up." Che Amirah then appealed, and the verdict was reversed in July 1950. In August, 13-year-old Maria married a 22-year-old teacher in a Moslem ceremony. Meanwhile, the custody case was again appealed. The court ruled that Maria's father had never consented to have the Amirahs raise the girl and that the Hertoghs would therefore have custody. The court also annulled Maria's marriage. While Che Amirah appealed this latest verdict, authorities decided to place Maria in the care of a convent. Newspaper pictures of Maria in a Christian convent aroused the antipathy of Singapore's Moslem population. On December 11, the court rendered its final decision, dismissing Amirah's appeal and confirming the Hertoghs' custody of Maria. After the verdict was announced, crowds of Moslems rioted outside the courthouse. By the time British military

police regained control of the streets three days later, 18 people had been killed and 173 injured.

6. THE CHICAGO SEVEN (1969–1970)

The case of the Chicago Seven, spawned in street rioting during the 1968 Democratic National Convention in Chicago, triggered a renewed round of protest after the jury verdict was delivered in 1970. The trial itself was chaotic: Black Panther leader Bobby Seale had to be bound and gagged to keep him quiet, and the wife of Yippie leader Abbie Hoffman warned the judge that she would dance on his grave. The seven defendants were acquitted of conspiracy, but five of them received maximum sentences (five years, plus fines and court costs) for their intent to incite a riot. The "jury of the streets" registered its immediate disapproval: Some 5,000 marchers protested the verdict in Boston, 3,000 assembled in Chicago, and in Washington, D.C., more than 500 demonstrators convened in front of the Watergate residence of U.S. attorney general John Mitchell. Students at the University of California in Santa Barbara burned down a local bank in protest, prompting Governor Ronald Reagan to threaten further antiriot prosecutions.

7. THE DAN WHITE CASE (1979)

At his trial for the murders of San Francisco mayor George Moscone and Supervisor Harvey Milk, Dan White claimed as a mitigating circumstance that he ate too much junk food. A former policeman and a member of the city's board of supervisors (he was elected with the slogan, "Crime is number one with me"), White had resigned from the board, then changed his mind. Angered by the mayor's refusal to reappoint him, he shot Moscone and Milk, leader of the city's large gay population, on November 27, 1978. White had suffered from depressions that were compounded by his overconsumption of Twinkies, his attorney argued. On May 21, 1979, when the jury returned a verdict of involuntary manslaughter due to "diminished capacity"—which meant the possibility of parole in five years—thousands of gays and their supporters rioted in the streets of San Francisco, torching 12 police cars and causing $1 million worth of property damage. As one gay leader announced, "Society is going to have to deal with us not as nice little fairies, who have hairdressing salons, but as people capable of violence." White committed suicide in 1985.

8. THE McDUFFIE RIOTS (May 17–19, 1980)

The verdict came down on a Saturday, exonerating four white Miami policemen accused of beating to death a 33-year-old black insurance salesman. Arthur McDuffie, who had been stopped for speeding on his motorcycle, died days later of injuries. Three police officers testified under immunity that their colleagues, the four men on trial, had beat

McDuffie over the head. "Street justice," the prosecutor called it. "They wanted to teach him a lesson. And boy, did they ever. He is not going to run from the police anymore." The night of the acquittal, violence broke out in Miami's black ghetto, and three white men were dragged from a passing car and beaten to death. By the time the smoke cleared away three days later, there were 14 dead in Miami and 300 injured.

9. **THE RODNEY KING BEATING TRIAL** (April 29–30, 1992)
In the early morning hours of March 3, 1991, motorist Rodney King was stopped by Los Angeles police officers following a three-mile high-speed chase. According to the arrest reports filed later, King refused orders to exit the car, then put up such a struggle that officers had to use batons and stun guns to subdue him. However, unknown to the police, the entire incident had been filmed by a nearby resident, and the video told a different story. On the tape, King appeared to offer little resistance as several officers kicked and beat him to the ground, while a dozen of their colleagues looked on. Public outrage led to a grand jury investigation that indicted four officers—Theodore J. Briseno, Stacey C. Koons, Laurence M. Powell, and Timothy E. Wind—for assault and the use of excessive force. Because of the massive publicity, the trial, when opened on March 4, 1992, was moved from Los Angeles to suburban Simi Valley. The prosecution presented several witnesses who testified that the officers—particularly Powell—were "out of control." However, defense attorney Michael Stone insisted, "We do not see an example of unprovoked police brutality. We see, rather, a controlled application of baton strikes for the very obvious reason of getting this man into custody." The jury clearly agreed. On April 29, they returned not guilty verdicts for all the defendants. The verdict rocked Los Angeles. Within hours, the city erupted in rioting that left 58 people dead and caused $1 billion in damages.

10. **THE JAMES KNIGHT HEARING** (November 13, 1996)
On October 24, 1996, two police officers stopped a speeding car in the predominantly black district of St. Petersburg, Florida. Police said that the driver, 18-year-old Tyron Lewis, refused to get out of the car, which then lunged forward at one of the officers. The officer, James Knight, fired several shots through the windshield, fatally wounding Lewis. Some eyewitnesses said that the car had barely moved toward Knight; others said that Lewis had been trying to surrender. The night of Lewis's death, riots broke out in a 20-block area, injuring 11 people.

On November 13, a grand jury exonerated Knight, declaring that the shooting was justifiable and not racially motivated. In its report, the jury concluded that the officer had been in danger of being run over by Lewis. However, a police review the same day found that Knight could have avoided the use of force and suspended him for 60 days with pay. The grand jury decision set off a new round of riots, in which 30 fires were set, concrete blocks were thrown at cars, and two law enforcement officers were shot and wounded.

C.D. & C.F.

22 Cases of Animals and Insects Brought Before The Law

There has been a long and shocking tradition of punishing, excommunicating, and killing animals for real or supposed crimes. In medieval times, animals were even put on the rack to extort confessions of guilt. Cases have been recorded and documented involving such unlikely creatures as flies, locusts, snakes, mosquitoes, caterpillars, eels, snails, beetles, grasshoppers, dolphins, and most larger mammals. In seventeenth-century Russia, a goat was banished to Siberia. The belief that animals are morally culpable is happily out of fashion—but not completely, for even now, such travesties and comedies occasionally occur.

1. CANINE CONVICT NO. C2559
   Rarely in American history has an animal served a prison term, but, incredibly, it happened as recently as 1924, in Pike County, Pennsylvania. Pep, a male Labrador retriever, belonged to neighbors of Governor and Mrs. Gifford Pinchot. A friendly dog, Pep unaccountably went wild one hot summer day and killed Mrs. Pinchot's cat. An enraged Governor Pinchot presided over an immediate hearing and then a trial. Poor Pep had no legal counsel, and the evidence against him was damning. Pinchot sentenced him to life imprisonment. The no doubt bewildered beast was taken to the state penitentiary in Philadelphia. The warden, also bewildered, wondered whether he should assign the mutt an ID number like the rest of the cons. Tradition won out, and Pep became No. C2559. The story has a happy ending: Pep's fellow inmates lavished him with affection, and he was allowed to switch cellmates at will. The prisoners were building a new penitentiary in Graterford, Pennsylvania, and every morning the enthusiastic dog boarded the bus for work upon hearing his number called. When the prison was completed, Pep was one of the first to move in. In 1930, after 6 years in prison (42 dog years), Pep died of old age.

2. THE RISING COST OF AIR TRAVEL
   In Tripoli in 1963, 75 carrier pigeons received the death sentence. A gang of smugglers had trained the birds to carry banknotes from Italy, Greece, and Egypt into Libya. The court ordered the pigeons to be

killed because "they were too well trained and dangerous to be let loose." The humans were merely fined.

3. TOO MUCH MONKEY BUSINESS

In 1905, the law against public cigarette smoking was violated in South Bend, Indiana. A showman's chimpanzee puffed tobacco in front of a crowd and was hauled before the court, where he was convicted and fined.

4. IT'S A DOG'S LIFE

In 1933, four dogs in McGraw, New York, were prosecuted to the full extent of the law for biting six-year-old Joyce Hammond. In a full hearing before an audience of 150, their lawyer failed to save them from execution by the county veterinarian. Proclaimed Justice A. P. McGraw, "I know the value of a good dog. But this is a serious case. . . . The dogs are criminals of the worst kind."

5. A HOOF FOR A HOOF

The Wild West custom of killing a horse responsible for the death of a human was reenacted by a group of Chicago gangsters in 1924. When the infamous Nails Morton died in Lincoln Park after being thrown from a riding horse, his buddies in Dion O'Banion's gang sought revenge. They kidnapped the animal from its stable at gunpoint and took it to the scene of the crime, where they solemnly executed it.

6. YOU REALLY GOT A HOLD ON ME

In 1451 in Lausanne, a number of leeches were brought into an ecclesiastical court. We can only imagine their distress as they listened to the reading of a document demanding that they leave town. When the tenacious leeches stuck to their guns, they were exorcised by the bishop-court.

7. DOGGED BY THE LAW

"Perverts transformed their stables into harems," wrote a French author in his legal history of the province of Lorraine. For centuries, bestiality was a regularly prosecuted crime, and as recently as 1940 a man was burned at the stake in Pont-à-Mousson, France, along with three cows. The case of Guillaume Guyart in 1606 contains a surreal twist. Guyart was sentenced to be hanged and burned for sodomy; his accomplice, a female dog, was to be knocked on the head and burned along with him. When Guyart managed to escape, the court decreed that his property be confiscated to pay for the costs of the trial. If the criminal was not caught, the judges ruled, the sentence would be carried out—a painting of Guyart would be hung from the scaffold. There is no record of the ultimate fate of man or dog.

8. THE BARNYARD BORDELLO

Puritan clergyman Cotton Mather left a rare account of an American buggery case. He wrote, "On June 6, 1662, at New Haven, there was a most unparalleled wretch, one Potter by name, about 60 years of age, executed for damnable Beastialities [sic]." Potter, it seems, began sodomizing animals at the age of 10 and never stopped. At the same time, he was a devout churchgoer, noted for his piety and for being "zealous in reforming the sins of other people." The man's wife, Mather wrote, "had seen him confounding himself with a bitch ten years before; and he had excused himself as well as he could, but conjured her to keep it secret." Potter then hanged the animal, presumably as an apology to his wife. Eventually, the law caught up with him, and he went to the gallows preceded by a cow, two heifers, three sheep, and two sows. Watching his concubines die one by one, Potter was in tears by the time he approached the scaffold.

9. I'M NOT THAT KIND OF GIRL

In Vanvres, France, in 1750, Jacques Ferron was caught in the act of love with a she-ass and sentenced to hang. Normally, his partner would have died, as well—but members of the community took an unprecedented step. They signed a petition that they had known the she-ass for four years, and that she had always been well behaved at home and abroad and had never caused a scandal of any kind. She was, they concluded, "in all her habits of life a most honest creature." As the result of this intervention, Ferron was hanged for sodomy, and the she-ass was acquitted.

10. JUVENILE DELINQUENTS?

The vast majority of prosecuted animals have been pigs. In the Middle Ages, they were frequently left unwatched, and they often harmed small children. Once arrested, they were usually placed in solitary confinement in the same jail with human criminals, registered as "so-and-so's pig," and publicly hung with all the formality of a typical medieval execution. In the annals of animal crime, there are many famous pig cases. One of the most fully documented and most unusual occurred in Savigny, France, in 1457. A sow and her six piglets were accused of "willfully and feloniously" murdering a five-year-old boy, Jean Martin. Found guilty, the sow was eventually hung by its hind legs from the gallows. But the matter was not so simple: Were the six piglets—who had been found stained with blood at the scene of the crime—also guilty? Their owner, Jean Bailly, was asked to post bail for them until a second trial and to take the accused back into his custody. Bailly said he didn't have the money, and furthermore, refused to make any promises about the piglets' future good behavior. Three weeks later, "the six little porklets" went to court. Because of their youth and the lack of firm evidence of their guilt, the court was lenient. The piglets were given to a local noblewoman; Bailly did not have to pay; and the porklets could hold their heads high.

11. AN IMPORTANT RULING

A significant pig case occurred in 1846 in Pleternica, Slavonia—it was one of the first times an animal's owner bore responsibility for damages. A pig ate the ears of a one-year-old girl and was given the usual death sentence. Its owner was sentenced to labor in order to provide a dowry for the earless girl, so that, despite her loss, she might someday find a husband.

12. MONKEYING AROUND

As recently as January 23, 1962, an animal was called into the courtroom. Makao, a young cercopithecoid monkey, escaped from his master's apartment in Paris and wandered into an empty studio nearby. He bit into a tube of lipstick, destroyed some expensive knickknacks, and "stole" a box (which was later recovered—empty). The victims of Makao's pranks filed a complaint, stating that the box had contained a valuable ring. The monkey's owner contended before the judge that his pet could not possibly have opened such a box. Makao was ordered to appear in court, where he deftly opened a series of boxes. His defense ruined, Makao's master was held liable for full damages.

13. A HAPPY TAIL

In 1877 in New York City, Mary Shea, a woman of Celtic origin, was bitten on the finger by Jimmy, an organ-grinder's monkey. Mary demanded retribution, but the judge said he could not commit an animal. Miffed, Mary stormed out of the courtroom, snarling, "This is a nice country for justice!" The monkey, who was dressed in a scarlet coat and velvet cap, showed his appreciation: He curled his tail around the gas fixture on the judge's desk and tried to shake hands with him. The police blotter gave this record of the event: "*Name:* Jimmy Dillio. *Occupation:* Monkey. *Disposition:* Discharged."

14. HARD-BOILED CRIMINAL

One of the most celebrated animal trials was that of the rooster in Basel, Switzerland, who was accused in 1474 of laying an egg (without a yolk, no less). It was a widely held belief that such eggs could be hatched by witches in league with Satan, giving birth to deadly winged snakes. The accused cock was in a tight spot, and even his defense attorney did not argue that the charges were false. He did argue that his client had no pact with the devil and that laying an egg was an unpremeditated and involuntary act. The judges were not impressed, and after a lengthy trial it was decided that the rooster was possessed by Satan. The bird and the egg were burned at the stake before a huge crowd. The subject was still being debated more than 200 years later, in 1710, when a Frenchman presented a paper before the Academy of Sciences stating that yolkless eggs were merely the occasional products of an ailing hen.

15. **WOMEN AND CHILDREN FIRST**
In Stelvio, Italy, in 1519, field mice (referred to in a German account as *Lutmäusse;* they may have been moles) were accused of damaging crops by burrowing. They were granted a defense attorney, Hans Grienebner, so that they could "show cause for their conduct by pleading their exigencies and distress." Grienebner claimed that his clients were helpful citizens who ate harmful insects and enriched the soil. The prosecutor, Schwartz Mining, argued that the damage they caused was preventing local tenants from paying their rents. The judge was merciful. Though he exiled the animals, he assured them of safe conduct "and an additional respite of 14 days to all those which are with young, and to such as are yet in their infancy."

16. **PUTTING THE BITE ON THE LANDLORD**
In the 1700s, an order of Franciscan friars in Brazil was driven to despair by the termites that were devouring not only the food and furniture, but also the very walls of the monastery. The monks pleaded with the bishop for an act of excommunication, and an ecclesiastical trial was held. When the accused defiantly failed to appear in court, they were appointed a lawyer. He made the usual speech about how all God's creatures deserved to eat, and he praised his clients' industry, which he said was far greater than that of the friars. Further, he argued that the termites had occupied the land long before the monks. The lengthy trial overflowed with complicated legal speeches and much passionate quoting of authorities. In the end, it was decided that the monks should give the termites their own plot of land. The judge's order was read aloud to the termite hills. According to a monk's document dated January 1713, the termites promptly came out of the hills and marched in columns to their new home. Wood you believe it?

17. **WHAT'S A MAYOR TO DO?**
In Ansbach, Germany, in 1685, it was reported that a vicious wolf was ravaging herds and devouring women and children. The beast was believed to be none other than the town's deceased mayor, who had turned into a werewolf. A typical politician, the wolf-mayor was hard to pin down but was finally captured and killed. The animal's carcass was then dressed in a flesh-colored suit, a brown wig, and a long gray-white beard. Its snout was cut off and replaced with a mask of the mayor. By court order, the creature was hung from a windmill. The weremayor's pelt was then stuffed and displayed in a town official's cabinet, to serve forever as proof of the existence of werewolves.

18. THE CRUEL DEATH OF "FIVE-TON MARY"

There are ancient records of the hangings of bulls and oxen, but there is only one known case of the hanging of an elephant—it happened in Erwin, Tennessee, on September 13, 1916. The Sparks Circus was stationed in Kingsport, Tennessee, when Mary, a veteran circus elephant, was being ridden to water by an inexperienced trainer, Walter Eldridge. On the way, Mary spotted a watermelon rind and headed for the snack. When Eldridge jerked hard on her head with a spear-tipped stick, Mary let out a loud trumpet, reached behind her with her trunk, and yanked the trainer off her back. She dashed Eldridge against a soft-drink stand and then walked over and stepped on his head. A Kingsport resident came running and fired five pistol shots into the huge animal. Mary groaned and shook but did not die—in fact, she performed in that night's show. The next day, the circus moved to Erwin, where "authorities" (no one is sure who) decreed that Mary should die on the gallows, to the great sorrow of her friends in the circus. She was taken to the Clinchfield railroad yards, where a large crowd was gathered. A 7/8-inch chain was slung around her neck, and a 100-ton derrick hoisted her 5 feet in the air. The chain broke. The next chain held, and Mary died quickly. Her five-ton corpse was buried with a steam shovel.

19. FREE SPEECH

Carl Miles exhibited Blackie, his "talking" cat, on street corners in Augusta, Georgia, and collected "contributions." Blackie could say two phrases: "I love you" and "I want my momma." In 1981, the city of Augusta said the enterprise required a business license and a fee, which Miles refused to pay. He sued the city council, arguing that the fee impinged on the cat's right to free speech. The judge actually heard Blackie say "I love you" in court. However, he ruled that the case was not a free speech issue. Since Blackie was charging money for his speech, the city was entitled to the fee. Miles paid $50 for the license, and Blackie went back to work. He died in 1992 at the age of 18.

20. LAST-MINUTE ESCAPE

On September 30, 1982, Tucker, a 140-pound bull mastiff, ran into a neighbor's yard and attacked the neighbor's black miniature poodle, Bonnie. Tucker's owner, Eric Leonard, freed the poodle from Tucker's mouth, but it had received critical injuries and died. A district court in Augusta, Maine, ruled that Tucker was a danger to other dogs and should be killed by intravenous injection. Leonard appealed to the Maine Supreme Court, but it upheld the lower court's ruling. In 1984, two days before his scheduled execution, the "National Doggie Liberation Front" removed Tucker from the shelter where he was being held. What happened to Tucker is unknown.

21. **DEATH-ROW DOG**
    The long arm of the law almost took the life of a 110-pound Akita named Taro, who got into trouble on Christmas Day of 1990. Owned by Lonnie and Sandy Lehrer of Haworth, New Jersey, Taro injured the Lehrers' 10-year-old niece, but how the injury occurred was in dispute. Police and doctors who inspected the injury said the dog bit the girl's lower lip. The Lehrers said the child provoked the dog and that while protecting himself, Taro scratched her lip. Taro had never before hurt a human being, but he had been in three dogfights and had killed a dog during one of the fights. A panel of local authorities ruled that Taro fell under the state's vicious-dog law and sentenced the Akita to death. A three-year legal nightmare ensued as the Lehrers fought their way through municipal court, superior court, a state appeals court, and finally the New Jersey Supreme Court. While the legal battle raged on, Taro remained on death row at Bergen County Jail in Hackensack, where he was kept in a climate-controlled cell and was allowed two exercise walks a day. By the time his execution day neared, the dog had become an international celebrity. Animal rights activist and former actress Brigitte Bardot pleaded for clemency; a businessman from Kenya raised money to save the dog. Thousands of animal lovers wrote to the Lehrers and offered to adopt the dog. Even the dog's jailer and the assemblyman behind the vicious-dog law interceded on behalf of Taro. But when the courts failed to free the dog, the final verdict fell to Governor Christine Todd Whitman. Although the governor did not exactly pardon the Akita, she agreed to release him on three conditions: Taro would be exiled from New Jersey; Taro must have new owners; Taro's new owners, or the Lehrers, must assume all financial liability for the dog's future actions. The Lehrers agreed, and the dog was released in February 1994, after spending three years in jail. The Lehrers found a new home for Taro in Pleasantville, New York. When all the costs of the canine death-row case were added up, the total exceeded $100,000. Taro died of natural causes in 1999.

22. **INTERNATIONAL INCIDENT**
    In January 2001, Dino, a five-year-old German shepherd, in Northampton, England, bit the hand of a Mrs. Coull, who was trying to break up a fight between her dog, Ralph, and Dino. Dino's owners, Bryan and Carole Lamont, paid a fine, but Dino was sentenced to death, anyway, according to the Dangerous Dogs Act. The Lamonts appealed, and the case dragged its way through the court system and was even heard before the European Court of Human Rights. Finally, in October 2004, it returned to the Northampton Crown Court. Since Dino had not bitten anyone in the three and a half years since the initial incident, the court gave him a reprieve.

                                                              A.W. & C.O.M.

Witticisms of 9 Condemned Criminals

1. GEORGE APPEL (electrocuted in 1928)
   As he was being strapped into the electric chair, Appel quipped, "Well, folks, you'll soon see a baked Appel."

2. JESSE WALTER BISHOP (gassed in 1979)
   The last man to die in Nevada's gas chamber, Bishop's final words were, "I've always wanted to try everything once. . . . Let's go!"

3. GUY CLARK (hanged in 1832)
   On the way to the gallows, the sheriff told Clark to speed up the pace. Clark replied, "Nothing will happen until I get there."

4. JAMES DONALD FRENCH (electrocuted in 1966)
   Turning to a newsman on his way to the electric chair, French helpfully suggested, "I have a terrific headline for you in the morning: 'French Fries.'"

5. ROBERT ALTON HARRIS (gassed in 1992)
   The last person to die in the gas chamber at San Quentin, Harris issued a final statement through the prison warden that stated, "You can be a king or a street sweeper, but everybody dances with the Grim Reaper." The quote was inspired by a line from the film *Bill and Ted's Bogus Journey*.

6. WILLIAM PALMER (hanged in 1856)
   As he stepped onto the gallows, Palmer looked at the trapdoor and exclaimed, "Are you sure it's safe?"

7. SIR WALTER RALEIGH (beheaded in 1618)
   Feeling the edge of the ax soon to be used on him, Raleigh said, "'Tis a sharp remedy but a sure one for all ills."

8. JAMES W. RODGERS (shot in 1960)
   Asked if he had a last request, Rodgers stated, "Why, yes—a bullet-proof vest."

9. FREDERICK CHARLES WOOD (electrocuted in 1963)
   Sitting down in the electric chair, Wood said, "Gentlemen, you are about to see the effects of electricity upon wood."

CHAPTER ELEVEN

War, Politics, and World Affairs

THE 10 MEN WHO CONQUERED THE MOST MILES

10 DEADLIEST WARS SINCE WORLD WAR II

18 SECRET ARMIES OF THE CIA

11 COMMANDERS KILLED BY THEIR OWN TROOPS

12 POLITICALLY INCORRECT TERMS
AND THEIR ALTERNATIVES

17 ACTORS WHO BECAME POLITICIANS

PERCENTAGE OF WOMEN
IN 30 NATIONAL LEGISLATURES

10 WORST DICTATORS CURRENTLY IN POWER

13 DEPOSED DICTATORS AFTER THE FALL

10 LARGEST ARMS EXPORTERS

10 LARGEST ARMS IMPORTERS

9 ORDINARY MEN WHO PLAYED KING

KIM JONG IL

The 10 Men Who Conquered
the Most Miles

1. **GENGHIS KHAN (1162–1227)**
   From 1206 to 1227, Mongol chieftain Genghis Khan conquered approximately 4,860,000 square miles. Stretching from the Pacific Ocean to the Caspian Sea, his empire included northern China, Mongolia, southern Siberia, and central Asia.

2. **ALEXANDER THE GREAT (356–323 BC)**
   From 334 to 326 BC, the Macedonian king Alexander the Great conquered approximately 2,180,000 square miles. His empire included the southern Balkan peninsula, Asia Minor, Egypt, and the entire Near East as far east as the Indus River.

3. **TAMERLANE (1336?–1405)**
   From 1370 to 1402, the Islamic Turkicized Mongol chieftain Tamerlane conquered approximately 2,145,000 square miles. His empire included most of the Near East, from the Indus River to the Mediterranean Sea and from the Indian Ocean north to the Aral Sea.

4. **CYRUS THE GREAT (600?–529 BC)**
   From 559 to 539 BC, the Persian king Cyrus the Great conquered approximately 2,090,000 square miles. He conquered the Median Empire, Babylonia, Assyria, Syria, Palestine, the Indus Valley, and southern Turkestan.

5. **ATTILA (406?–453)**
   From 433 to 453, Attila, the king of the Huns and the Scourge of God, conquered approximately 1,450,000 square miles. Although he failed in his attempt to conquer Gaul, he ruled an empire that encompassed central and eastern Europe and the western Russian plain.

6. **ADOLF HITLER (1889–1945)**
   From 1933 to the fall of 1942, Nazi dictator Adolf Hitler conquered 1,370,000 square miles, all of which he lost within three years. His Third Reich included most of continental Europe and extended from the English Channel to the outskirts of Moscow and from North Africa to Norway.

7. **NAPOLEON BONAPARTE (1769–1821)**
   From 1796 to the height of his power in 1810, Napoleon Bonaparte conquered approximately 720,000 square miles. His Grand Empire included France, Belgium, Holland, Germany, Poland, Switzerland, and Spain.

8. **MAHMUD OF GHAZNI (971?–1030)**
From 997 to 1030, Mahmud, the Muslim sultan and Afghan king of
Ghazni, conquered 680,000 square miles. His Near Eastern empire
extended from the Indian Ocean north to the Amu Darya River and
from the Tigris River east to the Ganges River in India.

9. **FRANCISCO PIZARRO (1470?-1541)**
From 1531 to 1541, Spanish adventurer Francisco Pizarro conquered
480,000 square miles. Employing treachery and assassination, and
taking advantage of internal discord, he subjugated the Inca Empire,
which extended from Ecuador south through the Andes to Bolivia.

10. **HERNANDO CORTES (1485–1547)**
From 1519 to 1526, Hernando Cortes, commanding a small Spanish
military expedition, conquered 315,000 square miles. Defeating the
Aztecs, he seized central and southern Mexico and later subjugated
Guatemala and Honduras to Spanish rule.

R.J.F.

10 Deadliest Wars Since World War II

Exact death totals for various wars are difficult to determine, primarily
because government estimates can be politically motivated and because many
victims are buried without being counted. In addition, some estimates are
based only on battle deaths, while others include civilian casualties and still
others add deaths caused by war-related diseases and famines. For more
information on estimates from various sources, see Matthew White's *Historical Atlas of the Twentieth Century* at http://users.erols.com/mwhite28/
20centry.htm.

War	Military and Civilian Deaths
1. CONGOLESE CIVIL WARS (1998–present) The International Rescue Committee estimates that there have been almost 4 million excess deaths, mostly in the eastern Congo, as the result of ongoing fighting among at least 11 armed groups.	3,900,000
2. KOREAN CIVIL WAR (1950–1953) North Korean death estimates range from 1.2 million to 3 million, South Korean totals from 500,000 to 1 million.	2,800,000

3. CHINESE CIVIL WAR (1945–1949)   2,500,000
   The ongoing civil war in China, temporarily interrupted
   by World War II, resumed in 1945 and continued until
   Communist forces gained a victory.

4. SECOND VIETNAM WAR (1965–1975)   2,000,000
   After evicting the French in 1954, Vietnam found itself
   the battleground for a surrogate war, as the United
   States and its allies supported South Vietnam and the
   USSR and China supplied North Vietnam, which
   emerged victorious in 1975. Meanwhile, the fighting
   had spread to Cambodia and Laos.

5. SUDANESE CIVIL WARS (1983–present)   1,900,000
   Sudan achieved independence in 1956 and has been in
   a state of war for all but 10 years since then, as the
   central government has tried to gain control over
   non-Islamic regions while fighting black followers of
   Islam in other regions.

6. AFGHANISTAN (1978–present)   1,800,000
   Since the invasion of Afghanistan by Soviet forces in
   1979, various warlords, religious militia, government
   forces, and foreign armies have battled for control of
   the country.

7. CAMBODIA (1975–1978)   1,600,000
   When the Khmer Rouge, led by Pol Pot, took power at
   the end of the Vietnam War, they massacred more
   than one and a half million people. They were finally
   overthrown by an invading Vietnamese army.

8. ETHIOPIAN WARS OF SECESSION (1962–1992)   1,400,000
   Most of the deaths were the result of attempts by
   Eritreans and others to gain independence. The
   Eritreans did form their own nation; the other ethnic
   groups did not. The majority of the victims died of
   famine and disease caused by the wars.

9. RWANDA AND BURUNDI (1959–1995)   1,350,000
   In 1994, Hutus in Rwanda massacred an estimated
   937,000 Tutsis. However, this was only the latest and
   worst of the massacres the two groups have committed
   against each other in both Rwanda and neighboring
   Burundi.

10. CREATION OF BANGLADESH (1971)   1,250,000
    West Pakistan and East Pakistan were physically
    separated by thousands of miles of India. When the
    easterners won a national election, the government
    attempted to crush the Bengalis of East Pakistan through
    massacres. India stepped in and drove out the Pakistanis,
    and East Pakistan established independent Bangladesh.

Note: Other wars that probably claimed 1 million lives are the Biafran War
of Secession in Nigeria (1966–1970), the Iran-Iraq War (1980–1988), and
the Mozambique Civil War (1975–1992).

18 Secret Armies of the CIA

1. UKRAINIAN PARTISANS
   From 1945 to 1952, the CIA trained and aerially supplied Ukrainian
   partisan units that had originally been organized by the Germans to
   fight the Soviets during World War II. For seven years, the partisans,
   operating in the Carpathian Mountains, made sporadic attacks. Finally,
   in 1952, a massive Soviet military force wiped them out.

2. CHINESE BRIGADE IN BURMA
   After the Communist victory in China, Nationalist Chinese soldiers fled
   into northern Burma. During the early 1950s, the CIA used these
   soldiers to create a 12,000-man brigade that made raids into Red
   China. However, the Nationalist soldiers found it more profitable to
   monopolize the local opium trade.

3. GUATEMALAN REBEL ARMY
   After Guatemalan president Jacobo Arbenz legalized that country's
   Communist Party and expropriated 400,000 acres of United Fruit
   banana plantations, the CIA decided to overthrow his government.
   Guatemalan rebels were trained in Honduras and backed up with a CIA
   air contingent of bombers and fighter planes. This army invaded
   Guatemala in 1954, promptly toppling Arbenz's regime.

4. SUMATRAN REBELS
   In an attempt to overthrow Indonesian president Sukarno in 1958, the
   CIA sent paramilitary experts and radio operators to the island of
   Sumatra to organize a revolt. With CIA air support, the rebel army
   attacked but was quickly defeated. The American government denied
   involvement, even after a CIA B-26 was shot down and its CIA pilot,
   Allen Pope, was captured.

5. KHAMBA HORSEMEN

After the 1950 Chinese invasion of Tibet, the CIA began recruiting Khamba horsemen—fierce warriors who supported Tibet's religious leader, the Dalai Lama—as they escaped into India in 1959. The Khambas were trained in modern warfare at Camp Hale, high in the Rocky Mountains near Leadville, Colorado. Transported back to Tibet by the CIA-operated Air America, the Khambas organized an army that numbered some 14,000 at its peak. By the mid-1960s, the Khambas had been abandoned by the CIA, but they fought on alone into 1970.

6. BAY OF PIGS INVASION FORCE

In 1960, CIA operatives recruited 1,500 Cuban refugees living in Miami, trained them at a base in Guatemala, and staged a surprise attack on Fidel Castro's Cuba. This small army—complete with an air force of B-26 bombers—landed at the Bay of Pigs on April 17, 1961. The ill-conceived, poorly planned operation ended in disaster, since all but 150 men of the force were either killed or captured within three days.

7. L'ARMÉE CLANDESTINE

In 1962, CIA agents recruited Meo tribesmen living in the mountains of Laos to fight as guerrillas against Communist Pathet Lao forces. Called L'Armée Clandestine, this unit—paid, trained, and supplied by the CIA—grew into a 30,000-man force. By 1975, the Meos—who had numbered a quarter million in 1962—had been reduced to 10,000 refugees fleeing into Thailand.

8. NUNG MERCENARIES

A Chinese hill people living in Vietnam, the Nung were hired and organized by the CIA as a mercenary force during the Vietnam War. Fearsome and brutal fighters, the Nung were employed throughout Vietnam and along the Ho Chi Minh Trail. The Nung proved costly since they refused to fight unless constantly supplied with beer and prostitutes.

9. PERUVIAN REGIMENT

Unable to quell guerrilla forces in its eastern Amazonian provinces, Peru called on the United States for help in the mid-1960s. The CIA responded by establishing a fortified camp in the area and hiring local Peruvians who were trained by Green Beret personnel on loan from the U.S. Army. After crushing the guerrillas, the elite unit was disbanded because of fears it might stage a coup against the government.

10. CONGO MERCENARY FORCE

In 1964, during the Congolese Civil War, the CIA established an army in the Congo to back pro-Western leaders Cyril Adoula and Joseph Mobutu. The CIA imported European mercenaries and Cuban pilots—exiles from Cuba—to pilot the CIA air force, composed of transports and B-26 bombers.

11. THE CAMBODIAN COUP

For over 15 years, the CIA had tried various unsuccessful means of deposing Cambodia'a left-leaning Prince Norodom Sihanouk, including assassination attempts. However, in March 1970, a CIA-backed coup finally did the job. Funded by U.S. tax dollars, armed with U.S. weapons, and trained by American Green Berets, anti-Sihanouk forces called Kampuchea Khmer Krom (KKK) overran the capital of Phnom Penh and took control of the government. With the blessing of the CIA and the Nixon administration, control of Cambodia was placed in the hands of Lon Nol, who would later distinguish himself by dispatching soldiers to butcher tens of thousands of civilians.

12. KURD REBELS

During the early 1970s, the CIA moved into eastern Iraq to organize and supply the Kurds of that area, who were rebelling against the pro-Soviet Iraqi government. The real purpose behind that action was to help the shah of Iran settle a border dispute with Iraq favorably. After an Iranian-Iraqi settlement was reached, the CIA withdrew its support from the Kurds, who were then crushed by the Iraqi Army.

13. ANGOLA MERCENARY FORCE

In 1975, after years of bloody fighting and civil unrest in Angola, Portugal resolved to relinquish its hold on the last of its African colonies. The transition was to take place on November 11, with control of the country going to whichever political faction controlled the capital city of Luanda on that date. In the months preceding the change, three groups vied for power: the Popular Movement for the Liberation of Angola (MPLA), the National Front for the Liberation of Angola (FNLA), and the National Union for the Total Independence of Angola (UNITA). By July 1975, the Marxist MPLA had ousted the moderate FNLA and UNITA from Luanda, so the CIA decided to intervene covertly. More than $30 million was spent on the Angolan operation, the bulk of the money going to buy arms and pay French and South African mercenaries, who aided the FNLA and UNITA in their fight. Despite overwhelming evidence to the contrary, U.S. officials categorically denied any involvement in the Angolan conflict. In the end, it was a fruitless military adventure, for the MPLA assumed power and controls Angola to this day.

14. AFGHAN MUJAHIDEEN

Covert support for the groups fighting against the Soviet invasion of Afghanistan began under President Jimmy Carter in 1979 and was stepped up during the administration of Ronald Reagan. The operation succeeded in its initial goal, as the Soviets were forced to begin withdrawing their forces in 1987. Unfortunately, once the Soviets left, the United States essentially ignored Afghanistan as it collapsed into a five-year civil war followed by the rise of the ultra-fundamentalist Taliban. The Taliban provided a haven for Osama bin Laden and al-Qaeda, the perpetrators of the 9/11 terrorist attacks in 2001.

15. SALVADORAN DEATH SQUADS

As far back as 1964, the CIA helped form ORDEN and ANSESAL, two paramilitary intelligence networks that developed into the Salvadoran death squads. The CIA trained ORDEN leaders in the use of automatic weapons and surveillance techniques, and placed several leaders on the CIA payroll. The CIA also provided detailed intelligence on Salvadoran individuals who were later murdered by the death squads. During the civil war in El Salvador from 1980 to 1992, the death squads were responsible for 40,000 killings. Even after a public outcry forced President Reagan to denounce the death squads in 1984, CIA support continued.

16. NICARAGUAN CONTRAS

On November 23, 1981, President Ronald Reagan signed a top-secret National Security Directive authorizing the CIA to spend $19 million to recruit and support the Contras, opponents of Nicaragua's Sandinista government. In supporting the Contras, the CIA carried out several acts of sabotage without congressional intelligence committees giving consent—or even being informed. In response, Congress passed the Boland Amendment, prohibiting the CIA from providing aid to the Contras. Attempts to find alternate sources of funds led to the Iran-Contra scandal. It may also have led the CIA and the Contras to become actively involved in drug smuggling. In 1988, the Senate Subcommittee on Narcotics, Terrorism, and International Operations concluded that individuals in the Contra movement engaged in drug trafficking; that known drug traffickers provided assistance to the Contras; and that "there are some serious questions as to whether or not U.S. officials involved in Central America failed to address the drug issue for fear of jeopardizing the war effort against Nicaragua."

17. HAITIAN COUPS

In 1988, the CIA attempted to intervene in Haiti's elections with a "covert action program" to undermine the campaign of the eventual winner, Jean-Bertrand Aristide. Three years later, Aristide was overthrown in a bloody coup that killed more than 4,000 civilians. Many of the leaders of the coup had been on the CIA payroll since the mid-1980s. For example, Emmanuel "Toto" Constant, the head of FRAPH, a brutal gang of thugs known for murder, torture, and beatings, admitted to being a paid agent of the CIA. Similarly, the CIA-created Haitian National Intelligence Service (NIS), supposedly created to combat drugs, functioned during the coup as a "political intimidation and assassination squad." In 1994, an American force of 20,000 was sent to Haiti to allow Aristide to return. However, even after that, the

CIA continued working with FRAPH and the NIS. In 2004, Aristide was overthrown again and claimed that U.S. forces had kidnapped him.

18. **VENEZUELAN COUP ATTEMPT**
On April 11, 2002, Venezuelan military leaders attempted to overthrow the country's democratically elected left-wing president, Hugo Chavez. The coup collapsed after two days as hundreds of thousands of people took to the streets and units of the military joined with the protestors. The administration of George W. Bush was the only democracy in the Western Hemisphere not to condemn the coup attempt. According to intelligence analyst Wayne Madsen, the CIA had actively organized the coup: "The CIA provided Special Operations Group personnel, headed by a lieutenant colonel on loan from the U.S. Special Operations Command at Fort Bragg, North Carolina, to help organize the coup against Chavez."

R.J.F. & C.F.

11 Commanders Killed by Their Own Troops

1. **COL. JOHN FINNIS (1804–1857), English**
On the morning of May 10, 1857, in Meerut, India, Colonel Finnis, commander of the 11th Native Regiment of the British Indian Army, was informed that his troops had occupied the parade grounds and were in a state of mutiny. He mounted his horse, rode to the parade grounds, and began lecturing his troops on insubordination. The inflamed Indian soldiers—known as sepoys—promptly fired a volley at Finnis and killed him. This violent action triggered the Sepoy Mutiny.

2. **CAPT. YEVGENY GOLIKOV (?–1905), Russian**
On June 13, 1905, the crew of the Russian cruiser *Potemkin* mutinied after an unsuccessful protest challenging the quality of meat served on the ship. Captain Golikov, the ship's commander, was seized by the mutineers and flung overboard. This incident was dramatized in the classic film *Battleship Potemkin* (1925), directed by Sergei Eisenstein.

3. **KING GUSTAVUS II (1594–1632), Swedish**
In 1632, at the Battle of Lützen during the Thirty Years' War, King Gustavus Adolphus was shot in the back while leading his cavalry in a charge against the Catholic armies of the Holy Roman Empire. Who actually killed him remains an unanswered question. However, many historical authorities insist that Gustavus must have been killed by one of his own men, if not accidentally, then intentionally by a traitor.

4–5. **LT. RICHARD HARLAN and LT. THOMAS DELLWO (?–1971), U.S.**
In the early morning hours of March 16, 1971, an enlisted man at the U.S. Army base in Bienhoa, Vietnam, cut a hole through the screen covering a window in the officers' quarters and threw a fragmentation grenade inside. Two lieutenants—Richard Harlan and Thomas Dellwo—were killed. Private Billy Dean Smith was arrested and court-martialed for the crime but later was declared innocent. The real murderer was never found.

6. **GEN. THOMAS "STONEWALL" JACKSON (1824–1863), U.S. (Confederate)**
On the night of May 2, 1863, at the Battle of Chancellorsville during the U.S. Civil War, Confederate general Thomas "Stonewall" Jackson went on a scouting mission ahead of his lines to find a way to attack the rear of the Union forces. When he returned, he was fired upon by a North Carolina Confederate regiment that thought he and his staff were Yankee cavalrymen. He died eight days later.

7. **CAPT. LASHKEVITCH (?–1917), Russian**
On March 12, 1917, in Petrograd (now St. Petersburg), Russian soldiers of the Volynsky Regiment refused to fire on street demonstrators and, instead, shot their commanding officer, Captain Lashkevitch. This marked a major turning point in the Russian Revolution, because after killing Lashkevitch, the Volynsky Regiment—the first Russian unit to mutiny—joined the revolutionary forces.

8. **COL. DAVID MARCUS (1901–1948), U.S.**
In 1948, U.S. Army colonel David Marcus resigned his post at the Pentagon and enlisted in the newly formed Israeli Army. On the night of June 10, 1948, after overseeing the construction of a relief road from Tel Aviv to besieged Jerusalem during the Israeli war for independence, he was shot and killed while urinating in a field. One of his own sentries had mistaken him for an Arab because he had a bedsheet wrapped around him.

9. **NADIR SHAH (1688–1747), Persian**
A Turkish tribesman who became a Persian general and then king of the Persian Empire, Nadir Shah was a highly successful conqueror who defeated the Afghans, Mongols, Indians, and Turks. In 1747, his own military bodyguard murdered him. His death met with widespread approval in Persia because of the harshness and cruelty of his rule.

10. **CPL. PAT TILLMAN**
Tillman, a member of the Arizona Cardinals football team, gave up a lucrative contract extension to join the U.S. Army in 2002. On April 22, 2004, he was killed while leading a team of Army Rangers up a hill

in southeastern Afghanistan to knock out enemy fire that had pinned down other soldiers. The army posthumously awarded him the Silver Star, its third-highest honor. One month later, the army announced that Tillman had been killed by fellow Americans in a "friendly fire" accident, a fact that it had known immediately. Tillman's parents later accused the army of covering up the circumstances of their son's death in order to exploit his memorial service for recruiting purposes.

11. CAPT. PEDRO DE URZÚA (?–1561), Spanish
In 1559, Captain Pedro de Urzúa led an expedition of Spanish soldiers from coastal Peru across the Andes to the Amazon Basin in search of El Dorado. Two years later, while still searching unsuccessfully for gold, de Urzúa was killed by his own men when they mutinied under the leadership of Lope de Aguirre. De Urzúa's death and the fate of the mutineers were depicted in the 1973 movie *Aguirre, the Wrath of God*.

R.J.F.

12 Politically Incorrect Terms and Their Alternatives

1. BORING—Differently interesting; charm-free.
2. DEAD—Terminally inconvenienced.
3. DISHONEST—Morally different; ethically disoriented.
4. DRUNK—Sobriety-deprived.
5. HERPES—His 'n' herpes.
6. MAFIOSO—Member of a career-offender cartel.
7. MEAT—Processed animal carcasses; scorched corpses of animals.
8. OLD JOKE—Previously recounted humorous narrative.
9. PANHANDLER—Unaffiliated applicant for private-sector funding.
10. SHOPLIFTER—Nontraditional shopper.
11. SNOWMAN—Person of snow.
12. WHITE (person)—Melanin-impoverished.

Source: The Official Politically Correct Dictionary and Handbook by Henry Beard and Christopher Cerf. Copyright 1992 by Henry Beard and Christopher Cerf. Reprinted by permission of Villard Books, a division of Random House, Inc.

17 Actors Who Became Politicians

1. HELEN GAHAGAN DOUGLAS
A Broadway star, Gahagan moved to Hollywood after marrying film actor Melvyn Douglas. Her brief movie career was highlighted by her

leading role in the cult classic *She* (1935). After several years' involvement in Democratic Party politics, she was elected to Congress in 1944 and served three terms. Gahagan Douglas ran for the U.S. Senate in California in 1950, facing up-and-coming right-winger Richard Nixon. Nixon scared voters by calling her "red hot" and "pink right down to her underwear" and by insinuating that she had slept with President Truman. Nixon won the election and went on to further political success. Gahagan Douglas never ran for office again.

2. CLINT EASTWOOD
The star of such films as *A Fistful of Dollars* (1964), *Dirty Harry* (1971), and *Sudden Impact* (1983), Eastwood took time off from his film career to serve two years as mayor of Carmel, California (pop. 4,800). Elected on a prodevelopment platform in 1986, he nonetheless stopped greedy developers from buying the 22-acre Mission Ranch, by using a tactic not available to most politicians: He bought the ranch himself for $5 million.

3. JOSEPH ESTRADA
Known as the "Filipino Ronald Reagan" because he starred in so many B movies, Estrada built his reputation by playing the role of the common man fighting the system. Elected mayor of San Juan, a suburb of Manila, Estrada moved on to become the only senator without a college degree. In 1992, he was elected vice president of the Philippines, and in 1998, he was elected president. In 2000, he was impeached by the Philippine Congress on charges of corruption and bribery. He resigned on January 20, 2001, in the face of a bloodless "people's revolt." He has since served time in prison for perjury.

4. CHARLES FARRELL
During the late 1920s and the early 1930s, Farrell and Janet Gaynor made 12 pictures together and were known as "America's Favorite Lovebirds." When his career began to decline, Farrell became a land developer in Palm Springs, California, and served as the city's mayor from 1947 to 1955. Television showed him an opportunity to stage a successful comeback as an actor. He costarred in *My Little Margie* (1952–1957) and starred in *The Charlie Farrell Show* (1956–1960) before retiring again to the desert.

5. FRED GRANDY
Although he has appeared on Broadway and in the movies, Grandy, a Harvard graduate, is best known for his portrayal of Gopher in the TV series *The Love Boat* (1977–1986). In 1986, he returned to his earlier interest in politics, winning election from Sioux City, Iowa, to the U.S. House of Representatives. A Republican, Grandy describes himself as a "knee-jerk moderate."

6. **GLENDA JACKSON**

Jackson won two Academy Awards for her performances in *Women in Love* (1970) and *A Touch of Class* (1972). Running as a Labour Party candidate, the bricklayer's daughter won election to Parliament in 1992 in the Hampstead and Highgate sections of north London.

7. **BEN JONES**

Best known for his portrayal of the mechanic Cooter Davenport in *The Dukes of Hazzard*, Jones, a Georgia Democrat, won election to the U.S. Congress in 1988. He was reelected in 1990, but in 1992 he was defeated in the Democratic Party primary.

8. **SHEILA KUEHL**

Kuehl played Zelda Gilroy on the TV series *The Many Loves of Dobie Gillis* from 1959 to 1963. After the series ended, she went to law school and became an attorney specializing in feminist issues. In 1994, she was elected speaker pro tem of the California State Assembly, the first woman to hold that position. In 2000, she was elected to the State Senate. Kuehl was the first openly gay or lesbian politician to be elected to the California legislature.

9. **MELINA MERCOURI**

The star of *Never on Sunday* (1959), Mercouri entered Greek politics as soon as democracy was restored in 1974. A member of the Pan-Hellenic Socialist movement, she was elected to Parliament in 1977 and has represented the working-class district of Piraeus ever since. She also served as minister of culture from 1981 until 1990. In 1990, she ran for mayor of Athens but was defeated.

10. **GEORGE MURPHY**

After several years on Broadway, Murphy moved to Hollywood, where he specialized in musicals such as *Little Miss Broadway* (1938) and war films such as *This Is the Army* (1943), in which he appeared with Ronald Reagan. From 1944 to 1946, he served two terms as president of the Screen Actors Guild. A Democrat turned Republican, Murphy was elected U.S. senator from California in 1968. An ineffective legislator, he was defeated when he ran for reelection in 1974.

11. **ALESSANDRA MUSSOLINI**

No one was surprised or upset when the beautiful niece of actress Sophia Loren became a film actress herself, appearing in such films as *White Sister* (1973) and *A Special Day* (1977). But she did cause a stir when, at the age of 30, she followed in the footsteps of her grandfather, dictator Benito Mussolini, by entering politics. In 1992, she was elected to Parliament as the representative of the neo-Fascist party from Naples.

12. **N. T. RAMA RAO**

Known as the Saffron Caesar because he usually appeared in an orange costume, Rama Rao, the star of more than 300 Indian films, capitalized on his widespread popularity to enter politics. He rose to become chief minister of Andhra Pradesh state. After leaving office, he remained the leader of the Telegu Desam Party, and in 1991, at the age of 69, he was arrested in the midst of a hunger strike to protest an attack on his house by supporters of the ruling Congress Party.

13. **RONALD REAGAN**

Like George Murphy before him, Reagan was a movie actor, a president of the Screen Actors Guild, and a Democrat-turned-Republican. When he announced that he planned to run for governor of California in 1966, studio head Jack Warner commented, "No, no, no! Jimmy Stewart for governor, Ronald Reagan for best friend." When he won the election, Reagan was asked what he planned to do when he took office. "I don't know," he replied, "I've never played a governor." He was reelected in 1970 and later served two terms as president of the United States (1981–1989). Nevertheless, he never lost his basic actor's mentality. At the 1987 economic summit in Venice, Italy, Reagan startled the leaders of the world's industrial nations by showing up with cue cards, not just for important meetings, but even at an informal cocktail party.

14. **ARNOLD SCHWARZENEGGER**

The bodybuilder-turned-actor rose to stardom in such films as *Conan the Barbarian* (1982) and *The Terminator* (1984). By the end of the 1980s, he was Hollywood's top action hero. After he married into the Kennedy clan (his wife, broadcast journalist Maria Shriver, is the daughter of Eunice Kennedy Shriver), speculation grew about a possible political career. He saw his chance in 2003, when Republicans launched a drive to recall California's Democratic governor Gray Davis from office. In true Hollywood fashion, Schwarzenegger announced his candidacy to Jay Leno on *The Tonight Show* on August 7, 2003. Two months later, California voters chose to oust Davis and replace him with Schwarzenegger.

15. **ILONA STALLER**

Hungarian-born pornographic film star Ilona Staller, better known by her stage name, Cicciolina, was elected to the Italian Parliament in 1987. A member of the Radical Party and the Party of Love, she represented her Rome constituency until retiring in 1992.

16. **FRED THOMPSON**

A veteran character actor, Thompson had prominent roles in the movies *The Hunt for Red October* (1990) and *In the Line of Fire*

(1993). A Republican from Tennessee, he was elected to the U.S. Senate in 1994. In the fall of 2002, he joined the cast of the NBC series *Law and Order*, becoming the first serving U.S. senator with a regular television acting job. Thompson left the Senate when his term ended in January of 2003.

17. **JESSE VENTURA**
    Jesse "The Body" Ventura first emerged as a star in the World Wrestling Federation. He parlayed that fame into a movie career, appearing with Arnold Schwarzenegger in *Predator* (1987) and with Sylvester Stallone in *Demolition Man* (1993). In 1998, he was elected governor of Minnesota as the candidate of the upstart Reform Party. He drew fire from critics for appearing as a TV commentator for the short-lived XFL (Extreme Football League) and being a celebrity referee at a WWF event while still in office. He served one term, choosing not to run for reelection in 2002.

                                                                    D.W. & C.F.

Percentage of Women in 30 National Legislatures

The Inter-Parliamentary Union, an international organization that works to foster representative government and world peace, reports that women are appallingly underrepresented in their national parliaments. Although they account for more than 50 percent of the world's population, in June 30, 2005 the number of female legislators stood at only 15.7 percent. The figures below are for February 2005. (The IPU can be contacted at www.ipu.org or by writing to 5 chemin du Pommier, Case postale 330, CH-1218 Le Grand-Saconnex, Geneva, Switzerland.

THE 10 NATIONS WITH THE HIGHEST PERCENTAGE OF WOMEN IN THEIR LEGISLATURES . . .

1.	Rwanda	48.8%
2.	Sweden	45.3
3.	Norway	38.2
4.	Finland	37.5
5.	Denmark	36.9
6.	Netherlands	36.7
7.	Cuba	36.0
	Spain	36.0
9.	Costa Rica	35.1
10.	Mozambique	34.8

11. Belgium	34.7
12. Austria	33.9
13. Argentina	33.7
14. Germany	32.8
South Africa	32.8
16. Iraq	31.5
17. Pakistan	21.3
18. Canada	21.1
19. China	20.2
20. United Kingdom	19.7
21. United States	15.2
22. Israel	15.0
23. South Korea	13.0
24. France	12.2
25. Italy	11.5
26. Russia	9.8
27. India	8.3
28. Japan	7.1
29. Kuwait	0.0
Saudi Arabia	0.0

Source: "Women in National Parliaments: World Classification," Inter-Parliamentary Union.

10 Worst Dictators Currently in Power

This list was prepared after consultation with human rights groups that have not hesitated to expose the policies of dictatorships of both the left and the right: Human Rights Watch, Freedom House, Amnesty International, and Reporters Without Borders.

1. OMAR AL-BASHIR, Sudan—in power since 1989
   Sudan, the largest country in Africa, has been in the news lately because of the humanitarian tragedy in its Darfur region that has claimed the lives of 70,000 people and uprooted 2 million. Most of the deaths have been caused by the activities of government-supported militia. This is nothing new in Sudan. The nation's dictator, Omar al-Bashir, has used the same tactics in other parts of the country ever since he seized power in a military coup that overthrew an elected government in 1989. Sudan has more internally displaced people than any other nation in the world: 6 million. A former paratrooper who fought against Israel in 1973, Bashir attempted to impose Islamic Shari'a law in southern Sudan, where the population practices Christianity and

traditional religions. Because of his limited education, al-Bashir was long thought to be a front man for Islamist intellectual Hasan al-Turabi. However, in 2001, Bashir had Turabi arrested, and he has maintained a firm grip on power ever since. His campaign against the south, which has included aerial bombing of villages and abduction and enslavement of women and children, was seen by some as a war between Muslims and Christians. But the people he has victimized in Darfur, in western Sudan, are Muslims. On January 9, 2005, Bashir's government signed a ceasefire agreement with southern Sudan's largest rebel group. As encouraging as this sounds, it is worth noting that Bashir has used previous ceasefires to gain time and reorganize his troops. Indeed, the new ceasefire agreement does not allow southerners to vote for independence for another six years. The agreement also guarantees Bashir's party a majority of all executive positions in a future government.

2. KIM JONG IL, North Korea—in power since 1994
   Reporters Without Borders ranks North Korea in last place in its international index of press freedom, and North Korea earned Freedom House's worst possible score for political rights and civil liberties for the thirty-third straight year, a dubious record unequaled by any other country. All citizens of North Korea are monitored by the Ministry of People's Security, which places informers in workplaces and neighborhoods to report anyone who criticizes the regime, even at home. All radios and televisions are fixed so that they receive only government stations. Among the crimes for which one may be punished are disloyalty to The Great Leader (Kim Jong Il's late father, Kim Il Sung) or to The Dear Leader (Kim Jong Il), an offense that includes allowing pictures of Kim Jong Il or his father to gather dust and allowing pictures of the Kims that appear in magazines or newspapers to be torn or folded. Authorities divide the entire population into three categories of "loyalty groups." About a third of North Koreans belong to the "hostile class." In addition to receiving the worst jobs and housing, the hostiles are not allowed to live in the capital city of Pyongyang. Below the hostile class are the estimated 250,000 people who are held in prison camps, some of them for alleged crimes committed by relatives. Executions are often performed in public, sometimes in crowded marketplaces.

3. THAN SHWE, Burma—in power since 1992
   In 2004, General Than Shwe resolved an ongoing power struggle with Prime Minister Khin Nyunt by having him arrested. In an attempt to satisfy international opinion, Than Shwe released 9,000 prisoners, but hopes of liberalization faded quickly when it became clear that all but 40 of the prisoners were common criminals rather than political detainees, of whom more than 1,000 are still in custody. In fact, Than Shwe extended the house arrest of Nobel Peace Prize winner

Aung San Suu Kyi, whose party won 80 percent of the vote in the last open election (in 1990). And in December 2004, the government began arresting opposition members once again. Than Shwe's military continues to use as soldiers an estimated 70,000 boys under the age of 18. In fact, one quarter of all underage soldiers in the world are in Burma. Freedom of expression in Burma is not allowed, and even unlicensed possession of a fax machine or a modem is punishable by 15 years in prison. In its ongoing campaign to forcibly relocate members of ethnic minorities, the Burmese army has destroyed almost 3,000 villages. There are currently one million Burmese who have been driven from their homes but remain in Burma, and several hundred thousand more who are refugees in neighboring countries. In December, in a landmark case, Unocal Corp. of California agreed to pay damages to Burmese villagers whose family members were raped, murdered, or forced to work on a natural gas pipeline by soldiers supporting Unocal's operations. Than Shwe is a generally reclusive dictator who surfaces on rare occasions to give speeches warning of the threat from "neocolonialists."

4. HU JINTAO, China—in power since 2002
After spending 39 years slowly working his way up the hierarchy of the Communist Party of China, Hu Jintao became president of China in 2003. In September 2004, he completed his control of all the country's major positions by taking over as chairman of the Central Military Commission. Despite China's economic liberalization, the Chinese government remains one of the most repressive in the world. An estimated 250,000 Chinese are serving sentences in "reeducation and labor" camps. Hu's government controls all media in China, and, with the help of spyware technology provided by Cisco Systems, it has developed a sophisticated system of controlling Internet use that has become the model for other dictatorships. China executes more people than all other nations combined, and most of those executions are for nonviolent crimes. Among the crimes that can bring the death penalty in China are burglary, embezzlement, counterfeiting, bribery, and killing a panda. Amnesty International has reported that schoolchildren have been bused to public executions as field trips. According to Human Rights Watch, defense lawyers may be disbarred or even imprisoned if they advocate their clients' rights too vigorously. If members of a minority group, such as Tibetans or Uighurs, speak out for autonomy, the Chinese government labels them "terrorists" even if their protests are nonviolent, and they are subject to imprisonment and torture.

5. KING ABDULLAH, Saudi Arabia—in power since 1995
Crown Prince Abdullah has been the acting leader of Saudi Arabia since his half brother, King Fahd, suffered a stroke in 1995. He and his family have absolute power. Responding to tremendous international

pressure, Saudi Arabia held its first elections in 40 years in 2005. Of course, they were only municipal elections, and only half the seats were contested. No women were allowed to vote, much less run for office. The Saudi government explained that women were excluded because of "technical difficulties": Most Saudi women do not have the photo IDs required to register, and even if they did, there were not enough female officials to register them. Male officials are not allowed to register women because in Saudi Arabia the sexes are forbidden from mingling in public places. In 2004, the United States State Department added Saudi Arabia to its list of eight nations in which religious liberty is severely violated. The Saudi royal family practices an extreme form of Islam known as Wahhabism, which considers other Muslims "infidels." King Abdullah has used oil revenues to fund Wahhabi religious schools around the world. If it seems strange that the U.S. government has been tolerant of the human rights excesses of the Saudi royal family, it is worth noting that U.S. companies export more than $6.5 billion worth of goods and services to Saudi Arabia each year, and Saudis own $250 billion worth of investments in the United States. Saudi Arabia is also the second-biggest source of oil for the United States.

6. **MU'AMMAR AL-QADDAFI, Libya**—in power since 1969
Increasingly annoyed by other Arab leaders, Qaddafi has gone to great lengths to reestablish links with the West. He turned over one perpetrator of the 1988 terrorist bombing of an American commercial flight over Lockerbie, Scotland, and he made substantial payments to the survivors of the Lockerbie victims and to the victims of another plane bombing aimed against the French. He also gave up his nuclear weapons development program. Sanctions against Libya have been lifted, and Qaddafi is opening his nation's economy to foreign investment. However, it should not be forgotten that domestically, Qaddafi still runs a brutal dictatorship in which he maintains complete control over all aspects of Libyan life. "Collective guilt" can lead to the punishment of entire families, tribes, and even towns, and freedom of speech, assembly, and religion are harshly restricted. People can be arrested for "opposition." "Crimes against the state" include the all-inclusive "damaging public or private institutions or property."

7. **PERVEZ MUSHARRAF, Pakistan**—in power since 1999
General Pervez Musharraf seized power in a military coup that overthrew an elected government. He appointed himself president of Pakistan in 2001 and then attempted to legitimize his rule by being elected in 2002. However, the election was heavily boycotted and did not come close to meeting international standards. Musharraf agreed to step down as head of the military at the end of 2004, but then he changed his mind, claiming that the nation needed to unify its political and military elements and that he could provide this unity. He justified

his decision by stating, "I think the country is more important than democracy." Prior to September 11, 2001, Musharraf was an ardent supporter of Afghanistan's Taliban regime. Yet his greatest transgression concerns Pakistan's role in the spread of nuclear technology. In early 2004, it was revealed that Abdul Qadeer Khan, the head of Pakistan's nuclear weapons development program, had been selling nuclear technology to the dictatorships of North Korea, Libya, and Iran. Musharraf claimed, rather unconvincingly, that he knew nothing about that dangerous and illicit trade, but he also gave Khan an unconditional pardon. According to a Pakistani law known as the Hudood Ordinance, a woman who has been raped may present her case only if she can produce four Muslim men who witnessed the attack.

8. SAPARMURAT NIYAZOV, Turkmenistan—in power since 1990
    Over the last 15 years, Niyazov, the ruler of this former Soviet republic in Central Asia, has developed an outrageous personality cult. He has built statues of himself throughout the country, put his picture on all denominations of money, and even renamed the month of January after himself. He controls all media, and it is illegal to criticize any of his policies. In 2004, Niyazov claimed that he was toning down his personality cult, but you would hardly know it from his actions. He renamed Turkmenistan's highest mountain after himself, and he published part two of his guide to living: *Rukhnama* (*Book of the Soul*). A copy of the book is presented to every couple when they marry, so that they can follow Niyazov's version of family values. All candidates for a driver's license must also pass an exam based on the book's spiritual teachings. It is against the law to smoke or to listen to loud music while driving. Niyazov has also inserted himself into the world of fashion. He ordered women news presenters to wear less makeup, and he demanded that female students wear their hair in braids. He also forbade young men from wearing beards or long hair or from getting gold tooth caps. In October 2004, Turkmenistan's legislature asked Niyazov to remain in office for the rest of his life. As one legislator put it, "You are given to us by God, and therefore any talk about presidential elections should be stopped."

9. ROBERT MUGABE, Zimbabwe—in power since 1980
    After leading a successful anticolonial war of liberation, Robert Mugabe was elected independent Zimbabwe's first president. It was hoped that, like Nelson Mandela in South Africa, he would guide Africa to a new era of democracy. But with each year that has passed, he has turned increasingly dictatorial, and he has run his country into the ground. Zimbabwe now has the lowest life expectancy in the world—33 years. Among the many repressive laws enforced by Mugabe is one that makes it a crime for any citizen to make an "abusive, indecent, or obscene statement" about Mugabe even if the speaker is not in Zimbabwe. In a recent case, a Zimbabwean named Arnold Bunya told his brother, while

the two were riding a bus, "Do not be thickheaded like Mugabe."
Overheard by a government security agent, Bunya was sentenced to two
weeks in jail. Mugabe continues to hold elections, but the opposition is
greatly restricted. In May and June of 2005, Mugabe's government
bulldozed the homes of more than 300,000 people, and two months later
Mugabe changed the constitution to allow confiscation of private
property without legal recourse, as well as revocation of passports
without appeal.

10. **TEODORO OBIANG NGUEMA**, Equatorial Guinea—in power since 1979
The tiny West African nation of Equatorial Guinea (pop. 500,000) was
catapulted onto the international scene when major reserves of oil were
discovered there in 1995. Since then, U.S. oil companies have poured
$5 billion into the country, but the majority of Equatoguineans live on
less than a dollar a day—the bulk of the oil income goes directly to
President Obiang and members of his family. The U.S. State Department has accused Obiang's government of committing torture, and
other branches of the U.S. government are investigating American oil
companies for improprieties involving Obiang. For example, Exxon
Mobil and Amerada Hess Corp. paid $1 million to a private security
firm headed by Obiang's brother, whom the State Department has
identified as a torturer. Amerada Hess also paid $500,000 to Obiang's
14-year-old son. And in May 2004, the U.S. Treasury Department fined
Riggs Bank of Washington, D.C., $25 million for its mishandling of
Obiang's accounts. In November 2004, 20 people, including 11 foreign
nationals, were sentenced to prison for an alleged coup attempt after a
trial that Amnesty International characterized as "grossly unfair." The
defendants were not allowed to meet with lawyers until two days before
the trial, and the only evidence against them was confessions extracted
through torture. For the record, it is estimated that Equatorial
Guinea's oil will be completely pumped out by 2020.

13 Deposed Dictators After the Fall

1. **IDI AMIN** (Uganda)
Amin seized power in 1971 and launched a reign of terror that led to
the deaths of an estimated 300,000 people. Deposed in 1979, he was
offered asylum in Saudi Arabia, with all living expenses paid. In 1989,
he tried to return to Uganda using a false passport. He got as far as the
Congo, where he was recognized and arrested and then sent back to
Saudi Arabia. He died in 2003 at age 78. Ugandan president Yoweri
Museveni vetoed a suggestion to give Amin a state funeral in order to
win votes in Amin's home region: "I would not bury Amin. I will never
touch Amin. Never. Not even with a long spoon."

2. **JEAN-BEDEL BOKASSA (Central African Republic)**
   Bokassa seized power in 1965. In 1976, he declared himself emperor, and a year later he staged an elaborate coronation celebration that used up one fourth of the nation's annual earnings. He was overthrown in 1979, but not before he had committed a series of horrible outrages, including ordering the massacre of schoolchildren who refused to buy uniforms made in a factory owned by Bokassa's wife. After his ouster, he lived lavishly in Paris. Then, incredibly, he returned to the CAR, where he was arrested upon arrival and charged with murder and cannibalism. He was convicted of the former charge and placed in "comfortable confinement" in the capital city of Bangui. Bokassa was set free in 1993, when General Andre Kolingba, the country's latest dictator, ordered all the nation's convicts released. He died in 1996.

3. **JEAN-CLAUDE DUVALIER (Haiti)**
   When longtime Haitian dictator François "Papa Doc" Duvalier died in 1971, the mantle of power passed to his 19-year-old son Jean-Claude, better known as "Baby Doc," who also inherited the dreaded Tonton Macoutes secret police. Baby Doc was finally forced from office in 1986 after widespread protest and flown out of the country on a U.S. Air Force plane. Baby Doc and his wife, Michelle, not content with stuffing an Air Haiti cargo plane with plunder, bumped 11 passengers off their escape flight—including Michelle's grandparents—to make room for more loot. The Duvaliers settled on the French Riviera and spent millions of dollars a year before divorcing in 1990.

4. **ERICH HONECKER (East Germany)**
   As head of East German security, Honecker supervised the construction of the Berlin Wall in 1961. Ten years later, he assumed leadership of the Communist Party. Among his most odious acts was ordering all border areas to be mined and equipped with automatic shooting devices. With the fall of communism in 1989, Honecker was put under house arrest. In 1991, he was flown from a Soviet military hospital near Berlin to Moscow itself. However, on July 29, 1992, the 79-year-old Honecker was expelled from the Chilean embassy, where he had sought refuge, and was flown back to Berlin to face charges of corruption and manslaughter. Because he was diagnosed as dying from liver cancer, Honecker was allowed to leave for Chile in January 1993. He died of liver cancer on May 29, 1994.

5. **SADDAM HUSSEIN (Iraq)**
   Saddam Hussein took power in 1979. A ruthless dictator, with help from the United States, he subjected the Iraqi people to a bloody eight-year war with neighboring Iran. He managed to survive in power despite losing the first Gulf War with a United States–led coalition in 1991. In 2003, the United States led a "preemptive" war against Iraq.

As Baghdad swiftly fell, Saddam disappeared. He remained elusive until December 13, 2003, when U.S. forces found him in a 6-foot-deep hole on a farm outside of his hometown of Tikrit. He offered no resistance, telling the American soldiers in English, "My name is Saddam Hussein. I am the president of Iraq, and I want to negotiate." He is currently being held in Iraq, awaiting trial on war crimes and other charges.

6. MENGISTU HAILE MARIAM (Ethiopia)

Mengistu was a member of the military junta that ousted Haile Selassie in 1974. By 1977, he had consolidated his personal power. While the Ethiopian people were suffering through a series of droughts and famines, Mengistu concentrated on brutally suppressing his opponents. Bodies of political prisoners who had been tortured to death were displayed in public and shown on television. Mengistu's ability to beat back various secessionist armies finally failed, and on May 21, 1991, he resigned and fled the country. He settled in Zimbabwe, where he was welcomed by that country's dictator, Robert Mugabe.

7. MOBUTU SESE SEKO (Congo)

After taking power in 1965, Mobutu amassed a huge fortune through economic exploitation and corruption, leading some observers to dub the government a "kleptocracy." He stole more than half of the $12 billion in aid that his country received from the International Monetary Fund during his 32-year-reign, saddling the country with a crippling debt. On May 18, 1997, Mobutu fled the country as rebel forces led by Laurent Kabila seized the capital. For his exile, Mobutu could choose among luxury residences in Morocco, South Africa, France, Belgium, Spain, and Portugal. He chose Portugal, and the wine collection at his castle there was worth an estimated $23 million. Mobutu didn't have much time to enjoy his ill-gotten luxuries: He died on September 7, 1997, of prostate cancer.

8. MANUEL NORIEGA (Panama)

Noriega was raised in a poor family of Colombian background. Something of an ugly duckling, he found his place in the military. He rose rapidly to become head of Panama's intelligence service. In 1983, he took command of the national army and, with it, the nation. A devious manipulator who played all sides, Noriega cooperated with the U.S. government and the CIA while at the same time making huge profits from drug trafficking, money laundering, and racketeering. When he refused to abide by the results of a free election, the first President Bush ordered the invasion of Panama, and troops seized Noriega and brought him back to Miami to stand trial. He was convicted and sentenced to 40 years in prison. But in December 1992, U.S. District Court judge William Hoeveler declared Noriega a prisoner of war, entitled to the rights guaranteed by the third Geneva Convention. He will be eligible for parole in 2006; however, the Panamanian government has sought his extradition because in 1995 he was tried in absentia and found guilty of murder.

9. AUGUSTO PINOCHET (Chile)

As commander in chief of Chile's armed forces, Pinochet led the 1973 coup that overthrew the elected government of Salvador Allende. For the next 17 years, he ruled Chile with an iron fist, suspending Parliament and ordering the abduction and murder of 2,000 political opponents. He did agree to democratic elections, which he lost, in 1988. In 1990, he stepped down as president but retained control of the armed forces, a position that he still holds. Pinochet was arrested in Great Britain in 1998 and held under house arrest while the British government considered extradition requests from four countries. During his house arrest, he lived at Wentworth, an exclusive estate outside of London, at a cost of $10,000 per month. In May 2000, he was returned to Chile on medical grounds, but after his arrival he was arrested, and more than 200 charges were filed against him. In 2002, all charges were dropped after the Chilean Supreme Court declared him unfit to stand trial. However, the case against him was reopened after he appeared lucid during a television interview, and a Chilean judge discovered that he retained the mental capacity to manage more than $12 million that he was hiding in secret bank accounts. In January 2005, Pinochet was formally charged with one murder and nine kidnappings.

10. POL POT

Pol Pot was one of the few modern dictators whose genocidal policies were so horrible that they rivaled those of Adolf Hitler. As leader of the notorious Khmer Rouge, Pol Pot launched a four-year reign of terror (1975–1979) that turned the country into one large forced-labor camp and led to the death of an estimated one million people. When Vietnamese forces finally drove the Khmer Rouge from power, Pol Pot and his followers set up shop in Thailand and northern Cambodia, where, with the encouragement of the government of the United States, he continued to be supported by the governments of China and Thailand. As late as 1996, Pol Pot was still executing Khmer Rouge opponents. He finally died of heart failure on April 15, 1998.

11. ALFREDO STROESSNER (Paraguay)

Stroessner seized power in a 1954 military coup and held on for over 34 years, setting a record as the longest-ruling head of state in the Western Hemisphere. He was finally deposed in February 1989. He flew to exile in Brazil, with one of his sons, while the rest of his family moved to Miami. In April 2004, the Paraguayan government paid compensation to 34 victims of Stroessner's repression.

12. SUHARTO (Indonesia)

Shortly after seizing the presidency in a 1965 coup, Suharto launched an anti-Communist and anti-Chinese campaign that killed at least 500,000 people. In 1975, the Indonesian army invaded the former Portuguese colony of East Timor and killed 200,000 people—more than a quarter of the island's population. Despite those genocides, the United States supported Suharto as an anti-Communist throughout the Cold War. The recession that hit East Asia in 1997 sent the Indonesian economy into free fall. As increasing numbers of demonstrators took to the streets, Suharto was forced out of office in May of 1998. In April 2000, he was put on trial for misappropriating $571 million from various charities that he controlled. But, in September, a panel of judges dismissed the charges, concluding that Suharto, who had suffered several strokes, was medically unfit to stand trial. They also lifted a house arrest that had been imposed on Suharto. The decisions led to rioting in the streets. Unable to prosecute Suharto himself, Indonesian authorities arrested his son, Tommy, and convicted him of murder.

13. CHARLES TAYLOR (Liberia)

In 1989, Taylor launched a revolt against the Liberian government, beginning 14 years of nearly constant civil war. In 1997, he was elected president, drawing 75 percent of the vote from a populace hoping his election would end the warfare. His regime became increasingly repressive and brutal. He was notorious for using child soldiers, organized into "Small Boy Units." Even as civil war resumed in Liberia, Taylor participated in conflicts in nearby Guinea, Côte d'Ivoire, and Sierra Leone. His soldiers were repeatedly accused by human rights groups of widespread looting, rape, torture, forced labor, and summary killings. By 2003, Taylor controlled little but the downtown of the Liberian capital, referred to derisively by rebels as the Federal Republic of Central Monrovia. On August 11, 2003, he accepted an asylum offer from Nigeria and fled Liberia, taking along $1 billion, emptying the national treasury. As he settled into a luxury villa in the Nigerian city of Calabar, a United Nations tribunal indicted him on charges of committing war crimes in Sierra Leone. Although the Nigerian journalists' union and bar association have both called for Taylor to be handed over to Sierra Leone, Nigerian president Olusegun Obasanjo has said he will not extradite the former warlord.

D.W. & C.F.

10 Largest Arms Exporters

Country	Millions of U.S. Dollars (2000–2004)
1. Russia	26,925
2. USA	25,930
3. France	6,358
4. Germany	4,878
5. United Kingdom	4,450
6. Ukraine	2,118
7. Canada	1,692
8. China	1,436
9. Sweden	1,290
10. Israel	1,258

Source: Stockholm International Peace Research Institute (*SIPRI Yearbook 2005*).

10 Largest Arms Importers

Country	Millions of U.S. Dollars (2000–2004)	Major Supplier
1. China	11,667	Russia
2. India	8,526	Russia
3. Greece	5,263	USA
4. United Kingdom	3,395	USA
5. Turkey	3,298	USA
6. Egypt	3,103	USA
7. South Korea	2,755	USA
8. United Arab Emirates	2,581	USA
9. Australia	2,177	USA
10. Pakistan	2,018	USA

Source: Stockholm International Peace Research Institute (*SIPRI Yearbook 2005*).

9 Ordinary Men Who Played King

1. **GIUSEPPE BARTOLEONI (1780?–1848?), king of Tavolara**
   One day in 1833, Carlo Alberto (1798–1849), king of Sardinia, instructed the captain of his ship to leave him on the island of Tavolara—located off

the coast of Sardinia—for a few hours of solitary hunting. After a short time, the king was approached by a huge man more than 7 feet tall. The man was the sole inhabitant of the island, and the king was so impressed with his harmonious lifestyle that he declared him king of Tavolara. The hermit identified himself as Giuseppe Bartoleoni, a shepherd from Maddalena, an island north of Sardinia. Carlo Alberto found that hard to believe. Most people of the time—especially peasants—were illiterate, but Giuseppe was fluent in several languages and extremely well educated. He was also the head of two families that lived on two other islands. He sent for both families to live with him in his new kingdom, and, because he was sovereign, the Italian government failed in its attempt to prosecute him for bigamy. Paolo, his eldest son, was named his successor upon his father's death in the late 1840s. When Paolo died 50 years later, the inhabitants of Tavolara proclaimed it a republic.

2. **PATRICK WATKINS** (fl. c. 1810), king of the Galápagos
Watkins, a redheaded Irish seaman, left his British whaling ship for the isolation of the Galápagos Islands off the coast of Ecuador and crowned himself king. He grew potatoes and pumpkins, which he sold to ships that stopped at the islands. He considered all of the Galápagos his domain and even pressed some unsuspecting sailors into slavery. To share his throne, he picked up a "queen" in Payta, Peru. Unfortunately, local police there found him hiding on board a ship and put him in prison, where he eventually died.

3. **ORÉLIE-ANTOINE DE TOUNENS** (1825–1878), king of Araucanía and Patagonia
Tounens, an adventuresome French lawyer, succeeded in winning the favor of the Araucanían Indians, a belligerent agrarian people of southern Chile. He was crowned Orélie-Antoine I. After a time, de Tounens was arrested and chased back to France. Upon his death, he left the throne to his secretary, Gustave Achille Laviarde, who took the name Achille I and "ruled in exile" from Paris, where he became known as Achille the Jovial.

4. **DAVID O'KEEFE** (?–1901), king of Yap
In 1871, O'Keefe, an Irish immigrant who had settled in Savannah, Georgia, said good-bye to his wife and daughter and left for China. En route he was shipwrecked on Yap, an island in the West Pacific Ocean southwest of Guam. Adjusting well to island life, he acquired real estate from local chiefs and, in a few short years, became king. He even designed a royal emblem (an American flag waving over the letters *OK*) and erected a mansion on a small island in the harbor. Not forgetting Mrs. O'Keefe, he sent money home to Savannah twice a year. His tranquil reign was upset one day when the tribal chiefs presented him with a suitable queen. Ever mindful of Mrs. O'Keefe, he tried to sidestep this

bigamous marriage. But the chiefs were insistent. Reluctantly, King David accepted Queen Dollyboy—reluctantly at first, that is, since the royal couple eventually produced seven children. In 1901, O'Keefe sent word to wife number one that he was coming home. With two of his Yapese sons, he boarded the ship *Santa Cruz*. It was lost at sea.

5. **BARON JAMES A. HARDEN-HICKEY (1854–1898), king of Trinidad**
"I propose to take possession of the Island of Trinidad under a maxim of international law which declares that anybody may seize and hold waste land that is not claimed by anybody else." So declared Baron Harden-Hickey—the Francophile American novelist, Catholic-turned-Buddhist Theosophist, and author of a how-to book on suicide—in 1893 as he prepared to assume the throne as King James I. Although his kingdom was not *the* Trinidad in the West Indies, but rather a small uninhabited island 700 miles off the coast of Brazil, Harden-Hickey fully expected to be welcomed into the family of nations. But it was not to be. While he recruited suitable subjects and issued fancy postage stamps and 1,000-franc bonds from a Manhattan office, Great Britain and Brazil haggled over possession of the South Atlantic rock. In 1896, Great Britain abandoned its claim. Brazil, assured of no further British occupation, left the island to the turtles. And lost in the shuffle was the would-be king, his crown gathering dust in a trunk. Two years later, taking a page from his own book, Baron Harden-Hickey committed suicide in El Paso, Texas.

6. **JOHN DAVIS MURRAY (1870?–?), king of Christmas Island**
In 1891, Murray, a mechanical engineer who graduated from Purdue University, went to work for the British-owned Phosphate Mining and Shipping Company. The firm first dispatched him to Christmas Island, southwest of Java, to oversee its phosphate mines there. Since most of the miners were native islanders, it was decided that the surest way to get things done was to make Murray king, complete with full executive and judicial powers. In 1910, while in London, he met a young woman and decided to marry. The prospect of royal life on a remote island held little appeal for the bride, so King John dutifully relinquished his throne.

7. **CARL HAFFKE (fl. 1900), king of the Ilocanos**
A German immigrant, Haffke first found work as a Western Union messenger in Omaha, Nebraska. He later joined the navy and, serving under Admiral Dewey during the Spanish-American War, ended up in the Philippines, where he was a court stenographer. In due time, he became acquainted with various Ilocano chieftains. When a cholera epidemic wiped out the royal family, Haffke was offered the crown. He accepted, but not before making sure that the venture would turn a profit: He demanded up front a one-time six-figure tribute from the tribe, a 5 percent cut of all tribal profits, and the customary royal perks, including servants. In exchange for this, he agreed to serve as

sovereign, purchase farm machinery, and teach the natives modern agricultural techniques. After a year on the throne, King Carlos I, longing for the Cornhusker State, visited his home. He looked up an old girlfriend while there and, failing to convince her of the charms of the Philippines, abdicated to practice law in Nebraska.

8. EDWARD THOMPSON (?–1910?), king of Naikeva
Dumped by his girlfriend in his hometown of Albion, Illinois, Thompson sought solace at sea and wound up in the Fijis. On Naikeva Island, he rebounded into the arms of Princess Lakanita, the king's daughter. Still, he pressed on to other adventures on other islands. Then one day, a messenger from Naikeva brought him word that insurgents on the island were threatening to topple the monarchy. He hastily returned to Naikeva and joined the battle. Although the king died in action and Thompson was wounded, loyalists managed to put down the rebellion. While convalescing, Thompson rekindled his romance with Princess Lakanita and decided, after all, to settle down. He assumed the throne and ruled Naikeva until his death 25 years later.

9. FAUSTIN E. WIRKUS (1897–1948), king of La Gonave
In 1925, Wirkus, a 28-year-old U.S. Marine Corps sergeant stationed in Haiti, volunteered for the post of district commander on the island of La Gonave, just 40 miles from the mainland. The position entailed supervising the collection of taxes to be paid to the capital of Port-au-Prince. He was warned that his job would be complicated by the islanders' occult customs—including voodoo—but Wirkus was intent on his mission. When he landed, by an incredible coincidence, the people opened their hearts to him and proclaimed him King Faustin II. (It appeared that in 1849 a black man named Soulouque had become emperor of Haiti and its surrounding islands. He had declared himself King Faustin I. Why he chose the name Faustin, no one knows.) When Wirkus arrived on La Gonave, he learned from Queen Ti Memenne the legend that Faustin I would return. Even though Wirkus was white, the natives believed him to be the fulfillment of the prophecy and crowned him king a few weeks later. Wirkus retained his post of district commander and his title of king for four years, until his duty was officially terminated in 1929. He returned to a hero's welcome in the United States in the early 1930s, lived in New York for a brief time lecturing and writing about voodoo, and then rejoined the Marines when World War II began. He died of cancer in a New York military hospital.

W.A.D. & L.O.

CHAPTER TWELVE

Travel

7 PLACES WITH UNLIKELY NAMES

16 PLACES WHOSE NAMES WE EAT OR DRINK

11 UNUSUAL JOURNEYS

12 MUSEUMS OF LIMITED APPEAL

12 OF THE ODDEST ITEMS FOUND
AT LONDON TRANSPORT

9 UNUSUAL DISASTERS

25 CASES OF BIZARRE WEATHER

13 POSSIBLE SITES FOR THE GARDEN OF EDEN

THE 7 WONDERS OF THE ANCIENT WORLD

THE 15 LEAST POPULOUS INDEPENDENT NATIONS

BLUE WHALE EXHIBIT AT
THE ICELANDIC PHALLOLOGICAL MUSEUM
Courtesy of and © the Icelandic Phallological Museum
(www.ismennt.is/not/phallus/ens.htm)

7 Places with Unlikely Names

1. **CAPE OF GOOD HOPE**
   When the Portuguese explorer Bartholomeu Dias rounded the southern tip of Africa in 1488, he found the seas so rough he called it the Cape of Storms. The epithet was hardly likely to encourage traffic through this new gateway to India, so Portugal's King John II changed it to the Cape of Good Hope.

2. **GHANA**
   The former British West African colony known as the Gold Coast became the Republic of Ghana when it combined with Togoland and achieved independence in 1957. The name Ghana was chosen to recall the glory of the famous Ghana Empire of a thousand years earlier. Despite politicians' claims, historians have found no direct connection between modern Ghana and old Ghana, which straddled present-day Mauritania and Mali, 500 miles to the north.

3. **GREENLAND**
   This great, snow-covered island is a tenth-century example of false advertising. Eric the Red hoped to attract settlers from the more clement Iceland.

4. **IDAHO**
   When a name was needed for a new territory in the Pike's Peak mining area in 1860, lobbyist and eccentric George M. Willing suggested the Indian word *idaho,* which he said meant "gem of the mountains." Just before Congress made its final consideration, it was discovered that Willing had invented the term as a hoax. The territory was quickly named Colorado. However, two years later, when it came time to name another mining territory in the Pacific Northwest, the controversy had been forgotten, and on March 4, 1863, the territory of Idaho was established. The name was retained when statehood was achieved in 1890.

5. **NOME**
   A classic geographical mistake, "Nome" was miscopied from a British map of Alaska on which "? Name" had been written around 1850.

6. **PACIFIC OCEAN**
   Magellan had the remarkable luck of crossing this ocean without encountering a storm, so he called it *Mar Pacifico*—"the calm sea." The Pacific in fact produces some of the roughest storms in the world.

7. SINGAPORE

This name derives from the Sanskrit for "city of the lion." Its exact origin is a mystery, since lions are not indigenous to the region. Legend has it that a visiting prince from Sri Vijayan mistook a local animal for a lion.

R.K.R.

16 Places Whose Names We Eat or Drink (Not Including Cheeses)

Place	Food or Drink
1. Alaska, USA	baked Alaska
2. Bologna commune, Italy	bologna or baloney
3. Brussels, Belgium	brussels sprouts
4. Cantalupo town and papal villa, Italy	cantaloupe
5. Cayenne, French Guiana	cayenne pepper
6. Corinth, Greece	currants
7. Daiquiri, Cuba	daiquiri
8. The Florida Keys, USA	key lime pie
9. Frankfurt am Main, West Germany	frankfurters
10. Hamburg, Germany	hamburger
11. Linz, Austria	linzentorte
12. Port Mahon, Menorca, Spain	mayonnaise
13. Tabasco river and state, Mexico	Tabasco sauce
14. Tangier, Morocco	tangerines
15. Turkey	turkey (mistaken for Turkish guinea fowl)
16. Worcestershire, England	Worcestershire sauce

11 Unusual Journeys

Adventure is the result of poor planning. —Colonel Blatchford Snell

1. OVERLAND FROM PARIS TO NEW YORK

Parisian Harry De Windt's plan had been to find a route for railroad service between Paris and New York. After a failed attempt at the trek in 1896, he set out again in December of 1901. His route took him through Europe and Asia and across almost the whole of Siberia, a distance of more than 11,000 miles; by the time he had reached the Bering Strait, he noted that he had employed the labors of 808 horses,

887 reindeer, and 114 dogs. When De Windt arrived at East Cape, the easternmost point in Asia, he was forced to stay for a month with the Chukchi people until a ship arrived that could take him across the Bering Strait. The remainder of the journey, down through Alaska and the Pacific Coast to San Francisco and then across country to New York, was far less arduous. He arrived in New York on August 25, 1902, having covered a total distance of 18,494 miles. His journey had been for naught, however—by the time he passed through the crushing ice hazards of the Bering Strait, he realized the impossibility of his dream.

2. CRAWLING FROM TEXAS TO WASHINGTON
Many people have made use of odd and sometimes peculiar methods in order to get to Washington, D.C., but perhaps none was as basically strange as that of Hans Mullikin. The logger and sometime Baptist minister crawled the entire distance from his home in Marshall, Texas, to the gates of the White House, a journey that took him two and a half years and ended on November 23, 1978. Mullikin's was not a continuous journey; in the winters he returned home to work to finance the odyssey. His mode of travel was to go a certain distance on his knees (equipped with goalie kneepads donated by the Dallas Blackhawks hockey team), then jog back to his car and bring it up to his stopping point—repeating that process over and over. His avowed purpose, said Mullikin, was to "show America that we need to get on our knees and repent." He had hoped to meet with President Jimmy Carter, but this could not be arranged. "A lot of people," said Mullikin, smiling, "tell me I'm crazy."

3. BACKWARD WALK FROM SANTA MONICA TO ISTANBUL
On April 15, 1931, a 36-year-old man named Plennie L. Wingo set out from his home in Santa Monica, California, on a journey to Istanbul, Turkey, intenting to walk the entire distance backward. His basic technical problem—of seeing where he was going as well as where he had been—was solved when he saw advertised a pair of sunglasses fitted with rearview mirrors. His route, which took him across the United States and much of Europe, covered a distance of more than 8,000 miles and took more than 18 months to complete. Wingo had hoped to walk backward around the world but was barred from entering Pakistan because of a civil war then in progress.

4. A JOURNEY THROUGH "UNIMPORTANT NATIONS"
Travel writer John Sack, apparently having decided that the popular destinations of the world's tourists had received too much attention, decided to visit countries that were so small or obscure that most travelers bypassed them. His purposefully odd journey took him first to Lundy—a small country in the Bristol Channel off England—thence to

Sark, another island in the Channel, and at the time of Sack's visit, the only feudal state in all of Europe, presided over by the Dame of Sark, a lady named Sybil Hathaway, who collected the annual taxes in chickens. Next came Andorra, the tiny country between France and Spain given its independence by Charlemagne in 784; Sack noted that its principal industries then appeared to be tobacco, tourism, and smuggling. After a brief stop in Monaco—too popular to hold his interest for long—he continued through tiny Lichtenstein and San Marino to the SMOM, short for the Sovereign Military Order of Malta. This country can be found in the center of Rome and is approximately the size of half a football field; it had diplomatic relations with several countries, and its population, at the time of Sack's visit, was two people. Sack's next stop was Athos, and it was only an accident of birth that allowed him to visit; no females are allowed in that monastic land, a rule that includes not only people but all other fauna. Other countries visited included Sharja, on the Persian Gulf; Swat, near Afghanistan; Amb, in the center of Pakistan; and Punial and Sikkim, both in the Himalayas. A collection of Sack's articles on those countries was published in 1959 under the title *Report from Practically Nowhere*; it is not known whether the book caused an upsurge in tourism.

5. FIRST WALKS AROUND THE WORLD
In 1970, brothers David and John Kunst of Minnesota began a journey in which the two planned to walk completely around the world. They walked across much of the United States and Europe and passed through Monaco, where they were received by Princess Grace. Their journey was tragically interrupted in Afghanistan, where they were set upon by bandits who murdered John and left David for dead.

After taking his brother's body back to Minnesota, David returned and continued the journey, this time with brother Peter accompanying him for much of the distance. The walk, which was intended to raise money for UNICEF, took Kunst more than four years to complete; he averaged about 40 miles a day and covered 14,450 miles.

Nearly ten years later, in 1983, Steven Newman, 28, set out on a similar journey, beginning at his home in Bethel, Ohio. His journey, like Kunst's, took four years and is the only authenticated solo walk around the world. Newman traveled through Northern Ireland, crossing the Channel to Belgium, then down through France, Spain, Algeria, and Morocco, through Italy and Turkey, across Asia to Thailand and Australia, and finally back to the United States.

6. BOWING FOR BUDDHA
Following the Buddhist tradition of a particular kind of religious journey known as a bowing pilgrimage, two American Buddhist monks—Hung Ju and Hung Yo—set out in 1973 to make such a pilgrimage from San Francisco to Seattle, in the cause of world peace. After every third step of

the 1,100-mile journey, each made a bow. This was not a simple nod of the head but a bow in which the monk went to his knees and brought his forehead down almost to the pavement. The pilgrimage began in October 1973 and ended in August 1974.

A similar journey was undertaken by two other American Buddhist monks in 1977. Heng Chau and Heng Sure set out from Los Angeles for a Buddhist monastery located near Ukiah, California. This journey, like the earlier one, included bowing with full prostration every third step and took several months to complete.

7. AROUND THE WORLD ON A BET
In 1958, three latter-day Phileas Foggs—cousins Bertrand and Marc d'Oultremont, and Abel Armand, Belgian counts all—set off on a round-the-world journey to win a bet made with their friend Dino Vastapane, the stakes being the expenses of the journey. To make things a bit more difficult, Vastapane allowed them only 30 days rather than Fogg's 80—and they had to win "points" at each stop by acquiring various items, ranging from a button from a flight attendant's jacket (easy) to an Alcatraz prison uniform (almost impossible) to a skull from the Parisian catacombs (completely impossible). Vastapane's challenges were difficult, but not insurmountable, and the three counts won their bet when they returned to Belgium with literally minutes to spare.

8. AFRICA TO GREENLAND
Born in Togo in Africa, Tété-Michel Kpomassie learned in a French-run school of the wonders of the outside world, and Greenland and its Eskimos exercised a strange fascination on the young man. At the age of 16, in 1958, he ran away from home and spent six years making his way to Greenland, where he lived a fish-out-of-water existence among the inhabitants for a dozen years. Kpomassie traveled across the country to Baffin Bay, and eventually left to settle in France, where his writings earned him literary awards.

9. AMPHIBIAN JOURNEY ACROSS THE ATLANTIC
In 1950, Australian Ben Carlin, with his wife, Elinore, set out from Montreal in an amphibious jeep; the craft took to the water off Nova Scotia and crossed the entire Atlantic Ocean, making landfall at the Canary Islands after a stop in the Azores. The Carlins continued their journey by land, eventually stopping in England and going to Malmo, Sweden. Carlin tried to interest British auto manufacturers in his heavily modified vehicle, but there were no takers.

10. A JOURNEY AROUND INDIA
In 1969, a strange bequest from one of its former residents allowed the 40 villagers of a tiny Bengali town to tour their country; most had never

been more than a few miles from their birthplace, and the landowner who left the bequest explained that she wanted her townspeople to see that India was "very big and very beautiful." The 9,300–mile trip took seven months and is the subject of a book—*Third-Class Ticket*—by Canadian author Heather Wood.

11. **FROM PEKING TO PARIS BY AUTOMOBILE**
Those who recall the 1965 Tony Curtis–Jack Lemmon film *The Great Race* may wonder if the notion of a car race through various countries was just the fantasy of a screenwriter; in fact, such races did take place, and one of the earliest was from Peking (now Beijing), China, to Paris, France—a 10,000-mile journey. The race was suggested first in the French newspaper *Le Matin*, and more than two dozen drivers applied—but when a large money deposit was required, the field narrowed to five. Of those vehicles, three were French, ranging from 6 to 10 horsepower; one was Dutch, with a 15-horsepower engine; and the last was Italian and boasted 40 horsepower. The cars were shipped by boat to Peking, and, in June 1907, the overland journey began. Prince Scipione Borghese, owner of the Italian car, had set up elaborate preparations, but the going was extremely difficult, the roads often only mud paths, and sometimes not even that. It was actually a relief to the travelers to encounter the Gobi Desert, for its flat bleakness was ideal for the vehicles. The autos progressed through Siberia and Russia, encountering rough terrain and officials eager for bribes. Sixty days after departing Peking, Prince Borghese arrived in Paris; the rest of the "race" contestants staggered in three weeks later. If the contest proved little, it probably caught the popular imagination and paved the way for more general acceptance of the horseless carriage.

T.A.W.

12 Museums of Limited Appeal

1. **THE MUSEUM OF BAD ART**, 580 High St., Dedham, MA, USA; www.glyphs.com/moba/
Founded in 1993, MOBA is located in the basement of the Dedham Community Theater eight miles south of Boston. Its motto is "Art too bad to be ignored." Although the bulk of the collection has been acquired at thrift shops, many of the finest pieces were fished out of rubbish bins.

2. **STRIPTEASE MUSEUM**, 29053 Wild Rd., Helendale, CA, USA; www.exoticworldusa.org/
Officially titled Exotic World Burlesque Hall of Fame and Museum, it is the domain of former exotic dancer Dixie Evans, whose specialty was

imitating Marilyn Monroe. Items on display include breakaway se-
quined gowns, tasseled pasties, and Gypsy Rose Lee's black velvet
shoulder cape.

3. **THE MARIE DRESSLER MUSEUM**, 212 King St. W., Cobourg, Ont.
K9A 2N1, Canada; 416/372-5831
Exhibits include five wax cylinders of songs by Dressler; a waxworks recreation of part of the set of *Min and Bill,* the film for which Dressler
won the 1931 Academy Award; and the lace-trimmed dress she wore
when she accepted the award.

4. **THE MÜTTER MUSEUM**, College of Physicians of Philadelphia, 19 South
22nd St., Philadelphia, PA, USA; www.collphyphil.org/muttpg1.shtml
This stunning collection of medical oddities and instruments includes
the Chevalier Jackson collection of foreign bodies removed from the
lungs and bronchi, the Sappey collection of mercury-filled lymphaticus,
the B. C. Hirot pelvis collection, and medical tools from Pompeii.
Individual items include Florence Nightingale's sewing kit; the joined
liver of Chang and Eng, the original Siamese twins; bladder stones
removed from U.S. Chief Justice John Marshall; a piece of John Wilkes
Booth's thorax; a wax model of a six-inch horn projecting from a
woman's forehead; and a cheek retractor used in a secret operation on
President Grover Cleveland, as well as the cancerous tumor that was
removed from his left upper jaw.

5. **THE DOG COLLAR MUSEUM**, Leeds Castle, Maidstone, Kent ME17
1PL, United Kingdom; www.leeds-castle.com/content/visiting_the_castle/
dog_collar_museum/dog_collar_museum.html
Housed in the Gate Tower of Leeds Castle, the museum features
medieval and ornamental dog collars spanning four centuries. Included
are numerous spiked collars designed for dogs used in hunting and
bull- and bear-baiting. The gift shop offers tea towels and key chains.

6. **KIM IL SUNG GIFT MUSEUM**, Mount Myohyang, North Korea
Housed in a 120-room, six-story temple north of Pyongyang, the
museum is home to 90,000 gifts that have been given to Kim Il Sung, the
late dictator of Communist North Korea, and to his son, Kim Jong Il,
the current dictator. Included are Nicolae Ceausescu's gift of a bear's
head mounted on a blood-red cushion, a Polish machine gun, and a
rubber ashtray from China's Hwabei Tire factory. Twenty rooms are
devoted to gifts given to Kim Jong Il, including an inlaid pearl and
abalone box from the Ayatollah Khomeini and a pen set from the
chairman of the journalist association of Kuwait.

7. ANTIQUE VIBRATOR MUSEUM, 603 Valencia, San Francisco, CA, USA; www.goodvibes.com/cgi-bin/sgdynamo.exe?HTNAME=museum/index.html The museum has collected more than 100 vibrators going back to 1869. Antique models include a hand-crafted wooden vibrator that works like an egg-beater and another that advertises "Health, Vigor and Beauty" to users. The museum's collection is displayed in Good Vibrations, a feminist sex toy emporium.

8. AMERICAN ACADEMY OF OTOLARYNGOLOGY MUSEUM, One Prince St., Alexandria, VA, USA; www.entnet.org/museum/index.cfm Devoted to the world of head and neck surgery, the museum displays special exhibits dealing with such topics as the history of the hearing aid and the evolution of tracheotomies. The diseases of famous people are examined, including Oscar Wilde's ear infections and Johannes Brahms's sleep apnea. The gift shop sells holiday decorations in the shape of ear trumpets.

9. SULABH INTERNATIONAL MUSEUM OF TOILETS, Mahavir Enclave, Palm Dabri Marg, New Delhi, India; www.sulabhtoiletmuseum.org The Sulabh International Social Service Organization was created to bring inexpensive but environmentally safe sanitation to poor rural areas. On the grounds of its headquarters, an indoor and outdoor museum that presents the history of toilets around the world has been built. One panel reprints poetry relating to toilets, and another gives examples of toilet humor from around the world.

10. BRITISH LAWNMOWER MUSEUM, 106–114 Shakespeare St., Southport, Lancashire PR8 5AJ, United Kingdom The museum includes 400 vintage and experimental lawn mowers, highlighting the best of British technological ingenuity. Of particular interest are the 1921 ATCO Standard 9 Blade, a solar-powered robot mower, and unusually fast or expensive mowers.

11. MARIKINA CITY FOOTWEAR MUSEUM, Manila, Philippines Former Philippine first lady Imelda Marcos, the world's most notorious shoe collector, donated the collection that made possible the opening of this footwear museum on February 16, 2001. The displays at the museum include several hundred of the pairs of shoes left behind at the presidential palace when Imelda and her husband, Ferdinand, fled the country in disgrace in 1986. Other shoes at the museum were donated by local politicians and film stars.

12. ICELANDIC PHALLOLOGICAL MUSEUM, Laugavegur 24, Reykjavík, Iceland The world's only museum for genitalia, the Icelandic Phallological Museum contains more than 200 preserved penises, as well as speci-

mens that have been pressed into service as purses, walking sticks, and pepper pots. The museum's holdings represent nearly all of Iceland's land and sea mammals, with the 47 whale species making for the most impressive viewing. As yet, the museum has no human specimen, but an elderly man has pledged his privates in a legally binding letter of donation.

12 of the Oddest Items Found at London Transport's Lost Property Office

1. Two human skulls in a bag
2. A vasectomy kit
3. Breast implants
4. A 14-foot boat
5. An urn filled with ashes
6. Dead bats in a container
7. A jar of sperm from a prize bull
8. A stuffed eagle
9. A lawn mower
10. A skeleton
11. A double bed
12. A box of false eyeballs (claimed by a hospital after six years)

9 Unusual Disasters

1. ST. PIERRE SNAKE INVASION
   Volcanic activity on the "bald mountain" towering over St. Pierre, Martinique, was usually so inconsequential that no one took seriously the fresh steaming vent holes and earth tremors during April 1902. By early May, however, ash began to rain down continuously, and the nauseating stench of sulfur filled the air. Their homes on the mountainside made uninhabitable, more than 100 fer-de-lance snakes slithered down and invaded the mulatto quarter of St. Pierre. The 6-foot-long serpents killed 50 people and innumerable animals before they were finally destroyed by the town's giant street cats. But the annihilation had only begun. On May 5, a landslide of boiling mud spilled into the sea, followed by a tsunami that killed hundreds, and, three days later, May 8, Mt. Pelee finally exploded, sending a murderous avalanche of white-hot lava straight toward the town. Within three minutes, St. Pierre had been completely obliterated. Of its 30,000 population, there were only 2 survivors.

2. THE SHILOH BAPTIST CHURCH PANIC

Two thousand people, mostly African Americans, jammed into the Shiloh Baptist Church in Birmingham, Alabama, on September 19, 1902, to hear an address by Booker T. Washington. The brick church was new. A steep flight of stairs, enclosed in brick, led from the entrance doors to the church proper. After Washington's speech, there was an altercation over an unoccupied seat, and the word "fight" was misunderstood as "fire." The congregation rose as if on cue and stampeded for the stairs. Those who reached them first were pushed from behind and fell. Others fell on top of them until the entrance was completely blocked by a pile of screaming humanity 10 feet high. Efforts by Washington and the churchmen down in front to induce calm were fruitless, and they stood by helplessly while their brothers and sisters, mostly the latter, were trampled or suffocated to death. There was neither fire nor even a real fight—but 115 people died.

3. THE GREAT BOSTON MOLASSES FLOOD

On January 15, 1919, the workers and residents of Boston's North End, mostly Irish and Italian, were out enjoying the noontime sun of an unseasonably warm day. Suddenly, with only a low rumble of warning, the huge cast-iron tank of the Purity Distilling Company burst open and a great wave of raw black molasses, two stories high, poured down Commercial Street and oozed into the adjacent waterfront area. Neither pedestrians nor horse-drawn wagons could outrun it. Two million gallons of molasses originally destined for rum engulfed scores of persons—21 men, women, and children died of drowning or suffocation, while another 150 were injured. Buildings crumbled, and an elevated train track collapsed. Those horses not completely swallowed were so trapped in the goo they had to be shot by the police. Sightseers who came to see the chaos couldn't help but walk in the molasses. On their way home they spread the sticky substance throughout the city. Boston smelled of molasses for a week, and the harbor ran brown until summer.

4. THE PITTSBURGH GASOMETER EXPLOSION

A huge cylindrical gasometer—the largest in the world at that time—located in the heart of the industrial center of Pittsburgh, Pennsylvania, developed a leak. On the morning of November 14, 1927, repairmen set out to look for it—with an open-flame blowlamp. At about 10 o'clock they apparently found the leak. The tank, containing five million cubic feet of natural gas, rose in the air like a balloon and exploded. Chunks of metal, some weighing more than 100 pounds, were scattered great distances, and the combined effects of air pressure and fire left a square mile of devastation. Twenty-eight people were killed, and hundreds were injured.

5. THE GILLINGHAM FIRE "DEMONSTRATION"

Every year, the firemen of Gillingham, in Kent, England, would construct a makeshift house out of wood and canvas for the popular fire-fighting demonstration at the annual Gillingham Park fete. Every year, too, a few local boys were selected from many aspirants to take part in the charade. On July 11, 1929, nine boys—aged 10 to 14—and six firemen, costumed as if for a wedding party, climbed to the third floor of the "house." The plan was to light a smoke fire on the first floor, rescue the "wedding party" with ropes and ladders, and then set the empty house ablaze to demonstrate the use of the fire hoses. By some error, the real fire was lit first. The spectators, assuming the bodies they saw burning were dummies, cheered and clapped, while the firemen outside directed streams of water on what they knew to be a real catastrophe. All 15 people inside the house died.

6. THE EMPIRE STATE BUILDING CRASH

On Saturday morning, July 28, 1945, a veteran army pilot took off in a B-25 light bomber from Bedford, Massachusetts, headed for Newark, New Jersey, The copilot and a young sailor hitching a ride were also aboard. Fog made visibility poor. About an hour later, people on the streets of midtown Manhattan became aware of the rapidly increasing roar of a plane and watched with horror as a bomber suddenly appeared out of the clouds, dodged between skyscrapers, and then plunged into the side of the Empire State Building. Pieces of plane and building fell like hail. A gaping hole was gouged in the seventy-eighth floor. One of the plane's two engines hurtled through seven walls and came out the opposite side of the building; the other engine shot through an elevator shaft, severing the cables and sending the car plummeting to the basement. When the plane's fuel tank exploded, six floors were engulfed in flame, and burning gasoline streamed down the sides of the building. Fortunately, few offices were open on a Saturday, and only 11 people—plus the 3 occupants of the plane—died.

7. THE TEXAS CITY CHAIN REACTION EXPLOSIONS

On April 15, 1947, the French freighter *Grandcamp* docked at Texas City, Texas, and took on some 1,400 tons of ammonium nitrate fertilizer. That night, a fire broke out in the hold of the ship. By dawn, thick black smoke had port authorities worried, because the Monsanto chemical plant was only 700 feet away. As men stood on the dock watching, tugboats prepared to tow the freighter out to sea. Suddenly, a ball of fire enveloped the ship. For many, it was the last thing they ever saw. A great wall of flame radiated from the wreckage, and within minutes the Monsanto plant exploded, killing and maiming hundreds of workers and any spectators who had survived the initial blast. Most of the business district was devastated, and fires raged along the waterfront, where huge tanks of butane gas stood imperiled. Shortly after midnight, a second freighter—also carrying nitrates—exploded, and the whole sequence began again. More than 500 people died, and another 1,000 were badly injured.

8. THE BASRA MASS POISONING
In September 1971, Cargill Corporation of Minneapolis shipped 95,000 metric tons of seed grain for planting to the Iraqi port of Basra. The American barley and Mexican wheat, which had been chemically treated with the fungicide methylmercury to prevent rot, were sprayed a bright pink to indicate their lethal coating, and clear warnings were printed on the bags—but only in English and Spanish. The grain, which was not allowed to be sold in the United States, was sent on to Kurdish areas in the north. But before the bags could be distributed to the farmers, they were stolen, and the grain was sold as food to the starving populace. The Iraqi government, embarrassed at its criminal negligence or for other reasons, hushed up the story, and it was not until two years later that an American newsman came up with evidence that 6,530 hospital cases of mercury poisoning were attributable to the unsavory affair. Officials would admit to only 459 deaths, but total fatalities were probably more like 6,000, with another 100,000 suffering such permanent effects as blindness, deafness, and brain damage.

9. THE CHANDKA FOREST ELEPHANT STAMPEDE
In the spring of 1972, the Chandka Forest area in India—already suffering from drought—was hit by a searing heat wave. The local elephants, who normally were no problem, became so crazed by the high temperatures and lack of water that the villagers told authorities they were afraid to venture out and to farm their land. By summer, the situation had worsened. On July 10, the elephant herds went berserk and stampeded through five villages, leaving general devastation and 24 deaths in their wake.

N.C.S.

25 Cases of Bizarre Weather

1. NEW ENGLAND'S DARK DAY
The sun did rise in New England on May 19, 1780, but by midday the sky had turned so dark that it was almost impossible to read or conduct business, and lunch had to be served by candlelight. The phenomenon was noted as far north as Portland, Maine, and as far south as northern New Jersey. General George Washington made mention of the spectacle in his diary. At Hartford, Connecticut, there was great fear that the Day of Judgment had arrived, and at the state legislature a motion was made to adjourn. Calmer heads prevailed, and when the sky cleared the

following day, it was generally concluded that the problem had been caused by smoke and ash from a fire "out west."

2. **THUNDER AND LIGHTNING DURING SNOWSTORM**

During the night of February 13, 1853, the residents of Mt. Desert Island, Maine, were frightened by the freak attack of a thunderstorm during a snowstorm. Bolts of purple lightning flashed to the ground, and balls of fire entered homes, injuring several people. Fortunately, no one was killed.

3. **GIANT SNOWFLAKES**

Huge snowflakes, 15 inches across and 8 inches thick, fell on the Coleman ranch at Fort Keogh, Montana, on January 28, 1887. The size of the flakes, which were described as "bigger than milk pans," was verified by a mail carrier who was caught in the storm.

4. **TURTLE HAIL**

Included in a severe hailstorm in Mississippi on May 11, 1894, was a 6-by-8-inch gopher turtle, which fell to the ground, completely encased in ice, at Bovina, east of Vicksburg.

5. **SUDDEN TEMPERATURE RISE**

On February 21, 1918, the temperature in Granville, North Dakota, rose 83 degrees in 12 hours—from – 33°Fahrenheit in the early morning to 50 degrees in the late afternoon.

6. **FOURTH OF JULY BLIZZARD**

Patriotic celebrants were stunned in 1918 when a major blizzard swept across the western plains of the United States, disrupting Fourth of July festivities in several states. Independence Day began with the usual picnics and parties, but in the afternoon the temperature dropped suddenly and rain began to fall, followed by hail, snow, and gale-force winds.

7. **HEAVIEST SNOWFALL**

On April 5 and 6, 1969, 68 inches of snow fell on Bessans, France, in only 19 hours.

8. **SUDDEN TEMPERATURE DROP**

On December 24, 1924, the temperature in Fairfield, Montana, fell 84 degrees in 12 hours, from 63°Fahrenheit at noon to −21°Fahrenheit at midnight. In one 24-hour period on January 23–24, 1916, the temperature in Browning, Montana, dropped 100 degrees, from 44 degrees Fahrenheit to −56 degrees.

9. **SLOWEST HAIL**

On April 24, 1930, at 2:30 p.m., hail began to fall at Hinaidi, Iraq, at the remarkably slow speed of 9 mph. A clever observer was able to determine the speed by timing the fall of several specimens against the side of a building.

10. **GREATEST TEMPERATURE FLUCTUATION**
The most bizarre temperature changes in history occurred at Spearfish, South Dakota, on January 22, 1943. At 7:30 a.m., the thermometer read −4°F. By 7:32 a.m., the temperature had risen 53°, to 49°F. By 9:00 a.m., it had drifted up to 54°F. Then, suddenly, it began to plunge, 58° in 27 minutes, until, at 9:27 a.m., it had returned to -4°F.

11. **MOST RAIN IN ONE MINUTE**
The most rain ever recorded in one minute was 1.5 inches at Barot on the Caribbean island of Guadeloupe on November 26, 1970.

12. **CURIOUS PRECIPITATION AT THE EMPIRE STATE BUILDING**
While rain was falling in the street in front of the Empire State Building on November 3, 1958, guards near the top of the building were making snowballs.

13. **POINT RAINFALL**
An extreme case of localized rainfall occurred the night of August 2, 1966, one and a half miles northeast of Greenfield, New Hampshire. Robert H. Stanley reported that rain began to fall at 7:00 p.m., reaching great intensity from 7:45 p.m. until 10:15 p.m. When he awoke the next morning, Mr. Stanley found that his rain gauge had filled to the 5.75-inch mark. However, his neighbor three tenths of a mile away had collected only a half inch in his rain gauge. Walking around the area, Stanley discovered that the heavy rainfall was limited to no more than a half mile in any direction.

Another strange case of point rainfall took place on November 11, 1958, in the backyard of Mrs. R. Babington of Alexandria, Louisiana. Although there were no clouds in the sky, a misty drizzle fell over an area of 100 square feet for two and a half hours. Mrs. Babington called a local reporter, who confirmed the phenomenon. The Shreveport weather bureau suggested the moisture had been formed by condensation from a nearby air conditioner, but that theory was never proved.

14. **SNOW IN MIAMI**
At 6:10 a.m. on January 19, 1977, West Palm Beach reported its first snowfall ever. By 8:30 a.m., snow was falling in Fort Lauderdale, the farthest south that snow had ever been reported in Florida. The snow continued south to Miami, and some even fell in Homestead, 23 miles south of Miami International Airport. The cold wave was so unusual that heat lamps had to be brought out to protect the iguanas at Miami's Crandon Park Zoo.

15. HIGHEST TEMPERATURE

On September 13, 1922, the temperature in Azizia, Libya, reached 136.4 degrees Fahrenheit—in the shade.

16. LOWEST TEMPERATURE

On July 21, 1983, the thermometer at Vostok, Antarctica, registered −128.6 degrees Fahrenheit. Vostok also holds the record for consistently cold weather. To reach an optimum temperature of 65 degrees Fahrenheit, Vostok would require 48,800 "heating degree days" a year. By comparison, Fairbanks, Alaska, needs only 14,300.

17. EXTREME TEMPERATURES

Temperatures in Verkhoyansk, Russia, have ranged from 98 degrees Fahrenheit down to 90.4 degrees Fahrenheit, a variance of 188.4 degrees.

18. LONGEST HOT SPELL

Marble Bar, Western Australia, experienced 160 consecutive days of 100-degree-Fahrenheit temperatures from October 31, 1923, to April 7, 1924.

19. FASTEST FOOT OF RAIN

Holt, Missouri, received 12 inches of rain in 42 minutes on June 22, 1947.

20. THE RAINIEST DAY

On March 16, 1952, 73.62 inches of rain—more than 6 feet—fell at Cilaos on Réunion Island east of Madagascar. Another 24 inches fell during the 24 hours surrounding March 16.

21. MOST RAIN IN FIFTEEN DAYS

Cherrapunji, Assam, India, received 189 inches of rain between June 24 and July 8, 1931. Back in 1861, Cherrapunji received 366.14 inches of rain in one month and 905.12 inches for the calendar year.

22. NO RAIN

The driest place on earth is Arica, Chile, in the Atacama Desert. No rain fell there for more than 14 years, between October 1903 and December 1917. Over a 59-year period, Arica averaged three hundredths of an inch of rain a year.

23. SNOWIEST DAY

The largest snowfall in a 24-hour period was 75.8 inches—more than 6 feet—recorded at Silver Lake, Colorado, on April 14–15, 1921.

24. SNOWIEST SEASON

Paradise Ranger Station on Mt. Rainier in Washington State recorded 1,122 inches of snow in 1971–1972. The average there is 582 inches.

25. CHAMPION HURRICANE

Hurricane John, which flourished in August and September of 1994, was notable for two reasons. It lasted for all or part of thirty-one days, making it the longest-lived tropical storm on record. It also crossed over the International Date Line twice, changing its name from Hurricane John to Typhoon John and back to Hurricane John.

13 Possible Sites for the Garden of Eden

And the Lord God planted a garden eastward in Eden. . . . And a river went out of Eden to water the garden; and from thence it was parted, and became into four heads. The name of the first is Pison: that is it which compasseth the whole land of Havilah, where there is gold; And the gold of that land is good: there is bdellium and the onyx stone. And the name of the second river is Gihon: the same is it that compasseth the whole land of Ethiopia. And the name of the third river is Hiddekel: that is it which goeth toward the east of Assyria. And the fourth river is Euphrates.

—Genesis 2:8–14

1. SOUTHERN IRAQ

Many biblical scholars believe that the Garden of Eden, the original home of Adam and Eve, was located in Sumer, at the confluence of the Euphrates and Tigris (or Hiddekel) rivers in present-day Iraq. They presume that the geographical references in Genesis relate to the situation from the ninth to the fifth centuries BC and that the Pison and Gihon were tributaries of the Euphrates and Tigris that have since disappeared. In fact, they may have been ancient canals.

2. EASTERN TURKEY

Other students of the Bible reason that if the four major rivers flowed *out* of the garden, the garden itself must have been located far north of the Tigris-Euphrates civilization. They place the site in the mysterious northland of Armenia in present-day Turkey. This theory presumes that Gihon and Pison may not have been precise geographical designations, but rather vague descriptions of faraway places.

3. NORTHERN IRAN

British archaeologist David Rohl claims that Eden is a lush valley in Iran, located about 10 miles from the modern city of Tabriz. He suggests that the Gihon and Pison are the Iranian rivers Araxes and Uizhun. He also identifies nearby Mt. Sahand, a snow-capped extinct volcano, as the prophet Ezekiel's Mountain of God.

4. ISRAEL
There are those who say that the garden of God must have been in the Holy Land and that the original river that flowed into the garden *before* it split into four separate rivers must have been the Jordan, which was longer in the days of Genesis. The Gihon would be the Nile, and Havilah would be the Arabian Peninsula. Some supporters of this theory go further, stating that Mt. Moriah in Jerusalem was the heart of the Garden of Eden and that the entire garden included all of Jerusalem, Bethlehem, and Mt. Olivet.

5. EGYPT
Supporters of Egypt as the site of the Garden of Eden claim that only the Nile region meets the Genesis description of a land watered, not by rain, but by a mist rising from the ground, in that the Nile ran partially underground before surfacing in spring holes below the first cataract. The four world rivers, including the Tigris and the Euphrates, are explained away as beginning far, far beyond the actual site of Paradise.

6–7. EAST AFRICA AND JAVA
Since Adam and Eve were the first humans, and since the oldest human remains have been found in East Africa, many people conclude that the Garden of Eden must have been in Africa. Likewise, when archaeologists discovered the remains of Pithecanthropus in Java in 1891, they guessed that Java was the location of the Garden of Eden.

8. SINKIANG, CHINA
Tse Tsan Tai, in his work *The Creation, the Real Situation of Eden, and the Origin of the Chinese* (1914), presents a case for the garden's being in Chinese Turkestan in the plateau of eastern Asia. He claims that the river that flowed through the garden was the Tarim, which has four tributaries flowing eastward.

9. LEMURIA
In the mid-nineteenth century, a theory developed that a vast continent once occupied much of what is now the Indian Ocean. The name Lemuria was created by British zoologist P. L. Sclater in honor of the lemur family of animals, which has a somewhat unusual range of distribution in Africa, southern India, and Malaya. Other scientists suggested that Lemuria was the cradle of the human race; thus, it must have been the site of the Garden of Eden.

10. **PRASLIN ISLAND, SEYCHELLES**

General Charles "Chinese" Gordon supported the theory that Africa and India used to be part of one massive continent. While on a survey expedition for the British government in the Indian Ocean, he came upon Praslin Island in the Seychelles group. So enchanted was he by this island, and by its Vallée de Mai in particular, that he became convinced that this was the location of the original Garden of Eden. The clincher for Gordon was the existence on Praslin of the coco-de-mer, a rare and exotic tree, which is native to only one other island of the Seychelles and which Gordon concluded was the tree of the knowledge of good and evil.

11. **MARS**

In his book *The Sky People*, Brinsley LePoer Trench argues that not only Adam and Eve but also Noah lived on Mars. He states that the biblical description of a river watering the garden and then parting into four heads is inconsistent with nature. Only canals can be made to flow that way, and Mars, supposedly, had canals. So the Garden of Eden was created on Mars as an experiment by Space People. Eventually, the north polar ice cap on Mars melted, and the descendants of Adam and Eve were forced to take refuge on earth.

12. **GALESVILLE, WISCONSIN, USA**

In 1886 the Reverend D. O. Van Slyke published a small pamphlet that expounded his belief that Eden was the area stretching from the Allegheny Mountains to the Rocky Mountains and that the Garden of Eden was located on the east bank of the Mississippi River between La Crosse, Wisconsin, and Winona, Minnesota. When the Deluge began, Noah was living in present-day Wisconsin, and the flood carried his ark eastward until it landed on Mt. Ararat.

13. **JACKSON COUNTY, MISSOURI, USA**

While traveling through Daviess County, Missouri, Mormon church founder Joseph Smith found a stone slab that he declared was an altar that Adam built shortly after being driven from the Garden of Eden. Declaring, "This is the valley of God in which Adam blessed his children," Smith made plans to build a city called Adam-ondi-Ahram at the site. The Garden of Eden itself, he determined, was located 40 miles south, near the modern-day city of Independence.

The 7 Wonders of the Ancient World

Who created one of the earliest and most enduring of all lists, a list that arbitrarily named the seven most spectacular sights existing in the world 150 years before the birth of Jesus Christ? The list was created by a most respected Byzantine mathematician and traveler named Philon. In a series of arduous trips, Philon saw all of the Western civilized world there was to see in his time, and then he sat down and wrote a short but widely circulated paper entitled *De Septem Orbis Spectaculis* (*The Seven Wonders of the World*).

1. **THE GREAT PYRAMID OF CHEOPS (Egypt)**
   Begun as a royal tomb in c. 2600 BC, standing in splendor 2,000 years before any of the other Seven Wonders were built, this largest of Egypt's 80-odd pyramids is the only Wonder to have survived to this day. Located outside of Cairo, near Giza, the burial tomb of King Cheops was made up of 2.3 million blocks of stone, some of them 2½ tons in weight. The height is 481 feet, the width at the base 755 feet on each side, large enough to enclose London's Westminster Abbey, Rome's St. Peter's, and Milan's and Florence's main cathedrals.

2. **THE HANGING GARDENS OF BABYLON (Iraq)**
   They were not hanging gardens, but gardens on balconies or terraces. When Nebuchadnezzar brought home his new wife, a princess from Medes, she pined for the mountains and lush growth of her native land. To please her, in 600 BC, the king started to build a man-made mountain with exotic growths. Actually, it was a square climbing upward, each level densely planted with grass, flowers, and fruit trees, and irrigated from below by pumps manned by slaves or oxen. Inside and beneath the gardens, the queen held court amid the vegetation and artificial rain. Due to the erosion of time and the influx of conquerors, the Hanging Gardens had been leveled and reduced to wilderness by the time Pliny the Elder visited them before his death in 79 AD.

3. **THE STATUE OF ZEUS AT OLYMPIA (Greece)**
   The multicolored Temple of Zeus, in the area where the Greek Olympic Games were held every fourth year, contained the magnificent statue of Zeus, king of the gods. Sculptured by Phidias (who had made Athena for the Parthenon) sometime after 432 BC, the statue was 40 feet high, made of ivory and gold plates set on wood. Zeus, with jewels for eyes, sat on a golden throne, feet resting on a footstool of gold. Ancients came from afar to worship at the god's feet. A Greek writer, Pausanias, saw the statue intact as late as the second century AD. After that, it disappeared from history, probably the victim of looting armies and fire.

4. **THE TEMPLE OF DIANA AT EPHESUS (Turkey)**
   Summing up his Seven Wonders, Philon chose his favorite: "But when I saw the temple at Ephesus rising to the clouds, all these other wonders were put in the shade." The Temple, a religious shrine built after 350 BC, housed a statue of Diana, goddess of hunting, symbol of fertility. The kings of many Asian states contributed to the construction. It was 225 feet wide and 525 feet long, supported by 127 marble columns

60 feet high. St. Paul, in the New Testament, railed against it. He is believed to have said, "the temple of the great goddess Diana should be despised, and her magnificence should be destroyed, whom all Asia and the world worshippeth." The craftsmen of the temple disagreed: "And when they heard these sayings, they were full of wrath, and cried out saying, Great is Diana of the Ephesians." Ravaged and brought down by invaders, the temple was rebuilt three times before the Goths permanently destroyed it in 262 AD. In 1874, after 11 years of digging, the English archaeologist J. T. Wood unearthed fragments of the original columns.

5. **THE TOMB OF KING MAUSOLUS AT HALICARNASSUS** (Turkey)
King Mausolus, conqueror of Rhodes, ruled over the Persian province of Caria. His queen, Artemisia, was also his sister. When he died in 353 BC, he was cremated and his grieving widow drank his ashes in wine. As a memorial to him, she determined to build the most beautiful tomb in the world at Halicarnassus, now called Bodrum. She sent to Greece for the greatest architects and sculptors, and by 350 BC the memorial was completed. There was a rectangular sculptured marble tomb on a platform, then 36 golden-white Ionic columns upon which sat an architrave, which in turn held a pyramid topped by a bronzed chariot with statues of Mausolus and Artemisia. The monument survived 1,900 years, only to tumble down in an earthquake. What remains of it today is the word *mausoleum*.

6. **THE COLOSSUS OF RHODES ON THE ISLE OF RHODES** (Aegean Sea)
To celebrate being saved from a Macedonian siege by Ptolemy I, the Rhodians, between 292 and 280 BC, erected a mammoth statue to their heavenly protector, the sun god Apollo. Chares, who had studied under a favorite of Alexander the Great, fashioned the statue. The nude Colossus was 120 feet tall, with its chest and back 60 feet around, built of stone blocks and iron and plated with thin bronze. It did not stand astride the harbor, with room for ships to pass between the legs, but stood with feet together on a promontory at the entrance to the harbor. In 224 BC, it was felled by an earthquake. It lay in ruins almost 900 years. In 667 AD, the Arabs, who controlled Rhodes, sold the 720,900 pounds of broken statue for scrap metal to a Jewish merchant. When the merchant hauled his purchase to Alexandria, he found that it required 900 camel loads.

7. **THE LIGHTHOUSE ON THE ISLE OF PHAROS** (off Alexandria, Egypt)
On orders of Ptolemy Philadelphus, in 200 BC, the architect Sostratus of Cnidus constructed a *pharos*, or lighthouse, such as the world had not seen before. Built on a small island off Alexandria, the tiers of the marble tower—first square, then round, each with a balcony—rose to a

height of 400 feet. At the summit, a huge brazier with an eternal flame was amplified by a great glass mirror so that the fire could be seen 300 miles at sea. Half the lighthouse was torn down by occupying Arabs, who hoped to find gold inside the structure. The rest of the structure crashed to the ground when an earthquake struck in 1375.

I.W.

The 15 Least Populous Independent Nations

Nation	Population
1. Tuvalu	11,636
2. Nauru	13,048
3. Palau	20,303
4. San Marino	28,880
5. Monaco	32,409
6. Liechtenstein	33,717
7. Saint Kitts and Nevis	38,958
8. Marshall Islands	59,071
9. Antigua and Barbuda	68,722
10. Dominica	69,029
11. Andorra	70,549
12. Seychelles	81,188
13. Grenada	89,502
14. Kiribati	103,092
15. Micronesia	108,105

Source: U.S. Census Bureau, International Data Base, April 26, 2005.

CHAPTER THIRTEEN

Books

8 UNLIKELY HOW-TO BOOKS

11 NOTABLE BOOK DEDICATIONS

THE ORIGINAL TITLES OF 31 FAMOUS BOOKS

28 GREAT BEGINNINGS TO NOVELS

11 LAST LINES OF NOVELS

15 BEST-SELLING BOOKS REJECTED
BY 12 OR MORE PUBLISHERS

MARGARET ATWOOD'S 10 ANNOYING THINGS
TO SAY TO WRITERS

32 BAD REVIEWS OF FAMOUS WORKS

31 NOTABLE BANNED BOOKS

14 POETS AND HOW THEY EARNED A LIVING

7 CURIOUS POETRY ANTHOLOGIES

17 UNUSUAL BOOK TITLES FROM THE LIBRARY
OF *THE BOOK OF LISTS*

11 INCREDIBLE LIPOGRAMS

44 CURIOUS HISTORIES AND ESOTERIC STUDIES FROM
THE LIBRARY OF *THE BOOK OF LISTS*

BRIAN ENO'S 18 MIND-CHANGING BOOKS

BENJAMIN SPOCK'S 10 GREATEST CHILDREN'S BOOKS

MAURICE SENDAK'S 10 FAVORITE CHILDREN'S BOOKS

29 CELEBRITIES WHO WROTE CHILDREN'S BOOKS

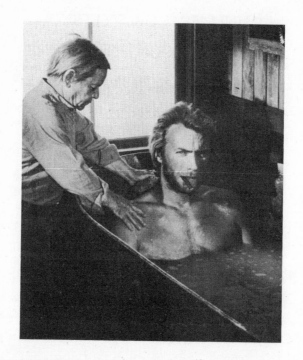

EXTRACTED FROM THE BOOK *MOVIE STARS IN BATHTUBS* BY JACK SCAGNETTI (1975). DOES EXACTLY WHAT IT SAYS ON THE TIN.

8 Unlikely How-to Books

1. *How to Be Happy Though Married,* by "A Graduate in the University of Matrimony." London: J. Fisher Unwin, 1895.

2. *How to Rob Banks Without Violence,* by Roderic Knowles. London: Michael Joseph, 1972.

3. *How to Shit in the Woods,* by Kathleen Meyer. Berkeley, Calif.: Ten Speed Press, 1989.

4. *How to Become a Schizophrenic,* by John Modrow. Everett, Wash.: Apollyon Press, 1992.

5. *How to Speak with the Dead: A Practical Handbook,* by "Sciens." New York: E. P. Dutton, 1918. The author is identified as also having written "recognized scientific text-books."

6. *How to Start Your Own Country,* by Erwin S. Strauss. Port Townsend, Wash.: Loompanics Unlimited, 1984.

7. *How to Avoid Huge Ships,* by Captain John W. Trimmer. Seattle, Wash.: Captain John W. Trimmer, 1983.

8. *How to Be Pretty Though Plain,* by Mrs. Humphry. London: James Bowden, 1899.

11 Notable Book Dedications

1. ARTHUR ASHE, with Neil Amdue
   "To that nameless slave girl off HMS *Doddington,* and her daughter Lucy, her granddaughter Peggy, her great-grand-daughter Peggy, and her great-great-grandson Hammet, all of whom were born, lived and died as slaves."
   —*Off the Courts,* 1982

2. BENNETT CERF
   There is a young lady from Fife
   Whom I never have seen in my life.
   So the devil with her;
   Instead I prefer
   To dedicate this to my wife.
   —*Out on a Limerick,* 1961

3. MAURICE CHEVALIER

"To all my American friends. Having been liked for such a long time in America is the pride of my life."

—I Remember It Well, 1971

4. AGATHA CHRISTIE

"To all those who lead monotonous lives in the hope that they may experience at second hand the delights and dangers of adventure."

—The Secret Adversary, 1922

5. JOHN CLARMONT

"To no one in particular."

—Did I Do That?, 1987

6. BUCHI EMECHETA

"I dedicate this work to the memory of many relatives and friends who died in this way, especially my eight-year-old niece, Buchi Emecheta, who died of starvation, and her four-year-old sister Ndidi Emecheta, who died two days afterwards of the same Biafran disease at the CMS refugee centre in Ibuza; also my aunt Ozili Emecheta and my maternal uncle Okolie Okwuekwu, both of whom died of snake bites as they ran into the bush the night the federal forces bombed their way into Ibuza. I also dedicate *Destination Biafra* to the memory of those Ibuza women and their children who were roasted alive in the bush at Nkpotu Ukpe. May the spirit of Umejei, the Father founder of our town, guide you all in death, and may you sleep well."

—Destination Biafra, 1982

7. JEROME K. JEROME

"To the very dear and well beloved friend of my prosperous and evil days. To the friend, who, though in the early stages of our acquaintanceship, he did ofttimes disagree with me, has since come to be my very warmest comrade. To the friend who, however often I may put him out, never (now) upsets me in revenge. To the friend who, treated with marked coldness by all the female members of my household, and regarded with suspicion by my very dog, nevertheless, seems day by day to be more drawn by me, and in return, to more and more impregnate me with the odour of his friendship. To the friend who never tells me of my faults, never wants to borrow money, and never talks about himself. To the companion of my idle hours, the soother of my sorrows, the confidant of my joys and hopes, my oldest and strongest Pipe, this little volume is gratefully and affectionately dedicated."

—The Idle Thoughts of an Idle Fellow, 1886

8. SEAN O'CASEY
"To the gay laugh of my mother at the gate of the grave."
—*The Plough and the Stars*, 1926

9. ALBERT PIERREPOINT
"To Anne, my wife, who in forty years never asked a question, I dedicate this book with grateful thanks for her loyalty and discretion."
—*Executioner: Pierrepoint*, 1974
(Pierrepoint was Britain's last hangman.)

10. STEPHEN PILE
"To Quin Xiang-Yi, who in 1846 was given the title 'distinguished failure' in recognition of his 20 years spent failing the Chinese Civil Service entrance exams. Buoyed up by this honour, he went on to fail several times more."
—*The Return of Heroic Failures*, 1988

11. JAMES RONALD
"To my creditors, whose increasing impatience has made this book necessary."
—*This Way Out*, 1940

Source: Bloomsbury Dictionary of Dedications by Adrian Room (London: Bloomsbury, 1990).

The Original Titles of 31 Famous Books

1. Original title: *First Impressions*
Final title: *Pride and Prejudice* (1813)
Author: Jane Austen

2. Original title: *Mag's Diversions*; also *The Copperfield Disclosures, The Copperfield Records, The Copperfield Survey of the World as It Rolled,* and *Copperfield Complete*
Final title: *David Copperfield* (1849)
Author: Charles Dickens

3. Original title: *Alice's Adventures Underground*
Final title: *Alice's Adventures in Wonderland* (1865)
Author: Lewis Carroll

4. Original title: *All's Well That Ends Well*
Final title: *War and Peace* (1866)
Author: Leo Tolstoy

5. Original title: *The Sea-Cook*
   Final title: *Treasure Island* (1883)
   Author: Robert Louis Stevenson

6. Original title: *The Chronic Argonauts*
   Final title: *The Time Machine* (1895)
   Author: H. G. Wells

7. Original title: *Paul Morel*
   Final title: *Sons and Lovers* (1913)
   Author: D. H. Lawrence

8. Original title: *Stephen Hero*
   Final title: *A Portrait of the Artist as a Young Man* (1916)
   Author: James Joyce

9. Original title: *The Romantic Egotist*
   Final title: *This Side of Paradise* (1920)
   Author: F. Scott Fitzgerald

10. Original title: *The Village Virus*
    Final title: *Main Street* (1920)
    Author: Sinclair Lewis

11. Original title: *Incident at West Egg*; also *Among Ash Heaps and Millionaires, Trimalchio in West Egg, On the Road to West Egg, Gold-Hatted Gatsby,* and *The High-Bounding Lover*
    Final title: *The Great Gatsby* (1925)
    Author: F. Scott Fitzgerald

12. Original title: *Fiesta*; also *The Lost Generation, River to the Sea, Two Lie Together,* and *The Old Leaven*
    Final title: *The Sun Also Rises* (1926)
    Author: Ernest Hemingway

13. Original title: *Tenderness*
    Final title: *Lady Chatterley's Lover* (1928)
    Author: D. H. Lawrence

14. Original title: *Twilight*
    Final title: *The Sound and the Fury* (1929)
    Author: William Faulkner

15. Original title: *O Lost*
    Final title: *Look Homeward, Angel* (1929)
    Author: Thomas Wolfe

16. Original title: *Bar-B-Q*
    Final title: *The Postman Always Rings Twice* (1934)
    Author: James M. Cain

17. Original title: *Tomorrow Is Another Day*; also *Tote the Weary Load, Milestones, Jettison, Ba! Ba! Black Sheep, None So Blind, Not in Our Stars*, and *Bugles Sang True*
    Final title: *Gone with the Wind* (1936)
    Author: Margaret Mitchell

18. Original title: *The Various Arms*; also *Return to the Wars*
    Final title: *To Have and Have Not* (1937)
    Author: Ernest Hemingway

19. Original title: *Something That Happened*
    Final title: *Of Mice and Men* (1937)
    Author: John Steinbeck

20. Original title: *Proud Flesh*
    Final title: *All the King's Men* (1946)
    Author: Robert Penn Warren

21. Original title: *Salinas Valley*
    Final title: *East of Eden* (1952)
    Author: John Steinbeck

22. Original title: *The Tree and the Blossom*
    Final title: *Peyton Place* (1956)
    Author: Grace Metalious

23. Original title: *Interzone*
    Final title: *Naked Lunch* (1959)
    Author: William S. Burroughs

24. Original title: *Catch-18*
    Final title: *Catch-22* (1961)
    Author: Joseph Heller

25. Original title: *The Fox*
    Final title: *The Magus* (1966)
    Author: John Fowles

26. Original title: *A Jewish Patient Begins His Analysis*
    Final title: *Portnoy's Complaint* (1969)
    Author: Philip Roth

27. Original title: *Come and Go*
    Final title: *The Happy Hooker* (1972)
    Author: Xaviera Hollander with Robin Moore and Yvonne Dunleavy

28. Original title: *The Summer of the Shark*; also *The Terror of the Monster* and *The Jaws of the Leviathan*
    Final title: *Jaws* (1974)
    Author: Peter Benchley

29. Original title: *Before This Anger*
    Final title: *Roots: The Saga of an American Family* (1976)
    Author: Alex Haley

30. Original title: *The Shine*
    Final title: *The Shining* (1977; altered because King learned that "shine" is a derogatory term for African Americans, stemming from employment shining shoes, and a black man is a central character in the novel)
    Author: Stephen King

31. Original title: *Harry Potter and the Doomspell Tournament*
    Final title: *Harry Potter and the Goblet of Fire* (2000)
    Author: J. K. Rowling

                                                                    R.J.F. & the Eds.

28 Great Beginnings to Novels

1. "Somewhere in La Mancha, in a place whose name I do not care to remember, a gentleman lived not long ago, one of those who has a lance and ancient shield on a shelf and keeps a skinny nag and a greyhound for racing." —*Don Quixote*, Miguel de Cervantes

2. "For a long time I used to go to bed early." —*In Search of Lost Time*, Marcel Proust

3. "Call me Ishmael." —*Moby-Dick, The Whale*, Herman Melville

4. "Mr. Sherlock Holmes, who was usually very late in the mornings, save upon those not infrequent occasions when he was up all night, was seated at the breakfast table." —*The Hound of the Baskervilles*, Sir Arthur Conan Doyle

5. "Lolita, light of my life, fire of my loins." —*Lolita*, Vladimir Nabokov

6. "Whether I shall turn out to be the hero of my own life, or whether that station will be held by anybody else, these pages must show." —*David Copperfield*, Charles Dickens

7. "She was so deeply imbedded in my consciousness that for the first year of school I seem to have believed that each of my teachers was my mother in disguise." —*Portnoy's Complaint*, Philip Roth

8. "He was an old man who fished alone in a skiff in the Gulf Stream and he had gone eighty-four days now without taking a fish." —*The Old Man and the Sea*, Ernest Hemingway

9. "Last night I dreamt I went to Manderley again." —*Rebecca*, Daphne du Maurier

10. "Many years later, as he faced the firing squad, Colonel Aureliano Buendía was to remember that distant afternoon when his father took him to discover ice." —*One Hundred Years of Solitude*, Gabriel García Márquez

11. "It was a queer, sultry summer, the summer they electrocuted the Rosenbergs, and I didn't know what I was doing in New York." —*The Bell Jar*, Sylvia Plath

12. "It is a truth universally acknowledged, that a single man in possession of a good fortune must be in want of a wife." —*Pride and Prejudice*, Jane Austen

13. "The past is a foreign country: they do things differently there." — Prologue, *The Go-Between*, L. P. Hartley

14. "Maman died today. Or yesterday maybe, I don't know." —*The Stranger*, Albert Camus

15. "It was love at first sight. The first time Yossarian saw the chaplain he fell madly in love with him." —*Catch-22*, Joseph Heller

16. "All happy families are alike; each unhappy family is unhappy in its own way." —*Anna Karenina*, Leo Tolstoy

17. "Tom!" —*The Adventures of Tom Sawyer*, Mark Twain

18. " 'Christmas won't be Christmas without any presents,' grumbled Jo, lying on the rug." —*Little Women*, Louisa May Alcott

19. "3 May. Bistritz. Left Munich at 8:35 p.m., on 1st May, arriving at Vienna early next morning; should have arrived at 6:46, but train was an hour late." —*Dracula*, Bram Stoker

20. "Someone must have been telling lies about Joseph K., for without having done anything wrong he was arrested one fine morning." —*The Trial*, Franz Kafka

21. "When he was nearly thirteen my brother Jem got his arm badly broken at the elbow." —*To Kill a Mockingbird*, Harper Lee

22. "Amerigo Bonasera sat in New York Criminal Court Number 3 and waited for justice; vengeance on the men who had so cruelly hurt his daughter, who had tried to dishonor her." —*The Godfather*, Mario Puzo

23. "In eighteenth-century France there lived a man who was one of the most gifted and abominable personages in an era that knew no lack of gifted and abominable personages." —*Perfume*, Patrick Suskind

24. "It was a bright cold day in April, and the clocks were striking thirteen." —*1984*, George Orwell

25. "If you really want to hear about it, the first thing you'll probably want to know is where I was born, and what my lousy childhood was like, and how my parents were occupied and all before they had me, and all that David Copperfield kind of crap, but I don't feel like going into it, if you want to know the truth." —*Catcher in the Rye*, J. D. Salinger

26. "It was about eleven o'clock in the morning, mid-October, with the sun not shining and a look of hard wet rain in the clearness of the foothills. I was wearing my powder-blue suit, with dark blue shirt, tie and display handkerchief, black brogues, black wool socks with dark blue clocks on them. I was neat, clean, shaved and sober, and I didn't care who knew it. I was everything the well-dressed private detective ought to be." —*The Big Sleep*, Raymond Chandler

27. "People are afraid to merge on freeways in Los Angeles." —*Less Than Zero*, Brett Easton Ellis

28. "All nights should be so dark, all winters so warm, all headlights so dazzling." —*Gorky Park*, Martin Cruz Smith

The Eds. & S.C.B.

11 Last Lines of Novels

1. "It is a far, far better thing that I do, than I have ever done; it is a far, far better rest that I go to, than I have ever known." —*A Tale of Two Cities*, Charles Dickens

2. "Yes," I said. "Isn't it pretty to think so?" —*The Sun Also Rises*, Ernest Hemingway

3. "It was not until they had examined the rings that they recognized who it was." —*The Portrait of Dorian Gray*, Oscar Wilde

4. "He is a gorilla." —*Planet of the Apes*, Pierre Boulle

5. "And however superciliously the highbrows carp, we the public in our heart of hearts all like a success story; so perhaps my ending is not so unsatisfactory after all." —*The Razor's Edge*, W. Somerset Maugham

6. "After all, tomorrow is another day." —*Gone with the Wind*, Margaret Mitchell

7. "The Martians stared back up at them for a long, long silent time from the rippling water. . . ." —*Martian Chronicles*, Ray Bradbury

8. "Then with a profound and deeply willed desire to believe, to be heard, as she had done every day since the murder of Carlo Rizzi, she said the necessary prayers for the soul of Michael Corleone." —*The Godfather*, Mario Puzo

9. "He loved Big Brother." —*1984*, George Orwell

10. "And out again, upon the unplumb'd, salt, estranging sea." —*The French Lieutenant's Woman*, John Fowles

11. "On the way downtown I stopped at a bar and had a couple of double Scotches. They didn't do me any good. All they did was make me think of Silver Wig, and I never saw her again." —*The Big Sleep*, Raymond Chandler

S.C.B & Eds.

15 Best-Selling Books Rejected by 12 or More Publishers

1. *ZEN AND THE ART OF MOTORCYCLE MAINTENANCE*, Robert Pirsig (Morrow, 1974)
Pirsig's story of a cross-county motorcycle journey with his 11-year-old son was rejected by 121 agents, editors, and publishers. Then, as Pirsig noted in the afterword to the tenth anniversary edition, "One lone editor offered a standard three-thousand-dollar advance. He said the book

forced him to decide what he was publishing for, and added that although this was almost certainly the last payment, I shouldn't be discouraged. Money wasn't the point with a book like this." The book became a cult classic that sold more than four million copies over the next 25 years.

2. *CHICKEN SOUP FOR THE SOUL*, Mark Victor Hansen and Jack Canfield (Health Communication, Inc., 1993)
This collection of stories by inspirational speakers Hansen and Canfield was turned down by 33 publishers. Although Health Communication owner Peter Vegno agreed to publish *Chicken Soup* after he cried when he read it, he thought it would sell 20,000 copies at most. Published in the summer of 1993, the book hit the best-seller lists by fall. It started a series of *Chicken Soup* titles that have collectively sold more than 34 million copies.

3. *AND TO THINK THAT I SAW IT ON MULBERRY STREET*, Theodor Geisel aka Dr. Seuss (Vanguard, 1937)
Geisel was on his way home with the manuscript and illustrations for his book after it had been rejected by the twenty-third publisher when he ran into an old college friend walking on Madison Avenue. The friend, who happened to be an editor of children's books for Vanguard Press, was interested in seeing Geisel's work. Twenty minutes later, "Dr. Seuss" had a contract for his book, which has since gone into more than 20 printings.

4. *DUBLINERS*, James Joyce (Grant Richards, 1914)
Joyce would not allow any changes to be made in his book of 15 short stories that depict Dublin in its most sordid light. Consequently, it was rejected by 22 publishers. In a letter to Bennett Cerf, Joyce described what happened after his book was finally published by Grant Richards: "When at last it was printed some very kind person bought out the entire edition and had it burnt in Dublin—a new and private auto-da-fé." The stories have since been hailed as the work of a genius.

5. *M*A*S*H*, Richard Hooker (William Morrow, 1968)
For seven years, Hooker worked over his humorous war novel under the close tutelage of an optimistic literary agent, only to see it shot down by 21 publishers before Morrow bought it. A hugely successful film version helped push the book to runaway best-sellerdom. Several sequels followed, and a long-running TV series based on the *M*A*S*H* characters was launched in 1972.

6. *HEAVEN KNOWS, MR. ALLISON*, Charles Shaw (Crown, 1952)
Shaw's humorous novel about an American Marine in the South Pacific was rejected by virtually every Australian publisher and by about 20 British firms over a three-year period. Finally, Shaw found an

American agent, who quickly sold the book to Crown. Paperback and foreign editions soon followed, and the book was made into a popular film in 1957.

7. *KON-TIKI*, Thor Heyerdahl (Rand McNally, 1950)
Twenty publishers decided Heyerdahl's story of his Pacific crossing on a raft wasn't worth publishing before Rand McNally accepted it. The book made top-10 nonfiction best-seller lists in 1950 and again in 1951, when Heyerdahl's Oscar-winning documentary film of his trip was released. Total sales have since reached the multimillion mark.

8. *JONATHAN LIVINGSTON SEAGULL*, Richard Bach (Macmillan, 1970)
Bach's 10,000-word story about a fast-flying seagull seemed so unprom- ising that 18 publishers turned it down before Macmillan accepted it and quietly issued 7,500 copies. Rapidly mounting sales led to the book's adoption by the Book-of-the-Month Club in 1972, a $1 million paperback sale to Avon, many foreign editions, and a 1973 film version. By 1975, more than 7 million copies of the book had been sold in the United States alone.

9. *LORNA DOONE*, Richard Doddridge Blackmore (Sampson Low, 1869)
The 18 publishers who rejected Blackmore's novel of seventeenth- century England appeared vindicated when Sampson Low's three- volume edition flopped in 1869. Two years later, however, a single-volume edition proved a big success. Harper's pirated the book in the United States, where it became the number one best seller in 1874. The book has remained in print ever since, and three film versions have been produced.

10. *AUNTIE MAME*, Patrick Dennis (Vanguard, 1955)
Some 17 publishers rejected this novel about a free-spirited older woman before Vanguard accepted it. An immediate hit, the book was soon adapted for the stage. After a successful run on Broadway, the play was made into a popular film starring Rosalind Russell. Ten years later, a musical version of the play, called *Mame*, started a long Broad- way run. The film *Mame* was released in 1974. Total book sales have been around two million copies.

11. *LUST FOR LIFE*, Irving Stone (Longmans Green, 1934)
Seventeen publishers rejected Stone's novel about Vincent van Gogh. Once the book was published, however, sales became spectacular, and Doubleday eventually took over publication. *Lust for Life* has sold more than 24 million copies in 70 editions. Kirk Douglas starred in a popular film version in 1956.

12. *THE PETER PRINCIPLE*, Laurence Peter (William Morrow, 1969)
Sixteen publishers rejected Peter's now-famous book about the rise of
individuals to their level of incompetence. However, after Peter wrote a
newspaper article on the subject, the same publishers flocked to his
door, contracts in hand, and Morrow bought the much-rejected manuscript. The book has sold six million copies, paving the way for *The
Peter Plan, Peter's Quotations*, and *Peter's People.*

13. *A CONFEDERACY OF DUNCES*, John Kennedy Toole (Louisiana
State University Press, 1980)
Toole sent his picaresque Dickensian novel to Simon & Schuster, and
although editor Robert Gottlieb expressed initial enthusiasm, he
ultimately passed, declaring that the book "isn't really about anything."
Toole never attempted to find another publisher. Having become
increasingly despondent, he committed suicide in 1968. Toole's mother,
Thelma, spent the next eight years trying to find a publisher, receiving
an additional 15 rejections. In 1976, she convinced novelist Walker
Percy to read her son's manuscript. Initially skeptical, he fell in love
with the novel and convinced the Louisiana State University Press to
publish it. *A Confederacy of Dunces* won a Pulitzer Prize in 1980 and
sold 1.5 million copies.

14. *DUNE*, Frank Herbert (Chilton, 1965)
Herbert's massive science fiction tale was rejected by 13 publishers
with comments such as "too slow" and "confusing and irritating." The
persistence of Herbert and his agent, Lurton Blassingame, finally paid
off. *Dune* won the two highest awards in science fiction writing and has
sold over 10 million copies. David Lynch directed a film version in
1984.

15. *A TIME TO KILL*, John Grisham (Wynwood Press, 1988)
The 12 publishers and 16 agents who rejected Grisham's first novel
seemed to be justified when *A Time to Kill* sold only 5,000 copies in its
first edition. When it was reissued in the early 1990s, the book sold 8
million copies, and the film rights sold for $6 million. Grisham became
the top-selling author of the 1990s.

Note: If these examples are not enough to prove that the experts aren't
always right, here is a final one that will surely encourage would-be writers.
In 1977, freelance writer Chuck Ross submitted a freshly typed copy of
Jerzy Kosinski's 1969 National Book Award winner, *Steps*, to 14 publishers
and 13 literary agents as an unsolicited manuscript. All 27 failed to recognize Kosinski's work, and all 27 rejected the book.

R.K.R., K.H.J. & C.F.

Margaret Atwood's
10 Annoying Things to Say to Writers

What to Say	What Writer Hears
1. a) I always wait for your books to come in at the library.	b) I wouldn't pay money for that trash.
2. a) I had to take you in school.	b) Against my will. Or: And I certainly haven't read any of it since! Or: So why aren't you dead?
3. a) You don't look at all like your pictures!	b) Much worse.
4. a) You're so prolific!	b) You write too much, and are repetitive and sloppy.
5. a) I'm going to write a book too, when I can find the time.	b) What you do is trivial, and can be done by an idiot.
6. a) I only read the classics.	b) And you aren't one of them.
7. a) Why don't you write about _____ ?	b) Unlike the boring stuff you do write about.
8. a) That book by _____ (add name of other writer) is selling like hotcakes!	b) Unlike yours.
9. a) So, do you teach?	b) Because writing isn't real work, and you can't possibly be supporting yourself at it.
10. a) The story of MY life—now THAT would make a good novel!	b) Unlike yours.

Margaret Atwood was born in Ottawa, Canada, in 1939 and grew up in northern Quebec and Ontario, and later in Toronto. She is the author of more than 30 books, including novels, collections of short stories, poetry, literary criticism, social history, and children's books. Her most popular novel is *The Handmaid's Tale* (1985) and her most recent novel is *Oryx and Crake* (2003).

32 Bad Reviews of Famous Works

1. *The Monkey Wrench Gang*—Edward Abbey, 1975
   "The author of this book should be neutered and locked away forever."
   —*San Juan County Record*

2. *Counting the Ways*—Edward Albee, 1977
   "The play sounds like George Burns and Gracie Allen trying to keep up
   a dinner conversation with Wittgenstein. . . . I have never seen such
   desperately ingratiating smiles on the faces of actors." —*Newsweek*

3. *Les Fleurs du Mal*—Charles Baudelaire, 1857
   "In a hundred years the history of French literature will only mention
   [this work] as a curio." —Emile Zola, in *Emile Zola*, 1953

4. *Malloy; Malone Dies; The Unnameable*—Samuel Beckett, 1959 (three
   novels in one volume)
   "The suggestion that something larger is being said about the human
   predicament . . . won't hold water, any more than Beckett's incontinent
   heroes can." —*The Spectator*

5. *The Man Who Knew Kennedy*—Vance Bourjaily, 1967
   "The man who knew Kennedy didn't know him very well. I'm almost as
   intimate with Lyndon Johnson. I met him once." —Webster Schott, *The
   New York Times Book Review*

6. *Naked Lunch*—William Burroughs, 1963
   ". . . the merest trash, not worth a second look." —*The New Republic*

7. *Nova Express*—William Burroughs, 1964
   "The book is unnecessary." —Granville Hicks, *Saturday Review*

8. *In Cold Blood*—Truman Capote, 1965
   "One can say of this book—with sufficient truth to make it worth saying:
   'This isn't writing. It's research.'" —Stanley Kauffmann, *The New Republic*

9. *The Deerslayer*—James Fenimore Cooper, 1841
   "In one place *Deerslayer*, and in the restricted space of two-thirds of a
   page, Cooper has scored 114 offences against literary art out of a
   possible 115. It breaks the record." —Mark Twain, *How to Tell a Story
   and Other Essays*, 1897

10. *An American Tragedy*—Theodore Dreiser, 1925
    "His style, if style it may be called, is offensively colloquial, common-
    place and vulgar." —*Boston Evening Transcript*

11. *Absalom, Absalom!*—William Faulkner, 1936
"The final blowup of what was once a remarkable, if minor, talent."
—Clifton Fadiman, *The New Yorker*

12. *The Great Gatsby*—F. Scott Fitzgerald, 1925
"What has never been alive cannot very well go on living. So this is a
book of the season only. . . ." —*New York Herald Tribune*

13. *Madame Bovary*—Gustave Flaubert, 1857
"Monsieur Flaubert is not a writer." —*Le Figaro*

14. *The Recognitions*—William Gaddis, 1955
"*The Recognitions* is an evil book, a scurrilous book, a profane, a
scatalogical book and an exasperating book. . . . What this squalling
overwritten book needs above all is to have its mouth washed out with
lye soap." —*Chicago Sun Times*

15. *Catch-22*—Joseph Heller, 1961
"Heller wallows in his own laughter . . . and the sort of antic behavior
the children fall into when they know they are losing our attention."
—Whitney Balliett, *The New Yorker*

16. *The Sun Also Rises*—Ernest Hemingway, 1926
"His characters are as shallow as the saucers in which they stack their
daily emotions. . . ." —*The Dial*

17. *For Whom the Bell Tolls*—Ernest Hemingway, 1940
This book offers not pleasure but mounting pain. . . ." —*Catholic
World*

18. *Brave New World*—Aldous Huxley, 1932
"A lugubrious and heavy-handed piece of propaganda." —*New York
Herald Tribune*

19. *Lives of the English Poets*—Samuel Johnson, 1779–1981
"Johnson wrote the lives of the poets and left out the poets."
—Elizabeth Barrett Browning, *The Book of the Poets*, 1842

20. *Finnegans Wake*—James Joyce, 1939
"As one tortures one's way through *Finnegans Wake* an impression
grows that Joyce has lost his hold on human life." —Alfred Kazin, *New
York Herald Tribune*

21. *Babbitt*—Sinclair Lewis, 1929
"As a humorist, Mr. Lewis makes valiant attempts to be funny; he
merely accedes in being silly." —*Boston Evening Transcript*

22. *Lolita*—Vladimir Nabokov, 1958
    "Any bookseller should be very sure that he knows in advance that he is selling very literate pornography." —*Kirkus Reviews*

23. *The Moviegoer*—Walker Percy, 1961
    "Mr. Percy's prose needs oil and a good checkup."—*The New Yorker*

24. *A Midsummer Night's Dream*—William Shakespeare, performed in London, 1662
    "The most stupid ridiculous play that I ever saw in my life." —Samuel Pepys, *Diary*

25. *Hamlet*—William Shakespeare, 1601
    "One would imagine this piece to be the work of a drunken savage."
    —Voltaire (1768) in *The Works of M. de Voltaire*, 1901

26. *Gulliver's Travels*—Jonathan Swift, 1726
    ". . . evidence of a diseased mind and lacerated heart." —John Dunlop, *The History of Fiction*, 1814

27. *Anna Karenina*—Leo Tolstoy, 1877
    "Sentimental rubbish . . . Show me one page that contains an idea."
    —*The Odessa Courier*

28. *Breakfast of Champions*—Kurt Vonnegut, 1973
    "From time to time it's nice to have a book you can hate—it clears the pipes—and I hate this book." —Peter Prescott, *Newsweek*

29. *Leaves of Grass*—Walt Whitman, 1855
    "Whitman is as unacquainted with art as a hog is with mathematics."
    —*The London Critic*

30. *The Waves*—Virginia Woolf, 1931
    "The book is dull." —H. C. Hardwood, *Saturday Review of Literature*

31. *The Jungle*—Upton Sinclair, 1906
    "So perverted that the effect can be only to disgust many honest, sensible folk."—*The Bookman*

32. *Dictionary*—Samuel Johnson, 1755
    "The confidence now reposed in its accuracy is the greatest injury to philology that now exists." —Noah Webster, letter, 1807

31 Notable Banned Books

1–2. *SLAUGHTERHOUSE-FIVE* AND *DELIVERANCE* (1973)
In Drake, North Dakota, these novels by Kurt Vonnegut, Jr., and James Dickey were removed from the public schools because they allegedly contained profanity. All 32 copies of the Vonnegut book were consigned to a school furnace. The five school board members who voted for the ban had not read either book.

3. *THE AMERICAN HERITAGE DICTIONARY* (1976, 1977)
The Cedar Lake, Indiana, and Eldon, Missouri, school boards ordered this dictionary removed from their high schools after parents pointed out at least 80 offensive definitions. The criticized entries included such words as "bed," "shack," "rubber," "hot," "horny," and "slut." One Eldon parent made a sincere albeit mind-boggling comment: "If people learn words like that, it ought to be where you and I learned it—in the street and in the gutter."

4. *THE BELL JAR* (1977)
Sylvia Plath's book was only one of the volumes banned by the Warsaw, Indiana, school board. (Others included *The Stepford Wives* and *Go Ask Alice*.) Copies of these books were burned by members of the Warsaw Senior Citizens Club, who applauded the school board's decision to rid the high school of "filth."

5. *DADDY WAS A NUMBERS RUNNER* (1977)
The superintendent of schools in Oakland, California, removed this highly acclaimed autobiographical novel by Louise Meriwether from junior high school library shelves after an African American father complained about it. The book describes a 12-year-old African American girl growing up in a Harlem tenement. Ironically, the school superintendent was formerly a director of the National Right to Read program.

6. *IN THE NIGHT KITCHEN* (1977)
Copies of the Maurice Sendak storybook, available in kindergarten classes in Springfield, Missouri, were doctored with a felt-tip pen. A pair of shorts was placed on a drawing of a naked boy. The director of elementary education explained, "We felt [the book] was a good story. . . . As far as nudity is concerned, I guess I'm an old fogey, but I think it should be covered."

7. *OF MICE AND MEN* (1977)
In Oil City, Pennsylvania, the school board removed copies of John Steinbeck's classic from the school library and had the books burned. This action was inspired by parental contentions that the novel "uses

the Lord's name in vain, refers to prostitution, and takes a retarded person and makes a big issue of it."

8. *CATCHER IN THE RYE* (1978)
The school board of Issaquah, Washington, voted to remove the J. D. Salinger classic from the optional reading list of a high school literature class after an elderly citizen complained that the book "brainwashes students" and represents "part of an overall Communist plot." She testified that the book "has 222 'hells,' 27 'Chrissakes,' and 7 'hornys.'"

9. *OUR BODIES, OURSELVES* (1978)
This women's health book was permanently removed from school libraries in Helena, Montana, after Marc Racicot, a member of the state attorney general's staff, informed the school board that "any person distributing it to a child under the age of 16 could be subject to criminal charges." The Helena chapter of the Eagle Forum had first brought the book to Racicot's attention. They felt, and he agreed, that the book by the Boston Women's Health Collective "assists, promotes, and encourages the reader to engage in sexual conduct." Racicot stated to the press, "I'm sick and tired of hearing the cry of censorship. We've genuflected at the altar of free speech far too long."

10. *FATHER CHRISTMAS* (1979)
Raymond Briggs's popular children's book was removed from all elementary classrooms in Holland, Michigan, when several parents complained that it portrayed Santa Claus as having a negative attitude toward Christmas.

11. *THE BIBLE* (1980)
In North Carolina, the Columbus County library forbade children to check out the Bible unless they had obtained parental permission to bring home "adult books." The librarian said the Bible was classified as "adult" not because it was considered racy, but because it was thought to be too difficult for children to read easily.

12. *DEENIE* (1980)
This Judy Blume book was one of four titles (including Elia Kazan's *Acts of Love*, Tom Sullivan's *If You Could See What I Hear*, and Mora Stirling's *You Would If You Love Me*) removed from the state library's bookmobile in Brigham City, Utah. A member of the Citizens for True Freedom claimed that the books contained "the vilest sexual descriptions" and if read by "the wrong kid at the wrong time [they would] ruin his life."

13. *THE GRAPES OF WRATH* (1980)
John Steinbeck's novel was banished from sophomore English classes at two Kanawha, Iowa, high schools after a parent complained that the

book was "profane, vulgar, and obscene." The president of the local school board taking the action said that the United States was "going pell-mell downhill" morally and that Kanawha was reversing the trend by banning the book.

14. *DEATH OF A SALESMAN* (1981)
The principal of Springs Valley High School in French Lick, Indiana, proscribed reading this Arthur Miller play in an English class after some ministers complained that the drama included the words "bastard," "goddamn," and "son-of-a-bitch." Students became so curious about the play's contents that they quickly checked out all the local public library copies.

15.–16. *THE BOOK OF LISTS* and *THE BOOK OF LISTS 2* (1981)
Adhering to complaints about *The Book of Lists* from several parents in Glen Rose, Arkansas, a faculty committee at Glen Rose High School recommended removing only those portions dealing with "sexual perversion." The rest of the best seller by David Wallechinsky, Irving Wallace, and Amy Wallace was allowed to remain intact on the library shelf. Superintendent Don Henson insisted that the action was not censorship, since the book was available—unedited—outside the school. Henson said, "If people want to read these books—fine. But we're not going to provide them." During 1981, Saudi Arabia dealt more severely with *The Book of Lists 2*. The entire book was banned because it contained critical comments about the Saudi government.

17. *THE LIVING BIBLE* (1981)
Burned in Gastonia, North Carolina, because it was allegedly "a perverted commentary of the King James Version."

18. *DORIS DAY: HER OWN STORY* (1982)
Removed from two high school libraries in Anniston, Alabama, due to its "shocking" contents, particularly "in light of Miss Day's All-American image." It was later reinstated on a restricted basis.

19. *WORKING* (1983)
Studs Terkel's oral history of Americans and their jobs was removed from an optional reading list at the South Kitsap, Washington, high school because the chapter about a prostitute "demeaned marital status and degraded the sexual act." It was also deleted from the seventh- and eighth-grade curriculum by the Washington, Arizona, school district with the following explanation: "When we require idealistic and sensitive youth to be burdened with despair, ugliness and hopelessness, we shall be held accountable by the Almighty God."

20. *AMERICAN FOREIGN POLICY, VOL. II* (1984)

Thomas Paterson's textbook was banned by the school board of the Racine, Wisconsin, unified school district for containing "judgment writing" and, in the words of one board member, "a lot more funny pictures of Republicans and nicer pictures of Democrats." It was returned to the curriculum one week later.

21. *THE ADVENTURES OF TOM SAWYER* (1985)

Removed from the school libraries in parts of London by the Inner London Education Authority, who accused Mark Twain's classic of being "racist" and "sexist."

22. *ENCYCLOPEDIA BRITANNICA* (1986)

Banned and pulped in Turkey for spreading "separatist propaganda."

23. *THE SATANIC VERSES* (1988)

Banned in India, Pakistan, Saudi Arabia, Egypt, Somalia, Sudan, Malaysia, Qatar, Indonesia, and South Africa for allegedly blaspheming Islam and the Koran. In Iran, Ayatollah Khomeini sentenced to death author Salman Rushdie and anyone else involved in the publication of the book. Khomeini also offered a substantial cash reward to whoever assassinated Rushdie.

24. *CERBERUS (MONSTERS OF MYTHOLOGY)* (1990)

Bernard Evslin's story of the guardian of the Underworld was removed from elementary school library shelves in the Francis Howell school district in St. Peters, Missouri, for being graphic and gruesome and because the illustrations were "pornographic." The illustrations were drawings by Michelangelo and other masters. The book was also said to "encourage Satanism."

25. *MY FRIEND FLICKA* (1990)

Mary O'Hara's beloved children's story of a boy and a horse was pulled from optional reading lists for fifth and sixth graders in Clay County, Florida, because the book uses the word "bitch" to refer to a female dog.

26. *FAHRENHEIT 451* (1992)

School officials in Irvine, California, ordered teachers at Venado Middle School to use black markers to obliterate all of the "hells," "damns," and other words considered "obscene" in Ray Bradbury's novel before giving copies to students as required reading. After local papers ran stories about the irony of a book that condemns book burning being censored, school officials announced that they would no longer use the expurgated copies.

27. *JAMES AND THE GIANT PEACH* (1995)
Roald Dahl's story was removed from classrooms in Stafford County, Virginia, and placed in restricted access in the school libraries. According to complainants, the book contains crude language and encourages children to disobey their parents.

28. *TWELFTH NIGHT* (1996)
Removed from the school curriculum in Merrimack, New Hampshire, after the school board passed a "prohibition of alternative lifestyle instruction" act. William Shakespeare's romantic comedy apparently ran afoul of the new rule because one of its characters is a young woman who disguises herself as a boy. In 1999, the school board members who had passed the act were voted out of office, in large part due to the uproar their censorship had caused. The play then returned to Merrimack's classrooms.

29. *THE COLOR PURPLE* (1997)
The Jackson County, West Virginia, school board ordered 16 books taken from the shelves of school libraries pending a review. But it decided not to bother reviewing *The Color Purple* before ordering Alice Walker's Pulitzer Prize–winning novel banned. School board member Bernard King declared, "It could lead to different sex games and violence and other things."

30. *HARRY POTTER AND THE SORCERER'S STONE* (1999)
Responding to parental complaints, Geary Feenstra, the superintendent of schools for Zeeland, Michigan, ordered all of J. K. Rowling's Harry Potter books off the library shelves in elementary and middle schools, banned the reading of the books in classrooms, and halted the purchase of future books in the series. One of the ban's supporters, the Reverend Lori Jo Schepers, suggested that the books could lead to violence, like the shooting at Columbine High School in Colorado in 1998: "As we expose our kids to the occult, we expose our kids to blood, to violence, and desensitize them to that. What I can expect is those kids, as they mature, have a very good chance of becoming the next Dylan Klebold and those guys in Columbine." A year later, a 14-member panel of parents and teachers recommended that the school district reverse most of Feenstra's orders, leaving in place only the ban on reading the books aloud in the classroom.

31. *SOPHIE'S CHOICE* (2001)
William Styron's National Book Award–winning story of a Holocaust survivor was removed from the library and the approved reading list of La Miranda High School in California following a complaint by one student's parent about sexual passages in the novel. The book was returned to the library shelves after the American Civil Liberties Union

of Southern California and the National Coalition Against Censorship sent a letter to school administrators urging them to "respect the First Amendment as well as the intelligence of students."

R.T. & C.F.

14 Poets and How They Earned a Living

1. **WILLIAM BLAKE (1757–1827), English poet and artist**
   Trained as an engraver, Blake studied art at the Royal Academy but left to earn a living engraving for booksellers. For a few years he was a partner in a print-selling and engraving business. He then worked as an illustrator, graphic designer, and drawing teacher, but it became increasingly hard for Blake to earn a living. He had a patron for a few years but essentially lived in poverty and obscurity, only occasionally receiving an art commission. He was later recognized as one of England's finest engravers.

2. **ROBERT BURNS (1759–1796), Scottish poet**
   Raised on a farm in Ayrshire, Burns was a full-time laborer on the land at 15. He tried to become a surveyor, but ill health forced him to give it up. Next he lived with relatives who ran a flax-dressing business, until their shop burned down. Farming barely paid his bills, so Burns published *Poems, Chiefly in the Scottish Dialect* in 1786 to get money for passage to Jamaica, where he had a job offer as an overseer. The book was so successful that he used the money to visit Edinburgh instead. Returning to the farm, he took a job as a tax inspector, trying unsuccessfully to juggle three occupations. He lost the farm but moved to Dumfries and continued as a tax inspector and a poet.

3. **JOHN KEATS (1795–1821), English poet**
   Keats was trained as a surgeon and apothecary in Edmonton and later moved to London to work as a dresser in a hospital. For a year or so, he had his own surgeon-apothecary practice, and at the same time, he began publishing his poetry. His first major work, *Poems*, appeared in 1817, and that year he gave up medicine for the literary life. Charles Armitage Brown became his patron, providing him with a house in Hampstead, outside London. Keats spent his last few years there, writing his best works while dying of tuberculosis.

4. **WALT WHITMAN (1819–1892), American poet**
   Whitman had a checkered career in newspaper work, starting as a printer's assistant and eventually becoming an editor in New York throughout the 1840s. After 10 years, he gave up journalism for carpentry and verse. During the Civil War, Whitman moved to Washington,

D.C., took a job in the paymaster's office, and spent his spare time nursing the wounded. In 1865, he became a clerk at the Department of the Interior's Bureau of Indian Affairs but was soon fired for being the author of the scandalous *Leaves of Grass*. He then clerked in the attorney general's office until a paralytic stroke forced him to retire in 1873.

5. SIDNEY LANIER (1841–1881), American poet
After graduation from Oglethorpe University in Georgia, Lanier worked as an English tutor at the university until the Civil War broke out. A Confederate volunteer, he was taken captive and contracted tuberculosis in a Union prison camp. He held various jobs after the war, including hotel clerk, high school principal, and law practitioner in Georgia, even though he had not been admitted to the bar. In 1873, he became a flutist for the Peabody Orchestra in Baltimore. Just a few years before his death, he was appointed lecturer in English literature at Johns Hopkins University.

6. ARTHUR RIMBAUD (1854–1891), French poet
Rimbaud's lover Paul Verlaine supported him for a while in Paris; after their separation, Rimbaud lived in London, working at various menial jobs until poverty or ill health or both caused his return to France. In 1876, he joined the Dutch colonial army and went to Indonesia, but he deserted and again returned to France. From there, he joined a circus en route to Scandinavia; went to Cyprus as a laborer and later as a builder's foreman; and finally gave up his wandering in Harar, Ethiopia. There he worked for a coffee exporter and later tried (unsuccessfully) to become an independent arms dealer. In 1888, he was managing a trading post, dealing in coffee, ivory, arms, and possibly slaves.

7. CARL SANDBURG (1878–1967), American poet and biographer
The son of a blacksmith's helper, Sandburg began working at the age of 11, sweeping floors and cleaning cuspidors in a law office. He quit school at age 13 and took a full-time job delivering milk. Over the next few years, he worked at a series of odd jobs, including harvesting ice at a frozen lake, moving scenery at a theater, shining shoes, washing dishes, and working at a racetrack. He also harvested wheat in Kansas; apprenticed to a housepainter; served in the U.S. Army, in 1898; and worked as a fireman while attending college. After leaving Lombard College without graduating, Sandburg worked as an advertising manager for a department store, as a stereoscope salesman, and as secretary to Milwaukee's socialist mayor. Late in 1912, he moved to Chicago and landed a job as a feature writer for the *Daily Socialist*. For the next 16 years, he supported himself and his family with a series of newspaper jobs, mostly as a reporter for the *Chicago Daily News*. After achieving success as a poet and biographer of Abraham Lincoln, Sandburg lectured, sang folk songs, and bred and raised goats.

8. **WALLACE STEVENS** (1879–1955), American poet
After leaving Harvard University without a degree, Stevens was a reporter for the *New York Herald Tribune* for a year. He then attended New York University Law School, passed the bar in 1904, and for the next 12 years practiced law in New York. In 1916, he joined the legal department of the Hartford Accident and Indemnity Company in Connecticut; by 1934, he was vice president of the company.

9. **WILLIAM CARLOS WILLIAMS** (1883–1963), American poet
Williams earned a medical degree from the University of Pennsylvania in 1906, interned at a hospital in New York City, and for a year did postgraduate work in pediatrics at the University of Leipzig in Germany. He established a medical practice in his hometown of Rutherford, New Jersey, in 1910, and until the mid-1950s, maintained both a medical and a literary career. An appointment to the chair of poetry at the Library of Congress in 1952 was withdrawn because of Williams's radical politics. He spent his last 10 years lecturing at many American universities.

10. **PABLO NERUDA** (1904–1973), Chilean poet
In recognition of his poetic skills, the Chilean government awarded Neruda a nonpaying position as Chile's consul in Burma in 1927. Eventually he graduated to a salaried office, serving in Ceylon, the Dutch East Indies, Argentina, and Spain. With the outbreak of the Spanish Civil War in 1936, Neruda, without waiting for orders, declared Chile on the side of the Spanish republic. He was recalled by the Chilean government and later reassigned to Mexico. In 1944, he was elected to the national senate as a member of the Communist Party. He later served as a member of the central committee of the Chilean Communist Party and as a member of the faculty of the University of Chile.

11. **KENNETH REXROTH** (1905–1982), American poet
The son of a wholesale druggist, Rexroth worked as a pharmacy apprentice after school and during summers. He rejected the opportunity offered to him in the pharmaceutical business and decided to pursue art and writing. In the 1920s, he moved to Chicago using an inheritance from his maternal grandmother. After a few years, he began traveling around the country, sometimes supporting himself by passing the hat at poetry readings, sometimes speaking from soapboxes for the International Workers of the World, sometimes working one of a variety of odd jobs that included horse wrangler, sheep herder, forest ranger, fruit picker, and short-order cook. Eventually, Rexroth settled in San Francisco, working as a trade unionist. During World War II, he was too old for the draft, but declared himself a conscientious objector and was assigned work as an attendant in a psychiatric hospital. In the 1950s, Rexroth became known as the "Godfather of the Beat Genera-

tion" and gave poetry readings with jazz accompaniment at clubs in San Francisco and Greenwich Village. He also cofounded the Poetry Center at San Francisco State University, hosted a weekly radio show devoted to literary criticism, and wrote a column for the *San Francisco Examiner*. In 1968, he moved to Santa Barbara and served as a special lecturer at the University of California.

12. **ALLEN GINSBERG** (1926–1997), American poet
In 1945, while suspended from Columbia University for a year, Ginsberg worked as a dishwasher in a Times Square, New York restaurant, as a merchant seaman, and as a reporter for a newspaper in New Jersey. He returned to Columbia and graduated with a BA in literature in 1948. Far more influential was his off-campus friendship with a number of figures in the future Beat movement, including Jack Kerouac, Neal Cassady, and William S. Burroughs. In 1949, Ginsberg was arrested for letting one of the friends, Herbert Huncke, use his apartment to store stolen property. For his sentence, Ginsberg was committed to a psychiatric hospital for eight months. Upon his release, he went home to Paterson, New Jersey, to live with his father. After a few years, he completely changed his lifestyle. He moved to San Francisco and led a life of middle-class respectability. He had a high-paying job in market research, a live-in girlfriend, and an upscale apartment. He was also miserable and began seeing a therapist. "The doctor kept asking me, 'What do you want to do?' Finally, I told him—quit. Quit the job, my tie and suit, the apartment on Nob Hill. Quit it and go off and do what I wanted, which was to get a room with Peter [Orlovsky], and devote myself to writing and contemplation, to Blake and smoking pot, and doing whatever I wanted." Ginsberg wrote a memo to his boss explaining how his position could be eliminated, and then he left. In 1955, shortly after devoting himself to poetry, he created a sensation with the first public reading of his poem "Howl," considered the birth of the Beat revolution. Ginsberg and his companion, Peter Orlovsky, were able to live off Ginsberg's royalties, money Ginsberg earned at poetry readings, and disability checks Orlovsky received as a Korean War veteran.

13. **MAYA ANGELOU** (1928–), American poet and memoirist
In her youth, Angelou worked as a cook and a waitress, and as the first African American female fare collector with the San Francisco Street-car Company. In the 1950s she became a nightclub performer, special-izing in calypso songs and dances. She also performed in *Porgy and Bess* on a 22-country tour of Europe and Africa organized by the U.S. State Department in 1954 and 1955. During the 1960s, Angelou was the northern coordinator of Martin Luther King's Southern Christian Leadership Council, associate editor of an English-language newspaper in Cairo, features editor of a paper in Ghana, and assistant administra-tor at the University of Ghana. She acted in Jean Genet's play *The*

Blacks, wrote songs for B. B. King, wrote and produced educational television series, and acted on Broadway (for one night in 1973) and on television in 1977—as Kunta Kinte's grandmother in *Roots.* In 1972, she wrote the script for *Georgia, Georgia,* the first original screenplay by an African American woman to be produced. She continues to be a university professor and a popular lecturer.

14. ROD McKUEN (1933–), American poet, singer, and songwriter
McKuen dropped out of high school and left home at age 11. He drifted through the western United States, working various odd jobs, including ranch hand, lumberjack, shoe salesman, and cookie puncher in a Nabisco factory. At age 16, he settled down in San Francisco and became a late-night disc jockey. His program *Rendezvous with Rod* was one of the most popular radio shows in the Bay Area for three years, until he was drafted in 1953. He spent his first year in the army in Tokyo as a public information specialist, writing psychological warfare scripts, and as a writer, producer, and entertainer for Special Services. After a year, he was sent to Korea as an American aid administrator. After his discharge, he returned to San Francisco and became a folksinger, performing during intermissions between nightclub headliners. He went to Hollywood, snuck past the guard at Universal Studios, wrangled a screen test, and signed a two-year contract. He appeared in such low-budget quickies as *Rock, Pretty Baby.* When his film contract expired, he went to New York City, pursuing a songwriting career. To make ends meet, he sold pints of his blood and crashed cocktail parties for free food. Lean times ended when he got a job composing musical themes for the *CBS Television Workshop.* In 1961, he cowrote and performed a novelty dance tune, "Mister Oliver Twist." McKuen promoted the song by touring bowling alleys coast-to-coast. During this adventure, he blew out his voice, which changed his tenor to a gravelly baritone. Recovered, he moved to Paris, sang like a French chansonnier, and his popularity grew. In 1966, his album *Seasons in the Sun* won the Grand Prix du Disque as best popular album of the year. That same year, unable to find a publisher for his poetry collection *Stanyan Street and Other Sorrows,* he self-published and distributed it. The book sold 65,000 copies through mail order before Random House took over the publishing. He was soon selling millions of volumes of his poetry, recording gold albums, starring in his own television specials, and selling out Carnegie Hall.

7 Curious Poetry Anthologies

1. *A Little Book of Ping-Pong Verse* (Boston: Dana Estes, 1902)
This charming volume was published at the height of the Ping-Pong craze that began in 1900. Among the 83 selections included are

"The Rubaiyat of Ping-Pong," "The Ping-Pong Ankle," "The Ponger and the Pingstress," and 16 different poems entitled "Ping-Pong."

How does the nimble little ball
Enjoy each "ping" and "pong!"
It also loves to talk a fall
And roll the floor along;
It will lead you then a merry race,
As any maiden coy,
And should it find a hiding-place,
It hugs itself with joy.
—Thomas Dykes Beasley, "Only a Ping-Pong Ball"

2. *The Vampire in Verse: An Anthology*, edited by Steven Moore (New York: Dracula Press, 1985)
A publication of the Count Dracula Fan Club, this anthology includes works by Byron, Keats, Kipling, Baudelaire, Yeats, and F. Scott Fitzgerald.

From my grave betimes I have been driven,
I seek the good I lost, none shall me thwart,
I seek his love to whom my teeth was given,
And I have sucked the lifeblood from his hearth.
If he dies, I will
Find me other, still
With my fury tear young folk apart.
—Johann Wolfgang von Goethe, "The Bride of Corinth"

3. *The Poetry of Chess*, edited by Andrew Waterman (London: Anvil Press Poetry, 1981)
Sixty-nine chess poems divided into six sections, including "The Game," "Players," and "Personal Relations."

Men tend to think in a prosaic way,
Identify the ends and find the means,
And chess to them is somewhat like a play
With all the plotting done behind the scenes,
But chess to women is like everyday
Only even more so, and Kings and Queens
Are you and me, in an odd sort of way.
(They think of knights as horses though, it seems.)
—Simon Lowy, "On Her Taking My Queen at Chess"

4. *The Poetry of Geology*, edited by Robert M. Nagen (London: George Allen & Unwin, 1982)
All selections are from eighteenth- and nineteenth-century English and American literature. Titles include "A Meditation on Rhode-Island Coal," "The Nautilus and the Ammonite," and "To a Fossil Fern." Especially noteworthy is the work of John Scafe,

who in 1820 published *A Geological Primer in Verse*, as well as "King Coal's Levee," a 1,145-line poem about the succession of stratification in England and Wales.

> *Of Feldspar and Quartz a large quantity take,*
> *Then pepper with Mica, and mix up and bake.*
> *This Granite for common occasions is good;*
> *But on Saint-days and Sundays, be it understood,*
> *If with bishop and lords in the state room you dine,*
> *Then sprinkle with Topaz, or else Tourmaline.*
>
> —John Scafe, "To Make Granite"

5. *Mary Queen of Scots: An Anthology of Poetry*, chosen by Antonia Fraser (London: Eyre Methuen/Greville Press, 1981)
Poems both by and about Mary Queen of Scots, the sixteenth-century queen of Scotland who was executed by her cousin, Queen Elizabeth I of England. Featured poets include Lope de Vega, Algernon Swinburne, William Wordsworth, Edith Sitwell, and Boris Pasternak.

> *O! soon, to me, may summer-suns*
> *Nae mair light up the morn!*
> *Nae Mair, to me, the autumn winds*
> *Wave o'er the yellow corn!*
> *And in the narrow house o' death*
> *Let winter round me rave;*
> *And the next flowers, that deck the spring,*
> *Bloom on my peaceful grave.*
>
> —Robert Burns, "Lament of Mary Queen
of Scots on the Approach of Spring"

6. *Gems from an Old Drummer's Grip*, compiled by N. R. Streeter (New York: Groton, 1889)
A collection of poems by and about traveling salesmen, or "drummers," as well as a few verses that, although not about traveling salesmen, have been enjoyed by traveling salesmen.

> *It was two rival drummers,*
> *The merit they did blow*
> *Of safes were in St Louis made*
> *And safes from Chicago.*
> *They chanced upon a merchant*
> *Who fain a safe would buy,*
> *And in the praise of their houses' wares*
> *The drummers twain did ire,*
> *Each striving to see which could construct*
> *The most colossal lie.*
>
> —N. R. Streeter, "The Rival Drummers"

7. *All Shook Up: Collected Poems About Elvis*, edited by Will Clemens. (Fayetteville: The University of Arkansas Press, 2001)
According to editor Will Clemens, this anthology "invites readers to experience the connection between the historical and mythical status of Elvis, on the one hand, and the poetic imagery, on the other." Among the more well-known contributors are Charles Bukowski ("Elvis Lives"), Joyce Carol Oates ("Waiting on Elvis"), and Diane Wakoski ("Blue Suede Shoes").

> *We've been out for an hour*
> *and caught nothing much,*
> *talking about lures and the lie*
> *of the water. Finally*
> *I tell him I have friends*
> *who like his music.*
> Are any of them black?
> I want them to forgive me.
> *I tell him to forgive himself.*
>
> —Dabney Stuart, "Fishing with Elvis"

17 Unusual Book Titles from the Library of *The Book of Lists*

1. *Engineering for Potatoes*, B. F. Cargill. (St. Joseph, Mich.: American Society of Agriculture Engineers, 1986)

2. *Holiday Retreats for Cats and Dogs in England*, Scarlett Tipping (Lewes, Sussex, England: Temple House, 1987)

3. *Learning from Salmon*, Herman Aihara (Oroville, Calif.: George Ohsawa Macrobiotic Foundation, 1980)

4. *Maternal Behavior in the Rat*, Berthold P. Weisner and Norah M. Sheard (Edinburgh: Oliver and Boyd, 1933)

5. *Sodomy and the Pirate Tradition*, B. R. Burg (New York: New York University Press, 1984)

6. *The Chinese Classics of Tongue Diagnosis in Color*, Henry C. Lu (Vancouver, B.C., Canada: Academy of Oriental Heritage, 1980)

7. *You Can Make a "Stradivarius Violin*," Joseph V. Reid (Chicago: Popular Mechanics Press, 1955)

8. *Electricity and Christianity*, Crump J. Strickland (Charlotte, N.C.: Elizabeth Publishing, 1938)

9. *Old Age: Its Cause and Prevention*, Sanford Bennett (New York: Physical Culture Publishing, 1912). Mr. Bennett, "the man who grew young at 70," also authored the book *Exercising in Bed*.

10. *Carnivorous Butterflies*, Austin H. Clark (Washington, D.C.: U.S. Government Printing Office, 1926)

11. *The Dynamics of Psychosomatic Dentistry*, Joseph S. Landa (Brooklyn, N.Y.: Dental Items of Interest Publishing, 1953)

12. *My Duodenal Ulcer and I*, "Dr. Stuart Morton" (London: Christopher Johnson, 1955). Fans of this book might also enjoy the more grammatically satisfying *My Prostate and Me* by William Martin (Cadell and Davies, 1994).

13. *The Magic of Telephone Evangelism*, Harold E. Metcalf (Atlanta, Ga.: Southern Union Conference, 1967)

14. *Practical Candle Burning*, Raymond Buckland (St. Paul, Minn.: Llewellyn Publications, 1970)

15. *Your Destiny in Thumb: Indian Science of Thumb Reading*, R. G. Rao (Bangalore, India: The Astrological Office, 1971)

16. *Careers in Dope*, Dan Waldorf (Englewood Cliffs, N.J.: Prentice-Hall, 1973)

17. *Correct Mispronunciations of Some South Carolina Names*, Claude and Irene Neuffer (Columbia: University of South Carolina Press, 1983)

11 Incredible Lipograms

A form of verbal gymnastics, lipograms are written works that deliberately omit a certain letter of the alphabet by avoiding all words that include that letter. *Lipo* actually means "lacking"—in this case, lacking a letter. An example of a contemporary lipogram is the nursery rhyme "Mary Had a Little Lamb," rewritten without the letter *s*:

> *Mary had a little lamb*
> *With fleece a pale white hue,*
> *And everywhere that Mary went*
> *The lamb kept her in view;*

To academe he went with her,
  Illegal, and quite rare;
It made the children laugh and play
  To view a lamb in there.

—A. Ross Eckler

1. **JACQUES ARAGO—AN A-LESS BOOK**
   The French author's book *Voyage Autour du Monde Sans la Lettre A* debuted in Paris in 1853. However, 30 years later, in another edition, he admitted letting one letter *a* sneak by him in the book—he had overlooked the word *serait*.

2. **GYLES BRADRETH—HAMLET WITHOUT ANY *I*'s**
   A contemporary British lipogrammarian, Brandreth specializes in dropping a different letter from each of Shakespeare's plays. All *i*'s were excluded from *Hamlet*, rendering the famous soliloquy: "To be or not to be; that's the query." He proceeded to rewrite *Twelfth Night* without the letters *l* and *o*, *Othello* without any *o*'s, and *Macbeth* without any *a*'s or *e*'s.

3. **GOTTLOB BURMANN—*R*-LESS POETRY**
   Bearing an obsessive dislike for the letter *r*, Burmann not only wrote 130 poems without using that letter, but also omitted the letter from his daily conversation for 17 years. This practice meant that the eccentric eighteenth-century German poet never said his own last name.

4. **A. ROSS ECKLER—LIPOGRAM NURSERY RHYMES**
   Eckler's specialty is rewriting well-known nursery rhymes such as "Little Jack Horner," excluding certain letters. His masterpiece was "Mary Had a Little Lamb," which he re-created in several versions, omitting in turn the letters *s*, *a*, *h*, *e*, and *t* (as in the *t*-less "Mary Had a Pygmy Lamb").

5. **PETER DE RIGA—A LIPOGRAM BIBLE**
   Summarizing the entire Bible in Latin, the sixteenth-century canon of Rheims Cathedral in France omitted a different letter of the alphabet from each of the 23 chapters he produced.

6. **TRYPHIODORUS—A LIPOGRAM ODYSSEY**
   The Greek poet Tryphiodorus wrote his epic poem *Odyssey*, chronicling the adventures of Ulysses, excluding a different letter of the alphabet from each of the 24 books. Thus, the first book was written without alpha, the second book contained no betas, etc.

7. **LOPE DE VEGA CARPIO—5 NOVELS WITHOUT VOWELS**
   Known as Spain's first great dramatist, he reputedly wrote 2,200 plays.

This sixteenth-century author wrote five novels that were lipograms. Each book omitted one of the five vowels *a, e, i, o,* and *u* in turn.

8. ERNEST VINCENT WRIGHT—NOVEL WITHOUT AN *E*
By tying down the *e* key on his typewriter to make sure one didn't slip in, Wright, a graduate of MIT, wrote a credible 50,110-word novel, *Gadsby* (1939), totally excluding the most frequently used letter of the English alphabet. "Try to write a single ten-word sentence without an *e*," said the Los Angeles *Times*, "and you will get some idea of the task he set himself." Wright's novel concerned the effort of a middle-aged man named John Gadsby to make his hometown of Branston Hills more progressive and prosperous by turning over its administration to an Organization of Youth. Wright, a 67-year-old Californian, undertook his *e*-less novel to prove such a feat could be done. He wrote the book in 165 days. He employed no tricks, such as coining words or substituting apostrophes for *e*'s. His greatest difficulty, he claimed, was avoiding the use of verbs ending with *ed*. Thus, he was forced to use "said" for "replied" or "asked" and to avoid pronouns such as *he, she,* and *they.* Wright died on the day of his book's publication—but the $3 novel remains his monument. Today it sells at rare-book dealers for more than $1,000 a copy with a jacket.

9. GEORGES PEREC—*E*-LESS AND *E*-FULL NOVELS
Perec (1936–1982) was a member of the literary group Oulipo (a French abbreviation for "workshop of potential literature"), the members of which experimented with constrained writing. His most notable work in this regard is his novel *La Disparation* (1969), written without the letter *e*. It was translated into English without *e*'s by Gilbert Adair under the title *A Void*. Another Perec novel, *Les Revenentes* (1972), is a sort of opposite: The letter *e* is the only vowel used.

10. CHRISTIAN BÖK—VOWEL-LESS POETRY
Bök, an experimental Canadian poet, wrote *Eunoia*, a work in which each chapter is missing four of the five vowels. The fourth chapter, for example, does not contain *a, e, i,* or *u*. A sample from that chapter is: "Profs from Oxford show frosh who do post-docs how to gloss works of Wordsworth." *Eunoia* won the Griffin Poetry Prize in 2002 and became one of the best-selling works of Canadian poetry.

11. MARK DUNN—AN INCREASINGLY LIPOGRAMMATIC BOOK
Dunn's *Ella Minnow Pea* (2001) is subtitled "A Progressively Lipogrammatic Epistolary Fable." The story concerns a small country that begins to outlaw the use of various letters. As each letter is banned within the story, it is no longer used in the book.

L.K.S. & C.F.

44 Curious Histories and Esoteric Studies from the Library of *The Book of Lists*

1. *MANUALE DI CONVERSAZIONE: ITALIANO-GROENLANDESE,*
   Ciro Sozio and Mario Fantin (Bologna, Italy: Tamari Editori, 1962).
   One of the least used dictionaries in the world, this slim 62-page booklet
   translates Italian into the language of the Greenland Eskimos. Collec-
   tors of obscure dictionaries will also appreciate Vladimir Marku's
   seminal work *Fjalori I Naftës* (1995), which translates 25,000 oil
   industry–related terms from English into Albanian.

2. *STURGEON HOOKS OF EURASIA*, Géza de Rohan-Csermak
   (Chicago: Aldine Publishing, 1963).
   An important contribution to the history of fishhooks. Some of the
   chapter titles: "The Character of Sturgeon Hooks," "Hooks in Eastern
   Europe," and "Life Story of Hooks of the Samolov Type."

3. *THE EVOKED VOCAL RESPONSE OF THE BULLFROG: A STUDY
   OF COMMUNICATION BY SOUND,* Robert R. Capranica (Cambridge,
   Mass.: MIT Press, 1965).
   This monograph details the responses of caged bullfrogs to the recorded
   sound of mating calls of 34 kinds of frogs and toads. The author's
   academic career was made possible by a fellowship awarded by Bell
   Telephone Laboratories.

4. *THE PEOPLE MACHINE*, Dennis R. Cooper (Tampa: General Telephone Company of Florida, 1971).
   An illustrated history of the telephone on the central west coast of Florida.

5. *WHY BRING THAT UP?* Dr. J. F. Montague (New York: Home Health
   Library, 1936).
   A guide to and from seasickness by the medical director of the New
   York Intestinal Sanitarium.

6. *CLUCK!: THE TRUE STORY OF CHICKENS IN THE CINEMA,*
   Jon-Stephen Fink (London: Virgin Books, 1981).
   At last, a fully illustrated filmography of every movie in which a
   chicken—living, dead, or cooked—appears. Films in which the word
   "chicken," "hen," or "rooster" is mentioned are also included.

7. *ON THE SKULL AND PORTRAITS OF GEORGE BUCHANAN*, Karl
   Pearson (Edinburgh: Oliver and Boyd, 1926).
   Buchanan, one of Scotland's greatest scholars and historians, died in
   poverty in 1582. This publication was part of a series that included

Phrenological Studies of the Skull and Endocranial Cast of Sir Thomas Browne of Norwick by Sir Arthur Keith and *The Relations of Shoulder Blade Types to Problems of Mental and Physical Adaptability* by William Washington Graves.

8. *COMMUNISM, HYPNOTISM, AND THE BEATLES*, David A. Noebel (Tulsa: Christian Crusade, 1979).
   This 15-page diatribe contends that the Beatles were agents of communism sent to America to subvert its youth through mass hypnosis "The Beatles' ability to make teenagers take off their clothes and riot is laboratory tested and approved," states Noebel. He supports his theory with no less than 168 footnotes.

9. *CAMEL BRANDS AND GRAFFITI FROM IRAQ, SYRIA, JORDAN, IRAN, AND ARABIA*, Henry Field (Baltimore: American Oriental Society, 1952).
   The publication of this study was made possible by the generosity of an anonymous donor.

10. *ICE CARVING PROFESSIONALLY*, George P. Weising (Fairfield, Conn: Self-published, 1954).
    An excellent textbook by a master ice sculptor. Weising gives instructions for carving such items as Tablets of the Ten Commandments Delivered by Moses (for bar mitzvahs); Rudolph, the Red-Nosed Reindeer; and the Travelers Insurance Company Tower in Hartford, Connecticut.

11. *THE HISTORY OF THE SELF-WINDING WATCH: 1770–1931*, Alfred Chapuis and Eugène Jaquet (Neuchâtel, Switzerland: Éditions du Griffon, 1952; English adaptation by Renée Savarè Grandvoinet.)

12. *THE ONE-LEG RESTING POSITION (NILOTENSTELLUNG) IN AFRICA AND ELSEWHERE*, Gerhard Lindblom (Stockholm: Statens Ethnografiska Museum, 1949).
    A survey of cultures in which people commonly rest while standing by placing one foot on or near the knee of the other leg. Contains 15 photographs from Africa, Sri Lanka, Romania, Australia, and Bolivia, as well as a foldout locator map of Africa.

13. *DIRT: A SOCIAL HISTORY AS SEEN THROUGH THE USES AND ABUSES OF DIRT*, Terence Mclaughlin (New York: Stein and Day, 1971).
    Readers who are drawn to dirty books might also enjoy *Smut: An Anatomy of Dirt* by Christian Engnensberger (New York: Seabury, 1972); *The Kingdom of Dust* by J. Gordon Ogden (Chicago: Popular Mechanics, 1912); and *All About Mud* by Oliver R. Selfrige (Reading, Mass.: Addison-Wesley, 1978).

14. *GOLDEN QUOTATIONS OF OUR FIRST LADY*, Julio F. Silvero (Caloocan City, Phillipines: National Book Store, 1978). Three hundred "golden" quotations from the speeches of Imelda Marcos, including "Reality: You can only wear one dress, one pair of shoes at a time."

15. *BIRDS ASLEEP*, Alexander F. Skutch (Austin: University of Texas Press, 1989). A detailed and surprisingly readable study by an ornithologist resident in Costa Rica. A 12-page bibliography is included for serious students. Less pacific readers might prefer *Birds Fighting* by Stuart Smith and Erik Hosking (London: Faber and Faber, 1955), which includes numerous photos of real birds attacking stuffed birds.

16. *KNIGHT LIFE: JOUSTING IN THE UNITED STATES*, Robert L. Loeffelbein (Lexington Park, Md.: Golden Owl, 1977). A fully illustrated account of the history of jousting tournaments in the United States, with emphasis on modern contests, records, rules, and heroes.

17. *HOW TO CONDUCT A MAGNETIC HEALING BUSINESS*, by A. C. Murphy (Kansas City, MO.: Hudson-Kimbery, 1902). A nuts-and-bolts account, including advertising tips and postal rules and regulations, as well as discussion of such difficult topics as "Should a lady healer employ a gentleman assistant?"

18. *I DREAM OF WOODY*, Dee Burton (New York: William Morrow, 1984). Burton presents the cases of 70 people from New York and Los Angeles who have dreamed about Woody Allen. Fans of books on people who dream about famous people will also want to track down *Dreams about H.M. the Queen* by Brian Masters (Frogmore, St. Albans, Herts: Mayflower, 1973), a collection of dreams about Queen Elizabeth II and other members of the British royal family; *I Dream of Madonna* by Kay Turner (San Francisco: Collins, 1993); *Dreams of Bill* by Judith Anderson-Miller and Bruce Joshua Miller (New York: Citadel Press, 1994), a collection of dreams about Bill Clinton; and *Dreaming of Diana: The Dreams Diana, Princess of Wales, Inspired* by Rita Frances (London: Robson Books, 1998).

19. *LITTLE-KNOWN SISTERS OF WELL-KNOWN MEN*, Sarah G. Pomeroy (Boston: Dana Estes, 1912). A review of the lives of eight little-known sisters, including Sarianna Browning, Sarah Disraeli, and Sophia Thoreau, as well as two known sisters of English writers, Dorothy Wordsworth and Mary Lamb.

20. *THE ROYAL TOUCH: SACRED MONARCHY AND SCROFULA IN ENGLAND AND FRANCE*, Mark Bloch (London: Routledge and Kegan Paul, 1973).
This book, written in 1923, examines the unusual custom of curing the disease of scrofula, a form of tuberculosis, with a touch from the king of France or the king of England. The practice died out after 1825.

21. *LUST FOR FAME: THE STAGE CAREER OF JOHN WILKES BOOTH*, Gordon Samples (Jefferson, N.C.: McFarland, 1982).
A biography that ignores Booth's assassination of Abraham Lincoln and deals instead, for 234 pages, with his career as an actor, which continued until four weeks before he killed the president of the United States.

22. *OUT OF OUR KITCHEN CLOSETS: SAN FRANCISCO GAY JEWISH COOKING* (San Francisco: Congregation Sha'ar Zahav, 1987).
One hundred and fifty recipes submitted by the members, families, and friends of a gay and lesbian synagogue. Seventeen of the recipes are for kugel.

23. *LEWIS CARROLL, PHOTOGRAPHER OF CHILDREN: FOUR NUDE STUDIES*, Morton N. Cohen (New York: Clarkson Potter, 1979).
A slim (32-page) treatise on a little-known aspect of the life of the author of *Alice's Adventures Underground* and *Through the Looking Glass*. For many years Carroll's hobby was photographing little girls under the age of 10. The four hand-colored photographs reproduced in this volume are the only nude studies he did not destroy before his death.

24. *THE HISTORY AND ROMANCE OF ELASTIC WEBBING*, Clifford A. Richmond (Easthampton, Mass.: Easthampton News Company, 1946).
A lively account of the birth and growth of the elastic webbing industry in the nineteenth century. In the words of the author, once a man has "got the smell of rubber in his nostrils . . . he either stays with rubber or is thereafter ever homesick to get back into the rubber industry."

25. *CANADIAN NATIONAL EGG LAYING CONTESTS*, F. C. Elford and A. G. Taylor (Ottawa, Canada: Department of Agriculture, 1924).
A report of the first three years of the Canadian national egg laying contests, from 1919 to 1922, as well as a preliminary contest held on Prince Edward Island in 1918–1919. The work consists almost entirely of charts comparing production and costs by owner, bird, and year. In 1921–1922, one of the birds belonging to Lewis N. Clark of Port Hope, Ontario, produced 294 eggs.

26. *THE RHINOCEROS FROM DÜRER TO STUBBS: 1515–1799*, J. N. Clarke (London: Sotheby's, 1986).
The first rhinoceros to be brought to Europe from India arrived in Lisbon in 1515. This book details the depiction of the single-horned Indian rhinoceros in European art from the sixteenth century through the end of the eighteenth century. It also tells the story of the travels of various rhinoceroses across the continent during that period. Fans of traveling rhinoceroses should check out *Clara's Grand Tour: Travels with a Rhinoceros in Eighteenth-Century Europe* by Glynis Ridley (New York: Atlantic Monthly Press, 2004).

27. *THE DIRECTION OF HAIR IN ANIMALS AND MAN*, Walter Kidd (London: Adam and Charles Black, 1903).
In his preface, Dr. Kidd states, "No doubt many of the phenomena here described are intrinsically uninteresting and unimportant." However, if you have ever yearned for a book that analyzes the direction in which hair grows on lions, oxen, dogs, apes, tapirs, humans, asses, anteaters, sloths, and other animals, you won't be disappointed.

28. *A STUDY OF SPLASHES*, A. M. Worthington (London: Longmans, Green, 1908).
This pioneering classic makes use of 197 photographs to help answer the question "What actually happens when a drop falls and splashes?" Worthington's book was considered so valuable to students of physics that it was reissued as recently as 1963.

29. *THE QUICK BROWN FOX*, Richard G. Templeton, Jr. (Chicago: At the Sign of the Gargoyle, 1945).
Thirty-three examples of sentences that include all 26 letters of the English alphabet. Included are classics such as "The quick brown fox jumps over the lazy dog" and "Pack my bags with five dozen liquor jugs," as well as the less well-known "The July sun caused a fragment of black pine wax to ooze on the velvet quilt" and "Very careful and exact knowledge should be emphasized in adjudging a quadrant."

30. *PAINTINGS AND DRAWINGS ON THE BACKS OF NATIONAL GALLERY PICTURES*, Martin Davies. (London: National Gallery Publications, 1946).
A rare opportunity to view the flip side of 42 famous works of art.

31. *THE ANTS OF COLORADO*, Robert E. Gregg (Boulder, Colo.: University of Colorado Press, 1963).
The author traveled 15,500 miles over a 16-year period in his search for the 165 kinds of ants found within the borders of the state of Colorado. The book is 792 pages long and contains a locator map for each species and subspecies.

32. *EARLY UNITED STATES BARBED WIRE PATENTS*, Jesse S. James (Maywood, Calif.: Self-published, 1966).
A definitive listing of 401 barbed-wire patents filed between the years 1867 and 1897.

33. *MANHOLE COVERS OF LOS ANGELES*, Robert and Mimi Melnick (Los Angeles: Dawson's Book Shop, 1974).
Despite its title, this book's scope is not limited to manhole covers—it also deals with handhole covers, which provide access to valves and meter boxes. There are 144 photographs. The authors lament the standardization of manhole cover making, which has put an end to the creative designs of the early part of the twentieth century.

34. *MOVIE STARS IN BATHTUBS*, Jack Scagnetti (Middle Village, N.Y.: Jonathan David Publishers, 1975).
One hundred and fifty-six photographs of movie stars in bathtubs. There are also numerous shots of actors, actresses, and animals in showers and steambaths.

35. *AMERICA IN WAX*, Gene Gurney (New York: Crown Publishers, 1977).
A complete guidebook to wax museums in the United States, with 678 illustrations, including Brigitte Bardot, Nikita Khrushchev, and the Battle of Yorktown.

36. *THE GENDER TRAP*, Chris Johnson and Cathy Brown with Wendy Nelson (London: Proteus, 1982).
The autobiography of the world's first transsexual parents. Chris and Cathy began life as Anne and Eugene. Anne was a social worker who wished she were a man; Eugene was a Kung Fu instructor who wished he were a woman. They fell in love; Anne gave birth to a baby girl, Emma; and then Anne and Eugene switched sexes. Anne, now Chris, became Emma's father, and Eugene, now Cathy, took over the role of mother.

37. *MISFITS! THE CLEVELAND SPIDERS IN 1899*, J. Thomas Hetrick (Jefferson, N.C.: McFarland and Co., 1991).
The 1899 the Cleveland Spiders were the worst team in the history of major league baseball. They got off to a bad start, winning only 3 of their first 23 games. Then they settled down to a terrible midseason streak before collapsing completely and losing 40 of their last 41 games. In a 12-team league, the Spiders' final record of 20 wins and 134 losses left them 35 games behind the eleventh-place team. Their average home attendance was 150. In fact, fan support was so anemic that the Spiders gave up playing in Cleveland and played 113 of their games on the road.

38. *SELL YOURSELF TO SCIENCE*, Jim Hogshire (Port Townsend, Wash.: Loompanics Unlimited, 1992).
The subtitle says it all: "The Complete Guide to Selling Your Organs, Body Fluids, Bodily Functions, and Being a Human Guinea Pig." If you are reasonably healthy, but have no job skills, this is the book for you. Hogshire explains how to earn $100 a day as a subject for drug studies and other scientific experiments, and how to sell your blood, sperm, hair, breast milk, and bone marrow.

39. *THE LIFE AND CUISINE OF ELVIS PRESLEY*, David Adler (New York: Crown, 1993).
In exquisite detail, Adler traces the evolution of what Elvis ate from the time he was a baby (corn bread soaked in buttermilk) through his years in the army, Las Vegas, Hollywood, and Graceland, and finally the bingeing that weakened his health. Elvis gobbled a dozen honey doughnuts in a cab before a visit to the White House and once ate five chocolate sundaes for breakfast before passing out. Included are recipes for fried squirrel, peanut butter and American cheese sandwich, and Elvis's last supper, which was ice cream and cookies. Elvis was also known to send a private plane to a favorite restaurant, in order to aquire and devour his favorite peanut-butter-and-jelly sandwiches.

40. *THE MUSEUM OF BAD ART: Art Too Bad to Be Ignored*, Tom Stankowicz and Marie Jackson (Needham, Mass.: Backyard Computing, 2003).
The Museum of Bad Art is a real place. Its permanent gallery is located at 580 High Street, Dedham, Massachusetts. This book brings together 39 of the worst pieces from the museum's collection. Fans of little-appreciated art should also look for *Thrift Store Paintings* (1990), edited by Jim Shaw.

41. *GENTLE SWASTIKA: RECLAIMING THE INNOCENCE*, ManWoman (Cranbrook, B.C., Canada: Flyfoot Press, 2001).
The author points out that the swastika has a long history as a religious symbol that predates its adoption by Adolf Hitler and the Nazis by thousands of years. He or she illustrates the pre-Nazi use of the swastika with 400 photographs and drawings from around the world. ManWoman proposes that the swastika should be reclaimed by humanity and no longer be ruined by its association with Hitler.

42. *THE DENTIST IN ART*, J. J. Pindborg and L. Marwitz. (Chicago: Quadrangle Books, 1960).
Translated from Danish, this volume displays 60 works of art dealing with dentistry and other tooth-related subjects. Although the artists represented include da Vinci, Rembrandt, Goya, and Breughel, the most impressive pieces are those by the French dentist and surrealist

painter David Solot, whose work includes *The Revolt of the Molars* and *The Family of Forceps.*

43. *THE ALIEN ABDUCTION SURVIVAL GUIDE: How to Cope with Your ET Experience,* Michelle LaVigne (Newberg, Ore.: Wild Flower Press, 1995).
Unlike most books that deal with alien abduction, LaVigne's treatise is a practical guide that helps abductees control their fear and "take control" of the experience. The author smashes various myths such as "The ETs have no lips, and do not open their mouths," "All ETs who are called greys are gray," and "The ETs have long tentacle-like fingers covered with suction cups, similar to those found on an octopus."

44. *PIE ANY MEANS NECESSARY: The Biotic Baking Brigade Cookbook* (Edinburgh: AK Press, 2004).
The *BBB* presents the history of pie throwing as a political act and includes several recipes for easy-to-throw pies. Also included are photographs of such celebrities as Bill Gates being pied.

Brian Eno's 18 Mind-Changing Books

Brian Eno's career encompasses music, writing, lecturing, teaching, and the visual arts. He has released a series of critically acclaimed solo albums and has collaborated with the likes of John Cale, Nico, Robert Fripp, David Bowie, and the band James. His award-winning production work spans from Gavin Bryars and Talking Heads to U2 and Laurie Anderson. A pioneer in tape looping, electronics, and other forms of sonic manipulation with an unusual, strategic approach to music making, he has an ability to help artists explore new areas. His audio-visual installation work has been shown around the world, a total of 80 or so exhibitions to date. His writings on politics, culture, and communications have been widely published. He is the author of *A Year with Swollen Appendices,* published by Faber and Faber in 1996.

1. *Brain of the Firm*—Stafford Beer
The most approachable book about the self-organizing nature of complex systems.

2. *Silence*—John Cage
Music as philosophy (with lots of Zen wit).

3. *The Evolution of Cooperation*—Robert Axelrod
How time changes relationships: a message of hope.

4. *The Clock of the Long Now*—Stewart Brand
   Why we need to think long.

5. *Managing the Commons*—Garrett Hardin
   Structural observations about shared resources.

6. *A New Kind of Science*—Stephen Wolfram
   Controversial and exciting new approach to the genesis of complex systems.

7. *Grooming, Gossip and the Evolution of Language*—Robin Fox
   The origins and limits of human community.

8. *The Mystery of Capital*—Hernando de Soto
   Why capitalism can't be planted just anywhere.

9. *Labyrinths*—Jorge Luis Borges
   The ultimate "what if?" book.

10. *Africa: A Biography of the Continent*—John Reader
    The story of Africa beginning 4½ billion BC.

11. *Animal Architecture*—Karl von Frisch
    One of the best "beauty of nature" books, academic jaw-dropper.

12. *Contingency, Irony and Solidarity*—Richard Rorty
    A great work of modern pragmatism: the antidote to Derrida.

13. *Peter the Great*—Robert K. Massie
    Superb biography of a giant located somewhere between Genghis Khan, Abraham Lincoln, and Joseph Stalin.

14. *Roll, Jordan, Roll: The World the Slaves Made*—Eugene Genovese
    The unexpected richness and lasting importance of slave culture in America.

15. *Folk Song Style and Culture*—Alan Lomax
    An extraordinary theory that singing style is indicative of social structure by the pioneer collector of world music.

16. *The Selfish Gene*—Richard Dawkins
    Even if you think you know what this is about it's worth reading. The atheists' defense.

17. *Democracy in America*—Alexis de Tocqueville
    He guessed at the best of it, warned of the worst of it, and was right on both counts.

18. *Guns, Germs and Steel*—Jared Diamond
    Compelling account of the physical factors shaping world history.

Benjamin Spock's
10 Greatest Children's Books

Born in New Haven, Connecticut, on May 2, 1903, Dr. Benjamin Spock had been a pediatrician for 17 years before his best-selling book, *The Common Sense of Baby and Child Care* (1946), which put forth then revolutionary ideas on child-rearing, became a bible to the new mothers of the post–World War II baby boom. In addition to his medical career, Dr. Spock was also a deeply committed political activist, campaigning for Presidents John F. Kennedy and Lyndon Johnson, protesting the Vietnam War and the proliferation of nuclear weapons, and running as the People's Party candidate for the U.S. presidency in 1972. Spock died on March 15, 1998. He contributed the following list to *The Book of Lists* in 1983:

1. *Tom Sawyer*, by Mark Twain
2. *Huckleberry Finn*, by Mark Twain
3. *Treasure Island*, by Robert Louis Stevenson
4. *Black Arrow*, by Robert Louis Stevenson
5. *A Tale of Two Cities*, by Charles Dickens
6. *Oliver Twist*, by Charles Dickens
7. *Nicholas Nickleby*, by Charles Dickens
8. *Westward, Ho!*, By Charles Kingsley
9. *Ivanhoe*, by Sir Walter Scott
10. The Babar books

Maurice Sendak's
10 Favorite Children's Books

Born in Brooklyn, New York, in 1928, Maurice Sendak worked as an illustrator before becoming an international success by writing and illustrating the classic *Where the Wild Things Are* (1963). Among his other works are *In the Night Kitchen* (1970), *Outside Over There* (1981), and *The Sign on Rosie's* Door (2002). Sendak is the recipient of the Caldecott Medal, the Hans Christian Andersen Illustration Award, and the Laura Ingalls Wilder Award for his "substantial and lasting contribution to children's literature." He is also the designer of many opera sets and costumes and in 1979 wrote the libretto for an opera version of *Where the Wild Things Are*. With fellow

children's writer and playwright Arthur Yorinks, Sendak cofounded
the groundbreaking Night Kitchen Theater Company, a not-for-profit
children's theater. His most recent book, *Bumble Ardy*, was published in
2004.

1. *The Pirate Twins*, by William Nicholson
2. *Clever Bill*, by William Nicholson
3. *Little Tim and the Brave Sea Captain*, by Edward Ardizzone
4. *Tim and Charlotte*, by Edward Ardizzone
5. *Roly Poly Pudding*, by Beatrice Potter
6. *Two Bad Mice*, by Beatrice Potter
7. *Hey Diddle Diddle*, by Randolph Caldecott
8. *Baby Bunting*, by Randolph Caldecott
9. *The Story of Babar*, by Jean de Branhoff
10. *The Tale of Peter Rabbit*, by Beatrice Potter

29 Celebrities Who Wrote Children's Books

1. JULIE ANDREWS (EDWARDS), actress
   Mandy (1973), the story of a little girl who lives in a city orphanage and
   discovers the country, and *The Last of the Really Great Whangdoodles*
   (1973), about two children who visit a land of wise and magical creatures.

2. ALAN ARKIN, actor
   Tony's Hard Work Day (1972), about a boy who builds his own house,
   and *The Lemming Condition* (1976), about a young lemming who learns
   to ask questions instead of blindly conforming.

3. GWENDOLYN BROOKS, poet
   Bronzeville Boys and Girls (1956) and *The Tiger Who Wore White
   Gloves: or What You Are You Are* (1974). Poems about the experiences
   of children.

4. DAVID BYRNE, singer and composer
   Stay Up Late (1988), based on one of Byrne's songs about the excite-
   ment that strikes a family when a new baby is brought home.

5. JIMMY CARTER, U.S. president
   The Little Baby Snoogle-Fleejer (1995), the story of young Jeremy,
   who can't walk and finds a kindred spirit in a young sea monster. The
   story was illustrated by his daughter, Amy.

6. CHARLES, PRINCE OF WALES
   The Old Man of Lochnagar (1980), the story of an old man who leaves
   his comfortable cave to explore the surrounding Scottish countryside.

7. BILL COSBY, comedian and actor
   A series of "Little Bill" books designed to help children cope with tough
   social situations. Titles include *The Meanest Thing to Say* (1997), *One
   Dark and Scary Night* (1999), and *The Day I Saw My Father Cry*
   (2000).

8. KATIE COURIC, talk show host
   The Brand New Kid (2000), about the arrival at school of a new kid
   with an accent.

9. BILLY CRYSTAL, comedian and actor
   I Already Know I Love You (2004), about the author's anticipation of
   the birth of his first grandchild.

10. JAMIE LEE CURTIS, actress
    A series of books with illustrator Laura Cornell, including *When I Was
    Little: A Four-Year-Old's Memoir of Her Youth* (1993), *Tell Me Again
    About the Night I Was Born* (1996), and *Where Do Balloons Go? An
    Uplifting Mystery* (2000).

11. SARAH FERGUSON, DUCHESS OF YORK
    Budgie, the Little Helicopter (1989), about a helicopter who rescues a
    little girl from kidnappers; and three other stories starring Budgie.

12. WHOOPI GOLDBERG, comedienne and actress
    Alice (1992), a retelling of *Alice in Wonderland* set in New Jersey and
    New York City.

13. KEN KESEY, novelist
    Little Fricker the Squirrel Meets Big Double the Bear (1990), about a
    smart squirrel who outwits a bully of a bear, and *The Sea Lion: A Story
    of the Sea Cliff People* (1991), about a small boy who saves his tribe
    from an evil spirit.

14. LARRY KING, talk show host
    With his daughter Chaira, he cowrote *Daddy Day, Daughter Day*
    (1997), an account of divorce and parenting told from both a child's
    and father's viewpoints.

15. SPIKE LEE, film director
    Please Baby Please (2002), about parents pleading with an energetic
    toddler blasting through a busy day.

16. **JAY LENO**, comedian and talk show host
If Roast Beef Could Fly (2004), based on a true story from his childhood.

17. **JOHN LITHGOW**, actor
A series of songs and stories on book-CD sets. Titles include *Marsupial Sue* (2001), about a discontented kangaroo; *Micawber* (2002), about an art-loving squirrel; and *I'm a Manatee* (2003), about a boy dreaming of being a manatee.

18. **LL COOL J**, rapper
And the Winner Is . . . (2002), about a young basketball player who learns the importance of winning and losing graciously.

19. **MADONNA**, singer
Mr. Peabody's Apples (2003), a tale about the dangers of gossip, based on a 300-year-old Ukrainian story transferred to small-town America; and *The English Roses* (2003), a story about jealousy.

20. **LeANN RIMES**, country singer
Jag (2003), the story of a young jaguar who dreads her first day at school.

21. **SALMAN RUSHDIE**, novelist
Haroun and the Sea of Stories (1990), about a fanatic cult that tries to wipe out storytelling and human speech.

22. **JERRY SEINFELD**, comedian
Halloween (2002), a nostalgic look at Halloweens past, especially the candy.

23. **JANE SEYMOUR**, actress
Splat! The Tale of a Colorful Cat (2001) and *Yum! The Tale of Two Cookies* (2003), two stories about twin kittens named "This One" and "That One."

24. **MARIA SHRIVER**, broadcast journalist
What's Heaven? (1999) and *What's Wrong with Timmy?* (2001), about dealing with difficult questions asked by kids.

25. **CARLY SIMON**, singer and songwriter
Amy the Dancing Bear (1989), about a bear who would rather dance than sleep, and *Fisherman's Song* (1991).

26. **WILL SMITH**, actor and rapper
Just the Two of Us (2001), based on Smith's hit record; a celebration of a father's love for his son.

27. **JOHN TRAVOLTA**, actor
Propeller One-Way Night Coach: A Story (1997), about an eight-year-old's first plane ride.

28. **BOB WEIR**, guitarist and singer
Panther Dream (1991), about the African rain forest. Proceeds from the book support reforestation and educational projects in Africa.

29. **VIRGINIA WOOLF**, novelist
Nurse Lugton's Curtain (1924), about the animals on a curtain who come alive when its seamstress falls asleep; and *The Widow and the Parrot* (1988), published posthumously, in which a parrot leads a Yorkshire widow to hidden treasure.

The Eds. & C.F.

CHAPTER FOURTEEN

Literary Favorites

HENRY MILLER'S 10 GREATEST WRITERS

DORIS LESSING'S 10 FAVORITE WRITERS OF ALL TIME

IRVING WALLACE'S 9 FAVORITE AUTHORS

JOE KANON'S 10 FAVORITE THRILLER WRITERS

VÁCLAV HAVEL'S 4 FAVORITE AUTHORS

ELMORE LEONARD'S 10 FAVORITE NOVELS

KEN KESEY'S 10 BEST AMERICAN NOVELS

WILLIAM BURROUGHS'S 10 FAVORITE NOVELS

KEN FOLLETT'S 10 FAVORITE NOVELS

WILLIAM STYRON'S 10 FAVORITE NOVELS

PETER STRAUB'S 10 GREAT GENRE NOVELS

TOM CLANCY'S 6 GREATEST WAR NOVELS

BRIAN ALDISS'S 10 FAVORITE SCIENCE FICTION NOVELS

MICHAEL ONDAATJE'S 12 TWENTIETH-CENTURY
CLASSICS IN TRANSLATION

MICHAEL ONDAATJE'S 12 TWENTIETH-CENTURY
CLASSICS IN ENGLISH

ROALD DAHL'S 5 BOOKS TO TAKE TO A NEW PLANET

SIDNEY SHELDON'S 10 ALL-TIME FAVORITE BOOKS

COLEMAN BARKS'S 11 FAVORITE POEMS

DR. SEUSS'S 10 BEST CARTOON CHARACTERS

CHARLES DICKENS.

CHARLES DICKENS

Henry Miller's
10 Greatest Writers

One of the most controversial and innovative American writers of the twentieth century, Henry Miller was born in New York City on December 26, 1891. He spent much of the 1930s as an expatriate in Paris, where he met Anais Nïn and wrote his two most famous novels, *Tropic of Cancer* (1934) and *Tropic of Capricorn* (1939). The books were banned for many years in English-speaking countries before being published in the UK in 1963 and the U.S. in 1964 after a landmark obscenity trial. His other works include *Black Spring, Colossus of Maroussi*, and *The Rosy Crucifixion* trilogy of *Sexus, Plexus*, and *Nexus*. Miller died in Pacific Palisades, California, on June 7, 1980. He contributed the following list to *The Book of Lists* in 1977:

1. Lao-tzu
2. François Rabelais
3. Friedrich Nietzsche
4. Rabindranath Tagore
5. Walt Whitman
6. Marcel Proust
7. Élie Faure
8. Marie Corelli
9. Fyodor Dostoyevsky
10. Isaac Bashevis Singer

Note: Élie Faure (1873–1937) was a French art historian who published a five-volume *History of Art* between 1909 and 1921. He had studied medicine and brought a scientific approach to his examinations of art history. London-born Marie Corelli (1855–1924), whose real name was Mary Mackay, wrote 28 books, most of them lurid romances, many dealing with psychic or religious events, and all enormously popular. Critics held her in disdain (once, in retaliation, she refused to send them review copies), but Queen Victoria adored her work. Among Corelli's most widely read books are *The Sorrows of Satan* and *The Murder of Delicia*.

Doris Lessing's
10 Favorite Writers of All Time
(Not Necessarily in This Order)

Born Doris May Taylor on October 22, 1919, in Persia (Iran), and raised in Rhodesia (Zimbabwe). Lessing's childhood experiences provided her with the material for many books, including her first published novel, *The Grass Is Singing*, and a five-volume series entitled *Children of Violence*. Her other works include *The Golden Notebook, Memoirs of a Survivor*, and *The Fifth Child*.

1. The sage Mahmud Shabestari
2. Marcel Proust
3. Anton Chekhov
4. Idries Shah
5. Henry David Thoreau
6. Gerard Manley Hopkins
7. al-Ghazali of Persia
8. Leo Tolstoy
9. Jalal ud-Din Rumi
10. Ibn al-Arabi

Irving Wallace's
9 Favorite Authors

On June 29, 1990, Irving Wallace, one of the coauthors of *The Book of Lists*, died in Los Angeles at the age of 74. His nearly three dozen books have sold an estimated 200 million copies and have been read by 1 billion people worldwide. He wrote 18 novels, including *The Prize, The Man*, and *The Word*. Shortly before his death, he compiled a list of his all-time-favorite authors:

1. W. Somerset Maugham—*Of Human Bondage*, because of its compelling characterization, narrative drive, crystal-clear prose; *The Summing Up*, for clarity, cynicism, philosophy; and *The Moon and Sixpence*.

2. F. Scott Fitzgerald—*Tender Is the Night*.

3. Arthur Koestler—*Arrival and Departure* and *Darkness at Noon*.

4. Arthur Conan Doyle—the Sherlock Holmes books; pure pleasure, nothing more. Also, *The Lost World*.

5. James Hilton—*Lost Horizon* and *Without Armor*.

6. Raymond Chandler.

7. Graham Greene.

8. John le Carré—*The Little Drummer Girl*.

9. Nelson DeMille—*Word of Honor* and *By the Rivers of Babylon*.

Joe Kanon's
10 Favorite Thriller Writers
(with a Top Pick for Each)

Joseph Kanon was educated at Harvard and Trinity College, Cambridge, then embarked on a distinguished career in publishing, which included serving as president and CEO of E. P. Dutton. In 1995, he published his first novel, *Los Alamos*, a mystery set against the historical background of the creation of the first atomic bomb, which became a *New York Times* best seller and won the Mystery Writers of America's prestigious Edgar Award for Best First Novel. His follow-ups—1998's *The Prodigal Spy*, 2001's *The Good German*, and 2005's *Alibi*—have all been successful thrillers of such exceptional literary quality that the *New York Times Book Review* was prompted to comment that "Kanon is fast approaching the complexity and relevance not just of Le Carré and Greene, but even Orwell." Kanon lives in New York City with his wife and children.

1. John le Carré—*Tinker, Tailor, Soldier, Spy*
2. Graham Greene—*Brighton Rock*
3. Elmore Leonard—*La Brava* or *Freaky Deaky*
4. Raymond Chandler—*Farewell, My Lovely*
5. Alan Furst—*Night Soldiers*
6. Patricia Highsmith—*The Talented Mr. Ripley*
7. Dashiell Hammett—*Red Harvest*
8. James M. Cain—*Double Indemnity*
9. Josephine Tey—*The Daughter of Time*
10. Eric Ambler—*Cause for Alarm*
Bonus selection: Carl Hiaasen—*Skinny Dip*

Václav Havel's
4 Favorite Authors

Czech playwright, poet, and statesman Václav Havel was often arrested during the 1970s for his stand against his nation's repressive government. His works include *The Memorandum* (1965), *A Private View* (1975), and an adaptation of Tom Stoppard's *Largo Desolato* (1987). When Havel's works were spirited out of the country, he was persecuted for that, too. In 1989, he helped lead the "Velvet Revolution," which resulted in the overthrow of Soviet-style communism in Czechoslovakia and led to the split between the Czech and Slovak republics. In 1993, he became the first president of the Czech Republic. He left office after the end of his second term, in February 2003.

1. Samuel Beckett
2. Eugène Ionesco
3. Tom Stoppard
4. Harold Pinter

Note: Havel notes that his favorite play is *The Guard* by Pinter.

Elmore Leonard's
10 Favorite Novels

Born on October 11, 1925, in New Orleans, Louisiana, Elmore "Dutch" Leonard began writing novels while working as an advertising executive. His first successes were Westerns, including *The Bounty Hunters* (1953) and *Hombre* (1961), before he turned to crime fiction with such best sellers as *Stick* (1983), *Glitz* (1985), and *Killshot* (1989). His novels have been the basis for many hit movies, including Barry Sonnenfeld's *Get Shorty* (1995), Quentin Tarantino's *Jackie Brown* (1997), and Steven Soderbergh's *Out of Sight* (1998). His most recent works include his first children's book, *A Coyote's in the House*, and the thriller *Mr. Paradise*, both published in 2004. Leonard makes his home outside of Detroit, Michigan (the locale for many of his novels).

1. *All Quiet on the Western Front* by Erich Maria Remarque
   The first book that made me want to write, when I was still in grade school.

2. *For Whom the Bell Tolls* by Ernest Hemingway
   A book I studied almost daily when, in '52, I began to write with a purpose.

3. *A Stretch on the River* by Richard Bissell
   The book that showed me the way I should be writing: not taking it so seriously.

4. *Sweet Thursday* by John Steinbeck
   The book that showed me the difference between honest prose and show-off writing.

5. *The Friends of Eddie Coyle* by George V. Higgins
   Twenty years ago George showed how to get into a scene fast.

6. *Paris Trout* by Pete Dexter
   An awfully good writer.

7. *The Heart of the Matter* by Graham Greene
   Especially moving at the time it was written. I like everything he did, from *The Power and the Glory* to *Our Man in Havana*.

8. *The Moviegoer* by Walker Percy
   Walker, the old pro.

9. *Legends of the Fall* by Jim Harrison
   Wonderful prose writer and great poet.

10. Collected short stories of Hemingway, Annie Proulx, Raymond Carver, and Bobbie Ann Mason
    Have studied and I hope learned from all of them.

Ken Kesey's
10 Best American Novels

Born September 17, 1935, in La Junta, Colorado, author Ken Kesey is best known for his 1962 novel *One Flew Over the Cuckoo's Nest,* which became a modern literary classic and was the basis for a hugely successful 1975 movie adaptation starring Jack Nicholson. Kesey's other works include *Sometimes a Great Notion, Demon Box,* and *Sailor Song.* He was also the leader of the "Merry Pranksters," whose antiestablishment attitudes and use of psychedelic drugs made them one of the key influences on 1960s counterculture lifestyles. Kesey died on November 10, 2001, following surgery for cancer of the liver. He contributed the following list to *The Book of Lists* in 1980:

1. *Moby-Dick* by Herman Melville
2. *DeFord* by David Shetzline

3. *Huckleberry Finn* by Mark Twain
4. *A Farewell to Arms* by Ernest Hemingway
5. *As I Lay Dying* by William Faulkner
6. *The Grapes of Wrath* by John Steinbeck
7. *The Dune Trilogy* by Frank Herbert
8. *On the Road* by Jack Kerouac
9. *From Here to Eternity* by Jack Jones
10. The Westerns of Zane Grey

William Burroughs's
10 Favorite Novels

Born in 1914 in St. Louis, Missouri, the rebellious William Seward Burroughs II grew up to be the disinherited heir of the Burroughs Adding Machine Corporation, a multimillion-dollar concern. During a drunken party game in Mexico, he accidentally killed his wife, Joan, as he aimed to shoot a glass off her head. Norman Mailer once termed Burroughs "the only American novelist living today who may conceivably be possessed by genius." A former private investigator, reporter, and exterminator, Burroughs earned a cult following with his novel *Naked Lunch* (1956), a surrealistic account of his experiences as a heroin addict. He wrote or collaborated on more than 35 books, including *Queer* and *Nova Express*. Toward the end of his life, he became a great lover of cats and wrote *The Cat Inside*. He died in Lawrence, Kansas, in 1997 at the age of 83. He contributed this list to *The Book of Lists* in 1980.

1. *The Process* by Brion Gysin
2. *The Satyricon* by Petronius
3. *In Youth Is Pleasure* by Denton Welch
4. *Two Serious Ladies* by Jane Bowles
5. *The Sheltering Sky* by Paul Bowles
6. *Under Western Eyes* by Joseph Conrad
7. *Journey to the End of the Night* by Louis-Ferdinand Céline
8. *Querelle de Brest* by Jean Genet
9. *The Unfortunate Traveller* by Thomas Nashe
10. *The Great Gatsby* by F. Scott Fitzgerald

Note: The Process (1969) by Brion Gysin (1916–1986) follows the bizarre adventures of a black American professor traveling across the Sahara Desert. English writer Denton Welch (1915–1948) explored an English schoolboy's sexual fears and fantasies in his second novel, *In Youth Is Pleasure* (1945). Thomas Nashe (1567–1601), English pamphleteer and dramatist, anticipated the English adventure novel with *The Unfortunate Traveller*.

Ken Follett's
10 Favorite Novels

Born June 5, 1949, in Cardiff, Wales, Ken Follett worked as a rock music columnist and publishing house editor, writing 10 books in his spare time until the success of his 11th, the spy thriller *Eye of the Needle* (1978), allowed him to quit his day job. A prolific author; his other novels include *The Pillars of the Earth, Hornet Flight*, and *Whiteout*. He also authored *On the Wings of Eagles*, a nonfiction account of the Ross Perot–financed rescue of two American hostages from Iran. He is married to Member of Parliament Barbara Follett.

1. *Martin Chuzzlewit* by Charles Dickens
   This contains my favorite character in all fiction, Sairy Gamp.

2. *Lonesome Dove* by Larry McMurtry
   The best book of my favorite living writer.

3. *From Russia with Love* by Ian Fleming
   I began to read James Bond stories when I was about 12 years old.

4. *Middlemarch* by George Eliot
   The pinnacle of Victorian fiction.

5. *Summer Lightning* by P. G. Wodehouse
   Wodehouse is the cleverest plotter in all fiction.

6. *Foundation* by Isaac Asimov
   This and the other two books in the trilogy are among the few that I reread every 10 years or so.

7. *Salem's Lot* by Stephen King
   Still his best book, although *Needful Things* comes close.

8. *The Warden* by Anthony Trollope
   I love Trollope and I'm so glad he wrote 47 novels.

9. *The Banker* by Leslie Waller
   Uptight WASP falls in love with sexy Jewish girl and blows his cool.

10. *The Pillars of the Earth* by Ken Follett
    Pretty darn good, though I say it myself.

William Styron's
10 Favorite Novels

Born June 11, 1925, in Newport News, Virginia, William Styron was educated at New York's New School for Social Research and made his literary debut at age 26 with *Lie Down in Darkness* (1951), which earned him the American Academy's Prix de Rome. His other works include the Pulitzer Prize–winning *Confessions of Nat Turner* (1967), *Sophie's Choice* (1979), and *Darkness Visible* (1990), an acclaimed memoir recounting Styron's struggle with depression.

1. *The Adventures of Huckleberry Finn* by Mark Twain
   Still the glorious American classic.

2. *Madame Bovary* by Gustave Flaubert
   No greater craft in a novel or keener insight into a woman's mind.

3. *Light in August* by William Faulkner
   Among the master's most accomplished works, its tragic vision harrowing and dark.

4. *The Stranger* by Albert Camus
   Defines once and for all the stoic courage of the existential vision.

5. *Anna Karenina* by Leo Tolstoy
   One of literature's greatest creations—a woman eventually doomed but triumphantly alive.

6. *1984* by George Orwell
   An incomparably skilled satire of the totalitarian spirit.

7. *An American Tragedy* by Theodore Dreiser
   Ponderous and often crude, but a shattering chronicle of murder and puritanical guilt.

8. *Look Homeward, Angel* by Thomas Wolfe
   A lyrical and youthful celebration of small-town life in early twentieth-century North Carolina. Still gorgeous.

9. *Lolita* by Vladimir Nabokov
   A great and scathing satire on America and a tragicomedy of sexual obsession.

10. *All the King's Men* by Robert Penn Warren
    About an American provincial dictator. One of the finest political novels ever written.

Peter Straub's
10 Great Genre Novels

Born in Milwaukee, Wisconsin, in 1943, Peter Straub studied literature at the University of Wisconsin and University College in Dublin. He soon set aside his academic studies in favor of fiction and poetry, publishing his first novel, *Marriages*, in 1973. His 1979 horror classic, *Ghost Story*, was the first in a string of best sellers that includes *Floating Dragon*, *Shadowland*, the Blue Rose trilogy of *Koko*, *Mystery*, and *The Throat*, and his most recent novel, *lost boy, lost girl.* He has also written two massively successful collaborations with Stephen King, *The Talisman* and *Black House*, as well as two books of short fiction and two collections of poetry. An avid jazz fan and prolific storyteller, Straub lives in New York City with his wife, Susan, director of Read to Me, a public service program encouraging teen mothers to read to their babies.

1. *The Long Goodbye*, Raymond Chandler
2. *The Lord of the Rings*, J. R. R. Tolkien
3. *The Shining*, Stephen King
4. *The Maltese Falcon*, Dashiell Hammett
5. *Little, Big*, John Crowley
6. *Dahlgren*, Samuel R. Delaney
7. *Dracula*, Bram Stoker
8. *His Dark Materials*, Philip Pullman
9. *The Lady in the Lake*, Raymond Chandler
10. *Rebecca*, Daphne du Maurier

Tom Clancy's
6 Greatest War Novels

A former insurance broker, Tom Clancy's best-selling first novel, *The Hunt for Red October* (1984), was proclaimed a "perfect yarn" by President Ronald Reagan. His numerous other books include the novels *Patriot Games*, *Clear and Present Danger*, *The Sum of All Fears*, and *Red Rabbit*, along with several works of nonfiction on the workings of the modern military. Four hit films have been adapted from his novels, and he has lent his name and plotting skills to the series of Tom Clancy's Splinter Cell and Tom Clancy's Ghost Recon video games.

1. *Run Silent, Run Deep* by Captain Edward L. Beach
   Adventures of a submarine patrol in the Pacific during World War II.

2. *The Third World War: August 1985* by General Sir John Hackett
   Politically and technically detailed "historical" account of a future war
   between NATO and Warsaw Pact powers.

3. *HMS Ulysses* by Alistair MacLean
   Men aboard a British cruiser in dangerous Arctic waters during World
   War II are tested to limits of heroism and endurance.

4. *The Cruel Sea* by Nicholas Monsarrat
   True story of two British ships and their crews in the North Atlantic
   during World War II.

5. *Fields of Fire* by James Webb
   Marine platoon experiences horrors of jungle warfare in Vietnam.

6. *The Caine Mutiny* by Herman Wouk
   Officers aboard U.S. Navy ship during World War II mutiny against
   their neurotic and exhausted captain, and are then court-martialed.

Brian Aldiss's
10 Favorite Science Fiction Novels

One of the legendary figures in the science fiction genre, Brian W. Aldiss
was born in 1925, served with the signal corps in the British army, then
spent nine years as a bookseller before becoming a full-time writer in 1956.
His works include *Frankenstein Unbound, Moreau's Other Island,* and the
groundbreaking Helliconia trilogy (*Helliconia Spring, Helliconia Summer,
Helliconia Winter*). His short story *Supertoys Last All Summer Long* was a
longtime dream project for the legendary director Stanley Kubrick, and was
eventually filmed after Kubrick's death as *A.I.: Artificial Intelligence* by
Steven Spielberg in 2001. A prolific writer, Aldiss lives in Oxford, England.
His most recent novel is *Super-State,* published in 2003.

1. *Frankenstein, or The New Prometheus* Mary Shelley
2. *The Twentieth Century* Albert Robida
3. *The Time Machine* H. G. Wells
4. *The War of the Worlds* H. G. Wells
5. *Star Maker* Olaf Stapledon
6. *The Paradox Men* Charles Harness
7. *Galapagos* Kurt Vonnegut
8. *Bill The Galactic Hero* Harry Harrison
9. *Martian Time-Slip* Philip K. Dick
10. *Mythago Wood* Robert Holdstock

Michael Ondaatje's
12 Twentieth-Century Classics in Translation

Michael Ondaatje is an internationally acclaimed novelist and poet. His novels include *Anil's Ghost, The English Patient, Coming Through Slaughter*, and *In the Skin of a Lion*. He has written a memoir, *Running in the Family*, and his books of poetry include *Handwriting* and *The Cinnamon Peeler*.

1. *Le Grand Meaulnes*—Henri Alain-Fournier (France, 1913)
2. *My Mother's House*—Colette (France, 1922)
3. *The Man Without Qualities*—Robert Musil (Austria, 1930)
4. *The Radetzky March*—Joseph Roth (Austria, 1932)
5. *The Street of Crocodiles*—Bruno Schulz (Poland, 1934)
6. *The Master and Margarita*—Mikhail Bulgakov (Russia, 1939)
7. *Pedro Pèramo*—Juan Rulfo (Mexico, 1955)
8. *Collected Stories*—Isaac Babel (Russia, 1955)
9. *The Devil to Pay in the Backlands*—João Guimarães Rosa (Brazil, 1956)
10. *The Baron in the Trees*—Italo Calvino (Italy, 1957)
11. *Beauty and Sadness*—Yasunari Kawabata (Japan, 1965)
12. *The Rings of Saturn*—W. G. Sebald (Germany, 1995)

Michael Ondaatje's
12 Twentieth-Century Classics in English

1. *Kim*—Rudyard Kipling (England, 1901)
2. *Victory*—Joseph Conrad (England, 1915)
3. *The Professor's House*—Willa Cather (USA, 1925)
4. *To the Lighthouse*—Virginia Woolf (England, 1927)
5. *Wolf Solent*—John Cowper Powys (USA, 1929)
6. *Light in August*—William Faulkner (USA, 1932)
7. *Call It Sleep*—Henry Roth (USA, 1934)
8. *An Imaginary Life*—David Malouf (Australia, 1978)
9. "The Three Lives of Lucy Cabrol" from *Pig Earth*—John Berger (England, 1979)
10. *So Long, See You Tomorrow*—William Maxwell (USA, 1980)
11. *Blood Meridian*—Cormac McCarthy (USA, 1985)
12. *The Selected Stories of Mavis Gallant*—Mavis Gallant (Canada, 1996)

Roald Dahl's
5 Books to Take to a New Planet

Born in Llandaff, Wales, in 1916, Roald Dahl served as a Royal Air Force fighter pilot during World War II before becoming a multitalented writer of novels (*My Uncle Oswald*), short story collections (*Someone Like You* and *Kiss, Kiss*), screenplays (the James Bond film *You Only Live Twice*), and hugely influential juvenile works (*Charlie and the Chocolate Factory* and *James and the Giant Peach*, which both became highly successful films). Although Dahl was much beloved for his children's books (his preferred form, he said, because "adults are much too serious for me"), a dysfunctional marriage to Academy Award–winning actress Patricia Neal, as well as accusations of anti-Semitism, have made him a controversial figure since his death in 1990. Dahl contributed this list to *The Book of Lists* in 1983:

1. *Price's Textbook of the Practice of Medicine* (Oxford University Press)
   Reason: A professional medical textbook covering the description, diagnoses, and treatment of virtually every known disease or illness.
2. *The Greater Oxford Dictionary*
3. *The Pickwick Papers*—Dickens
4. A book containing all of Beethoven's piano sonatas
5. Johann Sebastian Bach's B Minor Mass

Sidney Sheldon's
10 All-Time Favorite Books

Sidney Sheldon set out to become a composer but switched to screenwriting and won an Academy Award for his screenplay *The Bachelor and the Bobby-Soxer* (1947) and Screen Writers Guild awards for *Easter Parade* (1948) and *Annie Get Your Gun* (1950). He created *The Patty Duke Show* and *I Dream of Jeannie* for television. He turned to writing novels in the 1970s and proved to be a best-selling author with such books as *The Other Side of Midnight* (1974) and *Rage of Angels* (1980). His most recent novel is *Are You Afraid of the Dark?* (2004).

1. *Rebecca* by Daphne du Maurier

2. *Johnny Got His Gun* by Dalton Trumbo

3. *Act One* by Moss Hart
   One of the best autobiographies ever written about show business.

4. *Look Homeward, Angel* by Thomas Wolfe
   Written by a man who loved language.

5. *Roosevelt and Hopkins* by Robert Sherwood
   A spotlight on World War II.

6. Anything by James Thurber

7. *For Whom the Bell Tolls* by Ernest Hemingway

8. *Of Human Bondage* by W. Somerset Maugham

9. Anything by Booth Tarkington

10. *The Rise and Fall of the Third Reich* by William Shirer
    Brilliant and revealing.

Coleman Barks's
11 Favorite Poems

Born and raised in Chattanooga, Tennessee, poet and translator Coleman Barks taught creative writing at the University of Georgia for 30 years. A dedicated student of Sufism since 1977, he is the author of numerous works, including an acclaimed series of translations of the Islamic mystical poet Rumi (1207–1273), several of which were selected to appear in the prestigious *Norton Anthology of World Masterpieces*. Collections of Barks's own poetry include *Tentmaking: Poems and Prose Paragraphs* and *Club: Granddaughter Poems*. The father of two grown children, and the grandfather of three, Coleman Barks lives in Athens, Georgia.

1. *Sir Gawain and the Green Knight*

2. William Blake's *The Marriage of Heaven and Hell*

3. William Shakespeare's *Hamlet* and *The Tempest*

4. Walt Whitman's *Song of Myself*

5. Geoffrey Chaucer's "Prologue" to the *Canterbury Tales* and the "Miller's Tale" and the "Nun's Priest's Tale"

6. Emily Dickinson, the poems of 1863, all she wrote

7. Gerard Manley Hopkins, a hefty selection of the shorter poems

8. John Keats odes

9. T. S. Eliot's *Four Quartets*

10. D. H. Lawrence's *Birds, Beasts, and Flowers,* most of it and some selected others

11. William Carlos Williams' 37-page "Asphodel" and some others

Barks notes: I have chosen only poetry written in English, no translations, only things long enough to be collected in a book of about 80 pages, and only my favorites during this particular 30-minute period, 8:00 p.m. to 8:30 p.m., June 17, 2004. The next 30 minutes would produce a different list.

Dr. Seuss's
10 Best Cartoon Characters

Born Theodor Seuss Geisel March 2, 1904, Dr. Seuss began his career as a cartoonist. During World War II, he served in the U.S. Army, writing for Frank Capra's Armed Forces Motion Picture Unit. He began writing children's books in the 1930s and finally achieved a popular breakthrough in 1957 with the classic *The Cat in the Hat.* Despite never having any children of his own, the name Dr. Seuss became synonymous with great works for young readers; among his best-known books are *Green Eggs and Ham, How the Grinch Stole Christmas,* and *The Lorax.* Dr. Seuss died on September 24, 1991. He contributed the following list to *The Book of Lists* in 1980:

1. Winsor McKay's Little Nemo
2. George Herriman's Krazy Kat and Ignatz Mouse
3. Percy Crosby's Skippy
4. Bill Mauldin's Willie and Joe
5. Sidney Smith's Andy Gump
6. David Low's Colonel Blimp
7. Claire Briggs's Mr. and Mrs.
8. Milton Caniff's Terry and the Pirates
9. Rollin Kirby's Prohibition
10. Dr. Moose's Mouse in the Hat

CHAPTER FIFTEEN

Words

SO TO SPEAK—THE TRUTH BEHIND
16 COMMON SAYINGS

13 SAYINGS OF WOODY ALLEN

18 SAYINGS OF OSCAR WILDE

16 WELL-KNOWN SAYINGS ATTRIBUTED
TO THE WRONG PERSON

17 PAIRS OF CONTRADICTORY PROVERBS

8 PEOPLE WHO ATE THEIR OWN—OR OTHERS'—WORDS

33 NAMES OF THINGS YOU NEVER KNEW HAD NAMES

7 WORDS IN WHICH ALL THE VOWELS APPEAR
IN ALPHABETICAL ORDER

17 UNTRANSLATABLE WORDS

22 OBSCURE AND OBSOLETE WORDS

13 COLORFUL "ANIVERBS"

33 WORDS RARELY USED IN THEIR POSITIVE FORM

LEO ROSTEN'S 13 FAVORITE YIDDISH WORDS
OR PHRASES

WILLARD R. ESPY'S 10 UGLIEST WORDS
IN THE ENGLISH LANGUAGE

Columella Nasi

COLUMELLA NASI
© Paul Glover

So to Speak—The Truth Behind
16 Common Sayings

1. AT A SNAIL'S PACE
   The fastest land snail on record is a garden snail named Archie, who won the 1995 World Snail Racing Championship in Longhan, England, by covering 13 inches in 2 minutes. Archie's pace was .0062 mph.

2. JUST A MOMENT
   According to an old English time unit, a moment takes 1½ minutes. In medieval times, a moment was either $1/40$ or $1/50$ hour, but by rabbinical reckoning a moment is precisely $1/1,080$ hour.

3. ALL THE TEA IN CHINA
   The United Nations Food and Agricultural Organization estimates that all the tea in China in 2004 amounted to 861,000 metric tons.

4. BY A HAIRBREADTH
   Although the breadth of a hair varies from head to head, the dictionary definition of hairbreadth is $1/48$ inch.

5. ONLY SKIN DEEP
   The depth of human skin ranges from $1/100$ inch on the eyelid to $1/5$ inch on the back.

6. EATS LIKE A HORSE
   A 1,200-pound horse eats about 15 pounds of hay and 9 pounds of grain each day. This amounts to $1/50$ of its own weight each day, or 7 times its own weight each year. The real gluttons in the animal kingdom are birds, who consume more than 90 times their own weight in food each year.

7. A PICTURE IS WORTH A THOUSAND WORDS
   The amount paid by magazines for photographs and for written articles varies widely. Both *Travel & Leisure* magazine and *Harper's* magazine pay an average of $350 for a photograph and $1 a word for articles. Based on that scale, a picture is worth 350 words. When *The Book of Lists* first studied this matter in 1978, a picture was worth 2,000 words.

8. QUICK AS A WINK
   The average wink, or corneal reflex blink, lasts $1/10$ second.

9. **QUICKER THAN YOU CAN SAY "JACK ROBINSON"**
When members of *The Book of Lists* staff were asked to say "Jack Robinson," their speed varied from ½ to 1 second. It is acknowledged that this may not be a representative sample of the world population.

10. **SELLING LIKE HOTCAKES**
Sales figures for the International House of Pancakes show that their 1,186 U.S. restaurants sold a total of more than 700 million pancakes in 2004.

11. **SINCE TIME IMMEMORIAL**
Time immemorial is commonly defined as beyond the memory of any living person, or a time extending so far back as to be indefinite. However, for the purposes of English law, a statute passed in 1275 decreed that time immemorial was any point in time prior to 1189, the year Richard I began his reign.

12. **KNEE HIGH TO A GRASSHOPPER**
According to Charles L. Hogue of the Los Angeles County Museum of Natural History, this figure necessarily depends upon the size of the grasshopper. For the average grasshopper, the knee-high measurement would be about ½ inch.

13. **HIGH AS A KITE**
The record for the greatest height attained by a single kite on a single line is 14,509 feet. The kite was flown by a group headed by Richard Synergy at Kincardine, Ontario, Canada, on August 12, 2000.

14. **FASTER THAN A SPEEDING BULLET**
The fastest bullet is a caliber .50 Saboted Light Armor Penetrator-Tracer M962. Used in M2 machine guns, it travels 4,000 feet per second. The fastest nonmilitary bullet is the .257 Weatherby Spire Point, which travels 3,825 feet per second.

15. **BLOOD IS THICKER THAN WATER**
In chemistry, water is given a specific gravity, or relative density, of 1.00, because it is used as the standard against which all other densities are measured. By comparison, blood has a specific gravity of 1.06—only slightly thicker than water.

16. **A KING'S RANSOM**
The largest king's ransom in history was raised by Richard the Lion-Hearted to obtain his release from the Holy Roman emperor Henry VI in 1194. The English people were forced to contribute almost 150,000 marks to free their sovereign. Nearly as large a ransom was raised by Atahualpa, king of the Incas, when he offered Pizarro a roomful of gold

and two roomfuls of silver for his release in 1532. At today's prices, that ransom would be worth more than $7 million. Unfortunately, it was not sufficient to buy Atahualpa his freedom; he was given a mock trial and executed.

13 Sayings of Woody Allen

Born Allen Konigsberg in Brooklyn on December 1, 1935, Allen began writing quips for gossip columnists at age 15. After graduating from high school, he landed a job writing for Sid Caesar's classic television comedy series *Your Show of Shows*. In 1961 he branched out from writing to stand-up comedy. He also wrote plays and screenplays before directing his first film, *What's Up, Tiger Lily?* in 1966. Among his many hits are *Annie Hall* (1977), *Manhattan* (1979), and *Hannah and Her Sisters* (1986).

1. "It seemed the world was divided into good and bad people. The good ones slept better . . . while the bad ones seemed to enjoy the waking hours much more." (*Side Effects*, 1981)

2. "Don't listen to what your schoolteachers tell you. Don't pay attention to that. Just see what they look like and that's how you know what life is really going to be like." (*Crimes and Misdemeanors*, 1990)

3. "[Intellectuals] are like the Mafia. They only kill their own." (*Stardust Memories*, 1980)

4. "Sun is bad for you. Everything our parents told us was good is bad. Sun, milk, red meat, college." (*Annie Hall*, 1977)

5. "The prettiest [girls] are almost always the most boring, and that is why some people feel there is no God." (*The Early Essays*, 1973)

6. "Sex alleviates tension and love causes it." (*A Midsummer Night's Sex Comedy*, 1982)

7. "There's nothing sexier than a lapsed Catholic." (*Alice*, 1990)

8. "Love is deep; sex is only a few inches." (*Bullets over Broadway*, 1994)

9. "I thought of that old joke. You know, this guy goes to a psychiatrist and says, 'Doc, my brother's crazy. He thinks he's a chicken.' And the doctor says, 'Why don't you turn him in?' And the guy says, 'I would but I need the eggs.' Well, I guess that's pretty much how I feel about relationships. You know, they're totally irrational and crazy and

absurd . . . but I guess we keep going through it because most of us need the eggs." (*Annie Hall*, 1977)

10. "To you, I'm an atheist . . . to God, I'm the loyal opposition." (*Stardust Memories*, 1980)

11. "I don't want to achieve immortality through my work. I want to achieve it through not dying."

12. "Someone once asked me if my dream was to live on in the hearts of my people, and I said I would like to live on in my apartment. And that's really what I would prefer." (1987)

13. "There's this old joke. Two elderly women are in a Catskills Mountain resort and one of 'em says: 'Boy, the food at this place is really terrible.' The other one says, 'Yeah, I know, and such small portions.' Well, that's essentially how I feel about life. Full of loneliness and misery and suffering and unhappiness, and it's all over much too quickly." (*Annie Hall*, 1977)

18 Sayings of Oscar Wilde

Born in Dublin and educated at Oxford, Wilde (1856–1900) wrote one novel, *The Picture of Dorian Gray*, and a number of successful plays, including *Lady Windermere's Fan* and *The Importance of Being Earnest*. Considered the master of social comedy, he was an expert of witty sayings and paradoxes. Even on his deathbed, as he sipped champagne, he quipped, "I am dying beyond my means."

1. Murder is always a mistake. One should never do anything that one cannot talk about after dinner.

2. I don't recognize you—I've changed a lot.

3. Always forgive your enemies—nothing annoys them so much.

4. The idea that is not dangerous is unworthy of being called an idea at all.

5. To love oneself is the beginning of a lifelong romance.

6. Anybody can sympathize with the sufferings of a friend, but it requires a very fine nature to sympathize with a friend's success.

7. When one is in love, one always begins by deceiving oneself: and one always ends by deceiving others. That is what the world calls a romance.

8. To get back my youth I would do anything in the world, except take exercise, get up early, or be respectable.

9. I can resist everything except temptation.

10. What is a cynic? a man who knows the price of everything and the value of nothing.

11. Experience is the name everyone gives to their mistakes.

12. We are all in the gutter, but some of us are looking at the stars.

13. There is a luxury in self-reproach. When we blame ourselves, we feel that no one else has a right to blame us.

14. Only dull people are brilliant at breakfast.

15. A cigarette is the perfect type of a perfect pleasure. It is exquisite, and it leaves one unsatisfied. What more can one want?

16. Nothing succeeds like excess.

17. In this world there are only two tragedies. One is not getting what one wants, and the other is getting it.

18. Education is an admirable thing, but it is well to remember from time to time that nothing that is worth knowing can be taught.

16 Well-Known Sayings Attributed to the Wrong Person

1. *Saying:* "Anybody who hates children and dogs can't be all bad."
Attributed to: W. C. Fields
Actually said by: Leo Rosten (at a dinner, introducing Fields): "Any man who hates dogs and babies can't be all bad."

2. *Saying:* Go west, young man!"
Attributed to: Horace Greeley
Actually said by: John Soule (article, *Terre Haute Express*, 1851)

3. *Saying:* "Everybody talks about the weather, but nobody does anything about it!"
Attributed to: Mark Twain

Actually said by: Charles Dudley Warner (editorial, *Hartford Courant*, August 24, 1897)

4. *Saying:* "Survival of the fittest."
   Attributed to: Charles Darwin
   Actually said by: Herbert Spencer (*Principles of Biology* and earlier works)

5. *Saying:* "That government is best which governs least."
   Attributed to: Thomas Jefferson
   Actually said by: Henry David Thoreau (who put it in quotation marks in "Civil Disobedience" and called it a motto)

6. *Saying:* "Cleanliness is next to godliness."
   Attributed to: Bible
   Actually said by: John Wesley (*Sermons*, no. 93, "On Dress")

7. *Saying:* "A journey of a thousand miles must begin with a single step."
   Attributed to: Confucius
   Actually said by: Lao-tzu (*Tao Te Ching*)

8. *Saying:* "God helps those who help themselves."
   Attributed to: Bible
   Actually said by: Aesop ("The gods help them that help themselves.")

9. *Saying:* "God is in the details."
   Attributed to: Ludwig Mies van der Rohe
   Actually said by: François Rabelais ("The good God is in the details.")

10. Saying: "If you can't stand the heat, get out of the kitchen."
    Attributed to: Harry S. Truman
    Actually said by: Harry Vaughn (Truman's friend, whom Truman was quoting)

11. *Saying:* "Promises are like pie crust, made to be broken."
    Attributed to: V. I. Lenin
    Actually said by: Jonathan Swift (*Polite Conversation:* "Promises are like pie crust, leaven to be broken.")

12. *Saying:* "Wagner's music is better than it sounds."
    Attributed to: Mark Twain
    Actually said by: Bill Nye

13. *Saying:* "When I hear the word *culture,* I reach for my gun."
    Attributed to: Hermann Göring
    Actually said by: Hanss Johst (1933 play *Schlageter:* "Whenever I hear the word 'culture,' I reach for my Browning.")

14. *Saying:* "Winning isn't everything, it's the only thing."
    Attributed to: Vince Lombardi
    Actually said by: Red Sanders (UCLA football coach; quoted in *Sports Illustrated*, 1955)

15. *Saying:* "Spare the rod and spoil the child."
    Attributed to: Bible
    Actually said by: Samuel Butler (*Hudribras*, 1664)

16. *Saying:* "Float like a butterfly, sting like a bee. Your hands can't hit what your eyes can't see."
    Attributed to: Muhammad Ali
    Actually said by: Drew "Bundini" Brown (Ali's good friend)

                                                                    C.F. & K.A.

17 Pairs of Contradictory Proverbs

1. Look before you leap.
   He who hesitates is lost.

2. If at first you don't succeed, try, try again.
   Don't beat your head against a stone wall.

3. Absence makes the heart grow fonder.
   Out of sight, out of mind.

4. Never put off till tomorrow what you can do today.
   Don't cross the bridge till you come to it.

5. Two heads are better than one.
   Paddle your own canoe.

6. Haste makes waste.
   Time waits for no man.

7. You're never too old to learn.
   You can't teach an old dog new tricks.

8. A word to the wise is sufficient.
   Talk is cheap.

9. It's better to be safe than sorry.
   Nothing ventured, nothing gained.

10. Don't look a gift horse in the mouth.
    Beware of Greeks bearing gifts.

11. Do unto others as you would have others do unto you.
    Nice guys finish last.

12. Hitch your wagon to a star.
    Don't bite off more than you can chew.

13. Many hands make light work.
    Too many cooks spoil the broth.

14. Don't judge a book by its cover.
    Clothes make the man.

15. The squeaking wheel gets the grease.
    Silence is golden.

16. Birds of a feather flock together.
    Opposites attract.

17. The pen is mightier than the sword.
    Actions speak louder than words.

J.Ba.

8 People Who Ate Their Own—or Others'—Words

1. **EMPEROR MENELIK II**
   Menelik was one of the greatest rulers in African history and the creator
   of modern Ethiopia. Born in 1844, he was captured during an enemy raid
   and held prisoner for 10 years. Escaping, he declared himself head of the
   Province of Shewa. He began conquering neighboring kingdoms and
   developed them into modern Ethiopia with himself as emperor. When
   Italy tried to take over Ethiopia, Menelik's army met and crushed the
   Italians at the Battle of Aduwa. This victory, as well as his efforts to
   modernize Ethiopia (with schools, telephones, railroads), made Menelik
   world-famous. The emperor had one little-known eccentricity. Whenever
   he was feeling ill, he would eat a few pages of the Bible, insisting that that
   always restored his health. One day in December 1913, recovering from a
   stroke and feeling extremely ill, he ate the entire Book of Kings torn from
   an Egyptian edition of the Bible, ate every page of it—and died. Too
   much of the Good Book had proved a bad thing.

2. **PHILIPP ANDREAS OLDENBURGER**
   This celebrated seventeenth-century German law instructor and
   political historian wrote a pamphlet that offended the authorities. He

was arrested and sentenced to eat his own writings. To make matters worse, "he was also flogged during his repast, with orders that the flogging should not cease until he had swallowed the last crumb."

3–4. TWO PAPAL DELEGATES

In 1370, the pope sent two of his delegates to Bernabò Visconti to serve him with a rolled parchment bearing a leaden seal and wrapped in a silk cord, informing him that he had been excommunicated. So infuriated was Bernabò Visconti that he put the two papal delegates under arrest and released them only after he had made them consume the parchment of excommunication, the leaden seal, and the silken cord.

5. THEODOR REINKING

Reinking was a Danish author at the time when Denmark was suffering oppression under Swedish rule. In 1644, he wrote a book in Latin, *Dania ad exteros de perfidia Suecorum,* that blasted the Swedes for the damage they had done to the Danes. The Swedes wasted no time in throwing Reinking into prison. After he had languished in prison several years, his jailors were ready to mete out his real punishment. He was given a choice: either eat his words or lose his head. Happily, Reinking kept his head—and ate his words, consuming the pages of his book "boiled in broth."

6. ERNST TOLLER

Born in 1893 in Samotschin, Prussia (now Poland), Toller studied law in France. With the outbreak of World War I, he fought for Germany, was wounded, and became an active pacifist. He was jailed for treason. Upon his release, he became a Communist, helped overthrow the Bavarian monarchy, and established a German soviet. When this fell apart, Toller was arrested again and sentenced to five years behind bars. In prison, he began to write and became one of Germany's leading playwrights with such dramas as *The Machine Wreckers, Hinkemann,* and *Hoppla! Such a Life!* He also wrote two autobiographical books, *I Was a German* and *Through the Bars.* Free of prison at 30, he saw the rise of Adolf Hitler and toured Russia and the United States making anti-Fascist speeches. In 1933, back in Germany, he was detained by the Nazis. Recalled Toller, "It was terrible and inhuman. The guards forced me to swallow almost a complete volume of one of my latest books." Exiled, Toller wound up in New York. Alone (his wife had left him for another man) and impoverished (he had given all his money to Spanish Civil War refugees), he committed suicide in his hotel room on May 22, 1939.

7. ISAAC VOLMAR

Author Volmar wrote several booklets in which he satirized the life and activities of Bernhard, Duke of Saxe-Meiningen. Not amused, the duke invited his writer-antagonist to dinner. At the table, according to Frederic R. Marvin, who recorded the incident in 1910, Volmar "was not allowed the courtesy of the kitchen, but was forced to swallow his literary productions uncooked."

8. BOB METCALF
People who make predictions that don't pan out are often said to eat their words. Metcalf, the founder of 3Com Corporation, is one of the few to take that phrase literally. In the December 1995 issue of *Info-World* magazine, he declared, "The Internet will collapse within a year." A year later, with the Internet busier than ever, Metcalf took his article, liquefied it in a blender, and ate it with a spoon.

I.W.

33 Names of Things You Never Knew Had Names

1. *AGLET*—The plain or ornamental covering on the end of a shoelace.

2. *ARMSAYE*—The armhole in clothing.

3. *CHANKING*—Spat-out food, such as rinds or pits.

4. *COLUMELLA NASI*—The bottom part of the nose between the nostrils.

5. *DRAGÉES*—Small beadlike pieces of candy, usually silver-colored, used for decorating cookies, cakes, and sundaes.

6. *FEAT*—A dangling curl of hair.

7. *FERRULE*—The metal band on a pencil that holds the eraser in place.

8. *HARP*—The small metal hoop that supports a lampshade.

9. *HEELTAP*—A small amount of liquid remaining in a glass after drinking.

10. *HEMIDEMISEMIQUAVER*—A 64th note. (A 32nd note is a demisemiquaver, and a 16th note is a semiquaver.)

11–14. *JARNS, NITTLES, GRAWLIX*, and *QUIMP*—Various squiggles used to denote cussing in comic books.

15. *KEEPER*—The loop on a belt that keeps the end in place after it has passed through the buckle.

16. *KICK* or *PUNT*—The indentation at the bottom of some wine bottles. It gives added strength to the bottle but lessens its holding capacity.

17. *MINIMUS*—The little finger or toe.

18. *OBDORMITION*—The numbness caused by pressure on a nerve; when a limb is "asleep."

19. *OCTOTHORPE*—The sound symbol on a telephone handset. Bell Labs' engineer Don Macpherson created the word in the 1960s by combining *octo-* (because the symbol has eight points) with the name of one of his favorite athletes, 1912 Olympic decathlon champion Jim Thorpe.

20. *OPHRYON*—The space between the eyebrows on a line with the top of the eye sockets.

21. *PEEN*—The end of a hammer head opposite the striking face.

22. *PHOSPHENES*—The lights you see when you close your eyes hard. Technically, the luminous impressions are due to the excitation of the retina caused by pressure on the eyeball.

23. *PURLICUE*—The space between the thumb and extended forefinger.

24. *RASCETA*—Creases on the inside of the wrist.

25. *ROWEL*—The revolving star on the back of a cowboy's spurs.

26. *SADDLE*—The rounded part on the top of a matchbook.

27. *SCROOP*—The rustle of silk.

28. *SNORKEL BOX*—A mailbox with a protruding receiver to allow people to deposit mail without leaving their cars.

29. *SPRAINTS*—Otter dung.

30. *SWARF*—Metallic particles removed by a cutting, grinding, or filing tool.

31. *TANG*—The projecting prong on a tool or instrument.

32. *WAMBLE*—Stomach rumbling.

33. *ZARF*—A holder for a handleless coffee cup.

S.B. & D.W.

7 Words in Which All the Vowels Appear in Alphabetical Order

1. *Abstemious*—Practicing temperance in living.
2. *Abstentious*—Characterized by abstinence.
3. *Annelidous*—Of the nature of an annelid.
4. *Arsenious*—Of, relating to, or containing arsenic.
5. *Casesious*—Having a blue color.
6. *Facetious*—Straining to be funny, especially at the wrong time.
7. *Fracedinous*—Productive of heat through putrefaction.

C.R.M.

17 Untranslatable Words

Here are 17 words and phrases that have no equivalent in English; edited by *Book of Lists* authors from Howard Rheingold's *They Have a Word for It*, published by Sarabande Books, and used by permission of the author.

1. *BILITA MPASH* (Bantu)
   This denotes blissful dreams. In English, we have nightmares but no word for waking feeling happy. In Bantu, the word is further defined as a "legendary, blissful state where all is forgiven and forgotten." The Afro-American equivalent for bilita mpash is "beluthathatchee," believed to be traced to Afro-American slang from its Bantu roots.

2. *BIRITULULO* (Kiriwana, New Guinea)
   Comparing yams to settle disputes. In New Guinean culture, the code of behavior is that nobody talks about what everybody knows concerning sensitive subjects. Breaking this code results in violent disputes. They present their yams at these moments. Yams are so important in Kiriwana that people boast about their own supply, to the point of violence. Settling the fights with yam displays calms everyone down.

3. *CAVOLI RISCALDATI* (Italian)
   The attempt to revive a dead love affair. Literally, "reheated cabbage." The result of such a culinary effort is usually unworkable, messy, and distasteful.

4. *DOHADA* (Sanskrit)
   Unusual appetites and cravings of pregnant women. *Dohada* is a word older than the English language. There is a scientific basis for dohada:

Women who want to eat dirt (a condition called pica) or chalk, for example, attempting to ingest essential minerals.

5. *DRACHENFUTTER* (German)
A gift brought home from a husband to his wife after he has stayed out late. Literally, "dragon fodder." In decades past, men went to bars on Saturday night with the wrapped gifts prepared in advance. This word can also be used for all gifts or acts performed out of guilt for having too much fun, such as gifts from employees to bosses, children to parents, and students to teachers.

6. *ESPRIT DE L'ESCALIER* (French)
The brilliantly witty response to a public insult that comes into your mind only after you have left the party. Literally, "the spirit of the staircase." Observes author Rheingold, "Sometimes, this feeling about what you ought to have said at a crucial moment can haunt you for the rest of your life."

7. *HARI KUYO* (Japanese)
A hari kuyo is a shrine for broken sewing needles. In Japan's Wakayama Province, every village has a shrine where a periodic service is performed for the broken needles. The belief is that the sewing needles worked hard all their lives and died in the service of those who used them. When they break, they are put to rest on a soft bed of tofu.

8. *KATZENJAMMER* (German)
A monumentally severe hangover. The inspiration for the early American comic strip "The Katzenjammer Kids." On New Year's Eve, it is common for one German to remark to another, "You're setting yourself up for a real Katzenjammer." (The party in question may require some Drachenfutter.)

9. *KYOIKUMAMA* (Japanese)
A mother who pushes her children into academic achievement. A derogatory term that literally means "education mama." The pressure on Japanese students is severe and intense—but they are hardly the only victims of parental pushing. The American fad for using flashcards to create infant prodigies, for example, is practiced by fathers and mothers.

10. *NAKHES* (Yiddish)
A mixture of pleasure and pride, particularly the kind that a parent gets from a child. It is something one relishes, as in "May you only get nakhes from your son!"

11. *ONDINNONK* (Iroquoian)
This is a noun that describes the soul's innermost desires; the angelic parts of human nature. Listening to one's inner instinct to perform a kindly act is letting our ondinnonks be our guide.

12. *PALAYI* (Bantu)
A mythical monster that scratches at the door. The very same monster is said to haunt the doors of South Carolina, America, and West Africa.

13. *QUALQUNQUISMO* (Italian)
This describes an attitude of indifference to political and social issues. It is derived from a satirical political journal called "L'umo qualcune": The man in the street. For example, a great many people believe that the U.S. president is elected by a majority of the voting-age population. In fact, only 30 percent of Americans aged 18 or older voted for George Bush in 2004.

14. *SALOGOK* (Eskimo)
Salogok is young black ice. It is a famous fact that Eskimos have 17 different words for kinds of snow. In *Hunters of the Northern Ice*, a book by Richard K. Nelson, there is an appendix on Eskimo ice words titled "Eskimo Sea-Ice Terminology." A sample from this work is "*Salogok:* nilas, or black young ice: a thin, flexible sheet of newly formed ice which will not support a man, is weak enough to enable seals to break through it with their heads to breathe, and breaks through with one firm thrust of the unaak."

15. *SCHADENFREUDE* (German)
The literal translation is "shameful joy." It is the joy one feels as a result of someone else's misfortune, like seeing a rival slip on a banana peel. Schadenfreude is not as strong as taking revenge, because it's a thought or a feeling, not an action. But when your noisy neighbor's car breaks down, and you're secretly pleased—that's schadenfreude.

16. *TARTLE* (Scottish)
To hesitate in recognizing a person or thing, as happens when you are introduced to someone whose name you cannot recall. A way out of this social gaffe is to say, "Pardon my sudden tartle!"

17. *ZALATWIC* (Polish)
Zalatwic means using acquaintances to accomplish things unofficially. It means going around the system to trade, to avoid exchanges in cash. Since shortages seem to be a fact of social life, these exchanges can range from the profound (a new apartment) to the menial (a new pair of sneakers or trainers).

22 Obscure and Obsolete Words

The average adult recognizes 30,000 to 50,000 words, but uses only 10,000 to 15,000. However, there are actually about a million words in the English language, some of which—although obscure, forgotten, or rarely used—are worth reviving.

1. *BOANTHROPY*—A type of insanity in which a man thinks he is an ox.

2. *CHANTEPLEURE*—To sing and weep at the same time.

3. *DIBBLE*—To drink like a duck, lifting up the head after each sip.

4. *EOSOPHOBIA*—Fear of dawn.

5. *EUGERIA*—Normal and happy old age.

6. *EUNEIROPHRENIA*—Peace of mind after a pleasant dream.

7. *EYESERVICE*—Work done only when the boss is watching.

8. *FELLOWFEEL*—To crawl into the skin of another person so as to share his feelings; to empathize with.

9. *GROAK*—To watch people silently while they are eating, hoping they will ask you to join them.

10. *GYNOTIKOLOBOMASSOPHILE*—One who likes to nibble on a woman's earlobes.

11. *HEBEPHRENIC*—A condition of adolescent silliness.

12. *IATROGENIC*—Illness or disease caused by doctors or by prescribed treatment.

13. *LAPLING*—Someone who enjoys resting in women's laps.

14. *LIBBERWORT*—Food or drink that makes one idle and stupid, food of no nutritional value, "junk food."

15. *MEUPAREUNIA*—A sexual act gratifying to only one participant.

16. *NEANIMORPHIC*—Looking younger than one's years.

17. *ONIOCHALASIA*—Buying as a means of mental relaxation.

18. *PARNEL*—A priest's mistress.

19. *PILGARLIC*—A bald head that looks like a peeled garlic.

20. *PREANTEPENULTIMATE*—Fourth from last.

21. *RESISTENTIALISM*—Seemingly spiteful behavior manifested by inanimate objects.

22. *SUPPEDANEUM*—A foot support for crucifix victims.

13 Colorful "Aniverbs"

Human behavior can often be described most vividly by using a verb derived from the name of an animal. The following is a list of 13 animals that have become "aniverbs":

1. *APE*—To mimic.
   A small child sometimes will ape his parents' worst actions, much to their chagrin.

2. *BADGER*—To harry or pester.
   The housewife finally badgered her husband into taking out the garbage by dumping it in his lap.

3. *CROW*—To exult, gloat, or brag.
   After unexpectedly beating his son at tennis, the old man crowed about it to anyone who would listen.

4. *DOG*—To track or trail persistently.
   Whenever he appears in public, the president is dogged by reporters.

5. *FOX*—To trick by using ingenuity or cunning.
   The 15-year-old boy foxed his way into the theater to see the X-rated movie by wearing a fake mustache and beard.

6. *HORSE*—To engage in rowdy, prankish play.
   The children horsed around the pool all day and succeeded in getting the adults thoroughly wet.

7. *MONKEY*—To play or tamper with something.
   The two little boys monkeyed with their mother's watch until it was damaged beyond repair.

8. *PIG*—To eat ravenously or to gorge oneself.
   After his disappointment, the young boy pigged out on pizza and chocolate ice cream.

9. *RAT*—To betray one's associates by giving information.
   The thief ratted out his buddies to the police in exchange for a promise that he would not be arrested.

10. *SNAKE*—To move, crawl, or drag with a snakelike movement.
    The peeping Tom snaked his way through the bushes in order to get a better view.

11. *WEASEL*—To be evasive.
    Politicians often weasel their way out of answering tough questions by asking another question.

12. *WHALE*—To thrash.
    The young lady whaled the young man for making improper advances on their first date.

13. *WOLF*—To eat voraciously.
    He overslept this morning, so he wolfed down a doughnut and a cup of coffee before leaving for work.

F.H.

33 Words Rarely Used in Their Positive Form

Positive Form	Negative Form
1. *Advertent* (giving attention; heedful)	*Inadvertent*
2. *Algesia* (sensitiveness to pain)	*Analgesia*
3. *Biotic* (of or relating to life)	*Antibiotic*
4. *Canny* (Scot.: free from weird qualities or unnatural powers)	*Uncanny*
5. *Clement* (of weather: mild)	*Inclement*
6. *Conscionable* (conscientious)	*Unconscionable*
7. *Consolate* (consoled, comforted)	*Disconsolate*
8. *Corrigible* (correctable)	*Incorrigible*
9. *Couth* (marked by finesse, polish, etc.; smooth)	*Uncouth*
10. *Delible* (capable of being deleted)	*Indelible*
11. *Descript* (described; inscribed)	*Nondescript*
12. *Domitable* (tamable)	*Indomitable*
13. *Effable* (capable of being uttered or expressed)	*Ineffable*

14. *Evitable* (avoidable) — Inevitable
15. *Feckful* (efficient, sturdy, powerful) — Feckless
16. *Furl* (to draw in and secure to a staff) — Unfurl
17. *Gruntle* (to put in good humor) — Disgruntle
18. *Gust* (inclination, liking) — Disgust
19. *Infectant* (an agent of infection) — Disinfectant
20. *Kempt* (neatly kept, trim) — Unkempt
21. *Licit* (not forbidden by law; allowable) — Illicit
22. *Maculate* (marked with spots; besmirched) — Immaculate
23. *Nocuous* (likely to cause injury; harmful) — Innocuous
24. *Odorant* (an odorous substance) — Deodorant
25. *Peccable* (liable or prone to sin) — Impeccable
26. *Pervious* (of a substance that can be penetrated or permeated) — Impervious
27. *Placable* (of a tolerant nature; tractable) — Implacable
28. *Ruly* (orderly) — Unruly
29. *Ruthful* (full of compassion or pity) — Ruthless
30. *Sipid* (affecting the organs of taste; savory) — Insipid
31. *Speakable* (capable of being spoken) — Unspeakable
32. *Vincible* (capable of being conquered) — Invinicle
33. *Wieldy* (strong, manageable) — Unwieldy

R.A.

Leo Rosten's
13 Favorite Yiddish Words or Phrases

Born April 11, 1908, Leo Rosten was a novelist, journalist, humorist, social scientist, essayist, and social commentator. He served as professor and lecturer at various universities and authored numerous screenplays in the 1940s and 1950s. His love of language, especially verbal humor, is evident in many of his books: *The Education of Hyman Kaplan, The Mischief of Language, Leo Rosten's Treasury of Jewish Quotations, The Joys of Yiddish,* and *The Joys of Yinglish.* Leo Rosten died February 19, 1997. He contributed the following list to *The Book of Lists* in 1993.

ROSTEN NOTES: Many of my favorite Yiddish words are already part of demotic English—due to television, movies, talk shows, etc. For example: *bagel, chutzpa, noodge, blintz, shtik, yenta,* and *lox* are found in many recent English dictionaries and in the trade argot of Broadway, the badinage of nightclub routines, and (most important) television. Yiddish words continue to infiltrate English (and American English) simply because they convey a flavor, an irony, a nuance or colorful, sarcastic tone not found in their nearest English equivalent. Examples:

1. *SHMOOZ* (or *shmooze,* or *shmues*)—Formally, unimportant gossip; but briskly used as a wholly unstructured, lingering, heart-to-heart exchange of intimate news, confidences, complaints, etc. "We had a good long shmooz about the children and Harry and Celia—and *did* you notice the way she decorated her new living room?"

2. *TUMMLER*—An energetic, ever-active stirrer-up of things. A go-getter, often out for his own *gelt.* One who stirs things up. A *makher* or *macher* (maker of things happening). A live wire. A noisemaker. A clown.

3. *FONFER*—Originally, one who talks through his (or her) nose. More common these days, a blabbermouth, a promiser who does not come through, an exaggerator, a constant gossip and tale spreader; usually, an unsuccessful optimist.

4. *SACHEL* (or *tsachel*)—Sense, common sense, good judgment. "Jack has the imagination, but for real *sachel,* listen to what Sam suggests." *Sachel* is an exceptionally rare attribute—especially in a complicated world.

5. *KLUTZ*—From German meaning "a leg." A heavy-handed, clumsy, oaflike character, lacking in sensitivity, charm, wit, or ingenuity. Never take a klutz to a ballet.

6. *PASKUDNYAK*—I have searched for decades for a word remotely like *paskudnyak* (or its adjectival derivative *paskudne*) with woeful results. This word describes a thoroughly unpleasant, uncouth, unreliable perpetrator of the tactless or the tasteless. He can ruin any dinner party or offend even the most gracious hostess. He is often a guiltless liar, a cheat—in any case, a thoroughly undesirable, offensive no-goodnik.

7. *NARR*—A simple enough word with, oh, such a panoply of meaning! A *narr* is a fool. In our circles, he was more likely to be a fool's fool. Unlike the gallery of characters above, *narr* may convey sympathy, or regret—but not any of the tactless, foolish, gormless (walk down Piccadilly) traits that flourish in a community where *naronim* (plural) are simply simpleminded souls. A Talmudic gloss tells me "Against a *narr,* even the Lord Himself is helpless."

8. *CHAUCHEM* (Hebrew)—A wise man; a real expert, authority, man of judgment.

9. *KOCHLEFFEL* (German)—A stirrer-up of things; a hot potato; mischief maker.

10. *K'NOCKER*—A big shot who acts like one, shows off, puts on an egotistical show of importance that turns out to be mostly braggadocio.

11. *KVETCH*—Literally, to squeeze. As used, a chronic complainer, alibiist; a perpetual wet blanket; this is a marvelously mimetic word for anyone who frets, gripes, derides, and sour-pusses—for no reason other than psychological necessity. His function in life seems to be to darken the mood, or decrease the pleasure, of everyone else.

12. *FARTOOST* (a pip from German)—Mixed-up, confused, befuddled. An excellent synonym for *farchadat, farmisht, tsedoodelt.*

13. *KOSHER* (or not kosher)—According to dietary laws; strictly ethical; honest, honorable, reliable; right on the mark. "Not kosher" means something is awry—not strictly legal, cutting corners, tricky, deceptive.

Willard R. Espy's
10 Ugliest Words in the English Language
That Are Not Indecent

Born December 11, 1910, Willard R. Espy had a multifaceted career as a reporter, editor, publisher, radio interviewer, public relations manager for *Reader's Digest,* and panelist on the *Harper Dictionary of Contemporary Usage.* His books include *The Game of Words* (1972), *O Thou Improper, Thou Uncommon Noun* (1978), *The Garden of Eloquence* (1983), *Words Gotten Out* (1989), and *Skullduggery on Shoalwater Bay* (1998). Espy died in 1999. He contributed the following list to *The Book of Lists* in 1993.

MR. ESPY NOTES: A while back, A. Ross Eckler, editor of the journal of linguistics *Word Ways,* asked his readers to send me what they considered to be the 10 ugliest words in English. Dozens obliged. I made a list of their choices and forwarded them—more than 200 reeking specimens—to knowledgeable friends for additions and a vote. The vote was lopsided—and every one of the 10 winning candidates was a word that until recently was taboo in polite conversation.

That is not the way I had planned things. I turned to the 10 runners-up, only to find almost all of them equally indecent. I determined then to confine my quest to words that were innocuous in meaning, however they sounded. These ranked far down the list—but here they are.

I think there is a lesson to be drawn. Clearly, meaning eclipses sound (gutturals, clashing consonants, and the like) in the measurement of a word's ugliness. *Gonorrhea* and *diarrhea* would ring like church chimes in our ears if we did not know what they signified. A single suggestive syllable—the *fruc* in *fructify*, for instance, or the *pus* in *crepuscular*—can turn an otherwise charming sound into an insult to the eardrums. *Yearn*, *kiss*, and *shrine* are worshipful; the nearly indistinguishable *urine*, *piss*, and *slime* are loathsome.

Mind you, the 10 words listed below are quite ugly enough for most of us:

1. *FRUCTIFY*—To make fruitful.
2. *KUMQUAT*—A kind of small yellow to orange citrus fruit.
3. *QUAHOG*—A thick-shelled American clam.
4. *CREPUSCULAR*—Relating to or like twilight.
5. *KAKKAK*—A small bittern of Guam.
6. *GARGOYLE*—A gutter spout shaped like a grotesque figure.
7. *CACOPHONOUS*—Harsh-sounding.
8. *AASVOGEL*—An African vulture.
9. *BROBDINGNAGIAN*—Marked by tremendous size.
10. *JUKEBOX*—A cabinet player and records activated by inserting a coin.

CHAPTER SIXTEEN

Sports

7 BIZARRE SPORTS EVENTS

10 OLYMPIC CONTROVERSIES

13 OLYMPIC MEDALISTS WHO ACTED IN MOVIES

COACH JOHN WOODEN'S 10 RULES TO LIVE BY

ARNOLD PALMER'S 18 BEST GOLF HOLES IN THE U.S.

6 NON-BOXERS WHO TOOK ON THE CHAMPIONS

6 FAMOUS PEOPLE WHO INVENTED GAMES

6 UNUSUAL DUELS

TOMMY SMITH AND JOHN CARLOS
© Bettman/Corbis

7 Bizarre Sports Events

1. ROCK, PAPER, SCISSORS

The venerable sport of rock, paper, scissors (rock smashes scissors; scissors cuts paper; paper wraps rock) finally found its place on the world calendar in 2002, with the inauguration of the first international championships. Held in Toronto, Canada, the 2004 competition was won by Canadian Lee Rammage. For information, see www.rpschamps.com.

2. ROBOT SOCCER

RoboCup 2005, held in Osaka, Japan, brought together dozens of robot soccer teams from nations as far afield as Iran, Latvia, Chile, China, Australia, and the United States, although most of the leading entries were from Germany and Japan. Robot teams compete in four senior divisions, including Four-Legged Robot League and Humanoid League, the only category in which the robots are guided by humans with hand-held controllers. For information, see www.robocup.org.

3. ONE-HOLE GOLF TOURNAMENT

The annual Elfego Baca golf tournament (named after a colorful New Mexico lawyer and politician) consists of only one hole—but it's not your typical hole. The tee is placed on top of Socorro Peak, 7,243 feet above sea level. The hole, which is actually a patch of dirt 60 feet in diameter, is two and a half miles away and 2,550 feet below. The course record, 9, is held by Mike Stanley, who has won the tournament 15 times. The first competition was held in 1960. The 2005 competition was won by Caleb Gonzales with 13 shots. For information, write to New Mexico Tech Golf Course, 801 Leroy Place, Socorro, NM 87801 USA.

4. LAWN MOWER RACING

The first national lawn mower racing championship was held in Grayslake, Illinois, during the Labor Day weekend of 1992. The event was surprisingly controversial. The outdoor Power Equipment Institute, a trade association that represents lawn mower manufacturers, formally opposed the concept of lawn mower racing because it does not promote "the effective and safe use of outdoor power equipment." Nonetheless, 3,000 spectators had a good time, and the proceeds from admissions went to fight Lou Gehrig's disease. Since then, lawn mower racing has spread throughout North America. For information, write to the U.S. Lawn Mower Racing Association, 1812 Glenview Rd., Glenview, IL 60025, USA, or see www.letsmow.com.

5. STONE THROW

The Unspunnen Festival celebrating Swiss costume and folklore has been held irregularly since 1805. One of the highlights of the festival is the throwing of the 185-pound (83.5-kilogram) Unspunnen Stone. The record throw is 11 feet 2 inches (3.61 meters), set by Josef Küttel of Vitznau at the 1981 festival. The most recent festival was held in September 2005. For information, write to Schweizerisches Trachten und Alphirtenfest, Unspennen Geschäftsstelle, P.O. Box Harderstrasse, 3800 Interlaken, Switzerland or see www.unspunnenfest.ch.

6. NONVIOLENT HUNTING TOURNAMENT
Archers who don't like to kill animals can enter the National Field Archery Association's 3-D tournaments held throughout the United States. Competitors take aim at life-size dummies of deer, bears, mountain lions, wild pigs, and wild turkeys. There are numerous divisions for men and women of all ages, using equipment ranging from traditional—with no sights, stabilizers, wheels, and cams—to compound bow, which allows sights, stabilizers, wheels, and cams. For information, write to National Field Archery Association, 31407 Outer I-10, Redlands, CA 92373, USA, or see www.fieldarchery.org.

7. WATERLESS REGATTA
The Henley-on-Todd Regatta is held each October at Alice Springs in the Northern Territory of Australia as an alternative to England's famous Henley-on-Thames Regatta. The main difference between the two events is that Alice Springs is almost a thousand miles from the nearest large body of water. The canoes are bottomless, allowing the crew members to run along the dry riverbed. For more information, write to Scott Boocock, Action EnterprisesPromotions & Marketing Henley on Todd, PO Box 1385, Alice Springs NT 0871, Australia.

10 Olympic Controversies

1. CRUISING TO THE FINISH LINE (1904 marathon)
The first runner to enter the Olympic stadium at the end of the 1904 marathon was Fred Lorz of New York. He was hailed as the winner, photographed with the daughter of the president of the United States, and was about to be awarded the gold medal when it was discovered that he had stopped running after nine miles and hitched a ride in a car for eleven miles before returning to the course. Lorz was disqualified, and the victory was given to Thomas Hicks. Although this was only the third Olympic marathon, Lorz was not the first person to cheat in this way. In the inaugural marathon in 1896, Spiridon Belokas of Greece crossed the finish line in third place but was disqualified when it was discovered that he had ridden part of the way in a carriage.

2. **WITH TOO MUCH HELP FROM HIS FRIENDS** (1908 marathon)
Italian Dorando Pietri was the first marathon runner to enter the
stadium in London in 1908, but he was dazed and headed in the wrong
direction. Track officials pointed him the right way. But then he
collapsed on the track. He rose but collapsed again . . . and again and
again. Finally, the officials, fearful that "he might die in the very
presence of the Queen," carried him across the finish line. This aid led
to his disqualification, and the gold medal went to John Hayes of the
United States.

3. **CHAMPION WITH A DARK SECRET** (1932 and 1936 women's
100 meters)
Competing for Poland, Stella Walsh won the 100 meters in 1932,
equaling the world record three times in the process. Four years later,
at the Berlin Olympics, she was beaten into second place by American
Helen Stephens. A Polish journalist accused Stephens of being a man in
disguise. German officials examined her and issued a statement that
Stephens was definitely a woman. Forty-four years later, in 1980,
Walsh, by then an American citizen living in Cleveland, was shot to
death when she stumbled into the middle of a robbery attempt at a
discount store. An autopsy concluded that although Helen Stephens
may not have had male sexual organs, Stella Walsh did. All the while
she was winning medals and setting records in women's events, she was,
by today's rules, a man.

4. **CLOCK VS. EYES** (1960 100-meter freestyle)
Swimmer Lance Larson of the United States appeared to edge John
Devitt of Australia for first place in the 1960 100-meter freestyle. Devitt
congratulated Larson and left the pool in disappointment. Larson's
official time was 55.1 seconds, and Devitt's was 55.2 seconds. Of the
three judges assigned the task of determining who finished first, two
voted for Larson, but the three second-place judges also voted 2–1 for
Larson. In other words, of the six judges, three thought Larson had won
and three thought Devitt had won. The chief judge gave the victory to
Devitt, and four years of protests failed to change the results.

5. **THE FOG OF WAR** (1968 slalom)
French skier Jean-Claude Killy, competing at home in Grenoble, had
already won two gold medals and needed only to win the slalom to
complete a sweep of the men's Alpine events. His main challenge was
expected to come from Karl Schranz of Austria. But something curious
happened as Schranz sped through the fog. According to Schranz, a
mysterious figure in black crossed the course in front of him. Schranz
skidded to a halt and demanded a rerun. His request was granted, and
he beat Killy's time and was declared the winner. But two hours later, it

was announced that Schranz had been disqualified because he had missed two gates before his encounter with the mysterious interloper. At a four-hour meeting of the Jury of Appeal, the Austrians said that if Schranz missed a gate or two it was because a French soldier or policeman had purposely interfered with him. The French claimed that Schranz had made up the whole story to cover up the fact that he had missed a gate. The jury voted 3–1 for Killy with one abstention.

6. **EXTRA SHOT** (1972 basketball)
Since basketball was first included in the Olympic program in 1936, teams from the United States had gone undefeated, winning 62 straight games over a 36-year period . . . until the 1972 final against the USSR. In an era before professionals were allowed in the Olympics, and with most of the best American college players taking a pass, the U.S. team was hard-pressed against the seasoned veterans of the Soviet squad. The Americans trailed throughout and did not take their first lead, 50–49, until there were only three seconds left in the game. Two seconds later, the head referee, noting a disturbance at the scorer's table, called an administrative time-out. The officials in charge had failed to notice that the Soviet coach, Vladimir Kondrashkin, had called a time-out. With one second on the clock, the USSR was awarded its time-out. When play resumed, they inbounded the ball, and time ran out. The U.S. players began a joyous celebration, but then R. William Jones, the British secretary-general of the International Amateur Basketball Federation, ordered the clock set back to three seconds, the amount of time remaining when Kondrashkin originally tried to call time-out. Ivan Edeshko threw a long pass to Sasha Belov, who scored the winning basket. The United States filed a protest, which was heard by a five-man Jury of Appeal. Three members of the jury were from Communist countries, and all three voted to give the victory to the USSR. With the final vote 3–2, the United States lost an Olympic basketball game for the first time.

7. **WIRED FOR VICTORY** (1976 team modern pentathlon)
The favored team from the USSR was fencing against the team from Great Britain when the British pentathletes noticed something odd about Soviet army major Borys Onyshchenko. Twice the automatic light registered a hit for Onyshchenko even though he had not touched his opponent. Onyshchenko's sword was taken away to be examined by the Jury of Appeal. An hour later, Onyshchenko was disqualified. Evidently, he had wired his sword with a well-hidden push-button circuit breaker that enabled him to register a hit whenever he wanted. He was forever after known as Borys Dis-Onyshchenko.

8. **THE UNBEATABLE PARK SI-HUN** (1988 light-middleweight boxing)
The 1988 Summer Olympics were held in Seoul, South Korea, and the

Koreans were determined to win gold medals in boxing, one of their strongest sports. This determination turned excessive in the case of light-middleweight Park Si-Hun. Park made it to the final with a string of four controversial victories, including one in which he disabled his opponent with a low blow to the kidney. In the final, he faced a slick, 19-year-old American named Roy Jones, Jr. Jones dominated all three rounds, landing 86 punches to Park's 32. Yet three of the five judges awarded the decision to Park, who won the gold medal. Park himself apologized to Jones. Accusations of bribery lingered for years, and it was not until 1997 that an inquiry by the International Olympic Committee concluded that no bribe had occurred.

9. **SCORING SCANDAL SYNCS SWIMMER** (1992 solo synchronized swimming)
In 1992, the two leading synchronized swimmers were Sylvie Fréchette of Canada and Kristen Babb-Sprague of the United States. The competition included a round of figures that counted for 50 percent of the final score. Fréchette, who was strong in figures, hoped to pick up points to offset the gains that Babb-Sprague was expected to make with her free routine. But one of the five judges, Ana Maria da Silviera of Brazil, gave Fréchette's albatross spin of 180° the unusually low score of 8.7. She immediately tried to change the score, claiming she had pushed the wrong button. But before the referee could be notified, the judges' scores were displayed, and, according to the rules, that meant they could not be changed. When the free routine was completed the next day, it turned out that da Silviera's low score provided the margin of victory that gave the gold medal to Babb-Sprague. Fourteen months later, the International Swimming Federation awarded Fréchette a belated gold medal, while allowing Babb-Sprague to retain hers.

10. **IMPAIRED JUDGMENT** (2002 pairs figure skating)
The sport of figure skating has a long history of judging controversies, but the problem reached a head at the Salt Lake City Olympics. Russian skaters had won 10 straight Olympic championships in the pairs event. In 2002, Russians Elena Berezhnaya and Anton Sikharulidze were in first place after the short program, with Jamie Salé and David Pelletier of Canada in second. In the free skate, the Russians made a series of technical errors, while the Canadians skated a clean program. Nonetheless, the judges voted 5–4 to award the gold medals to Berezhnaya and Sikharulidze. The ensuing outrage expressed by the North American media was so great and so prolonged that the International Olympic Committee pressured the International Skating Union into giving a second set of gold medals to Salé and Pelletier. Subsequent investigations revealed behind-the-scenes deals among judges and even possible involvement of organized crime figures. Lost in the uproar was the possibility that the five judges who voted for the Russian pair simply

preferred their traditional balletic style and considered the exuberance of Salé and Pelletier's performance to be glitzy and too "Hollywood."

13 Olympic Medalists Who Acted in Movies

1. **JOHNNY WEISSMULLER** (4 golds; 1924 and 1928 swimming)
   While swimming at a club on Sunset Boulevard in Hollywood, Weissmuller was invited to try out for the part of Tarzan. In 1932, he made his film debut in *Tarzan, the Ape Man*. He eventually starred in 11 more Tarzan films.

2. **HERMAN BRIX** (silver; 1928 shot put)
   Brix changed his name to Bruce Bennett and pursued a successful career that included performances in *Mildred Pierce* (1945) and *The Treasure of the Sierra Madre* (1948). He also acted in such clunkers as *The Alligator People* (1959) and *The Fiend of Dope Island* (1961).

3. **BUSTER CRABBE** (gold; 1932 400-meter freestyle)
   Crabbe won his gold medal by one tenth of a second. He later recalled that that tenth of a second led Hollywood producers to discover "latent histrionic abilities in me." In 1933, he made his film debut as Karpa the Lion Man, in *King of the Jungle*. He eventually appeared in 53 movies but is best known for his roles as Flash Gordon and Buck Rogers.

4. **HELENE MADISON** (gold; 1932 100-meter freestyle)
   Madison, who once set 16 world records in 16½ months, was invariably described by sportswriters as "shapely." After her Olympic triumph, she played an Amazon captain of the guards in the 1933 satire *The Warrior's Husband*. Unfortunately, her performance was undistinguished, and she never acted again.

5. **SONJA HENIE** (3 golds; 1928, 1932, and 1936 figure skating)
   Henie's first film, *One in a Million* (1937), was a box-office winner, and nine more followed. Although her acting was never as smooth as her skating, her Hollywood career brought her great financial success.

6–7. **GLENN MORRIS** (gold; 1936 decathlon) and **ELEANOR HOLM** (gold; 1932 100-meter backstroke).
   Tarzan's Revenge (1938) starred two Olympic champions as Tarzan and Jane. Unfortunately, Holm was described as looking "bored" throughout the film, and reviewers found Morris's performance "disappointing" and "listless." Holm never acted again.

8. HAROLD SAKATA (silver; 1948 light-heavyweight weightlifting)
   After the Olympics, Sakata pursued a successful career as a professional wrestler and then moved on to acting. He appeared in eight films, but it was his first role that gained him international stardom—the evil Oddjob in *Goldfinger* (1964).

9. CAROL HEISS (gold; 1960 figure skating)
   Heiss, described by *Variety* as "a fetching lass," made her film debut in the title role in *Snow White and the Three Stooges* (1961). The film was panned, but she received praise for her acting, her singing, and, of course, her skating. However, she never appeared in another movie.

10. JEAN-CLAUDE KILLY (3 golds; 1968 Alpine skiing)
    Killy costarred as a con-man ski instructor in the mediocre 1972 film *Snow Job.*

11. CORNISHMAN V (2 golds; 1968 and 1972 three-day event)
    The only nonhuman Olympic medalist to pursue a successful film career, Cornishman V helped two different riders to victory in equestrian events. He later appeared in *Dead Cert* (1974), based on a Dick Francis novel, and *International Velvet* (1978).

12. BRUCE JENNER (gold; 1976 decathlon)
    Jenner's one and only film appearance was in the loud and awful 1980 film *Can't Stop the Music*. He played a staid lawyer who is drawn into the irresistibly fun New York disco scene.

13. MARK BRELAND (gold; 1984 welterweight boxing)
    Breland is one of the few athletes to appear in a movie before he appeared in the Olympics. In 1983, he received good reviews for his role in *The Lords of Discipline*. He played the first black cadet at a southern military academy.

Note: Among the dozens of other Olympic athletes who have appeared in movies are 1924 pole-vault champion Lee Barnes, who served as a stand-in stuntman for Buster Keaton in *College* (1972); 1948 and 1952 decathlon champion Bob Mathias, who appeared in four films, including *It Happened in Athens* (1962) with Jayne Mansfield; and 1952 and 1956 triple jump champion Adhemar Ferreira da Silva, who appeared in the internationally acclaimed film *Black Orpheus* (1958). Ken Richmond, who won a bronze medal as a wrestler in 1952, was better known as the muscleman who struck the gong at the beginning of J. Arthur Rank films.

Coach John Wooden's
10 Rules to Live By

John Wooden, head basketball coach at UCLA from 1948 to 1975, once defined success as the peace of mind "that comes from knowing you did your best to become the best that you are capable of becoming."

1. 1 Corinthians 13. (This Bible chapter addresses the importance of charity—love—and ends with the verse, "And now abideth faith, hope, charity, these three; but the greatest of these is charity.")

2. Make each day your masterpiece.

3. Drink deeply from good books.

4. Freedom from desire leads to inner peace. (Lao-tzu)

5. Failure to prepare is preparing to fail. I will get ready and then, perhaps, my chance will come.

6. Ability may get you to the top, but it takes character to keep you there. (Abraham Lincoln)

7. Help others.

8. It is better to trust and be disappointed occasionally than to distrust and be miserable all the time.

9. Almost anyone can stand adversity, but to test a person's character, give them power. (Abraham Lincoln)

10. Be more interested in your character, which is what you really are, than in your reputation, which is what others perceive you to be.

Arnold Palmer's
18 Best Golf Holes in the U.S.

Born September 10, 1929, legendary golfer Arnold Palmer first came to prominence on the links with his 1954 victory in the U.S. Amateur Championship, which led him to turn pro just a few months later. From 1960 to 1963, he won 29 of his titles and collected over $400,000; he was voted Athlete of the Decade in 1969 by the Associated Press. Palmer is the author of several books, including *Arnold Palmer's Golf Book* (1961) and *Play Great Golf* (1987).

1. 12th hole, Augusta National Golf Club, Augusta, Georgia
2. 15th hole, Oakmont Country Club, Oakmont, Pennsylvania
3. 18th hole, Laurel Valley Golf Club, Ligonier, Pennsylvania
4. 12th hole, Southern Hills Country Club, Tulsa, Oklahoma
5. 11th hole, Composite Course, The Country Club, Brookline, Massachusetts
6. 8th hole, Pebble Beach Golf Links, Pebble Beach, California
7. 17th hole, Cypress Point Club, Pebble Beach, California
8. 13th hole, East Course, Merion Golf Club, Ardmore, Pennsylvania
9. 17th hole, Bay Hill Club, Orlando, Florida
10. 13th hole, Augusta National Golf Club, Augusta, Georgia
11. 2nd hole, No. 3 Course, Medinah Country Club, Medinah, Illinois
12. 16th hole, Oakland Hills Country Club, Birmingham, Michigan
13. 15th hole, Seminole Golf Club, Palm Beach, Florida
14. 14th hole, Champions Golf Club, Houston, Texas
15. 4th hole, Lower Course, Baltusrol Golf Club, Springfield, New Jersey
16. 16th hole, South Course, Firestone Country Club, Akron, Ohio
17. 17th hole, Cherry Hills Country Club, Denver, Colorado
18. 16th hole, Lake Course, Olympic Club, San Francisco, California

6 Non-Boxers Who Took On the Champions

1. LORD BYRON (1788–1824), English poet
   Byron sparred with John "Gentleman" Jackson, the former bare-knuckled champion, in the poet's Bond Street rooms. Both men wore "mufflers" (mittenlike gloves used for sparring in the early days). The poet boxed in a dressing gown, Jackson in knee breeches and a shirt. With his legendary temper, Byron was reputedly a tough customer in the ring.

2. HESSIE DONAHUE (fl. 1890s), U.S. housewife
   John L. Sullivan, world heavyweight champion from 1882 to 1892, invited Hessie and her husband, a boxing instructor, to join his entourage, which was staging boxing exhibitions in theaters around the country. As part of an act they worked out, Hessie, wearing boxing gloves and dressed in a blouse and bloomers, would climb into the ring after Sullivan had disposed of his male challengers, and the two would go at it. During one of their sparring sessions, Sullivan inadvertently hit Hessie in the face, and she countered with a right to the jaw that sent him to the canvas for a full minute. The audience was so delighted that Hessie and Sullivan decided to make a "knockout" part of their regular routine.

3. PAUL GALLICO (1897–1976), U.S. author
   Gallico, author of *The Poseidon Adventure*, was a cub reporter in 1923, assigned to Jack Dempsey's camp at Saratoga Springs, New York, prior to the heavyweight champion's title bout with Luis Firpo. Against his better judgment, Gallico asked Dempsey to spar with him for one round. It was, for Gallico, a vivid and somewhat terrifying experience, as he was "stalked and pursued by a relentless, truculent professional destroyer." He never saw the punch that flattened him; he was aware only of an explosion in his head, and the next instant he was sitting on the canvas grinning stupidly. He struggled to his feet and finished the round propped up in a clinch with Dempsey, absorbing those taps to the neck and ribs that had seemed so innocuous to him as an observer.

4. J. PAUL GETTY (1892–1976), U.S. entrepreneur
   The billionaire oil magnate met Jack Dempsey in 1916, when Dempsey was an up-and-coming young fighter, and the two became good friends. Getty, who kept fit in the fully equipped basement gym in his parents' mansion, used to spar with Dempsey. Dempsey once claimed that, in an altercation over a girl, Getty knocked him out with a left uppercut—the only time he was KO'd by anyone.

5. ERNEST HEMINGWAY (1899–1961), U.S. author
   During visits to Hemingway's Havana home, former heavyweight champion Gene Tunney would occasionally allow himself to be talked into sparring bare-fisted with the writer, especially if the two had just downed a thermos of frozen daiquiris. Once Hemingway, in a rambunctious mood, tagged Tunney with a hard punch. Incensed, Tunney feinted his friend's guard down and then faked a menacing punch to the face, as he issued a stern warning: "Don't you ever do that again!"

6. GEORGE PLIMPTON (1927–2003), U.S. journalist and author
   One of Plimpton's early experiments in "participatory journalism" was taking on Archie Moore, the former light-heavyweight champ, in January 1959. The fight lasted only three rounds, during which Moore cuffed Plimpton around gently, bloodying his nose. The referee called it a draw. Moore was asked how long it would have taken him to polish off his opponent, had time been a factor. Moore told Plimpton, "'Bout the time it would take a tree to fall on you, or for you to feel the nip of the guillotine."

6 Famous People Who Invented Games

1. LEWIS CARROLL (1832–1898), British author and mathematician
   A wizard at conventional games such as chess and billiards, the creator of *Alice in Wonderland* was a genius at inventing mazes,

ciphers, riddles, magic tricks—even a paper pistol that popped when waved through the air. Wherever he traveled, especially to seaside resorts, Carroll carried a black bag filled with delectable toys and games to enchant prospective female child-friends. His Game of Logic, published as a book in 1886, was an attempt to teach a dry academic subject in a humorous, innovative way. Using "propositions," "syllogisms," and "fallacies," the game, though fairly complicated, was lively and filled with clever statements on everything from dragons and soldiers to pigs, caterpillars, and hard-boiled eggs. One of Carroll's syllogisms:

Some new Cakes are unwholesome;
No nice Cakes are unwholesome.
Therefore, some new Cakes are not nice.

2. MARK TWAIN (1835–1910), U.S. author
Mark Twain's Memory-Builder, a Game for Acquiring and Retaining All Sorts of Facts and Dates, was a particularly appropriate game for Twain, who was known for his absentmindedness. Played on a pegboard divided into 100 rectangles (representing the 100 years in a century), the history game tested players' abilities to remember dates of worldwide "accessions" (to thrones and presidencies), "battles," and "minor events" (such as important inventions). A player called out a date and event (such as 1815, Waterloo), then stuck a pin (each player had a set of colored pins) in the corresponding year and category ("battle"). Penalties were imposed when a player gave an incorrect date, and a point system determined the winner. Twain sold the game in 1891 and later revised it, hoping to organize nationwide clubs to compete for prizes. But the overhauled memory-builder proved too complex and was a commercial failure.

3. ROBERT LOUIS STEVENSON (1850–1894), Scottish novelist and essayist
The author of *Treasure Island* invented a German-style war game in the winter of 1881–1882 while residing in Davos, Switzerland, with his wife, Fanny, and 13-year-old stepson, Lloyd. After clearing ample floor space in the lower story of their chalet, Stevenson, armed with *Operations of War* (a military strategy book), methodically set up a "theater of war" and carefully positioned opposing armies of lead soldiers. To shoot down the enemy, players used popguns—ingeniously loaded with "ems" from Lloyd's small printing press. Face-down cards provided the element of luck in the game, serving up valuable military secrets. The war game never had an official name, nor was it marketed, but Stevenson did write a long magazine article about it, which was published in 1898. One reader, H. G. Wells, was so captivated by the game that he created his own—called Little Wars.

4. **(HELEN) BEATRIX POTTER (1866–1943), British author and illustrator**
A shy and repressed little girl, Beatrix Potter turned to animals for companionship. Secreted in her nursery was a menagerie of rabbits, mice, frogs, snails—even bats and a tame hedgehog. Years later, many of her most popular animal characters—Peter Rabbit, Squirrel Nutkin, Jemima Puddle-Duck, and Jeremy Fisher—became playing pieces on a board game, Peter Rabbit's Race Game, marketed in 1920. To play, you would choose a character, then roll a die and advance on a path of 122 squares (each player had a separate path) toward the winning goal, "The Meeting Place in the Wood." Just one of the obstacles waiting to impede Squirrel Nutkin: "Nutkin meets his friends and loses a turn while talking." But there were chances to jump ahead: Square 96 said, "Old Mr. Brown suddenly bites off Nutkin's tail and in terror he bounds off to 98."

5. **H. G. WELLS (1866–1946), British novelist and historian**
Wells's book-game Little Wars (1913) had simple rules but required an elaborate battleground. Players made houses, churches, castles, and sheds by gluing together wallpaper, cardboard, and corrugated packing paper; the structures (some over 1 foot high) were handsomely painted to show various details, such as windows and rainwater pipes. H. G. liked to play on an 18-foot battlefield with 200 soldiers and 6 brass cannon (that could fire 1-inch wooden cylinders 9 yards) per side. Playing the game was a serious event for Wells, a boisterous, red-faced commander always ready to rally his troops to anticipated victory. As one friend commented: "I have seen harmless guests entering for tea, greeted with the injunction, 'Sit down and keep your mouth shut'. . . . It was a game which began at ten and only ended at seven-thirty, in which Wells had illegitimately pressed noncombatants into his army— firemen, cooks, shopkeepers, and the like—and in which a magnificent shot from the other end of the floor destroyed a missionary fleeing on a dromedary—the last representation of a nation which had marched so gaily into battle so many hours before."

6. **EDGAR CAYCE (1877–1945), U.S. clairvoyant and psychic healer**
Known for his health "readings" (in self-induced trances, he prescribed treatments for more than 14,000 patients) and psychic powers (among his correct predictions were the stock market crash of 1929 and the beginnings and ends of both World Wars), Cayce was a simple Kentucky farmboy who dropped out of school in the ninth grade. While working as head clerk in a bookstore in Bowling Green, Ohio, in 1903, he invented a card game called The Pit, or Board of Trade. The 64 cards, dealt to two or more players, represented various commodities listed on the New York Stock Exchange, and the object of the game was "to corner the market." After the parlor game became popular at the

local YMCA, Cayce sent it to a reputable game company in Massachusetts, which bought it and successfully sold it throughout the United States.

C.O.M.

6 Unusual Duels

1. **COMTE JACQUES DE LÉVIS DE QUELUS AND SIEUR DE DUNES (1578)**
   This duel suddenly erupted into a full-fledged battle when the two sets of seconds the French noblemen had brought along spontaneously joined the fray. The duel had barely begun when one pair of seconds began fighting, and the second, apparently shamed by their noncombatant status, then turned on each other. The final toll: Quelus died, De Dunes was wounded, three of the seconds also died, and the fourth was disfigured for life.

2. **JOHANN MATTHESON AND GEORGE FREDERICK HANDEL (1704)**
   During a performance of Handel's opera *Antony and Cleopatra,* Mattheson allowed the visiting composer Handel to take over as conductor for a while. Later in the performance, Mattheson wished to resume conducting, but Handel refused to leave the podium. Mattheson challenged him to a duel. The performance ceased, and the audience gathered in the street in front of the Hamburg opera house to watch the fight. Mattheson was a skilled swordsman, while Handel was a rank amateur. However, Handel was dressed in a heavy coat featuring large wooden buttons. The point of Mattheson's sword lodged firmly in one of those buttons and remained there until friends separated the composers and sent them on their way.

3. **M. DE GRANDPRÉ AND M. LE PIQUE (1808)**
   After quarreling over a lady, the two gentlemen agreed to fight a duel while riding in balloons high over Paris. Two balloons exactly the same size and shape were constructed, and on the designated date each man armed himself with a blunderbuss and then ascended over the Tuileries gardens. M. le Pique missed his shot, but M. de Grandpré punctured his opponent's balloon. Le Pique and his second plunged half a mile to their deaths.

4. **HENRI D'EGVILLE AND CAPTAIN STEWART (1817)**
   This unusual encounter was staged in a grave near Kingston, Jamaica. D'Egville, a hot-tempered French Creole duelist, used an imagined slight as an excuse to challenge Stewart to a duel. Stewart, a Scotsman, hated dueling, but nevertheless agreed to fight the arrogant D'Egville

on one condition—that the fight be held in an open grave. D'Egville agreed, and the two men entered a large grave that had been freshly dug. But as the two men prepared to fire their pistols, D'Egville's courage deserted him, and he fainted. Stewart sneered an insult and walked away.

5. ELLA ZEIGLIN AND MRS. DAUGHSON (1902)
The two Newkirk, Oklahoma, neighbors had been feuding for a long time, but when Ella Zeiglin bragged to her neighbor Mrs. Daughson that she could lure her husband away any time she felt like doing so, Mrs. Daughson decided to take action. She went to court and charged Zeiglin with trespassing and inciting trouble. The court levied a $300 fine against Zeiglin; she paid it and immediately rushed to Mrs. Daughson's house and challenged her to a duel. The two women wasted no time— they faced off with revolvers at 50 feet Each fired three shots, but none of them found its mark. Then Mrs. Daughson fired again and hit her opponent in the breast—twice. Zeiglin was taken to the hospital, and reportedly both women's husbands and friends were seen preparing their own guns to carry on the conflict.

6. SERGE LIFAR AND THE MARQUIS DE CUEVAS (1958)
Lifar was a choreographer, the marquis was the head of a ballet company appearing in Paris. Despite a court order and Lifar's strong objections, the marquis's company performed one of Lifar's ballets. The two men argued during the intermission, and Lifar challenged the marquis to a duel with swords. They fought in front of an audience of 50 journalists a few miles outside Paris. Lifar's arm was nicked, and after it was bandaged, the two men embraced and declared their mutual admiration.

E.F.

CHAPTER SEVENTEEN

Death

8 ALMOST INDESTRUCTIBLE PEOPLE

16 CASES OF PEOPLE KILLED BY GOD

9 PEOPLE WHO DIED LAUGHING

5 PEOPLE WHO DIED PLAYING CARDS

29 STRANGE DEATHS

12 TIMELY DEATHS

10 CELEBRATED PEOPLE WHO READ
THEIR OWN OBITUARIES

PRESERVING OUR HERITAGE: 29 STUFFED
OR EMBALMED HUMANS AND ANIMALS

REMAINS TO BE SEEN: 14 PRESERVED PARTS

PRESERVING OUR HERITAGE: JEREMY BENTHAM
Courtesy of University College London Library Services

8 Almost Indestructible People

1. **GRIGORY RASPUTIN**

   The Russian mystic and orgiast held enormous political power at the court of the Romanovs from 1905 until his murder in 1916. That this decadent, vulgar peasant should hold such sway over the Empress Alexandra infuriated a group of five power-hungry aristocrats, who set out to destroy him. They arranged for Rasputin to take midnight tea at the home of Prince Felix Yussupov. Some accounts say that Rasputin drank voluminous amounts of poisoned or opiated wine and remained unaffected, to Yussupov's great consternation. The frightened prince contrived an excuse to go upstairs, where the waiting gang furnished him with a gun, then followed him downstairs. According to Rasputin's daughter, Maria, the men assaulted her father and "used him sexually." Then Yussupov shot him. Again, according to Maria, they viciously beat Rasputin and castrated him, flinging the famed penis across the room. One of the conspirators—a doctor—pronounced the victim dead; but Yussupov, feeling uneasy, began to shake the body violently. The corpse's eyelids twitched—and opened. Suddenly, Rasputin jumped to his feet and gripped Yussupov by the shoulders. Terrorized, Prince Felix pulled himself free; Rasputin fell to the floor, and the other men dashed upstairs. In the midst of the brouhaha that followed, they heard noises in the hallway: Rasputin had crawled up the stairs after them. Two more shots were fired into him, and again he was beaten with harrowing violence. The men (still doubting his death) bound his wrists. They carried him to a frozen river and they thrust his body through a hole in the ice. Rasputin was still alive. The icy water revived him, and he struggled against his bonds. When his body was found two days later, his scarred wrists and water-filled lungs gave this proof. It was rumored that he was able to free his right hand, which was said to have been found frozen in a sign symbolizing the cross.

2. **SAMUEL DOMBEY**

   Dombey was a black gravedigger in post–Civil War New Orleans. Because he worked for such low rates, his fellow gravediggers decided to put an end to their competition. They called upon a certain Dr. Beauregard, reputed to have magical powers, to use his $50 "supreme curse" involving an owl's head. The next morning, as Dombey began to dig a new grave, he heard a loud explosion. Someone, apparently injured, staggered away from a nearby clump of bushes. There Dombey found a gun which, overloaded with buckshot, had blown up. Later, a much bandaged Dr. Beauregard threatened to curse anyone who questioned him. The gravediggers took matters into their own hands. They placed a keg of explosive powder under the cot in the tool shed where Dombey took his daily nap and lit it while he slept. The explosion blasted Dombey out the doorway and plopped him 20 feet away. The tool shed was completely destroyed, but Dombey was unhurt. The local police nicknamed him Indestructible Sam. But the best (or worst) was yet to come: Indestructible Sam was soon captured by masked men and taken in a boat to Lake Pontchartrain. His hands and feet were tied, and he was dumped into the depths of the lake. These particular depths, however, turned out to be only two feet; Sam wriggled free of his bonds and walked ashore. Next, his foes tried arson—and as Dombey ran from his burning home, he received a full load of buckshot in his chest. Firemen saved the house and rushed him to the hospital, where he lived up to his nickname. Sam had the last laugh. He continued to dig graves and died at 98, having outlived every one of his jealous competitors.

3. MICHAEL MALLOY

In 1933, a down-and-out drunken Irishman became the victim of an extraordinary series of murder attempts. Malloy was a bum who frequented the speakeasy of one Anthony Marino in the Bronx. Marino and four of his friends, themselves hard up, had recently pulled off an insurance scam, murdering Marino's girlfriend and collecting on her policy; pitiful Michael Malloy seemed a good next bet. The gang took out three policies on him. Figuring Malloy would simply drink himself to death, Marino gave him unlimited credit at the bar. This scheme failed—Malloy's liver knew no bounds. The bartender, Joseph Murphy, was in on the plot and substituted antifreeze for Malloy's whiskey. Malloy asked for a refill and happily put away six shots before passing out on the floor; after a few hours, he perked up and requested another drink. For a week, he guzzled antifreeze nonstop. Straight turpentine worked no better, and neither did horse liniment laced with rat poison. A meal of rotten oysters marinated in wood alcohol brought Malloy back for seconds. In a moment of culinary inspiration, Murphy devised a sandwich for his victim: spoiled sardines mixed with carpet tacks. Malloy came back for more. The gang's next tactic was to dump the drunk into a bank of wet snow and pour water over him on a night when the temperature had sunk to -14°F. No luck. So Marino hired a professional killer, who drove a taxi straight at Malloy at 45 mph, throwing him into the air—and then ran over him again for good measure. After a disappearance of three weeks, Malloy walked into the bar, told the boys he'd been hospitalized because of a nasty car accident, and was "sure ready for drink." Finally, the desperate murderers succeeded—they stuffed a rubber hose into Malloy's mouth and attached it to a gas jet until his face turned purple. The scheme was discovered, and four members of the five-man "Murder Trust" (as the tabloids dubbed Marino & Co.) died in the electric chair. One New York reporter speculated that if Mike Malloy had sat in the electric chair, he would have shorted out every circuit in Sing Sing.

4. DR. ARTHUR WARREN WAITE'S FATHER-IN-LAW AND MOTHER-IN-LAW

Dr. Waite was a New York dentist whose wife was the only daughter of a rich drug manufacturer in Grand Rapids, Michigan. Waite decided to remove the only two obstacles in his path to riches: his parents-in-law. The doctor's efforts are neatly chronicled in Carl Sifakis's book *A Catalogue of Crime:* "Setting to work on his mother-in-law, Waite took her for a drive in a heavy rain with the windshield open. He put ground glass in her marmalade. He introduced into her food all sorts of bacteria and viruses—those that cause pneumonia, influenza, anthrax, and diphtheria. The lady did catch a cold, but that was all. In disgust, Waite shifted his attention to his father-in-law, trying the same disease producers—with absolutely no effect. He filled the old man's rubbers with water, dampened his sheets, opened a container of chlorine gas in his bedroom while he slept. Nothing. Then he tried giving the old man calomel, a purgative, to weaken him, and then a throat spray loaded with typhoid bacteria. People started commenting on how well the old man looked. Waite got off the disease kick and switched to arsenic. Amazingly, the poison failed. Finally, Waite polished off the old man by smothering him with a pillow. By now, however, other relatives were suspicious, and an autopsy on the father-in-law's body was ordered. Heavy traces of arsenic were found; although this was not the cause of death, the arsenic was traced to Waite and he finally confessed to his crime."

5. HERBERT "THE CAT" NOBLE

This Dallas racketeer earned his nickname after the first nine attempts on his life. He was shot at so often that he was also called "The Clay Pigeon." His third moniker was "The Sieve" because he had been riddled by so many bullets. The murder attempts were made by another Dallas gangster, the crude, illiterate "Benny the Cowboy" Binion. A retired police captain revealed the details of their rivalry to Ed Reid and Ovid Demaris, authors of the *Green Felt Jungle,* an exposé of Las Vegas crime. Binion was taking a 25 percent cut of Noble's crap games and wanted to up it to 40 percent. Noble refused, and the fireworks began. In a dramatic car chase, Binion's thugs splattered Noble's car with bullets, and one slug lodged in Noble's spine. He survived, and moved to Las Vegas, but the feud continued long distance—Benny wanted to save face by employing hired killers to nail Noble. Hollis "Lois" Green, a depraved murderer, succeeded in wounding Noble on his third attempt. The following year, in 1949, explosives were found attached to Noble's car, and he was soon shot again. Real tragedy struck when Noble's beloved wife, Mildred, was literally blown to bits by an explosion of nitrogelatin planted in his car. The loss unhinged Noble's mind—his prematurely gray hair (he was 41) turned snow white, he lost 50 pounds, and he began to drink heavily.

Another shooting put him in the hospital, where he was fired upon from across the street. Noble's attempts at retaliation included equipping a plane with bombs to drop on Binion's home, but Noble was shot again before he could carry out his plan. Next, he miraculously survived the bombing of his business and a nitroglycerin explosion in one of his planes. Binion finally killed Herbert the same gruesome way he killed Mildred—with nitrogelatin hidden near Noble's mailbox. On August 7, 1951, the top part of Noble's body was blown clear over a tree—there was nothing left of the bottom. The retired police captain who revealed all this commented, "I think Noble had more downright cold-blooded nerve than anyone I've ever known. He was ice in water in a tight place."

6. DAVID HARGIS

The 23-year-old Marine drill instructor was murdered in San Diego on July 21, 1977—but it wasn't easy. His wife, Carol, 36, took out an insurance policy on her husband to the tune of $20,000. Her accomplice was 26-year-old Natha Mary Depew. First, the ladies went to the woods to find a rattlesnake; instead, they found a tarantula, which they made into a pie. David didn't really like the taste of the tarantula pie, so he ate only a few pieces. The women then tried to (1) electrocute him in the shower, (2) poison him with lye, (3) run him over with a car, and (4) make him hallucinate while driving by putting amphetamines in his beer. Their plan to inject a bubble into his veins with a hypodermic needle—thereby causing a heart attack—failed when the needle broke. They considered putting bullets into the carburetor of his truck, but Depew objected because she wanted to keep the truck after his death. Frustrated, they resorted to a more old-fashioned method—they beat him over the head with a 6½-pound metal weight while he slept. This worked. The murderesses were apprehended while trying to dump the body into a river. Depew told the jury, "If it had not been for Carol I would never have touched him. . . .He looked so beautiful lying there sleeping."

7. BERNADETTE SCOTT

Between 1979 and 1981, Peter Scott, a British computer programmer, made seven attempts to kill his 23-year-old wife after taking out a $530,000 insurance policy on her. First he put mercury into a strawberry flan, but he put in so much that it slithered out. Next, he served her a poisoned mackerel, but she survived it. Once in Yugoslavia and again in England, Peter tried to get her to sit on the edge of a cliff, but she refused. When she was in bed with chicken pox, he set the house on fire, but the blaze was discovered in time. His next arson attempt met with the same result. Bernadette had her first suspicion of foul play when Peter convinced her to stand in the middle of the street while he drove their car toward her, saying he wanted to "test the suspension."

He accelerated, but he swerved away moments before impact. "I was going to run her over, but I didn't have the courage," he later confessed to the police. Pleading guilty to several charges, he was jailed for life. The Scotts had been married for two years.

8. **ALAN URWIN**
   According to the *Daily Mirror*, after his wife left him, Urwin, a 46-year-old former miner from Sunderland, England, made seven suicide attempts in a three-month period in 1995. Having survived three drug overdoses, he wound an electrical wire about his body, got into a tub of water, and plugged the wires into an outlet. The fuse blew out, and he suffered a minor electric shock. He then tried to hang himself with the same piece of wire, but it snapped and he fell to the floor, very much alive. For his sixth attempt, he broke a gas pipe in his bedroom and lay next to it. When this didn't kill him, he lit a match. The explosion blew away the gable end of his semidetached house, along with the windows and part of the roof. He was pulled out of the wreckage suffering nothing worse than some flash burns. He was convicted of arson and placed on two years' probation. A few months later, he was on speaking terms with his ex-wife and was considerably more cheerful.

16 Cases of People Killed by God

1. **ENTIRE WORLD POPULATION EXCEPT NOAH AND 7 RELATIVES** (Genesis 6, 7)
   Transgression: Violence, corruption, and generalized wickedness
   Method of execution: Flood

2. **ENTIRE POPULATIONS OF SODOM AND GOMORRAH EXCEPT LOT, HIS WIFE, AND THEIR 2 DAUGHTERS** (Genesis 19)
   Transgression: Widespread wickedness and lack of respect for the deity
   Method of execution: Rain of fire and brimstone

3. **LOT'S WIFE** (Genesis 19)
   Transgression: Looked back
   Method of execution: Turned into a pillar of salt

4. **ER** (Genesis 38)
   Transgression: Wickedness
   Method of Execution: Unknown

5. **ONAN** (Genesis 38)
   Transgression: Refused to make love to his brother Er's widow
   Method of execution: Unknown

6. ALL THE FIRSTBORN OF EGYPT (Exodus 12)
   Transgression: Egypt was cruel to the Jews
   Method of execution: Unknown

7. PHARAOH AND THE EGYPTIAN ARMY (Exodus 14)
   Transgression: Pursued the Jews
   Method of execution: Drowned

8. NADAB AND ABIHU (Leviticus 10)
   Transgression: Offered strange fire
   Method of execution: Fire

9. KORAH, DATHAN, ABIRAM, AND THEIR FAMILIES (Numbers 16)
   Transgression: Rejected authority of Moses and started own congregation
   Method of execution: Swallowed by earth

10. 250 FOLLOWERS OF KORAH (Numbers 16)
    Transgression: Supported Korah
    Method of execution: Fire

11. 14,700 ISRAELITES (Numbers 16)
    Transgression: Murmured against Moses and his brother Aaron
    following execution of Korah and his supporters
    Method of execution: Plague

12. UNKNOWN NUMBER OF RETREATING AMORITE SOLDIERS
    (Joshua 10)
    Transgression: Fought the Israelites
    Method of execution: Hailstones

13. UZZAH (2 Samuel 6)
    Transgression: Touched the ark of God after oxen shook it while
    pulling it on a cart
    Method of execution: Unknown

14. 70,000 PEOPLE (2 Samuel 24)
    Transgression: King David ordered a census of the population
    Method of execution: Plague

15. 102 SOLDIERS OF KING AHAZIAH (2 Kings 1)
    Transgression: Tried to capture Elijah the Tishbite
    Method of execution: Fire

16. ANANIAS AND SAPPHIRA (Acts 5)
    Transgression: Land fraud
    Method of execution: Unknown

9 People Who Died Laughing

1. CALCHAS (Greek soothsayer, c. 12th century BC)
   Calchas, the wisest soothsayer of Greece during the Trojan War,
   advised the construction of the notorious wooden horse. One day he
   was planting grape vines when a fellow soothsayer wandered by and
   foretold that Calchas would never drink the wine produced from the
   grapes. After the grapes ripened, wine was made from them, and
   Calchas invited the soothsayer to share it with him. As Calchas held a
   cup of the wine in his hand, the soothsayer repeated the prophecy. This
   incited such a fit of laughter in Calchas that he choked and died.
   Another version of his death states that he died of grief after losing a
   soothsaying match in which he failed to predict correctly the number of
   piglets that a pig was about to give birth to.

2. ZEUXIS (Greek painter, 5th century BC)
   It is said that Zeuxis was laughing at a painting of an old woman that he
   had just completed, when his breathing failed and he choked to death.

3. PHILEMON (Greek poet, 362 BC–263 BC)
   This writer of comedies became so engulfed in laughter over a jest he
   had made that he died laughing.

4. CHRYSIPPUS (Greek philosopher, 3rd century BC)
   Chrysippus is said to have died from a fit of laughter on seeing a
   donkey eat some figs.

5. PIETRO ARETINO (Italian author, 1492–1556)
   Aretino was laughing at a bawdy story being told to him by his sister
   when he fell backward in his chair and died of apoplexy.

6. THOMAS URQUHART (Scottish writer and translator, 1611–1660)
   Best known for his translation into English of Rabelais's *Gargantua*,
   the eccentric Sir Thomas Urquhart is said to have died laughing upon
   hearing of the restoration to the throne of Charles II.

7. MRS. FITZHERBERT (English widow, ?–1782)
   On a Wednesday evening in April 1782, Mrs. Fitzherbert of
   Northamptonshire went to Drury Lane Theatre with friends to see
   The Beggar's Opera. When the popular actor Mr. Bannister made his
   first appearance, dressed outlandishly in the role of "Polly," the
   entire audience was thrown into uproarious laughter. Unfortunately,
   Mrs. Fitzherbert was unable to suppress the laugh that seized her,
   and she was forced to leave the theater before the end of the second
   act. As the *Gentleman's Magazine* reported in its issue of the

following week: "Not being able to banish the figure from her memory, she was thrown into hysterics, which continued without intermission until she expired Friday morning."

8. ALEX MITCHELL (English bricklayer, 1925–1975)
Mr. and Mrs. Mitchell of Brockley Green, Fairstead Estate, King's Lynn, were watching their favorite TV comedy, *The Goodies*. During a scene about a new type of self-defense called "Ecky Thump," Mr. Mitchell was seized by uncontrolled laughter. After a half hour of unrestrained mirth, he suffered a heart attack and died. His wife, Nessie, wrote to *The Goodies* thanking them for making her husband's last moments so happy.

9. OLE BENTZEN (Danish physician, ?–1989)
An audiologist who specialized in developing hearing aids for people in underdeveloped countries, Bentzen went to see the film *A Fish Called Wanda*. During a scene featuring John Cleese, Bentzen began laughing so hard that his heartbeat accelerated to a rate of between 250 and 500 beats a minute, and he was seized by a heart attack and died.

5 People Who Died Playing Cards

1. JOHN G. BENNETT (perfume agent)
Mr. Bennett and his wife, Myrtle, lived in a fashionable apartment in Kansas City. One unfortunate Sunday afternoon in the autumn of 1929, the Bennetts sat down with their neighbors, the Hoffmans, to play a friendly game of bridge. Mrs. Hoffman later explained, "As the game went on, the Bennetts' criticisms of each other grew more caustic." Finally, Bennett dealt and bid one spade on a hand that better deserved a pass. Mr. Hoffman overcalled with two diamonds, and Mrs. Bennett, overeager for a contract, jumped to four spades. In the play of the hand, Bennett was set one. His wife taunted him, and they began arguing. John reached across the table and slapped Myrtle, whereupon she told him he was a bum, thus goading him further. He threatened to leave, and Myrtle suggested that the Hoffmans depart, as well. But before they could go, Myrtle ran into her mother's bedroom, grabbed the family automatic, dashed back, and shot her husband twice, killing him. It is worth noting that if Bennett had established his club suit before drawing trumps, he might have survived the evening.

2. JAMES BUTLER HICKOK (gunfighter)
When "Wild Bill" Hickok entered Deadwood, South Dakota, in June of 1876, he had a premonition that he would never leave the gulch alive. On August 2, he was playing poker with three friends in a saloon,

laughing and having a good time. Normally Hickok sat with his back to the wall, but that afternoon Charlie Rich had taken Bill's seat to tease him and had refused to give it up. Jack McCall, whom Hickok had defeated at poker earlier that day, entered the saloon, drew a .45-caliber Colt, and shot Wild Bill Hickok through the back of the head, killing him instantly. Wild Bill, who was 39 years old, was holding two pairs, aces and eights, a hand that has since been known as "the dead man's hand." He died with a smile on his face.

3. AL JOLSON (entertainer)
Jolson suffered a heart attack while playing gin rummy with friends in his room in San Francisco's St. Francis Hotel on the night of October 23, 1950. He was 64 years old.

4. BUSTER KEATON (comedian)
Keaton was stricken by a seizure late in the afternoon of January 31, 1966, while playing poker at his home in Hollywood. He expired the following morning at the age of 70.

5. ARNOLD ROTHSTEIN (gambler)
The man who fixed the 1919 World Series was playing poker in the suite Hump McManus occupied at the Park Central Hotel in New York City when he was shot in the stomach. Rothstein, who owed McManus $320,000 from a previous poker game, stumbled out of the building and was rushed to a hospital, where he refused to name the gunman before he died on November 4, 1928.

29 Strange Deaths

1. THE FATEFUL BATH
Pat Burke of St. Louis, Missouri, took his first bath in 20 years on August 23, 1903. It killed him. Burke was the second victim of cleanliness in a week at the city hospital, and the third in its history. The first was Billy O'Rourke, who had been bathed on the previous Tuesday. Both men had been scrubbed with a broom.

2. DROWNED AT A LIFEGUARDS' PARTY
On August 1, 1985, lifeguards of the New Orleans recreation department threw a party to celebrate their first drowning-free season in memory. Although four lifeguards were on duty at the party, and more than half the 200 partygoers were lifeguards, when the party ended, one of the guests, Jerome Moody, 31, was found dead on the bottom of the recreation department pool.

3. THE PERFECT LAWYER

Clement L. Vallandigham was a highly controversial Ohio politician who engendered much hostility by supporting the South during the Civil War. Convicted of treason, he was banished to the Confederacy. Back in Ohio after the war, Vallandigham became an extremely successful lawyer, who rarely lost a case. In 1871, he took on the defense of Thomas McGehan, a local troublemaker who was accused of shooting Tom Myers to death during a barroom brawl. Vallandigham contended that Myers had actually shot himself, attempting to draw his pistol from his pocket while trying to rise from a kneeling position.

On the evening of June 16, Vallandigham was conferring in his hotel room with fellow defense lawyers when he decided to show them how he would demonstrate his theory to the jury the next day. Earlier in the day, he had placed two pistols on the bureau, one empty and one loaded. Grabbing the loaded one by mistake, Vallandigham put it in his trouser pocket. Then he slowly pulled the pistol back out and cocked it.

"There, that's the way Myers held it," he said, and pulled the trigger. A shot rang out and Vallandigham explained, "My God, I've shot myself!" He died 12 hours later. Vallandigham's client, Thomas McGehan, was subsequently acquitted and released from custody.

4. THE ELECTRIC GUITARIST

Keith Relf, who gained fame as the lead singer of The Yardbirds, a 1960s blues-rock group, was found dead at his home in London on May 14, 1976. The cause of death was an electric shock received while playing his guitar. Relf was 33 years old.

5. THE BURDEN OF MATRIMONY

William Shortis, a rent collector in Liverpool, England, and his wife, Emily Ann, had not been seen for several days. Worried friends and a policeman entered their house on August 13, 1903, and were horrified to discover William, dazed and dying, at the foot of the staircase pinned to the floor underneath the body of his 224-pound. wife. A coroner's jury concluded that the elderly couple had been walking up the stairs when Emily Ann fell backward, carrying her husband with her, but William remained in his unfortunate position for three days, too seriously injured to be able to extricate himself.

6. THE FATAL SNOOKER SHOT

Mr. Raymond Priestley of Melbourne, Australia, was playing snooker in a garage with a friend when he met his doom. He had climbed onto a crossbeam in the ceiling to attempt a trick shot and was hanging upside down by his legs when he slipped. He crashed down on the concrete floor headfirst and later died from brain damage.

7. REVENGE OF THE PLANT KINGDOM

On February 4, 1982, 27-year-old David M. Grundman fired two shotgun blasts at a giant saguaro cactus in the desert outside Phoenix, Arizona. Unfortunately for Grundman, his shots caused a 23-foot section of the cactus to fall on him, and he was crushed to death.

8. A WISH FULFILLED

American revolutionary patriot James Otis often mentioned to friends and relatives that as long as one had to die, he hoped that his death would come from a bolt of lightning. On May 23, 1783, the 58-year-old Otis was leaning against a doorpost in a house in Andover, Massachusetts, when a lightning bolt struck the chimney, ripped through the frame house, and hit the doorpost. Otis was killed instantly.

9. A FATAL TEMPER

On April 15, 1982, 26-year-old Michael Scaglione was playing golf with friends at the City Park West Municipal Golf Course in New Orleans. After making a bad shot on the thirteenth hole, he became angry with himself and threw his club against a golf cart. When the club broke, the club head rebounded and stabbed Scaglione in the throat, severing his jugular vein. Scaglione staggered back and pulled the metal piece from his neck. Had he not done so, he might have lived, since the club head could have reduced the rapid flow of blood.

10. THE WORST NIGHTMARE OF ALL

In 1924, British newspapers reported the bizarre case of a man who apparently committed suicide while asleep. Thornton Jones, a lawyer, woke up to discover that he had slit his own throat. Motioning to his wife for a paper and pencil, Jones wrote, "I dreamt that I had done it. I awoke to find it true." He died 80 minutes later.

11. A DAREDEVIL'S FINAL FALL

Bobby Leach was a colorful character who first became famous in 1911 when he went over Niagara Falls in a barrel. He continued to perform dangerous exploits, including parachuting over the falls from an airplane. In April 1926, Leach was walking down a street in Christchurch, New Zealand, when he slipped on a piece of orange peel and broke his leg so badly that it had to be amputated. Complications developed and he died.

12. KILLED BY JAZZ

Seventy-nine-year-old cornetist and music professor Nicolas Coviello had had an illustrious career, having performed before Queen Victoria, Edward VII, and other dignitaries. Realizing that his life was nearing its end, Coviello decided to travel from London to Saskatchewan to pay a final visit to his son. On the way, he stopped in New York City to bid farewell to his nephews, Peter, Dominic, and Daniel Coviello. On June

13, 1926, the young men took their famous uncle to Coney Island to give him a taste of America. The elder Coviello enjoyed himself but seemed irritated by the blare of jazz bands. Finally, he could take it no longer. "That isn't music," he complained, and he fell to the boardwalk. He was pronounced dead a few minutes later. Cause of death was "a strain on the heart."

13. AMONG THE MANY DANGERS OF THE MATERIAL WORLD— PART ONE
Yousouf Ishmaëlo was a colorful Turkish behemoth who visited the United States in 1897, defeated former wrestling champion Evan Lewis easily, and then won over Greco-Roman champion Ernest Roeber. Ishmaëlo converted all his winnings into gold coins, which he kept—day and night—in a belt around his waist. He was returning home on *Le Bourgogne* in 1898, when his ship collided with a British vessel off Nova Scotia and began to sink. Ishmaëlo refused to discard his money belt, and, still wearing it, he went overboard. Although a good swimmer, he was too weighted by gold coins to stay afloat. He sank to his death at the bottom of the sea.

14. AMONG THE MANY DANGERS OF THE MATERIAL WORLD— PART TWO
A Brinks armored-car guard, Hrand Arakelian, 34, of Santee, California, was crushed to death by $50,000 worth of quarters. Arakelian was guarding a load of 25-pound coin boxes in the back of a truck traveling down the San Diego Freeway on February 3, 1986, when the driver braked suddenly to avoid a car that swerved in front of him. When he pulled over to check on his partner, he found Arakelian completely covered by boxes of coins.

15. STRANGLED BY A GARDEN HOSE
Thirty-five-year-old Richard Fresquez of Austin, Texas, became drunk on the night of May 7, 1983. He tripped on a garden hose, became tangled in it, and strangled to death while trying to break free.

16. PERFECT RE-CREATION
On April 23, 1991, Yooket Paen, 57, of Angton, Thailand, slipped in some mud, grabbed a live wire, and was electrocuted. Later that day, her 52-year-old sister, Yooket Pan, was showing some neighbors how the accident happened when she slipped, grabbed the same live wire, and was also electrocuted.

17. KILLED BY ART
In 1991 Bulgarian environmental artist Christo erected 1,760 yellow umbrellas along Southern California's Tejon Pass and another 1,340

blue umbrellas in Ibaraki Prefecture north of Tokyo. Each of the umbrellas weighed 488 pounds. On October 26, Lori Jean Keevil-Mathews, a 30-year-old insurance agent, drove out to Interstate 5 to view the California umbrellas. Shortly after Keevil-Mathews and her husband got out of their car, a huge gust of wind tore one of the umbrellas loose from its steel screw anchors and blew it straight at Keevil-Mathews, crushing her against a boulder. Christo immediately ordered the dismantling of all the umbrellas in both countries. However, on October 30, another umbrella-related death occurred when 57-year-old crane operator Wasaaki Nakaruma was electrocuted by a power line in Japan as he prepared to take down one of the umbrellas.

18. **SELF-INDUCED CAPITAL PUNISHMENT**
    Michael Anderson Godwin was convicted of murder and sentenced to the electric chair, but in 1983 his sentence was changed to life in prison. On March 5, 1989, Godwin, 28 years old, was trying to fix a pair of earphones connected to the television set in his cell at the Central Correctional Institution in Columbia, South Carolina. While sitting on a steel toilet, he bit into a wire and was electrocuted.

19. **AMONG THE MANY DANGERS OF THE SPIRITUAL WORLD—PART ONE**
    John Edward Blue, 38, of Dorchester, Massachusetts, was being baptized in Natick's Lake Cochituate on August 13, 1984, when he and the minister performing the baptism slipped and fell backward into deep water. The minister survived, but Blue drowned.

20. **AMONG THE MANY DANGERS OF THE SPIRITUAL WORLD—PART TWO**
    Seventy-five-year-old Maddalena Camillo was crossing the main square in her hometown of Sant Onofrio, Italy, on September 22, 2004, when an iron crucifix fell from a monument that was being restored and landed on her head, killing her.

21. **THE PERILS OF POLITICS**
    Nitaro Ito, 41, a pancake shop operator in Higashiosaka City, Japan, concluded that he needed an extra edge in his 1979 campaign for the House of Representatives. He decided to stage an attack on himself and then draw sympathy by campaigning from a hospital bed. Ito's scheme was to have an employee, Kazuhiko Matsumo, punch him in the face on the night of September 17, after which Ito would stab himself in the leg. After Matsumo had carried out of his part of the plan, Ito stabbed his right thigh. Unfortunately, he cut an artery and bled to death before he could reach his home, 50 meters away.

22. KILLED BY A ROBOT

Ford Motor Company's casting plant in Flat Rock, Michigan, employed a one-ton robot to fetch parts from a storage rack. When the robot malfunctioned on January 25, 1979, 25-year-old Robert Williams was asked to climb up on the rack and get the parts. While he was performing the task, the robot suddenly reactivated and hit Williams in the head with its arms. Williams died instantly. Four years later a jury ordered Unit Handling Systems, the manufacturer of the robot, to pay Williams's family $10 million. Williams is believed to have been the first person killed by a robot.

23. AW CHUTE

Ivan McGuire was an experienced parachutist who spent the afternoon of April 2, 1988, in Louisburg, North Carolina, videotaping parachuting students as they jumped and jumping with them. On his third trip up, McGuire dropped from the airplane and began filming the instructor and student who followed him a second later. McGuire reached back and discovered that he had forgotten to put on his parachute. His videotape, which was shown on the news in nearby Raleigh, recorded his final words: "Uh-oh."

24. WHAT A WASTE TO GO—PART ONE

The 70-year-old mayor of Betterton, Maryland, Monica Myers, considered it part of her duties to check the sewage tanks at the municipal facility. On the night of March 19, 1980, she went to the Betterton treatment plant to test for chlorine and sediment. Unfortunately, she slipped on a catwalk, fell into a tank of human waste, and drowned.

25. WHAT A WASTE TO GO—PART TWO

Carl Theuerkauf, Sr., and his family ran the largest dairy farm in Michigan's Upper Peninsula. Elmbrook Farm had been in the Theuerkauf family for 108 years. On the fateful day of July 27, 1989, Carl Sr.'s son Tom climbed through a narrow hole and down a ladder into a manure pit filled with 12 inches of liquefied manure. He was trying to clear a blocked drain. Unbeknownst to Tom, odorless but lethal methane gas had built up during a deadly heat wave. He lost consciousness and fell back into the manure. Tom's nephew Dan sent for help and then went down into the pit. Then Carl Sr.'s cousin Bill Hofer went down to help. When he was overcome, Carl Sr. tried to rescue his family. Finally, Carl Jr. followed. By the time others on the farm could haul everyone out, it was too late—five men had died.

26. WHAT A WASTE TO GO—PART THREE

During a routine parachute jump on December 2, 1990, Army reservist Private Martin St. Eskew overshot the drop zone and landed in a pool of liquefied manure. A group of 13 reservists formed a human chain to retrieve the unconscious soldier from the pool. Two medics on the scene then tried to revive Eskew, but he had died from asphyxiation.

27. A FISHY TALE
In July 1996, Nathan do Nascimento was fishing by the Maguari River south of Belem, Brazil. Like many fishermen, he was very relaxed. While he was in the middle of a long yawn, a six-inch fish suddenly leapt out of the river and into his mouth. It lodged deep in his throat. Two fellow fishermen tried to pull out the fish but couldn't reach it, and Nascimento choked to death.

28. THE WORLD'S SLOWEST MURDER
Sixty-year-old M. C. Russell died in January of 1998 from the effects of a bullet that had lodged in his spine when his wife shot him more than 20 years earlier. His death was classified as a homicide, but investigators closed the case quickly: Russell's wife, Lois, had died four years earlier. Russell's sister, Imogene Evans, who cared for him after the shooting, said that Russell declined to press charges against his wife and never acted bitter toward her. "He said if he pressed charges against her, he was not leaving anything for God to do," noted Evans.

29. SILENCED BY THE LAMBS
Betty Stobbs, 67, put a bale of hay on her bike and went out to feed the sheep at her family farm in Stanhope, England on January 26, 1999. Forty sheep rushed toward her and began jumping up on the bike to reach the hay, knocking Stobbs into the 100-foot-deep Ashes Quarry. Alan Renfry witnessed the incident from his home and was convinced that the sheep were responsible for Stobbs's death.

12 Timely Deaths

We read so often in the newspapers about "untimely deaths" that it makes one wonder if anyone ever died a "timely death." Well, people have, and here are some examples.

1. DOMITIAN (51–96 AD), Roman emperor
Early astrological predictions had warned that he would be murdered on the fifth hour of September 18, 96 AD. As the date approached, Domitian had many of his closest attendants executed to be on the safe side. Just before midnight marked the beginning of the critical day, he became so terrified that he jumped out of bed. A few hours later, he asked the time and was told by his servants (who were conspiring against him) that it was the sixth hour. Convinced that the danger had passed, Domitian went off to take a bath. On the way he was informed

that his niece's steward, Stephanus, was waiting for him in the bedroom with important news. When the emperor arrived, Stephanus handed him a list of conspirators and then suddenly stabbed him in the groin. Domitian put up a good fight, but he was overcome when four more conspirators appeared. He died as predicted, on the fifth hour of September 18, 96 AD.

2. THOMAS JEFFERSON (1743–1826), U.S. president
The 83-year-old former president was suffering badly from diarrhea, but he had hopes of lasting until July 4, 1826, the fiftieth anniversary of the signing of the Declaration of Independence. From his sickbed, he asked, "This is the Fourth?" When he was informed that it was, he died peacefully.

3. JOHN ADAMS (1735–1826), U.S. president
Adams, like Jefferson, held on until July 4, 1826, before dying at the age of 90. He is reported to have said, "Thomas Jefferson survives. . . . Independence forever," unaware that his old friend had died a few hours earlier.

4. DR. JOSEPH GREEN (1791–1863), English surgeon
While lying on his deathbed, Dr. Green looked up at his doctor and said, "Congestion." Then he took his own pulse, uttered the single word "Stopped," and died.

5. HENRIK IBSEN (1828–1906), Norwegian dramatist
On May 16, 1906, Ibsen was in a coma in his bedroom, surrounded by friends and relatives. A nurse told the others in the room that the famed playwright seemed to be a little better. Without opening his eyes, Ibsen uttered one word: *"Tvertimod"* ("On the contrary"). He died that afternoon without speaking again.

6. MARK TWAIN (1835–1910), U.S. humorist
Born in 1835, the year of Halley's Comet, Twain often stated that he had come into the world with the comet and would go out of the world with it as well. Halley's Comet next returned in 1910, and on April 21 of that year Twain died.

7. ARNOLD SCHÖNBERG (1874–1951), Austrian composer
Schönberg's lifelong fascination with numerology led to his morbid obsession with the number 13. Born in 1874 on September 13, he believed that 13 would also play a role in his death. Because the numerals 7 and 6 add up to 13, Schönberg was convinced that his seventy-sixth year would be the decisive one. Checking the calendar for 1951, he saw to his horror that July 13 fell on a Friday. When that day

came, he kept to his bed in an effort to reduce the chance of an accident. Shortly before midnight, his wife entered the bedroom to say good night and to reassure him that his fears had been foolish, whereupon Schönberg muttered the word *harmony* and died. The time of his death was 11:47 p.m., 13 minutes before midnight on Friday, July 13, in his seventy-sixth year.

8. **LEONARD WARREN (1911–1960), U.S. opera singer**
Warren was performing in Verdi's *La Forza del Destino* on the stage of the Metropolitan Opera in 1960. He had just begun the aria "O fatal urn of my destiny." When he reached the word *fatal*, he suddenly pitched forward, dead of a heart attack.

9. **ELIZABETH RYAN (1892–1979), U.S. tennis player**
Elizabeth Ryan won 19 Wimbledon tennis championships between 1914 and 1934—a record that stood for 45 years. On July 6, 1979, the day before Billie Jean King broke her record by winning a twentieth Wimbledon title, the 87-year-old Ryan became ill in the stands at Wimbledon. She collapsed in the clubhouse and died that night.

10. **CHARLES DAVIES (1927–1995), British singer**
Davies, age 67, was giving a solo rendition of the old soldiers' song "Good-bye" at the annual dinner of the Cotswold Male Voice Choir in Echington, England, on January 3, 1995. He finished with the words, "I wish you all a last good-bye." As the crowd applauded, Davies collapsed and died.

11. **CHARLES SCHULZ (1922–2000), U.S. cartoonist**
In 1999, Schulz, the creator of the popular comic strip *Peanuts*, announced his decision to retire because of poor health. He died on February 12, 2000, the night before the last original *Peanuts* ran in the Sunday newspapers. The timing was "prophetic and magical," said close friend and fellow cartoonist Lynn (*"For Better or for Worse"*) Johnston. "He made one last deadline. There's romance in that."

12. **GEORGE STORY (1936–2000), U.S. journalist**
In 1936, the premier issue of *Life* featured a picture of newborn baby George Story under the headline "Life Begins." Over the years, the magazine periodically updated readers about the *"Life* baby," as Story married twice, had children, and retired. On April 4, 2000, just days after *Life* announced that it would cease publication, Story died of heart failure. The final issue of *Life* featured one last article about Story. The headline: "A Life Ends."

D.W. & C.F.

10 Celebrated People Who Read Their Own Obituaries

1. **HANNAH SNELL**

   Her husband walked out on her and joined the British army. To find him, Hannah Snell also enlisted, posing as a man. During surgery, her true sex was discovered. She became a celebrity, and, once out of the army, she performed in public houses as the Female Warrior. On December 10, 1779, when she was 56, she opened a copy of the *Gentlemen's Magazine* and read her own obituary, which informed her that she had died on a Warwickshire heathland. Perhaps she was superstitious, because reading her death notice snapped something in her mind. Her mental health slowly deteriorated, and in 1789 she was placed in London's Bethlehem Hospital. She remained there insane until she expired in 1792.

2. **DANIEL BOONE**

   The great American frontiersman had retired and settled down in Missouri. In 1818, an American newspaper in the eastern United States trumpeted the news that the renowned hunter had been found dead near a deer lick, kneeling behind a tree stump, his rifle resting on the stump, a fallen deer a hundred yards away. The obituary was picked up across the nation. Daniel read it and laughed. Although he could still trap, he was too old and weak to hunt and could no longer hit a deer, even close up. Two years later, aged 86, Boone finally did die. His best obituary was seven stanzas devoted to him in Lord Byron's *Don Juan*.

3. **LADY JANE ELLENBOROUGH**

   She was one of the most beautiful women in history. Her name was Jane Digby. At 17 she married Lord Ellenborough, Great Britain's lord of the privy seal, then left him to run off with an Austrian prince. During her colorful career she was the mistress of novelist Honoré de Balzac, King Ludwig of Bavaria, and Ludwig's son, King Otto of Greece. Her last marriage of 26 years was to Sheik Medjuel, an erudite Bedouin, head of the Mezrab tribe in the Syrian desert. Returning from a desert trip with Medjuel, the 66-year-old Lady Ellenborough learned that she was dead. Her obituary appeared prominently in *La Revue Britannique*, published in Paris in March 1873. It began: "A noble lady who had made a great use—or abuse—of marriage has died recently. Lady Ellenborough, some 30 years ago, left her first husband to run off with Count von Schwarzenberg. She retired to Italy, where she married six consecutive times." The obituary, reprinted throughout Europe, called her last husband "a camel driver." The next issue of the publication carried a eulogy of Lady Ellenborough written by her friend Isabel

Burton, the pompous and snobbish wife of Burton of Arabia. Mrs. Burton claimed she had been authorized to publish the story of Lady Ellenborough's life, based on dictated notes. Appalled, Lady Ellenborough vehemently wrote the press denying her death—and having dictated an "authorized" book to Mrs. Burton. Lady Ellenborough outlived her obituary by eight full years, dying of dysentery in August 1881.

4. **JAMES BUTLER HICKOK**
In March 1873, "Wild Bill" Hickok, legendary sheriff and city marshal in the Midwest and a constant reader of Missouri's leading newspaper, the *Democrat*, picked up a copy and learned that he was a corpse. Hickok read: "The Texan who corralled the untamed William did so because he lost his brother by Bill's quickness on the trigger." Unsettled by his supposed demise, Wild Bill took pen in hand and wrote a letter to the editor: "Wishing to correct an error in your paper of the 12th, I will state that no Texan has, nor ever will, 'corral William.' I wish to correct your statement on account of my people. Yours as ever, J. B. Hickok." Delighted, the editor of the *Democrat* printed Hickok's letter and added an editorial: "We take much pleasure in laying Mr. Hickok's statement before the readers of the *Democrat*, most of whom will be glad to learn from his pen that he is 'still on the deck.' But in case you should go off suddenly, William, by writing us the particulars we will give you just as fine an obituary notice as we can get up, though we trust that sad pleasure may be deferred for years." Three years later, Hickok was murdered while playing poker.

5. **ALFRED NOBEL**
As the inventor of dynamite, Alfred Nobel, a moody, idealistic Swede, had become a millionaire. When his older brother, Ludwig, died of heart trouble on April 12, 1888, a leading French newspaper misread the report and ran an obituary of Alfred Nobel, calling him "a merchant of death." Upon seeing the obituary, Nobel was stunned, not by the premature announcement of his passing but by the realization that in the end he would be considered nothing more than a merchant of death. The printed summary of his life reflected none of his hopes for humanity, his love of his fellow beings, his generosity. The need to repair that false picture was one of several factors that led Alfred Nobel to establish, in his will, the Nobel Prize awards to be given to those who did the most to advance the causes of peace, literature, and the sciences.

6. **P. T. BARNUM**
At 80, the great American showman was ailing and knew that death was near. From his sickbed, he told a friend that he would be happier if he had "the chance to see what sort of lines" would be written about him after he was dead. The friend relayed this wish to the editor of the

Evening Sun of New York City. On March 24, 1891, Barnum opened his copy of the *Evening Sun* and read: "Great and Only Barnum. He Wanted to Read His Obituary; Here It Is." According to the preface, "Mr. Barnum has had almost everything in this life, including the wooly horse and Jenny Lind, and there is no reason why he should not have the last pleasure which he asks for. So here is the great showman's life, briefly and simply told, as it would have appeared in the *Evening Sun* had fate taken our Great and Only from us." There followed four columns of Barnum's obituary, illustrated by woodcuts of him at his present age, of him at 41, of his mother, of his deceased first wife Charity, and of the Swedish singer Jenny Lind. Two weeks later, Barnum was dead.

7. LEOPOLD VON SACHER-MASOCH

This police commissioner's son, born in Galicia, raised in Austria, was fascinated by cruelty and loved pain and degradation. His first mistress, Anna von Kottowitz, birched him regularly and enjoyed lovers that Sacher-Masoch found for her. His second mistress, Fanny Pistor, signed a contract with him agreeing to wear furs when she beat him daily. She fulfilled the contract and treated him as a servant. He had become a famous writer when he met and married a woman named Wanda. She thrashed him with a nail-studded whip every day of their 15-year marriage and made him perform as her slave. After she ran off, Sacher-Masoch married a simple German woman named Hulda Meister. By now he was slipping into insanity, and he tried to strangle her. In 1895 she had him secretly committed to an asylum in Mannheim and announced to the world that he had died. The press published obituaries praising his talent. Undoubtedly, in lucid moments, he read some of his death notices. He finally did die 10 years later in 1905. Because of Sacher-Masoch's life, psychiatrist Richard von Krafft-Ebing coined the word *masochism.*

8. MARK TWAIN

In 1897, the noted American author and humorist was in seclusion, grieving over a death in his family, when he learned that he, too, had been declared dead. A sensational American newspaper had headlined his end, stating that he had died impoverished in London. A national syndicate sent a reporter to Mark Twain's home to confirm the news. Twain himself appeared before the bug-eyed reporter and issued an official statement: "James Ross Clemens, a cousin of mine, was seriously ill two or three weeks ago in London, but is well now. The reports of my illness grew out of his illness. The reports of my death are greatly exaggerated." Twain finally lived up to his premature obituaries in 1910.

9. BERTRAND RUSSELL

Once in the 1930s, while the English philosopher was visiting Beijing, he became very ill. Japanese reporters in the city constantly tried to see

Russell, but were always denied access. The journalists decided he must be dead and notified their newspapers of his demise. Word of his death went around the world. Wrote Russell, "It provided me with the pleasure of reading my obituary notices, which I had always desired without expecting my wishes to be fulfilled. One missionary paper had an obituary notice of one sentence: 'Missionaries may be pardoned for heaving a sigh of relief at the news of Mr. Bertrand Russell's death.' " All this inspired Russell to compose his own obituary in 1937 for the *Times* of London. He wrote of himself: "His life, for all its waywardness, had a certain anachronistic consistency, reminiscent of the aristocratic rebels of the early 19th century. . . . He was the last survivor of a dead epoch." He told the *Times* to run it in 1962, the year in which he expected to die. The *Times* did not need it until 1970.

10. EDWARD V. RICKENBACKER

This auto-racing driver-turned-fighter pilot emerged from World War I as America's leading ace with 26 confirmed kills. In peacetime, he was an executive in the automobile and aviation industries. With the onset of WWII, Rickenbacker volunteered to carry out missions for the U.S. War Department. In October 1942, on an inspection tour, his B-17 went down somewhere in the Pacific Ocean. An intensive air search was made of the area. There was no sign of survivors. Newspapers across the U.S. declared Rickenbacker dead. The following month, on Friday the thirteenth of November, there were new headlines. Rickenbacker and seven others were spotted alive in the Pacific. They had survived on a raft for 23 days. Waiting for Rickenbacker when he returned home was a pile of his obituaries. One, in the *New York Daily News*, was a cartoon showing a black wreath floating on water, with the caption "So Long, Eddie." Another, in the *New York Journal*, bore the headline "End of the Roaring Road?" Grinning, Rickenbacker scrawled across it, "Hell, no!"

Note: These 10 are the editor's favorite cases, but numerous other celebrated persons read of their deaths while they were alive, among them U.S. president Thomas Jefferson, magician Harry Houdini, dancer Josephine Baker, singer Jeanette MacDonald, novelist Ernest Hemingway, and foreign correspondent Edgar Snow. Also, there have been many famous people who, if they did not read about their deaths, heard rumors or announcements that they had gone to the Great Beyond. The modern living dead have included singer Paul McCartney, vague hints of whose demise were supposedly traced to several Beatles records; actress Bette Davis, whose attorney told her that word of her death was spreading throughout New York, to which Miss Davis replied, "With the newspaper strike on, I wouldn't consider it"; and India's elderly political dissenter J. P. Narayan, who heard Prime Minister Morarji Desai mistakenly deliver a eulogy over his still warm body in April 1979.

I.W.

Preserving Our Heritage: 29 Stuffed or Embalmed Humans and Animals

1. **TUTANKHAMEN**
   In 1922, while excavating in the Valley of the Kings, English archaeologist Howard Carter discovered the tomb of Tutankhamen, a king of the Eighteenth Dynasty of Egypt who flourished about 1348 BC. The mummy of the pharaoh was encased in a 6-foot coffin containing 2,448 pounds of gold. Over the bandages on the king's face was a lifelike gold mask inlaid with precious jewels. A dazzling assortment of rings, necklaces, amulets, and other exquisite ornaments were found among the body wrappings. The internal organs of the king had been removed, embalmed, and placed in a separate alabaster chest. The mummy, coffin, and other valuables from the tomb have toured the world and are currently diplayed at the Egyptian Museum in Cairo.

2. **CHARLEMAGNE**
   This ruler of the Holy Roman Empire died in 814. Embalmed, he was dressed in his royal robes, a crown placed on his head, a scepter placed in his hand, and thus he was propped up in a sitting position on his marble throne. His preserved body remained on that throne for 400 years. At last, in 1215, Holy Roman Emperor Frederick II removed the corpse, which was found to be in excellent condition. It was buried in a gold and silver casket in the cathedral at Aix-la-Chapelle.

3. **EL CID (Rodrigo Díaz de Vivar)**
   Spanish leader in the war against the Moors, El Cid established the independent kingdom of Valencia. Wounded in battle in 1099 and dying, his last wish was that his body be embalmed and then seated on his horse, Babieca, during the next battle. When the next battle came—an attack on Valencia by King Bucar of Morocco—and the Spanish were on the verge of defeat, the preserved corpse of El Cid, mounted on his horse, appeared at the head of the troops. Heartened, the Spanish troops rallied and were victorious.

4. **INÉS DE CASTRO**
   When King Pedro of Castile was a young prince, he fell in love with Inés de Castro. His father, fearing political complications, trumped up a charge against Inés and had her beheaded. Pedro waited until he had become king after his father died and then had the assassins' hearts torn out and ordered Inés's body exhumed. Her corpse was dressed, placed on the throne, and officially crowned queen. All dignitaries were forced to pay homage by kissing her hand and treating her like a living monarch. Pedro died in 1369.

5. **RICHARD II**

This English king was deposed in 1399 and probably murdered in 1400. In 1413, Henry V had Richard's body embalmed and put on public display in full royal regalia. Three days later Henry was the chief mourner at Richard's second funeral, during which Richard was interred in Westminster Abbey. At one time, there was a hole in the side of the tomb through which visitors could put their hands to touch the king's head. In 1776, an enthusiastic schoolboy thrust in his hand and stole Richard's jawbone. The boy's descendants kept the relic until 1906, when it was finally restored to its rightful resting place.

6. **CATHERINE OF VALOIS**

Henry V's queen died in 1437. Her grandson, Henry VII, made major alterations to Westminster Abbey which involved moving her embalmed body. She was placed in a crude coffin constructed of flimsy boards and left above ground. There she remained a public spectacle for over 200 years. Vergers used to charge a shilling to take off the lid so curious visitors could view her corpse. But seeing wasn't enough for Samuel Pepys, who went to the abbey on his thirty-sixth birthday. "I had the upper part of her body in my hands, and I did kiss her mouth, reflecting upon that I did first kiss a Queene." The body was finally removed from public view in 1776.

7. **DUKE OF MONMOUTH**

This English rebel was beheaded in 1685 in one of history's messiest executions (it took "five chopps"). The body and head were dispatched for burial, but at the last moment it was realized that no portrait existed of the duke. Since he had been the out-of-wedlock son of King Charles II, it was considered important to have one painted. Body and head were returned, sewed back together, dressed—and finally painted. The portrait hangs in the National Portrait Gallery, London.

8. **CHARLES BYRNE**

This Irish giant lived from 1761 to 1783. He feared that his huge body would be dissected for study, so he paid a group of friends to bury him at sea. But the famous anatomist John Hunter, who owned a collection of human oddities, was not to be cheated. When Byrne died, Hunter bribed the friends to deliver the body to him. He immediately set about boiling the remains before anyone discovered what had happened. The speed with which he boiled the bones turned them brown. Hunter kept his acquisition secret for more than two years but finally put it on display. Byrne can still be seen in the Hunter Museum at the Royal College of Surgeons in London.

9. **"THE PRESERVED LADY"**

Martin van Butchell was an English eccentric who lived from 1735 to 1812. In his marriage contract there was a clause stating he could own certain articles only "while [his wife] remained above ground." When she died, he retained title to the property by having her embalmed, dressed in her wedding clothes, and placed in a glass-topped case in his drawing room. "The Preserved Lady" became a great attraction, with Butchell always introducing her as "My dear departed." When he remarried, his new wife—irritated by the competition—insisted the corpse be removed. In keeping with the provision that she remain above ground, Butchell presented her to the Royal College of Surgeons, where she remained on public view until she was cremated by a German bomb during a Luftwaffe raid in May 1941.

10. BARRY

When the fabled Swiss St. Bernard who rescued so many travelers trapped in Alpine snowstorms died in 1814, a taxidermist stuffed and mounted him. He may be seen today, remarkably lifelike, standing in the National Museum, Bern, Switzerland.

11. JEREMY BENTHAM

English philosopher and the "Father of Utilitarianism," Bentham, who died in 1832 at he age of 84, willed his entire estate to the University College Hospital in London—on condition that his body be preserved and placed in attendance at all of the hospital's board meetings. Dr. Southward Smith was chosen by Bentham to prepare the philosopher's corpse for viewing. Smith constructed the skeleton and affixed a wax likeness of Bentham's head to it, then attired the body in an appropriate suit and hat. According to Smith, "The whole was then enclosed in a mahogany case with folding glass doors, seated in his armchair and holding in his hand his favorite walking stick. . . ." Thus, for the next 92 years, Jeremy Bentham never missed a board meeting.

12. JULIA PASTRANA

A professional freak, Pastrana (1834–1860), a bearded Mexican Indian described as the ugliest woman in history, was exhibited all over the world. Her manager married her "for myself alone" and when she became pregnant, made a fortune selling tickets to witness the delivery. The child was stillborn and deformed like his mother. Julia died soon after. Her husband had both mother and child embalmed and placed in a glass case, which he immediately began exhibiting around the world. Her body, still on display, was in Norway at last report.

13. JUMBO

Phineas T. Barnum's famous giant elephant, 10 feet 9 inches at the shoulder, was hit by a freight train and killed in 1885. The showman had Jumbo's carcass stuffed—sending his skeleton to the Smithsonian Institution in Washington, D.C.—and put the mounted animal on permanent exhibit in Barnum Hall, Tufts University, Medford, Massachusetts. In April 1975, a fire swept Barnum Hall and destroyed Jumbo's remains.

14. COMANCHE
When the U.S. Army horse who survived Custer's Last Stand died a national hero, it was decided to preserve and mount him. A University of Kansas naturalist, Professor Lewis Dyche, was paid $450 to do the job. Comanche's insides were given a military funeral. His outsides were preserved, shown at the Columbian Exposition in Chicago in 1893, then permanently placed in the University of Kansas Museum of Natural History in Lawrence. In 1947, General Jonathan Wainwright tried to get Comanche back to be a U.S. Army exhibit in Fort Riley, but failed. In 1950, to save his hide from expanding and contracting, Comanche was placed in an airtight glass case with humidity control and set against an artificial "sunbaked" setting of soil and grass.

15. TIM
Tim was a small mongrel dog who came to Paddington Station in London in 1892 to meet the trains. Attached to his collar was a collection box into which departing passengers dropped coins for a British railroad's fund for widows and orphans. After a decade's work, Tim died in 1902. He was stuffed, and his preserved body—complete with collar and collection box—was placed in a glass case in Paddington Station to continue his good works.

16. ANDERSON McCREW
In 1913, a one-legged African American hobo died after falling off a moving freight train in Marlin, Texas. Anderson (also known as Andrew) McCrew was dead, but he did not rest in peace for 60 years. The morning after his death, he was taken to a funeral parlor and embalmed. When no one appeared to claim the body, a traveling carnival purchased it and displayed McCrew as "The Amazing Petrified Man— The Eighth Wonder of the World." When the troupe disbanded 55 years later, McCrew remained in storage until a Dallas widow, Elgie Pace, discovered him. She wanted to give him a decent burial because, as she said to her sister, "He's a human being. You just can't throw a body in a ditch." However, she was unable to afford the cost of burial, so she nicknamed him "Sam" and kept him in the basement. Eventually, a local black undertaker volunteered to give McCrew a funeral. The service was "beautiful, and very dignified," reported Elgie, and Anderson McCrew was finally laid to rest. Several months later, folksinger Don McLean wrote a song, "The Legend of Andrew McCrew," which inspired a radio listener to purchase a gravestone for McCrew. The stone reads: "Andrew McCrew, 'The Mummified Man,' Born 1867/Died 1913/Buried 1973."

17. VLADIMIR ILYICH LENIN

On January 21, 1924, Lenin died, reportedly of a stroke, but possibly of poisoning. The deification process began at once. Lenin's brain was removed and cut into 20,000 sections for study by the Soviet Brain Institute, and then his body was embalmed. It was a poor job, and the face became wrinkled and shrunken. By 1926, a Russian doctor, using new embalming fluid, which he claimed was based on that used by the ancient Egyptians, reembalmed the body. A younger, more ascetic look was restored to the face. In 1930, a mausoleum composed of red Ukrainian granite and Karelian porphyry was built in Red Square to contain Lenin's body, enclosed in a glass sarcophagus. In a poll taken in April 2004, 56 percent of Russians wanted Lenin buried, while 30 percent preferred that he remain above ground.

18. EVA PERÓN

When the wife of Argentine president Juan Perón died in 1952, her husband had her body embalmed. He planned to build a mausoleum for his wife, but his government was overthrown in 1955 and he was forced into exile in Spain. Eva Perón's body disappeared, and it was assumed that she was buried in an Italian cemetery under a different name. However, by 1971, Juan Perón had retrieved the body, and, according to a friend who dined with him, the body was present every evening at the dinner table along with Perón and his new wife, Isabel. In late 1974, at Isabel's request, Eva Perón was returned to Argentina, where she was placed in an open casket beside the closed casket of her husband. After being briefly displayed, her body was buried in the Duarte family tomb in La Recoleta Cemetery in Buenos Aires.

19. TRIGGER

The world's most famous animal actor, Trigger costarred with Roy Rogers in 88 motion pictures and 100 television shows. An unusually intelligent horse, he was able to untie knots with his teeth and count to 20. Upon his death in 1965 at the age of 33, Trigger was stuffed and mounted. He is on display at the Roy Rogers Museum in Victorville, California, as is Dale Evans's horse, Buttermilk, and their German shepherd, Bullet.

20. MAO ZEDONG

After Mao, chairman of the Chinese Communist Party, died at 82 on September 9, 1976, he was embalmed. His corpse was placed in a crystal sarcophagus to be displayed permanently to the public in a mausoleum in Tiananmen Square in Beijing. At night, after visitors have gone home, Mao is lowered into an earthquake-proof chamber below the square.

21. ST. BERNADETTE

In 1858, at the age of 14, Bernadette Soubirous saw several visions of the Virgin Mary at a spring in Lourdes, France. Bernadette later joined the Sisters of Notre-Dame of Nevers, and today the site of the apparitions is one of the most famous Catholic shrines. After her death at age 35, Bernadette's body was buried and exhumed three separate times in the next 45 years in attempts to verify the incorruptibility of her corpse (according to Catholic tradition, a sign of sainthood). Although there has been some decomposition, owing in part to numerous examinations, Bernadette's remains are remarkably intact. Her body has been on display in the chapel of the Convent of St. Gildard at Nevers since August 3, 1925.

22. ENRICO CARUSO

During the six years that followed his death in 1921, the great Italian tenor surely qualified for the "best-dressed corpse" list. Each year solicitous friends ordered a new outfit for Caruso's body, which lay on public display in a crystal casket. In 1927, his widow decided enough was enough and had a white granite slab placed over the casket. It now remains sealed and undisturbed, with Caruso in old clothes, at Del Planto Cemetery near Naples, Italy.

23. BUSHMAN

More than three million people viewed the huge, chest-thumping gorilla in Chicago's Lincoln Park Zoo over a period of 20 years. While alive Bushman often became moody when zoo-goers ignored him. In death, his stuffed and mounted carcass continues to awe visitors at Chicago's Field Museum of Natural History, where he glares from a sealed glass case filled with insecticidal gases.

24. VU KHAC MINH

When Vu, a Buddhist monk, was nearing death in 1639, he asked his followers to leave him alone for 100 days so he could meditate. When his disciples eventually returned, they reportedly found his perfectly preserved body still in the lotus position. Believing that he had reached nirvana, they preserved his remains with red lacquer. In 2002, monks at his pagoda began restoring the cracked lacquer. X-rays showed that the body was still intact after more than three centuries. Thich Thanh Nhung, the head monk at the pagoda, said that Vu's incorruption "illustrates the ability of the body to acquire a new level of grace through Buddhist teachings."

25. "EL NEGRO"

"El Negro" was the name given to an anonymous Bushman stolen from his grave in 1830 by two French taxidermists, Jules and Eduoard Verraux. The body was displayed in a Parisian shop for 50 years before

being given to a museum in the town of Banyoles in Spain. The presence
of "El Negro" in Spain led several African nations to threaten a boycott
of the 1992 Summer Olympics in Barcelona. In 2000, the embalmed
body was returned to Gabarone, Botswana, and given a burial with
military honors.

26. BREDO MORSTOEL

Morstoel died of heart failure at age 89 in his native Norway in 1989.
His grandson, Trygve Bauge, had the body frozen at a cryogenics
facility in California, then had it stored in a shed at Bauge's unfinished
house in Nederland, Colorado. In 1994 Bauge lost a battle with immi-
gration authorities and was deported to Norway. He arranged to pay
$674 per month to locals to deliver dry ice to keep Morstoel from
thawing out. Four years later, Morstoel became the subject of a short
film, *Grandpa's in the Tuff Shed,* directed by Robin Beeck. Tom Plant,
Nederland's representative in the state legislature, tried in 2002 to have
March 9 declared "Frozen Dead Guy Day," pointing out that "Grandpa
Bredo" had been "a model citizen, never giving the cold shoulder to
anyone." Many representatives were not amused, and the motion lost,
35 votes to 27. Despite this setback, Nederland held a festival honoring
Morstoel on the weekend of March 9–10. The main events were a
showing of *Grandpa's in the Tuff Shed* and a coffin race. A longer
sequel, *Grandpa's Still in the Tuff Shed,* was released in 2003.

27. TED WILLIAMS

After the Hall of Fame baseball player died at age 83 in 2002, he was
taken to the Alcor Life Extension Foundation's cryogenic facility in
Scottsdale, Arizona. The decision was challenged by Williams's oldest
daughter, Bobby Jo, since his will stated that he wanted to be cremated
and have his ashes scattered off the coast of Florida. Williams's son
John Henry produced a note in which he, Ted, and Ted's daughter
Claudia entered into a pact to freeze themselves after death. The
handwritten pact, signed by all three, read, "JHW, Claudia and Dad all
agree to be put in Bio-stasis after we die. This is what we want, to be
able to be together in the future, even if it is only a chance." The suit
was settled in December of 2002, and Ted Williams will remain indefi-
nitely in one of Alcor's liquid nitrogen–filled cryogenic tanks.

28. DOLLY

Dolly the sheep was famous as the first mammal successfully cloned
from an adult. Her birth in 1996 was heralded as a scientific breakthrough but also triggered heated debate about the ethics of cloning.
Dolly was put to sleep on February 13, 2003, after developing a fatal
lung disease. Her preserved remains were placed on display at the
Royal Museum in Edinburgh, Scotland.

29. JOSEPH PAUL JERNIGAN

In 1993, convicted murderer Joseph Paul Jernigan was executed in Texas. Because he had donated his body to science, his body was frozen and shipped to the University of Colorado, where it was "sliced" into 1,800 cross-sections. Two years later, a 59-year-old Maryland woman was similarly sliced, but into 5,000 segments. These two became the subjects of the Visible Human Project, the first computerized library of human anatomy, to be made available to medical researchers around the world.

I.W., J.Be., C.F. & the Eds.

Remains to Be Seen: 14 Preserved Parts

1. SAARTJE BAARTMAN'S BRAIN AND SEXUAL ORGANS

Baartman was born in the Cape Colony (part of modern-day South Africa) in 1789. Around 1810, she was taken to London by a British navy doctor, who exhibited her in Britain and France as the "Hottentot Venus." People paid to gawk at her unusually large buttocks and elongated labia. Baartman was also studied by racial theorists seeking to support notions of the inherent superiority of European races. After she died in poverty at age 27, her brain and sexual organs were preserved and put on display at the Musée de l'Homme (Museum of Man) in Paris. After the fall of apartheid, the government of South Africa began requesting the return of Baartman's remains. In April 2002, the preserved organs, Baartman's skeleton, and a plaster cast of her body that had been on display were handed over at the South African embassy. "She has recovered her dignity, albeit after many years, with a ceremony that has celebrated her as a true person, and I am very happy about it," announced Bernard Chevassus-au-Louis, director of the French Museum of Natural History.

2. ST. BONAVENTURE'S HEAD

This great Catholic theologian and philosopher is one person who definitely did not rest in peace. Almost 300 years after his death in 1274, his remains were caught in the middle of a French religious war that pitted the Roman Catholic Church against the Protestant Huguenots. In 1562, St. Bonaventure's tomb at Lyons was plundered. While his body was publicly burned, the head—said to be perfectly preserved—was saved and hidden by one of the faithful. It disappeared, however, during the French Revolution and has not been seen since.

3. PAUL BROCA'S BRAIN

In one of the less frequented corners of the Musée de l'Homme (Museum of Man) in Paris are numerous bottles containing human brains. Some belonged to intellectuals, others to criminals. But perhaps the most distinguished of the specimens is that of Paul Broca, a nineteenth-century physician and anthropologist who was the father of modern brain surgery.

4. DEL CLOSE'S SKULL

Close was an improvisational comedian who trained John Belushi, Bill Murray, and Mike Myers. Upon his death in 1999, he willed his skull to Chicago's Goodman Theatre to be used as Yorick's skull in productions of *Hamlet*. Close's former improv partner, Charna Halpern, noted, "It's not the starring role. But Del was always willing to take smaller parts." Close was not the only actor to continue his profession after he died. Irish-born actor George Frederick Cooke died in 1812, but his skull was used in productions of *Hamlet* before being retired to the Thomas Jefferson University Medical School library in Philadelphia.

5. BARON PIERRE DE COUBERTIN'S HEART

Lausanne, Switzerland, and Olympia, Greece, are the two most revered sites of the modern Olympic movement. Baron Pierre de Coubertin, the founder of the movement, left a part of himself in each place. His will requested that his body be buried at Lausanne, the site of the International Olympic Committee headquarters. But first his heart was to be removed and placed in a marble column at Olympia, where the ancient games were held.

6. ALBERT EINSTEIN'S BRAIN

What might have been the greatest brain of the twentieth century was not buried with the body that housed it. Albert Einstein asked that after his death his brain be removed for study. And when the great physicist died in 1955, this was done. The brain—which was neither larger nor heavier than the norm—was photographed, sectioned into 240 blocks, and sent around the country to be studied by specialists. His parietal lobes were discovered to be unusually large.

7. GALILEO'S FINGER

The great astronomer died in 1642, but his body was not interred in its final resting place until 1737. During that final transfer to a mausoleum at the Church of Santa Croce in Florence on March 12, an intellectual admirer, Anton Francesco Gori, cut off Galileo's middle finger as a keepsake. After passing through various hands, it was acquired by Florence's Museum of the History of Science, where it is now encased in glass and pointing skyward.

8. JOSEPH HAYDN'S HEAD

The Austrian composer died in 1809. Soon after his burial, a prison warden who was an amateur phrenologist—a person who tries to correlate head bumps with character traits—hired grave robbers to steal the head. The warden examined the skull, then gave it to an acquaintance, and a remarkable 145-year odyssey began. The theft of the skull was discovered in 1820, when the family of Haydn's patron had the body disinterred. Eventually they got a skull back, but it wasn't Haydn's. The real item was passed from one owner to another, some of them individuals, others organizations. Finally, it found a home in a glass case at Vienna's Society of Friends of Music. In 1932, the descendants of Haydn's patrons once again tried to get it back. But WWII and then the Cold War intervened—the body was in Austria's Soviet quarter, but the skull was in the international zone. It wasn't until 1954 that body and skull were finally reunited.

9. MAJOR JOHN W. POWELL'S BRAIN
    Geologist John W. Powell donated his brain to the Smithsonian Institution, of which he was an official, in order to settle a bet with an associate over whose brain was larger. Although Powell's gray matter is still in the museum collection, that of his associate is nowhere to be found, which makes Powell the winner by default.

10. JOSÉ RIZAL'S VERTEBRA
    José Rizal, the national hero of the Philippines, was accused of sedition, executed by the Spanish in 1896, and buried without a coffin. He was exhumed in August 1898, after the Americans took Manila. Most of Rizal's remains are interred beneath the Rizal Monument in Luneta—all except one of his cervical vertebrae; the vertebra is enshrined like a holy relic in Fort Santiago.

11. DAN SICKLES'S LEG
    Sickles was a colorful New York congressman who organized and led a brigade of volunteers at the outbreak of the Civil War. He was involved in some of the bloodiest fighting at Gettysburg, losing his right leg in the battle. That trauma, however, apparently did not diminish Sickles's personal flair. He had the leg preserved and sent to Washington, where it was exhibited in a little wooden coffin at the medical museum of the Library of Congress. Sickles frequently visited it himself.

12. LAZZARO SPALLANZANI'S BLADDER
    When Italian biologist Spallanzani died in 1799, his diseased bladder was excised for study by his colleagues. It is currently on display in the Scarpa Room at the University of Pavia in Italy, where it remains a monument to the inquisitive mind.

13-14. GEORGE WASHINGTON'S HAIR AND TOOTH
    In June 1793, George Washington gave a locket containing a clipping of his hair to his aide-de-camp, Colonel John Trumbull. When

Trumbull died, he willed the lock of hair to a first cousin of the president's, Dr. James A. Washington, who passed it along to his family as a sort of "hairloom." George Washington's dentist, John Greenwood, managed to acquire another collectible that the president shed from his person—the last of his natural teeth. Washington mailed the tooth to Greenwood to use as a model in making a new set of dentures. The dentist kept the tooth as a souvenir, and it remained in the Greenwood family for generations.

E.F. & M.J.T.

Miscellaneous

LONG NOSE CHAMPION MEHMET OZYUREK

21 IGNOBLE PRIZES

The Ignobel Prize Award Ceremony was begun in 1991 and has continued to grow in popularity. According to the Ignobel Prize Committee. "The winners have all done things that first make people laugh, then make them think." More information is available in the book *Ig Nobel Prizes*, by Marc Abrahams (London: Orion, 2002).

1. In 1991, the BIOLOGY award went to Robert Klark Graham, for his pioneering development of the Repository for Germinal Choice, a sperm bank that accepts donations only from Nobellians and Olympians.

2. In 1992, the ARCHAEOLOGY award went to the Eclaieurs de France, a Protestant youth group whose name means "those who show the way," fresh-scrubbed removers of graffiti, for erasing the ancient paintings from the walls of the Meyrieres Cave near the French village of Bruniquel.

3. In 1993, the MATHEMATICS award went to Robert Fraid of Greenville, South Carolina, for calculating the exact odds (710,609,175,188,282,000 to 1) that Mikhail Gorbachev is the Antichrist.

4. In 1993, the PEACE award went to the Pepsi-Cola Company of the Philippines, for sponsoring a contest to create a millionaire, then announcing the wrong winning number, thereby inciting and uniting 800,000 riotously expectant winners, and bringing together warring factions for the first time in the nation's history.

5. In 1993, the LITERATURE prize was given to E. Topol, R. Califf, F. Van de Werf, P. W. Armstrong, and their 972 coauthors, for publishing a medical research paper with 100 times as may authors as pages. The study was published in *The New England Journal* of *Medicine*, vol. 329, no 10, September 2. 1993, pp. 673–82.

6. In 1994, the BIOLOGY prize was awarded to W. Brian Sweeney, Brian Krafte-Jacobs, Jeffrey W. Britton, and Wayne Hansen, for their breakthrough study, "The Constipated Serviceman: Prevalence Among Deployed U.S. Troops," and especially for their numerical analysis of bowel movement frequency. Published in *Military Medicine*, vol. 158, August 1993.

7. In 1995, the NUTRITION award went to John Martinez of J. Martinez & Company in Atlanta, Georgia, for Luak Coffee, the world's most expensive coffee, made from beans ingested and excreted by the luak, a bobcatlike animal native to Indonesia.

8. In 1996, the BIOLOGY prize was given to Anders Barheim and Hogne Sandvik of the University of Bergen, Norway, for their report, "Effects of Ale, Garlic and Soured Cream on the Appetite of Leeches," published in the *British Medical Journal*, vol. 309, 1994.

9. In 1996, the PUBLIC HEALTH prize went to Ellen Kleist of Nuuk, Greenland and Harald Moi of Oslo, Norway, for their cautionary medical report, "Transmission of Gonorrhea Through an Inflatable Doll," published in *Genitourinary Medicine*, vol. 69, 1993.

10. In 1997, the ENTOMOLOGY award went to Mark Hostetler of the University of Florida, for his scholarly study, "That Gunk on Your Car," which identifies the insect splats that appear on automobile screens and windows.

11. In 1998, the BIOLOGY winner was Peter Fong of Gettysburg College, Gettysburg, Pennsylvania, for contributing to the happiness of clams by giving them Prozac. Published in the *Journal of Experimental Zoology* as "Induction and Potentiation of Parturition in Fingernail Clams (Sphaerium striatinum) by Selective Serotonin ReUptake Inhibitors (SSRI's)," Peter F. Fong, Peter T. Huminski, and Lynette M. D'urso, 1998.

12. In 1999, the ENVIRONMENTAL PROTECTION award went to Hyuk-ho Kwon of Kolon Co. of Seoul, Korea, for inventing the self-perfuming business suit.

13. In 1999, the LITERATURE prize was given to the British Standards Institution for its six-page specification (BS-6008) of the proper way to make a cup of tea.

14. In 1999, the MEDICINE award went to Dr. Arvid Vatle of Stord, Norway, for collecting, classifying, and contemplating which kinds of containers his patients chose when submitting urine samples. Paper published in the *Journal of the Norwegian Medical Association.*

15. In 1999, the CHEMISTRY prize went to Takeshi Makino, president of the Safety Detective Agency in Osaka, Japan, for his work on S-Check, an infidelity detection spray that wives can apply to their husbands' underwear.

16. The 2000 ECONOMICS prize went to the Reverend Sun Myung Moon, for bringing efficiency and steady growth to the mass-marriage industry. From a 36-couple wedding in 1960, Moon went on to a 6,000-couple wedding in 1982, a 30,000-couple wedding in 1992, a 360,000-couple wedding in 1992, and so on, culminating (so far) in a 36,000,000-couple wedding in 1997.

17. In 2001, the PEACE prize went to Viliumas Malinauskus of Grutas, Lithuania, for creating an amusement park known as "Stalin World."

18. In 2001, the LITERATURE prize was awarded to John Richards of Boston, England, founder of the Apostrophe Protection Society, for his efforts to promote, protect, and defend the differences between plural and possessive.

19. The 2002 HYGIENE prize was received by Eduardo Segura of Lavakan de Aste, who in Tarragona, Spain, invented a washing machine for cats and dogs.

20. The 2003 ECONOMICS award was given to Karl Schwarzler and the nation of Liechtenstein, for making it possible to rent the entire country for corporate conventions, weddings, bar mitzvahs, and other gatherings.

21. The 2003 PHYSICS prize was given to six Australian scientists for their breakthrough report: "An Analysis of the Forces Required to Drag Sheep over Various Surfaces."

10 Famous Noses

1. RUDOLF I OF HAPSBURG (German king and Holy Roman emperor, 1218–1291)
   According to one historian of anatomy, Rudolf "had so large a nose that no artist would ever paint its full dimension."

2. MICHELANGELO (Italian artist, 1475–1564)
   Michelangelo's nose was so squashed against his face that, in the words of one historian, "his forehead almost overhangs the nose." As a boy, Michelangelo had mercilessly teased the painter Pietro Torrigiano while Torrigiano was trying to study some art inside a church. Angered, Torrigiano turned on young Michelangelo and, in his own words, "dealt him such a blow on the nose that I felt the bone and the cartilage yield under my fist as if they had been made of crisp wafer. And so he'll go with my mark on him to his dying day."

3. MATTHEW PARKER (English clergyman, 1504–1575)
   Matthew Parker's name entered the English language as "Nosey" Parker—meaning someone who pokes his nose into other people's business. Parker was archbishop of Canterbury under Queen Elizabeth I. Though shy and modest, he was overinquisitive about church matters, and his enemies began to call him "Nosey."

4. **TYCHO BRAHE** (Danish astronomer, 1546–1601)
   Brahe lost the bridge of his nose in a swordfight when he was 20 years old and replaced it with a silver one.

5. **CYRANO DE BERGERAC** (French poet and soldier, 1619–1655)
   He really was a living person. He is said to have fought a thousand duels over insults concerning his enormous nose.

6. **THOMAS WEDDERS** (English circus freak, 1700s)
   Wedders had the longest known nose of any human being in history. It measured 7½ inches in length. He was exhibited throughout England and was said to be mentally retarded.

7. **JOSEF MYSLIVEČEK** (Czech composer, 1737–1781)
   Nicknamed the Bohemian, Mysliveček was known for his operas *Armida* and *Il Bellerofonte* and for the fact that he had no nose. In 1777, suffering from a venereal disease, he went to a third-rate doctor who told him that the only way to cure the disease was to remove his nose. So off it came. This led to the collapse of his career, and he died in poverty.

8. **KATE ELDER, alias FISHER** (American brothel owner, 1870s)
   Elder was famous in the Wild West as "Big Nose" Kate. Her nose was of the bulbous variety. She ran a house of ill fame in Dodge City, Kansas, and was the mistress of badman Doc Holliday. Once when Holliday, in an argument over a poker hand, slit his opponent's throat and was about to be arrested, Kate set the livery stable afire, creating a distraction that allowed her lover to escape.

9. **JIMMY "SCHNOZZOLA" DURANTE** (American entertainer, 1893–1980)
   Durante parlayed his elongated proboscis into a show business fortune as he became a song-and-dance comic star of stage, screen, and television.

10. **MEHMET OZYUREK** (Longest Nose Contest Winner)
    Ozyurek is the only two-time winner of the Longest Nose competition in Rize, Turkey. Proudly displaying his 3½-inch nose, he won the inaugural contest in 1997 and then regained the title in 2000.

                                                                    I.W. & J.Be.

Bruce Felton's *What Were They Thinking?* 14 of the Worst Ideas In History

Bruce Felton is the coauthor of *The Best, Worst & Most Unusual: Note-worthy Achievements, Events, Feats & Blunders of Every Conceivable*

Kind and *Felton and Fowler's Famous Americans You Never Knew Existed* and the author of *What Were They Thinking? Really Bad Ideas Throughout History.*

1. **SENATOR SOUP**
   Victor Biaka-Boda, the Ivory Coast's representative in the French Senate, returned to his home district in January 1950 to campaign for reelection. It wasn't a smart career move. Later that month, his belongings and bones were found near the village of Bouafle. The leftovers were shipped to police labs in Paris for analysis, but it was plain that Biaka-Boda had ended his days in a tureen. Until the facts were in, however, a successor could not be named, and his constituents had to forgo representation. It took the French Overseas Ministry two years to acknowledge officially that Biaka-Boda had been eaten. Only then could the vacancy be filled. As the *New York Times* delicately put it, "You cannot have your senator and eat him too."

2. **THE PLOT TO KILL HITLER'S MUSTACHE**
   In a study of Adolf Hitler's health and habits during World War II, the Office of Strategic Services—forerunner of the CIA—found that the Führer was "close to the male-female line," according to Stanley Lovell, wartime director of research and development for the OSS. "A push to the female side might make his mustache fall out and his voice become soprano," turning Hitler into a national laughingstock and driving him from power. To make it happen, the OSS bribed Hitler's personal gardener to inject estrogen into the Führer's food. Inevitably, this absurd "destabilization program" failed. Lovell speculates that either Hitler's official tasters noticed something funny about the carrots, or, more likely, the gardener was a double-crosser who kept the bribe and discarded the hormones.

3. **JUST THE FAX, MA'AM**
   When residents of Seoul, South Korea, complained that police emergency phone lines were often busy, the Metropolitan Police Administration added two emergency fax lines.

4. **BADGE OF EXCELLENCE**
   The U.S. Consumer Product Safety Commission paid $1,700 for 80,000 promotional buttons with the slogan "Think Toy Safety" in the 1970s. But the buttons turned out to be more of a menace than any toy concocted by the most socially irresponsible toy manufacturer. The metal tags had sharp edges and metal tab fasteners that broke off easily and were a sure bet to be swallowed by small children. Also, the buttons were coated with lead paint. Eventually, the commission recalled the buttons with an eye to recycling them or just scuttling the lot.

5. GUILT TRIP

Novelist Thomas Wolfe was once injured jumping off a moving train as it pulled out of New York's Grand Central Station. Wolfe was on the way to spend a weekend at the Connecticut home of his editor, Maxwell Perkins, when he suddenly decided that he should be back in Brooklyn writing.

6. THE HILLS ARE ALIVE WITH THE SOUND OF SPLICING

A movie theater manager in Seoul, South Korea, decided that the running time of *The Sound of Music* was too long. He shortened it by cutting out all the songs.

7. FINANCIAL AID FOR THE DIFFERENTLY HANDED

Juniata College, in Huntingdon, Pennsylvania, offers a scholarship to left-handed students with financial need. The stipend was established by alumni Frederick and Mary Francis Beckley, who were dropped from the college tennis team in 1919 solely because of their left-handedness. Other excessively specialized scholarships include:

- The International Boar Semen Scholarship, a $500 stipend earmarked for the study of swine management at the undergraduate level. IBS is a division of Universal Pig Genes, Inc.
- The $500 NAAFA-NEC Scholarship, awarded to obese college-bound high school seniors by the New England Chapter of the National Association to Advance Fat Acceptance.
- The Zolp Scholarship, available exclusively to Loyola University (Chicago) students named "Zolp."

8. BALLOON TALK

In 1917, more than a decade before the first talking motion pictures, inventor Charles Pidgin patented a breakthrough way to simulate speech on screen. Before filming, balloons "made of rubber or any other suitable material" are concealed in each performer's mouth. The balloons are imprinted with dialogue; characters simply blow up their balloons on cue, allowing their lines to be read just as if they were comic strip figures.

9. HONK IF YOU LOVE RADIATION SICKNESS, BIRTH DEFECTS, AND THE END OF CIVILIZATION AS WE KNOW IT

The Nevada state legislature authorized a new license plate in 2002 depicting a mushroom cloud from an atomic explosion. The design symbolized the 928 nuclear weapons tests conducted in the Nevada desert from 1945 through 1992. Ultimately, the Nevada Department of Motor Vehicles rejected the concept, noting that "any reference on a license plate to weapons of mass destruction is inappropriate and would likely offend our citizens."

10. **BIG SPENDER**

In the fourteenth century, Mansa Musa held sway over the Mali Empire, among the most powerful and far-reaching Islamic kingdoms of its time. Musa was an enlightened leader who sought peace with his neighbors, fostered the arts, and built majestic structures. He also liked to have a good time. In 1324, he led 60,000 followers on a pilgrimage to Mecca; a retinue of 500 slaves bearing solid gold scepters accompanied them. Along the way, Musa stopped off in Cairo for a few months of revels and relaxation. He spent so much gold in the Egyptian capital that the national economy collapsed. Musa and his followers continued to Mecca and returned to Mali all but broke; it was years before Egypt recovered from the emperor's excesses.

11. **SCHUMANN'S FINGER-RACK**

As a young man, composer Robert Schumann (1810–1856) showed great promise as a concert pianist. Unfortunately, the middle and fourth fingers of his right hand lacked suppleness and agility. To whip some discipline into the wayward digits, he invented a device that held them in place and stretched them while the others played freely. Schumann's homemade finger-rack turned out to be so effective that he wound up crippling his fingers. On doctor's orders, he marinated his hand regularly in a restorative bath of warm animal guts, but the injury was permanent, and Schumann never played seriously again.

12. **THE ANNALS OF ACADEME**

At its 1989 commencement ceremonies, Ohio's Central State University awarded boxer Mike Tyson an honorary doctorate in humane letters.

13. **GAME CALLED ON ACCOUNT OF HEIDI**

On the evening of November 17, 1968, millions of American football fans were watching the New York Jets battle the Oakland Raiders in a game aired over NBC. At 7:00 p.m., with a minute left to go in the fourth quarter and the Jets protecting a 32–29 lead, NBC programmers aborted the telecast to begin a regularly scheduled showing of the movie *Heidi*. Viewers must have thought they were hallucinating when their TV pictures suddenly morphed from football to postcard scenes of Alpine meadows. When it became known that the Raiders had scored two last-minute touchdowns to pull out a 43–32 victory, the tide of enraged phone calls swamped the NBC switchboard and the circuits went dead. Those who couldn't get through to NBC called the New York City Police Department. NBC executives later claimed that as Oakland started its remarkable comeback, they considered cutting back to the game. But before they could make up their minds, the clock ran out.

14. **BRINGING STARLINGS TO AMERICA**

Screechy and aggressive, starlings gather in noisy flocks, befouling the nation's byways, decimating wheat fields, and terrifying nicer birds.

Worse, America would be starling-free had it not been for one man's misguided obsession with the plays of Shakespeare. In Manhattan's Central Park in 1890, a wealthy New Yorker named Eugene Scheifflin released 40 pairs of starlings imported from Europe. No starling had ever entered U.S. airspace before; the launching of these 80 was part of Scheifflin's grand scheme to introduce in this country specimens of every bird mentioned in Shakespeare. ("I'll have a starling that shall be taught to speak nothing but 'Mortimer'": *Henry IV*.) While most of the other Old World birds brought over by Scheifflin died out, his starlings bred like bunnies. Sizable colonies were spotted as far away as Connecticut by 1898 and in Pennsylvania, Delaware, and upstate New York by 1910. By 1947, they had spread to the West Coast. Today, they're everywhere. And, like cockroaches and magazine blow-in cards, there's no getting rid of them. The U.S. Army has tried to downsize the starling population with blasts of Tergitol, a potent detergent that washes away the protective coating of oil that keeps the birds from freezing to death. But so far, Scheifflin's babies are doing just fine.

Jeremy Beadle's
20 Not-So-Easy Quiz Questions

Writer and TV presenter Jeremy Beadle first came to major public attention in 1981 when he cohosted *Game for a Laugh*. Among the other series he has presented are *Beadle's About*, *You've Been Framed*, and *Win Beadle's Money*. But before all that, he was the European editor of *The Book of Lists*. He has a personal library of 25,000 volumes. Here Beadle displays his passion for quizzes in typical style.

1. What color are the breasts of blue tits?

2. To which planet do Abbott and Costello travel in *Abbott & Costello Go to Mars*?

3. How long does morning last on the moon?

4. The Caspian Sea is the world's largest what?

5. Where would you go to have a meal in Le Restaurant de la Tour Eiffel?

6. In England what day followed September 2 in 1752?

7. How far down a flagpole should a flag be if it is flying at half mast?

8. Where does Juliet stand during the famous balcony scene of *Romeo and Juliet?*

9. What religion was Britain's only Jewish prime minister?

10. What type of creature was Buffalo Bill famous for killing?

11. Is the Upper Nile north, south, east, or west of the Lower Nile?

12. It was predicted Henry IV would die in Jerusalem, and he did. In which town did he die?

13. In the 1948 London Olympics, what stroke was used by the first seven finishers in the 200-meter breaststroke final?

14. At the time of writing, the world's population is estimated at 6,222,336,610. Approximately how many of them live on the surface of the earth?

15. Who wrote *The Autobiography of Malcolm X?*

16. In which city was the Plymouth Brethren founded?

17. What was the name of the character played by Clint Eastwood in the 1973 film *The Man with No Name?*

18. On what side of the moon is the Eastern Sea?

19. *The Hitchhiker's Guide to the Galaxy* is a trilogy of how many parts?

20. Including Queen Elizabeth II, how many Queen Elizabeths of England have there been?

ANSWERS
1. Yellow.
2. Venus.
3. A week.
4. Lake.
5. New Orleans, Louisiana. The dismantled restaurant was originally on the first level of the Tower, from 1937 to 1981.
6. September 14, 1752—the country adopted the Gregorian calendar.
7. Only the distance equal to its depth; i.e., the top edge is placed where the bottom edge should rest.
8. On a floor beside an upper window. There is no mention of a balcony.
9. Christian; Benjamin Disraeli was baptized into the Church of England at the age of 12.
10. None; he shot bison—buffalo are found in Africa and India.

11. South; it's higher—more elevated—hence its name.
12. London. He died in the Jerusalem Chapel in Westminster Abbey in 1413.
13. Butterfly.
14. Exactly none. The actual surface of the earth, as defined by astronomers, is the outer edge of the atmosphere, about 100 miles above our heads.
15. Alex Haley.
16. Dublin, in about 1827 by the Reverend John Darby.
17. Joe.
18. West. Originally on the east, but owing to a policy decision by the International Astronomical Union reversing lunar east and west, the Eastern Sea is now on the western limb of the moon.
19. Five.
20. Five. Edward IV's consort, Henry VII's consort, Queen Elizabeth I, George VI's consort, and Queen Elizabeth II.

15 Strange Stories

The *Fortean Times, the Journal of Strange Phenomena*, is a monthly magazine of news, reviews, and research on all types of unusual phenomena and experiences. It was named after philosopher Charles Fort (1874–1932), who thought that data that did not fit the scientific norm should not be excluded or ignored by the scientific community. (To subscribe, write to Fortean Times, PO Box 2409, London NW5 4NP, United Kingdom.) These stories were selected by Paul Sieveking, coeditor of the *Fortean Times*.

1. BEES PAY THEIR RESPECTS
   Margaret Bell, who kept bees in Leintwardine, about seven miles from her home in Ludlow, Wales, died in June 1994. After her funeral, mourners were astonished to see hundreds of bees settle on the corner of the street opposite the house where Mrs. Bell had lived for 26 years. The bees stayed for about an hour before buzzing off over the rooftops. The local press ran a photograph of the bees, hanging on the wall in a cluster.

2. PHANTOM CAR CRASH
   On December 11, 2002, two motorists called police to report seeing a car veer off the A3 trunk road with headlights blazing at Burpham in Surrey. A thorough search uncovered a car concealed in dense undergrowth and the long-dead driver nearby. It turned out that the crash had happened five months earlier; the driver, Christopher Chandler, had been reported missing by his brother.

3. **ENIGMATIC EARTH DIVOT**

   An irregularly shaped hole, about 10 by 7 feet with 2-foot vertical sides, was found on remote farmland near Grand Coulee, Washington, in October 1984. It had not been there a month earlier. "Dribblings" of earth and stones led to a three-ton, grass-covered earth divot 75 feet away. It was almost as if the divot had been removed with a "gigantic cookie cutter," except that roots dangled intact from the vertical sides of both hole and displaced slab. There were no clues such as vehicle tracks, and a seismic cause was thought very unlikely, although there had been a mild quake 20 miles away a week before the hole's discovery.

4. **BALLOON BUDDIES**

   Laura Buxton released a helium-filled balloon during celebrations for her grandparents' gold wedding anniversary in Blurton, Staffordshire, in June 2001. Attached to the balloon were her name and address and a note asking the finder to write back. Ten days later, she received a reply. The balloon had been found by another Laura Buxton in the garden hedge of her home in Pewsey, Wiltshire, 140 miles away. Both Lauras were aged ten, and both had three-year-old black Labradors, a guinea pig, and a rabbit. "I hope we can become best friends," said the Staffordshire Laura.

5. **HUM MISTY FOR ME**

   A noise a bit like amplifier feedback had been heard for three years coming from the right ear of a Welsh pony called Misty, according to the *Veterinary Record* (April 1995). It varied in intensity but stayed at a constant pitch of 7 kilohertz. Hearing a buzzing in one's ears is called subjective tinnitus; very much rarer is when other people can hear the noise, a condition called objective tinnitus, the cause of which is a matter of debate.

6. **WHIRLWIND CHILDREN**

   A nine-year-old Chinese girl was playing in Songjiang, near Shanghai, in July 1992, when she was carried off by a whirlwind and deposited unhurt in a treetop almost 2 miles away. According to a wire report from May 1986, a freak wind lifted 13 children in the oasis of Hami in western China and deposited them unharmed in sand dunes and scrub 12 miles away.

7. **RIVERSIDE MYSTERY**

   Gloria Ramirez, 31, died of kidney failure at Riverside General Hospital, California, in February 1994, after being rushed there with chest pains. Emergency room staff were felled by "fumes" when a blood sample was taken. A strange oily sheen on the woman's skin and unexplained white crystals in her blood were reported. A doctor suffered liver and lung damage and bone necrosis; at least 23 other people were affected. One hypothesis was that Ramirez, who had cervical cancer, had taken a cocktail of medicines that combined to make an insecticide (organophosphate), but exhaustive tests yielded no clues. The hospital was later demolished. The episode remains a mystery 10 years later.

8. BOULDERS IN TREES

In April 1997, a turkey hunter in Yellowwood State Forest, Indiana, came upon a huge sandstone boulder wedged between three branches of an oak tree about 35 feet from the ground. The arrow-shaped rock was estimated to weigh 500 pounds. Subsequently, four more large boulders were found wedged high up in trees elsewhere in the forest. All were in remote areas. None of the trees was damaged, there were no signs of heavy equipment being used or of tornado damage, and no one recalled any mishaps involving dynamite anywhere nearby.

9. HELPFUL VOICES

While on holiday, a woman, referred to in the *British Medical Journal* (December 1997) as AB, heard two voices in her head identifying themselves as staff from the Great Ormond Street Children's Hospital in London and telling her to return home immediately. Once she was back in London, the voices gave her an address that turned out to be a hospital's brain scan department. They told her to ask for a scan, as she had a brain tumor and her brain stem was inflamed. Though she had no symptoms, medical staff reluctantly agreed to a scan, and she did indeed have a tumor. After an operation in May 1984, AB heard the voices again. "We are pleased to have helped you," they said. "Good-bye." AB made a full recovery and never heard the voices again.

10. LA MANCHA NEGRA

A hazard unique to Venezuelan highways is a slippery goo called *la mancha negra*, which means "black stain," although it's more of a sludge with the consistency of chewing gum. Although the government has spent millions of dollars in research, no one knows what the goo is, where it comes from, or how to get rid of it. It first appeared in 1987 on the road from Caracas to the airport, covering 50 yards, and it has spread inexorably every year. By 1992, it was a major road hazard all around the capital; it was claimed that 1,800 motorists had died after losing control because of it. The problem remains.

11. POSTCARD FAREWELL

When Jim Wilson's father died in Natal, South Africa, in April 1967, both Jim, living in England, and his sister Muriel, living in Holland, were informed. Muriel contacted her husband, who was on business in Portugal, and he flew to South Africa right away. Changing planes at Las Palmas airport in the Canary Islands, he bought a postcard showing holiday makers on Margate Beach in Natal and sent it to Muriel. It was she who noticed that the photograph showed her father walking up the beach.

12. NOTECASE FROM THE SKY

In October 1975, Mrs. Lynn Connolly was hanging washing in her garden in The Quadrant, Hull, in England, when she felt a sharp tap on the top of her head. It was caused by a small silver notecase, 2½ inches by 1½ inches, hinged, containing a used notepad with 13 sheets left. It was marked with the initials "SE," "C8," "TB" (or "JB") and "Klaipeda," a Lithuanian seaport. No one claimed it at the police station, so it was returned to Mrs. Connolly. It seems likely it fell only a short distance, but from where? If it had dropped from a plane, it would have given her more than a tap.

13. FIERY PERSECUTION

The village of Canneto di Caronia on Sicily's north coast has been plagued by mysterious fires. The trouble began on January 20, 2004, when a TV caught fire. Then things in neighboring houses began to burn, including washing machines, mobile phones, mattresses, chairs, and even the insulation on water pipes. The electricity company cut off all power, as did the railway company, but the fires continued. Experts of all kinds carried out tests, but no explanation was found. The village was evacuated in February, but when people began returning in March, the fires resumed. Police ruled out a pyromaniac after they saw wires bursting into flames. Father Gabriel Amorth, the Vatican's chief exorcist, was quoted as blaming demons.

14. BOVINE ENIGMA

On June 28, 2002, in the middle of a spate of unexplained cattle mutilations in Argentina, something macabre was found in a field near Suco, west of Rio Cuarto in San Luis province. Nineteen cows were stuffed into a sheet-metal water tank, closed with a conical cap. Nine were drowned; the rest were barely alive, having endured freezing temperatures, not to mention the shock of their lives.

15. BOY TURNS INTO YAM

Three pupils of the Evangelist Primary School in the northern Nigerian town of Maiduguri rushed into the headmistress's office in March 2000 and said that a fellow pupil had been transformed into a yam after accepting a sweet from a stranger. The headmistress found the root tuber and took it to the police station for safekeeping. Following local radio reports, hundreds of people flocked to see the yam, and police were hunting for the sweetgiver. What happened next failed to reach the wire services.

27 Things That Fell from the Sky

1. HAY

   A great cloud of hay drifted over the town of Devizes in England at tea time on July 3, 1977. As soon as the cloud reached the center of town, it all fell to earth in handful-size lumps. The sky was otherwise clear and cloudless with a slight breeze. The temperature was 79°F.

2. GOLDEN RAIN

   When yellow-colored globules fell over suburban Sydney, Australia, in late 1971, the ministry for health blamed it on the excreta of bees, consisting mostly of undigested pollen. However, there were no reports of vast hordes of bees in the area and no explanation as to why they would choose to excrete en masse over Sydney.

3. BLACK EGGS

   On May 5, 1786, after six months of drought, a strong east wind dropped a great quantity of black eggs on the city of Port-au-Prince, Haiti. Some of the eggs were preserved in water and hatched the next day. The beings inside shed several layers of skin and resembled tadpoles.

4. MEAT

   The famous Kentucky meat shower took place in southern Bath County on Friday, March 3, 1876. Mrs. Allen Crouch was in her yard making soap when pieces of fresh meat the size of large snowflakes began to fall from the cloudless sky. Two gentlemen who tasted it said that it was either mutton or venison. Scientists who examined the material found the first samples similar to lung tissue from either a human infant or a horse. Later samples were identified as cartilage and striated muscle fibers. The local explanation was that a flock of buzzards had disgorged as a group while flying overhead.

5. A 3,902-POUND STONE

   The largest meteorite fall in recorded history occurred on March 8, 1976, near the Chinese city of Kirin. Many of the 100 stones that were found weighed over 200 pounds; the largest, which landed in the Haupi Commune, weighed 3,902 pounds. It is, by more than 1,000 pounds, the largest stony meteorite ever recovered.

6. MONEY

   On October 8, 1976, a light plane buzzed the Piazza Venezia in Rome and dropped 500-lire, 1,000-lire, and 10,000-lire banknotes on the startled people below. The mad bomber was not found.

7. SOOT
   A fine blanket of soot landed on a Cranford park on the edge of London's Heathrow Airport in 1969, greatly annoying the local park keepers. The official report of the Greater London Council said the "soot" was composed of spores of a black microfungus, *Pithomyces chartarum*, found only in New Zealand.

8. FIVE HUNDRED BIRDS
   About 500 dead and dying blackbirds and pigeons landed in the streets of San Luis Obispo, California, over a period of several hours in late November 1977. No local spraying had occurred, and no explanation was offered.

9. FIRE
   On the evening of May 30, 1869, the horrified citizens of Greiffenberg, Germany, and neighboring villages witnessed a fall of fire, which was followed by a tremendous peal of thunder. People who were outside reported that the fire was different in form and color from common lightning. They said they felt wrapped in fire and deprived of air for some seconds.

10. WHITE FIBROUS BLOBS
    Blobs of white material up to 20 feet in length descended over the San Francisco Bay area in California on October 11, 1977. Pilots in San Jose encountered them as high as 4,000 feet. Migrating spiders were blamed, although no spiders were recovered.

11. LUMINOUS GREEN SNOW
    In April 1953, glowing green snow was encountered near Mt. Shasta, California. Mr. and Mrs. Milton Moyer reported that their hands itched after touching it and that "a blistered, itching rash" formed on their hands, arms, and faces. The Atomic Energy Commission denied any connection between the snow and recent A-bomb tests in nearby Nevada.

12. MYSTERIOUS DOCUMENTS
    The July 25, 1973, edition of the *Albany (NY) Times Union* reported the unusual case of Bob Hill. Hill, the owner of radio station WHRL of North Greenbush, New York, was taking out the station garbage at 4:15 p.m. when he noticed "twirling specks" falling from a distance higher than the station's 300-foot. transmitter. He followed two of the white objects until they landed in a hayfield. They turned out to be papers with two sets of formulas and accompanying graphs, which apparently explained "normalized extinction" and the "incomplete Davis-Greenstein orientation." No explanation has been made public. The Davis-Greenstein mechanism is used in astrophysics.

13. BEANS

Rancher Salvador Targino of João Pessoa, Brazil, reported a rain of small beans on his property in Paraíba State in early 1971. Local agricultural authorities speculated that a storm had swept up a pile of beans in West Africa and dropped them in northeastern Brazil. Targino boiled some of the beans but said they were too tough to eat.

14. SILVER COINS

Several thousand rubles' worth of silver coins fell in the Gorki region of the USSR on June 17, 1940. The official explanation was that a landslide had uncovered a hidden treasure, which was picked up by a tornado, which dropped it on Gorki. No explanation was given for the fact that the coins were not accompanied by any debris.

15. MUSHROOM-SHAPED THINGS

Traffic at Mexico City airport was halted temporarily on the morning of July 30, 1963, when thousands of grayish, mushroom-shaped things floated to the ground out of a cloudless sky. Hundreds of witnesses described these objects variously as "giant cobwebs," "balls of cotton," and "foam." They disintegrated rapidly after landing.

16. HUMAN BODY

Mary C. Fuller was sitting in her parked car with her eight-month-old son on Monday morning, September 25, 1978, in San Diego, California, when a human body crashed through the windshield. The body had been thrown from a Pacific Southwest Airlines jetliner, which had exploded after being hit by a small plane in one of the worst flight disasters in U.S. history. Mother and son suffered minor lacerations.

17. TOADS

Falls of frogs and toads, though not everyday occurrences, are actually quite common, having been reported in almost every part of the world. One of the most famous toad falls happened in the summer of 1794 in the village of Lalain, France. A very hot afternoon was broken suddenly by such an intense downpour of rain that 150 French soldiers (then fighting the Austrians) were forced to abandon the trench in which they were hiding to avoid being submerged. In the middle of the storm, which lasted for 30 minutes, tiny toads, mostly in the tadpole stage, began to land on the ground and jump about in all directions. When the rain let up, the soldiers discovered toads in the folds of their three-cornered hats.

18. OAK LEAVES

In late October of 1889, Mr. Wright of the parish of Penpont, Dumfries, Scotland, was startled by the appearance of what at first seemed to be a flock of birds, which began falling to the ground. Running toward them, he discovered the objects to be oak leaves, which eventually covered an area 1 mile wide and 2 miles long. The nearest clump of oak trees was 8 miles away, and no other kind of leaf fell.

19. JUDAS TREE SEEDS
    Just before sunset in August 1897, an immense number of small, blood-colored clouds filled the sky in Macerata, Italy. About an hour later, storm clouds burst and small seeds rained from the sky, covering the ground to a depth of half an inch. Many of the seeds had already started to germinate, and all of the seeds were from the Judas tree, which is found predominantly in the Middle East and Asia. There was no accompanying debris—just the Judas tree seeds.

20. FISH
    About 150 perchlike silver fish dropped from the sky during a tropical storm near Killarney Station in Australia's Northern Territory in February 1974. Fish falls are common enough that an "official" explanation has been developed to cover most of them. It is theorized that whirlwinds create a waterspout effect, sucking up water and fish, carrying them for a distance, and then dropping them.

21. ICE CHUNKS
    In February of 1965, a mass of ice plunged through the roof of the Phillips Petroleum plant in Woods Cross, Utah. In his book *Strangest of All*, Frank Edwards reported the case of a carpenter working on a roof in Kempten—near Düsseldorf, Germany—who was struck and killed in 1951 by an icicle 6 feet long and 6 inches around, which shot down from the sky.

22. PEACHES
    On July 12, 1961, unripe peaches were scattered over a small portion of Shreveport, Louisiana, from a cloudy sky.

23. DEADLY WHITE POWDER
    On Saturday, July 10, 1976, the citizens of Seveso, Italy, were startled by a sudden loud whistling sound coming from the direction of the nearby Icmesa chemical factory. The sound was followed by a thick, gray cloud, which rolled toward the town and dropped a mist of white dust that settled on everything and smelled horrible. It was 10 days before the people of Seveso learned that the white dust contained dioxin, a deadly poison far more dangerous than arsenic or strychnine. By then it was too late. The effects of dioxin poisoning had already begun. The area was evacuated, surrounded by barbed wire, and declared a contaminated zone. All exposed animals were killed, ugly black pustules formed on the skin of young children, babies were born deformed, and older people began to die of liver ailments. The full extent of the tragedy has still not been felt.

24. SPACE JUNK

In September 1962, a metal object about 6 inches in diameter and weighing 21 pounds crashed into a street intersection in Manitowoc, Wisconsin, and burrowed several inches into the ground. The object was later identified as part of *Sputnik IV*, which had been launched by the USSR on May 15, 1960. Since 1959, approximately 9,000 parts of spacecraft have fallen out of orbit, and many of them have reached the surface of the earth. On July 11, 1979, Skylab, the 77-ton U.S. space station, fell out of orbit over the South Indian Ocean and western Australia. The largest piece of debris to reach land was a one-ton tank.

25. THE LARGEST METEORITE

The largest known iron meteorite, weighing more than 60 tons, crashed to earth in late 1920, landing on a farm in the Hoba district west of Grootfontein in northern Namibia. It has since been declared a national monument and is visited by more than 20,000 tourists a year. A minor international incident occurred in 1989 when 36 Malaysian soldiers serving in a UN peacekeeping force tried to cut pieces from the boulder for souvenirs.

26. HUMAN WASTE

On Sunday, October 18, 1992, Gerri and Leroy Cinnamon of Woodinville, Washington, were watching a football game on TV in their den with Gerri's parents when something crashed through the roof of their living room. "I expected to see Superman soar through the hole," said Leroy. Instead. they found several baseball-sized chunks of greenish ice. As it melted, it began to smell bad. Two days later, the Federal Aviation Administration confirmed that the Cinnamons' roof had been damaged by frozen human waste from a leaky United Airlines sewage system. "It's a good thing none of us was killed," reflected Leroy. "What would you put on the tombstone?"

Unfortunately, falls of waste blobs are not uncommon. On April 23, 1978, for example, a 25-pound chunk landed in an unused school building in Ripley, Tennessee. Other attacks have occurred in Denver and Chicago. And then there's the story of the unfortunate Kentucky farmer who took a big lick of a flying "Popsicle" before he discovered what it was.

27. NONDAIRY CREAMER

White powder of a more innocuous kind began falling on the small town of Chester, South Carolina, in 1969—shortly after the Borden company started production of a corn syrup–based nondairy creamer in its local plant. Whenever the plant's exhaust vents clogged, the creamer spewed into the air and landed on people's homes and cars. Although basically harmless, the powder would mix with dew and rain and cause a sticky mess. Said homeowner Grace Dover, "It gets on your windows and you can't see out. It looks like you haven't washed your windows for a hundred years." In 1991, Borden paid a $4,000 fine for releasing Cremora beyond plant boundaries. By that time, the company had already taken steps to reduce the low-fat rain.

26 Things That Are Not What They Seem

1. A firefly is not a fly—it's a beetle.

2. A prairie dog is not a dog—it's a rodent.

3. India ink is not from India—it's from China and Egypt.

4. A horned toad is not a toad—it's a lizard.

5. A lead pencil contains no lead—it contains graphite.

6. A Douglas fir tree is not a fir—it's a pine.

7. A silkworm is not a worm—it's a caterpillar.

8. A peanut is not a nut—it's a legume.

9. A panda bear is not a bear—it's a raccoon relative.

10. A *cor anglais*, or English horn, is not English and not a horn—it's an alto oboe from France.

11. A guinea pig is not from Guinea and is not a pig—it's from South America, and it's a rodent.

12. Shortbread is not a bread—it's a thick cookie.

13. Dresden china is not made in Dresden—it's made in Meissen.

14. A shooting star is not a star—it's a meteor.

15. A funny bone is not a bone—it's the spot where the ulnar nerve touches the humerus.

16. Chop suey is not a native Chinese dish—it was invented by Chinese immigrants in California.

17. A bald eagle is not bald—it's got flat white feathers on its head and neck when mature, dark feathers when young.

18. A banana tree is not a tree—it's an herb.

19. A cucumber is not a vegetable—it's a fruit.

20. A jackrabbit is not a rabbit—it's a hare.

21. A piece of catgut is not from a cat—it's usually made from sheep intestines.

22. A Mexican jumping bean is not a bean—it's a seed with a larva inside.

23. A Turkish bath is not Turkish—it's Roman.

24. A koala bear is not a bear—it's a marsupial.

25. A sweetbread is not bread—it's from a calf's or lamb's pancreas or thymus.

26. A prairie oyster is not an oyster—it's a calf's testicle.

I.W. & W.D.

21 Bad Predictions

1. THE SUBMARINE
   I must confess that my imagination, in spite even of spurring, refuses to see any sort of submarine doing anything but suffocating its crew and floundering at sea.
   —H. G. Wells, British novelist, *Anticipations*, 1901

   The development of the submarine proceeded rapidly in the early twentieth century, and by World War I, submarines were a major factor in naval warfare. They played an even more important role in World War II. By the 1960s and 1970s, submarines were considered among the most important of all strategic weapons.

2. AIRCRAFT
   We hope that Professor [Samuel] Langley will not put his substantial greatness as a scientist in further peril by continuing to waste his time, and the money involved, in further airship experiments. Life is short, and he is capable of services to humanity incomparably greater than can be expected to result from trying to fly. . . . For

students and investigators of the Langley type there are more useful
employments.

—*New York Times*, December 10, 1903

Exactly one week later, the Wright brothers made the first successful
flight at Kitty Hawk, North Carolina.

I confess that in 1901, I said to my brother Orville that man would not
fly for fifty years. . . . Ever since, I have distrusted myself and avoided
all predictions.

—Wilbur Wright, U.S. aviation pioneer, 1908

The popular mind often pictures gigantic flying machines speeding
across the Atlantic and carrying innumerable passengers in a way
analogous to our modern steamships. . . . It seems safe to say that such
ideas must be wholly visionary, and even if a machine could get across
with one or two passengers the expense would be prohibitive to any
but the capitalist who could own his own yacht.

Another popular fallacy is to expect enormous speed to be ob-
tained. It must be remembered that the resistance of the air increases
as the square of the speed and the work as the cube. . . . If with 30
horse-power we can now attain a speed of 40 miles per hour, then in
order to reach a speed of 100 miles per hour we must use a motor
capable of 470 horse-power. . . . It is clear that with our present
devices there is no hope of competing for racing speed with either our
locomotives or our automobiles.

—William H. Pickering, U.S. astronomer, c. 1910,
after the invention of the airplane

The first transatlantic commercial scheduled passenger air service was
June 17 to 19, 1939, New York to England. The fare one way was $375,
round trip $675—no more than a first-class fare on an ocean liner at
the time. On October 14, 1922, at Mount Clemens, Michigan, a plane
was flown 216.1 miles per hour.

3. HIGHWAYS
The actual building of roads devoted to motor cars is not for the near
future, in spite of many rumors to that effect.

—*Harper's Weekly*, August 2, 1902

Conceived in 1906, the Bronx River Parkway, New York, when completed
in 1925, was the first auto express highway system in the United States.

4. RADIO
[Lee] De Forest has said in many newspapers and over his signature
that it would be possible to transmit the human voice across the

Atlantic before many years. Based on these absurd and deliberately
misleading statements, the misguided public . . . has been persuaded
to purchase stock in his company.
     —A U.S. district attorney prosecuting inventor Lee De Forest
      for selling stock fraudulently through the U.S. mails
       for his Radio Telephone Company, 1913

The first transatlantic broadcast of a human voice occurred on December 31, 1923, from Pittsburgh, Pennsylvania, to Manchester, England.

5. BOLSHEVISM
What are the Bolsheviki? They are representatives of the most
democratic government in Europe. . . . Let us recognize the truest
democracy in Europe, the truest democracy in the world today.
   —William Randolph Hearst, U.S. newspaper publisher, 1918

6. ROCKET RESEARCH
That Professor Goddard and his "chair" in Clark College and the
countenancing of the Smithsonian Institution does not know the
relation of action to reaction, and of the need to have something better
than a vacuum against which to react—to say that would be absurd. Of
course he only seems to lack the knowledge ladled out daily in high
schools.
       —*New York Times*, January 12, 1920

The *New York Times* printed a formal retraction of this comment some 49 years later, on July 17, 1969, just prior to the *Apollo* landing on the moon.

The proposals as outlined in your letter . . . have been carefully
reviewed. . . . While the Air Corps is deeply interested in the research
work being carried out by your organization . . . it does not, at this
time, feel justified in obligating further funds for basic jet propulsion
research and experimentation.
    —Brigadier General George H. Brett, U.S. Army Air Corps,
      in a letter to rocket researcher Robert Goddard, 1941

7. AIR STRIKES ON NAVAL VESSELS
The day of the battleship has not passed, and it is highly unlikely that
an airplane, or fleet of them, could ever successfully sink a fleet of
navy vessels under battle conditions.
   —Franklin D. Roosevelt, U.S. assistant secretary of the navy, 1922

As far as sinking a ship with a bomb is concerned, you just can't do it.
    —Rear Admiral Clark Woodward, U.S. Navy, 1939

8. JAPAN AND THE UNITED STATES

Nobody now fears that a Japanese fleet could deal an unexpected blow on our Pacific possessions. . . . Radio makes surprise impossible.

—Josephus Daniels, former U.S. secretary
of the navy, October 16, 1922

A Japanese attack on Pearl Harbor is a strategic impossibility.

—George Fielding Eliot, "The Impossible War with Japan,"
American Mercury, September 1938

The Hawaiian Islands are over-protected; the entire Japanese fleet and air force could not seriously threaten Oahu.

—Captain William T. Pulleston, former chief of U.S. Naval
Intelligence, *Atlantic Monthly*, August 1941

Pearl Harbor will never be attacked from the air.

—Admiral Charles H. McNorris, December 3, 1941

See newspaper headlines for December 7, 1941.

9. COMMERCIAL TELEVISION

While theoretically and technically television may be feasible, commercially and financially I consider it an impossibility, a development of which we need waste little time dreaming.

—Lee De Forest, U.S. inventor and "father of the radio," 1926

[Television] won't be able to hold on to any market it captures after the first six months. People will soon get tired of staring at a plywood box every night.

—Darryl F. Zanuck, head of Twentieth Century-Fox, 1946

10. REPEAL OF PROHIBITION

I will never see the day when the Eighteenth Amendment is out of the Constitution of the United States.

—William Borah, U.S. senator, 1929

The Eighteenth Amendment was repealed in 1933. Borah was alive to see the day; he did not die until 1940.

11. HITLER

In this column for years, I have constantly laboured these points: Hitler's horoscope is not a war-horoscope. . . . If and when war comes, not he but others will strike the first blow.

—R. H. Naylor, British astrologer for
the *London Sunday Express*, 1939

12. THE ATOMIC BOMB

That is the biggest fool thing we have ever done. . . . The bomb will never go off, and I speak as an expert in explosives.

—Admiral William Leahy, U.S. Navy officer
speaking to President Truman, 1945

13. LANDING ON THE MOON

Landing and moving around the moon offers so many serious problems for human beings that it may take science another 200 years to lick them.

—*Science Digest,* August 1948

It took 21 years.

14. ATOMIC FUEL

It can be taken for granted that before 1980 ships, aircraft, locomotives, and even automobiles will be atomically fueled.

—David Sarnoff, U.S. radio executive
and former head of RCA, 1955

15. THE VIETNAM WAR

The war in Vietnam is going well and will succeed.

—Robert McNamara, U.S. secretary
of defense, January 31, 1963

We are not about to send American boys 9,000 or 10,000 miles away from home to do what Asian boys ought to be doing for themselves.

—Lyndon B. Johnson, U.S. president, October 21, 1964

Whatever happens in Vietnam, I can conceive of nothing except military victory.

—Lyndon B. Johnson, in a speech at West Point, 1967

16. FASHION IN THE 1970s

So women will wear pants and men will wear skirts interchangeably. And since there won't be any squeamishness about nudity, see-through clothes will only be see-through for reasons of comfort. Weather permitting, both sexes will go about bare-chested, though women will wear simple protective pasties.

—Rudi Gernreich, U.S. fashion designer, 1970

17. THE FALL OF THE BERLIN WALL

Liberalization is a ploy. . . . The Wall will remain.

—George Will, columnist for the *Washington Post,*
November 9, 1989—the day the Berlin Wall fell.

18. **COLLAPSE OF THE SOVIET UNION**

We must expect the Soviet system to survive in its present brutish form for a very long time. There will be Soviet labor camps and Soviet torture chambers well into our great-grandchildren's lives.

—Newt Gingrich, U.S. representative (and future speaker of the house), 1984

19. **INVASION OF IRAQ #1**

There is a minimal risk of conflict.

—Heino Kopietz, senior Middle East analyst, on the possibility of Iraq invading Kuwait, in the *Times* of London, July 26, 1990

Iraq invaded Kuwait five days later.

20. **9/11**

Who cares about a little terrorist in Afghanistan?

—Paul Wolfowitz, U.S. deputy secretary of defense, dismissing concerns about al-Qaeda at an April 2001 meeting on terrorism

21. **INVASION OF IRAQ #2**

I have no doubt we're going to find big stores of weapons of mass destruction.

—Kenneth Adelman, Defense Policy Board member, in the *Washington Post*, March 23, 2003

[The war] could last six days, six weeks. I doubt six months.

—Donald Rumsfeld, U.S. secretary of defense, to U.S. troops in Aviano, Italy, February 7, 2003

My belief is we will, in fact, be greeted as liberators. . . . I think it will go relatively quickly, weeks rather than months.

—Dick Cheney, U.S. vice president, March 16, 2003

We are dealing with a country that can really finance its own reconstruction, and relatively soon.

—Paul Wolfowitz, U.S. deputy secretary of defense, to the House Budget Committee, February 27, 2003

K.H.J. & C.F.

Barbara Walters's
5 Events in History I Would Like to Have Seen

Prominent TV journalist Barbara Walters made broadcasting history in 1976 when she joined the *ABC Evening News* to become the first female coanchor of a network news program. In 1979, she joined ABC's nighttime news show *20/20*, and she currently cohosts the daytime talk show *The View*. She is perhaps best known for her lively and probing interviews with figures ranging from world leaders to movie stars. Her *Barbara Walters Specials* routinely generate top ratings.

1. MOSES PARTING THE RED SEA (c. 14th century BCE)

2. JESUS PERFORMING THE LOAVES AND FISHES MIRACLE (1st century AD)

3. AMELIA EARHART'S LAST HOURS (disappeared July 2, 1937)

4. REAL ROMAN ORGY (to watch, not to participate)

5. HITLER'S LAST DAY IN THE BUNKER (April 30, 1945)

Ronald Reagan's
6 People in History Whose Life
I Would Like to Have Lived

Actor Ronald Reagan's six years as president of the Screen Actors Guild whetted his appetite for politics. After doing a political turnabout from liberal to conservative, he won the governorship of California in 1966 and was reelected in 1970. He vied for the Republican presidential nomination in 1968 and again in 1976. He gained it on his third try. Reagan was elected president of the United States in 1980 and reelected in 1984. He contributed this list to *The Book of Lists* in 1980:

1. Adam (It would have been wonderful to see the world begin.)
2. Cortés
3. Balboa
4. Lewis and/or Clark
5. Father Junípero Serra

6. And any number of those men who first crossed the plains in the opening of the West. In other words, I'm fascinated by those who saw this new world when it was virtually untouched by man.

Truman Capote's
11 People in History Whose Life I Would Like to Have Lived

Born in New Orleans in 1924, Truman Capote became a literary phenomenon (Somerset Maugham called him "the hope of modern literature") with the publication of his first book, the coming-of-age novel *Other Voices, Other Rooms* (1948). He followed it with *The Grass Harp* (1951) and the short novel *Breakfast at Tiffany's* (1958), which became a hit movie starring Audrey Hepburn in 1961. His 1966 book *In Cold Blood,* concerning the real-life murder of a family in rural Kansas, invented a new literary form—the nonfiction novel. In the wake of his successes, Capote became a jet-setting pop-culture figure. He died on August 24, 1984, leaving behind an unfinished novel, *Answered Prayers,* which was published posthumously in 1987. He contributed the following list to *The Book of Lists* in 1980:

1. Caligula
2. Catherine the Great
3. Stalin
4. Sigmund Freud
5. Rasputin
6. Cleopatra
7. Henry VII
8. Madame de Pompadour
9. Alcibiades
10–11. J. Edgar Hoover and Clyde Tolson

George Plimpton's
10 People in History Whose Life I Would Liked to Have Lived

A modern renaissance man and popular "participatory journalist," George Plimpton was born on March 18, 1927, in New York City. His remarkable achievements include cofounding the literary journal the *Paris Review* and infiltrating the world of professional sports (recounted in best-selling memoirs such as *Out of My League* and *Paper Lion*). He also appeared in small parts in a number of movies (he dubbed himself "the Prince of Cameos"), including *Reds, Nixon,* and *Good Will Hunting.* He died on September 26, 2003, of natural causes. He contributed the following list to *The Book of Lists* in 1983.

1. Richard Haliburton
2. Amelia Earhart
3. Captain of the *Mary Celeste*
4. Ambrose Bierce
5. Judge Crater
6. James Hoffa
7–10. And four of the leaders of the lost tribes of Israel

NOTE: The *Mary Celeste* was discovered floating in the Atlantic in November 1872 with no one aboard. Captain Benjamin Briggs, his wife, baby daughter, and seven-man crew had vanished; their fate has never been discovered. Judge Joseph Crater (1889–?), a New York Supreme Court justice, disappeared on August 6, 1930. It was speculated that he was involved in political corruption through Tammany Hall and possibly murdered or that he decided to leave his old life and begin anew somewhere else. He has never been found.

Marcel Marceau's
10 People in History Whose Life
I Would Like to Have Lived

Acclaimed as the world's greatest mime, Marcel Marceau was born in Strasbourg, France, on March 22, 1923. Influenced as a child by silent film stars such as Charlie Chaplin and Buster Keaton, he studied at the Sarah Bernhardt Theater in Paris. In 1947, he developed his mime persona, the white-faced clown Bip. In addition to his live performances, Marceau has appeared in a number of films, most notably the 1976 Mel Brooks spoof *Silent Movie* (in which he has the only speaking part). In 2002, he served as a Goodwill Ambassador for the United Nations Second World Assembly on Aging. His full company production of *Les Contes Fantastiques* (*Fantasy Tales*) played to great acclaim at the Theater Antoine in Paris.

1. Jesus Christ
2. Moses
3. Michelangelo

4. Leonardo da Vinci
5. Siddhartha (Buddha)
6. Mozart
7. Aristotle
8. Shakespeare
9. Einstein
10. Tolstoy

8 Onlies

1. **THE ONLY PRESIDENT TO GET STUCK IN THE WHITE HOUSE BATHTUB**
   William Howard Taft, U.S. president from 1909 until 1913, weighed more than 300 pounds. After getting stuck in the White House bathtub, he ordered a new one installed, large enough for four men. When he visited the Panama Canal Zone engineers built him a dining room chair reinforced with steel. Jokes about Taft's size were common, and he took them with good humor. According to Paul L. Boller, Jr., in *Presidential Anecdotes*, Taft was once swimming off Cape Ann, Massachusetts, when two neighbors walked by and one said, "We'd better wait. The president is using the ocean."

2. **THE ONLY PRESIDENT TO WEIGH UNDER 100 POUNDS**
   James Madison, the fourth president of the United States (1809–1817), stood 5 feet 4 inches and weighed 98 pounds. Had he lived in the twentieth century he probably could not have gotten elected—although the average American male is 5 feet 9 inches tall, in 22 of the last 24 presidential elections, the taller candidate has won the popular vote.

3. **THE ONLY FOOT DEODORANT ELECTED TO PUBLIC OFFICE**
   In the early 1970s, during an election campaign in Ecuador, a foot deodorant manufacturer used the advertising slogan "Vote for any candidate, but if you want well-being and hygiene, vote for Pulvapies." The day before the election, the manufacturer distributed a leaflet reading, "For Mayor: The Honorable Pulvapies." Voters in the coastal village of Picoaza (pop. 4,100), unimpressed with the alternatives, elected Pulvapies by a clear majority.

4. **THE ONLY ENGLISH MONARCH NEVER TO SET FOOT IN ENGLAND**
   Berengaria, the daughter of King Sancho VI of Navarre, married King Richard the Lion-Hearted and was crowned queen—in Cyprus—in 1191. She never visited England and spent most of her eight-year reign in Italy and France.

5. **THE ONLY BONE IN THE HUMAN BODY NOT CONNECTED TO ANOTHER**
The hyoid is a V-shaped bone located at the base of the tongue between the mandible and the voice box. Its function is to support the tongue and its muscles.

6. **THE ONLY 7–LETTER WORD THAT CONTAINS ALL 5 VOWELS**
The word is *sequoia*, referring to the giant trees of California. The sequoia is named after the Cherokee Indian scholar who created a written alphabet for the Cherokee language.

7. **THE ONLY BASEBALL PLAYER TO GET A HIT FOR 2 DIFFERENT TEAMS IN 2 CITIES ON THE SAME DAY**
Joel Youngblood began August 4, 1982, as the starting right fielder for the New York Mets in their game against the Chicago Cubs. He singled in the third inning, but was immediately pulled from the game and told that he had been traded to the Montreal Expos. Youngblood flew to Philadelphia, took a taxi to Veterans Stadium, put on a Montreal uniform, and entered the game in the sixth inning. In his only at-bat, he singled again.

8. **THE ONLY NONHUMAN LAND ANIMAL THAT COMMONLY MATES FACE TO FACE**
Two-toed sloths typically mate vertically while hanging by their arms from a tree branch.

Source: One of a Kind by Bruce Felton (New York: William Morrow, 1992).

16 Famous Events That Happened in the Bathtub

1. **POISONING OF PELIAS**
According to Greek mythology, Medea murdered Jason's uncle (Pelias, king of Thessaly) by giving him a bath in a vat of deadly poison, which she falsely claimed would restore his lost youth.

2. **MURDER OF AGAMEMNON**
Shortly after his return from the Trojan War, the Greek hero Agamemnon was murdered by his wife, Clytemnestra, who struck him twice with an ax while he was relaxing in the tub.

3. **ARCHIMEDES' DISCOVERY**
While soaking in the bathtub, the Greek scientist Archimedes formulated the law of physics—known as the Archimedean principle—that a body

immersed in fluid loses weight equal to the weight of the fluid it displaces. He became so excited about his discovery that he rushed out stark naked into the streets of Syracuse, Sicily, shouting "Eureka!" ("I have found it!")

4. BURNING OF ALEXANDRIA

When the Arabs conquered Alexandria, they were alleged to have burned the 700,000 books in the library to keep up the fires in the city's 4,000 public baths.

5. QUEEN ANNE'S BURNING BATH

Anne, queen of Denmark, was the wife of James I of England. In 1615, gases from her mineral bath momentarily ignited, causing Her Majesty great consternation.

6. FRANKLIN'S PASTIME

Benjamin Franklin is reputed to have imported the first bathtub into America. He improved its design, and contemporary reports indicate that he carried on much of his reading and correspondence while soaking in the tub.

7. MARAT'S ASSASSINATION

Jean-Paul Marat played an active part in the French Revolution. As editor of the journal *L'Ami du people*, he became known as an advocate of extreme violence. The moderate Girondists were driven out of Paris and took refuge in Normandy. There, some of them met and influenced a young woman, Charlotte Corday. Convinced that Marat must die, she went to Paris and bought a butcher knife. When she arrived at Marat's house on July 13, 1793, he was taking a bath. (He spent many hours in the tub because of a painful skin condition.) Overhearing Corday, he asked to see her. They discussed politics for a few minutes; then Corday drew her knife and stabbed Marat to death in the bathtub.

8. THE BONAPARTES' ARGUMENT

While Napoleon was taking a bath one morning in 1803, his brothers Joseph and Lucien rushed in, seething with rage because they had just heard of his plan to sell Louisiana to the Americans. They were furious because he refused to consult the legislature about it. Lucien had worked hard to make Spain return the colony to France, and now his work would be for naught. Joseph warned Napoleon that he might end up in exile if he carried out his plan. At that, Napoleon fell back angrily in the tub, splashing water all over Joseph. Napoleon's valet, who was standing by with hot towels over his arm, crashed to the floor in a dead faint.

9. WAGNER'S INSPIRATION

Composer Richard Wagner soaked in a tub scented with vast quantities of Mild of Iris perfume for several hours every day while working on his final opera, *Parsifal* (1882). He insisted that the water be kept hot and heavily perfumed so that he could smell it as he sat at his desk, clad in outlandish silk and fur dressing gowns and surrounded by vials and sachets of exotic scents.

10. MORPHY'S DEATH

Paul Morphy of New Orleans defeated famous chess players when he was still a child. As an adult, he could play eight games simultaneously while blindfolded. Some people consider him the greatest chess player who ever lived, but from the age of 22 until his death on July 10, 1884, at 47, he played no more chess. Believing that people were trying to poison him or burn his clothes, Morphy became a virtual recluse. On one oppressively hot day, he returned from a walk and took a cold bath. In the tub, he died from what doctors described as "congestion of the brain or apoplexy, which was evidently brought on by the effects of the cold water on his overheated body."

11. ROSTAND'S WRITING

Edmond Rostand, French poet and playwright, hated to be interrupted while he was working, but he did not like to turn his friends away. Therefore, he took refuge in the bathtub and wrote there all day, creating such successes as *Cyrano de Bergerac* (1898).

12. SMITH'S MURDERS

George Joseph Smith of England earned his living by his almost hypnotic power over women. In 1910, he met Bessie Mundy, married her (without mentioning that he already had a wife), and disappeared with her cash and clothes. Two years later, they met by chance and began living together again. After Smith persuaded Bessie to write a will in his favor, he took her to a doctor on the pretense that she suffered from fits. (Both she and the doctor took his word for it.) A few days later, she was found dead in the bathtub, a cake of soap clutched in her hand. Everyone assumed she had drowned during an epileptic seizure. Smith married two more women—Alice Burnham and Margaret Lofty—took out insurance policies on their lives, and described mysterious ailments to their doctors. They, too, were found dead in their bathtubs. When Alice Burnham's father read of Margaret Lofty's death, he was struck by the similarity to his daughter's untimely end. The police were notified, and Smith was tried for murder and sentenced to be executed. His legal wife, Edith, testified at the trial that she could remember only one occasion when Smith himself took a bath.

13. CARROLL'S ORGY

America was shocked by reports of an orgy on February 22, 1926, at the Earl Carroll Theatre in New York after a performance of Carroll's *Vanities*. To climax a midnight party on stage, a bathtub was filled with champagne and a nude model climbed in, while the men lined up and filled their glasses from the tub. This was during the Prohibition era, so a federal grand jury immediately began an inquiry into whether the tub really did contain liquor and, if so, who had supplied it. The producer who staged the party, Earl Carroll, was convicted of perjury for telling the grand jury that no wine had been in the bathtub. He was sentenced to a year and a day in prison, plus a $2,000 fine. After he suffered a nervous breakdown on the way to the penitentiary, his fellow prisoners were ordered never to mention bathtubs in his presence.

14. KING HAAKON'S FALL

On June 29, 1955, the reign of King Haakon VII, who had ruled Norway from the time of its independence in 1905, effectively came to an end when the beloved monarch fell in the royal bathtub at his palace in Oslo. The elderly king lingered for over two years before succumbing on September 21, 1957, to complications resulting from his fall.

15. GLENN'S CAREER

The momentum of what contemporary experts considered to be an unstoppable political career was interrupted in 1964 when astronaut hero John Glenn fell in the bathtub and had to withdraw from his race for senator from Ohio. He was finally elected to the Senate in 1974.

16. MORRISON'S DEATH

Rock 'n' roll idol Jim Morrison was living in exile in an apartment in Paris. On the morning of July 3, 1971, he was found dead in his bath-tub. The cause of death was ruled "heart failure." He was 27 years old.

P.S.H., L.B. & J.Be.

12 Amazing Attic Events

1. THE RESIDENCE OF MADAME DE POMPADOUR (1745–1750)

Madame Jeanne-Antoinette d'Etoiles was known throughout Paris as one of the most beautiful and cultured women of her day. In 1745, she met King Louis XV of France. The two immediately fell in love, and Madame d'Etoiles obtained a legal separation from her husband. She was then given the title of the Marquise de Pompadour and installed in the attic apartment of Versailles as the king's mistress. Her apartment became known as the meeting place for some of the most celebrated people of France, and her guests were assisted in the steep 100-stair ascent by an elementary lift dubbed the "flying chair." But her private life with the king was less than ideal. After two blissful years together, Pompadour lost her physical passion for the king. She feared losing him and believed that a diet of vanilla, truffles, and celery would stimulate her desire for sexual activity. It only worsened her already weak physical condition. After she spent five years in the attic, the king moved her to a flat on the ground floor of the palace. It was clear he had taken new mistresses. Pompadour, however, retained her powerful position as his political and artistic adviser until her death in 1764.

2. THE SUICIDE OF THOMAS CHATTERTON (1770)

As a boy, Thomas Chatterton was a prodigious poet and scholar and an early Romantic who at age 10 wrote on a par with his adult contemporaries. His family was poor, his mother a widowed seamstress, and privacy was difficult to come by in their small Bristol home. So young Thomas set up a writing room in the attic, which he jealously guarded as his secret domain. In the attic room, among his books and papers, stood Ellinor, a life-size doll made of woven rushes, which his mother used for dress fittings. Thomas loved Ellinor and always took care to powder her face and fix her hair. However, when he moved to London to pursue his literary career, he left his beloved Ellinor behind. He rented a garret reminiscent of his attic study at home, and thereafter suffered repeated personal and professional disappointments, including failure to sell a series of forgeries he claimed had been written by a fifteenth-century monk, Chatterton took arsenic and died at the age of 17.

3. THE LITERARY GARRET OF EDMOND DE GONCOURT (1885–1896)

Edmond and his brother Jules were French novelists. Both are best remembered for the detailed journals they kept on literary people of the late nineteenth century. Jules died in 1870, and in 1885, Edmond turned the two attic rooms of the house into a salon. Each Sunday afternoon, he would entertain such notables as Guy de Maupassant and Émile Zola. The following are some excerpts from Edmond's journal on those afternoons:

- *February 1, 1885*, on the French poet Robert de Montesquieu-Fezenac: "Somebody described his first love affair with a female ventriloquist who, while [he] was straining to achieve his climax, would imitate the drunken voice of a pimp."
- *May 24, 1885*, on Zola's reaction to the recent death of Victor Hugo: "He walked around the room as if relieved by his death and as if convinced he was going to inherit the literary papacy."
- *April 19, 1896*, a description of the removal of Paul Verlaine's death mask: "The conversation turned to Verlaine's alcoholism and the softening effect it had had on his flesh. . . . [Stéphane] Mallarmé had said he would never forget the wet, soggy sound made by the removal of the death mask from his face, an operation in which his beard and mouth had come away too."

4. **MARCONI INVENTS THE WIRELESS TELEGRAPH (1894–1896)**
   Guglielmo Marconi was 20 years old when he began experimenting in earnest with radio waves. Because his father took a dim view of such "childish" pursuits as physics and even went so far as to destroy his son's electronic equipment, young Marconi had to set up a secret laboratory in the attic of their villa in Bologna. There, among his mother's trays of silkworms, Marconi determined that radio waves could carry a message in Morse code across the room. In time, he proved that his invention was not bound by the four attic walls and could transmit messages over great distances.

5. **THE CONSTRUCTION AND DEMONSTRATION OF THE FIRST TELEVISION (1922–1926)**
   In 1922, British scientist John Logie Baird rented an attic room above an artificial flower shop at 8 Queen's Arcade in Hastings to continue research on his primitive television sets. He used a tea chest as the base for his motor, a biscuit tin to house the projection lamp, and held the whole contraption together with darning needles, scraps of wood, string, and sealing wax. In 1924, he took his "working" apparatus to London. There he rented two attic rooms at 22 Frith Street in Soho. He struggled for another two years before he gave the first demonstration of true television on January 26, 1926, for an audience of 50 scientists. The British Broadcasting Corporation inaugurated Baird's system in 1929 and used it until 1935, when a more sophisticated system was adopted.

6. **ADOLF HITLER'S ATTEMPTED SUICIDE (1923)**
   After the failure of his Beer Hall Putsch in Munich, Germany, Hitler hid in an attic bedroom at Uffing, the country estate of his follower Ernst "Putzi" Hanfstängl. Hitler tried to commit suicide by shooting himself when the police came to arrest him. A police agent managed to disarm him before he could pull the trigger.

7. **ESPIONAGE AT PEARL HARBOR, HAWAII (1939–1941)**
   Ruth Kühn was only 17 years old when she became the mistress of Nazi leader Joseph Goebbels. But like all of his mistresses, she was soon discarded. When the affair ended in 1939, Goebbels decided to send Ruth out of Germany. He arranged for her and her parents, Bernard and Friedel, to move to Hawaii and act as espionage agents for the Japanese. Ruth set up a beauty parlor in Honolulu, which became her chief source of information, since it was frequented by American military wives. The next step was to figure out a way of transmitting information to the Japanese. The Kühns devised a simple code system and sent signals from the attic window of their small house overlooking Pearl Harbor. On December 7, 1941, toward the end of the Japanese surprise attack, their signals were noticed by two American naval

officers. The U.S. Navy Shore Patrol arrested the family, and all were imprisoned for espionage.

8. ANNE FRANK WRITES HER DIARY (1942–1944)

Forced into hiding when the Nazis overran the Netherlands, Anne Frank, her parents and sister, and four other Jews shared a musty Amsterdam attic above a warehouse and office building. They hid there for two years, obtaining food and other necessities from Gentiles on the floor below. Anne, a precocious girl in her early teens, kept a diary in which she chronicled not only the details of their imprisonment, but also her feelings about life, love, the future, and her budding sexual awareness. In August 1944, the Gestapo, acting on a tip by Dutch informers, raided the hiding place. All the Franks died in concentration camps (Anne of typhus), except Otto Frank, the father. He returned to the attic after the war and found his daughter's diary, which was published under the title *The Diary of a Young Girl*.

9. THE DISCOVERY OF FRANZ SCHUBERT'S LOST PIANO SCORE (1969)

The score for a fantasy for piano by Franz Schubert was discovered in an attic in Knittlefield, Austria, in 1969. The piece is believed to have been written by the Viennese composer in 1817.

10. THE DISCOVERY OF FRÉDÉRIC CHOPIN'S LOST WALTZES (1978)

Several waltzes dedicated to Clementine de la Panouse were discovered by Vicomte Paul de la Panouse in the attic of the family chateau near Paris in 1978. They were stored in a heavy trunk belonging to the French aristocratic family. During World War II, they were hidden— along with many other documents—in various locations prior to the German invasion of France.

11. THE DISCOVERY OF SCHINDLER'S LIST (1998)

When a German couple found an old gray suitcase in a loft belonging to the husband's late parents in Hildesheim, they didn't think much about it, until they saw the name on the handle: O. Schindler. Inside were hundreds of documents, including a list of the names of Jewish laborers that factory owner Oskar Schindler gave the Nazis during World War II. By giving Jewish workers fake jobs and otherwise manipulating the system, Schindler saved 1,200 Jews from extermination. His story inspired Thomas Keneally's novel *Schindler's Ark* (1982) and the movie *Schindler's List* (1993). The documents had apparently been stored in the loft by friends of Schindler's and then forgotten. In 1999, the suitcase and its contents were donated to the Yad Vashem Holocaust Museum in Jerusalem.

12. **THE DISCOVERY OF AARON COPLAND'S LAST FILM SCORE** (2003)

Aaron Copland's last film score was for the 1961 movie *Something Wild*. Because the film failed at the box office, plans for a soundtrack album were canceled. Film score researcher Mark Leneker learned that Copland had put together a 35-minute album and distributed it to friends. Forty years later, in 2003, Leneker tracked down the film's director, Jack Garfein, in Paris. Garfein's wife discovered a sealed copy of the album in her attic. It was then digitally transferred and released to the public.

L.O. & M.J.T.

Stephen Spender's
10 People He'd Like to Invite to Lunch

Spender, who was born in London and educated at Oxford, was one of the handful of young writers who revolutionized English poetry in the 1930s by including images of everyday life in their work. *Poems for Spain* (1937), *Trial of a Judge* (1938), and *European Witness* (1946) describe his early observations and experiences in Spain and Germany. Later works include *The Generous Days* (1971), *Letter to Christopher: Stephen Spender's Letters to Christopher Isherwood 1929–1939* (1980), *Collected Poems 1928–1985* (1986), and *The Temple* (1988). Spender, who was knighted in 1983, died in 1995 at the age of 86. A famous quote from his work: "I think of those who were truly great. The names of those who in their lives fought for life, who wore at their hearts the fire's centre." He contributed this list to *The Book of Lists* in 1993:

1. Alcibiades without Socrates
2. Francis Beaumont without John Fletcher
3. James Boswell without Samuel Johnson
4. George Gordon, Lord Byron, without his "last attachment"
5. Oscar Wilde without "Bosie" [Lord Alfred Douglas]
6. Gustave Flaubert without George Sand
7. Algernon Charles Swinburne without Theodore Watts-Dunton
8. Gertrude Stein without Alice B. Toklas
9. Alice B. Toklas without Gertrude Stein
10. Jesus Christ without Andrew Lloyd Webber

Paul Bowles's
10 Favorite Dinner Guests in History

First published at the age of 16, Bowles wrote novels, short stories, and poetry. His fiction was characterized by exotic locales (often Morocco) and existential concerns. His best-known novel, *The Sheltering Sky*, was made into a movie in 1990. Also a composer, Bowles wrote music for plays, operas, films, and ballets. He died of a heart attack in Morocco November 18, 1999, at the age of 88. He prepared this list for *The Book of Lists* in 1993:

1. Gautama Buddha
2. Isabelle Eberhardt
3. Judas Iscariot
4. Dr. Carl Jung
5. Petronius Arbiter
6. Joseph Conrad
7. Isidore Ducasse (Comte de Lautréamont)
8. Erik Satie
9. Jeanne d'Arc
10. Anton Chekhov

MR. BOWLES ADDS: It will be noted that the guest list flouts the rules of etiquette, there being included only two women, as against eight men, but since both of the females habitually dressed as men, the occasion could have been referred to as a "stag dinner" without causing unfavorable comment.

Arthur Koestler's
10 Favorite Dinner Guests from All History

Born in Budapest, Hungary, in 1905, Arthur Koestler was a novelist, historian, political activist, philosopher, social critic, and autobiographer. A true renaissance man, he was fluent in five languages. A youthful Communist Party member, one of his main themes became anticommunism. He was imprisoned during the Spanish Civil War, joined the French Foreign Legion, and fought in the British army. The most famous of his books, *Darkness at Noon*, has been translated into 33 languages. His most controversial best seller was *The Thirteenth Tribe*, in which he brought to popular attention the argument that Jews today are the descendants of the Khazars, a people of the Caucasus who eventually adopted forms of Judaism in the eighth century and were later forced to migrate west into what is now Poland and Russia. Koestler supported the statehood of Israel while opposing the idea of a Diaspora Jewish culture. He was so profoundly interested in mysticism that he left a large portion of his estate to the study of parapsychology at Edinburgh University. Koestler and his wife were advocates of euthanasia, and, when he contracted Alzheimer's disease at the age of 77, they peacefully committed joint suicide in London in 1983. Koestler contributed this list to *The Book of Lists* in 1977:

1. Pharaoh Akhenaton
2. King Solomon
3. Queen Cleopatra
4. Lucius Licinius Lucullus
5. Genghis Khan
6. Martin Luther
7. Benjamin Franklin
8. Madame de Pompadour
9. George-Jacques Danton
10. Benjamin Disraeli

Polonius's 10 Pieces of Advice to Laertes

1. Give thy thoughts no tongue,
   Nor any unproportion'd thought his act.

2. Be thou familiar, but by no means vulgar . . .

3. Those friends thou hast, and their adoption tried,
   Grapple them unto thy soul with hoops of steel . . .

4. But do not dull thy palm with entertainment
   Of each new-hatch'd, unfledg'd comrade.

5. Beware of entrance to a quarrel, but, being in,
   Bear't that th' opposed may beware of thee.

6. Give every man thy ear, but few thy voice . . .

7. Take each man's censure, but reserve thy judgment.

8. Costly thy habit as thy purse can buy,
   But not express'd in fancy; rich, not gaudy;
   For the apparel oft proclaims the man . . .

9. Neither a borrower nor a lender be;
   For loan oft loses both itself and friend,
   And borrowing dulls the edge of husbandry.

10. This above all: to thine own self be true,
    And it must follow, as the night the day,
    Thou canst not then be false to any man.

Source: Hamlet, Act 1, Scene 3, lines 59–79.

Miss Manners's 10 Worst Faux Pas

According to Miss Manners (Judith Martin), she was "born a perfect lady in an imperfect society" and "considers it her duty and privilege to lead the way to a more civilized—and cheerful—society." Since 1978, she has been giving etiquette and relationship advice in her "Miss Manners" column, written for the *Washington Post* and syndicated in numerous newspapers. She has also written many books, including *Miss Manners' Guide for the Turn-of-the-Millennium* and *Miss Manners' Guide to Excruciatingly Correct Behavior, Freshly Updated.*

1. HONESTY
   When what this means is insulting other people to their faces, and then, when they are hurt, insulting them again by inquiring whether they don't believe in honesty.

2. HELPFULNESS
   When this consists of minding other people's business by volunteering, unasked, your opinion of how they should lead their lives.

3. HEALTH CONSCIOUSNESS
   When this is an excuse for spoiling other people's dinners by telling them that what they are eating, or serving their guests, is poison.

4. IDEALISM
   When this leads to humiliating other people for unexceptional activities—pointing at strangers who are using two sheets of paper towels to dry their hands, for example—that violate your own resolutions.

5. BEING TRUE TO YOUR OWN FEELINGS
   When this is cited as a reason for neglecting your duties toward others, such as writing thank-you letters or attending funerals, that you happen to find distasteful.

6. SELF-ASSERTIVENESS
   When this means elbowing others out of the way so you can get what you want.

7. FRIENDLINESS
   When this is held to be the motivation for taking unauthorized liberties with others, such as addressing strangers by their first names or making personal remarks to acquaintances.

8. SPONTANEITY
   When this translates into not being willing to answer invitations or honor acceptances because you feel like doing something else on the night of the party.

9. HOSPITALITY
   When this consists of inviting your own guests to someone else's wedding or party, or telling your guests that they are expected to supply the meal or pay for what they ate.

10. CREATIVITY
    When fostering this is cited as an excuse for allowing your children to destroy other people's property or peace of mind.

Vidal Sassoon's
10 Historical Characters He Would Like to Have Made Up or Styled

Born on January 17, 1928, in London's East End, Vidal Sassoon began cutting hair at the age of 14. In 1948, he enlisted in the fight for the establishment of Israel, returning to London afterward to start his first salon. He came to prominence in the early 1960s when he cut the hair of fashion designer Mary Quant; since then, he has been the hair stylist for countless celebrities. He is also the founder of Vidal Sassoon, Inc., which operates boutiques and beauty salons throughout the world.

1. Delilah
2. Nikita Khrushchev
3. Albert Einstein
4. Eleanor Roosevelt
5. Tallulah Bankhead
6. George Washington
7. Mona Lisa
8. Buffalo Bill
9. Orphan Annie
10. Rasputin

16 Tips for Removing Household Stains

1. **CHOCOLATE**

   If dropped on upholstery: (1) Let melted chocolate harden, then scrape off as much as possible with blunt knife. (2) Lather gently with carpet shampoo. (3) Wipe off foam with damp sponge; when dry, lift off traces with liquid stain remover.

2. **RED WINE**

   Move fast with red wine: (1) Blot with paper towels. Sponge with clear warm water, to dilute stain. Repeat. (2) Sprinkle with talcum powder if necessary. Leave powder for a few minutes. Clean off with a soft brush. Repeat blotting till stain is gone.

3. **BLACK COFFEE**

   Sponge with cold water and liquid shampoo.

4. **FRUIT JUICE**

   Sponge immediately with cold water, then blot dry till fabric is barely damp. For stubborn juice stains, use commercial liquid stain remover.

5. **COLA DRINKS**

   Blot with paper towels, then sponge repeatedly with cold water. Blot dry.

6. **NAIL POLISH AND LIPSTICK**

   Blot with paper tissues or paper towels. After testing a small area, use a non-oily nail polish remover soaked in a damp cloth.

7. **CHEWING GUM**

   Do not try to pick it off. Melt gum by placing brown paper over fabric and heat with a warm iron. Remove any traces with denatured alcohol. On clothes, place garment in a plastic bag, put in freezer, and gum will usually break off. (Author note: If you get chewing gum in your hair, remove by covering with peanut butter.)

8. **FELT-TIP PEN**

   Act quickly. Blot light marks with cotton swabs, larger ones with paper towels. If needed, try spraying with denatured alcohol and a stain remover.

9. **PET HAIR AND URINE**

   Use adhesive tape to remove pet hair from any fabric, about a three-fingers-width worth of tape. Brush tape over fabric till hair is gone. Repeat if necessary. Sponge fresh urine stains with clear, cold water. Blot thoroughly with a dab of one tablespoon vinegar to two cups warm water. Old stains must be taken to a cleaners.

10. **HOT DRINKS ON BLANKET WHILE READING IN BED**
Rinse stained blanket quickly in a lot of warm water. If the stain has dried, try careful bleaching with a solution of one part hydrogen peroxide to six parts water. Old stains must be taken to a cleaners.

11. **BEER AND ALE**
Blot well, then sponge with clean, damp cloth. Treat persistent stains with an aerosol remover. Sponge dried stains on natural fabrics with a mild solution of white vinegar.

12. **CANVAS SNEAKERS OR TRAINERS**
Lift dirt from shoes by scrubbing fabric with a clean toothbrush dipped in rug shampoo. Sponge away foam. For grass stains, use a harder brush dipped in a mix of dishwashing liquid and warm water. Machine-dry on low heat or dry naturally.

13. **COMPUTER KEYBOARD**
Clean tops of keys with cotton swabs dipped in turpentine. Use dry cotton swabs to dust between keys.

14. **BOOKS**
Be sure books aren't too tightly packed together—this causes mildew. To remove mildew from hardbound books, sprinkle with cornstarch and leave for a few days, then brush off. For greasy finger marks, lay a sheet of blotting paper over the marks and press with a warm iron.

16. **PIANO KEYS**
Leave piano lid open on sunny days; sun will bleach keys white. For dirty marks, use toothpaste on a soft, damp cloth, gently rubbing one key at a time; then rinse with a cloth dipped in milk—and ring out cloth before wiping, so milk won't trickle between the keys. Buff keys dry with a soft cloth.

Source: 101 Tips for Removing Household Stains by Cassandra Kent (New York: DK Publishing, 1997).

12 Prodigious Savants

Savant syndrome is a rare condition in which people suffering from mental retardation, autism, or schizophrenia nonetheless possess an unusual ability in a single field, most often relating to music, art, or numbers.

1. **THOMAS "BLIND TOM" BETHUNE (1849–1908)**
Although his vocabulary was limited to less than a hundred words, Blind Tom could play more than 5,000 pieces on the piano, an

instrument he had mastered as a four-year-old slave on a Georgia plantation. At age eleven, he performed at the White House for President James Buchanan. He learned each piece after hearing it only once; his repertoire included Mozart, Beethoven, Bach, and Verdi.

2. ELLEN BOUDREAUX (1957–)
A California resident, Boudreaux, also blind, shares with Blind Tom Bethune the ability to learn a musical piece after hearing it once. Despite an IQ of only 50, she can play rock 'n' roll songs in minuet form and vice versa. She performs on both piano and guitar.

3. ALONZO CLEMONS (1959–)
Clemons, who has an IQ of 40 (the average IQ is 100), lives in a home for the developmentally disabled in Boulder, Colorado. An exceptionally talented sculptor, he has sold hundreds of pieces, including one for $45,000. Many buyers have purchased his work unaware that it was created by a mentally handicapped artist.

4–5. GEORGE AND CHARLES FINN (1939–)
Known as the Bronx Calendar Twins, they first attracted national attention when they were featured in a 1966 *Life* magazine article. The brothers can give the day of the week for any date over a period of 80,000 years. They can also recall, in detail, the weather for any day of their lives.

6. THOMAS FULLER (1710–1790)
Born in Africa, Fuller was brought to Virginia as a slave in 1724. He was a calculating wonder who could easily multiply nine-digit numbers. At the age of 78, Fuller, who was never able to learn to read or write, was asked, "How many seconds has a man lived who is seventy years, seventeen days, and twelve hours old?" Ninety seconds later, he gave the answer—2,210,500,800. Informed that he was wrong, Fuller corrected his interrogator by pointing out that the man had forgotten to adjust for leap years.

7. LESLIE LEMKE (1952–)
Like many prodigious savants, Leslie is blind, was born prematurely, and possesses an extraordinary memory. He sings and plays the piano and has appeared on numerous television shows, including *60 Minutes* and *Donahue*. He has also been the subject of two films, *An Island of Genius* and the Emmy-winning *Woman Who Willed a Miracle*.

8. JONATHAN LERMAN (1987–)
Lerman, who was diagnosed as autistic at age 3, has a tested IQ of 53. He began drawing at age 10, shortly after the death of his maternal

grandfather, Burt Markowitz, who had always insisted that Jonathan had promise. His charcoal drawings, which critics have compared to the works of George Grosz and Francis Bacon, sell for $500 to $1,200. A book of his art work, *Jonathan Lerman: The Drawings of a Boy with Autism*, was published in 2002.

9. KIM PEEK (1951–)
A mathematical savant, Peek, who lives in Salt Lake City, Utah, was the inspiration for the character played by Dustin Hoffman in the 1988 Academy Award–winning film *Rain Man*. His true story is told in the book *The Real Rain Man* (1997).

10. CHRISTOPHER PILLAULT (1982–)
Born in Iran, Pillault is unable to talk, walk, or feed himself. He discovered painting in 1993, using his hands, since he can't use his fingers functionally. His paintings, featuring striking, ethereal figures, have been exhibited in France, Italy, Japan, and the United States. He is also a member of several artists' societies.

11. RICHARD WAWRO (1952–)
Wawro, who is autistic and moderately retarded, started drawing at age 3. He held his first exhibition in Edinburgh, Scotland, when he was 17. Most of his works are landscapes and seascapes based on images that he has seen just once in books or on television. He can remember where and when he drew each picture. He was the subject of the documentary *With Eyes Wide Open* (1983).

12. STEPHEN WILTSHIRE (1974–)
Although Wiltshire, who lives in London, has the IQ of someone half his age, he is able to glance briefly at a building and then draw it in exquisite detail. He has produced three books of drawings, one of which, *Floating Cities*, was a number one best seller in Great Britain.

NOTE: The best book on savant syndrome is *Extraordinary People,* by Darold Treffert, M.D. It is also worth noting that there exists a school—Hope University, in Anaheim, California—devoted solely to educating gifted developmentally challenged adults.

The Eds. & C.F.

Marshall McLuhan's
10 Most Potent Extensions of Man

"The medium is the message." With those words, Marshall McLuhan (born Herbert Marshall McLuhan in Edmonton, Alberta, Canada, on July 21,

1911) changed the way the world related to its vastly expanding mass media. One of the most influential, challenging thinkers and philosophers of the twentieth century, he also popularized the term *global village*. His most famous work is *Understanding Media: The Extensions of Man,* which expounded on the concepts of "Hot" and "Cold" media in modern life. He died in Toronto on December 31, 1980. McLuhan contributed this list to *The Book of Lists* in 1977 . . . before the creation of the Internet:

1. Fire
2. Clothing
3. The wheel
4. The lever (Archimedes: "Give me but one firm spot on which to stand, and I will move the earth.")
5. Phonetic alphabet (extension of language)
6. The sword
7. Print
8. Electric telegraph (predecessor of telephone)
9. Electric light
10. Radio and TV (extensions of the central nervous system)

Professor McLuhan adds: "It is very difficult to restrict the extensions of man to these 10, but they may prove controversial and interesting."

10 Good Things That Happened on Friday the Thirteenth

1. **Alfred Dreyfus reinstated (July 13, 1906)**
    The French government restored Dreyfus, a Jewish officer, to the army 12 years after he had been wrongly convicted of treason and banished to Devil's Island.

2. **ASCAP organized (February 13, 1914)**
    The American Society of Composers, Authors, and Publishers was formed in New York City to collect royalties when copyrighted music is performed in public for profit.

3. **First woman flight instructor licensed (October 13, 1939)**
    After completing 200 hours of flight, Evelyn Pinchert Kilgore received the first instructor's license ever issued to an aviatrix. During World War II, she trained pilots in Pomona, California.

4. **Greek patriots retake Athens (October 13, 1944)**
    On this day, the three-and-a-half-year Nazi occupation of Athens ended.

5. Return of the *Kitty Hawk* announced (February 13, 1948)
   Orville and Wilbur Wright gave their famous flying machine to the Science Museum in London in 1928. Twenty years later, the museum sent it to the United States for permanent display at the Smithsonian Institution.

6. President Lyndon Johnson cracks down on sex discrimination (October 13, 1967)
   President Lyndon Johnson signed an executive order designed to rid the United States government of sex bias.

7. *Spycatcher* vindicated (March 13, 1987)
   In a victory for press freedom, an Australian judge ruled that the memoirs of a British spy could be published in Australia. The British government had for months tried to prevent their publication for "security" reasons; further attempts to thwart its release failed. It soon became a best seller.

8. Poland privatizes companies (July 13, 1990)
   Poland's lower house of Parliament passed legislation to privatize 80 percent of the national economy, allowing workers to purchase shares in the companies for which they worked. The senate approved the bill two weeks later.

9. Palestinians take control of security in Jericho (May 13, 1994)
   Israel handed over security and administrative control of the area of Jericho to Palestinian police and officials, and the first joint Israeli-Palestinian patrols of the main road began.

10. First all-female crew wins an America's Cup qualifying race (January 13, 1995)
    Led by Leslie Egnot and J. J. Isler, the 16-woman crew of *America3* defeated Dennis Conner's *Stars & Stripes* in the opening match of the U.S. America's Cup trials.

Mark Twain's
List of 27 People and Things to be Rescued from a Boardinghouse Fire

1. Fiancées
2. Persons toward whom the rescuer feels a tender sentiment but has not yet declared himself

3. Sisters
4. Stepsisters
5. Nieces
6. First cousins
7. Cripples
8. Second cousins
9. Invalids
10. Young-lady relations by marriage
11. Third cousins and young-lady friends of the family
12. The unclassified
13. Babies
14. Children under 10 years of age
15. Young widows
16. Young married females
17. Elderly married ditto
18. Elderly widows
19. Clergymen
20. Boarders in general
21. Female domestics
22. Male ditto
23. Landlady
24. Landlord
25. Firemen
26. Furniture
27. Mothers-in-law

Source: Bernard De Voto, ed., *Mark Twain: Letters from the Earth.*
Copyright 1962 by Mark Twain Company. Reprinted by permission of
Harper & Row Publishers, Inc.

Henny Youngman's
10 Favorite One-Liners

The King of the One-Liners, most famous for quipping, "Take my wife . . .
please!" Henry "Henny" Youngman was born in London in 1906 and moved
to New York with his parents when he was six months old. He began his
career as a printer before being discovered by Milton Berle, thanks to
"Comedy Cards" written and printed by Youngman. By the 1940s, he was
averaging nearly 200 nightclub appearances a year. Henny Youngman died
on February 24, 1998, of complications from the flu. Typical of Youngman, he
offered up a comedic "will" of sorts, years before his death, saying that he was
leaving his body to Julia Roberts, but "if she can't wait, she can have it now."
He contributed the following list to *The Book of Lists* in 1980:

1. Take my wife . . . please.
2. My grandson, 22 years old, keeps complaining about headaches. I've told him a thousand times, "Larry, when you get out of bed, it's feet first."
3. My grandson was so ugly when he was born, the doctor slapped his mother.
4. I once wanted to become an atheist, but I gave up—they have no holidays.
5. A doctor gave a man six months to live. He couldn't pay his bill . . . so the doctor gave him another six months.
6. My wife, Sadie, just had plastic surgery—I cut up her credit cards.
7. I made a killing in the market—I shot my broker.
8. When I go to Israel in Milton Berle's honor, I will have a tree uprooted.
9. My wife is a light eater . . . as soon as it's light, she starts to eat.
10. I said to my wife, "Where do you want to go for your anniversary?" She said, "I want to go to somewhere I've never been before." I said, "Try the kitchen."

8 Last Facts

1. BABE RUTH'S LAST HOME RUN
   Ruth hit his 714th and last major league home run, a towering out-of-the-park drive off of Pittsburgh Pirates pitcher Guy Bush, on May 25, 1935. However, 11 years later, the owner of the Veracruz Blues of the Mexican League hired the famous slugger for $10,000 to come and bat once in a game against the Mexico City Reds. The pitcher, Ramon Brazana, threw three balls and was removed from the game. A reliever was brought in and threw his first pitch straight down the middle. The 51-year-old Ruth hit it deep into the right-field bleachers, much to the delight of 10,000 Mexican fans.

2. THE LAST AMERICAN KILLED IN THE VIETNAM WAR
   Kelton Rena Turner, an 18-year-old Marine from Los Angeles, was killed in action on May 15, 1975, two weeks after the evacuation of Saigon, in what became known as the Mayaguez incident. His body was never recovered.

3. THE LAST VICTIM OF SMALLPOX
   On October 26, 1977, Ali Maow Maalin, a hospital cook in Somalia, became the last person to contract smallpox through natural transmission when he chose to tend an infected child. The child died but Maalin survived. In September 1978, Janet Parker, an English medical photographer, was exposed to smallpox as the result of a laboratory accident. She died. The virologist in charge of the lab felt so guilty that he committed suicide. On May 8, 1980, the World Health Organization declared smallpox eradicated, but some samples remain in laboratories in Atlanta and Moscow.

4. THE LAST PLAYBOY CLUB
The final day of business for the Lansing, Michigan, Playboy Club, the last Playboy Club in America, was July 30, 1988. The last international club closed in Manila in 1991.

5. THE LAST CRANK PHONE IN THE UNITED STATES
On July 12, 1990, America's last hand-cranked, party-line telephone system was replaced by private-line, touch-tone technology. The system had serviced the 18 year-round residents of Salmon River Canyon, near North Fork, Idaho.

6. THE LAST MISS CANADA
In 1991, women's groups successfully lobbied to have the Miss Canada contest canceled, claiming that it was degrading to women. The last Miss Canada, Nicole Dunsdon, completed her reign in October 1992.

7. THE LAST VOLKSWAGEN BEETLE
The VW Beetle, little changed since its debut in 1936, became the most popular automobile in history, with 21,529,464 cars rolling off the assembly lines. Production of the car ceased in Germany in 1978 but continued in Mexico, where the Beetle was particularly popular as a taxi. After 2000, sales dropped in Mexico due to free trade agreements that flooded the market with a variety of inexpensive cars with better gas mileage. A decision by Mexico City's local government to grant future licenses only to taxis with four doors helped seal the two-door Beetle's fate. The last Beetles were produced at a plant in Pueblo, Mexico, on July 30, 2003. The very last car was sent to a museum at Volkswagen headquarters in Wolfsburg, Germany.

8. THE LAST MESSAGE FROM THE AUTHORS TO THE READERS
We hope you have enjoyed *The Book of Lists*. If you have any comments or suggestions, please write to viciousgnu@aol.com.